WALLACE STEVENS

By Joan Richardson
WALLACE STEVENS:
The Early Years,
1879–1923

WALLACE STEVENS

The Later Years
1923–1955

JOAN RICHARDSON

BTB
BEECH TREE BOOKS
WILLIAM MORROW
New York

Grateful acknowledgment is made to Alfred A. Knopf, Inc., for permission to reprint previously published material from: *The Collected Poems of Wallace Stevens*, copyright 1954 by Wallace Stevens; *Opus Posthumous: Poems, Plays, Prose* by Wallace Stevens, edited by Samuel French Morse, copyright © 1954 by Elsie Stevens and Wallace Stevens; *The Necessary Angel* by Wallace Stevens, copyright 1951 by Wallace Stevens; *Letters of Wallace Stevens*, selected and edited by Holly Stevens, copyright © 1966 by Holly Stevens; *Souvenirs and Prophecies: The Young Wallace Stevens* by Holly Stevens, copyright © 1966, 1976 by Holly Stevens.

Grateful acknowledgment is also made to The Huntington Library, San Marino, California, for permission to reproduce previously unpublished material and photographs (previously published and unpublished) from The Wallace Stevens Collection, and to Nigel Nicolson for the estate of Vita Sackville-West for permission to quote from *Seducers in Ecuador*.

Library of Congress Cataloging-in-Publication Data
(Revised for volume 2)

Richardson, Joan, 1946-
Wallace Stevens.

Bibliography: v. 1, p.
Includes index.
Contents: [1]. The early years, 1879-1923 —
[2]. The later years, 1923-1955.
1. Stevens, Wallace, 1879-1955—Biography.
2. Poets, American—20th century—Biography.
PS3537.T4753Z758 1986 811'.52 [B] 86-5393
ISBN 0-688-05401-3 (v. 1)
ISBN 0-688-06860-X (v. 2)

Printed in the United States of America

First Edition

1 2 3 4 5 6 7 8 9 10

BOOK DESIGN BY MARIE-HÉLÈNE FREDERICKS

BTB

The word "book" is said to derive from *boka*, or beech.
The beech tree has been the patron tree of writers since ancient times and represents the flowering of literature and knowledge.

To a new life

A Note on Abbreviations and Other Technical Details

References to the following books have been included in the text:

- *CP* — *The Collected Poems of Wallace Stevens.* New York: Alfred A. Knopf, 1955.
- *OP* — *Opus Posthumous: Poems, Plays, Prose by Wallace Stevens,* ed. Samuel French Morse. New York: Alfred A. Knopf, 1957.
- *NA* — *The Necessary Angel: Essays on Reality and the Imagination.* New York: Vintage, 1951.
- *L* — *The Letters of Wallace Stevens,* ed. Holly Stevens. New York: Alfred A. Knopf, 1966.
- *SP* — *Souvenirs and Prophecies: The Young Wallace Stevens,* ed. Holly Stevens. New York: Alfred A. Knopf, 1977.

Sources for primary material are given in parentheses following the quoted passages. In the case of material quoted from letters or notebooks in the Wallace Stevens Collection at the Huntington Library (in San Marino, California), the date of the letter or entry is given in parentheses while the addressee or notebook title is indicated in the text and/or heading. Only in the few instances where no date is given is the library's catalog number given; this represents a simplifying difference from the method of Volume I, where in all cases both catalog number and date were given. Within the quoted material most of Stevens's peculiarities of punctuation—erratic uses of commas, for example, or two instead of three dots for ellipses—as well as his solecisms, such as failing to use the conditional in hypothetical sentence constructions, have been allowed to remain without *sic* indications. Only in the circumstances where the typesetter or printer might be blamed for carelessness have *sic* notes been inserted.

Again, I would like to thank all who have gone before me in pursuing Stevens's studious ghost and those whose ongoing practical help have made this biography a reality.

New York
January 1988

CONTENTS

INTRODUCTION

Wallace Stevens made silk dresses out of worms. This is what poets do, as he noted in his "Adagia." From the gray particular of everyday life he wove a fabric of shimmering colors. It became his "cloak of China, cap of Spain," the purple raiment Hoon wore. Like the magical veil Ino gave Odysseus, it enabled him to survive.

The first volume of this biography traced the course of the poet's development. This second and final volume follows him through his maturity to the final "Good night" he spoke softly to his daughter from his deathbed. The news of her coming birth opens this volume; her helping her father in death closes it. Between these two moments Stevens lived in a different way than he had before. With his exquisite sensibility he attended more carefully to how to live, what to do.

Stevens never spoke at length (on the basis of available evidence) of how the birth of his child affected him. But it is abundantly clear that after her arrival there was a significant change in spirit that reflected itself most directly in the tone of his second volume of poems, *Ideas of Order.* As the following chapters will show, the difference was equally apparent in the way he lived his life. It was not so much that quotidian details changed—as they must to accommodate a new member of the household—but that Stevens's attitude, the posture he assumed toward life, changed fundamentally.

The distinction in tone between *Harmonium* and *Ideas of Order* has long been a subject of critical discussion. By the time Stevens returned to writing poetry after the six-year interruption that came following the birth of his daughter and the publication of *Harmonium,* he had blunted his cynical edge and sharpened his eye. What Harriet Monroe once metaphorically referred to in describing his early style as his "gargoyle grin" was replaced by the comedian's smile. Over the years even that expression eased into the Buddha-like mien that characterizes Stevens's favorite portrait of himself, the photograph reproduced on the dust jacket here and on the editions of the *Collected Poems* and *Opus Posthumous.* The pages to follow unfold the story of this transformation that began as Stevens in mid-life greeted a new life.

These last five chapters, or ways of looking at Stevens, reveal aspects that were not known, or seen, before. They oppose the image of the poet as ponderously serious and politically conservative and present, rather, a man who delighted in delighting and who, in fact, openly described himself as belonging "to the left." The fiction Stevens wove about his life deceived, confused, contradicted. In this he belongs with those other supreme versers of the American Sublime, Ralph Waldo Emerson and Walt Whitman. In "Self-Reliance" Emerson wrote: "Suppose you should contradict yourself; what then? . . . With consistency a great soul has simply nothing to do." Whitman, who described himself as "simmering, simmering, simmering" until Emerson brought him "to a boil," echoed his "Master" in "Song of Myself":

> Do I contradict myself?
> Very well then I contradict myself,
> (I am large, I contain multitudes.)

Stevens, too, came to know himself as a "great soul" and to "contain multitudes." He knew because he had forged that soul through work, his work. He slowly realized himself, took on the knowledge of his power, as he wove the grand design of his intention into words that became facts under the pressure of reality he exerted on them. From the vantage point of seventy-five years he looked back at what he had done and he saw that it was good. He had succeeded in solving the "greatest problem of his age," the "will to believe," at least for himself. As Richard Poirier has elegantly pointed out in closing his recent *The Renewal of Literature: Emersonian Reflections,* Stevens learned *how* to live, while facing, as William James put it in *The Varieties of Religious Experience,* into the "pit of insecurity beneath the surface of life." Poirier goes on:

> Against the doubt of existence, one does not posture a "self" but only a "belief," and not even a belief in the self so much as a belief in life. "Because that life *is* worth living," he [James] advises in *The Will to Believe,*" and your belief will help create the fact." So far as any human self goes, it may be willed into and willed out of existence without loss of consciousness or loss of subjective life, and any act of belief, in the self or in its dissolution, is no more than a modification in the stream of thought.[1]

I agree wholly with Poirier here and in his reading of Stevens's equanimity—an equanimity sometimes moving toward exhilaration and bordering on joy—as he contemplated personal dissolution.

> Ariel was glad he had written his poems.
>
> . . . .
>
> It was not important that they survive.
> What mattered was that they should bear
> Some lineament or character,

> Some affluence, if only half-perceived,
> In the poverty of their words,
> Of the planet of which they were part.

Stevens's ability to celebrate even total annihilation derived from the basic strength of his temperament. His announcement of it in the voice of the necessary angel of reality represented an act of will. He could have chosen otherwise, but he chose to offer a sacrament of praise to the "Nothing that is not there and the nothing that is," our imperfect paradise. This is why we read him.

I

THE SEA OF SPUMING THOUGHT

1923–1933

FOR THE SAKE OF GOODNESS AND LOVE,
MAN SHALL LET DEATH HAVE
NO SOVEREIGNTY OVER HIS THOUGHTS.

—THOMAS MANN,
The Magic Mountain

The sea is a form of ridicule.

—from "The Man with the Blue Guitar," *Collected Poems* (p. 180)

Though Stevens's project for the "Grand Poem" represented a highly individualized perception, the comedian's intelligence grew, as he had discovered, from his soil. That soil was just as much the energy of words touching him as was the earth he walked and smelled. An avid reader of French and English as well as American periodicals, Stevens easily assimilated timely and germinal ideas together with the particular words and images associated with them. "Fact" and "fiction," the two major terms of his theoretical vocabulary, were such ideas and they reflected the age's spiritual tension. "Fact" carried the weight with which William James had charged it when he spoke of the unconscious as the container of the deep recesses of feeling where real facts are made. James had thus equivocated the leftover nineteenth-century positivist position without denying the central significance of "facts." Out of this ambiguity American pragmatism built a foundation strong enough to offer a resting place for postwar European intellectuals, until then unimpressed by what their children in the new world could teach them. "Fact" was also the central term in Ludwig Wittgenstein's vocabulary. Similarly, "fiction" brought with it Hans Vaihinger's expansion of Henri Poincaré's apprehension of the hypothetical relation between facts and reality. In the journals Stevens read in the late 1910s and 1920s these terms provided anchorages of thought where minds found shelter from the threatening clouds of irrationality darkening the century's horizon.

Having completed the survey of his experience's compass and curriculum, like Crispin, arrived in a new world, Stevens was now extremely sensitive to knowing that he didn't know, to seeing "how much/ Of what he saw he never saw at all" (*CP* 36). His coming to this point coincided with the birth of the Vienna Circle and particularly with Wittgenstein's disturbing illumination of the limits of understanding:

> . . . he who understands me finally recognizes them [propositions] as senseless, when he has climbed out through them, on them, over them. (He must so to speak throw away the ladder, after he has climbed up on it.)
>
> He must surmount these propositions; then he sees the world rightly.
>
> Whereof one cannot speak, thereof one must be silent.[1]

Stevens sensed the rightness of this and realized, too, that for the sake of "goodness and love" he could not continue to let death have the sovereignty over his thoughts that it had had in the last twelve years. Though this preoccupation had been the spring of his poems—"Death is the mother of beauty"—now on the other side of middle age he understood how necessary it was to "celebrate the faith of forty" and beyond. He recognized that repeatedly representing his clashing against what was with weapons of words that killed even the possibility of hope made him just as guilty of self-indulgence as T. S. Eliot had been found to be by Robert McAlmon, a current correspondent-friend of Stevens. (He could not have known at this moment that Eliot, too, was turning toward something that would suffice, that would give joy in spite of the seeming futility of human effort through history.) But before Stevens could speak of his new faith, he had to give himself to life as he never had before. He had to practice not allowing death to dominate his thoughts. This required silence.

Silence was chosen by many during these years. The decade of the twenties marked "a kind of caesura, a period of summing up, as the 1890's had been a period of innovation."[2] The time of intellectual triumph in the immediate postwar years—the years that saw Stevens succeed in various new journals the beginnings of which attested to the excitement of the age—was succeeded by a pause in creativity. But this long, deep breath of thought was taken mostly by Europeans. This was true of Luigi Pirandello, André Gide—for whom the silence would lead to a severe emotional crisis—and Sigmund Freud, among others. Freud published *The Ego and the Id* in the same year that Stevens published *Harmonium.* From 1923 on Freud "simply modif[ied] details"[3]; similarly, after *Harmonium,* Stevens modified the details of individually important words and images set down in his basic work. And just as, after the late twenties, the master rabbi turned his speculative attention to society and religion, so Stevens preoccupied himself with how to forge a viable religion for himself and his society.

Stevens's silence during the twenties also had to do with the sharp break in philosophical tradition before and after the war. Stevens was very much in tune with the prevailing prewar tone set by William James with his version of pragmatism.[4] James redefined "facts" so that he could at the same time satisfy the materialist needs of the thinkers of his age and offer the tonic of the all-important will to believe. His notes rang as loudly through the European cultural air as they did in the Harvard Yard, where Stevens had first heard them. But the war disturbed this harmony, and in the years after it was the work Alfred North Whitehead and Bertrand Russell had been doing from 1910 to 1913, the *Principia Mathematica,* that set the standard by which thinkers measured the weight of their thoughts. With his proclivity to the metaphysical, Stevens needed time to consider the new, scientifically limited analytic approach; he had to learn, too, how to use symbolic language in a different way. In the years between 1923 and 1933 he moved from a fascination with language as expressive form, understood in a primarily *symboliste* musical way, to the formulation he expressed most directly in his "Adagia": "The exquisite environment of fact. The final poem will be the poem of fact in the language of fact. But it will be the poem of fact not realized before" (*OP*

171). The change was from seeing language as the "mere medium or instrument" of poetry to seeing it as the "material of poetry" (*OP* 171).

Though his intellect applied the laws of this new logic to himself and his forms, Stevens's emotions remained tied to aspirations of an earlier time. These could not be easily analyzed. Both his familial background and the exposure during his college years to those thinkers like George Santayana, William James, Josiah Royce, Charles Eliot Norton, and others who nostalgically yearned for "something sacred to believe in" had prepared Stevens to be sympathetic to the approaches of philosophers like Henri Bergson and Benedetto Croce. Reflecting an optimistic attitude, these representatives of the leading French and Italian schools were still linked to the thought of the eighteenth century.[5] Stevens's sense of kinship with these figures led him to immerse himself in the history of the eighteenth century and to follow up on Bergson's and George Meredith's direct and indirect references to the prime Western examples of the comic spirit. Unlike the postwar technicians of the mathematical-logical method of Whitehead and Russell, Stevens was unwilling to abandon questions of feeling, value, and metaphysics. He wanted both to see things as they were and to understand why and how these things, these "facts," interacted with feeling to create such irrational manifestations as God, desire, hope, and fear.

At the same time as the poet opened himself to musing about these various problems, Edmund Husserl on one side and Martin Heidegger on the other, without ignoring the faith in intuition that Stevens found so appealing, offered alternatives to Croce's and Bergson's optimistic views. Both phenomenology and existentialism offered practical approaches for dealing with the postwar world. Husserl's method of devoting meticulous attention to the minutest detail of experience was protection from the assault of anger and impotence that one had to feel when considering the broader world picture during and after the Great War. And Heidegger's tragic view of existence, opposing the Enlightenment's "progressive" tradition—an attitude inherited from Sören Kierkegaard—was far more in keeping with "things as they were" than was any lingering meliorist position. From these two closely related schools Stevens learned as well. He weighed what made sense without ignoring facts of feeling.

It was against this intellectual background that *Harmonium* appeared. The hard facts of experience that had created this climate marked the last phases of Stevens's labor. Between 1920 and 1923, the years of recovery from the terrors of World War I, signs of the next catastrophe were already encroaching. In Germany Adolf Hitler announced his twenty-five-point program at a beer hall in Munich shortly before the mark began its fateful plunge; just after its rate dropped to 4 million to 1 U.S. dollar, he attempted the coup d'état that failed. At the same time in America Ku Klux Klan activities in the South made the 1919 Chicago race riots seem mild; the organization, nonetheless, gained more and more political power. Nicola Sacco and Bartolomeo Vanzetti were arrested, tried, and found guilty of murder. The Teapot Dome oil scandal hearings seriously called into question the survival-of-the-fittest values of the Calvinist work ethic. The mass-scale economic polarization of society was well under way, as the stock market boom that began in 1922 indicated. The differences between the haves and have-nots had never been so clear. In spite of revolutions fought under rhetorical banners of freedom from class oppression, it was the Industrial Revolution that had determined the changes most affecting people at all levels of society. The thought that went into the development of unthinking machines, in not having taken account of feelings and values, had created the monster that prophets had been warning against for generations.

As Stevens disarmingly disclosed to various individuals later in his life, when both his careers, as poet and as insurance executive, were more than successful, his tastes for the better things of life were too insistent for him not to have seriously entered the battle to become one of the "haves." In a 1937 letter to Ronald Lane Latimer he made this especially clear, relating the indulgence of his needs to his giving up poetry after *Harmonium:*

> DEAR MR. LATIMER,
>
> Giving up the Alcestis Press must be to you what giving up any idea of writing poetry would be to me. Nevertheless, a good many years ago, when I was really a poet in the sense that I was all imagination, and so on, I deliberately gave up writing poetry because, much as I loved it, there were too many other things I wanted not to make an effort to have them. I wanted to do everything that one wants to do at that age: live in a village in France, in a hut in Morocco, or in a piano box at Key West. But I didn't like the idea of being bedeviled all the time about money and I didn't for a moment like the idea of poverty, so I went to work like anybody else and kept at it for a good many years.
>
> If you could do that sort of thing, it would not mean anything more than turning away temporarily. For instance, there is a man who runs a press at Greenwich. This is not much of a story without being able to remember the name of the press, but the man that I have in mind is a member of Lazard Freres [*sic*]. He has now made enough money to do the sort of thing that you would like to do; my impression is that he has about half a dozen people constantly employed. While I don't like his books, that is merely a difference in taste; the principle is the same. It is not at all unlikely that, if you got down to business, whatever it might be, and attended to it exclusively for, say, the next twenty-five years, you would have a thoroughly good time and would be able to come back to all this the better for your life away from it. One does not change a great deal; you would not be the same person, but you would be pretty much the same person. (*L* 320)

Though he ironically exaggerated the period of time Latimer might safely give up his passion in favor of making himself secure, Stevens was sincere in his advice. A concern with material things had been with him all his life. As a high school friend remembered, ". . . he had long contemplated a career as a lawyer because he liked financial security and desired to live graciously and have expensive things."[6] It was not only his father, then, who thought law school was important. Though Stevens's talent for "painting pictures in words" persistently lured him from the straight and narrow money-making path that would allow him to smoke big cigars and buy French paintings, like the bachelor uncle he as a boy had admired so, the temptation was never strong enough for him to risk what he most feared: that he might, in the absence of financial security, break down as his father had. The one image Stevens would never shatter was that a "real man" was a solid provider and that to be "man number one" required even more. "Things" were signs of this. They were also distractions that screened the deeper need to fulfill an image he had set for himself long before, waiting for approval that never came from the father he saw as a sphinx. But, too, not having to think about where or how to earn next month's rent meant that he would be able to give his attention to what pleased him without the concern, as he had once expressed in a bitter moment of his youth, "of whether it avail[ed] or not."

In addition to all he read of the "literary life" and times, the scientific developments of the still-young century attracted his imagination—I borrow one of his comparisons—like "flypaper . . . a fly." The explorations Freud led into the unconscious were rivaled by the various explorations to the North and South poles during the century's first and second decades as well as by those to sites once thought lost or fictitious. Sir Arthur Evans's digging in Crete, following Heinrich Schliemann's earlier expeditions to Troy and Mycenae, made myths seem more accurate descriptions of reality than the new, precise logical analyses of the Vienna Circle. Similarly, but contradictorily, the observations in 1919 of the total eclipse of the sun, which bore out Albert Einstein's theory of relativity, made the unobservable, wholly abstract mathematical descriptions of reality the basis for whatever could be known. While Ernest Rutherford demonstrated that the atom was not the final building block of the universe, and while the true structure of the Milky Way was observed for the first time (in 1920, in an early application of photography to the discovery of asteroids),[7] Stevens and those around him, witnessing with exhilaration what reason was accomplishing, sensed its importance in dealing with the irrational element, now so evident a part of life. As Edith Wharton's Pulitzer Prize–winning novel commemorated, the "Age of Innocence" was over, the "age of confusion" begun.

Various individuals attempted to remedy or soothe their personal feelings of confusion in different ways. H. G. Wells produced his *Outline of History;* if he could not order his present he would order the past. His subjective views at least offered some kind of foil to Oswald Spengler's pessimistic perception of *The Decline of the West* two years before. Others simply mourned the past. Paul Valéry composed himself composing *Le Cimetière Marin,* while others suggested there were more pressing concerns than the self with its nostalgic attachment to dreams of lost paradises. John Reed's *Ten Days That Shook the World* countered the sentiment Valéry expressed in the same year, 1920. Reed's overriding commitment to an ideal also offered the perfect antithesis to F. Scott Fitzgerald's mucking around in the real in *This Side of Paradise,* published in 1920 as well. The extremes they represented mirrored the alternatives of American life. It was not surprising that most preferred to follow Fitzgerald who echoed Mallarmé: "The flesh is weak, alas, and I have read all the books."

Stevens could have muttered this line to himself as he prepared for one of his "Frenchiest" experiences that fall of 1923. After the publication of *Harmonium* on September 7, but wisely before the first reviews, Stevens left with Elsie on the only extended holiday they had taken since their marriage fourteen years before. On October 18 they sailed in a beautiful sea-keen ship, appropriately named—for one who loved puns—the *Kroonland* (*L* 241). "Paradisal green/ Gave suavity to the perplexed machine/Of ocean" (*CP* 99) and to Stevens for these two weeks that began a two-month suspension from the cares of the everyday world.

After this, things would never be the same. As Stevens commemorated in "Sea Surface Full of Clouds," a poem that has been celebrated as the most perfect example of a "pure poem"[8] (John Crowe Ransom also noted, without knowing the poem's occasion, that to contemplate it was to become happy), "In that November off Tehuantepec," their only child was conceived.[9] Spooning and crooning one night when the "slopping of the sea grew still" (*CP* 100) Wallace and Elsie, like "the sea/ And heaven rolled as one and from the two/ Came fresh transfigurings of freshest blue" (*CP* 102) in the eyes of the girl they named Holly nine months later. Out of this voyage into nothingness came a new beginning. By the time they arrived back in Hartford, after their stays in California and New Mexico (where they stopped to see Witter Bynner), Elsie, now thirty-seven, knew she was pregnant. Her husband, prudent in the most usual of circumstances, felt concern.

Elsie was with child; she was not young; they would need a larger house; they would need help; the child would have to have a secure future and a good education, be exposed to beautiful things to shape its spirit. Certainly he was pleased, but there were so many things to think of and attend to. He, now forty-four, "past meridian," as he put it, had to think of his health, be as strong as he could be. Elsie and the child would need him. His "self" now mattered only as providing-protecting machine. It was natural that happy, "tranced" (*CP* 100), with the idea of the child to come, but weighted with all these considerations, he became a "perplexed" and "tense machine" (*CP* 99). And his health—he was an "obese machine" (*CP* 102), and would have to take care. No time now for the "indulgences that in moonlight [had] their habitude" (*CP* 35). Poetry, his greatest indulgence, would have to wait—not that there weren't other good reasons, as he knew, for his withdrawal.

There was one more poem, however, written shortly after "Sea Surface" and which appeared almost at the same time, in August 1924's *Measure.* "Red Loves Kit" (*OP* 30) is a bitter companion piece to "Sea Surface." Submitting them simultaneously, but to different magazines, Stevens must have felt a twinge of satisfaction in getting back at Elsie, who grew more and more difficult with her pregnancy. She no doubt had begun to feel, though without being able to articulate it, her deep ambivalence about motherhood. Elsie acted out her doubts and fears with hostility and seeming arbitrariness. Her feelings were not simply temporary results of hormone changes or reactions to discomfort. Holly Stevens's memory of her mother's prohibition against being called Mommy (*SP* 137) evidences the painful associations Elsie must have had—associations that could easily explain what Stevens had early perceived as her "coyness" in response to his advances. After fourteen years of marriage he addressed it directly, though couched in the "fiction" of "Red Loves Kit": "Your yes her no. . . ." Elsie's pregnancy, of course, provided her with an understandable excuse for denying "Red" (another of Stevens's early nick-names); perhaps, then, this rejection did not bite as deeply as her earlier "no, no," the two killing words which had prompted the angry burst that opened "Le Monocle de Mon Oncle."[10] But it bit enough for him to address the situation once more:

RED LOVES KIT

I

Your yes her no, your no her yes. The words
Make little difference, for being wrong
And wronging her, if only as she thinks,
You never can be right. You are the man.
You brought the incredible calm in ecstasy,
Which, like a virgin visionary spent
In this spent world, she must possess. The gift
Came not from you. Shall the world be spent again,
Wasted in what would be an ultimate waste,
A deprivation muffled in eclipse,
The final theft? That you are innocent
And love her still, still leaves you in the wrong.
Where is that calm and where that ecstasy?
Her words accuse you of adulteries
That sack the sun, though metaphysical.

II

A beautiful thing, milord, is beautiful
Not only in itself but in the things
Around it. Thus it has a large expanse,
As the moon has in its moonlight, worlds away.
As the sea has in its coastal clamorings.
So she, when in her mystic aureole
She walks, triumphing humbly, should express
Her glory in your passion and be proud.

Her music should repeat itself in you,
Impelled by a convulsive harmony.
Milord, I ask you, though you will to sing,
Does she will to be proud? True, you may love
And she have beauty of a kind, but such
Unhappy love reveals vast blemishes.

III

Rest, crows, upon the edges of the moon,
Cover the golden altar deepest black,
Fly upward thick in numbers, fly across
The blueness of the half-night, fill the air
And darken it, make an unbroken mat
Out of the whirl and denseness of your wings,
Spread over heaven shutting out the light.
Then turn your heads and let your spiral eyes
Look backward. Let your swiftly-flying flocks
Look suddenly downward with their shining eyes
And move the night by their intelligent motes.
Make a sidereal splendor as you fly.
And you, good galliard, to enchant black thoughts
Beseech them for an overpowering gloom.
It will be fecund in rapt curios.

Cleverly playing in key lines with spondees (feet of two long syllables, spondees originally accompanied the pouring of a libation), Stevens elliptically described Elsie's delayed reaction to the outpouring that resulted in her pregnancy as well as her now generalized reaction to his outpouring in the words of poems. He had brought "the incredible calm in ecstasy" that he described in the thick marine imagery of "Sea Surface Full of Clouds," but now "Her words accuse[d] [him] of adulteries/ That sack[ed] the sun." How could he think of writing poems while she suffered the weight both of increasing size through the hot summer months and of the countless considerations for the future?

In trying to understand her, he attempted to rationalize what she must have felt: "The gift/ Came not from [him]." The gift, this child she had thought she wanted so much during the first years of their marriage, was a product of chance, of Providence. With this explanation he would be neither blamed nor praised. With her desire become fact, he would have thought "She should reflect/ Her glory in [his] passion and be proud." He would have thought she "should express/Her beauty in [his] love," but instead, their "Unhappy love reveal[ed] vast blemishes."

In spite of his own pain, Stevens was more sympathetic to Elsie's feelings now than he had been years before, when she had first expressed her resentment about his writing and publishing poems. This sensitivity gave him his final reason for invoking a period of silence. He called to Apollo's birds, symbols of poetic inspiration, to "Rest . . . [,] darken" the air, shut out the light from the varying reflections out of which he made his poems, as he had most recently and specifically in "Sea Surface." If she had winced at his exposing feelings about her in his publishing early poems from the "June Books" and in "Le Monocle," how much more she must have reacted to what he revealed in "Sea Surface." For her, who had experienced with him what had happened "In that November off Tehuantepec," the "true subject" was blatant. She could not know that others could not see it through the beautiful "poetry of the subject" he had woven. No wonder she accused him of "adulteries," of betrayal. Seeing intimacies treated as subject matter could not be pleasing for someone who did not understand the subject itself, and Elsie never had and never would understand herself as subject.

Stevens consciously made the decision not to write; he knew that this dark time would be his own period of gestation, that out of it new life would come. This is clear in the last line of "Red Loves Kit": "It will be fecund in rapt curios." During the five years that passed before he penned "Metropolitan Melancholy" (*OP* 32), in which he began to play with the devices he developed fully nine years after that in "The Man with the Blue Guitar," Stevens did not stop being a poet. Quite the contrary, it was as though those years were his personal "dark age," his metaphoric as well as his real "middle age," during which the classical language he had learned to speak and imitate evolved into his own romance vernacular, a language combining French and English and the remembered inflections of the Pennsylvania Dutch farmers. "Metropolitan Melancholy" exhibited this with its "purple woman with a lavender tongue" saying "hic . . . hac . . . ha" in a parody of declining Latin. This new language was also apparent in the next poem he wrote about a year later, "Annual Gaiety" (*OP* 32); its "melanchole," a kind of Mallarméan invention, suited Stevens's purpose of becoming a "priest of the invisible" (*OP* 169).

❧

"Rapt into future times, the bard begun." Alexander Pope's line described Stevens's situation perfectly. By the time he would reemerge with his new idiom, the "man-poet" would have gone through a change of life. The sounds of his child's cooings and gagas would be transformed into hard-shaped syllables of meaning. But for now the sounds of automobile, truck, and trolley traffic as it passed on the busy street where the Stevenses rented an apartment at 735 Farmington Avenue; the radio's new magical noises; the voices of the landlord's children screaming, singing, and playing downstairs made up a confused but constant background. Above this din it was difficult to hear the sounds of birds or trees shivering in winter wind, out of which the poet had made so much years before. The pressures of the everyday world could not now be escaped. Attending to these concerns, which began immediately on the couple's return from their long holiday, also distracted Stevens from the sting of some of the reviews of *Harmonium,* which had begun to appear while he was away. By the time he wrote Harriet Monroe in July 1924 that his "royalties for the first half of 1924 amounted to $6.20," he had enough distance from the lukewarm to cold reception with which many had greeted his first volume to look at the situation with humor. He closed his note to Monroe with the comment that with his royalties he would "charter a boat and take [his] friends around the world" (*L* 243).

Of the early reviews, two were of particular importance. Naturally Stevens would be most interested in the first impressions of his work presented in the *Nation* and *Poetry*. Because he was a longtime subscriber to the *Nation* and felt himself attuned to the views it presented, Stevens's heart must have raced as he found the page in the October 10 issue on which Mark Van Doren's review began. "Poets and Wits" ambiguously introduced the critic's reaction. *Harmonium* was the first of three volumes Mr. Van Doren's incisive intelligence addressed; the others were Alfred Kreymborg's *Less Lonely* and Robert Graves's *Whipperginny*.

Reading the first paragraph, Stevens breathed a sigh of relief:

> Mr. Stevens' most famous poem, "Peter Quince at the Clavier," appeared in "Others" as long as seven years ago, and he has continued ever since to dance like a tantalizing star through magazines and anthologies. But there was no volume until now. While some admirers called for one rather loudly, the rest were content that Mr. Stevens should exist in bright fragments, being afraid perhaps that he might not glitter in the bulk. "Harmonium" will dissolve their doubt, for it places its author high among those wits of today who are also poets—T. S. Eliot, Ezra Pound, Maxwell Bodenheim, Alfred Kreymborg, William Carlos Williams, Aldous Huxley, Sacheverell Sitwell, and Robert Graves. . . .

Reading through the second paragraph, Stevens must have caught his breath intermittently, as though punctuating the critic's more biting perceptions:

> His wit, of course, has nothing of the Augustan about it. It is not clear; it is not the expression of common sense. It is tentative, perverse and superfine; and it will never be popular. What public will care for a poet who strains every nerve every moment to be unlike anyone who ever wrote, who writes a remarkable spiritual autobiography no line of which is transparent and calls it "The Comedian as the Letter C," who writes not about a blackbird but about Thirteen Ways of Looking at a Blackbird; who gives his pieces such titles as Le Monocle de Mon Oncle, Hibiscus on the Sleeping Shores, Homunculus et La Belle Étoile, The Emperor of Ice-Cream, Exposition of the Contents of a Cab, and who offers this under Bantams in Pine Woods,
>
> Chief Iffucan of Azcan in caftan
> Of tan with henna hackles, halt!

Damned universal cock, as if the sun
Was blackamoor to bear your blazing tail.

Fat! Fat! Fat! Fat! I am the personal.
Your world is you. I am my world.

You ten-foot poet among inchlings, Fat!
Begone! An inchling bristles in these pines,

Bristles, and points their Appalachian tangs,
And fears not portly Azcan nor his hoos.

> Mr. Stevens will never be much read. But someday there will be a strong monograph on him and his twentieth century kin who ranged their restless faculties over all the deserts and hill-tops of the world to inaugurate a new era of what Dryden once called "wit-writing"—an era which may be short and may be long. . . .

Then, Stevens's heart and breath eased into regularity again with the strong sentences of praise for his style, so well matched in Van Doren's mind to the spirit of the age:

> That monograph will pay particular tribute to the pure phrasing of Mr. Stevens, to his deliberately enunciated melody, his economy, his clipped cleanliness of line, his gentle excellence. And it will not be wrong if it finds him more durable, even with all his obscurity, than much of the perfect sense and the perfect rhyme that passed for poetry in his day; if it represents his work as drifting permanently, like frozen chords, through certain memories—the overtone of our droll, creedless time.

But by the third paragraph, which introduced Kreymborg in comparison to him, Stevens must have felt the encroachment of that old catastrophe, felt the renewed movement of his up and down between two elements now described by someone observing him: "It was Mr. Kreymborg who introduced Mr. Stevens into 'Others' and the two names are often mentioned together. But Mr. Kreymborg is not the poet Mr. Stevens is, whatever he may genuinely be. Both men write nonsense, but the pages of Mr. Kreymborg lack tension and vibrancy and so cannot appeal to the ear. . . ."

He was a poet but a witty poet who wrote beautiful and vibrantly tense nonsense. That Kreymborg, in the eyes of the reviewer, was unquestionably bad and that Graves, whom he went on to consider, was also seen ambivalently—though with no praise for skill—did not mitigate the effect. What mattered was that Van Doren had not perceived the semblance of the thing Stevens had in mind behind the well-wrought wit. He had sensed the strain but not what occasioned it. Stevens's deep personal struggle with his creedless time was missed, and what appeared to Van Doren was simply true wit to advantage dressed.

Receiving December's *Poetry* after this, Stevens could not but have been eagerly expectant to find what the reviewer in this journal, so long his primary support, would present. No doubt feeling that it would be thought less than objective if she were to review the work of her own discovery and longtime favorite, Harriet Monroe assigned the task to Marjorie Allen Seiffert. It isn't difficult to imagine the anxious and excited anticipation with which Stevens flitted through the pages of the issue. Again, the contradictoriness of his spirit confronted him. Entitled "The Intellectual Tropics," the review reflected the same ambivalence Van Doren had expressed, though Seiffert cast her perception in a more positive, if no more promising, light in terms of how the work would be understood by those not well versed in arcana. What was clear to both Van Doren and Seiffert, she expressed in her opening sentence: "The authentic poet walks in his own world." But, she went on to point out, "there is a lot one never quite gets." It must have been hard for Stevens to go on reading: ". . . one regretfully assumes that perhaps Mr. Stevens doesn't mean to be any more illuminating than life itself, which offers a glorious amount of experience, much of which teaches us nothing. . . ."

Seiffert felt manipulated, as though she had been made to think she had constantly missed something in reading "The Comedian." She finally came to the conclusion that its last line—"So may the relation of each man be clipped"—if not the whole thing, was utterly "meaningless." Her general impression was that the poet had "put his tongue in his cheek at life." Nonetheless, she properly sensed the tragic tone of "Le Monocle de Mon Oncle." The "uncontestably beautiful" "Sunday Morning" she found "uncharacteristic," so much so that she believed that if it were taken out of the volume, it "could not be identified as his own."

After this it would have been almost impossible for Stevens to anticipate what forgiveness could follow, yet, as the piece progressed, Miss Seiffert relented; it was as though she sensed that she might never again review did she not also praise Miss Monroe's darling. Her taking on the opposing stance halfway through the review ironically yet perfectly mirrored the antithetical nature of the poetry itself and of the man who made it. Her transition into appreciation turned around her questioning of the poet's purpose:

> . . . sometimes the issue [is] left obscure, and the poet has contented himself with presenting a design, the meaning of which is not apparent. Perhaps such poems are constructed for design's sake alone. . . . But by far the greater number of the poems have both the "beauty of inflections" and the "beauty of innuendoes"; they delicately convey without plot or argument a theme and its significance, yet seem to remain wholly simple. . . .

Relaxing about the perplexity she at first criticized harshly, Seiffert went on to construct her own poetic periods in describing Stevens's most distinctive gift of evoking verbal action with adjectives. She attributed this skill to his handling his "matter without the *grand serieux*" and being "keen, subtle, and wary"; she then observed: "To attain certain effects he keeps wild adjectives in cages from which they flatly leap upon the startled noun and elope with it. . . . This is very stimulating to the reader." Reading on now, Stevens must have been pleased. He had made a conquest. The review reflected the situation between him and the ideal reader he imagined. This reader presented him with the possibility of satisfying through poetry what he could not satisfy in life. Initially resistant, even offended and defensively offensive, as women could be when first approached, this reader slowly yielded to the power of his seduction, the enchantment of his words, the inescapable rhythms he had been practicing for so long. That last sentence delighted him: "This is very stimulating to the reader."

Once she had entered his "fluent mundo," the seduction was complete. Since she had, as it were, taken on "his knowledge with his power," even something she might not have understood before was now clear to her. She had become "fluent" in his language. What might be judged by another as a decadent, overly extravagant indulgence in "purple" language, she was able to recognize accurately as belonging to an Oriental tradition:

> After this survey of Stevens' world, one retires to one's own to think it over. It is a brilliant country with tropic splendor beside which the real tropics seem faded and meagre [*sic*], a world in which the accustomed realities are concealed under scenery of luxuriant and intricate design, but a world which has, after all, a rocky substratum of reality. Sometimes one wishes Mr. Stevens would write more poems in the manner of "Ploughing on Sunday" or "The Snow Man" whose bare rigor is immensely effective. However, the tropics have a steamy sensuality about them, no sticky purple patches; rather they are curiously patterned like an East Indian painting. His emotion lurks behind the design. We must peer through thickets to catch a glimpse of that sky wary bird as it flits into obscurity. Distinctly, there is nothing homogeneous between Harmonium and our own back yard except that bird, which roosts so trustfully on one's own clothes-pole that one can recognize the color of his tail even in a tropic landscape.
>
> There is a background of gracious beauty behind Mr. Stevens' art that causes one to believe that he is as happy as a poet is permitted to be; and in his poems one divines that his revolt is not against his environment but rather against the limitations of the universe, and that it is a revolt tempered with modesty and appreciation, almost gratitude. There is nowhere irritation and distaste, everywhere a delicate and sensual perception of loveliness.

She detected "his emotion lurk[ing] behind the design," saw him as a "sky wary bird." She saw him. But as everyone caught in the web of romance is wont to do, she idealized what she saw. Closing her review in a tone as opposed to that with which she opened as B minor to C, she interpreted his railing to be against the limitations of the universe rather than against his own; she chose to see him as happy, and now she ignored the acrid notes of violence and mordant irony. For her, the poet who created the lush tropic where she lost herself had to be noble, his gratitude for things as they were totally obscuring anything but his "delicate sensual perception of loveliness."

Perhaps in reaction to seeing how he was being perceived in the various reviews, Stevens again began reading a great deal, as he noted to Harriet Monroe and others who continued to inquire about poems he might submit to them for the journals they represented. From what remains of his library, it seems that, among other things, he was "catching up on," as he put it, recently published volumes of poetry.[11] He wanted to compare his volume with others in an attempt to understand the kinds of criticism being voiced. While the early ambivalence toward his work became gradually more weighted on the positive side, as the months passed and his longtime acquaintances and appreciators added their estimates to the appraisal there was an underside to this praise. Because they knew him more intimately, these friendly reviewers were able to pinpoint sources of some of the tones of *Harmonium* that produced the uncomfortable ambivalence of other critics.

A good example of this was Marianne Moore's review, "Well-Moused Lion," which appeared in the *Dial* in January 1924. Even though the two poets had never met, Moore, having moved for years in the same circle as Stevens, was familiar with aspects of the personality of the "Giant"—as he was affectionately known by members of this group—that informed the poems. Moore was well versed in the group's intellectual background. She knew what excited them, knew about their heroes, shared their purpose. Consequently, she could recognize and specify certain notes in Stevens that others had not yet learned to hear. Moreover, she was a poet and could address Stevens and his work in appropriate language. Beginning with her title, Miss Moore dealt with Stevens on common ground. As much a mistress of language as he was a master, she was not at all intimidated by the flashing "poetry of the subject" that had bewildered others.

Moore pointed out his extraordinary richness of reference and skill in word arrangement; she focused, as did Seiffert, on his using adjectives like verbs and she called this effect a "triumph of explicit ambiguity." Moore then seized on the truly disturbing element of Stevens's work: his obsession with death and violence. She suggested this even in her title, where she drew on Shakespeare's use of "mouse"—"Death . . . mousing the flesh of men"—for the curious epithet with which she tagged him. Certainly her name also described the way he stealthily hunted for meaning's nourishment and toyed sadistically, it seemed, with his readers' attention. Yet there was, too, the underside hinted at by Shakespeare's lines, which she addressed without hesitation in her review:

> One resents the temper of certain of these poems. Mr. Stevens is never inadvertently crude; one is conscious, however, of a deliberate bearishness—

a shadow of acrimonious, unprovoked contumely. Despite the sweet-Clementine-will-you-be-mine nonchalance of the "Apostrophe to Vincentine," one feels oneself to be in danger of unearthing the ogre in "Last Looks at the Lilacs;" a pride of unserviceableness is suggested which makes it a macrocosm of cannibalism.

To make sure her readers would not miss the point, she closed with a sentence that again disturbingly evoked his savage, macabre aspect: "In the event of moonlight and a veil to be made gory, he would, one feels, be appropriate in this legitimately sensational act of a ferocious jungle animal."

Before coming to this conclusion, Moore planted some clues leading up to it. The clues placed Stevens in a particular environment which few could have properly recognized. This was the salon-studio of Walter Arensberg, where Stevens had spent the evenings of so many years. In that room was a dominating Rousseau, and Moore could easily see the parallels between it and the savagery of Stevens's hidden intent. In one sentence early in the review, Moore, tipping her readers off, explicitly compared the effect Stevens was trying to achieve with "Rousseau's paintings of banana leaves and alligators." It seemed more than fortuitous that two months later the *Dial* published Kenneth Burke's translation of a part of *Death in Venice*. Thomas Mann implicitly evoked Rousseau in describing Aschenbach's jungle hallucination, which was the prompt and signal for his impending self-destruction. Could Moore have been familiar with Burke's translation and so been associating Rousseau's tiger as drawn by Mann with the lion lying in her imagination as she composed her title-epithet:

It was the desire for travel, nothing more; although, to be sure, it had attacked him violently and was heightened to a passion, even to the point of an hallucination. His yearnings crystallized; his imagination, still in ferment from hours of work, actually pictured all the marvels and terrors of a manifold world which it was suddenly struggling to conceive. He saw a landscape, a tropical swampland under a heavy, murky sky, damp, luxuriant, and enormous, a kind of prehistoric wilderness of islands, bogs and arms of water, sluggish with mud; he saw, near him and in the distance, the hairy shafts of palms rising out of a rank lecherous thicket, out of places where the plant life was fat, swollen, and blossoming exorbitantly; he saw strangely misshapen trees sending their roots into the ground, into stagnant pools with greenish reflections; and here, between floating flowers which were milk-white and large as dishes, birds of a strange nature, high-shouldered, with crooked bills, were standing in the muck, and looking motionlessly to one side; between dense, knotted stalks of bamboo he saw the glint from the eyes of a crouching tiger—and he felt his heart knocking with fear and with puzzling desires. Then the image disappeared; and with a shake of his head Aschenbach resumed his walk along past the fences of the stone-masons' establishments.[12]

Moore understood the common intention linking Rousseau, Mann, and Stevens. A lush tropic with stagnant pools where new life bred was a perfect metaphor for the cultural situation. This imaginary landscape, with strongly sexual elements tinged always by decay or danger, represented a revised version of the Garden of Eden. It was a post-Darwinian paradise with monkeys and apes playing Adam and Eve, lions and tigers threatening the survival of the fittest, a disingenuously primitive world that replaced a 5,000-year-old myth with a new scientific view.

Moore heard Stevens's *Harmonium* describing this new world with all the threats it presented to old ideas of self, threats Freud had been making explicit over the previous twenty years. Stevens's world was full of these tensions. They had all to do with sexuality and death. With his leftover Christianity and his Victorian attitudes, part of him wanted to deny or hide sexuality, the clearest evidence of our animal nature. But another part wanted to celebrate it and simply move with the rhythms of things that could not be understood—the irrational element. His "relation" with the world in which he had been reared had to be "clipped," as he had shown in "The Comedian." *Harmonium* was the instrument on which he played the dirge for the death of the old order. Its homely, honky-tonk sound set the proper tone for this funeral—as specifically in "The Emperor of Ice-Cream"—which should have been a joyful occasion. But sensing ourselves as trivial is never easy. All this Stevens described, and Moore knew it. It was not surprising that most found it difficult or distasteful. Even for those who could come to terms with the death of the old order and welcome the new, there was still resistance against parodying mourning itself. The ponderous, mysterious, impenetrable, seeming high seriousness of Eliot's reaction or the angry declaiming of Pound was preferable to the comedian's complacent smile.

In her review Moore also indicated many of the sources from which Stevens had learned this attitude. She opened with an implicit comparison of Stevens's "achieved remoteness" to "Tu Muh's lyric criticism: 'Powerful is the pointing . . . and high is it hung on the spotless wall in the lofty hall of your mansion!'" The parallel drawn between the late T'Ang poet and Stevens was the first hint: Carefully consider the comedian's "cloak of China." She immediately moved on to an association to Honoré de Balzac: "The riot of gorgeousness in which Mr. Stevens' imagination takes refuge recalls Balzac's reputed attitude to money, to which he was indifferent unless he could have it 'in heaps or by the ton.'" Hint number two. Respectful as only a poet could be to the reader's delight in eventually discovering an echo or source, yet wanting to suggest the right direction, Moore properly but elliptically directed attention to *La Comédie Humaine* as another of Stevens's many models.

She was also careful along the way to specify Stevens's understanding of the weighty function of comedy, as he had learned of it from Bergson and Meredith. She noted that it was the result of being "disturbed by the intangible" that a "mind oppressed by the properties of the world" found relief in expertly "manipulating" it. She also observed that "one's humor is based on the most serious part of one's nature . . ." and that Stevens's "capacity for self-mockery . . . illustrated [his] disgust with mere vocativeness."

Nearing the end of her piece, she was even more direct about his Oriental influence: "In his positiveness, aplomb and verbal security, he has the mind and method of China." Moore was uncovering the model Stevens had set for himself. Whether or not he had openly articulated it to himself or to others at this point, by the time he gained full recognition years later, he had made it clear that what he desired most was that his work leave "an impression of something venerable, true and quiet" (*L* 742), like the impressions made by Oriental scrolls and poems. This was in spite of the disclaimers about the influence of Chinese or Japanese poetry on his work with which he later gently misled critics like Earl Miner, who got a little too precise about the provenance of individual poems like "Thirteen Ways of Looking at a Blackbird" (*L* 291 n.). The germ of interest in things Oriental that had begun during the poet's years at Harvard had developed into an integral part of his personality. As Stevens rightly recognized, personality was identical with style, so it was understandable that a reader as astute as Moore would isolate this important element.

Internalizing the Oriental attitude affected more than Stevens's poetic style. The most salient feature of the "mind and method of China" was that it focused on the minute particulars of experience. His imaginative immersion in the Eastern tradition allowed Stevens to transform the Puritan values with which he had been reared into a set of qualities that nurtured instead of starved his spirit. Industry, thrift, and sobriety became neutralized, collapsed, and metamorphosed into meticulous attention to detail, self-containment, quietness, which combined to produce the "angelic hilarity" he had idealized in his youth. The very same control and retentiveness that for the Puritans and their heirs, with their time-bound myth of progress, meant closure and deprivation, for the Orientals, with their sense of continuity in change, meant an openness to what surrounded them and a celebration of the fleeting. The ideas that in his Harvard years and later had still been only ideas, toys for his intellect, had now gathered the weight of emotional experience. Making this transition enabled Stevens to free himself finally from the Christian myth. It also prepared him for the years of spiritual quietude that lay ahead. All this Moore had implicitly recognized, yet, curiously, no reader following her would pick up these foreign clues. They did follow, however, some of the others closer to common experience.

Before closing, for example, she also noted a "sense of architectural diagram" that emerged from the poems, the "accomplishment in the use of reiteration," the "precise pattern." Each of these aspects developed in the hands of later readers into full critical analyses. Yet another clue, pointing to the parallelism between Stevens's use of words and rhythms and that of the biblical Hebrew poetry was something else that was later ignored. The very particular resonances of Stevens's spirit seemed to be detectable only to another poet, able to pinpoint the "true subject" beneath the "poetry of the subject" that he had gone to such trouble to fabricate. From the difference between her review and others Stevens realized that only another poetic sensibility could recognize his motive. This understanding contributed yet another reason he chose to keep silent until he had perfected a fluent speech that would be accessible to all who, he felt, were so badly in need of a new vulgate of experience. To them, as yet, he seemed a leftover aesthete, a dandy, not a "well-moused lion" but a lion unrecognizable beneath his sheep's clothing.

❧

For the present, then, Stevens devoted himself to things as they were. While McAlmon in France with William Carlos Williams wrote to thank him for *Harmonium* and to ask if he were "coming over" to circulate among the "Jewishly-minded, fashionable" people to whom his wife in her enthusiasm for the volume distributed copies—Havelock Ellis, Norman Douglas, Dorothy Richardson, André Gide, and others (*WAS* 1160 and 1161)—Stevens prepared himself for a new phase of domesticity. As he playfully wrote to Williams on his return from his European tour and his "visits to the pope, McAlmon and so on," his own job since Holly's birth was "to keep the fireplace burning and the music-box churning and the wheels of the baby's chariot turning and that sort of thing" (*L* 246). The easy transfer Stevens made, evidenced here, in applying his poetic gift to describing his new occupations indicates that he was happy about the change his child had brought. This was borne out by earlier and later accounts to various others in letters of how utterly enchanting his daughter was, how good-tempered, inquisitive, and responsive.

Stevens was not only a proud papa but an accommodating one. He didn't mind removing himself to the attic with his books; he would even sleep there rather than complain about the inconvenience of being awakened at feeding times. He would take on getting the laundry done—finding laundresses in town—and getting other help. And in recompense for his well-meaning adaptability, he saw no reason why he should not reward himself, tend to his own needs as well. A trip to his beloved Florida would be just the thing. He planned to leave in mid-January. Elsie and Holly, after all, were both in "corking condition" (*L* 243), and there were Elsie's mother and sister to be called on if necessary, in addition to the domestic help. In spite of his announcements to friends and editors about giving up literature for a while, the voice of the Muse whispered like a faraway siren. Perhaps even just a brief sojourn in Florida's "venereal soil" would breed new revelations of the beauty tinged with evil that characterized his work, as Lucy Calhoun, Harriet Monroe's sister (one of those to whom he had sent *Harmonium* in return for her kindness in sending him objects from China where she had been living), noted in her letter of thanks to him (May 24, 1924). In the presence of the child who smiled at him "like an angel," he could not possibly return the "gargoyle grin" that was his habit with his Muse. As he commented to Monroe, Holly and her heavenly antics were "a terrible blow to poor literature," though he added that there was "the radio to blame too" (*L* 244).

This new mechanical distraction opened up the world in a way that was as fascinating and as yet unknown as the world he imagined the infant perceiving from what he observed of her reactions. Responding to both of them, Stevens entered realms he could not leave since there was no fixity to the facts they presented. There was no way to stop the multiplication of propositions he could pose to explain what he heard from both the baby and the machine. He could not voyage into a poem without an anchorage of thought to which he could return, and for a while there was nothing to set his simmering, hissing mind to rest. Though he tried, as he related to Williams, in retiring to his attic, "to run through a book now and then, for, as the Chinese [said], two or three days without study and life [lost] its savor," most often he would fall asleep in the attempt, spent from the careful attention he was giving to the constantly changing and demanding worlds created by infant and radio. This was added to the attention he continued to give his work at the company. While before Holly he could relax on leaving the office and return to the unconscious order that habits of home life provided, now things required energetic vigilance. In addition, the news of the world with which the radio punctuated days and evenings meant he was as aware of the constant changing outside as well as inside his domain. Meeting these major shifts in key and tempo at forty-five was taxing. That lights went out every night at nine—because of the baby, as he wrote to Monroe in November 1925—was a relief. The pressures of reality were too great. "At present there are no poems, no reviews," he noted to Marianne Moore, who had written to ask that he review Williams's latest volume (*L* 246).

But among the books he did manage to stay awake to read was a slender volume he had picked up on one of his days in New York at the beginning of the year. In one of his favorite haunts, the Holliday Bookstore at 10 West Forty-seventh Street, after he had already perused the shelves of Scribner's and Gotham, both a stone's throw away, Stevens found a title that intrigued him, *Seducers in Ecuador* by Vita Sackville-West. "What could that be about?" Stevens must have wondered. It had, after all, a semblance to things he had in mind: "O Florida, Venereal Soil," and the Maya sonneteers he imagined in Yucatán. Seduced himself, wanting on this cold winter day at least the warmth of another's conjured tropical climate, he gently pulled the book from the shelf and began nosing into it. It was short enough to finish as he rode back through Connecticut in the coach car, sitting comfortably while icicles formed on the glass of the windows and transformed the passing landscape into abstractly refracting patterns, like early "barbaric" glass or like the paintings of Jacques Villon he so much liked. What a wonderful trip lay ahead!

Reading a page here and there decided it. Though the title prepared him for a voyage to South America, the pages he read set him afloat in the Mediterranean and left him in Egypt. Here was something close to his own heart, a subject belied by its title. Feeling a kinship already, he bought it and, unusually, did something he had stopped doing for a while: He inscribed his name, "New York," and the date, "1/9/25," in pencil on the flyleaf. Fitting it neatly into his pocket (it was slim enough for that), he went back out into the brisk city air. Off to the train and back home.

Seducers in Ecuador parodied both murder mysteries and the archaeological romances that were becoming increasingly popular during the century's beginning decades. The story's stated purpose was "to demonstrate the dangers of becoming involved in the lives of others without having previously tested the harmlessness of those others, and the dangers above all of constructing in middle-age a new habit liable to release those lions of folly which prowl about our depths and which it is the duty of every citizen to keep securely caged."[13] Here, once more, was the Rousseauean lion, but about to be tamed. Stevens must have been amused that there was another who confronted the problems of middle age, like him, now, with a humorous eye.

He continued, smiling silently at meeting the protagonist, Mr. Lomax, who found himself in the curious position of joining a yachting party of individuals whom he had just met. It was April, and they would sail from Southampton to Alexandria. The yacht's owner, Mr. Bellamy, wanted one more on board and so invited Lomax. Lomax accepted, delighted by the prospect of adventure. He was even more delighted by a new acquisition, a necessary addition for the blinding light of the Mediterranean sun and Egypt—a pair of blue glasses:

> . . . under the new influence of his spectacles he was living in a condition of ecstasy—a breathless condition, in which he was hurried along by his instincts, and precipitated into compromising himself before he had had time to remove his spectacles and consult his reason. Indeed, with a rapidity which he was never quite able to understand, he found himself in such a position that he no longer dared to remove his spectacles at all; he could not face a return to the daylight mood; realism was no longer for him. And the spectacles, having once made him their slave, served him well. They altered the world in the most extraordinary way. The general light was green instead of yellow, the sky and the desert both turned green, reds became purple, greens were almost black. It produced an effect of stillness, everything seemed muffled. The noises of the world lost their significance. Everything became at once intensified and remote. Lomax found it decidedly more interesting than the sights of Egypt. The sights of Egypt were a fact, having a material reality, but here was a phenomenon that presented life under a new aspect. Lomax knew well enough that to present life under a new aspect is the beginning and probably the end of genius; it is therefore no wonder that his discovery produced in him so profound and sensational an excitement. His companions thought him silent. . . . (pp. 10–11)

In the course of the journey Mr. Bellamy persuaded Lomax, who gave the impression, because of the serenity he took on when wearing the spectacles, of being a man to be depended upon in all circumstances, to do two things. The first was to marry one Miss Whitaker, another of the passengers aboard the

Nereid. She was, it seemed, pregnant with the child of a man who had seduced her in Ecuador. Lomax would be performing an act of chivalry to protect her honor. The second was that he, Lomax, should kill Bellamy, who, as he related to Lomax, was dying of a mortal disease. Lomax and he would arrange his papers and will so that Lomax would inherit his fortune. Lomax would then decide to use the fortune in some way that would be of good to humanity. Lomax agreed.

In spite of the requests of his fellow passengers that he remove the spectacles, Lomax kept them on continuously. He responded to the requests that he take them off by saying that he "should go mad" if he did, that "if he took them off, Miss Whitaker would immediately become intolerable." He said he had to keep "his common sense . . . divinely in abeyance" to ensure that indeed, she would "snare" her protector according to the plan Bellamy had arranged. She, in turn, maintained her stories, which "were marvellously coming true. Indeed, to her, they were always true; what else was worth while? But that the truth of fact should corroborate the truth of imagination!" (p. 17). The narrator added: "It did not occur to her that the truth was as likely to increase his attention as any fiction. She was not alone in this; for who stands back to perceive the pattern made by their own lives?" (p. 19). Lomax "reasoned" to himself that there could be no "better reason than that one had found a lonely woman in tears, and had looked on her through colored glasses" (p. 18). The first step was completed. They went from Alexandria to Cairo by train, were married, and then returned to Alexandria to sail back to England.

Sailing back, Lomax thought of the woman he had loved in England who had married another. Since she had, he thought, his marriage to Miss Whitaker was no problem. That he had done a good deed was rather a consolation. Finding himself thinking about home, however, he vaguely wondered when they would get "there" but then dismissed it since he did not know where "there" was. Instead, "he was content to hammock himself passively in the amplitude of enveloping time." Bellamy was taking them; Lomax and all the others acquiesced in all his decisions. Their only way of knowing where they were and what they saw was what he said. He named the isle they passed "Illyria," and they agreed to see it as Illyria.

In this state, at sea, Lomax mused, and the narrator blended her voice with his to elaborate the story's theme in a central passage:

> What of it anyway? There were quite a number of other communities in the world besides this little community, microscopic on the Mediterranean. Lomax saw the blue as it was not, the others saw or thought they saw the blue as it was, but unless and until our means of communication become more subtle than they at present are, we cannot even be sure that our eyes see colours alike. How, then, should we know one another? . . . The lives of friends touch here and there. . . , and the gap over the interval is never

> bridged, knowledge being but a splintered mirror which shall never gather to a smooth and even surface. (p. 7)

The voyage ended, and the killing of Bellamy was done once all had arrived safely at his home in England. The police came to investigate, and Lomax would tell things as they were—the truth—in spite of the attempt of Artivale, a scientist, another of the passengers, who sympathized with Lomax and wanted to persuade him that he should try to get away. At his last urging, as the police knocked, Lomax responded: "It's only a question of sooner or later . . . for everybody, you know; not only for me. If they let me keep the spectacles I don't mind. With them, I don't see things as they are. Or perhaps I do. It doesn't make much difference which. If you won't go and open the door, I shall go and open it myself" (p. 62). The inevitable, of course, occurred:

> They took Lomax away in a cab. He was not allowed to keep his spectacles. . . .
>
> It was only during the course of the trial that Lomax discovered how pitiable a weapon was truth. . . . Lomax in the days when he might meet fact with fantasy had been a contented man; now, when he tried to meet with fact the fantastical world which so suddenly and utterly swamped him, was a man confounded, a man floundering for a foothold. He had lost his spectacles. He had lost his attitude towards life. . . . If earth had turned to heaven and heaven to earth a greater chasm could not have resulted in his mind.
>
> The public see me in the dock; they do not see me in my cell. Let me look at the walls; they are white, not clouded with a nameless colour, as once they would have been! But I must remember: this is a prison cell. I have no means of turning it into anything else. I am a prisoner on trial for my life. That's fact. A plain man, suffering the consequences for the actions of a creature enchanted, now disappeared. The white walls are fact. Geometry is a fact,—or so they say,—but didn't someone suggest that in another planetary system the laws of geometry might be reversed? This cell is geometrical; square floor, square ceiling, square walls, square window intersected by bars. Geometrical shadows, Euclidean angles, white light. Did I or did I not do this, that, and the other? I did, but . . . No buts. Facts are facts. Yes or no. Geometrical questions require geometrical answers. If A be equal to B, then C . . . But either I am mad, or they are mad, or the King's English no longer means what it used to mean. (pp. 62–64)

At peace with himself throughout the trial because "he knew that his intentions had been honourable" (p. 68), Lomax maintained himself even when the evidence, piece by piece, revealed that things as they were were not as they were when he wore his blue glasses. The doctor's report showed that Bellamy had had no mortal disease and, more, that Miss Whitaker not only was not with child but was still a virgin. ("Things as they are/ Are changed upon the blue guitar.") Lomax realized that:

> . . . the [blue] spectacles were really responsible. . . . And now that he was deprived of [them]—was become again that ordinary man, Arthur Lomax getting through existence with only the information of that fantastic interlude, as though it concerned another man, the information rather than the memory, since it existed now for him in words and not in sensation,—now that he was returned to his pre-spectacle days, he could survey his story with cold hard sense and see that it could bear no relation to a world of fact. It was a mistake, to mix one's manner. (pp. 71–72)

Because he saw that in the end only cold facts mattered, his last comfort was that Artivale would inherit the fortune he had inherited from Bellamy. "Science would have the money; and science was a fact, surely incapable of caricature; absolute as mathematics was absolute. He had had enough of living in a world where truth was falsehood and falsehood truth."

But:

> Shortly after Lomax had been hanged, Bellamy's nearest relations, two maiden ladies who lived at Hampstead and interested themselves in the conversion of the heathen, entered a plea that Bellamy's will had been composed under the undue influence of Arthur Lomax. The case was easily proved, and it was understood that the bulk of the fortune would be placed by the next-of-kin as conscience money at the disposal of His Majesty's Treasury. (pp. 73–74)

Stevens closed the book on this last paragraph, sat back, and mused on the charmingly conjured but deeply disturbing aspects presented to his mind by Sackville-West's allegory: Bellamy = *bel ami* = God; Arthur Lomax, *lo*west and *max*imum of men, the ordinary man who wanted to be "man number one," seemingly enabled to fulfill his desire of becoming extraordinary by the blue spectacles; Lomax and the others, like those of Stevens's generation, at middle age finding themselves at sea in a world wholly changed, a Lewis Carroll world where the language of the past, "the King's English," no longer served to describe things as they were. In this world only the scientists, who had suggested that in other planetary systems different geometries obtained, were to be entrusted with the hope of providing something true for the future. Yet how could there now be any one thing true? The situation described the experience Stevens and his generation lived, but how disarmingly their condition had been presented! How much more effective, Stevens thought, to depict things as they were in the ridiculous way they had been drawn here. The beautiful explosion of reality during the trial when no reality could be fixed! Had Lomax imagined it all in the madness of his blue-spectacled eyes, or had the officials of the state persuaded the doctor and witnesses to give false evidence so that things as they were would not be disturbed?

Here was a comic prefiguring of the existential position described so weightily fifteen to twenty years later by Camus and Sartre. Laughing at it, with it, at himself in the same confusion of reality experienced by Lomax, Stevens let the story's elements sink into the reservoir of his being, as all the other elements of things that touched him. Ten years later, when he composed himself once more through devotion to a long poem, they reemerged the same yet changed. The images and phrases that moved him now "The Man with the Blue Guitar" repeated.

Like Lomax's, the guitarist's "day was green" (*CP* 165), seen through the blue of imagination. In the poem, too, a murder was committed that would make the speaker "man number one": "To drive the dagger in his heart,// To lay his brain upon the board" (*CP* 166), to kill the idea of God by discovering the workings of his brain—the intricate pattern of nature that science promised to reveal. Even the musings of "The Man with the Blue Guitar" paralleled those of Lomax as he contemplated the truth of his situation:

> Things as they are have been destroyed.
> Have I? Am I a man that is dead
>
> At a table on which the food is cold?
> Is my thought a memory, not alive?
> (*CP* 173)

Like the plot of Lomax's story, the poem's was played as "a duet/ With the undertaker" (*CP* 177)—it was an attempt to understand the nature of doing good, or of doing anything at all, in the face of inevitable death after which no heaven waits. The speaker's perception of what made things as they were was also like that of Lomax:

> And things are as I think they are
> And say they are on the blue guitar
> (*CP* 180)

And like Lomax, confronting finally the bare white of his prison walls—as later Meursault in *The Stranger* would confront the "benign indifference of the universe"—"The Man with the Blue Guitar" came to the same end:

> Throw away the lights, the definitions,
> And say of what you see in the dark
>
> That it is this or that it is that,
> But do not use the rotted names.
> (*CP* 183)

It would take Stevens ten years to arrive at this. During this time he came to know the well-intentioned part of Lomax much more intimately. The story he read now, to escape if only for a short while from his own pressing concern with things as they were, was transformed by his experience to resonate with the power of sound, part of the sensation Lomax felt with his glasses, but that was markedly absent from Sackville-West's insightful and wry, yet nonetheless cool and flat, presentation. Stevens recognized the importance of the themes she treated but realized, too, that the slim little volume that had given him an hour's pleasure would not survive in "the amplitude of enveloping time." For that, something that could be played on and with time's own rhythms was needed. The instincts Lomax felt wearing his blue spectacles had to be indulged in the very words used to describe the situation which he, like Stevens, experienced, the situation of all voyaging in the century's uncertain seas. Stevens's sympathy with Lomax, with all those he imagined spiritually at sea was, during the period when he read this story, deepened by his contact with those in his very real everyday world.

Under the extreme demands of this time and with his new accepting attitude, Stevens became increasingly responsive to others. The young, hispid misanthrope transformed himself into a patient, sympathetic helpmeet and friend, even to those beyond his family circle. This is clear, for example, from the evidence of a note of thanks sent to him by Archibald MacLeish on October 20, 1925, in which the other poet expressed that it meant a great deal to him that Stevens had listened to his outpouring for an hour a few days earlier. MacLeish felt that it must have been a "waste of time" for Stevens and that he had performed an act of "charity." He repaid his gratitude by offering to send the "Giant" his favorite "patisseries, candy or confections" from Paris, for which he was headed. He was also having a copy of his last book sent; he added, in closing, "Never mention it." The loving attention Stevens was now extending to people, rather than to the places and things of his imagination, was demanding and wearing, however.[14] In light of this, his hopes of returning to Florida for what the businessman in him called "R&R" was understandable. The freshening in the weather of his life that Holly brought, like the south wind to which he compared her (*L* 245)—as he had once compared Elsie—had made a tremendous difference in everything, even greater than the "tremendous difference" Harvard had made years earlier. To love this daughter with curls was truly a liberal education.

Whether Stevens did transport himself to the summer of Florida that winter of 1924–1925 as he had wanted to is uncertain, but he did manage to go the following winter. This trip lasted several weeks and was unusual for Stevens in that the entire time was spent cruising on a yacht. As he related to Harriet Monroe on his return, they "went from Miami to Key West, up the Gulf to Indian Key and to Everglades on the West Coast (including the Ten Thousand Islands, which [were] inaccessible except by yacht) then by way of Cape Sable to Long Key and back to Miami." He went on to say: "It was a glorious trip, which so far as [he] was concerned, could have gone on for several months without protest" (*L* 247). Here, too, a tremendous difference from the past was evident. Stevens had come a long way from the time he crouched below in the cabin to protect his clothes while out cruising on Long Island Sound years before. His easy adaptability to the new situations facing him now attested to how truly poetry could teach "how to live, what to do." These revolutions in being had come about not only under the pressure of facts to be faced—another might easily have reacted quite differently—but also because of what he had learned in composing himself through his poems, most explicitly as he had in "The Comedian as the Letter C." It was no accident that the attitude he described Crispin's taking on in the last two, late-added sections—"A Nice Shady Home" and "And Daughters with Curls"—was the same one he now exhibited, even if there was only one real daughter. It was as though in these sections he had prophetically fleshed out his wishes and dreams so that when they became a reality, he was more than ready. Poetry was indeed "a health," a "completion of life." Poetry had to function this way if what he believed about words being the only possible providers of truth in this uncertain world were to prove itself true. Not to have acted the way he envisioned his touchingly comic hero acted would have been to betray the "Great Work" and himself.

In the same note to Monroe in which he described the watery itinerary, which must have made him feel that he had truly become Crispin, nosing into pristine jungles under sail, he thanked her for the gift she had sent to Holly for Christmas. (Miss Monroe was particularly attentive to the Stevenses' new addition. She sent her a silver spoon for her first Christmas and now this second Christmas gift. She obviously felt closely tied, keeping the announcement of Holly's birth until her death, when it was returned to Stevens with a note from Anne Monroe.) The Stevenses reciprocated, making a special point of arranging a time when Miss Monroe could see the child on one of her trips east when Holly was only five months old. Now, in describing Holly's reaction to the gift, Stevens revealed how lovingly observant a father he was: "She was most curious about it for she has a strange eye for detail. If you show her a bush, she does not see it but will see a bird in it. If you show her a picture her finger goes straight to some particularity."

As Stevens followed the development of her perception, he tenderly identified with his daughter, again as he had once done with Elsie: Holly's eyes, like his, noticed the minutest aspects of things. At the same time he was implicitly reconstructing the development of his own perception. For a poet this was especially valuable. By the time he began writing poems again, it was clear that these exercises in imaginatively extending his consciousness into that of another—had held tremendous importance. The order of *Ideas of Order,* the next volume he was to publish, was not an intellectually applied one, not an artificial structuring designed to force readers to submit to it, as the order of *Harmonium* had been. It reflected, rather, his own submission to orders outside himself and mirrored his yielding to things as they were. For the first time he was unafraid and undefended against the "pathos" of reality. Eventually he would be able to recognize that even a violent disorder was an order, something that would declare its pattern if only attended to long and carefully enough.

The disorders to which Stevens submitted himself during this period were of many different kinds. One of the things he learned was complementary: that a great order was a disorder. His retreat into the attic, for example, did not mean that he found himself in a world undisturbed except for his own movements. Elsie's or the housekeeper's periodic cleaning expeditions into his lair resulted in the rearrangement of his papers, journals, and books; his own order was upset. This continued, and although it later sometimes caused him difficulty, he accepted what another might have railed against as simply part of the necessary ordering activity of Elsie's being. In the late 1930s Hi Simons, one of his longtime readers, wanted Stevens's help in compiling a bibliography. He needed to know in which issues of what journals Stevens's work had appeared. The poet put off gathering the information for a while because it depended on his going up into the attic (by that time at a different, his last, residence, at 118 Westerly Terrace), where his books and journals were misplaced each time cleaning was done. It was a difficult chore to go through randomly grouped items. Finally, after repeated requests from Simons, he did go up, found the material, and sent him both the information and the journals themselves, noting that he wanted them to be kept and well taken care of.

Another disorder Stevens learned to observe with equanimity was the world's. Once jostled this way and that by political and social changes (though not admitting it openly), stirred sometimes even to falling into one of the typical patterns of blaming the newest outsiders' infiltration for the latest ills or disturbances, he now looked at the world with the comedian's eye and saw the rest of the actors in reality, like himself, "merest minuscules in the gale." They were beings who elicited compassion and laughter rather than judgment and anger. He had abandoned the Christian myth and could now fully accept, as he was experiencing in himself, that human nature, and so the fate of society, were plastic, malleable. Both were changeable, not God-given, predetermined; it was neither hubristic nor sacrilegious to question or alter these forms. But only the comic attitude, as Bergson had carefully pointed out, could effect change without violence. Having persistently applied this attitude to his own being and having seen how he had changed, Stevens could now, with authority, extend it to others. In middle age he took the helm, like Crispin. He had voyaged into the sea of his unconscious, made up of all past voices and events that had shaped him, and he had steered his way safely to a new shore. It was naïvely, yet truly, an illustration of Freud's analytical purpose: Where id was, there ego shall be. Stevens had made his ego, an "I" that could "see-C," choose and shape, clip relations that did not serve, and fashion others.

Thus during his winter 1925–1926 visit to Florida, on seeing the place he once thought ideal for "exotic hermits now a jamboree of hoodlums," instead of mourning or uttering one of the misanthropic statements he would have years before, he merely expressed that things perhaps would change when the "boom [was] over." If not, there would still be "temples [to be] found in Tobago or in the mountains of Venezuela" (*L* 247). Similarly, in the more circumscribed literary world in which he now had a place, if he couldn't at present write, he did not despair or fear that he might never write again. He reacted with humorous responses to the many who wrote asking him for contributions. A good example is this reply to Louis Untermeyer's soliciting something for his yearly collection of the newest poetry:

November 8, 1926

DEAR MR. UNTERMEYER,

It doesn't in the least look as though I should have anything for your annual this year. At the present time all my attention is devoted to reducing, getting the week's washing done (not by me but by one of the ever-flitting laundresses of the town) etc.

I see a vast amount of nature, my source of supply, but I am obliged to see it at the rate of about six miles an hour, and not even a honey bee could do much business at that gait.

Yours very truly,
WALLACE STEVENS
(*L* 247)

As the twenties began to roar both in New York, less than 200 miles away, and more loudly in the Continental cafés where his expatriate contemporaries gathered, Stevens tended his garden and his nice, shady home. He tended himself as well. There was one disorder that had to be ordered. His mentioning to Untermeyer that he had to reduce was part of this. Two months earlier, apparently just before or during another trip to Florida in September on business (from the evidence of photos taken in Miami just before the 1926 hurricane, it seems that Elsie, the photographer in the family, made this trip with her husband), Stevens began experiencing blurring of vision. This frightened him both for himself and for the two who depended so much on him. There was an added irony in this. Just as he had begun to see how much of what he had seen he had never really seen at all (he could even see Elsie's difficulties and be accepting instead of angry), he feared that he might not continue to see well or, worse, continue to be. He was now well "past meridian" and, as he knew, had put "that monster, [his] body," through more than its share of punishment. He had already been warned years earlier that he might not live past forty (*L* 398). Having weathered that storm, he understood that he had to take serious precautions.

Early in October, then, back home, he consulted a Dr. Mittendorf, an optometrist in New York, who referred him to a Dr. Herrick, an internist who reported back to Mittendorf. The fact that he did not consult the eye doctor until this time, when he had first been disturbed by his vision problem early in September, suggests that he must have been away when the blurring began because it was not his habit to procrastinate. (Stevens answered even the least important bit of mail usually no later than the next day.)

Dr. William Herrick, one of the best "diagnosticians"—as Stevens described him when later recommending him to his friend Henry Church—was a descendant of Thomas Hooker, the Puritan clergyman who was the chief founder of Hartford, Connecticut. Stevens was impressed with his large and austere old New England bearing; accordingly, he took his counsel very seriously. As Herrick reported back to Mittendorf, Stevens's condition resulted from a combination of causes. He began by noting that there had been a history of "former smoking and of the occasional use of alcohol," and that "Mr. Stevens [had] traveled much and exercised little." He went on to observe that the poet had become "particularly sluggish in the last two or three years" and had "not restrained himself at the table." He had also "eaten much salt." Since his marriage Stevens had abandoned completely even his intermittent attempts at "clean living." Herrick related the details of Stevens's family health history that had also played their parts in contributing to his present state. He had had malaria as a boy and had a chronic discharge from his left ear. He suffered as well from nycturia (excessive urination as an adult). To complete the picture, most recently there had been an additional weight gain.

His diagnosis contained both expected and unexpected facts. First, and most obviously, Mr. Stevens was overweight at 229 pounds. Next, he was an "acromegalic type"—that is, he suffered from a condition in which the thorax, head, and extremities continue to grow long after normal development has stopped. The "Giant" Stevens had described and signed himself so often in seeming lightness was real. The feelings of being "grotesque" he had expressed, usually in poems, corresponded to something objectively perceptible, not just to some vague, subjectively distorted sense of himself. It is difficult to imagine precisely how Stevens felt on learning this. On the one hand, there was probably a kind of relief coming from the external confirmation of a view of himself that he had long had—a version of "So then I'm not crazy. I really am not like everyone else." On the other hand, it had to have been painful to accept that indeed, he was some sort of freak. Taking on his various comedic, clowning disguises obeyed some innately sensed knowledge of himself; they were not simply facilely adopted poses. In some way he did belong in a circus or traveling show. His reticence and embarrassment about his body were justified.

That Stevens did take this diagnosis deeply into himself is confirmed by the fact that nearly twenty years later, in the midst of his genealogical researches, he observed to his niece Jane MacFarland (daughter of his sister Elizabeth), who suffered from another version of hypertrophy, that it was probably from his great-grandfather, Garrett Barcalow, that they had inherited their thyroid ailments. There was some comfort at least in believing that his condition was something belonging to his family, not to him alone.[15] In the same letter he also tenderly observed a more positive aspect. Referring to the photo of Garrett Barcalow, he noted that his own eyes were like his. The desire to belong, to find and make a place for himself in the family with whom he shared no eponymous ties, in spite of his already having a secure place in the American pantheon of "man-poets," was still with him in 1944.

Herrick's report indicated additional signs of abuse and atrophy. There were sclerotic changes in the retinal vessels as a result of a series of hemorrhages. There were also slight atrophy of the heart, very high blood pressure, moderate hypoglycemia, and a trace of sugar indicating mild diabetes. On the positive side, there was no edema, and his lungs were fair. Summing up, Herrick listed the main problems to be attended to as "essential hypertension," a pituitary disturbance, and the diabetic condition. He recommended immediate weight loss (aided by a thyroid extract), taking in more water to help restore the carbohydrate and salt balance, and regular exercise, gradually increasing in exertion over a period of time.

Stevens was nothing if not a good patient. By the end of December, when he again visited Dr. Herrick, he had made a "great improvement over October." He was on normal ground as far as the blood and urine samples showed, though the salt content in his system had not yet been reduced to normal levels. The doctor advised him to continue being careful but was, in general, encouraging. Heartened by the result of his checkup, Stevens found himself in good humor the next day when he wrote to Marianne Moore. She had sent him a note requesting that he write the announcement of the *Dial* award for 1926 to William Carlos Williams. He responded that he simply didn't have the time but expressed his warm and enthusiastic "salutations to Carlos the Fortunate." In an unusual burst of effusiveness, he closed with *"I wish I had an inscribed copy of your poems"* (*L* 248). Carried away by his responsiveness to Williams's success and his appreciation of her work, he forgot to add the answer to the other request she had made in the same letter for some of his poems for the upcoming *Dial* issue. Five days later he caught up with himself in Florida, where he found himself for the third time in 1926. He expressed his thanks for her interest but regretted he had nothing at the moment, though he hoped "sooner or later to be able to submit something" (*L* 248).

He stayed in Florida for about two weeks, returning a few days before Christmas to Hartford, where he and Elsie carefully prepared for Holly's third winter holiday season. Things seemed to be going along better than they ever had. The ups and downs of his spirit and habits, which had contributed a large part to the strain his body evidenced, he had managed to translate into the simple movement of going up and down between North and South. He had been maintaining a steady course now for a while. Earlier, whenever he had begun to adjust his spirit, using his reasoned will to act differently, he had compensated for the downward movement he no longer indulged with others by depressing his body, making it "sluggish" with far too much food. Now he was addressing this, too. His personality had never been stronger. He was taking himself in tow, truly becoming the master of his being. He became his own craft. And as he ordered himself, the ideas of order that shaped his next volume were forming without his directing attention any longer to "being a poet."

This is clear in a note he wrote to Williams on January 15, 1927, where poetic elements burst spontaneously onto the page in the spirit of congratulation that guided his words. He playfully headed his missive "Hartford-le-Glacé." Just beneath he placed a long line between the numerals indicating the date, lines like those that ice skates would make across the frozen pond in Elizabeth Park, where his daughter later delighted in watching his large frame glide along smoothly. Then he went on:

> DEAR WILLIAMS:
>
> Alas, that I could not have celebrated the awarding of the award with you before it was all gone! The *Dial* gives its foster-children veritable fortunes. Your townsmen must whisper about you and, as you pass the girls, they surely nudge each other and say "The golden boy!" That is the award in terms of life. Anyhow, though I'm a little late about it, let me express the pleasure I felt when I heard of this. Mon Doo, why is there not a daily Dial [not italicized this time in Stevens's text], or a more liberal Pope or something to help you keep that wolf away while you put up your pungent preserves? To thee all things tend, quill-Williams. Congratulations.
>
> Always yours,
> WALLACE STEVENS
> (*L* 249)

The wordplay here was the comedian's, and it came from the deepest springs of his generosity. He ignored the fact that he was not writing; his concern was wholly with his friend. He wished that Williams would be the one free of the pressures of the everyday world so to be able to give himself completely to the Muse. This was far more than cordiality. It was genuine, heartfelt joy for the good fortune of another, and experiencing it made him feel the fullness of his own being. With the birth of his child Stevens had learned how to love, and it seemed that as she grew, so did his capacity for this most necessary of human emotions.

As his spirit expanded, his fortune did. He was slowly becoming more prosperous, fulfilling the need planted in him by his father and the tradition that made American soil rich. He began to be able to afford the things he wanted. His first indulgence was in finely printed and rare books. He ordered numerous catalogs from presses and dealers and began placing orders. Next, he looked for a place in the South more exotic than Florida, a new, foreign, and exciting locale, moreover, one where he could comfortably take Elsie and Holly with him. Perhaps from a telegram Elsie had sent him on his most recent trip to Florida in May 1927, he had realized that too many absences from home were beginning to bother Holly—if not Elsie: ". . . GLAD FOR YOUR WIRE IT MUST BE VERY PLEASANT THERE ALL WELL BUT ABLE TO

HAVE WOMAN FOR HOUSE CLEANING ONLY A HALF DAY ALL WEEK HOLLY MISSES YOU THIS TIME AND AT SUPPER TONIGHT SHE CHOSE A COOKIE FOR YOU COULDN'T UNDERSTAND WHY YOU DO NOT COME HOME LOVE E[LSIE]. V[IOLA].

In August, then, Stevens inquired about a house in Tobago, British West Indies. Though they did not go—for whatever reason, whether because the expense was still beyond his reach or because of his work schedule or because Elsie did not want to risk the possible dangers to health for her child in such an exotic landscape (Elsie was an overprotective mother)—the impulse to attend to his family was there, and this impulse gave rhythm to life.

Punctuating the regularity of its beats were more and more calls for Stevens to sound his spirit once more. In mid-August William Carlos Williams wrote, enclosing a card from Ezra Pound, who now seemed receptive to Stevens's voice. Williams strongly urged Stevens to send Pound "whatever verses [he could] bring [him]self to part with. Do this for Jesus' sake" (August 17, 1927), he exclaimed. Stevens responded with an account of his typical days:

> But believe me signor, I'm as busy as the proud Mussolini himself. I rise at day-break, shower, etc; at six I start to exercise; at seven I massage and bathe; at eight I dabble with a therapeutic breakfast; from eight-thirty to nine-thirty I walk down-town; work all day; go to bed at nine. How should I write poetry, think it, feel it. [*sic* punctuation] Mon Dieu, I am happy if I can find time to read a few lines, yours, Pound's, anybody's. I am humble before Pound's request. But the above is the above.[16]

At about the same time Marianne Moore wrote again, asking for a contribution. Stevens responded that he was sorry, that in spite of the immense pleasure the request gave him, there had been "a fever of work" and that "the extreme irregularity of [his] life [made] poetry out of the question for the present except for momentary violences." He assured her, however, that "when things [grew] quieter and [he had] time to do what [he wanted] to do," he would "try to submit something" (*L* 249). And in late September he received a copy of yet another volume in which he was anthologized: L. W. Payne's *Later American Writers: Part Two of Selections from American Literature* (*L* 249). One thing was certain for Stevens now: He was not forgotten. More, he was recognized.

Poetry was, for the present, out of the question because of the "extreme irregularity of [his] life." It seemed that only when his days and nights followed a predictable rhythm, like the movements of the earth in its rotation and orbit that accounted for the repetitions of light, darkness, and the seasons, could the poet view the world around him as if he were himself one of the heavenly orbs. The unpredictability of things now, which created a climate of constant storms that required full concentration, reduced him to an all too human condition. But even in this, he rose above, became captain of the imagined craft on which he carried the precious cargo of wife and child. In this, he became more than Crispin—"merest minuscule in the gales" (*CP* 29). He became "Capitán profundo" (*CP* 102). He became a figure who made his own order like the character he created in one of the poems he composed as the seas of his life stilled enough for him to begin writing again. It is important to keep in mind that it was during this turbulent time that Stevens learned to give his full attention to the facts of the quotidian. Its demands, as well as the insights he had gained in playing through the situations of his spiritual autobiography, "The Comedian as the Letter C," humanized him. After this he returned to a life of order and regularity but with a new, plain sense of things as they were and of himself as he was. He had "come down," as he had realized he had to years before while still at Harvard when he had first begun to get a sense of how distant he kept himself from the "affairs of people and places."

But even in the irregularity of his life, as he related to Miss Moore, there were "momentary violences," eruptions of feeling or perception he could not express except in lines that he would someday stitch together in more rhapsodies of rhythms and images. Occasionally assaulted by emotions he could not avoid—"Like jades affecting the sequestered bride" (*CP* 34)—he noted lines on scraps of paper. Later he transcribed these, usually in pencil, into odd, leftover examination book types of folios.[17] There he captured and kept them for future training. What prompted these outbursts can only be guessed at: perhaps flares of anger at Elsie; perhaps fears about his health, the child's, Elsie's, the future. Perhaps his insights into the beauty and fragility of human life grew out of watching his child develop greater consciousness each day, protected from the innumerable possible dangers in the world around her only by a delicately thin envelope of skin. A perception of this sort was enough to pierce him to the point of tears. His momentary violences were his way of mastering them. They would not reduce him; he would conquer them, transform them into verses of his sacrament of praise.

❧

Before the end of 1927 Stevens again visited Dr. Herrick. The physician's report showed that though Stevens's domestic life was irregular, he had, in spite of this and the "momentary violences," been so regular in his regimen of restoring his health that he had begun to move toward the opposite extreme of the condition that the doctor had first observed. The salt, sugar, and albumen levels of his blood and urine were satisfactory, but he had become slightly anemic, and he had lost so much weight that the doctor advised him to relax his diet and gain about five pounds. His co-workers at the insurance company noted that he had become irritable and more impatient because of his weight loss; his suits seemed to hang on his huge frame.[18] Dr. Herrick closed his letter noting that Mr. Stevens was "to be congratulated upon the very satisfactory results in the control of the tendency towards diabetes and high blood pressure which [he] had" (December 15, 1927). After this report Stevens felt renewed and soon relaxed more than his diet. His return to his old habits must have pleased his business associates. Within a few days of the doctor's report Stevens wrote to Pitts Sanborn about his recent book and added that he looked forward to a visit with him and to sipping some of his special brandy (December 22, 1927). More important, 1928 would see the poet shape some of his "momentary violences" into finished poems.

Holly was now just over three years old. The "south wind" mildness of her infancy had blown her into the terrible twos, when, like all children, she learned the wonderful power of noes. But this stage passed as well when she grew into the inquisitive charms of three and four. Intelligent and beautiful, she clearly was not a child whose presence could be ignored or forgotten. Stevens commented in a letter to Harriet Monroe about two months before Holly's fourth birthday, "Holly, dear duck, [another name for her that was identical to one he had earlier used for her mother] was "just too much trouble for words. The only thing that [kept] her in order [was] a fear of foxes, and next to that of being placed on top of the piano from which she [could] not get down." Quickly musing on the image he drew here for Monroe, he added, in closing, "What would she do with Mr. [Marc] Blitzstein at the instrument?" (June 12, 1928).

In spite of the rigorous demands of the life of father, Stevens had begun to make time for the "literary life" once more. In March 1928 he took time out to give attention to a long reply to L. W. Payne apropos of the poems he was anthologizing in his *Later American Writers.* This was an important moment for Stevens. It was the first time he found himself having to paraphrase the intent and meaning of his work. He expressed to Payne that it was "very difficult for [him] to change things from one category to another" and that he disliked doing so. "It *may or may not be* like converting a piece of mysticism into a piece of logic" (italics mine), he added, falling into one of the characteristic paradoxical phrases he began using in his letters as well as in the poems he soon started to compose again. Beneath the rhetorical feint, his comments were unexpectedly straightforward (*L* 250–52) and revealed an ingenuousness wholly unprepared for by the complexity of the poems themselves. Stevens wrote that he didn't mind if Payne repeated what was described about each of the poems but that he didn't want it to be quoted and wished these notes destroyed. Fortunately and ironically Stevens did not destroy his copy of his letter to Payne thus allowing us the privilege of seeing into yet another aspect of his ambivalent attitudes about revelation and disclosure.

These notes appear complete in *Letters,* and it is unnecessary to refer to them extensively here. But it is important to give attention to one or two of Stevens's comments. These shed light on the changing state of his consciousness vis-à-vis his relationship to the subject matter of his poems; on his reaction to reading through the poems of *Harmonium* as a volume for the first time; and on his present understanding of the relationship between imagination and reality.

First, in connection with "Sunday Morning" Stevens stated: "The poem is simply an expression of paganism." But he added, "I do not think I was expressing paganism when I wrote it." Remarkably frank in his offering to one he hoped would elucidate his meaning without disclosing the source of his knowledge, Stevens here provided a most important insight into the nature of his creative process. Finally both emotionally and intellectually past his religious crisis, he could look back and see that he had been celebrating an anti-Christian impulse when he wrote the poem, even though at the time that impulse, which shaped the images, sang its song beyond himself. The meaning expressed in the poem, then, preceded his rational understanding of it. Looking back, he could see that the poem had prefigured one of his later states.

This is another illustration of what was described earlier about the relationship between "The Comedian as the Letter C" and the being Stevens evolved in the months and years after its creation. As he made explicit in this letter to Payne, he now fully comprehended the function of poetry in his life. It was the necessary means in helping him see himself, know himself. He had to write his poems because in the absence of an interlocutor to whom he could speak as if he were truly speaking to a "second self"—someone as intelligent, as widely read, as sensitive as he and someone who would not qualify or judge what he said, a "second self" as he had early wanted Elsie to be—the poems were his only access to discovering his thought and feeling. The extreme self-consciousness of his youth had been totally purged of its romantic affectations and been transformed into an analytical tool. "Let the lamp affix its beam. . . . Let be be finale of seem." Thirteen years after voicing his feeling in "Sunday Morning," Stevens was able to say simply and directly, though observing that to do so rather than to couch it in a poem was "a frightful bore," that there was no purpose to human life; it was "as meaningless as dew." As his daughter grew, and he watched her, he felt secure in the biological knowledge of his continuity in the flesh. ("Beauty is momentary in the mind—/The fitful tracing of a portal;/But in the flesh it is immortal." These lines had also been preparations.) As a consequence, he also felt perfectly complacent uttering his absolute lack of religious faith. For this gift, too, he would be ever-thankful to Elsie, the "Beauty" who had engendered this new "Beauty."

Stevens's second important disclosure to Payne described his reaction to seeing his poems collected as a volume for the first time. "The reading of the proofs of the book gave me such a horror of it that I have hardly looked at it since it was published." Though this is a common experience with authors and their first products, the strength of Stevens's reaction was unusual. It was five years since the book had appeared, and he had hardly looked at it. His critics' reactions had no doubt played their part in contributing to his horror. But Payne's inquiry began to mitigate this deadening effect. It was perhaps out of gratitude for his positive interest and his desire to get things straight that Stevens helped him along.

In the third disclosure Stevens articulated for the first time in prose the theoretical underpinning of his work, the structure he had translated from the essential tension of his being, that had been part of his experience since the days of his childhood, when he alternately followed the examples offered by his parents. With his mother he shared imagination; by this time he might even have read her late poems, only found after her death. With his father he shared the hard facts of the real world. As he rephrased for Payne the import of "To the One of Fictive Music," he could have been describing the reaction of the child he had been: "But after living there [in a world of the imagination] to the degree the poet does, the desire to get back to the everyday world becomes so keen that one turns from the imaginative world in a most definite and determined way." At various moments, after being carried away across the wide water of his imagination to one of the fictional places he conjured as his mother read Bible stories or sang her hymns, he suddenly felt the need to stop floating and find his footing once more in the real world of people and places of which his father spoke after one of his long business days. Stevens went on to note to Payne that in spite of the necessity he felt for periodically turning to the "everyday world," the imaginative world was the "only real one after all."

The gloss Stevens provided on his poem, though valuable, is secondary to what he laid bare about the requirements of his own life. In an uncharacteristically open manner, he gave the answer here to the question critics and readers were still asking him more than twenty years later. As William Carlos Williams ironically expressed in his note congratulating his old rival and friend on his receiving the Bollingen Prize for 1949, "Can you tell me why you work so hard to earn a living?" (March 28, 1950). Stevens had answered the question long before. Work in the everyday world was his response to a feeling he had first sensed in childhood. He needed contact with the practical world of affairs to bring him down from his "Jovian atelier," the attic where during long evenings he lost himself with his Muse: "We must come down; we must use tooth and nail." Between writing poems on scraps of paper at night or on the way to work in the morning there were the demands of his desk to bring him down. Between seasons of writing poems there were seasons of reading and observing—as he noted to his correspondents in later years, in winter he read, and in spring he began writing again. So now, after the longest immersion in his "fluent mundo," the years from 1914 to 1923, when he composed the poems of *Harmonium,* there was this extended period of attention to the everyday world, a period about to come to an end. He had come up for a long breath and was ready to plunge once more.

Before Stevens publicly declared himself a poet again, he had to test the waters of current literary life. In midspring he attended a lecture on modern art given by his old Harvard friend Walter Pach (May 10, 1928). Stevens had also been reading the books he had ordered from the presses producing fine, rare copies and from those like Leonard and Virginia Woolf's Hogarth Press, which issued what was newest. Getting back into the swim of things didn't seem to disturb his newfound equilibrium, at least insofar as his latest medical report showed. In October 1928 Dr. Herrick gave him an almost clean bill of health. He was still somewhat anemic, but the prescribed remedy was mild.

As far as Stevens was concerned, it was "just what the doctor ordered": additional quantities of meat, green vegetables, and fruit.

By October 1929, a year later, Stevens was well on his way to being as deeply immersed in his imaginary world as ever. In his papers as they remain there is not even a mention of the stock market crash, the most pressing fact in the world outside at the moment. He corresponded with Pitts Sanborn about the latest of Sanborn's books that he was reading and about his friend's latest literary trips abroad, on his return from which he promised to bring Stevens many boxes of candy from Paris (WAS 1675–78). He caught up on the latest periodicals. And he sent off more verse, this time to Louis Untermeyer for his revised edition of *Modern American Poetry: A Critical Anthology.* Appropriately Stevens's submission was titled "Annual Gaiety." It announced the change in his spirit over the last five years:

> In the morning in the blue snow
> The catholic sun, its majesty,
> Pinks and pinks the ice-hard melanchole.
>
> Wherefore those prayers to the moon?
> Or is it that alligators lie
> Along the edges of your eye
> Basking in desert Florida?
>
> Père Guzz, in heaven thumb your lyre
> And chant the January fire
> And joy of snow and snow.
>
> (*OP* 32–33)

The mocking that went with the bitterness and self-deprecation of earlier poems, like "Le Monocle," was not attached to celebration. "Wherefore those prayers to the moon?" All that he knew or needed to know was within him, lying "along the edges of [his] eye." He didn't have to be in Florida; he now saw it as a "desert." The alligators there were lies; only in his imagination were they real. It was enough to be in the cold North with the sun "pink[ing] the ice-hard melanchole." He exulted in his newfound strength so much that he created a new word in the fashion of Mallarmé: "melanchole." It described him in such creative playfulness that it, a word only as real as the alligator, lied. It couldn't be taken seriously as a characterization of what he had become. Just as he had been transformed through the forms he had shaped, so the form of this word transformed its meaning and contradicted any sense of real melancholy. The last stanza of the poem reinforced this sense and made it clear. The self-addressing persona, "Père Guzz," and the "pinks, pinks," used as verbs, were attached to the primary new fact of his life, dressed in her pink dresses and bonnets.

On October 21 Dr. Herrick wrote that he couldn't report more favorably.

The only irregularity was a trifling anemic condition that would take care of itself.

Everything seemed to be taking care of itself. Stevens had finally learned, even if late (he was now fifty), to relax enough to understand that the only way to steer himself and his craft safely was to follow winds and currents. Though he had devoted the better part of his energies to the Hartford in the hope of significant advancement, he had not yet made it to vice president. By 1928 he abandoned hope that this would ever come to pass. Rather than rail, he continued to perform his duties competently and comprehensively. But because he had begun paying more attention to the currents of the literary world, he had also gathered some of the material out of which he wove the "poetry of the subject" around his "true" ones. With this he created the group of poems that were added to the 1931 edition of *Harmonium*. Ready again to heed the voices of those like Moore, Williams, Untermeyer, and others who were becoming increasingly insistent in their nudgings, he responded positively to Alfred Knopf's writing to him in spring of 1930 about reissuing his first volume with some new additions. Stevens planned to give the coming summer to poetry. Though the demands of the office kept him from plunging in as soon as he would have liked (on July 21, he wrote to Lincoln Kirstein, editor of *Hound and Horn,* answering his request for a contribution, and said that though he was "supposed to be writing poetry this summer," he was "doing anything but" [*L* 258]), by September he had written at least seven new poems. He built them out of the fragments of experience he had been collecting. These were parts of his everyday world at home and at work; parts of the world he heard of and read of around him; parts of quick trips to New York, where he caught up with old friends and French films; parts of his longer stays in Florida, including the last just a few months before.

The new poems—"The Revolutionists Stop for Orangeade," "Anatomy of Monotony," "The Public Square," "Sonatina to Hans Christian," "In the Clear Season of Grapes," "Two at Norfolk," and "Indian River" (*CP* 107–12); "The Sun This March" (which appeared in the *New Republic* in April 1930) and "Lunar Paraphrase" were also written during this time but not included in the new edition of *Harmonium* (appearing in *The Palm at the End of the Mind*)—reflected Stevens's new mind. This new mind, in turn, reflected some of the things he had ordered and read over the last two or three years. Among these was one carefully made slim volume from the Hogarth Press; its importance for Stevens was in direct counterproportion to its heft. This was Freud's *The Future of an Illusion,* which Stevens went through, marking sentences and paragraphs and adding, on the inside back flap of the dust jacket, in his characteristic manner, notes of central words and passages with the appropriate page number that he had penciled in the text. In this way, when later searching for an anchorage of thought on one of his imaginative voyages, he could always easily find it in the particular line or fact that had touched him.

Later in his life, playing another feint to puzzle an inquiring reader, Stevens admitted to having read only *The Interpretation,* as he put it. It had been one of the Arensberg circle's sacred texts. Stevens's disclaimer about having read more of Freud's work was the same kind of device he used when asked about his reading other poets. He usually disclosed that there was one figure, if he had been asked about a school or group, noting that he had liked Verlaine when asked about the symbolists, or one volume, if he had been asked about a poet, commenting that he was familiar with the poems of *Ara Vus Prec* when asked about Eliot, when, in fact, he was extensively familiar with the material being suggested. In the case of the symbolists, he knew not only the primary texts, the poems themselves, but in many cases the theoretical writings that had preceded, accompanied, or followed them. He not only had carefully read Mallarmé's verse but had at his fingertips, almost verbatim, significant passages from *Crise de Vers* and other expansions in prose of the French poet's intent. In connection with his knowledge of Arthur Rimbaud, he was comfortable enough to comment in fragmentary, cryptic notes to himself about the success of Edith Sitwell's translation of some of his *Illuminations.* And as for his reading of Eliot, whose *Waste Land* had appeared just as he was about to go over the proofs for his own first volume, his exchange of letters with McAlmon on the subject showed that while McAlmon had seen an early draft, Stevens knew the first published one.

In consistently pointing those curious about his relationship to what he read to something tangential or partial, Stevens was not being dishonest but simply engaging others in a game, though in most cases, this was well beyond their knowledge. Since he had established the rules of play for this game, and revealed neither them nor that there was a game afoot, the fact that his correspondents didn't realize the deception is not to their discredit. For Stevens, this was another extension of his early pleasure in playing practical jokes. It was perhaps connected as well to the way his father had played with poetry. Garrett, Sr., had often used Pennsylvania Dutch neologisms or idioms in designing challenges to the friends who read his work. They and he submitted poems anonymously to the local newspapers. Their game was to guess who the writer of "this one" was. For his son, this kind of engagement was developed to an extraordinary degree during his years with the Arensberg circle. This kind of playing was in the Renaissance tradition of punning and using complex anagrams that Walter Arensberg believed Francis Bacon to have practiced. Consequently, Arensberg encouraged exercising and polishing these cryptographic skills. When one of the members of the circle pulled off one of his or her plays, he or she "won"—won the attention of others in the group who tried to divine the solution to the puzzle being presented and won approval when the steps leading to the discovery were found to be woven into a brilliantly intricate design that, in fact, had been apparent all along but that showed its "true" meaning only with the uncovering of the key. One had to find the right key to play *Harmonium.* Marcel Duchamp and Walter Arensberg, playing seemingly endless and repeated games of chess, had to find the key to the other's strategy in order to win. The more elaborate and complicated the scheme, the more successful. The group was to use its collective pondering to bridge the gap between science and nature, as each member tested his or her ability against that of the others. Nothing could have pleased Stevens more. The man who had been so concerned about "winning all the prizes at school" and "gold medal boys" could prove himself with these tricks.

But beyond the personal enjoyment that this kind of endeavor provided, and beyond the immediate gratification that came with indulging the spirit of play as adults, there was a serious purpose, and Arensberg had not let any of them forget that. It was exemplified in his own work. The discipline he had required for his studies on the cryptography of Shakespeare and Dante and for his translation of the *Divine Comedy* was not academic. The aim had been neither to impose nor to abstract some artificially constructed intellectual pattern in order to display individual genius. He and his group had searched for the metaphorical philosopher's stone. They had sought the ultimate structure of reality, the particular configuration that was identical in matter and language (understood as all media of communication: paint, marble, etc.). Their assumption had been that the great works of art of the past, like the corpus of Shakespeare or Dante, were constructed on the same pattern as the forms of nature. To discover this structure in these works had been their purpose. Beneath this lay a deeper assumption that had directed their activities. They believed that the mind was made up out of the same matter as the sea out of which human life had come; they believed it was truly the "sea of spuming thought" that shaped consciousness. If the mind were exercised and expanded to its fullest possibilities, it should slowly disclose the human "bond to all that dust" (*CP* 15), the dust that was the stars and the earth on which humans crawled and out of which they were made. The game playing, the rigorous demands of chess, the study and application needed to create a word that would stretch their minds, the efforts to discover the hidden patterns that exceeded reason—all these had been exercises meant to facilitate the one "Great Work."

It is not at all surprising that this group formed when it did, was constituted by whom it was, and that Stevens was a part of it. In fact, its most salient feature was its naturalness. Stevens's almost sole direct disclosure of one of his most important sources—Goethe—pointed to the deepest roots of the group's search. The grounding idea of all of Goethe's work and life was *Organismus*. His commitment to understanding and applying it paralleled Francis Bacon's perception concerning the work that had to be done to bring together the various kinds of explorations into pure science, nature, and "humanistic" study. It was as though Goethe had taken up the thread Bacon had begun unraveling. Unfortunately the later romantic poets in the exuberance and unsophistication of their youth tangled up the thread and strangled themselves with it. In the strength of their reaction against reason, which they felt to have been the prison from which their spirits had recently escaped, they lost the skein that could lead them out of the maze of their time's confusion. Illustrating the problem Bacon underlined, these writers ran to nature and across continents to find or fight for freedom, or they lost themselves in the obscure woods of drugs, while pure-minded scientists applied reason to chain the natural forces to power the machines that would soon transform the planet into a system of grids and plots interrupted only by recalcitrant mountains and ever-fertile seas and jungles. Darwin alone, not formally trained as a scientist, made a major contribution that would eventually bring human beings closer to nature rather than drive them farther away from it. One of the forces contributing to the success of the conquest of nature and so to the rise of industrialization in the West, was religion. Crushing underfoot the serpent of nature, with all its chthonic power, was the inevitable manifestation of the myth of human progress and perfectability. That the most immediate effects of industrialization created situations that were unchristian to an extreme unparalleled in history—except perhaps on wartime occasions—was a consideration that would have to be tabled for a while. Eventually it would be rationalized into another system of paternalism and patronage whereby industrialists would, according to their power, establish funds for the care and education of the masses.

It was this development, with all its reverberations, that the generation of Henry Adams at Harvard had addressed, passing its legacy through the hands of Charles Eliot Norton, William James, and George Santayana to the lesser figures like Pierre LaRose, Barrett Wendell, and Charles Townsend Copeland with whom Stevens, Arensberg, Pach, and the rest of their Cambridge circle had come into regular contact. It was to the consequences of this same development, attenuated in the dying strains of the old order in Europe, that Freud attended. The Arensberg group's involvement with reality represented its generation's still-strong rebellion against the ideals of progressivism and materialism. The designs the members had elaborated in their organic complexity, harmonizing elements in the construction of their puzzles from as many diverse sources as they could, were antithetical to mechanical thinking. The only kind of machine that could be evolved from their approach was one illustrated by a Rube Goldberg drawing. (Some of Goldberg's designs appropriately appeared in issues of the more short-lived publications with which the Arensberg group was connected, *Rong-Rong* and *The Blind Man;* later Jean Tinguely would actually build some absurd machines of this order.

Something else the group had recognized was that, of the art forms of the romantic period, only one had escaped the sentimental distortion most apparent in poetry. This was music, and it had escaped largely because its production could not be judged profane or corrupting since there were no images or words to which such judgment could be attached. The secularization of musical production, from which Mozart, another extremely playful figure, had early profited, continued unchecked through the nineteenth century (at least, until Richard Wagner), so that composers did not have to break away from the order of the past. They could and did continue to develop inherited forms that were intrinsically involved with the most exquisite extensions and variations of pure, mathematically precise reason.

The French symbolists knew this—or felt it—as did the adherents of art for art's sake in England, the two groups most often noted in connection with Stevens's work by his early critics. All art should aspire to a condition of music: "It Must Be Abstract; It Must Change; It Must Give Pleasure." Stevens's formulations of these categories, which had begun when he was still a young man at Harvard heeding Barrett Wendell's words on the effectiveness of Wagner's music drama, had been further clarified during the countless evenings he had spent in Arensberg's studio. They took on yet another dimension—at the same time the broadest and most particular—as he read *The Future of an Illusion* sometime in late 1928 or 1929.

Though Freud's text had nothing to do with music, the argument he presented for the necessity of clearing away illusions of all kinds and committing emotions and intellect to the scientific spirit touched on each of the qualities Stevens later canonized as essential for the "Supreme Fiction." These same qualities characterize music. Moreover, at one central point in making his case, Freud used and elaborated an idea of "fiction" in terms that were echoed by Stevens. These were not, however, passages Stevens marked (as he did others that will be discussed shortly). The impression made on the poet by the paragraphs about "fictions" in Freud suggests that, at least in some cases, when Stevens disclaimed having been overtly influenced, he was not being disingenuous. The passages he did mark in the margin and list on the inside flap of the dust jacket left their imprint. (Stevens even used 'Ανάγκη [Ananke] in Freud's sense, which he had been careful to translate as "=external reality" in the margin and to note as a key term in his handy, back-flap index, in his own work [first in "Owl's Clover," *OP* 59].) But the more important idea of "fiction" remained suspended in the aureole of associations he later drew on as his own.

One reason why Stevens would not have consciously internalized the notion of "fiction" while reading *The Future of an Illusion* is that in the context in which it appeared, Freud was using it to illustrate yet another aspect of the outworn remnants of religious attachments. At the same time he was referring to it secondhand, calling into question the kind of approach to the problem of belief exemplified by thinkers like Hans Vaihinger (whom he singled out in his fostering of the philosophy of "as if") and William James. Stevens, having given himself to the logic of Freud's argument, at this moment did not take exception. But later in his life, having realized that he himself could not "stand up to a Freudian analysis," he went back to what he had learned from James and found comfort there. He then retrieved the unmarked passage about "fictions" that he now read in 1928 and 1929. Out of it he constructed the peristyle supporting his masque.

In the passage in question, Freud pointed out how the philosophy of "as if" was simply a more sophisticated version of the intellectually immature religious position:

> The second attempt is the one made by the philosophy of "As if." This asserts that our thought-activity includes a great number of hypotheses whose groundlessness and even absurdity we fully realize. They are called

> "fictions," but for a variety of practical reasons we have to behave "as if" we believed in these fictions. This is the case with religious doctrines because of their incomparable importance for the maintenance of human society. [Here Freud has a note citing Vaihinger.] This line of argument is not far removed from the *"Credo quia absurdum"*. But I think the demand made by the "As if" argument is one that only a philosopher could put forward. A man whose thinking is not influenced by the artifices of philosophy will never be able to accept it; in such a man's view, the admission that something is absurd or contrary to reason leaves no more to be said. It cannot be expected of him that precisely in treating his most important interests he shall forgo the guarantees he requires for all his ordinary activities. I am reminded of one of my children who was distinguished at an early age by a peculiarly marked matter-of-factness. When the children were being told a fairy story and were listening to it with rapt attention, he would come up and ask: "Is that a true story?" When he was told it was not, he would turn away with a look of disdain. We may expect that people will soon behave in the same way towards fairy tales of religion, in spite of the advocacy of "As if."[19]

After showing how these hypotheses functioned to keep human beings at a primitive or childlike stage of development, Freud pointed out how the cultivation of the scientific spirit, as a natural concomitant of better and broader education, inevitably would challenge the more naïve positions. But he also wisely indicated that this kind of education was not something that would immediately reach the "masses." If, then, there were not going to be an absolute revolt on their part against the scientific approach, which they saw from afar as depriving them of their pacifiers (their myths of security, protection, and ultimate justice), there would have to be a fundamental revision in the relationship between civilization and religion. Freud elucidated the line of thought presented here in three closely reasoned and well-illustrated paragraphs at the end of Chapter VII, which Stevens carefully marked.

The direction in which the above passage pointed Stevens was one he had already been following from the time, when he was still a young man, and he expressed the view that nature made a god of a man but that churches kept him only a man. It was the same theme that Vita Sackville-West had playfully translated into *Seducers in Ecuador.* The choices Leonard and Virginia Woolf (to whom *Seducers* was dedicated) made for their publications were clearly not determined by concern for marketability. They and their subscribers, of whom Stevens was one, understood the seriousness of their purpose.

The passage above from *The Future of an Illusion* which Stevens marked was a conclusion Freud arrived at after having meticulously described how human beings evolved the idea of a single, fatherlike God. He showed how this idea of God, as necessary and effective as it had been for a certain period in history, had outworn its purpose and was now inhibiting rather than nourishing. The change in the relationship between civilization and religion that Freud was suggesting had to do with freedom from the need for the idea of a protecting father and of the promise of perfection and an afterlife.

Stevens realized the necessity for this just as he understood how naturally the need to devise this kind of god had come about. For one of his key sections, Freud gave an explanation in terms that could just as easily have described the most critical moment in Stevens's early intellectual and spiritual maturation. This passage Stevens marked as well. Addressing an invented devil's advocate, against whom he tested his argument, Freud noted:

> Thus I must contradict you when you go on to argue that men are completely unable to do without the consolation of the religious illusion, that without it they could not bear the troubles of life and the cruelties of reality. That is true, certainly, of the men into whom you have instilled the sweet—or bitter-sweet—poison from childhood onwards. But what of the other men, who have been sensibly brought up? Perhaps those who do not suffer from the neurosis will need no intoxicant to deaden it. They will, it is true, find themselves in a difficult situation. They will have to admit to themselves the full extent of their helplessness and their insignificance in the machinery of the universe; they can no longer be the centre of creation, no longer the object of tender care on the part of a beneficient Providence. They will be in the same position as a child who has left the parental house where he was so warm and comfortable. But surely infantilism is destined to be surmounted. Men cannot remain children forever; they must in the end go out into "hostile life." We may call this *"education to reality"*. Need I confess to you that the sole purpose of my book is to point out the necessity for this forward step? (p. 81)

Under the pressure of what he felt to be his age's greatest problem, at the same time his own greatest problem, that of "belief," Stevens forged the elements Freud suggested as necessary here. Stevens understood that the first step toward weaning society from its outworn religious faith—it could not be done precipitously, as Freud pointed out and as he himself well knew from the difficulty he had had in accomplishing the same thing—was to replace the image of God the Father on which Western religion rested. "It Must Be Abstract" was, therefore, the basis for a new formula for belief. In the poems he wrote, Stevens gradually and consistently secularized and abstracted the sacred. He began early, for example, with an image of "snow" as "eyesight falling to earth" (*CP* 294). Here the perception was equivocally tied both to an image of God in early Renaissance panels as He looked down to earth with shining silvered beams and to the actual fact that it is human eyesight that sees snow falling and provides an imaginative representation. Finally, near the end of his career he gave an explicit statement of the same process in the "It Must Be Abstract" section of "Notes Toward a Supreme Fiction": ". . . The sun/Must bear no name, gold flourisher, but be/In the difficulty of what it is to be" (*CP* 381). Freud's insistence on accepting the difficulty of what it means to be human was no different.

The second step of Stevens's formula, "It Must Change," also followed in sequence and development the next series of passages he marked in his copy of *The Future of an Illusion.* Freud took up another of his imaginary opponent's objections—that any scientific method of education presented would suffer from the same dogmatic and delusionary quality attacked as belonging to religion—and pointed out the necessary characteristic of the inquiring scientific spirit to be nothing other than inevitable and constant change:

> But I hold fast to one distinction [between the scientific and religious methods]. Apart from the fact that no penalty is imposed for not sharing them, my illusions are not, like religious ones, incapable of correction. They have not the character of a delusion. If experience should show—not to me, but to others after me, who think as I do—that we have been mistaken, we will give up our expectations. . . .
>
> And there are two points that I must dwell on a little longer. Firstly, the weakness of my position does not imply any strengthening of yours. I think you are defending a lost cause. We may insist as often as we like that a man's intellect is powerless in comparison with his instinctual life, and we may be right in this. Nevertheless, there is something peculiar about this weakness. The voice of the intellect is a soft one, but it does not rest until it has gained a hearing. Finally, after a countless succession of rebuffs, it succeeds. This is one of the few points on which one may be optimistic about the future of mankind, but is in itself a point of no small importance. And from it one can derive yet other hopes. The primacy of the intellect lies, it is true, in a distant, distant future, but probably not in an *infinitely* distant one. It will presumably set itself the same aims as those whose realization you expect from your God (of course within human limits—so far as external reality, 'Ανάγκη, allows it), namely, the love of man and the decrease of suffering. This being so, we may tell ourselves that our antagonism is only a temporary one and not irreconcilable. We desire the same things, but you are more impatient, more exacting, and—why should I not say it?—more self-seeking than I and those on my side. You would have the state of bliss begin directly after death; you expect the impossible from it and you will not surrender the claims of the individual. Our God, Λόγος [the twin gods Λόγος (Logos: reason) and 'Ανάγκη (Ananke: necessity) of the Dutch writer Multatuli], will fulfill whichever of these wishes nature outside us allows, but he will do it very gradually, only in the unforeseeable future, and for a new generation of men. He promises no compensation for us, who suffer grievously from life. On the way to this distant goal your religious doctrines will have to be discarded, no matter whether the first attempts fail, or whether the first substitutes prove to be untenable. You know why: in the long run nothing can withstand reason and experience, and the contradiction which religion offers to both is all too palpable. Even purified religious ideas

cannot escape this fate, so long as they try to preserve anything of the consolation of religion. (pp. 93–94)

In addition to this argument, which Stevens duly noted, he bracketed the passage beginning with the sentence "The voice of the intellect is a soft one . . . ," and underlined the beginning of the sentence "We desire the same things. . . ." The first instance was a germ that later contributed to one of Stevens's favorite themes—"It can never be satisfied, the mind, never" (*CP* 247)—while the second instance provided him a moment of tender recognition from the time when he held his dialogue with an imagined interlocutor of the same persuasion as Freud's in "A High-Toned Old Christian Woman": "We agree in principle."

The final step of Stevens's formula, "It Must Give Pleasure," represented a synthesis of the first two steps as well as the last, distinct, and necessary part of the process. "Pleasure" was accordingly something that in Freud's text provided the underlying motive for the whole endeavor of attempting the task of reeducation required to change the relationship between civilization and religion. This motive, as Freud described it, was simply that people would be happier, and life more satisfying, civilization no longer oppressive. This would be the direct result of finally giving up "hankering after hymns" and "the need for some imperishable bliss." As Freud described in another of the passages Stevens marked:

> By withdrawing their expectations from the other world and concentrating all their liberated energies into their life on earth, they will probably succeed in achieving a state of things in which life will become tolerable for everyone and civilization no longer oppressive to anyone. Then, with one of our fellow-unbelievers, they will be able to say without regret:
>
> *Den Himmel überlassen wir*
> *Den Engeln und den Spatzen.*
> ["We leave Heaven to the angels and the sparrows."
> From Heine's poem *Deutschland*] (pp. 86–87)

Stevens responded strongly to this echo of his own earlier phrasing in "Sunday Morning" (when he, too, may have been thinking of Heine):

> The sky will be much friendlier then than now,
> A part of labor and a part of pain,
> And next in glory to enduring love,
> Not this dividing and indifferent blue.
> (*CP* 68)

❧

In contrast with his earlier poems, Stevens's new poems—that is, those written between 1927 and 1930 (as distinguished from poems that could have been included in the original edition of *Harmonium* but were not[20]—reflected sovereignty over death, the attitude he evolved over the long period of resolving the crisis of his middle age. It was not that the new poems ignored painful aspects that the earlier body of poems explored, but that these same aspects were now examined without the ironic distance that characterized his previous work. Stevens's omission of "The Silver Plough-Boy," his first explicitly ironic poem about death, from *Harmonium*'s second edition exemplified this. Moreover, in the new poems there was much less hiding. Both the lines connecting them to occasions in Stevens's actual experience and those connecting the development of his thought to what he read were far more distinct than they had been. But there was one element that was more hidden. In also deleting "Exposition of the Contents of a Cab" and "Architecture" from the new edition, Stevens secreted the key to unlock the cryptic nuances of the major poems of the volume. This was the importance of sexuality in understanding his corpus. The last lines of "Architecture" proclaimed it directly:

> Only the lusty and the plenteous
> Shall walk
> The bronze-filled plazas
> And the nut-shell esplanades.
> (*OP* 18)

In the same way, "Exposition" revealed too blatantly for his revisionary eye the connection between the tensions produced by Victorian morality and his particular situation with Elsie. Without these poems as part of his corpus, the suggestions of the same situations and positions as reflected in "Le Monocle de Mon Oncle," "A High-Toned Old Christian Woman," "Sunday Morning," "The Emperor of Ice-Cream," and "Peter Quince at the Clavier" would remain only as intimations of the personal.

In the new poems the same situations were explored, but impersonally. At the same time, because of the protective nonironic distance provided by references derived from what he had been reading during his years of silence, they were dealt with more tenderly and directly. It was as though the six new poems—"Anatomy of Monotony," "The Public Square," "Sonatina to Hans Christian," "In the Clear Season of Grapes," "Two at Norfolk," and "Indian River"—represented Stevens's first sustained attempt at fulfilling the requirement that "It Must Be Abstract." They were abstract not in relationship to nature or to lived experience but to his already existing body of poems now considered by him "Part of the res itself and not about it" (*CP* 473). As such, they functioned as a gloss on the earlier poems, a coda completing his first opus, like "Thirteen Ways" in relationship to the poems collected under the title of "In the Northwest" of the "Primordia" group. Looking back on what had been, reconsidering the salient elements of the past, and playing them in a new key—with his new attitude—Stevens was also illustrating how poetry "must change." Since the new attitude reflected his improved relationship with himself and with others, these poems were designed to "give pleasure" in a way the previous ones were not. In making those, he had been equally attentive to the sounds, rhythms, and images that would give pleasure, but in these irony was gone. Considered together, each of these subtle developments represented a major shift.

"Anatomy of Monotony" was an abstraction of "Sunday Morning," "The Snow Man," "The Man Whose Pharynx Was Bad," "Banal Sojourn," and "Le Monocle de Mon Oncle." The echoes of "Sunday Morning" were clearest since that was the poem in which the issues involved were originally made most explicit, even though as Stevens revealed in his disclosure to Payne about this poem, he did not know at the time he wrote it that it was the actual proclamation of paganism he later understood it to be. The new poem was a response to what he had then suggested, but now made with self-conscious acceptance, without the defensiveness that produced the ambiguities of voice in "Sunday Morning." In "Anatomy of Monotony" Stevens resolved the duality between man and nature expressed in "Sunday Morning" and generally running through the rest of the poems of the first edition of *Harmonium.* Though the speakers in those poems wanted to become one with the mind of winter and the other seasons, they could not. The sky remained an indifferent and dividing blue, and the first and foremost law of nature was felt to be in conflict with human desires. Nature, devised as the sleepless mother endlessly waiting, was always beyond, outside lived experience. She was death, that at that time Stevens could not accept.

"Anatomy of Monotony" presented exactly the opposite situation. First, there was no persona; the voice spoke as one with all: "we"; "our nature is her [the earth's] nature." The "it" of "Le Monocle"—"It comes, it blooms, it bears its fruit and dies"—that led into the grotesque distortion of "two gourds distended on [their] vines" (an image that makes the acceptance of aging impossible) was transformed here. Though the "Hence it comes" of "Anatomy" resonated with the earlier poem's words and set the stage for another excursion into the pain of growing old, an excursion that would similarly express the human refusal to admit our "bond to all that dust," by the very enunciation of it, Stevens now provided a simple, abstract description of the human condition that was *not separate* from the condition of earth:

> . . . Hence it comes,
> Since by our nature we grow old, earth grows
> The same . . .
>
> (*CP* 107–108)

The line continued to establish this identity by evoking the earlier figure of death as the mother he had imagined in "Sunday Morning": "We parallel the mother's death." The rest of the stanza completed the revision of "Sunday Morning." It was not only deer and quail that moved naturally about the autumn mountains but the "she" who now included all who read the poem. The wish that Stevens had unconsciously expressed to Elsie in one of those consciously self-disclosive letters in the months just before their marriage—

that he be able to bridge the duality he felt between "mind" and "monster" (the body tied to nature)—he fulfilled in this poem. Appropriately it was called "Anatomy of Monotony." Though residues of irony appeared in the title, which suggested that the poem would be another analysis of one of his black moods, like "The Snow Man" or "The Man Whose Pharynx Was Bad," it actually pointed directly and descriptively to the positive sense of human oneness with nature, the *monotone* of identification.

Completing the picture, the poem's second stanza (*CP* 108) established nature's unconscious sympathy with humanity. In a description that forced both the pathetic fallacy and anthropomorphism to transcend themselves as tropes, Stevens incorporated physical, scientific laws accounting for attraction and procreation: The sun implicitly heats bodies and prepares them to recognize the warmth they will feel when "covetous in desire." This now became the "first and foremost law" stated with the weight of the biblical phrasing of God's voice, "So be it." But the anthropomorphized sun that gave comfort out of "tenderness or grief" is part of "that fatal and that barer sky," and the spirit, one with the sun, feels, too, "aggrieved" that there will be death. Yet the grief is something to be accepted, part of human nature. No ironic turning away, no invention of Palestine across the wide water without sound here was necessary now.

This made perfect sense for Stevens at this point. Both his child and his first book were there to ensure his continuity. Death no longer had to be fought. It was simply something occasioning grief and was not incompatible with acceptance. There was grief because living in the world was such a pleasure, and contemplating that the experience would cease one day was painful. "And hard it is in spite of blazoned days" was rephrased to "And hard it is [because] of blazoned days."

Looking back at another aspect of his past involvement with reality as contained in earlier poems, Stevens fashioned "The Public Square" (*CP* 108–09). Its title pointed directly to what would be accomplished in its lines. What was once so personal as to be almost wholly unavailable to analysis would here be exposed, made "public," and then exploded. The specific first reference for this poem was "Anecdote of the Prince of Peacocks." The landscape was the same: a world of moonlight strangely characterized by modern structures. In the "Anecdote," the "blue ground/Was full of blocks/And blocking steel." Here there were "angular blacks," "pylon and pier." The difference was that the "Anecdote" clearly described a dream state, while "The Public Square" described a waking one made to seem dreamlike by a "coma of the moon." The "Berserk" of the "Anecdote," his name threatening the madness the poet feared, here was merely the memory of a janitor who, while walking through such a moonlit cityscape with his lantern, made it appear dreamlike with the "swooning" light of his lamp. The transformation of the scene paralleled the development of Stevens's personality.

In the "Anecdote" the moonlit plane where Berserk lived was, on one level, a metaphor for the unconscious experienced as a threat, setting traps in the midst of dreams. Here the same kind of moonlit scape was calmly considered and traversed by the observer who witnessed, and perhaps even caused, the collapse of the older structure of the unconscious. After this, "It turned cold and silent. Then/The square began to clear." Where id was, there ego shall be. Stevens's fear of being overwhelmed by the voices of others murmuring in the midst of dreams was gone. The square, like the poet over the last six or seven years, became silent. All that remained in the poem was the moon, carrying a classical reference and exhibiting its "porcelain leer." It suggested—following the ambiguity of describing that it was "last," though readers couldn't know what it was last to do—that there would be more poems.

In addition to the internal reference to an earlier perception, this poem reflected how Stevens transformed and combined elements from everyday experience with elements associated with things that appealed to his intellect and imagination. He had more than once seen, in the various cities he visited on business, the demolition of older structures to clear the way for new construction. The scene he painted in "The Public Square" touched on these memories but was also evocative of Alfred Stieglitz's or Charles Demuth's cityscapes, with which Stevens was familiar. The poem displayed the commonality of the poet's vision with the photographer's and painter's exquisite sensitivity to the changes modernity continued to bring to American cities. These changes themselves echoed a larger social movement toward rationality and balance. The "bushy plain" and outworn "edifices," beautiful as they were, had to be transformed to accommodate the changing order, simply to make life better for larger numbers. In focusing on the harmonies and rhythms of city lines, Stieglitz and Demuth were forcing attention on the beauty—the abstract beauty—of the contemporary city. They wanted, through their vision, to help others leave behind sentimental attachments to idealized views of nature and earlier ways of life. In this they expressed their Americanness, their commitment to a real democracy.

By the time Stevens wrote "The Public Square," he had come to realize how important it was to celebrate the ever-changing present, to demolish romantic ideas of the superior beauty of the past. The modern city, the New World, America, like the healthy personality, had constantly to evolve, destroy the old, and build anew. There was a hope for America. It was expressed by its artists and poets and by Freud, who, in the opening pages of *The Future of an Illusion,* exempted it from criticism, noting that in this new country everything was still to be expected. His desire was that his work would go toward making the experiment successful. In "The Public Square" these ideas played their part. Stevens was preparing his *Ideas of Order.*

Announcing his commitment to the American scene more loudly, "In the Clear Season of Grapes" represented revision of the perceptions expressed by both "The Doctor of Geneva" and "The Comedian as the Letter C." This was clearest in the poem's third stanza (the second quoted on the following page). It came after the poet had directed attention to the fact that the poem was what came of his having stopped and thought about the "point" of "This conjunction of mountains and sea and our lands" and after his first settling his mind on the minute particular of what all this meant:

> When I think of our lands I think of the house
> And the table that holds a platter of pears
> Vermilion smeared over green, arranged for show.
>
> But this gross blue under rolling bronzes
> Belittles those carefully chosen daubs.
> Flashier fruits! A flip for the sun and moon,
> (*CP* 110).

The figure perceiving this had become a naturalized American. He was no longer like the doctor of Geneva, sighing and crying, left speechless before the "visible, voluble delugings" of what his European "lacustrine" mind saw as "the wild, the ruinous waste." He was no longer like Crispin at the outset of his voyage, feeling the "merest minuscule" in the face of the "gross blue," desiring but unable to "stem verboseness in the sea." The figure here was no persona but the poet himself, as in the other poems of the group. He had learned, through the experience of "a nice shady home" and his daughter "with curls," to feel his place in his place. The clue that these facts helped occasion this new sense he carefully set at the end of the following stanza:

> If they mean no more than that. But they do.
> And the mountains and the sea do. And our lands
> And the welter of frost and the fox cries do.

After subtly evoking the memory of "The Snow Man"—the misery he heard in the sound of the winter trees now abstracted to just "the welter of the frost"—Stevens included the one thing (besides being placed on top of the piano) that startled Holly enough to keep her quiet and attentive: the fox (as he had related to Harriet Monroe in a letter referred to earlier in this chapter). Implicit in this blending of his consciousness with Holly's was his awareness of how he had extended himself, grown in spirit to include her and others in the compass and curriculum of his being. The last line completed this sense, with each man seen as contributing his part to the making of the sea, his first home: "And his nostrils blow out salt around each man."

This specific consciousness of the American condition was also explored in "Two at Norfolk" (*CP* 111–12), in which Stevens poetically developed a theme stated explicitly by Paul Rosenfeld in many of the pieces he wrote during the twenties which appeared in the periodicals Stevens regularly read. Rosenfeld repeatedly made a point of elaborating on the differences existing between generations in America. He noted that because of both immigration and the quick-paced changes in technological development, an unusually painful and difficult situation arose between parents and children. This mirrored the situation obtaining between America itself, seen as parent, and its nonnative children, continually arriving on its shores but unable to speak to it or even understand its language.

Each of the scenes presented in "Two at Norfolk" reflected this awareness: the contrast between the "darkies" tending the white people's cemetery; the reference to the man buried there whose moon had remained in Scandinavia and whose daughter was a foreign thing; the reference to the man who praised "Johann Sebastian" familiarly (not even using his last name) for his son's "natural" outpouring of music. The poem ended with the poignant creation of what could come of these strains: brother and sister still needing as adults to consummate their incestuous desires because it seemed only in such pairings that trust and ease could be established. But "these two [could] never meet in the air so full of summer." Without the political and economic levels added by Theodore Dreiser in his platter of prose, Stevens was exploring the very ground of the American tragedy.

The two remaining poems of the group, "Indian River" and "Sonatina to Hans Christian," were the most openly personal. They integrated specific elements from the poet's past and through them pointed to how very different things were now. The first was drawn from Stevens's memory of the long sailing trip he made shortly after Holly's birth. Indian River was one of the places on the itinerary he had noted in his letter to Harriet Monroe. His seeming celebration of the constancies of the trade wind jingles in Florida's various settings was offset by the last sentence—"Yet there is no spring in Florida, neither in boskage perdu, nor on the nunnery beaches"—with its curiously awkward Frenchiness and cryptic modifiers. Florida was no longer being praised for its "venereal soil." Stevens now saw "nunnery beaches" and felt loss in the face of the eternal summer he had once found to be a "radiant and productive atmosphere." Though the poem recalled the time of the Indian River trip, it seems that the change in the poet's attitude came somewhat later.

Stevens continued to make his yearly trips to Florida, joining Judge Arthur Powell and other friends (he often went more than once a year), but it was only during February 1931 that his letters home, now addressed to both Elsie and Holly, showed that he felt this difference. After commenting on the various flowers he had seen on the trip to Miami from Atlanta, he noted: "Yet this had none of the thrill that the same thing will have later on at home, because there is none of the feeling of Spring that ought to go along. Spring is an end of darkness and of ugliness and, much more, it is a feeling of new life and of the old activity of life returned, immense and fecund" (*L* 261). He felt at this point that there was "no spring" in Florida, no source of inspiration without "spring," the seasons' turning, change. Finally able to accept his own mortality, Stevens could also accept the necessity of change. This major shift in key completed the stage setting for the *Ideas of Order* soon to follow. Appropriately that volume began with his "Farewell to Florida."

There were many things that had contributed to this new outlook, which transformed spring from a season that brought on his depressions to the season that brought new life. The poet's feelings now were synchronized with nature. No longer ambivalent about his involvement with the Christian myth, he could see things as they were. The regularity of life with a child had contributed to this as well. There were even family holidays. One, to Atlantic City once again during the previous spring of 1930, seemed to prefigure the turnaround in his attitude about the spring. While he had never thought much of Atlantic City, as he related much later in a letter to a friend in which he described the alteration in his feelings that this trip had occasioned, the time spent there now, watching Holly play in sand and sea, walking through flower beds and gardens with Elsie, and reading the darkly curious tales of E.T.A. Hoffmann[21] during sparkling mornings and afternoons made him happy. He was surprised to find himself enjoying these things as much as he did, and the following trip to Florida paled by comparison. "Indian River" (*CP* 112), then, combined elements he had seen and loved in the past with a present consciousness that did not deprive them of their beauty yet nonetheless deromanticized them. He was well on the way to playing things as they were.

The last poem of the group, "Sonatina to Hans Christian" (*CP* 109–10), also dealt with things as they were, but not at one of those moments when some evasion by metaphor was unnecessary. Though things in his own being were more settled than they had ever been, there were aspects involving the others in his life that disturbed him. This was reflected in his poem. On the surface it was apparently just a playful musing on the fairy tale of the ugly duckling that Stevens had read years earlier and now reread or overheard being read to Holly. But as with "Sea Surface Full of Clouds" or "Le Monocle de Mon Oncle," the surface hid one of the poet's most moving experiences of other. However, while in the earlier poems, that other was the *one* other, Elsie, who expanded to include additional imagined beings in the poems' development, here the poet began with the consciousness of two others: Elsie and Holly. The first edition of *Harmonium* had been dedicated "To My Wife," while the 1931 edition was dedicated "To My Wife and Holly." In this short poem the nature of Stevens's involvement with what he imagined Holly had to have been feeling in relationship to her mother showed itself to have been most profound and gave its full weight to the dedication's addition, which might otherwise seem to have been merely perfunctory.

One clue to the direct linkings of the poem's figures with Elsie and Holly comes from having become familiar with earlier references in Stevens's vocabulary. The "duck" is recognizable as Holly from his having described her as "Holly, dear duck" in letters. This was reinforced by the second clue: the mother-daughter relationship established in the poem between "any duck" and "a mother." The occasion of the poem was Stevens's identification with Holly. He conjured her feeling "fluttering" helplessness in response to her mother's seeming, at least at times, "Regretful that she bore her." While this identification was the prompting of the poem's "true subject," the second identification—Stevens's projection into the consciousness of Hans Christian Andersen (here he omitted the last name, as in the case of "Bach" in "Two at Norfolk")—was the basis for the "poetry of the subject" woven around the "true" one to distract attention from it. Once he had done this, the "you" he addressed in the poem was ambiguously Hans Christian, the poet himself, and Elsie.

The hypothetical construction was a further elaboration of the poetry of the subject. Thinking about the various possibilities, the poet diffused the pain he felt at witnessing the situation of his child with her mother:

> If any duck in any brook,
> Fluttering the water
> For your crumb,
> Seemed the helpless daughter
>
> Of a mother
> Regretful that she bore her;
> Or of another,
> Barren, and longing for her;
>
> What of the dove,
> Or thrush, or any singing mysteries?
> What of the trees
> And intonations of the trees?
>
> What of the night
> That lights and dims the stars?
> Do you know, Hans Christian,
> Now that you see the night?

At first, in the face of the occasioning perception, the poet devised an obverse circumstance, the impossible, possible wish for Holly: that rather than be the unwanted daughter of a regretful mother, she be the child of a barren woman, who would want and love her to an extreme. This second impossibility worked to neutralize the actuality of the other. Then, distracting attention still more, the "dove" and "thrush," "any singing mysteries," and, finally, the "trees" and "night" were introduced for consideration. Moving slowly to the inanimate before ending with the "night," the most abstract, ungraspable aspect of the human environment, Stevens hoped to alleviate the immediacy of his sympathetic pang for Holly by making her, as each of these other things, "part of nature, part of us." No earthly mothers suckled them. Like Jove, they had their "inhuman birth." The "dear duck" was no worse off than they. Just as he had always earlier turned his attention to things in the world around him when touched by something that might have caused him to be "bathed in tears," so now he turned his daughter with curls into a duck and, in his imagination, protected her from pain by likening her to increasingly generalized things.

❧

As Stevens's sensibility gradually gained strength through these years of watching another's growth, the world around him was dying. Confidence in the future, already severely shaken by the First World War, finally collapsed after the deceptive boom of the twenties with the financial crisis of 1929. However, each new failure tolling the nation's bankruptcy ensured that those as talented as Stevens in settling insurance claims would be made increasingly secure in their positions and called on more and more to use their skills. As unemployment figures rose, building projects planned in the twenties were brought to completion. The Empire State Building was finished in 1931, while Rockefeller Center was just begun. And with the crisis, there were more failures; failures meant claims. Accordingly Stevens became busier and busier through the early thirties, again traveling often and being overwhelmed with work at the office.

Things were so pressed that after his desired return to poetry, which produced the group of new poems added to the 1931 edition of *Harmonium,* Stevens again found himself unable to make time to spend with his Muse. He wrote to Lincoln Kirstein in April 1931, responding to a request for a contribution to *Hound and Horn,* "Nothing short of a coup d'état would make it possible for me to write poetry now" (*L* 261). He added that he looked forward to seeing the article R. P. Blackmur had written about his work. There was at least satisfaction in knowing that his poems were receiving serious attention, especially in *Hound and Horn,* which had succeeded the *Dial* as "the official organ of the strictly-artistic advance guard."[22] Stevens particularly looked forward to the appearance of this piece because he had given Blackmur the key to understanding his poetic purpose, much in the same way that he had earlier given L. W. Payne central insights. In his correspondence with Blackmur about his planned article, which quoted extensively from the 1931 *Harmonium,* Stevens stressed "ambiguity" as the essential thing, "the *explicit* value of poetry" (December 2, 1931). Blackmur noted that both William Empson—following up on I. A. Richards's "Confucianism"—and Kenneth Burke were attempting to provide the theoretical groundwork for understanding this significant element. It reflected the uncertain nature of reality as it was being revealed to be since the turn of the century with the work of Einstein, Freud, and their followers. Blackmur observed as well that this was not just perceived by those who lived in the "atmosphere of science-impregnated minds." Such individuals understood falsely and wanted only precision and a one-to-one correspondence between things and signs; an example was a critic like Granville Hicks to whom "eloquence and ambiguity as precise instruments seem[ed] *nothing but* paradox." Blackmur's essay appeared in the issue for January–March 1932.[23]

Almost a year and a half later Stevens was still in the predicament of not being able to write, though it was clear that he wanted to. As he mentioned in a letter to Elsie on one of his trips to Florida, because of a temporary lull in business demands he hoped to give himself to what made life "really worthwhile." He had managed a few "scraps" ("The Woman Who Blamed Life on a Spaniard," in response to a request from *Contempo;* it appeared in the December 1932 issue), as he put it to Harriet Monroe in an August 1932 letter accompanying another "scrap" for *Poetry.* This was probably "Good Man, Bad Woman," a poem that dealt with the theme of disappointment and disillusionment in love, centering on "*her* indifference" (italics mine), as in "Le Monocle de Mon Oncle" and "Red Loves Kit," but now with the admission that this implicit rejection disturbed his world and caused him pain. Parts of both these "woman" poems had been composed around the time he was gathering things to add to the second edition of *Harmonium.* "The Woman Who Blamed Life on a Spaniard" also explored the theme of disappointment in love, its lines and images repeating those of the earlier poems. These two poems were the coda completing those pieces, as the other seven closed the major poems discussed above.

Section III of "The Woman Who Blamed Life on a Spaniard" was written, according to a letter dated December 26, 1930, for Harriet Monroe in celebration of her seventieth birthday. Stevens added that it was "for [her]self alone." That he later sent it to *Contempo* as part of a larger poem was curious in that it repeated the pattern Elsie complained of early in her husband's career, when he sent poems apparently for "her alone" to various journals. The section supposedly composed for Monroe, when seen together with the first two sections of the poem, announces itself as belonging with them. It is clear that it was written with them and not as a separate occasional piece for Miss Monroe. But in that section Stevens made the transition from the disturbing real female in his life to the Muse, so that, when it is seen alone, the section seems a self-contained figurative "musing" on the poetic process. A change he made in the version that appeared in *Contempo* revealed the subtlety of the connection between the actuality of the situation between him and Elsie and his covering it in imaginative language. In the original version the voice of the Muse, symbolized as "the fowl of Venus," was described as having a "destroying voice," a voice that would repeat the "no, no," the "two words that kill" in "Le Monocle." In the second version "destroying" became "decoying," a change signaling precisely the way Stevens disguised his "true subject" in the "poetry of the subject."

It is important to remember that "The Woman Who Blamed Life on a Spaniard" and "Good Man, Bad Woman" were written during the last phase of the *Harmonium* years, as were the others that formed the coda added to the second edition. After them, and the period of increased involvement with the business world during the first years of the Depression, Stevens stopped considering the pains of his personal life. These two poems were the last to deal specifically with the problems he experienced with his woman. In the same way Florida was left behind. The changes in the outside world were too great to be ignored. As one directly connected to the economic workings of that world, Stevens could not avoid being affected by what they meant.

While there had been booming expansion during the twenties, accompanied by equal expansion in political and social life, after 1929's "Black Thursday," October 24, an understandably strong contraction began. Each year of the century's third decade had brought exciting developments. In science work on the atom continued and yielded an entirely new understanding of the structure of matter. The work of Werner Heisenberg and Niels Bohr on quantum mechanics, formulated in 1925, brought Heisenberg the Nobel Prize in physics for his matrix theory in 1932. A year later, culminating their involvement over the previous ten years, Paul Dirac and Erwin Schrödinger discovered yet another form of atomic energy, and together won the physics prize. By 1929 Prince Louis Victor de Broglie, following up on the suggestions implicit in Einstein's theories, had discovered the wave nature of electrons. Abstracting from and applying these new perceptions, Max Planck, in 1931, came out with his *Positivism and the Real Outside World.*

At the same time as the microscopic level of reality was being revealed in more and more detail, on the macroscopic scale, similar work through the twenties prompted a better understanding of social groupings. Biologists produced evidence of the workings of the chromosomes in heredity. Anthropologists like Franz Boas published work illustrating the relativity of cultural mores—detailed explications of what Stevens had expressed poetically as his soil being man's intelligence. Ironically, just as this work—one specifically refuting the theory of the master race—was appearing, in Germany life was growing more violent. The war that would erupt in 1939, though generated by economic circumstances, would be a war fought for truly ideological reasons, not only verbally ideological ones. For the first time the "true cause" was supported by the hard facts of science. This became patent in 1933, the year Hitler was elected chancellor. Not only were all forms of "modernism" rejected in favor of superficial realism, but all books by non-Nazi and Jewish authors were banned, and Jews themselves were boycotted. But before this came to pass, much that would change the way the world looked had been developed in this country devastated almost twenty years before by the Great War. Not only had the most monumental scientific discoveries of the century been made here, but the most significant new movements in the arts had also grown on its wasted soil.

Having to rebuild after World War I, Germany found the most efficiently pleasing forms in the Bauhaus style. Though its makers and their compeers in painting and music would not be able to continue their work (in 1933 Paul Klee and Wassily Kandinsky, for example, having already created their expressionist "blue" styles, left for Switzerland and France, while Bruno Walter left for Vienna), the preparation was not lost. By the end of the decade the Bauhaus had found a new home in America as the Museum of Modern Art, opened in 1929, and the Daily News Building, in 1930, both attested in New York City. The German millionaires who backed the Nazi movement effected a purge of the very things that were establishing the identity of modernism in the twentieth century. Again, ironically, after the Second World War, largely because of the intellectual migration, it was the United States that profited most directly from the work that had been done in Germany as it recovered from the First War. This situation paralleled what had happened in New York around the time of the onset of that war, when Duchamp, Gleizes, and Picabia had left their homes in Europe to avoid or protest participation. Just as Stevens had benefited from that earlier exodus, so he would be enriched by this second, most directly from meeting Henry and Barbara Church, who fled Vichy France. But this meeting was still years ahead.

Along the way, however, Stevens had been preparing himself. He maintained his habit of keeping in touch with the intellectual and artistic developments on the Continent and in England by reading a selection of foreign periodicals. (In addition to those he subscribed to regularly, he was always quick to get copies of new ones as they appeared; from these samples he would decide which to add to his subscription lists.) He was aware of the major contributions through the twenties and early thirties. Among the most important of these for him were works that reflected the deepened concern with the nature of reality after the new understandings in science. Especially significant were those that explored moral or ethical questions in the face of the relativistic perception of the universe and man's place in it. Freud's *Civilization and Its Discontents* appeared in 1930. After winning the Nobel Prize for literature in 1927, Bergson particularized his study of human consciousness in connection with the larger natural background in *The Two Sources of Morality and Religion* in 1932. José Ortega y Gasset's *Revolt of the Masses* had already appeared in 1929, together with Martin Heidegger's *What Is Philosophy?* Simultaneous with the formal organization of the Vienna Circle, also in 1929, Alfred North Whitehead published *The Function of Reason,* following it up three years later with *Adventures of Ideas,* at the same time that James Joyce's *Ulysses* was finally allowed in the United States. (Stevens had already long had his copy, smuggled in for him shortly after its first appearance by Pitts Sanborn.) Exploring the nature and behavior of human beings, following up on Freud's work, but suggesting more drastic solutions, Wilhelm Reich published his *Character Analysis,* also in 1933.

Literature abroad reflected the excitement with the new consciousness of human beings and their place in the world. But it pointed out, too, the precariousness of the position as it variously manifested itself in individual perception—Marcel Proust's completed *Remembrance of Things Past,* for example, appeared posthumously in 1927—and in political and social life, as in Thomas Mann's *Magic Mountain* of 1924, Robert Musil's *Man Without Qualities* (also published in parts in *Mesures,* the journal edited by Henry Church and his circle in Paris, a journal to which Stevens subscribed from its first number), and André Malraux's *Man's Fate,* published in 1933. In addition, there were prophetic allegories of things to come now that the notion of "technocracy" had established its currency. Aldous Huxley's *Brave New World* was published in 1932, the same year in which Goethe's centenary was celebrated around the world. Stevens, feeling the full weight of what Goethe had imagined possible for human beings in their relation to nature with his idea of *Organismus* and feeling what the pull of technocracy promised, probably smiled sadly. Poets and scientists were also turning their attention to things as they were. Paul Valéry's *Regards sur le Monde Actuel* appeared in 1931, a year after Einstein's *About Zionism,* a specific address to a problem involving facts that could not be ignored, with racism in Germany becoming more vicious by the day and the situation in Palestine more than uneasy.

Painting and music as well reflected concern with the unseeable but "intuited" forces that were felt to move life. This was clear in the expressionist works of the "Blue Rider" group (formed in 1924 by Lyonel Feininger, Aleksey von Jawlensky, Kandinsky, and Klee) and in the surrealist works of figures like Salvador Dali (*Persistence of Memory* was completed in 1931) and Max Ernst. This concern also showed itself in the metaphysical paintings of Giorgio de Chirico, Giorgio Morandi, and others in the Italian school like Alberto Giacometti. (*The Palace at 4 A.M.* was completed in 1933, its theme echoing the bankruptcy of the old order in the same way as Mann's and Musil's work.) There were also the unaffiliated masters like Pablo Picasso, who began to explore the abstract in the twenties, and Henri Matisse, whose success with color and shape as expressions of feeling had already firmly established his reputation in America (the Barnes Foundation murals of *The Dance* were finished in 1931). At the same time there were works that reflected the increasingly threatening mechanization of life—the work of Fernand Léger, for instance, which extended also into film; his *Ballet Mécanique* was performed early in the decade, in 1923, the same year that *Harmonium* appeared with its faint echoes of the lost pastoral ideal squeaking through in haunting phrases. In music the expressionist mode was further explored by Igor Stravinsky, Kurt Weill, and, more extensively, Arnold Schönberg, while Edgard Varèse's *Ionisation* mirrored what he understood of the new scientific perception of reality.

While all this was going on abroad, the United States was just beginning to develop self-consciousness. Unlike the work of the English and Europeans, which during this period concerned itself with universal themes, here philosophy, music, painting, and literature for the most part reflected what was most native. John Dewey's work through the twenties and early thirties centered on the practical application of the pragmatic outlook, as in his 1927 book, *The Public and Its Problems.* Two years later, in *The Quest for Certainty,* he linked the epistemological problems of the century to their roots in the past while particularizing the present situation. Advancing technology offered seeming security in fixed solutions; in contrast, answers to ethical questions became increasingly ambiguous. He pursued this theme even further in *Philosophy and Civilization,* which appeared in 1931.

In music the work of Charles Ives and Aaron Copland (the first person to win a Guggenheim Fellowship in 1925) explored American themes to their fullest, opening new paths across frontiers of tonality and rhythm. The same tendency was apparent in the more popular forms, with musicals like Richard Rodgers and Lorenzo Hart's *Connecticut Yankee* or like Jerome Kern and Oscar Hammerstein II's *Show Boat* in 1927. These productions, which sentimentalized regional identities and the relations between North and South, stood in almost parodic counterpart to Weill and Bertolt Brecht's savage social criticism in *Mahagonny,* first performed in the same year. George Gershwin was more musically sophisticated but still evoked a programmatic aspect of the American experience, though this time abroad, with his *American in Paris.* At the same time technological advances in recording and radio (in 1924 there were 2.5 million sets in use in the United States) popularized jazz as a form equal in importance to "serious music"; it had the advantage of offering the pleasure of vocal and dance accompaniment. Duke Ellington and Jelly Roll Morton were star figures, and the Charleston became the 1925 dance craze, with flappers, their skirts high above their quick-moving knees, rustling whatever excitement the music alone didn't generate.

This was also the period during which Grant Wood produced his satirically naïve *American Gothic* (1930) and *Daughters of the American Revolution* (1932), and Charles Demuth's American cubist style memorialized the particularly American urban scene with skies filled with factory chimneys. Similarly, the first of William Faulkner's novels about Yoknapatawpha County, subtly and parodically echoing the distinctly American identity, appeared in 1929, the same year that Thomas Mann won the Nobel Prize in literature and that Robert Graves's *Goodbye to All That* mourned the inanity of the war that had destroyed illusions of human progress. In 1932 John Galsworthy won the Nobel Prize for his monumental *Forsyte Saga* (which had occupied Stevens's attention over years earlier, though without his great remark), and John Dos Passos published *1919.* Erskine Caldwell's work, revealing the rawness of certain aspects of American life, was popular. A year earlier, in 1931, the most American of America's twentieth-century poets, Robert Frost, won the Pulitzer Prize for his *Collected Poems,* just as Stevens, only four years his junior, was reissuing his first volume. In the same year the Pulitzer for biography went to Henry James for his quintessentially American study of Charles W. Eliot, the president who had made Harvard what it had been for Stevens and Frost. A year earlier it had been Conrad Aiken who won the Pulitzer for poetry, as Hart Crane published *The Bridge,* which carried across a Whitmanian sentiment to confront the new American scene. Reinforcing how seriously "old" America wanted to protect its developing identity, also in 1930, Boston banned all of Leon Trotsky's work. Comic strips, instead, reached their peak of popularity. Especially favored was *Blondie,* which appeared in the same year to celebrate in a tenderly mocking manner, too playful to be taken to heart, the typical American family, with Dagwood revealing a disorganized, ineffectually bumbling, but lovable figure who had to be guided and protected by his wife. The humorous treatment of the emasculated male was disclosing a great deal about the inherent problems of the American ideal.

The same problems were being treated seriously by another, however, who also illustrated paradigmatically in his life both the positive and the negative sides of the question of American male identity. This was Ernest Hemingway, who, with the physical distance of an ocean between him and his native soil, did not, like Pound, have his sleep troubled by the thought of what America would be like if the classics had a wide circulation. He concentrated instead on what life could be like without any reference to the classics. Rejecting the path prepared for him by his well-established family, precisely the path the still-new middle-class Stevens family struggled to open for its sons, Hemingway chose the adventuring life over the university and attempted to become in actuality Emerson's idealized man who could stand ever erect before nature. During the twenties he perfected a pure American speech in Parisian cafés and salons, listening to Gertrude Stein utter her sibylline sentences. He then set a standard that many would imitate for decades following, one so strong that even he, in his later years, would find it difficult to maintain; *Across the River and into the Trees,* for example, seemed a failed parody of his earlier work.

Edmund Wilson was one of the first critics to "discover" and praise Hemingway's work. In a review of *In Our Time,* which appeared in 1925, and, later, of *Men Without Women*—both of which Stevens, a regular reader of the *Partisan Review,* where they appeared, certainly had read—Wilson celebrated the purity and elegance of this new voice against the criticisms of more conservative readers who found the chiseled hardness of Hemingway's diction disturbing. Modernism in prose was no easier to accept than modernism in poetry; concern with form alone seemed threatening to those looking for a moral content or a romanticized view of some aspect of America's new history, like *The Forsyte Saga.* A concern with form pointed out the creator's separation from society, his entrance into and participation in the sacred precinct of art.

The strain between the two positions concerning the place and function of the artist in society was reflected as clearly in the response to Stevens's work during his period of silence through the twenties and in the reviews of the second edition of *Harmonium.* While his reputation had been growing steadily through the twenties, as illustrated by the various articles written between 1924 and 1929,[24] and though he became a model for younger poets to imitate, most of the reviews of the 1931 edition of *Harmonium* denounced his esotericism and his finely polished style.[25]

One exception was expressed in the *Boston Evening Transcript.* The reviewer praised the "rose harmonies" and perceived Stevens's "significant modern Weltanschauung. . . ." It was in the city Ezra Pound disliked for its Amy Lowells and others affecting Harvard airs that a voice that sang its ties to a European past could be appreciated. This voice was appreciated too by Morton Dauwen Zabel, who eventually succeeded Harriet Monroe as editor of *Poetry.* (Stevens once commented that Zabel's full name was like an exercise in comparative philology.) Zabel did not even think it necessary to compare Stevens with his contemporaries; he had passed far beyond them. Another voice of support came from Horace Gregory in the *New York Herald Tribune.* He astutely recognized the strong social commitment present in the volume others found decadent and effete. He compared Stevens to James A. McNeill Whistler:

> Wallace Stevens is secure in much the same fashion that Whistler remains intact within our memories. Like John Crowe Ransom, Wallace Stevens is the perfect example of the civilized artist thrust head first into modern society. He is not merely a connoisseur of fine rhythms and the precise nuances of the lyrical line, but a trained observer with an intelligent eye upon the decadence that follows the rapid acquisition of wealth and power.[26]

In spite of these strong evidences of recognition, Stevens still wanted to reach more than the circle of initiates who understood the avant-garde. He wanted this especially now, when society so needed to see itself in its ever-changing relation to the forms it created. He wanted his work to be sustaining in an uncertain universe. It was because of this desire that Stevens was so careful to stress to Blackmur "the *explicit* value of ambiguity" for poetry. Poetry had to have ambiguity as its essential element if it was going to be a part of things as they were.

It was, no doubt, partly because of the split in the reactions to the second edition of *Harmonium* that Stevens again withdrew into a short period of silence between 1931 and 1933. But then, too, the demands of the real world required almost all his attention. He was not untouched by the possible threat the general economic uncertainty presented, however vague, to his security, especially since he had recently bought the large house on Westerly Terrace where he was to spend the rest of his life. In letters to Elsie and business associates at various points between 1931 and 1933, when he was away working for the Hartford, he commented on the precariousness of others' positions and on the situation at the company. He prided himself on having helped prevent the unemployment of James Powers by having brought him to the Hartford when he did. He had met the talented young attorney in Miami four years earlier, when Powers was acting in behalf of J. C. Penney against Stevens, who was representing the Hartford. Stevens was so impressed by Powers that he persuaded him to come back to the home office as his assistant. Had he not, the failure of banks and businesses at the Depression's most frightening point would have meant disaster for Powers. He remained with the Hartford for two years, then returned to private practice, first in New York, later in Portland, Oregon, where he settled, but he always maintained regular contact with Stevens; the Powerses came east every year and in the fifties spent a summer in Cornwall, Connecticut. Stevens always saw them on their visits.

Under such extreme economic circumstances, with unemployment figures in the United States jumping from 4.5 million in 1931 to 13.7 million in 1932 (worldwide unemployment at 30 million showed that America was suffering the brunt of the disaster), it was natural that Stevens did not want to take the chance of being too distracted by what he would have to do in order to make his poetry accessible to all. For the while he had done what he could through Blackmur, and it would have its effect, at least on the poetry that Blackmur and some of the other younger poets were producing. As Alfred Kreymborg noted, Stevens had been an important influence on the poets of the "Secessionist group" and had been one of e. e. cummings's early models. Allen Tate echoed this, adding that Stevens had "intelligently" managed to bring into American poetry what was important from the Parnassians and symbolists.[27]

Stevens's inability to focus attention on writing at the peak moment of the American crisis was not helped by the fact that after having maintained his regimen of health fairly well over the years since 1926, on applying for life insurance in the spring of 1931, he was turned down. Dr. Herrick reported to the insurance company doctor in May of that year that "Mr. Stevens [had] continued to take good care of himself" and that his blood and urine chemistry were normal. But there were irreversible conditions evidenced by retinal arteriosclerosis and moderate cardiac hypertrophy. In addition, though he had not become again the "obese machine" he once was, he had gained 13 pounds since his lowest weight of 187 in 1927, when his blood pressure, too, at 130/75 was normal, as were his blood and urine. In 1929 there was a rise in blood pressure to 135–40/90, and by February 1931, the time of the latest examination, it had risen to 180/95. It was on the basis of this kind of fluctuation that insurance was refused. The company's doctor suggested that Stevens reapply the following year, provided he was able to stabilize his blood pressure and keep it below 150/90. He added, no doubt realizing that the changes in Stevens's condition were at least partially the result of his again yielding to indulgences: "The elimination of the use of any stimulants and a diet tending not to increase [his] weight [were] important." Though the eye condition that had first sent him to seek help seven years earlier had cleared up satisfactorily and he needed only reading glasses, knowing that he was a high-risk case at a time when business pressures were greatest was disturbing. At the same time he felt the added burdens of the house and Holly's education. (Holly attended private school and was also enrolled in special programs, like that at Vassar in euthenics, which she attended with her mother during the summer of 1931.)

More, there were now the finer things of life to be considered—things that Stevens had grown used to having. Over the last few years he had made a point of asking his correspondents in different parts of the world to send him items from daily life in those places in order to give him a concrete sense of life elsewhere. Whereas for a long time before, he had satisfied primarily his own desire with these objects and with fragrant teas from the East, as well as with books, journals, and other bibelots for his aesthetic appreciation, now he also wanted curios for Holly. In this Elsie participated. This was important for Stevens. He knew he had to preserve the security of the household so that she, too, could grow in following what was good for the child. While during the early years of their marriage her main involvement outside home and church had been her music—after she had joined the Hartford Musical Club, she sometimes performed (mirroring her husband's interest in the "new," she had played pieces by contemporary Italian composers for one program)—now, through and with Holly, she broadened her interests. At the same time she began to keep closer to home, as moving through menopause brought into greater relief the features of her personality that had caused her as a young girl to walk "straight and stiff, like a gendarme almost." Within a few years, the robust beauty of her Liberty head presence had withered into wizened eccentricity, and she dressed like a maiden schoolmarm of sixty. No doubt painfully aware of this change herself, the woman who had won a beauty contest in her youth, who had once been so attentive to fashion, perusing magazines and newspapers and making herself smart clothes, now saw a sterile old woman's face reflected in the mirror. Remembering what she once was when she posed for the sculptor who memorialized her, Elsie withdrew more and more, eventually becoming almost a total recluse. (As though mimicking this sad situation, the bust of her that Stevens had commissioned after Elsie had posed for the coins Adolph Alexander Weinman designed was finally lost in one of the moves made after Elsie sold and left the house on Westerly Terrace in the years after her husband died. She did not want the bust displayed and urged Holly to take it. Holly, feeling it belonged with her mother, did not. At some point, whether before or after her mother's death, it disappeared.)

The physical change in Elsie was something her husband could not help observing. It seemed to follow the change that had come over America between 1923 and 1933. Something had died, just as many of the important individuals of Stevens's youth had died. These figures, though he did not know them personally, had been centers around which his imagination and intelligence circled: Sarah Bernhardt (d. 1923), whose gesture accompanying "To be or not to be" as she performed Hamlet gave Stevens one of his earliest and strongest insights into the significance of symbols accompanying thought; Charles W. Eliot (d. 1926), whose pedagogical principles shaped life at Harvard and provided the necessary tension between others like himself and individuals like James, Santayana, and Charles Eliot Norton, who were Stevens's direct and indirect mentors (their manners, in spite of their intellectual difference from Eliot, ensured that Stevens and those like him would emerge as gentlemen in the courtliest sense of the word); Amy Lowell (d. 1925), who had early praised Stevens's strong new voice; Bliss Carman (d. 1929), whose songs from Vagabondia had solaced Stevens, supplied an imaginative bridge which he and Elsie could cross together, and provided one of the models for the "June Books"; Kenneth Grahame (d. 1932), another author who had touched Stevens, especially in relationship to Elsie during the years of their courtship; D. H. Lawrence (d. 1930), with whom, as later critics realized, Stevens shared an outlook concerning the pressure of the real on the possibilities of a life connected with nature and instinct. Something about each of these figures expressed an aspect of the old order before the idea of technocracy became the commonplace it now was. A natural grace, like Elsie's movement on the half dollar, had been lost to the machine pace of the modern industrial state, and with it, for the most part, had gone the sense of humor, the comic element that, as Bergson had made explicit, could neutralize its effects. Stevens and the others in Arensberg's circle had clearly understood the importance of the comic and all had tried to make it "part of the res." But the pressure of events directed by the limited logic of rational progress toward an ideal still bound to the Calvinist work ethic—with its stress on sobriety and diligence—did not allow the comic to continue as the important force it could have been.

This shift was mirrored in what happened, too, as mechanical means of communication and entertainment took over what had been the place of comic figures like Mark Twain earlier in the century, Will Rogers in the twenties, and the host of vaudeville comedians whose itinerant and improvised performances provided a healthy, spontaneous critique of things as they were. Like Marcel Duchamp, the vaudeville comedians dealt with sexuality in human situations. With the establishment of the film industry this changed. As the nation grew hungrier, the film industry boomed. The twenties and early thirties saw the move from silents to talkies, the beginning of color films, the start of Clark Gable's "star" career. These things occurred against an increasingly disintegrating reality that culminated in 1933. The newly elected Franklin Delano Roosevelt, given wide powers, closed banks by presidential order from March 6 to 9. The United States went off the gold standard. The Tennessee Valley Authority and Public Works Administration were established, and Prohibition was repealed. All these measures were attempts to rescue the quickly sinking economy. In sharp contrast, in 1933 the film industry produced 127 sound films, as opposed to 18 in 1929. There was also wide radio broadcasting. But the mass availability of film and radio meant censorship as well. This was inimical to the spontaneous improvisations on which the earlier popular comic forms had been based. It wouldn't be until the brilliant antics and asides of Groucho Marx and his brothers, whom Stevens appreciated even more than the French films he loved (in contrast with American films of this period, European films were not prudish about sexuality), that some of what had been lost with vaudeville and road comics found its way into film.

Stevens considered Groucho Marx one of the "greatest goods" (like ice cream and red-winged blackbirds). The way this comedian functioned in relationship to his brothers on-screen was very much like the way Stevens's "true subject" worked in relationship to the "poetry of the subject." While most of the audience responded to the ridiculous situations and bizarre behavior of the brothers as they played against one another and others in their roles in the plot—all combined, like the poetry of the subject—Groucho dropped his loaded verbal asides, striking sharp blows at the way things were, as he either spoke the lines himself or prompted Chico with his feigned Italian accent to bring their meaning—the "true subject"—across. "You can't-a-fool-a-me. There ain't-a-no Sanity Claus" was neutralized by their designed distractions for an audience that knew full well that the world had gone mad, that things were wholly out of control. No Santa Claus, no God, could restore the innocence that had been lost.

While films offered easy escape into other worlds where things as they were somehow remained as they were, the passage from innocence to experience was poignantly echoed by the change in the most popular songs from 1923 to 1933. Early in the decade songs like Irving Berlin's "April Showers" offered tunefully soothing promises that painful situations would be resolved, and others like "Yes, We Have No Bananas" playfully treated the immigrant experience with language and so lightened feelings of alienation and difference. However, by 1933 the despairing notes of "Brother, Can You Spare a Dime?" reflected the total collapse of the capitalist dream, in spite of the fact that through the Depression many people continued to amass fortunes and build personal empires.

But the time required that those who were worst off believe that even those who had made it were now in the same situation as they. Mass delusion compensated for mass illusion, and the artificial paradises created by films, songs, and other forms of popular entertainment, though not Edenic, reflected the greatest need of the age. These functioned to provide a sense of national unity far more than the adoption as national anthem in 1931 of Francis Scott Key's "Star-Spangled Banner" from the old English song "To Anacreon in Heaven." The progressions and rhythms of "Minnie the Moocher" were far easier to follow than the demanding spans of Key's piece. None had witnessed and few knew the details of the conflict that the anthem celebrated, but no member of the population—in 1933 nearly double its 1900 figure of 76 million—whether new immigrant, scion of first settlers, or child of slaves, did not recognize the figure and hear familiar strains in the popular song. In some way everyone had to "mooch," become a kind of criminal, break some commandment in order to survive. This was true not just of the gangster in Chicago. Everyone was culpable; the collapse of 1929 could be seen as just punishment for the collective loss of faith that by now had filtered down to even the uneducated masses.

The real advances of the decade that had brought appropriately enthusiastic responses—the conquering of the air marked by first Charles Lindbergh's and then Amelia Earhart's flight across the Atlantic; the synthesis of nylon, magically making material out of liquids and gases, a creation that promised the feeling of silken luxury to all; the completion of futuristic skyscrapers with spires still mimicking steeples and symbolizing the continued aspirations of the continent of builders; the opening of longer bridges and tunnels across and under broad spans of water (the George Washington Bridge opened in 1929, while work began on the Golden Gate in 1932; the Holland Tunnel opened in 1927); the mysterious but deceptive feeling of access to others through radio and films—all were counterbalanced by what went on beneath the surface polished by these technological miracles. In addition to the increasing economic and political disturbances occurring in Europe, Asia, and

South America and slowly being felt in the United States—it was Germany that first had huge levels of unemployment, bank failures followed by closings, and going off the gold standard, then Britain, then the United States—there were subtler, deeper, sociocultural problems being worked out as well. The Scopes trial in 1925 and Tennessee's forbidding sex education in schools during the same year pointed to how resistant the American people were to give up Victorian ideals and admit their ties to nature, about which more and more was being learned each day.

Those in the forefront, of course, understood the implications of what was being learned. It was not accidental that the new architectural styles instituted by the Bauhaus or exemplified by the designs of Le Corbusier (another person attached to the Henry Church circle) abandoned the points and spires that mimicked the myth of progress. There was no place in the world of things as they were now for decorative elements that suggested the separation of spirit from matter. Squared, geometric shapes, fitting together and following the contours of the environment, were what was most natural as well as most efficient. Valéry's 1924 dialogue, "Eupalinos, or the Architect," expressed specifically that a sense of time was essential in human creations. Though nature might evolve beautiful forms over centuries of process, man could imagine and shape them in his lifetime. When Stevens wrote a prologue for the Bollingen translation of this piece, as well as for "Dance and the Soul," shortly before he died, he read in Valéry's words the record of his own experience through this difficult decade. Living through this period required that the sensitive individual make peace with the transitoriness of all creations and at the same time derive pleasure from them as mere instants of the present, like the pattern of the wind's movement on the face of the waters. The point of seeing this now was not to imagine the spirit of God but to "bang from it a savage blue" (*CP* 166).

Exploring what this transitoriness meant, composers created improvisatory, stochastic progressions. Painters recorded their own movements, thoughts, and perceptions of time passing as shapes and figures yielding to one another; there was no illusion of fixed forms as lines moved like liquid cats across the canvas. And Stevens mused on how "It"—everything, all—"Must Change." Though Hitler's coming to power parodied the illusion of world unity represented in 1932 by the Olympics and in 1933 by the Chicago World's Fair, and though Japan took advantage of the economic chaos in the West by brutally undercutting prices, seen from a broader perspective, these events were simply "other makings of the sun" (*CP* 532). The important thing was to do all that was possible to make a more pleasing structure, one that would satisfy primary needs. In order to do this, one had to abstract from the details of experience, to become as familiar with as many of these details as possible in order to be able to deal with the broadest spectrum—the most salient, nourishing aspects, the lucid, inescapable rhythms, and the noble accents common to all through the ages of the imperfect.

This Stevens attempted. He observed details about himself as he went through his morning's regimen "like a machine." He watched the daily changes in the flowers, trees, and sky he passed on his walks to and from the office. He carefully described places he visited to Holly on series of postcards as he once had to Elsie. On a trip Stevens made to New Orleans in February 1933, he noted facts of nature and culture and taught Holly about Mardi Gras or "Fat Tuesday" and its Lenten function. In all these things Stevens reiterated his commitment to what was real. All thoughts and ideas had to begin from this. Those who had early recognized his gift, like Harriet Monroe and Marianne Moore, feared he would not continue to write and urged him even more pressingly not to "desert his job." Monroe, in August 1932, had put it this way, adding, "Is there anything—*anything*—I can do to keep you keen for it?" (WAS 35). Moore, taking a different, subtler tack, stressed how necessary his work was for "the young," as she put it in noting to him why someone younger had been chosen to review the 1931 edition of *Harmonium:* "The better the book the more important it is that it should be a text for the young" (January 3, 1933). But there was really nothing to fear. Stevens knew that he would write. His purpose was not "to be a poet" but to teach "how to live, what to do." For that he had to live and do what was necessary in the face of the real. Only in that way could his words resonate.

II

A GREAT ORDER IS A DISORDER

1933–1942

But with the objects which are
the work of man it is quite different,
their structure is . . . a disorder!

—The Shade of Socrates,
Paul Valéry, "Eupalinos"

. . . as we both know, being myself is the most difficult thing in the world.

—From a letter to Marianne Moore,
March 3, 1937 (Rosenbach Library)

But I am, in any case,
A most inappropriate man
In a most unpropitious place.

—From "Sailing After Lunch,"
The Collected Poems (p. 120)

Between 1933 and 1942 Stevens succeeded in applying his ideas of order to everyday life so that he could move through his days with ease. Within this order he could safely yield to poetry's disorder. He thus entered his most productive period. In 1935 *Ideas of Order* appeared; in 1936 *Owl's Clover* was published, and "The Irrational Element in Poetry" was delivered as a lecture; in 1937 came *The Man with the Blue Guitar and Other Poems;* in 1942, *Parts of a World, Notes Toward a Supreme Fiction,* and "The Noble Rider and the Sound of Words," also given as a lecture. Stevens also continued to be diligent in the world of business. In 1934 he was, finally, duly rewarded, by being made a vice president of the Hartford. Through these years, Stevens grew into an elder statesman of letters and a poet capable of speaking with the voice of "major-man." He had achieved the aims he had set for himself in the practical world of affairs, had fulfilled his father's expectations that he make a place for himself "on the front bench," and so settled into a steady rhythm around his understatedly stately home on Westerly Terrace. Now he could afford to indulge fully what he had gotten from his mother, the imagination with which he brought the world quite round.

The regularity he established was extreme. Its tempo was set by his responses to things as they were. He did not externally impose order from some notion of how things should be. Things as they were were the givens of his experience, things that could not be altered or controlled by him. Together these things constituted what Freud in *The Future of an Illusion* had included under the heading of Ananke, whatever had to be considered for survival. All things in this category had equal weight. Stevens's response to them was determined simply by their temporality. Some things had to be attended to each day: work at the office; meals; the family circle. Some things had to be attended to each week, each month; yet others, seasonally.

Reacting to these things provided the sustaining, bass rhythm of Stevens's life. Melody, harmony, and counterpoint came from events that were not predictable: changes in the weather; the movement of national and world affairs; contact with others, each with particular and different needs. The work of imagination was to order these "chance" elements against the ground established by the regularly occurring others. This would produce a pleasing whole, a symphony of psalms to the fact of merely circulating with the gift of consciousness. Effecting this meant transforming the self-consciousness that was, according to the dominant Christian myth of nearly 2,000 years, the cause of pain into an instrument on and with which a sacrament of praise for life could be composed.

During these years, after the long period of practice on the harmonium of his early career, Stevens came to understand the "ultimate Plato" as "the reddened flower, the erotic bird" (*CP* 253). He realized that the realm of the ideal was not, as it had been interpreted to be by the Christian fathers, a static "heaven" arrived at through hierarchical ordering of experience and individuals. The ideal was not imminent but immanent, ever-present, and always available. The importance of order was not to fix levels through which only certain individuals could move if guided. It was, rather, the product of reason working to establish a rhythmic and harmonic relation with things as they were, so that it would not be necessary to expend the mind's energy every day on the details of what, if not ordered, remained a chaos of demands requiring full attention. The more regular the order established, the freer the mind to exist in the simple and direct contemplation of whatever was, whatever the "sea of spuming thought" foisted up from the deep reservoirs of being.

Stevens came to understand that the sequence of these ideas could not be determined yet that the pattern they made was the only tie one had to knowing oneself and discovering the world. This was the great disorder that was an order. This was the ideal, made up of nothing else but what the word "idea" in its original etymology revealed, literally, "what was seen." "Sight is a museum of things seen" (*CP* 274), Stevens wrote near the end of this period. The poet saw how the elements gathered from experience and stored in memory disclosed him to himself and bound him to the actual. He realized the Platonic world of forms and appearances in its truly human aspect, not as the basis of a philosophy of pure spirit but as a method to achieve peace in the imperfect present. It was as though Stevens had fully imagined the world of classical Greece and had understood its commitment to democracy as a practical aim rather than as a cold-blooded concept. The possibility offered by Plato was open to all, just as citizenship was open to anyone who learned the language necessary to enter into dialogue and so to thresh out which were the common ideas, those required for continued participation with others and with nature.

It was in large measure Stevens's involvement with Eastern thought that had made this understanding of the "ultimate Plato" possible. In his imaginative reconstruction of the Greek world he had not forgotten to consider the news brought by traders to the sun-filled marketplaces about a prince who had given up all he had in order to meditate alone and blissfully high on a mountaintop about the nature of things as they were. The prince came down to move among people. He asked them questions that would help them see. Socrates, walking barefoot among the people in the agora and asking questions that forced them to clarify terms they used, was not different in spirit from the Indian prince. Stevens the insurance company executive, moving through his everyday world of associates and office workers and teasing them into questioning what he meant by one of his gnomic asides, and Stevens the poet, reading and writing in early morning and evening hours, musing on how best to shape language for his new vulgate of experience, were also not different from Buddha, the figure the Chinese named the "red-bearded barbarian from the West."

By 1935 Stevens had made this affinity explicit in the poems he wrote. Though he noted to correspondents who asked him for contributions that his involvement with poetry over the previous two years, after his long absence from it, was sporadic, the individual pieces, as they came now, were products of moments of intense concentration. He had found it difficult to return to a relationship with a constant and demanding mistress, but as he wrote to Morton Dauwen Zabel in March 1933, there were a good many requests for his poetry, and he did his best to respond to them. These requests were parts of the givens of his experience, and it was his intention to be sensitive to all these givens that struck their chords in him.

But the things he first wrote he did "not much like," as he also noted to Zabel. They seemed to reflect the difficulty he had in returning to his Muse. "Writing again after a discontinuance seems to take me back to the beginning rather than to the point of discontinuance" (*L* 265). Among the poems to which he was referring were some of those discussed at the end of the last chapter, those described as forming a coda for the earlier poems in *Harmonium.* "Good Man, Bad Woman" and "The Woman Who Blamed Life on a Spaniard," in their open treatments of old themes and not chosen by Stevens for inclusion in the second edition of *Harmonium,* seem the most likely candidates for what he did "not much like." He went on in his letter to Zabel to promise that because he would like to make a special effort for Miss Monroe, if he "accomplished anything that seem[ed] to be worthwhile," he would send it.

A year and a half later, in another note to Zabel (*L* 271), after commenting that the things that had appeared in other journals in the interim were "things more or less improvised" ("Snow and Stars" in *New Act* [June 1933]; "The Brave Man" and "A Fading of the Sun" in *Harkness Hoot* [November 1933]; "The Pleasures of Merely Circulating" in *Smoke* [Spring 1934]), he reiterated his promise to do something for *Poetry* within the next few months. This, "Like Decorations in a Nigger Cemetery," appeared in *Poetry* in February 1935. Reflecting his desire to do something special for the journal that had "always been so friendly" to him, the poem revealed Stevens's current major preoccupation and the position in which he now saw himself and the role of poetry. These aspects he also expressed in different forms around the same time: in his response to a six-part questionnaire which appeared in *New Verse* in October 1934; in an introduction to William Carlos Williams's *Collected Poems, 1921–1931;* and in a review of Marianne Moore's *Selected Poems,* which he wrote sometime in late spring or early summer of 1935. Each of these phrased in its own way the interweaving of Eastern and Western perception that he had managed to effect.

Stevens's responses to the "Enquiry" from *New Verse* were especially indicative of his new attitude:

> Q.1. Do you intend your poetry to be useful to yourself or others?
> A. Not consciously. Perhaps I don't like the word useful.
> Q.2. Do you think there can now be a use for narrative poetry?
> A. There can now be a use for poetry of any sort. It depends on the poet.
> Q.3. Do you wait for a spontaneous impulse before writing a poem; if so, is this impulse verbal or visual?
> A. Most often, while the immediate impulse is verbal, there is, no doubt, a group of impulses.
> Q.4. Have you been influenced by Freud and how do you regard him?
> A. No. I have not read Freud, except the *Interpretation.*
> Q.5. Do you take your stand with any political or politico-economic party or creed?
> A. I am afraid that I don't.
> Q.6. As a poet, what distinguishes you, do you think, from an ordinary man?
> A. Inability to see much point to the life of an ordinary man. The chances are the ordinary man himself sees very little point to it.

Stevens's answers were unexpectedly terse and evasive. He had learned this manner from the masters of the East. At least one was also deceptive: He had recently read Freud's *The Future of an Illusion.* (He did not want to give away that easily the provenance of one of the pivotal terms, Ananke, around which he was just now planning his "Decorations" [*CP* 150].)[1] On the surface it might have seemed to many that the poet was being arrogant. But beneath the surface Stevens was being true to his commitment to exclude "personality" from his work while pointing to what he felt to be the value of poetry. Poetry made him more than an ordinary man. In addition, there was an implicit judgment about Western life in general: It was not the political or economic reality, but poetry, art, that gave direction—"a point"—to life. This, too, was in keeping with the Eastern ideal. Stevens knew that in China, throughout the centuries of its history, every household had a copy of one of the classic anthologies from which something was read each day; to those members of the family who could not read, the lines were read aloud.[2] Considering the passing political or economic realities as having ultimate value was thought misguided. Accordingly, when asked about his political affiliation, Stevens responded negatively.

Stevens had arrived at a new stage of his life. He was secure. In addition to his responses to the *New Verse* "Enquiry," the other pieces he wrote during this period, as indicated above, reflected the ease he now felt. This was in great measure a result of the satisfaction he experienced at having fulfilled the expectations he had set for himself in his youth. These more mundane background details he revealed in letters to younger business associates like James Powers. Stevens sensed a particular closeness to Powers. It came both from his having recognized Powers's talents years earlier and from the fact that Powers was like a later version of Walter Butler, the friend of Stevens's New York years who, though younger, offered his older friend a figure to elicit and challenge his competitive spirit. With these men the leftover unresolved childhood tensions, attached to the time when Stevens had found himself in class with his younger brother, could be worked through.

His correspondence with Powers, like that with others who became regular in their responses, established yet another rhythm to syncopate both the faster, repeated beats of his days and nights and the slower ones of seasons and years. From these exchanges of letters, as much as from anything else, Stevens gleaned patterns and images for his poems. These were abstracted from elements that would endure, common elements that at the same time revealed the man in his relation to his particular world. This relation linked him in the chain that stretched from Homer and the poets of the Bible, back through the sages of the East, to the future poets he imagined as virile youths, able to whip from themselves a jovial hullabaloo among the spheres while still in the full flower of their manly power. Unlike these last, his power had come late, with and after much pondering about what had to be dealt with and shed before he could truly sing a song beyond himself.

Stevens opened a letter to Powers in May 1933 (*L* 266) noting his awareness of the rhythmic way he conceived his correspondence with him: "This is in the nature of a semi-annual statement." He appropriately borrowed terms from their business affiliation. He went on to talk about what he called "the best thing [he had] ever done," purchase the house on Westerly Terrace of which he enclosed a photograph. He added humorously that Powers would see that it was much like his own, with a declivity behind it, but "only, of course, much handsomer etc. . [*sic* punctuation]." He commented that it was expensive but that it prevented him from "throwing money away on unimportant things . . . in fact on anything." (Garrett, Sr., would have been proud.) He asked Powers if he recalled that Westerly Terrace was situated on the slopes of Prospect Hill, which, he noted, ran toward a public dump. Meditating on it from his position atop, observing it as part of his everyday life, like Stevenson's hero of counterpane whom he had conjured years earlier from atop a hill in Tennessee, he collected fragments of experience, his "soil," like the bits of wrappers and labels scattered below. He used these images. In his 1934 introduction to William Carlos Williams's *Collected Poems* Stevens concretized his meaning with examples drawn from what he had seen on the dump:

> What, then, is a romantic poet now-a-days? He happens to be one who still dwells in an ivory tower, but who insists that life would be intolerable except for the fact that one has, from the top, such an exceptional view of the public dump and the advertising signs of Snider's Catsup, Ivory Soap and Chevrolet Cars; he is the hermit who dwells alone with the sun and moon, but insists on taking a rotten newspaper. (*OP* 256)

A few years more of such observation produced a specific celebration. "The Man on the Dump" of 1938 abstracted questions from this experience:

> Is it a philosopher's honeymoon, one finds
> On the dump? Is it to sit among mattresses of the dead,
> Bottles, pots, shoes and grass and murmur *aptest eve:*
> Is it to hear the blatter of grackles and say
> *Invisible priest;* is it to eject, to pull
> The day to pieces and cry *stanza my stone?*
> Where was it one first heard of the truth? The the.
> (*CP* 203)

By the time he wrote this poem, he had also observed (as Holly Stevens notes) and identified with the man, said to be a Russian refugee, who built a shack out of old boxes, tin cans, and bottles on the dump and lived there as a semihermit for several years. The reality of the depression was not something Stevens avoided.

He went on with his description to Powers. He noted that the dump was surrounded by Jews and Jewesses—no doubt refugees as well, part of the hundreds of thousands fleeing Hitler's Germany and Stalin's Russia. He painted a picture in words of the "dank and dark" spots of the back grounds of his house, shaded by neighbors' "handsome manor-like trees" and of the garden plot he and Elsie had made for their irises and roses in front. He then related that because of the Depression, there were many burglars. As a result, the neighborhood was brilliantly lit at night, not only by streetlamps but by the householders who went to bed leaving lights burning all over the house to "fool the bums." He added, humorously describing his invented tactics, that "Holly and Mrs. Stevens [had] been trained in the event of a break, to offer to make breakfast and show any visitors round, whether [he was] absent or not." Completing the understated comic portrait, he commented, "I am afraid that if I hear burglars in the house, no one will be able to determine whether I am about or not."

The deflating comic manner of this description was characteristic of the way Stevens now dealt with himself, as was the homely detail he related about how because of the season's late frosts, he had been spraying his transplanted irises with cough compound. To the friend with whom he could be intimate through letter writing, as he had once been with Elsie, he painted a portrait of himself as a modern mock Candide, tending his garden with manufactured compounds. While he wrote of the idealized poet as the sun, "Like Walt Whitman walking along a ruddy shore/ . . . singing and chanting the things that are part of him" (*CP* 150), he presented himself in an everyday, banal aspect, like the attendants at the funeral in "The Emperor of Ice-Cream." This was important. It reflected a conscious commitment to offer consistently, from this point on, the antithetical aspects of whatever he considered. Just as the title "Like Decorations in a Nigger Cemetery" counterpointed the image of Walt Whitman walking that opened the poem, the most common feature of *Ideas of Order* as a volume was the setting up of explicit contrasts. This Stevens pointed out in a letter to Ronald Lane Latimer, who was to publish the volume: "The arrangement is simply based on contrasts; there is nothing rigid about it. Not every poem expresses a phase of order or an illustration of order: after all, the thing is not a thesis" (*L* 279).

His method was illustrated by the titling of juxtaposed poems: "Botanist on Alp (No. 1)" against "Botanist on Alp (No. 2)" and "Nudity at the Capital" against "Nudity in the Colonies." These pairings were designed to give directions about how all the poems should be read, about how the curious tension between the seeming ridiculousness of some of the titles and the seriousness of the content—in spite of the "gaiety" and playfulness of language—should be approached. The inconsistency pointed as well to the difference between the "poetry of the subject" and the "true subject." The disjunction was there to produce a space that would not exist if the seriousness of the "true subject" were matched by ponderous language and meditative titles. In that space the reader would be forced to muse on what could account for the strange marriages of weighty matter and lighthearted manner. Stevens was attempting—as he spelled out now in one of the volume's titles—to show "How to Live. What to Do" (*CP* 125) in order to develop an accepting attitude toward things as they were. Paradoxically, this was the only way of generating positive change. He fully integrated and made more explicit what he had learned from Bergson about the function of comedy. He added what he had learned from the Eastern sages about verbal forms that opened up consciousness to the multiplicity of possibilities rather than limit it to stringent logical dealings. Stevens constructed poems that were puzzles, riddles. They were to be like Japanese koans, which, when understood, produce in the moment of illumination the "angelic hilarity" Stevens, while still a youth, had found to be a goal most worthy of achieving.

This attitude was not confined to silent and solitary contemplation for Stevens. It dominated every aspect of his life. Of the situations where it showed itself most, from the evidence of remaining letters, one was in his relationship with Judge Arthur Powell and his circle. The "annual jaunts" to Florida, which had begun several years earlier, continued into the thirties. Though Stevens's sense of Florida as a place and as an imaginative construct had changed as the depression darkened the face of things and as Stevens developed new feelings about home and family, the relationship with Powell was central and belonged to Florida and the South. It would remain a given, part of the seasonal rhythm of his life.

In the same May 1933 letter to Powers, for example, Stevens reported that he and Powell had made their yearly visit to Key West. (Powers joined on some of these visits.) They were accompanied by two younger associates of the Hartford, C. L. Daughtry and Manning Heard, as well as others. Sometimes business had to be attended to, sometimes it did not, but always Stevens and Powell showed the younger men how to live and what to do much in the same way W. G. Peckham had shown Stevens when he was the young law clerk fresh out of school. All this was part of an American education. Stevens's role as preceptor to ephebes was not limited to poetic, virile youths; indeed, many of the younger people who worked under him remember Stevens's actively taking on this role, even helping them continue their educations. It was a natural part of what had to be done after coming down from the mountain.

However, what Stevens taught by his example in the everyday world and in poetry was not an application of Eastern ascetic modes of being. Though he had made his own the mind and method of the Oriental teachers, he knew that what America needed to learn had to be as naturally a part of its soil as sitting by mountain pools in solitude was to a place teeming with unnumbered numbers. As much as the Easterner needed to dismiss the appeal of man's material creations (because there was simply no possibility of attaining them with things as they were) and to find solitude amid the constant chaos of other people moving and talking, the American needed to learn to appreciate the things his fellows created—if the economic system as it was was not to collapse—and also needed to establish more social connections in order to break down the isolation and alienation attached to being a member of a particular cultural group rather than "an American." Stevens did not articulate these aims explicitly, but it was clear that he lived them and that they were aspects of a historical and social consciousness that also gave shape to his poetic corpus. This consciousness became prominent in the years of his relationship with Powell, as it did later in that with Henry Church.

Powell was archetypally southern and displayed the graciousness and aspirations associated with the Old South since the time of Jefferson. His gentlemanly qualities and courtly manner colored his keen interest in America's regional aspects and his sensitivity to forms that would preserve intrinsically American elements in the face of industrial technology's uniform march across the continent. Stevens valued him for these various gifts and for his speech, rich with images and sounds inseparable from the land. Powell also knew how to have a good time. Unlike the New Englander's typically astringent attitude toward indulgence and enjoyment, the southerner, bred by soothing weather, did not have the fear of profligacy that belonged to those ever aware of harsh winter's approach. This attitude was far closer to that of the old Greeks Stevens loved to imagine. For them, too, though seasons changed, there was never the threat of death from exposure to what nature brought to their part of the earth. In these more temperate climates, the mind was naturally freer to muse.

What Stevens recognized in moving through his time was that with the changes industrialization brought—changes he had mourned in his youth, when he saw sky and land he loved slowly transformed by factory smokestacks and "blocking steel"—the southerners' attitude toward life was appropriate to things as they were becoming. The stalwart New Englanders' stress on industry, thrift, and sobriety could be relaxed now that machines could provide what had earlier to be wrung with continual hard work and diligence. This shift was centrally important. If not made—if, that is, the values of the Calvinist work ethic continued to dominate—people's lives would be driven by unceasing striving, which would produce a gross excess of goods and equal excess of capital in the hands of those who were most industrious, sober, and thrifty. Only this driving would give meaning to life—a driving that could now become, if the new machines were properly used, unnecessary.

Together with this realization went another: The southerners' way of life could be equitable only if each member of the society recognized that the aim of life was not individual advancement—one of the puritanical New Englanders' signs of election—but communal enjoyment. The true gentleman in the new court of America, conceived in its ideal of liberty for all, would abandon all notions of hierarchy. (In direct connection with this, in a late lecture/essay Stevens stressed the importance of getting rid of the "hieratic" in everything; a priestly caste in special contact with revelation of any kind was particularly inimical, in the poet's mind, to ideas of freedom and democracy.) If this were achieved, the dream of the Jeffersonian democracy would be realized. The true gentleman would be constantly attentive to what could be done to help others arrive at the common plain where there was enough ease to enjoy sunsets and stars, the movements of birds and weather—the gifts of human experience on the planet.

In becoming aware of this, Stevens became a naïve socialist. Things he had read over the past ten years, from Bertrand Russell's *Icarus or the Progress of Science* to the various pieces in the *Partisan Review* that he began reading when the journal was born in 1934, had contributed to this understanding. Now, with the ravages of the depression, it became pressingly clear that the ethic that had dominated America with the promise of infinite progress had to be left behind. Pursuing what he saw, Stevens read more of Russell in the thirties. He felt and expressed his sympathy and closeness with the contributors to the *Partisan Review* and *New Republic.* He threaded out his ideas over drinks with friends like Powell and, later, Henry Church. And he acted personally on what he saw as necessary. Increasingly, through the thirties and until his death, Stevens was attentive to the material needs of those with whom he came in contact, whether family members or acquaintances whom he had not met but knew of. He often expressed his offering of help directly, without being asked, as he did in closing the same May 1933 letter to Powers: "I sincerely hope that things are going well with you, even if that only means well enough to enable you to keep going. If I can help you in any way, I shall always be glad to do so." While this could be construed to mean only that he would help him find another position or put him in contact with other business associates who might help him, it is evident from other correspondence that as Stevens became more prosperous, he shared his prosperity with others unstintingly. By the end of the decade he was a major supporter of his brother, Garrett, and his family; later he extended similar support, usually couched as Christmas gifts, to his widow, as well as to his surviving sister, Elizabeth, and her daughter whenever necessary.

Beyond the family there was the hungry, sickly poet who wrote periodically of his woes and who devised elaborate schemes for subscription offerings to elicit support from Stevens on the ground of being a great admirer and student of his work. Stevens good-humoredly and realistically dismissed the subscription schemes and simply sent money whenever he could afford it. In a less personal but nonetheless involved way, as the years of the thirties passed into the forties, he became an active supporter of efforts like the Alcestis Press and the Cummington Press, paying for copies of his own things that the presses wanted to give him. He also subscribed to new journals attempting to make their way. By the forties his reputation for extending help had reached to Europe, where through contacts like Winifred Bryher, he heard of Hermann Hesse's financial difficulties and made a quiet arrangement through her to buy some of the writer's watercolors. These acts of generosity were carried out with the greatest subtlety and grace. It was a case not of playing the munificent benefactor but of contributing to the communal effort of existing in a world made increasingly difficult by what Stevens called the "pressures of reality" (*NA* 20–27). He knew that under these circumstances it was not possible for an individual to perceive the exquisite beauty of things as they pass. As a poet, privileged through talent, accident, and hard work, knowing this aspect of life to an extraordinary degree, he wanted to help others know it too.

In terms of the development of his work and the form it took, the political, social, and cultural situations of the century that occasioned his burgeoning socialist attitude played other parts. Though desiring in his youth, largely for reasons of personality, to produce what would be the American epic in order to make a place for himself in his imagined pantheon of "man-poets," Stevens came to realize that to continue in the path Whitman had forged, to produce for the twentieth century an epic that echoed the communal, enlarged "I" themes of Whitman, was dangerous. Understanding that the only appropriate epic for the age would be the "epic of disbelief" (*CP* 122), Stevens remained committed to the lyric as his mode of expression. His beginning to elaborate on the importance of the "romantic" at this point in the early thirties—as in his review of Marianne Moore's *Selected Poems* and in his introduction to Williams's *Collected Poems* and in many of the letters he wrote in which he clarified his ideas—went together with this commitment. In the largest sense this attitude revealed a deep understanding of the forces in a nation that lead to war. Epics expressed national identities forged in response to war: the *Iliad* and *Odyssey;* the *Chanson de Roland;* the poem of the *Cid.* Whitman's work similarly reflected a consciousness shaped by the rending effects of the Civil War. To continue to idealize and celebrate the particularly American "I" as Whitman did was far too dangerous. The experience of World War I had been sufficient for Stevens to put to rest any residue of epic ambition. This he did with his comic mock epic "The Comedian as the Letter C."

What he had learned as part of the Arensberg circle had had a great deal to do with this, just as it offered him the model, in the figure of Francis Bacon, of maintaining a seemingly conservative position in the world of affairs while constructing his *Novum Organum,* "The Whole of Harmonium," the idea of whose shape never left him. In the same way that Bacon's work expressed a revolutionary world view, though dressed in language and form that cryptically hid his purpose from those on whom his continued access to information and support depended, Stevens's work provided a revolutionary world view for America, couched in a lyric mode that seemed to present no threat to things as they were. Abandoning the Christian myth, as Stevens had done, meant turning belief and attention away from the God who was always called on to lead the armies of Christian soldiers to this or that end. This meant there could be no godlike heroes, no God-given causes for battle, no epics.

But as Freud had clearly pointed out in *The Future of an Illusion,* to present such a view to a population still strongly attached to its mythic father would mean violent rejection. To effect the desired end, slow and patient education was necessary. If one of the figures who guided this education appeared to be one of the most solid of citizens, secure in his position in society, the teaching he offered would naturally be more easily accepted. This was the work Stevens cut out for himself and fostered in others. But knowing how long the whole process would take, he regarded what he offered as "Notes." Only in the future would it be possible for the poet to stand as virile youth, proudly naked and savage in his world rather than dressed in a three-piece suit behind an executive's desk. In the future it would be possible, Stevens hoped, for the poet to survive as a poet. Part of the tragedy of his time, as he expressed it in various pieces he wrote during the thirties and forties, was that as things were, the poet could exist only as a vagabond or in bondage to the world of merchants and bankers. But in the future imagined seeming and being would be one.

A final observation Stevens made to Powers in his May 1933 letter was that conditions in Key West were so low economically that a depression was "an impossibility." In one of his characteristically gnomic asides, he added, "If things go from bad to worse, I am either going to move to a farm in Sweden or a houseboat in Key West." The same kind of antithetical positioning of images and manner that he used to construct his poems was used here to spur his friend to figure out the connection between these seemingly unrelated and contradictory possibilities. On the one hand, a move to a farm in

Sweden was understandable as an escape from the economic disaster the United States was facing. Sweden symbolically offered a situation of self-sufficiency; notably this was a socialistic environment. But why offer as an equal possibility the move to Key West? And why a houseboat? Vague memories of John Kendrick Bangs's *A Houseboat on the Styx,* which he had read twenty-odd years before, blended with his recent correspondence with someone in Sweden from whom he was commissioning a rug to be woven for his new house, a rug in which a personal inscription would be worked into a design of trees. (Through this dealing he was also, as was his habit, learning about life in Sweden—habits, light, landscape.) What Sweden had in common with Key West was that it became, through this interchange, another place where the poet's imagination took up residence. In this juxtaposition of a place in the far North and a place in the far South, Stevens was expressing that he could now continue to be in either climate or situation; he carried his balance within himself.

Within a few months Stevens had composed "Lions in Sweden," a poem that appeared to be a product of pure fancy, a seeming escape from things as they were. Without the grounding provided by the facts concerning his purchase of the rug and his learning about things Swedish—including, naturally, the rate of exchange between the Swedish "sovereigns," kroner, and the asthenic American dollar—this is what it would remain. But brilliantly playing on the uses of "sovereign" in the poem, Stevens pointed to the important connection between money and the needs of the soul, a connection extremely pertinent to the inheritors of the Calvinist spirit and more pertinent now that the center had already fallen out in Germany.

LIONS IN SWEDEN

No more phrases, Swenson: I was once
A hunter of those sovereigns of the soul
And savings banks, Fides, the sculptor's prize,
All eyes and size, and galled Justitia,
Trained to poise the tables of the law,
Patientia, forever soothing wounds,
And mighty Fortitudo, frantic bass.
But these shall not adorn my souvenirs,
These lions, these majestic images.
If the fault is with the soul, the sovereigns
Of the soul must likewise be at fault, and first.
If the fault is with the souvenirs, yet these
Are the soul itself. And the whole of the soul,
    Swenson,
As every man in Sweden will concede,
Still hankers after lions, or, to shift,
Still hankers after sovereign images.
If the fault is with the lions, send them back

To Monsieur Dufy's Hamburg whence they came.
The vegetation still abounds with forms.
(*CP* 124–25)

The poem was addressed to an archetypal Swede, an everyman, to whom the speaker, "I," confessionally described his past commitment to the material aspect of Calvinism. Properly associating the images adorning coins with their belying spiritual nobility—Fides, Justitia, Patientia, Fortitudo—Stevens suggested how subtly the soul was bound to the counters actually incompatible with its nature. In the lines introducing the central argument, "But these shall not adorn my souvenirs,/These lions, these majestic images," the poet expressed his separation from this material attachment through the ambiguous opposition of "these lions, these majestic images." This contrast was designed to produce initial uncertainty as to whether the reference was to the "souvenirs" or to the "sovereigns of the soul" depicted on the sovereigns themselves. Consequently, his utterance at this point was confused. Completing his argument with the offered hypotheticals, however, the point was clarified as the "sovereigns" were reduced from their nominal to an adjectival state, illustrating the poet's understanding—together with "everyman in Sweden"—that the soul still yearned for the images of Fides, Justitia, etc. The suggestion was that these desires had to be separated from material. The "sovereigns" were "lions" because they threatened to devour the soul. The image of Raoul Dufy's Hamburg—then the center of the maddened hunt for quick capital gain—was a sweetened romanticization, a contemporary version of the images of Fides etc. on the coins. The lions had to be sent back to devour their source. Only in the vegetation, in ever-changing nature, would forms appropriate to the soul's real need for souvenirs be found.

Stevens's poetic involvement now was not at all isolated from the affairs of the world in which he lived, as many of his readers, unfamiliar with the intimate connection between what he read and what he wrote, complained. While it is true that he did not write with the social and political rhetoric of a W. H. Auden, to believe that he should have is to miss the essential feature of his life and work: that his poetry was the product of a man who participated fully in what it meant to be an American caught up in the network responsible for the nation's successes and failures. Though he now bemoaned the fact that the poet had to support himself as "a bustling merchant, farmer, lawyer, or the like," the fact was that had this not been the case for him, he would not have experienced, from the inside, the workings of the American machine.

This was not the case for any of the other major poets of his generation. Pound and Eliot had left America altogether; Frost, Aiken, and Moore supported themselves wholly outside the world of American business; and Williams, though he worked hard and every day, was a doctor, separated from a primary concern with profit-and-loss margins decorated by dollar signs. Similarly, the younger and minor poets were also separated, either living on the economic fringes of society or safely protected within walls of colleges and universities, where their only connection with the American business machine was as yet more subject matter. Stevens, on the other hand, was as involved in America's money-green world as he was in his green and fluent world of words, and he knew and felt both were necessary for him. He did not think that things should be otherwise so that he could give all his time to poetry. He recognized that because of all that had gone into shaping him, this would not make him happy. In his later life he expressed repeatedly that the work at the office satisfied him and was as integral a part of his life as poetry.[3] His having come to realize this meant that the old movement up and down between reality and imagination was no longer something that disturbed his equanimity.

Now that he had reached this point in his life, everything could be seen and considered. No more defenses or harsh judgments were necessary. The life Stevens had shaped now followed its own intrinsic ideas of order, and this order regarded and incorporated what came from outside. It made these various elements parts of its own rhythm if they were so suited; if they were not, it rejected them with ease. As a result, from this time on there would be no great change; there would be only the subtle and random variations that came as a natural part of his movement through time. Just as in his lifetime the scientific discoveries of the order of the universe reflected an understanding that both the laws of classical mechanics and those of quantum mechanics had to be applied in order for one to comprehend the behavior of both micro- and macrosystems—classical mechanics describing the repeating, timeless order and quantum laws describing the evolution through randomness and time—Stevens's ideas of order derived from what he knew could not be changed, played against and with the chance elements with which he came into contact in his own dance with time.

❧

This integration was naturally reflected in his work. In *Harmonium* Stevens had experimented with a variety of forms; it was as though each of these were a practice piece with which he trained his ear and mind. Later he developed these into major structural features: building stanzas around sound value; adopting the tercet of the *Divine Comedy* and extending its effect to other stanzaic forms of odd numbers of lines. But because of *Harmonium*'s variety of attempts, no overall rhythm of regularity or irregularity emerged. In *Ideas of Order,* on the other hand, just the opposite situation obtained. In place of the short line and irregular stanza form of free verse poems, of the thirty-six poems of this volume, twenty-eight are poems with stanzas repeating the same number of lines: seven with two-line stanzas; nine with three-line stanzas; seven with four-line stanzas; four with five-line stanzas; and one with ten-line stanzas. Of the remaining eight poems, two have only one stanza—"Lions in Sweden," with nineteen lines, and "Autumn Refrain," which, as appropriate to a refrain, has an even number of lines, fourteen. The other six poems have stanzas of various lengths, some with even and some with odd numbers of lines. Though the poems had been written, as Stevens put it, "mostly as improvisations" over the period from 1933 to 1935, they nonetheless expressed a formal statement when collected together as a volume, especially when seen against *Harmonium* and the volumes that followed. The irregular poems of *Ideas of Order* illustrated their maker's "rage against chaos" (*CP* 141). They reflected that there were certain things which could not be brought "quite round" by the power of imagination. Some of these were beyond the poet's understanding, or perhaps any man's. Some were too large or too pressing to be contained. At the same time, because of the order established by the preponderant number of rounded, regular poems, the irregular ones stand out. This foregrounding was intentional. If the intention is followed through, it points the way to central elements, keys, necessary for the reading of the rest of the work.

The volumes after *Ideas of Order* displayed gradually more regularity. By the end of *The Auroras of Autumn* almost every poem was in tercets, the form that slowly displayed its ascendancy over others, as was fitting for Stevens's desired vulgate of experience. The last two irregular poems of that volume served both to mimic the uncertainty of reality and to provide a transition to the next volume. In *The Auroras of Autumn* there is one other irregular poem, "Saint John and the Back-Ache," an adaptation of dialogue form; there are, then, a total of three poems with irregular stanzas in the volume (though in two of the poems with three-line stanzas the sections contain an odd number of stanzas). It was as though—and as Stevens indicated in his description of "A Thought Revolved"—in the autumn of his life his thought stretched like the light in autumn, allowing longer expansions and greater shades to emerge from the facts and elements he observed.

Plotting the changes in form in the volumes from *Harmonium* to *The Rock* as they were shaped for *The Collected Poems,* what becomes abundantly clear is the consciously evolved musical structure of Stevens's intended "Whole of Harmonium." *The Collected Poems* presents an elaborately conceived opera, which at the same time preserves classical sonata form. The early lessons Stevens learned from Barrett Wendell about the major importance and effectiveness of the music drama of Richard Wagner had not been forgotten. Nor had Stevens given up the symbolist aspiration to have all art approach the state of music. His appreciation of this was continually strengthened. He had also never lost interest in the pastiche forms of the commedia dell'arte, to which opera was connected. At the same time he remained curious about the formal developments in the serious music of his time. His contact during his New York years with friends who were music critics, like Carl Van Vechten and Pitts Sanborn, as well as with Louise Norton and Edgard Varèse, had sharpened his sense of music, as had his exposure, through them and others in the Arensberg circle, to Igor Stravinsky's and Erik Satie's explorations. From the time of *Harmonium* he had been interested in having musical settings composed for his poems, the first being the result of his inquiry. Furthermore, Elsie's work with the piano had continued, if intermittently. Listening to her practice and play had preceded and now occasionally supplemented his devotion to musical radio broadcasts and to recordings and attending concerts whenever he could.

The idea for "The Whole of Harmonium" was an abstracted musical form. In terms of the "Whole," *Harmonium* is the overture, presenting each of the themes and rhythms but in snatches and quick phrases sonorously overlapping and clashing together. The major theme is pointed to by the longest poem, "The Comedian as the Letter C." *Ideas of Order* is the first act; it develops the themes, expressed in the irregular poems of the volume, against the background of regular ones, which act like a bass or chorus repeating and echoing the major themes and rhythms with variations and improvisations. The irregular poems here and in later volumes are the recitatives and arias. "The Man with the Blue Guitar," following,is a long duet between the two main characters. Stevens provided one of the clearest clues for perceiving his musical idea in one of the poem's lines: It was "like a duet with the undertaker." Of the poems accompanying it, the first, "A Thought Revolved," restates some of the earlier themes of *Harmonium* and combines them with the developments in *Ideas of Order.* At the same time it picks up the developments of "The Man with the Blue Guitar," making the theme of the search for a leader more specific. The second, "The Men That Are Falling," serves as the entr'acte, providing a transition from the theme restated, developed, and introduced in the loosened form of "The Man with the Blue Guitar." It also provides a gloss on all that has gone before, pointing out the causes for escape into the world of imagination. But it also announces that the man of imagination has died. This accounts for the "duet with the undertaker" that has just been completed.

The next act, *Parts of a World,* opens with a poem in couplets echoing those of the previous duet and entr'acte. Here the two central themes develop and play against each other in an attempt at resolution. One theme is that in a world without imagination even the imagination itself has to be imagined. The other, complementary to it, has to do with what constitutes the heroic in a time of difficulty and war, a time which does not permit indulgence in imagination. Reflecting the equal importance of the two themes and their movement toward resolution, in this volume the number of regular and irregular poems roughly balances. This is appropriate since in *Ideas of Order* the dominating structure was provided by "ideas," not by working them out against reality's chaos. But after the death of the man of imagination who lived largely in this world of ideas, this is no longer possible. The tension of the drama reaches its climax following the poet's "rage against chaos" through the repeated juxtapositions of arias and recitatives against regular interludes that could, because of their repetitive form, be easily sung by a chorus. The various irregular pieces represent the different earlier personae of the poet, each offering a particular aspect of the subject and attempting to win the struggle.

In this context it is illuminating to note a perception Stevens had about his process of composition. He described this in the first draft of "The Figure of the Youth as Virile Poet" but omitted it in preparing the final version probably because it was too disclosive. Had he left it in, the structure of his work might be made too apparent and thus lose some of the essential puzzling quality that Stevens felt was primary to his purpose. He wanted his readers to "search for reality," a search "as momentous as/the search for god," as Professor Eucalyptus, the "well-hidden" (eu-kalyptos) poet as teacher in "An Ordinary Evening in New Haven" observes (*CP* 481). The more the work had to be puzzled out—meaning, pattern, clues looked for—the more training the reader would have in searching for reality.

"The Figure of the Youth" was written as a lecture to be delivered at the Entretiens de Pontigny conference held at Mount Holyoke College in summer of 1943. It reflected Stevens's understanding of the poetic process as he had come to know it during his most productive period. The passage edited out followed the opening of the lecture's fourth section in which Stevens spoke of how the "personal" entered into the creative process. He clarified that the "personal" was not to be taken in its "pejorative" sense (pointing back to how he specified the nonpejorative meaning of the "romantic" during the time he composed *Ideas of Order,* a discussion which will be picked up shortly). He suggested that poetry, because of the "personal," may be superior to philosophy as the instrument through which individuals could best comprehend their relation to the world. The beginning of this section as it appears in *The Necessary Angel* is presented below (*NA* 47–48); the omitted section (in the Huntington Library collection) is in italics:

> An attempt has been made to equate poetry with philosophy, and to do this with an indication of the possibility that an advantage, in the long run, may lie with poetry; and yet it has been said that poetry is personal. If it is personal in a pejorative sense its value is slight and it is not the equal of philosophy. What we have under observation, however, is the creative process, the personality of the poet, his individuality, as an element in the creative process; and by process of the personality of the poet we mean, to select what may seem to be a curious particular, the incidence of the nervous sensitiveness of the poet in the act of creating the poem and, generally speaking, the physical and mental factors that condition him as an individual. If a man's nerves shrink from loud sounds, they are quite likely to shrink from strong colors and he will be found preferring a drizzle in Venice to a hard rain in Hartford. Everything is of a piece. If he composes music it will be music agreeable to his nerves. Yet it is commonly thought that the artist is independent of his work. *We take a man like Picasso, for instance, and assume that here is Picasso and there is his work. This is nonsense, where the one is, the other is, this son of an intellectual and antiquarian, with his early imaginative periods, as inevitable in such a case as puberty, may sit in his studio, half-a-dozen men at once conversing together. They reach a conclusion and all of them go back into one of them who seats himself and begins to paint. Is it one of them within him that*

dominates and makes the design or rather could it be? Can Picasso choose? Free will does not go so far.

The illustration using Picasso was revealing in two ways. First, it showed that Stevens compared himself to the painter whose *Guernica* had recently reconfirmed his greatness in a way that included the world of politics and war. Secondly, it revealed that Stevens had imagined Picasso experiencing what he himself did as he composed with his earlier imaginative selves. The personae, the voices of previous poems, "conversed" before reaching a conclusion, when all of them went back into the one, who then seated himself and began to write. The poetic self conceived here was, at once, the multitude of his many voices. All of them met to discuss a particular subject, but each poem expressed one of them. The notion of free will was called into question since were there free will, active choice, the struggle for voicing against the pressure of external circumstance would not have the weight it did.

These various voices were the characters in Stevens's opera. Their battle was with the real, which intruded itself into imagination. Over time, however, accords were reached. Throughout the work these were represented by the regularly patterned poems. In evolving this mode of composition, Stevens hoped to make his readers witnesses to the scraping of his spirit against the real. He wanted to make them feel with their "nerves" his own. From the tight complexity of the regular poems Stevens made it clear that it was not because he could not that he did not formally resolve the irregularities that do appear. Rather, these were to stand out. They would catch the reader unexpectedly, after years of devoted study.

A prime instance of Stevens's surprise tactic is the last poem of *Parts of a World,* "Examination of the Hero in a Time of War." It is possible to read through the poem's sixteen stanzas countless times without realizing that one stanza has only thirteen rather than fourteen lines. With its at first apparently completely regular long stanzas, the poem seems to harmonize the volume's tension between the shorter, regular pieces and the longer, irregular meditations. Coming finally to recognize that the third stanza is imperfect, as it were, unfinished, is startling. On looking at it again and seeing that it has in its three central lines (5, 6, 7) the word "Sight" beginning a new sentence, which is then completed in the following line, the reader is forced to look again at what the poet has been communicating until now and to question all the other *seeming* regularities encountered. Were they really regular or has some other trick escaped notice? The state of uneasy curiosity experienced at this point emphasizes the condition in which human beings found and find themselves in this uncertain century. The readers' questioning voices enter the drama directly: "The common man is the hero" (*CP* 275).

It is important to realize how much Stevens wanted to force his public's participation in his management of form. His involvement with form was as far from the aestheticized art for art's sake conception and practice as it could be. Contrary to what some critics continued to feel, his work was not at all removed from things as they were, existing only in a self-referential radiant atmosphere. That it was not reflected itself as well in the change of tone apparent in *Ideas of Order* and the later volumes. His ironic "gargoyle grin" disappeared. This was appropriate to his desire to dissolve the narrowly conceived notion of self—the "romantic" in its "pejorative" sense. He replaced this with an idea of anonymity that reflected a conception of an enlarged self that was not heroic and epic but "common." "There is no image of the hero. . . . The hero is a feeling,"—here was the point. Stevens wanted to restore to individuals their birthright in an age when technology and industrialization robbed them of it more each day. Since earlier he had established, as one of the central themes of his overture, that "Music is feeling," he had provided the terms for the equation where the hero is music, the leader that will once more teach the importance of feeling. From this understanding came the significance of a musical structure.

Preparing the way for the growing regularity of *The Auroras of Autumn,* following the working through of the tensions of *Parts of a World,* and picking up on the central clue of "sight," *Transport to Summer* opens with a poem that begins with the direction to "Look round"; this suggestion is repeated three times. More, the idea of "three" is echoed at central points in lines like:

> Three times the concentred self takes hold, three
>   times
> The thrice concentred self, having possessed
>
> The object, grips it in savage scrutiny,
> Once to make captive, once to subjugate
> Or yield to subjugation, once to proclaim
> The meaning of the capture, this hard prize,
> Fully made, full apparent, fully found.
> (*CP* 376)

This tripling moves toward the general resolution into triadic groupings of stanzas and sections of later poems in the volume (as in "Credences of Summer" and "Notes Toward a Supreme Fiction"). In *Transport to Summer* there are only four irregular poems: "Certain Phenomena of Sound," fittingly mimicking the random nature of sounds that are *not* music and thus not *feeling* ("Music is feeling, then, not sound"); "Esthétique du Mal," which uneasily explores all forms, settling into tercets for only seven stanzas, the unresolved form thus reflecting that the imagination could not deal with the *mal* of reality and the mind except in those brief interludes; "Paisant Chronicle," in which the "must" that becomes the central motif in "Notes" is first introduced against "chance" but not yet successfully; and "Mountains Covered with Cats," in which again, the "invalid personality" bent by its *mal* is impotent to empower the imagination to confront reality. But the volume ends betokening final accords and prefiguring the predominant triadic form of *The Auroras of Autumn* with the "three times three" organization of "Notes."

In *The Auroras of Autumn* there are three irregular poems. But the last is only vaguely so, ending the volume with faint echoes of what was and reevoking, too, with its couplets, the central duet with the undertaker. Nonetheless, there is resolution. The drama is ended. The final poems of *The Rock* follow to provide the coda for the whole work. They appropriately represent in less elaborate forms the various explorations originally introduced by *Harmonium*'s overture. Appropriately, too, the volume repeats the gradual domination of the triple pattern.

Stevens's sensitivity to form was not something to which he had to give constant attention. After the long apprenticeship, during which he perfected his various forms, and with his lifelong and deep appreciation of Goethe, who had worked out a viable "romantic" form, it was enough that Stevens kept alive only an idea of the thing he had in mind in order to evolve the overall order of his work. After he had put together numbers of poems, it was in the selection and arrangement of them and of the volumes as they appeared, pruned and shaped in final form for *The Collected Poems,* that he determined the exquisite design of the whole. But what he was conscious of at all times was the underlying antithetical pattern that he resolved into dialectic with and after *Ideas of Order.* Reflecting his musical commitment and describing the processes of perception, thought, and history as he understood them from his own experience and from what he read, this pattern preserved the most characteristic features of sonata form that he extended from application to one movement in a musical piece to his whole work. The tension between imagination and reality was the basis on which the various tripartite expositions, developments, and recapitulations were woven. The final resolution of the second foreign theme by transposition into the key of the home theme was perfectly paralleled in the movement from *Harmonium*'s mimicking of the separation of imagination and reality—represented by the chaos of different forms—to *The Auroras of Autumn*'s and *The Rock*'s mimicking—in the domination of the tripartite scheme—that imagination and reality had now become fused. More, in having effected the initial transposition to another key, Stevens had perfectly illustrated Bergson's definition of how the comic operated (See note 40, Chapter VII, Vol. I). In the years beginning with 1933, with the composition of the antithetical pieces for *Ideas of Order,* Stevens mastered the sonata form. It became the core of what he meant when he defined the "romantic" in its positive sense.

❧

With his reputation firmly established in the thirties, Stevens was asked to contribute not only poems but introductions to and reviews of other poets' volumes. Those individuals or volumes about which he was ambivalent, he refused, always being careful to point out why. Such was the case, for instance, with a volume of Horace Gregory's he thought he would be asked to review for *Poetry.* He felt that Gregory's work, though exhibiting "power," unlike much of the writing of the time, was too "highly parenthetical" and too preoccupied with death (*L* 265–66). This judgment was significant coming from the poet whose first volume was so reflective of his own early obsession with death. This judgment confirmed in another way the turn that had come about since that time. Stevens wanted not only that death should have no sovereignty over *his* thoughts but also that he did not give an external sign—in the form of a review—that he had given attention to another whose work exhibited such a fixation. Similarly, about the poems constituting *Ideas of Order,* which he collected for Ronald Lane Latimer's Alcestis Press, he expressed concern that they might seem too "low and colorless." Before submitting what he wanted for the proposed volume, he set himself to write some pieces that would add "gaiety and lightness" to show that his mind was not "lamentable" (*L* 273). All effort was to go toward "indulging the instinct of joy" (*L* 296). This could be recognized only if there were feeling. If this awareness were achieved by all, there would be no question of war, the most extreme sign of devotion to a wholly intellectualized aim.

Even when asked to do introductions to or reviews of volumes by those he admired, Stevens sometimes refused, at least at first, when he thought the work might interfere with a poetic project of his own. While he did not hesitate to say no to doing an introduction to a volume by Ernest Dowson (to have been published by the Alcestis Press; no record of its publication exists), he was of two minds in the case of Marianne Moore's *Selected Poems,* which he was asked to review by T. C. Wilson of the *Westminster Magazine* in March 1935. He had by this time completed the poems he wanted to add to those he already had to make up *Ideas of Order,* but he was now involved with another long project—a group of poems about statues that would occupy some 700 lines. "The Old Woman and the Statue" and "Mr. Burnshaw and the Statue" of *Owl's Clover* were the first two of these. He completed them by November 1935 but not without relenting about his decision to do the Moore review (*OP* 247–53). In his reconsideration and in putting together the review, Stevens elaborated on what he felt was the "vital element of poetry": its freshness, preserved through a nonpejorative understanding of the "romantic." The word "pejorative," which had recently appeared in one of his letters, had also figured prominently in one of the latest poems he sent to Latimer, "Sailing After Lunch," which began, "It is the word *pejorative* that hurts" (*CP* 120). In this poem Stevens dealt with the unfortunate confusion of the sentimental strain of romanticism—represented by a poet like Alphonse de Lamartine or, later, Rimbaud—with the valuable, "true" romantic in his sense, who constantly touched what was with transcendence and made apparent the continually evolving newness of things. Part of his purpose in reviewing Marianne Moore's volume was to make this as explicit as he could. In this way his own poetic purpose would become clearer as he extolled Moore to be one like himself.

Each of the elements Stevens singled out for attention in Moore's work was one that was important to his poetic act: language that seemed "inapposite" to the content; lines that appeared to have no rhyme but that had "more intricate" order determined by "unconsciously" and "instinctively relate[d] sounds'; stanzas that flowed 'innocently' like "mechanisms," reflecting his recent observation, related to Latimer, that he had of late come to concentrate on the way each individual's instinctive sense of order manifests itself as an illustration of each being as essentially a "biological mechanism," organically a part of a larger natural order (echoing his commitment to Goethe's notion of *Organismus*); the hybridization of associations by negatives, which more than any other particular element bespoke, as he put it, "in a time like our own of violent feelings, equally violent feelings and the most skillful expression of the genuine" (*OP* 252). Stevens went on to observe that the overall effect of such a technique was "hilarious" and showed how this paralleled Aristotle's categorizing the "wonderful" above the merely "possible." Here Stevens was providing a classical grounding for his own commitment to puzzles, riddles, and charms[4] that "wonderfully" elicit laughter on being recognized and solved.

In a generous appreciation of a fellow poet who, unfortunately, would never himself be reciprocally open,[5] Stevens pointed toward T. S. Eliot as the "most brilliant instance" of the romantic in the sense he was defining. He noted that Eliot "incessantly revive[d] the past and create[d] the future." Other instances he indicated were the ideas of Hamlet in modern dress and the "playing of a well-known concerto by an unknown artist." Those capable of being such figures had to be unselfconscious in their work. Their involvement was with their craft. They did not care about being known as "writers" but wrote out of a "profound need." Stevens closed indicating that the true romantic was "an association of the true and the false. It [was] not the true. It [was] not the false. It [was] both." He then added the at first seemingly gnomic illustration that "the school of poetry that believe[d] in sticking to the facts would be stoned if it was not sticking to the facts in a world in which there [were] no facts: or some such thing."

In laying all this out, Stevens was describing the romantic as the essential third term in any conflict. As he pointed out in another letter to Latimer, it was not enough to destroy what was insufficient by taking an antithetical position. There had to be an implicit synthesis. For this reason, he would not adhere to any political platform, party, or position. Things were constantly changing. The romantic was the index and instrument of this process. Precisely because he described the ever-renewing face of things as they were, the poet was superior to the politician and the philosopher, who fashioned "isms" for themselves.

In his correspondence with Latimer—in which he clarified his political feelings in a way he avoided in his poetry, designed as it was to survive beyond the confines of his historical period—Stevens described the protean nature of his affiliation with the political realities of his time. It was not that he was being evasive. None of the categories naming commitments was sufficient, yet all were necessary, though only provisionally, especially for the men who were, as he now saw himself, leaders among men. Unfortunately those who were themselves firm adherents of one or another fixed position were quick to condemn Stevens as anything ranging from a mere aesthetic dabbler in words to a fascist. These judgments were made on the basis of some of the comments he made only in passing to illustrate the nonfixity of his position and the absurdity of the labels and names denoting fixity.

While, for example, Stevens observed that he was what could be called an "up-to-date capitalist" in Edward Albert Filene's sense, Filene's version of capitalism represents a movement toward socialism.[6] This was consistent with what Stevens observed to Latimer in connection with "Mr. Burnshaw and the Statue." This poem was his answer to Stanley Burnshaw's critique of *Ideas of Order* from a Communist point of view; the review appeared in the *New Masses* on October 1, 1935. Stevens noted that his response antithetically applied "the point of view of a poet to Communism" and that it was "a general and rather vaguely poetic justification of leftism." He added that his objection to strict Marxism was that "to the extent that the Marxians [were] raising Cain with the peacocks and the doves, nature [had] been ruined by them" (*L* 295). Even more explicitly, apropos of the review in the *New Masses,* Stevens expressed that he found it most interesting because "it placed [him] in a new setting." Significantly, he wrote:

> I hope I am headed left, but there are lefts and lefts, and certainly I am not headed for the ghastly left of *Masses*. The rich man and the comfortable man of the imagination of people like Mr. Burnshaw are not nearly so rich nor nearly so comfortable as he believes them to be. And what is more, his poor men are not nearly so poor. These professionals lament in a way that would have given Job a fever. . . . *Masses* is just one more wailing place and the whole left now is a mob of wailers. I do very much believe in leftism in every direction, even in wailing. These people go about it in such a way that nobody listens to them except themselves; and that is at least one reason why they get nowhere. They have the most magnificent cause in the world. (*L* 286–87)

In spite of his feelings about the *New Masses,* he was happy to have become involved with it. As he commented, being so involved "helped to make one's poetry truer." He closed saying that "merely finding [him]self in the milieu [of the *New Masses*] was an extraordinarily stimulating thing."

Why passages such as the above were largely ignored, while others that reinforced the image of the poet as archconservative resident in one of the nation's strongest financial institutions were distortedly taken out of context and fastened upon is important to consider. Doing so casts light on the implicit defensiveness of those maintaining fixed critical and political positions—something that began to have dangerous significance for the United States during the twenties—and on the consistency of Stevens's manner and method as they were involved both inside and outside poetry. Coming across the following parenthetical remark from a letter to Latimer (*L* 289–90), for example, ". . . (I am pro-Mussolini, personally*)"— the asterisk indicating an added postscript that seems, at first, even more scathing: "The Italians have as much right to take Ethiopia from the coons as the coons had to take it from the boa-constrictors" could produce two distinct effects. Both these effects had to have been imagined by the poet who was aware, from the earliest years of his correspondence, that he was leaving behind a record that would be read by others.

One kind of reader, going through Stevens's letters and looking for evidence of a particular view of the poet, would find such an aside the last bit of corroboration needed to confirm that indeed, the executive in the gray flannel suit had never escaped his bourgeois attachments and that these finally became petrified in the worst kind of racially fascist attitudes. This view was perfectly consistent with the writing of a leftover dandy, one of the descendants of the foppish decadents, involved only with form. Here was a poet wholly without moral concern. The idea conjured by the name Wallace Stevens, even today, evokes this for many who, under the banner of liberalism, are eager to ban from the new republic any poet who seems to suggest privilege, as clearly Stevens does.

But the privilege Stevens knew was and is accessible to all. Through education, first of the senses, then in arts and letters, Stevens believed that any individual could come to an awareness of what he called "nobility." The poet's belief in an "up-to-date capitalism" centered on this. As he expressed to Latimer in explaining the meaning of one of the poems he had recently submitted to him ("A Fading of the Sun"), "The point [is] that, instead of crying for help to God or to one of the gods, we should look to ourselves for help. The exaltation of human nature should take the place of its abasement. . . . the sense of its exaltation should take the place of its abasement" (*L* 295). For Stevens, being an "up-to-date capitalist" meant being self-sufficient and self-directed in a way that had been made explicit by Ralph Waldo Emerson a century before, a way that had made Stevens, his father, and his father before him the self-made men they were.

In expressing extreme statements like the one about Benito Mussolini, Stevens was playing with the same kind of antithesis he used in his poetry. Such statements (like the one, too, to Powers about moving to either a farm in Sweden or a houseboat in Key West) were meant to elicit questioning responses. One who did not respond, but who simply took one of these statements as fact, failed to enter into the essentially human relationship—the dialogue on which all directed change is based. The one who failed to respond would be the real conservative, seeing such utterances as fixed facts, as evidence to support a particular absolute view. Stevens's devil's advocate approach was an indirect but effective method to tease out from those immured behind their rhetorical walls the few with whom real dialogue was possible.

But there was another kind of reader as well, one who, on coming upon a comment such as that about Mussolini, would question the shock itself and then proceed to look for possible answers. In dropping the comment as he did to Latimer, Stevens was testing to see what kind of reader Latimer would be.

Would he pick up on this and continue a dialogue or drop it and think the poet a closed-minded fascist? Latimer proved to be a worthy interlocutor. His return letters to Stevens prompted not only the poet's clarifications about leftism and Marxism, some of which were noted above, but also this particular antithetical response to the Mussolini aside:

> While it is true that I have spoken sympathetically of Mussolini, all of my sympathies are the other way: with the coons and the boa-constrictors. However, ought I, as a matter of reason, to have sympathized with the Indians as against the Colonists in this country? A man would have to be very thick-skinned not to be conscious of the pathos of Ethiopia or China: or one of these days, if we are not careful, of this country. But that Mussolini is right, practically, has certainly a great deal to be said for it.
>
> I am going to skip your question about fascism. Fascism is a form of disillusionment with about everything else. I do not believe it to be a stage in the evolution of the state; it is a transitional phase. The misery that underlies fascism would probably be much vaster, much keener, under any other system in the countries involved at the present time. (*L* 295)

The key to understanding Stevens's meaning in this interchange about Mussolini is the closing of his review of Moore's *Selected Poems:* "It is not true. It is not false. It is both." He was being a romantic in the positive sense. In offering contradictory statements about Mussolini, he was presenting both extremes of the positions those about him held. He, on the other hand, considered himself one of the few who moved at a very high level, one of those on whom others depended (*L* 299). He was being representative at the same time as he was imagining the reality of Abyssinia and feeling the pathos of the situation there, just as, when still a young man, he had felt the pathos of the Wily sisters' situation or that of the parents of the two-headed child. His capacity for empathy had not left him. What had changed was that he could now face situations such as these without turning away.

Stevens could see that the problem of the "Abyssinians," or of the Indians of two or three centuries earlier, was a lack of system, an absence of "ideas of order." This lack was the result of a way of life that simply did not allow—because of the pressure of external reality—enough leisure for the musing and speculation out of which a society develops more effective and equitable patterns for living. This was something Stevens attempted to make clear in another letter to Latimer and in his favorite poem of *Ideas of Order,* "How to Live. What to Do."

Responding to a personal question Latimer had posed about whether Stevens himself was orderly, the poet answered that though he was, he had also become very interested in "disorder." He went on:

> What you don't allow for is the fact that one moves in many directions at once. No man of imagination is prim: the thing is a contradiction in terms.

> It is true that, if we are to eliminate systems as we go along (and it is obvious that everyone is fairly busy at that) we have got to replace them, unless we are to live like Abyssinians. System of some sort is inescapable; they have something even in Central Asia, where it is purely military. In New York it is purely political, and in your group it is purely something else.

He continued to clarify what he meant by using a homely illustration:

> I do very much have a dislike of disorder. One of the first things I do when I get home at night is to make people take things off the radiator tops. Holly subscribes to various magazines, collects stamps and carries on correspondence with unknown people about unknown things. She starts to tear the wrappers off at the front door and leaves them on chairs and on the floor and piles up her magazines wherever there is a ledge. Of course, all sorts of people do the same thing, even in their thoughts. I do confess to a dislike of that. . . . (*L* 300)

Without order and time for contemplation it is impossible for an individual or a society to design a system that could survive accidental changes. This was one of the general points of "How to Live. What to Do":

Last evening the moon rose above this rock
Impure upon a world unpurged.
The man and his companion stopped
To rest before this heroic height.

Coldly the wind fell upon them
In many majesties of sound:
They that had left the flame-freaked sun
To seek a sun of fuller fire.

Instead there was this tufted rock
Massively rising high and bare
Beyond all trees, the ridges thrown
Like giant arms among the clouds.

There was neither voice nor crested image,
No chorister, nor priest. There was
Only the great height of the rock
And the two of them standing still to rest.

There was the cold wind and the sound
It made, away from the muck of the land
That they had left, heroic sound
Joyous and jubilant and sure.

(*CP* 125–26)

The "heroic height" was "this rock [reality]/ Impure . . . a world unpurged" that could be recognized as heroic only if there were time to stop and rest before it, to consider it with the light of imagination (in the moonlight). Though the seekers left to find a "sun of fuller fire"—another intellectualized ideal—they found in the time of rest, with moonlight, the "heroic sound/ Joyous, jubilant and sure" of actuality, without "crested image . . . chorister [or] priest."

Stevens felt that what Mussolini offered the Ethiopians was practicable for two reasons. First, a system, even a foreign one, would mean increased possibilities for a population torn by tribal hostilities. Stevens saw the external imposition of an order, as he made clear, as a "transitional phase," a temporary solution. Secondly, in response to Mussolini and the introduction of a Western mode, the Ethiopians might themselves be forced to evolve a coherent and unifying government of their own, one derived from the intelligence of their own soil. Stevens was not speaking as the enlightened imperialist, rationalizing exploitation with facile meliorist arguments, though without our having read carefully through the endless qualifications and clarifications of his position that he expressed in his letters, it would be easy to think that he was. It is also important to remember that this was still 1935, before the extremity of Mussolini's position led to actions that made it impossible for Stevens to have any sympathy even with those who madly supported him—like Ezra Pound (see *L* 516–17).

In coming to know himself, Stevens recognized that every individual and every state "move[d] in many directions at once." He wanted to provide a coherent world view that centered on the acknowledgment of continual change. With his attention now focused on things in the outside world, he believed poetry had to become involved with these facts. As he indicated to Latimer, he was aware that his attitude toward the outside world, the function of poetry, and the kind of poetry he wrote were radically different from before and that this was so because the importance of current world events could not be ignored. He directed his imagination to work with the elements that he learned of about situations in different parts of the world and he developed mental schemes that mapped how these elements must have combined to account for what was happening. He then considered the various possible solutions. Here he was applying the same skills he used in his work as a claims attorney to come to terms with the facts of each case in order to settle it.

By engaging reality in this way, Stevens arrived at the same kind of realization about the conditions of less developed societies in relationship to modern, industrial powers as one of the century's most noted anthropologists, who during the same period was observing social conditions in India and South America. In a central passage of *Tristes Tropiques,* Claude Lévi-Strauss observed the following:

> One has to be very naive or dishonest to imagine that men choose their beliefs independently of their situation. Far from the forms of social exis-

> tence being determined by political systems, it is they which give meaning to the ideologies by which they are expressed. Ideologies are signs which only constitute a language in the presence of the objects to which they relate. At the moment, the misunderstanding between East and West is primarily semantic: the concepts or "signifiers" that we try to propagate in the East refer to "signifieds" which are different there or non-existent. On the other hand, if it were possible for circumstances to change, it would matter very little to their victims if this occurred within a framework that we Westerners would deem intolerable. They would not be conscious of being enslaved but, on the contrary, would feel that they had been liberated, if they graduated to forced labor, food rationing and regimented thought since this would be the historical development by virtue of which they would obtain work, food and some measure of intellectual life. Modalities, which appear to us to be forms of deprivation, would be cancelled out by the possibility of a proffered reality, which we had denied them on the grounds of its appearance.[7]

Similarly, from his close observation of groups in technologically backward areas, Lévi-Strauss came to understand the central role of the poet in all societies. Lévi-Strauss expressed this in terms almost identical with some of Stevens's statements, which the latter had derived, at least in part, from his own experience of moving from the town situation of Reading, caught in the throes of the Industrial Revolution, to the urban situation of modern twentieth-century life. Again in *Tristes Tropiques,* Lévi-Strauss made the point that in a town, as opposed to the huge, complicated mass of a city, ordered by seemingly rational systems, one could still witness man's irrationalities and the collective superstitions that control or drive them. He continued:

> But are they really superstitions? I see these preferences rather as denoting a kind of wisdom which savage races practiced spontaneously and the rejection of which, by the modern world, is the real madness. Savages have often succeeded in achieving mental harmony with a minimum of effort. What wear and tear, what useless irritation we could spare ourselves if we agreed to accept the true conditions of our human experience and realize that we are not in a position to free ourselves completely from its patterns and rhythms! Space has its own values, just as sounds and perfumes have colours, and feelings weight. The search for such correspondences is not a poetic game or a practical joke (as some critic has had the audacity to say it is, in connection with Rimbaud's "sonnet de voyelles," which is now a classic text for linguists who know the basis, not of the colour of phonemes—which is a variable depending on the individual—but of the relationship between these, which admits of only a limited scale of possibilities); it offers absolutely virgin territory for research where significant discoveries are still to be made. If, like the aesthete, fish divide perfumes into light and dark, and bees classify luminosity in terms of weight—darkness being heavy and

> brightness light—the work of the poet, painter or the musician, like the myths and symbols of the savage, ought to be seen by us, if not as a superior form of knowledge, at least as the most fundamental and the only one really common to us all; scientific thought is merely the sharp point, more penetrating because it has been whetted on the stone of fact, but at the cost of some loss of substance—and its effectiveness is to be explained by its power to pierce sufficiently deeply for the main body of the tool to follow the head.[8]

This point of view, expressed by Lévi-Strauss in the fifties, though culled from his work of the previous twenty years, Stevens voiced not only in letters and lectures later collected as his prose pieces but also in the poems of *Ideas of Order,* for example, in "Evening Without Angels":

> Let this be clear that we are men of sun
> And men of day and never of pointed night,
> Men that repeat the antiquest sounds of air
> In an accord of repetitions. Yet,
> If we repeat, it is because the wind
> Encircling us, speaks always with our speech.
> (*CP* 137)

The poems of *Ideas of Order* were products of Stevens's "rubbings against reality," but reality understood in a very different way from the years of the *Harmonium* poems. Reality then was largely internal, the product of all that had gone into making the man he was as he began to define himself against the past and face his personal crises. His purpose then, expressed in "The Comedian," was "to drive away/ The shadow of his fellows from the skies" (*CP* 37).

But now reality was external, present, and the material of *Harmonium* was the past to which he referred. In *Ideas of Order* Stevens used threads from *Harmonium* to rhapsodize the new elements he now considered. He had learned from the epic poets, beginning with Homer, the effectiveness of repetitions of themes, phrases, and epithets in making an audience feel it was a participant in the poetic process. "To rhapsodize" comes originally from the Greek, meaning "to sew." Stevens attempted to "bring a world quite round . . . [to] patch it" (*CP* 165) as he could with familiar strains.

All through the poems of *Ideas of Order,* Stevens echoed lines, stanzas, and rhythms of *Harmonium;* sometimes he even called up a name as he stitched together references to what he experienced, read about, and heard of through this most trying of historical moments. In "Anglais Mort à Florence" (*CP* 148)—the poem to which he was probably referring when he wrote to Latimer in January 1935 that he was imaginatively conjuring "a deathbed scene under the new regime" (*L* 273)—he recalled the movement of Hoon, as he did again, naming him specifically, in "Sad Strains of a Gay Waltz" (*CP* 121). In

"Mozart, 1935" (*CP* 131) he played on the rhythm, diction, and images of "The Emperor of Ice-Cream" (*CP* 64), blended with those of "The Snow Man" (*CP* 9) and "The Man Whose Pharynx Was Bad" (*CP* 96). In "Farewell to Florida" (*CP* 117) he reversed the themes and rhythms of all the earlier Florida poems. Stevens ran such repetitions throughout the volume. Against them he set present, timely references, some general, like the year 1935, some personal, as in "Lions in Sweden" (*CP* 124) or "A Postcard from the Volcano" (*CP* 158). This last he developed from musing on a postcard picturing a volcano which he had received from a friend traveling in Honduras in 1933 (WAS 410). "A Fish-Scale Sunrise" (*CP* 160) he addressed to Jim and Margaret Powers to commemorate a night out on the town with them on their first visit back east after they had moved to Oregon. Having spent the afternoon in New York together, Stevens and Powers met Mrs. Powers at about six. They all went to a couple of Stevens's favorite speakeasies, then to a restaurant where musicians played "La Paloma." Leaving there near midnight, Stevens, in one of his "impetuous" moods, as Margaret Powers put it, whisked them off to the newly opened Waldorf Roof, where the poet thoroughly enjoyed himself doing something he had never done, as he told Mrs. Powers—dancing. Before they left, he ordered pickled herring in cream. And before the evening was over, he did something else he had never done: kissed Margaret Powers. She reported that it was "the only time in his life—he wasn't that type."[9] Composing himself, later, in writing his poem, he memorialized more than his late-night fish treat and his "doggone good . . . sense of rhythm" that Mrs. Powers had so appreciated:

> Melodious skeletons, for all of last night's music
> Today is today and the dancing is done.
>
> Dew lies on the instruments of straw that you were playing,
> The ruts in your empty road are red.
>
> You Jim and you Margaret and you singer of La Paloma,
> The cocks are crowing and crowing loud,
>
> And although my mind perceives the force behind the moment,
> The mind is smaller than the eye.
>
> The sun rises green and blue in the fields and in the heavens.
> The clouds foretell a swampy rain.
>
> (*CP* 160–61)

Similarly, "Like Decorations in a Nigger Cemetery" (*CP* 150) began from a personal experience but broadened into cultural references. It was addressed to Arthur Powell, from whom Stevens had gotten the image and phrase for the title (as he had earlier borrowed the phrase naming "A High-Toned Old Christian Woman"). "Like decorations in a nigger cemetery" described his state of mind as he confronted things as they now were. The irregularity of the poem, its gnomic stanzas—reminiscent of "Thirteen Ways," "Six Significant Landscapes," and "New England Verses"—reevoked Stevens's Oriental forms. He brought this Eastern influence into contact with one of the most pressing realities of the time. In comparing his perceptions to "decorations in a nigger cemetery," Stevens was revealing his sympathetic identification with America's most obvious underclass.

This was also apparent in other poems of the period. "Nudity at the Capital" (*CP* 145), "Nudity in the Colonies" (*CP* 145), and "Some Friends from Pascagoula" (*CP* 126) also disclosed the poet entering the black man's skin. This was the same spirit that had conjured for himself, as an earlier persona, "Victoria Clementina, negress" in "Exposition of the Contents of a Cab." It was an aspect of the same spirit that identified, too, with "gold medal boys" the "little Jews" who grew to become "rabbis" in various poems. Stevens's conception of "an American poet," like Whitman's, included an attempt to identify with all groups within his society. At the same time, he felt, as the man he was in the circles in which he moved, ambivalence about certain minorities. Notably, however, in the poems of *Ideas of Order,* he resolved his ambivalence into a realization of the black man's insight and his advantage, in being symbolically "anonymous," of having a more primary and nourishing relationship with the natural world. This is clearest in the counterpointed "Nudity at the Capital" and "Nudity in the Colonies," in which the persona of the black man pointed to what should be sought:

> But nakedness, woolen massa, concerns an innermost atom.
> If that remains concealed, what does the bottom matter?

The white man, "massa," then admitted the truth:

> Black man, bright nouveautés leave one, at best, pseudonymous.
> Thus one is most disclosed when one is most anonymous.

Other references in the volume were more pointedly timely, like that to Ramón Fernández, addressed "unconsciously" (*L* 798 and 823) in "The Idea of Order at Key West" (*CP* 128). Stevens had read Fernández's criticism in some of the Paris weeklies he followed. When he composed his poem and looked for just a "common Spanish name," it was this one that came to him. Since shortly after he consciously addressed another critic of similar political sympathies in "Mr. Burnshaw and the Statue," it seems either that Stevens was being disingenuous when asked about this reference twenty years later (when he responded that it was not conscious) or that the unconscious address and weaving of "The Idea of Order at Key West" around it were a preparation for what he attempted in "Mr. Burnshaw and the Statue." Whichever the case, his choice of name reflected how deeply involved the poet had become with things outside himself. The Spanish critic's name seems to have become a part of Stevens's unconscious language as he began to be preoccupied with "anonymity" and the "common man."

As the process of loosening the boundaries of self continued, Stevens grew less concerned with his physical being. Though he had been "on the water wagon" for years before, as he indicated in a letter to Powers in June 1933, humorously suggesting that he do the same, he now began to climb down more than occasionally, once again indulging as he liked. This was naturally reflected in his health. A visit he made to Dr. Herrick in December 1934 revealed that his weight had been going up continually: From 200 pounds in 1931 he had gone up to 205 in 1932, 220 in early 1934, and he was now 234 and 3/4. In addition, as a result of the high blood pressure connected with his relaxed eating and drinking habits, he was suffering from "mild dental sepsis": His upper right molar was quite loose, and several other teeth were "suspicious." But these signs of decay—milder forms of which a few years before had set him to putting himself on a Draconian regime, complete with following exercise schemes in books every morning—did not now disturb his rhythms or his wryly complacent outlook. Much more important for the present was simply writing poetry. This concern dominated all others, as he revealed in a letter to Latimer within days of receiving Herrick's report. After a comic note about a "damsel" who had recently asked him to inscribe a copy of *Harmonium,* to whom he replied that an uninscribed copy would be a rarer object, he gave Latimer a glimpse, touched with homely humor, of a typical moment of composition: "I sit down every evening after dinner and after a little music, put my forefinger in the middle of my forehead and struggle with my imagination."

He then observed:

> One of the essential conditions of writing poetry is impetus. That is a reason for thinking that to be a poet at all one ought to be a poet constantly. It was a great loss to poetry when people began to think that the professional poet was an outlaw or an exile. Writing poetry is a conscious activity. While poems may very well occur, they had very much better be caused. If all this is true, then it may be that in a few weeks my imagination will be such a furnace that I can stroll home from the office and fill the house with the most iridescent notes while I am brushing my hair, say, or changing to the slippers that are so appropriate to the proper enjoyment of Beethoven and Brahms on the gramophone. (*L* 274)

In this description Stevens made a point of distinguishing his involvement with poetry from that of the romantic poet like Keats, who had expressed the thought that if poetry did not come as easily as leaves to a tree, it was better that it should not come at all. Stevens was now fully mature as a poet and recognized that for his time poetry had to be a "conscious activity." This did not mean that the poet should exclude the irrational element but that he perfect a holding form and rhythm to contain this element. Stevens found the forms and rhythms he sought in his earlier work, just as for that work he had found models in others' forms. While the *Harmonium* poems had been, in part, responses to "studious ghosts," the poems of *Ideas of Order* and later volumes were responses to his own other voices.

❧

Over the years Stevens came into direct and indirect contact with more of his contemporaries. The publication of the second edition of *Harmonium* had brought increased attention; new contacts established additional cycles of correspondence, set in motion by Stevens's quick responses to letters and inquiries. Rhythms were then maintained for varying periods, depending on his correspondents' tempos. Early in 1934, for example, after a performance in Hartford of Gertrude Stein's *Four Saints in Three Acts* (on February 8)—which Stevens found an "elaborate piece of perversity . . . if one excludes aesthetic self-consciousness from one's attitude, a delicate and joyous work all round" (*L* 267)—he noticed Winifred Bryher's name above the place where he signed his in the guest book for the party given by Harriet Monroe after the play. Bryher did not meet Stevens at the reception. As Stevens noted in a letter to Monroe (*L* 267), he had gotten caught up in a group of "pretty awful people," part of the "trainload from New York—of numerous asses of the first water . . . who walked round with cigarette holders a foot long." He added that "if there [was] any place under the sun that need[ed] debunking, it [was] the place where people of this sort [came] to and [went] to." But he was careful to exclude Bryher from this category. He reported that she had sent him a note which was "delightful to have." In it Bryher expressed her regret at not seeing him at the performance; she had been wanting to meet him from the time she first became aware of his work around 1920, she wrote, adding that she looked forward to another volume soon.

The world of imagined relations Stevens had been conjuring since the time when letters from McAlmon in Paris described evenings and afternoons with Bryher (whom he had married there), Joyce, and others was becoming real. Just as Stein's work was finding a place even in provincial Hartford, so Stevens found himself in demand as well.

Stevens's youthful dream of participating in the life of letters was becoming more and more of a reality. During the next winter's trip to Key West he spent time with Robert Frost. Frost had already won the Pulitzer Prize, thus establishing his place in America's pantheon of "man-poets." In addition to spending afternoons with Frost and inviting him to dinner (*L* 275), Stevens, with his friend Judge Powell, threw a cocktail party to which they asked him. As Stevens wrote to Harriet Monroe after his return to Hartford, the party, as "riotous" as any the two friends had ever hosted, had probably left Frost "purifying himself by various exorcisms ever since" (*L* 278). Stevens was comfortable with himself now. He was secure in both his professional and his poetic positions. Having been made a vice president of the Hartford the previous winter had put him "up in the air," as he had noted to Powers (*L* 269).

With everything bolstering his sense of self, it was easy for him to extend himself to those with whom he came into contact.

Following his "many pleasant meetings" with Frost on this trip, Stevens assumed a paternal role toward the "senior" poet. They shared observations about how they composed. After Stevens disclosed how entries in dictionaries often provided sources from which elaborations of the "poetry of the subject" could be drawn, he generously offered to send Frost his copy of one of his well-used tools, Lewis and Short's *A Latin Dictionary* (*L* 275). But later, in a short letter, he noted that rather than send his own copy he was "procuring" him a "fresh" one. He sent him, too, a copy of *Harmonium*. He closed the letter with a description of the "season after winter and before spring"—a fitting perception created for another poetic sensibility.

Sensitivity to others had become a major feature of Stevens's personality. The relationships revealed by his correspondence show the poet imagining the realities of those whose lives he touched, just as he imagined the realities of political and social situations. Whether for Holly or for a tea grower in Ceylon, he consistently attempted to provide in his letters and in gifts—like the dictionary to Frost—elements that would nourish the spirit. It was not, either, that he sent the same kind of thing to everyone. What he wrote and what he sent depended on what he knew of the individuals.

From his annual stays in Florida or trips to other cities on business he sent Holly series of postcards on which the places or things he mentioned in letters to her and her mother were depicted. Reflecting a parallel to the way he described images in poems, the postcards often showed the same scene viewed from many different angles and under various aspects. He also sent Holly objects to educate her in the earth's richness: one year, palmetto fronds; the next, a baby alligator that she could show at school and that later, he wisely noted, could be taken to the Elizabeth Park greenhouse, where it would be able to survive the North's weather. On a trip to New York from Hartford he made a special point of taking Holly to the Aquarium, which kept brown pelicans like the ones he described having seen in Key West.

To Philip May, another younger business associate, and James Powers he sent books on subjects that interested them. To Powers, who shared his taste for exotic teas, he also sent samples he ordered for himself. To all those of whom he made requests to send him items from the places they visited or lived, he was meticulously careful always to reciprocate. If he was not familiar enough with their tastes and curiosities to do this comfortably, he made sure to offer his services in acquiring whatever they might want or need from America. This included running errands or going to out-of-the-way shops in New York. He once even searched out a certain kind of handbag for Rosamund Cary, whom Elsie had met at Vassar during the summer of 1931, when both women were enrolled with their daughters in the Institute of Euthenics. Mrs. Cary, married to a missionary, was now in Japan.

And to Elsie, who was slowly shrinking into herself within the rhythm she established in their quiet, solitary home, Stevens offered, once more, when he was away, observations about the weather, people, landscape, and special leaves and blooms he saw. As of old, too, some of what he described for her he later developed into poems. "The crowds of men out of work" in Florida (February 18, 1935) became the subject of "Sad Strains of a Gay Waltz" (*CP* 121). When he was at home, he wrote letters requesting necklaces, kimonos, and other exquisite objects from faraway places as well as dried or candied fruit and other delicacies she liked. Though in reality she was no longer the "radiant bubble," in his imagination's "radiant and productive atmosphere" she came alive again. However, while there were difficulties, such that he could not extend invitations to their home—as he would have liked and as he had been able to do in the earlier years of their marriage before the uneasiness she felt about indulgent social behavior hardened into adamant intolerance—there were compensations.

He appreciated the peace she helped establish. She tended to things in the house, with or without help. She had learned how to make the roses and irises bloom. Most important, she had come to respect his need for solitude. As he noted to Powers after the first three years in their house, "I never really lived until I had a home, and my own room, say, with a package of books from Paris or London" (*L* 301). He added, just after, a sentence that showed that there was still an old feeling from his youth that hadn't been quite resolved (even though it no longer interfered with his productiveness or with his relations with others): "But then there is always the anxiety that follows over-indulgence." Did he mean "over-indulgence" as having acquired whatever he had wanted materially? Did this make him feel uneasy when the shadowy ghosts of his Puritan forebears occasionally whispered threats? Or did he mean that he felt guilty when he had actually been overindulgent in drinking—at least in Elsie's terms—when he returned home from one of his day or weekend trips to New York or from the longer jaunts to Florida or when he sipped wine alone in his room at night? The open-endedness of the sentence suggests that in his mind all these feelings were operative.

Since cases of wine sometimes had to be secreted into the house[10] and since he felt that he could be "hospitable" only to those who would enjoy a "pure 'joie de vivre'" without any imbibing of spirits (February 6, 1936 to Philip May) and that he could invite friends or associates for a martini only away from the house and "without Mrs. Stevens," his sense of "over-indulgence" probably did have something to do with drinking. But Stevens also felt the effects of a leftover Puritan conscience. He felt compelled, in at least one instance around the same time, to deny that his having stopped drinking was a matter of Puritanism. The fact was that because of his having "gone off the wagon" a few too many times in the previous two or three years and having given in too many times to his appetite for capon and fresh peach pie, he had continued to gain even more weight. The clothes he had tailored to fit his 234 pounds did not fit. So he noted to Philip May about a month before his mid-February 1936 trip to Florida: "At this moment I am on a diet and shall have to be fussy for some time to come. This makes all drinking out of the question, and, of course, that will also put out of the question any further discussion of the theological problem in which Scotch, all that sort of thing, always involves us" (January 1, 1936). A week later he added, somewhat guiltily but humorously:

> [It] looks as though [my] numerous exclusions might put the excursion on the blink. But in any case I leave it to you. After all, you must expect now and then to be agreeable, even to cripples. Any sort of hell-raising is simply out. . . . I don't, of course, object to the Rebout Club but the idea of knocking round the country with a couple of girls doesn't click a bit. . . .
>
> The trouble is, Phil, that every time I go down to Florida with judge Powell, while I never do anything particularly devilish, nevertheless I invariably do a good many things that I ought not to do. The result is that I always return feeling pretty much like a flagellant. I want to go down to the sea and the sun and to loaf, and that is all I want to do. Puritanism has nothing to do with it; I simply want to be myself as much in Florida as I am anywhere else. (*L* 307)

Following up on being himself, he suggested a visit with Judge Powell to some botanical gardens in the area, then restated his resolve:

> I am going to be inflexible about what I do this time. Judge Powell is a good old rummy and the three of us could have a wild time. But you and Judge Powell will have to have it together or, if he is not along, you will . . . have to . . . leave word at the hotel that you have a headache, although the truth is that we can have a riotously good time without the riot, unless I am very much mistaken.

He closed with a description of his diet, adding that it didn't matter what they ("you guys") ate; it wouldn't bother him.

On this trip, as on others, Stevens sent postcards back home to Holly. But this year they amounted to almost daily reports. They were brief but provided a day-by-day account of his movements. It was as though he were sending these as he had once sent daily letters to Elsie in order to alleviate uncertainties she had had about his company and whereabouts before their marriage. There were, however, no letters to Elsie from this trip. Since the following winter Stevens did not go to Florida at all, it seems that Elsie might have expressed displeasure about his annual jaunts with Powell and that this voicing, in part at least, prompted her husband's expressed desire to stick to his diet and not to indulge at all in alcohol. Seeing her once again as his conscience, he sent back, through Holly, these constant reminders that though he was away, his thoughts were at home. Paralleling a primary focus of his poetry, these brief reports most often mentioned the weather:

Monday 2/17/36

Driving Southward. A warm, bright day, a touch of summer.

DADDY

Four days and three postcards later (one, for Washington's Birthday, recorded that the card would "have been flying a long time when it reach[ed]" her, and bore a stamp depicting one of the new Flying Eagles):

A lovely
morning
here

Two days later the card he sent was all printed unevenly:

SUNDAY FEB 23/36

A high wind is
blowing TODAY
FroM a CLEAR
SKY.

DADDY. [*sic*]

The next day he sent another printed card, acknowledging one of Elsie's messages from home—not a letter, but a staccato telegram advising him simply that things were well. Stevens's response:

A WARM DAY, DELIGHTED TO
HAVE THIS MORNING'S WIRE
FROM HOMe.
LOVE TO BOTH.

DADDY. [*sic*]

Again the next day he sent another, his printing spread in misshapen letters:

TUESDAY 2/25/36

The sprig En-
CLOSED is A VARIETY
OF HOLLY NOW IN
BLOOM HERE.
LoVE tO YOU AND
TO MOTHER

DADDY

The following day, on two postcards in an envelope, now in script again, though shaky and rough, he sent the details of when he expected to arrive. He closed with "Love to mother and yourself."

When he did arrive home, both Elsie and Holly must have been quite surprised to see Stevens with remnants of a black eye and a broken hand. Hence, the badly printed cards. He reported that he had fallen down a flight of stairs,[11] but what had actually happened was that the fifty-five-year-old executive-poet had gotten involved in a drunken brawl. So much for his resolve that alcohol was "out of the question." In view of his knowledge of his weakness, his concern only a few weeks before about "over-indulgence" was understandable. Shortly after the incident Stevens spoke of having been "a fool to get so drunk" on that particular evening.[12] But the experience was not sobering enough to make him renew his broken resolve not to drink since he told the story of what had happened while having drinks with Judge Powell at the house of another Florida friend. It was the by now famous story of the Stevens-Hemingway fight.

The actual details of what prompted the incident and its outcome are not clear. According to Hemingway, Stevens had caused the fight and come off badly beaten. In the way Stevens remembered it, the cause and who won the round are blurry. Both versions present Stevens as having been "pretty well lit." It is also beyond question that the poet came out of the entanglement with a "puffy eye" and a broken hand. Again, according to Hemingway, Stevens suffered his hand injury from finally landing a punch on the mighty man's jaw. While Stevens related humorously to Judge Powell and his other Florida acquaintances that he and Hemingway had simply disagreed on particular issues and that the scene occurred because they both had had quite a bit to drink, Hemingway's version was far more particular.[13]

Stevens, he reported, had "spoken badly of him" at a cocktail party. Hemingway's sister had been present and had left the party and run to her brother "in tears" to tell him what the poet had said. Hemingway immediately went off to confront Stevens. He met him "just after Stevens had left the party boasting that if Hemingway had been there he would have flattened him with a single blow."[14] On seeing Hemingway, Stevens set himself to make his word deed, swung at him, and missed, at which point the great American male knocked down the "Giant" several times before Stevens managed to land the punch that shattered the hand with which he wrote. Stevens apparently, again according to Hemingway, made up with him before he left Key West, asking him not to say anything about the incident lest his insurance company colleagues get wind of it. The "official story" was to be that Mr. Stevens had fallen down a flight of stairs. Yet Stevens did relate his version of the story of the fight himself before he even got back to the office in Hartford, where at least one person, his assistant at the time, Manning Heard, already knew of it. He had been in Florida around the time and had been told the story. Neither he nor "Mr. Stevens" mentioned anything about it, however, when Stevens came into the office with his swollen eye and battered hand.

Years later, in 1951, Stevens told the story again with great good humor to some who gathered after hearing him deliver his lecture on "The Relations Between Poetry and Painting" at the Museum of Modern Art. Those listening included e. e. cummings and Monroe Wheeler, the museum's director. According to Wheeler, in this rendition Hemingway came out with "no glory" and Stevens was "the hero."[15] Because of the variety of the accounts and the nature of the personalities involved, it is impossible to know what really happened between Hemingway and Stevens. The incident was something Stevens never forgot. Though what it represented for him can't be known either. Even if he had actually come off as the hero, he had to have felt awkward dissembling guiltily before his wife and daughter, who stood as personifications of the conscience he had wanted so much to follow before leaving on the trip that was to be soberly different from previous ones. Here he was, not in imagination but in life, like "the sheep before the cottage door," as he had described himself after one of his "black moods" in the months before his marriage, but now the sheep had its tail between its legs.

Stevens had been making efforts over the previous seven or eight years to harmonize himself to Elsie's moods. Still, there were periods when there were "blow-ups of the nerves," as he later referred to them to Holly (*L* 422). In light of how much of himself he had to hide from Elsie, this is not surprising. One such period seems to have stretched all the way through 1935 and well into the beginning of 1936. What made this a particularly difficult time can only be guessed at. But the guesses have been educated by what is already known about Elsie Stevens and their common life.

In view of Elsie's early feelings of having been betrayed when her husband published poems that she thought belonged to her and the fact that the period during which they had arranged their common life into domestic rhythms that pleased both of them coincided with the longest time that Stevens did not write poetry, it is not farfetched to suggest that the resurgence of Stevens's feelings of anxiety about self-indulgence and his desire to change the nature of his participation on the trips to Key West with Powell were connected to what was going on at home during 1935. As he prepared his second volume, he fully entered, once again, into the life of letters. He began his long correspondence with Latimer and devoted the largest part of his attention at home to the planned sequence of poems about statues that ended up as *Owl's Clover.*

Elsie no doubt feared more public revelations about the nature of her husband's relationship with her in the new poems. Intermingled with those poems, which focused primarily on what went on in the world around him, there was at least one such "adultery," though voiced without the angry bitterness that had characterized earlier poems on similar themes:

GALLANT CHÂTEAU

Is it bad to have come here
And to have found the bed empty?

One might have found tragic hair,
Bitter eyes, hands hostile and cold.

There might have been a light on a book
Lighting a pitiless verse or two.

There might have been the immense solitude
Of the wind upon the curtains.

Pitiless verse? A few words tuned
And tuned and tuned and tuned.

It is good. The bed is empty,
The curtains are stiff and prim and still.
(*CP* 161)

Here the poet pointed to the opposition in his life. What Elsie would have called his "pitiless verse"—the earlier "adulteries that sack[ed] the sun" of which she had accused him—this betrayal of her with the Muse, robbed her and their child of his attention. But his compensation for the empty bed and the curtains "stiff and prim and still" was the product of his betrayal, his "pitiless verse." "A few words tuned/ And tuned and tuned and tuned" were better than finding a figure in the bed with "tragic hair" (no longer the "golden hair of [his] blond"), "bitter eyes, hands hostile and cold."

Stevens had made his adjustments. Everything he could do he did, including yielding to Elsie's prohibitions about his physical indulgences, at least while he was at home. But given these compromises, he had to do, too, at least sometimes, what gave him pleasure. What could not be completed in reality he completed in imagination: He returned to poetry. The correspondence of 1935 and the first quarter of 1936 reveals the nature of the compromises he made as well as the effects of some of these on the person in the household now old enough to be vulnerable to the underlying strain.

During 1935 Stevens had begun to make adjustments to his wife's injunctions about his indulgences. As he gave up alcohol, he became a true connoisseur of teas. Though he had for years enjoyed full and tasty exotic brews, he had not tasted all varieties and had not learned the intricacies of brewing. Nor had he inquired, as he did now, about typical accompanying condiments. From Benjamin Kwok, who had relatives with tea plantations, the poet learned how to steep optimally; he learned about the colors of various teas and how Chinese porcelain was glazed to compliment these colors best. Kwok sent him ginger candy and other treats that Stevens would have enjoyed if, as he put it, he were "sitting in Peking." At the same time Stevens renewed contacts with others in the East and asked for more objects that would sharpen his sense of what it felt like to be an Oriental. He religiously observed his tea ritual every day at three at the office.

This reopening of his interest in the East coincided with his giving up indulgences. His impulses had a healthful purpose and belonged to his desire to order life in ways that would be most beneficial to all in the family. However, it is not difficult to imagine how the subtle changes in his personality that accompanied such readjustments affected a sensitive child of eleven, who was, at the same time, slowly being asked to assume the position of mediator, as evidenced by Stevens's addressing to her his "report cards" from his winter 1936 trip.

This was a period of transition during which Stevens set in motion more rituals to structure life; these would absorb and deflect disturbances. He could then have more time to indulge his imagination. Though good for his work, these changes must have been trying for Holly. Just as she was approaching puberty and feeling more needful of her father's attention, he had again begun to give the greatest part of his free time to poetry. Simultaneously, his attempts to restrain himself from food and drink and to establish a climate conducive to meditation made him appear more removed. To make up for the loss she felt, Holly began overeating. Instead of growing to be more like the delicate creature her mother had been in her adolescence—as Stevens first remembered her (Holly took after Elsie in coloring and in the piercing beauty of her eyes)—she became like her father in one of his obese periods. This was painful both to her and to her father. While he would have wanted to dress her in things that flattered her beauty so that he could see her, in reality, completing a picture he kept in his imagination, her bulk frustrated his desire. In one of his letters to Rosamund Cary during 1935, responding to her inquiring about whether he would like her to send kimonos from Japan for Elsie and Holly, he noted that while the gift would be most appreciated for Elsie, Holly had "grown so large that, if somehow or other [he] managed to find out what size She [*sic*] would take, [she—Rosamund Cary] would think that [he] was really thinking of something for the Statue of Liberty" (June 19, 1935). He added that he would like, instead, some more gifts for "Mrs. Stevens," samples of Ainu weaving and pottery. Though he dealt with his daughter's weight problem somewhat humorously to Cary, it was not at all an easy situation. Nearing sixty, his own emotional ties to overindulgence still unresolved, the father of the budding adolescent did not quite know what to do, especially since he could not have a reasonable discussion with Elsie about the problems of young womanhood, her own difficulties with her own sexual identity having shaped her into someone who looked like an old maid.

Unsure about how to deal with the situation, Stevens seems to have shifted between treating Holly as the adult in the family on whom he could depend for understanding and treating her as a child, younger than her actual years. For Christmas 1935, for example, he and Elsie set up an electric train all over the living room and bought her, among other things, a set of dolls representing the Dionne quintuplets, each one with a dress of its own. At the same time Stevens observed (in the letter to Philip May in which he described the scene and thanked May for his gift of oranges for Holly)[16] that Holly moved among all this, holding a teddy bear while reading *Gone with the Wind* or some other "reasonably mature novel" (*L* 314). Tending to Holly's mature side, Stevens also bought her many books and her first typewriter. In addition, she received various objects from Japan that her father had requested from Rosamund Cary. These were more educational samples of the world. With them Stevens wanted to refine his daughter's sensibility.

What most excited Holly among these objects was a carved bear and another set of little dolls in Japanese silk dresses. Stevens commented to Mrs. Cary that Holly's appreciation of these things was based on her having "a good deal of taste in the sense that she quickly form[ed] likes and dislikes on the basis of what [was] fine and what [was] not fine: crude" (*L* 304). While this was no doubt partially true, her attraction to bears and dolls at this point in her own development—she also expressed desire for yet another set of "Classical [doll] figures" Cary had described—reflected that particular, gender-marked aspects of her education had been overly stressed, even for her generation. This focus, which left her with a late attachment to her teddy bear and with an extreme interest in dolls at the point when she was beginning to mature physically into a woman, later contributed to making it difficult for her to find in college an area of interest appropriate to her imaginative and intellectual skills. The troubles Stevens experienced with Holly through the years beginning with her time in college had begun long before. Her childhood had been marked by certain unfortunate facts centering largely on her mother's eccentricities, which were, in addition, contradictorily inconsistent. While, for example, Elsie enforced the strictest rules of etiquette, garnered from her extensive reading on the subject in her desire to act properly in the ways of the "upper" class, she also followed other kinds of "progressive" suggestions for child rearing, such as sending Holly out naked to play when she was younger and the family still lived on Farmington Avenue.[17] Holly's experience of these extremes was not helped by her father's reticence about dealing with these issues openly. He did not attempt to explain the nature of Elsie's engagement with her, with himself, or with the outside world. Private school, books, and all the curios from distant places could not mitigate the effects of this.

But adolescence offers parents a time when early mistakes can be corrected, as the child's sexuality reemerges and the personality is adjusted to that "first, foremost law." In order for Stevens to have addressed himself to this task directly, however, he would have had to have resolved his own relationship to sexuality. Moreover, he would have had to enter into a relationship with Holly that, ideally, her mother should have had with her. Stevens was clearly not the man who could have done this. So it was easier for all involved that instead of his openly acknowledging Holly's coming into womanhood, she was kept and seen as a precocious child with mature interests. In the strained atmosphere of indirection, it was natural that Holly developed an intimate and affectionate relationship with the Stevenses' housekeeper—who, from 1933 to 1935 (except for periods of interruption brought on by the stress of working for Mrs. Stevens), came in daily from nine to five-thirty and saw herself as Holly's full-time baby-sitter.

Sadly, in connection with Holly, Stevens seemed to stop his imagination from projecting possibilities. He seemed to be unable to consider the facts of his daughter's reality as she approached womanhood. Just as he had wanted to

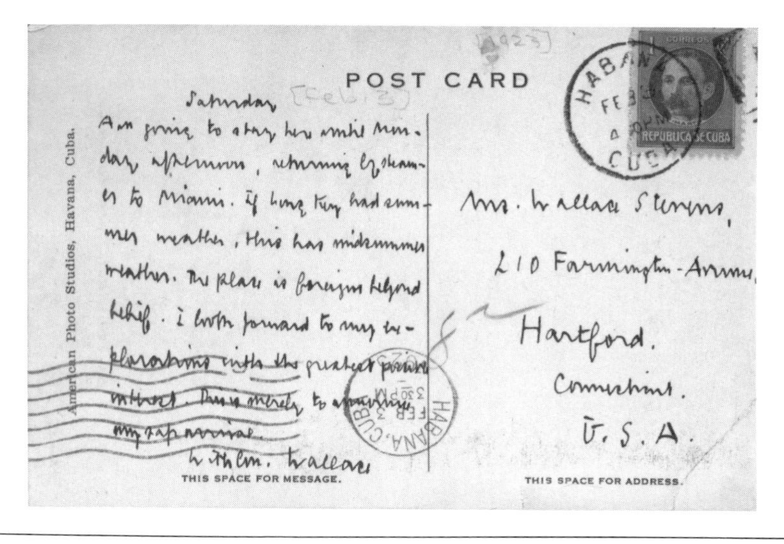
POST CARD

American Photo Studios, Havana, Cuba.

Saturday [Feb. 3]

Am going to stay here until Monday afternoon, returning by steamer to Miami. If Long Key had summer weather, this has midsummer weather. The place is foreign beyond belief. I look forward to my explorations with the greatest possible interest. This merely to announce my safe arrival.

With love, Wallace

THIS SPACE FOR MESSAGE.

Mrs. Wallace Stevens,
210 Farmington-Avenue,
Hartford.
Connecticut.
U.S.A.

THIS SPACE FOR ADDRESS.

Now, as this odd
Discoverer walked through the harbor streets
Inspecting the cabildo, the facade
Of the cathedral, making notes, he heard
A rumbling, west of Mexico, it seemed,
Approaching like a gasconade of drums.

THE COMEDIAN AS THE LETTER C

Stevens's postcard to his wife announcing his safe arrival in Havana, Cuba, February 3, 1923. Note his comment: "The place is foreign beyond belief."

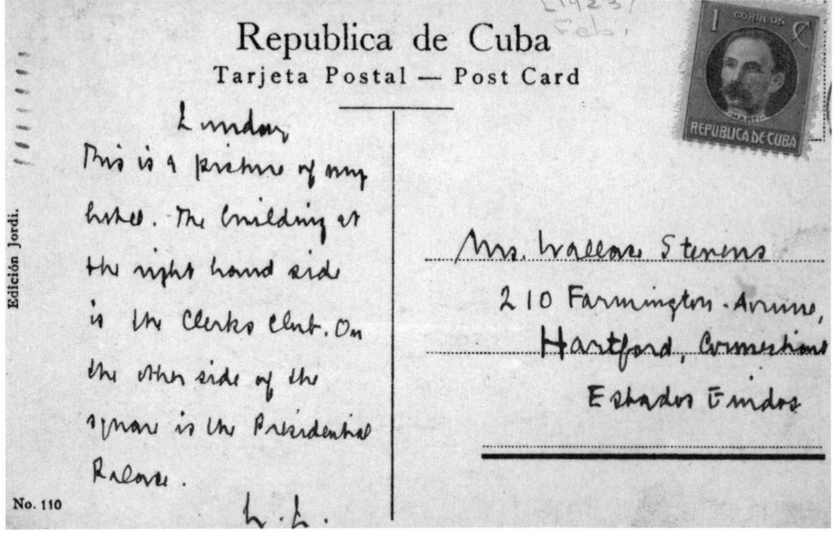

Republica de Cuba
Tarjeta Postal — Post Card

Edición Jordi.

Sunday
This is a picture of my hotel. The building at the right hand side is the Clerks Club. On the other side of the square is the Presidential Palace.
W. S.

No. 110

Mrs. Wallace Stevens
210 Farmington Avenue,
Hartford, Connecticut
Estados Unidos

Crispin knew
It was a flourishing tropic he required
For his refreshment, an abundant zone,
Prickly and obdurate, dense, harmonious,
Yet with a harmony not rarefied
Nor fined for the inhibited instruments
Of over-civil stops.

THE COMEDIAN AS THE LETTER C

Another postcard from Stevens to his wife, also from the February, 1923, trip. This one shows his hotel on the left.

How content I shall be in the North to which I sail
And to feel sure and to forget the bleaching sand . . .

FAREWELL TO FLORIDA

Elsie Stevens waited back in the North, in Hartford.

"Holly grows prettier and jollier every day. We have never had the least trouble with her—have never lost a wink of sleep. She babbles and plays with her hands and smiles like an angel. Such experiences are a terrible blow to poor literature" (*Letters,* p. 244).

Elsie and Holly Stevens, autumn, 1924.

First Crispin smiled upon
His goldenest demoiselle, inhabitant,
She seemed, of a country of the capuchins,
So delicately blushed, so humbly eyed,
Attentive to a coronal of things
Secret and singular.

THE COMEDIAN AS THE LETTER C

The poet and his daughter in 1925.

Where in the park is the dark spadille
   With scent of lavender sweet,
That never was held in the mad quadrille,
   And where are the slippered feet?
Ah! we'd have given a pound to meet
   The card that wrought our fall
The card that none other of all could beat—
   But where is the pink parasol?

Ballade of the Pink Parasol

Holly Stevens, c. 1928.

"Mother, my mother, who are you"

QUESTIONS ARE REMARKS

Elsie and Holly Stevens, c. 1929.

She made the motions of her wrist
The grandiose gestures
Of her thought.

INFANTA MARINA

Holly Stevens, c. 1929.

The air is full of children, statues, roofs
And snow

CHAOS IN MOTION AND NOT IN MOTION

Wallace Stevens, Holly (center), an unidentified child, and "The Snow Man" of 1929.

keep Elsie his "Little Girl," so he wanted to keep Holly a little girl. And just as he had made Elsie the embodiment of his "second self," on whom he depended for constancy and understanding and to whom he was accountable, so Holly was gradually being asked to take on this role. Under the pressure of these unspoken, opposing demands, it was no wonder Holly grew so heavy that it horrified her father. Some defense was necessary to protect her from being a woman since she had not been prepared to become one. Growing fat would keep her from being seen as a woman. At the same time it was a call for attention from her father as he removed himself into an involvement with poetry that she had not yet witnessed.

During this trying period Stevens experienced the effects of blocking his imagination in relationship to Holly. If things at home had been different, this time might have provided the climate in which he produced his most successful work. Reviews of *Ideas of Order* and broader comments about his poetry were making it clear that indeed, he was being considered a major figure. More, his influence was being acknowledged. He was delighted, for example, by both Marianne Moore's review (in the English *Criterion* of January 1936) and by Howard Baker's "extremely intelligent analysis" of his work in the autumn 1935 *Southern Review.*[18] In letters to Latimer, Monroe, and others he confirmed and clarified his attraction to Chinese and Japanese models. Monroe responded by noting that largely because of his influence, *Poetry* was devoting a special issue to Oriental poetry so as to stress its importance for younger American poets. As for the criticisms from the extreme left and from the pure Marxists, Stevens had expected these and was not disturbed when they appeared. The critiques from the left had begun with Stanley Burnshaw's review, to which Stevens had poetically replied and for which he was grateful because it had involved him, as he put it in the actual dialectical process of elucidating his ideas in the marketplace.

In spite of the sense of security as a poet that came from this public recognition, the work Stevens produced during this time was his least successful. By "devoting attention to one thing over a long period"—the theme of the statues that held together the poems of *Owl's Clover*—he had expected to repeat the experience he had had with "The Comedian as the Letter C." He described this kind of engagement as being like courting a woman for many years. Slowly all favors fell away from it, he noted, and it stood by itself, in bare relief. Notwithstanding this desire and his long application to the statue poems, none of them would have, in spite of the powerful "gaiety" of language, the effect of his strong poems. The rhythms, when not echoing earlier poems, were often stilted; images and references were not integrally woven into the "poetry of the subject." This group was Stevens's most extended composition, 700 to 800 lines as compared to the roughly 500 of "Comedian." Though the blank verse of *Owl's Clover* was praised as surpassing even Algernon Swinburne's, there was something missing.

All through 1935 and 1936 Stevens's attention to these poems was constant; their demands dominated all others. One reason he looked forward to his stay in Florida during the late winter of 1936 was that there, away, without distraction and without indulgences, as he had intended, he expected to complete one whole section (*L* 307). This was probably "A Duck for Dinner." The theme of the absence of "duck for dinner" for the "masses" echoed the fact that one night in Florida, though Stevens and his friends had hoped for it, there was no duck for dinner. This, in turn, echoed Stevens's desire to be abstemious on this trip: "no duck, no drink, no cake," etc. But this was not the only poem of the group that began from a sense of loss or privation. Each of the poems sequentially developed this theme, which was, at bottom, what the poet felt. He had lost some power of imagination. This was the unavoidable fact. Though he attributed this lack to the pressure of external events, his incapacity had also to do with what he was experiencing personally. He had lost a sense of inner strength in not keeping his resolve to refrain from drinking, and he had withdrawn even more from his relationship with Holly. It does not seem accidental that the figure he chose to describe her size was the *Statue* of Liberty and that this group of poems centered on the idea of a statue. In a sadly ironic way his inability to come to terms with his own childishly "indulgent" appetites and with his daughter's passage into maturity mimicked the situation of a world unable to mature. The ideas of the past, the adherence to a moral system fixed on the notion of God or gods, precluded one's being able to see things as they were in their constant changing. This theme was played out in all its variations in the poems of *Owl's Clover.*

The figure of the old woman of bitter mind in "The Old Woman and the Statue," the woman whose thought "repressed itself/ Without any pity in a somnolent dream" (*OP* 44), was a recasting of the youthful Eve-like figure in "Le Monocle de Mon Oncle," who, "without pity on [those] studious ghosts,/ [came] dripping in [her] hair from sleep" (*CP* 14). The figure in "Sunday Morning" that witnessed deer walking upon the mountains in the wilderness now walked in a "motionless place," though still thinking of "heaven and earth and herself" (*OP* 45). The idealized figure of "The Idea of Order at Key West" that sang a song beyond herself and of the sea now was "that tortured one," her "ear unmoved" (*OP* 44). She had become "So destitute that nothing but herself/ Remained and nothing of herself except/ A fear too naked for her shadow's shape" (*OP* 44). She was the inverted form of the figures of Crispin and Hoon, who found themselves "more truly and more strange." The address to the "High-Toned Old Christian Woman" was broadened in "Mr. Burnshaw and the Statue" to all, to "Mesdames" (*OP* 48). The angels that descended in "Le Monocle" appeared once again, but instead of heralding a "damsel heightened by eternal bloom" (*CP* 15), they came "to slay/ The black and ruin his sepulchral throne" (*OP* 55) in "The Greenest Continent." In the same poem "the diplomats of the cafés expound[ed]:/ Fromage and coffee and cognac and no gods./ It was a mistake to paint the gods" (*OP* 57), they thought, collectively echoing the situation of the naïvely misguided figure of "Sunday Morning," who, with her "late coffee and oranges," replaced the wine and bread of communion, but to no internal effect. There were many more such rephrasings in *Owl's Clover.* All served to illustrate that against things changing, old forms reappeared deceptively filled with new content that made it seem that the forms, too, had changed.

With his daughter approaching maturity, Stevens faced the same reticences and fell into many of the same patterns he recognized from more than twenty years earlier, when he had had to deal with Elsie in her nascent womanhood. Unable to master his responses, he came to know at first hand the power which in the last poem of *Owl's Clover,* "Sombre Figuration," he attributed to "subman under all/ The rest, to whom in the end the rest return,/ The man below the man below the man,/ Steeped in night's opium, evading day" (*OP* 66). Who was this figure if not the embodiment of the unconscious, the "irrational element" that was the subject of a piece Stevens composed as a preface to reading parts of *Owl's Clover* at Harvard in December 1936 (*L* 313)? On the day before he left for Cambridge he commented: "This is something I have never done before and I look forward to it the way one must look forward to one's first baby." He had just read some of the renewed attacks from the left that came in the form of reviews of *Owl's Clover.* But he was not fazed. As he expressed in a letter to Latimer apropos of having seen Ruth Lechlitner's piece in the *New York Herald Tribune,* his attitude reflected the same humor with which he had learned to regard himself and the world: "We are all much disturbed about a possible attack from the Left; I expect the house to be burned down almost any moment" (*L* 313).

He was not disturbed both because he had foreseen the misunderstanding that would come from any who held a fixed position and because he knew that whatever he wrote was transitional. His poems could only mirror the relationship he had with reality at the moment he was writing. Just as he had realized that *Ideas of Order* as a volume was not as successful "as poetry" as *Harmonium,* so he felt that what he had attempted in the poems of *Owl's Clover* resulted in being "rather boring" (*L* 308). What he had tried was "to apply [his] own sort of poetry . . . to what one reads in the papers . . . the commonplaces of the day." This effort was a continuation of his response to the reception of *Ideas of Order.* Not only "Mr. Burnshaw and the Statue" but all the poems of the group represented his desire to clarify the function of poetry in life. As he put it to Latimer in March 1936, answering his suggestion that *Ideas of Order* be submitted to the Pulitzer Prize committee, his interest was in "social reform and not in social revolution." He felt that because the major critical attitude of the time reflected a desire for revolution, *Ideas of Order* would be judged weak. In referring to the latest review of it, titled "A Stuffed Goldfinch" by Geoffrey Grigson (founder and editor of *New Verse*) he noted that Grigson was interested in propaganda. Stevens went on to elucidate his position and purpose by saying:

> [F]rom the point of view of social revolution, *Ideas of Order* is a book of the most otiose prettiness; and it is probably quite inadequate from any social point of view. However, I am not a propagandist. Conceding that the social

> situation is the most absorbing thing in the world today, and that those phases of it that you and I regret as merely violent have a strong chance of prevailing in the long run, because what now exists is so depleted, and because the other things are all that there are to look to, it is not possible for me, honestly, to take the point of view of the poet just out of school.

He closed, adding, ". . . it would be extraordinary if the Pulitzer Prize had anything to do with the sort of thing that I have just been talking about. It would be a feather in the cap of the Alcestis Press, not to speak of my own cap, but merely to have been asked to submit a book for consideration does not justify one's giving the thing another thought. . . ." (*L* 309).

In Stevens's mind, social reform could come about only if things as they were, the commonplaces of the day, no matter how horrifying, were considered from a different, distanced point of view, an ancient aspect had to touch the new mind of the century. His preferred title for *Owl's Clover,* "Aphorisms on Society," pointed to this. He wanted his readers to look at society in the same way he had looked at himself in "Le Monocle de Mon Oncle," from a point of view that translated the immediate violence of the situation back into its contributing causes, the ideas of the "studious ghosts" of the past. The disjunction between those outworn ideas and the pressing realities of the day, he hoped, would be made as clear as that resulting from the presence of the white man and his order in Africa, "The Greenest Continent" (*L* 307–08). Observing the events of the world and feeling the strain in his own being between the orders of the past that had shaped him and his inability to deal with certain immediate facts, Stevens had come to think that "intelligence" was inadequate to deal with what was. Something deeper, more primary and primal, had to be included in the way the present was addressed. This was what he named the "irrational element," the "subman" of "Sombre Figuration."

The level of understanding by "subman" could be best approached and experienced through rhythmic aphorisms—the aphorisms like snatches of the nightmarish social situation. Poetically removed from their newspaper context, beaten out in rhythms like messages on jungle drums, they could be felt in their connection to the deeper, irrational forces that propelled them. These forces were well beyond the forms intelligence had invented. The poet was applying to poetry the lesson about the purpose and operation of aphorisms that he had learned from his reading of Francis Bacon,[19] who, almost four centuries earlier had, for his time, chosen to imitate the aphoristic models of figures like Marcus Aurelius and Epictetus to challenge his readers to complete his meaning with their own imaginations. As Stevens put it in yet another letter to Latimer, in making the poetry of *Owl's Clover* he realized that the "orderly relations of society as a whole" could not be dealt with "flatly and explicitly." For that, "one would have to be a Lucretius of politics," he added (*L* 305).

While in the end Stevens felt that *Owl's Clover* had not succeeded in accomplishing his purpose, his working through the problems he faced in composing the poems of the volume led him to reflect on what constituted these problems. The result was one of his most important but largely ignored pieces, "The Irrational Element in Poetry" (*OP* 216–28). This, in turn, prepared the way for the central act of his music drama, "The Man with the Blue Guitar," which did accomplish what he had intended for *Owl's Clover.* In the later poem he beat out in noble accents and inescapable rhythms his central theme: the function of the poet and of poetry in society. This he illustrated by taking it upon himself to play out the "duet with the undertaker." If the fear of death could be acknowledged as a deep motivating factor, "commonplaces" could be seen in their proper light, as distractions from, at the same time as evidences of, the fear.

Between the time of writing *Owl's Clover* and "The Man with the Blue Guitar," Stevens broke through the imaginative block that had made the former less than satisfying. To a large degree, "The Irrational Element in Poetry" was the instrument he used to tear through the barriers he had set up. As such it is an extremely personal record and, since it elucidated the deepest level of his involvement with his work and the role he wanted it to play in the world, the first section of his public defense of poetry. Subsequent sections would follow in the form of later lectures.

In writing this piece, Stevens reopened the wounds of his past, the concerns and feelings that had first led him to write poetry. But he now considered these in light of what he had experienced and accomplished since then. That this reevaluation occurred at this point is not surprising. He was living on very shaky ground. He feared Elsie's reaction to his renewed involvement with poetry. He recognized the difficulties he had in dealing with his daughter's development. He realized that he had once again to impose an external order on himself in the form of diet and exercise. Experiencing these things, he had to admit to himself that his own irrational element, his unconscious, was not well tuned to reality. In attempting to understand why he had not achieved this attunement, Stevens saw himself as representative of all the external forces that had impinged on his generation. He dealt with his feelings in terms that interwove his most personal experience with that of the collectivity. He knew he feared most what all feared most: death, the ultimate unknown. He knew, too, that all human efforts were generated by the desire to know and control that unknown. Years before he had figured death as the eternal mother sleeplessly waiting—an association born out of extremely personal reactions. Now death was simply the "unknown." The "unknown," in turn, was the "irrational element," as he pointed out in his lecture.

In composing "The Irrational Element in Poetry," Stevens reexamined his still-unresolved relationship to his mother and his past. But he did this on a heightened level, a level that reflected how his instinctual needs had been sublimated so that his personal problems became, in his consciousness, those of his age. It is immaterial whether Stevens himself realized what he had accomplished in putting together this piece, though the fact that in it he named Freud "one of the greatest figures in the world" suggests that he had at least an "irrational" understanding of the connections between his public concerns and his private motivations. This lecture reflected all Stevens had read of the psychology of intuition and the unconscious. In addition to Freud, he cited Bergson and Charles Mauron. He had read deeply in major works of each of these figures; he had heavily marked and noted Mauron's *Aesthetics and Psychology* and read his *Nature of Beauty in Art and Literature* as well, both in his library, together with Bergson's *L'Intuition philosophique* (all now at The Huntington). He also made a point of referring to those literary figures most intensely immersed in the movements of the unconscious: Marcel Proust, James Joyce, and, in connection with a theoretical application to poetry itself, Henri Brémond.

He did not make more of Freud because he anticipated the resistance he would meet if he made explicit his commitment to understanding human motivation in the way that Freud's eye—"the microscope of potency"—had perceived. It was more prudent to focus on literary figures who shared this understanding but whose names did not, like Freud's, raise walls that made communication impossible. Doing this was exactly like dressing the "true subject" in the distracting "poetry of the subject" or like appearing the arch-conservative, dressed in a three-piece suit and moving toward the left. Each of these dualities was another form of what he had early on expressed to Elsie, his wish, borrowed from one of his "studious ghosts," to be one who could repeatedly do "one of the best things in life . . . to do good and to have it discovered by chance" (WAS 1789).

This desire also lay behind the many gifts he bestowed. After reading "The Irrational Element in Poetry" and parts of *Owl's Clover* at Harvard, he enclosed with his letter of thanks to his hosts, Theodore Spencer and Robert Hillyer, a manuscript letter of Charles Eliot Norton's, noting that it should be designated as an anonymous gift. The anonymous gift and the dialectic between the true subject and the poetry of the subject had a common ground. Both would force the individual who considered these facts to appreciate the appearance, the surface in and for itself. If the hidden aspect were revealed—the true subject beneath the poetry of the subject or the donor of the gift—it would have to be appreciated as the moving force, the spring beneath the apparent fact. Employing such devices would ultimately protect the donor/shaper from the possible effects of rejection. Those who did not appreciate the surface features would simply walk away, but those who did would remain long enough to see through them. Such individuals could not help valuing, too, the giver or shaper of the gift.

In describing the important difference between the true subject and the poetry of the subject, Stevens touched on all this. On the most intimate level, the issues he dealt with stemmed from the old conflict that had determined the structure of his life: the struggle between the external expectations he had set up for himself, following his father, and the internal demands of his spirit, forged by his mother's involvement with imagination. In returning to a wholehearted commitment to poetry after years devoted to making a place for himself "on the front bench," Stevens was finally resolving the two parts of his being into one.

Accepting and articulating publicly that as a poet he yielded to the "unknown" was an admission that the "other" moved in him. From his youth Stevens had felt that the "other" associated with "writing verses" was female, "lady-like." In wanting to know and see Elsie as his "other self," he had expressed his need to understand the nature of this "second self." He wanted to capture and control this "other." All these feelings about the female were reactivated as he fully immersed himself in poetry again and as his daughter was becoming a woman. In describing the central importance of the irrational element in poetry and, more generally, in life, Stevens was also announcing that he had now become one with the "other"—the female, night, imagination—and that it moved him beyond what he could understand: "You have somehow to know the sound that is the exact sound; and you do in fact know. Your knowledge is irrational. In that sense life is mysterious; and if it is mysterious at all, I suppose that it is cosmically mysterious" (*OP* 226).

It is extremely important to realize in understanding this level of meaning that as in the poems in which there are also personal references, this level does not provide *the meaning.* Such a view would be reductive. Becoming aware of this level, however, gives a sense of the complex extension that informs a consciousness as exquisitely refined and developed as Stevens's. What is being considered is the evolution of a sensibility through time. Specifically, what is being witnessed is the transformation of a desire unspoken from childhood to merge again with the mother, earth, nature. In Stevens's case it became a yearning for identification with a more abstract "female." Through the shift Stevens pointed out in this piece from wanting, like mystics—or like his mother—to approach God through poetry that was explicitly prayer to wanting to "write poetry to find the good which, in the Platonic sense, is synonymous with God . . . the good in what is harmonious and orderly . . . out of delight in the harmonious and orderly" (*OP* 222), what is perceived is the kind of sublimation on which the development of society depends. Stevens elucidated this again a few years later (1939) in a poetic setting in the second stanza of "The Woman Who Had More Babies Than That":

> Berceuse, transatlantic. The children are men, old men,
> Who, when they think and speak of the central man,
> Of the humming of the central man, the whole sound
> Of the sea, the central humming of the sea,
> Are old men breathed on by a maternal voice,
> Children and old men and philosophers,
> Bald heads with their mother's voice still in their ears.

> The self is a cloister full of remembered sounds
> And of sounds so far forgotten, like her voice,
> That they return unrecognized. The self
> Detects the sound of a voice that doubles its own,
> In the images of desire, the forms that speak,
> The ideas that come to it with a sense of speech.
> The old men, the philosophers, are haunted by that
> Maternal voice, the explanation at night.
> They are more than parts of the universal machine.
> Their need in solitude: that is the need,
> The desire, for the fiery lullaby.
>
> (*OP* 82)

Beneath the insecurities of Stevens's childhood and youth that produced the reticences and eccentricities of his personality, there was a profound sense of security and trust forged out of the residues of faith that had been instilled in him from his earliest days. Stevens's Calvinist virtues, mixed with his desire for approval from those who had taught him those virtues, kept him constantly striving to understand, to know all that he could know. He read and read, questioned and questioned. Eventually he was able to transform the desire for God, learned from his mother, into a desacramentalized version: the "delight in the harmonious and orderly." This offered, instead of the promise of heaven, "momentary existence on an exquisite plane" (*OP* 223).

As Stevens made certain to reiterate in closing this piece, the consideration of the irrational was central. He knew in 1936 that this "potent subject," as he called it, had not been adequately addressed. In the future the "figure of the youth as virile poet" would do this: "We must expect in the future incessant activity by the irrational and in the field of the irrational. The advances thus to be made would be all the greater if the character of the poet was [*sic*] not so casual and intermittent a character. . . . For the poet, the irrational is elemental" (*OP* 229). Freud was the "great figure in the world" who had made this understanding paramount in human experience. Without naming him again, Stevens expressed his acceptance of his importance for the century. Freud had been careful to point out that he had learned from the poets, and Stevens understood.

The implications of what he understood he made clear not only here but also in what he wrote about the "romantic" in its "non-pejorative" sense. These implications were also illustrated by the poetry he wrote after coming to terms with his imagination—through all its associations, to mother, night, the female, the unknown, God, the irrational, death—in "The Irrational Element in Poetry." This was something he made explicit in "The Man with the Blue Guitar." Dealing with the irrational meant, first, fully acknowledging its particular manifestations in the individual. In this lecture/essay Stevens was careful to indicate that all were moved by irrational forces and that each individual expressed these in particular ways: ". . . it is becoming easier to say every day that we are irrational beings; that all irrationality is not of a piece and that the only reason why it does not yet have a tradition is that its tradition is in progress" (*OP* 218). But there were, and are, always moments when the collective was, and is, moved by one voice and answers with one voice. Stevens cited the landslide results of the latest presidential election (in which Franklin Roosevelt was reelected by an overwhelming majority) to illustrate this example of what Freud theoretically explored in *Group Psychology and the Analysis of the Ego.*

In simple terms, what Freud had uncovered in *The Interpretation of Dreams,* which Stevens indicated he knew well, was the way externals, the accidents of an individual's movement through life, determine the specific *id*iom, the language of his or her unconscious. Common to all individuals are the biological, instinctual needs shared with animals: needs for warmth, shelter, sleep, food, drink, and sex. Together, these constitute the "first, foremost law," survival. This is also the fundamental law of the irrational. Shaping the particular id of each individual are forces of his or her culture forged out of adaptation to environment, the social structure, the events of a specific historical moment, the idiosyncrasies of other individuals in the family and in the extended societal order, and, finally, his or her reactions to each of these determinants. These reactions are encoded in associations to particular events and words as the infant moves through an imagistic, preverbal to a verbal stage. Because of the overlays of various associations connected with the preverbal child's expressions of its different instinctual needs, networks of images, sounds, rhythms, colors, sensations become bound to primal urgings. As the child grows into an adult, more associations attach themselves, with the difference that as society's language is learned and reason is developed, certain of these associations become repressed while the dominant modes of expression, necessary to preserve society's order, are formalized. Excluded earlier associations, then, become the particular id of each individual, the personal language in which his or her instinctual needs and fears announce themselves in the rebuslike images of dreams.

Following Freud's insight, part of the work of reason is to translate the language of the unconscious. This translation means being able to recognize associations attached to sources of satisfaction and dissatisfaction. Only after such recognition is it possible to negotiate against the demands of the society for the maximizing of pleasure. This must be done without infringing on the rights of others to do the same. In a self-contained, uniform society this work does not belong to the individual alone since the associations coming from the culture, society, the family, and the historical moment are largely communal. The emergence of psychology as a separate discipline, and Freud's emergence as its archarticulator during the last quarter of the nineteenth century, had to do with the beginning of a world-scale transformation of society. Until industrialization there had been various local groups attached to ritualized customs and constant forms. Then suddenly, societies became diverse and mobile, no longer rooted in soil that had nurtured families over generations.

It was not accidental that it was after his visit to America that Freud began to focus on the problems of civilization and groups rather than on the individual. The United States had been, before industrialization, a prototype, an experiment in what happens when the common language of associations born out of a long, shared past no longer ties together the individuals of the collective. In this situation analysis offers itself as a tool facilitating the individual's negotiation of personal needs against societal demands. It was also not accidental that in the opening pages of *The Future of an Illusion* Freud expressed hope for what might evolve in America, where, at least nominally, reason rather than religion formed the basis of the polity's communality.

Stevens, as meticulously observant a reader as he was a poet, understood Freud's perceptions and their implications. By the time of writing "The Man with the Blue Guitar," Stevens had realized that precisely because America had and has no common myth, no common religion—and so no common unconscious language—the population, wanting the security such communality provides, would be as eager as any other in which traditional forms were disintegrating (such as they had been, brutally, in Germany since its defeat in the First World War) for a leader who could speak with the voice of "major man" to quell fears and inspire hope. This figure would take on the function of Western religion's God-the-Father. FDR's landslide reelection was evidence of this for Stevens, as it certainly must have been for Freud. Aware of this need, Stevens wanted to pave the way for an idealized future poet who could provide a common language, one so universal that it could form part of the basic vocabulary of the world. "The Man with the Blue Guitar" was, in Stevens's mind:

> A poem like a missal found
> In the mud, a missal for that young man,
>
> That scholar hungriest for that book,
> The very book, or, less, a page
>
> Or, at the least, a phrase, that phrase,
> A hawk of life, that latined phrase:
>
> To know; a missal for brooding-sight.
> To meet that hawk's eye and to flinch
>
> Not at the eye but at the joy of it.
> I play. But this is what I think.
> (*CP* 177–78)

Rather than the personalized figures of religion or national heroes, it was the weather, the seasons, and the shape of the earth as it turned through light and night that Stevens believed should be celebrated. The rhythms in which this psalm of praise was to be sung were simple and primary—like nursery rhymes. This feature would allow them to be learned easily so that even words that were not at first understood would be remembered, prompted by internal rhymes. Just as children learn songs and rhymes before they understand what each word means and then one day ask about these unknown words one by one, so adults recalling lines or stanzas that caught them would ask themselves about this poet's mysterious words or "latined phrase[s]": "squamous," "Sudarium," Oxidia," "rattapallax," "gurrituck," "cloak of Spain," "prismatic reeks," "cata-sisters," "curule." In searching out these meanings, readers would be forced to add history to their feeling for the rhythms since each instance of Stevens's using such a word or phrase involved his understanding of the evolution of the forms of the words. In his poetry the sources of these histories are as diverse as the populations that came to settle these teeming shores. According to Stevens's view, the imagination of the major poet, sensitive to the mechanisms and function of language and to the range of possible associations, attempts to contain and represent as many of these associations as possible and with them to forge a common unconscious language particularized in the words but attached to universal moments. The intention behind the poet's desire, as expressed in "The Man with the Blue Guitar," to "bring a world quite round," echoed Plato's description of the purpose of education in *The Republic:* True education is "being turned around" so that things as they are are changed.

This poem illustrated what Stevens had come to understand about the necessary "conjunctions between things as they are and things imagined." The process of its composition revealed how reason works with and against imagination to make "a thing yet to be made" (*CP* 169): A language of "Poetry// Exceeding music must take the place/ Of empty heaven and its hymns,// Ourselves in poetry must take their place" (*CP* 167). Just as an individual can use reason to uncover his or her idiomatic language and sift through its words and images, translating into common forms those that will foster optimal communication, the poet, on a larger scale, does the same. In "The Man with the Blue Guitar" the poet was figured as a "shearsman of sorts" (*CP* 15); he was imagined to be like the epic poet, rhapsodist of episodes elaborated to hold the attention of an audience and shape it into one sympathetic identity. In this new work there were no heroes, no personal feelings, but rather a "million people on one string" (*CP* 166) and feelings generalized back into their "bond to all that dust" (*CP* 15), to nature, "feelings . . ./ Like a buzzing of flies in autumn air" (*CP* 166).

> I know my lazy, leaden twang
> Is like the reason in a storm;
>
> And yet it brings the storm to bear.
> I twang it out and leave it there.
> (*CP* 169)

Stevens's ability to play things in the way he did against the voices of opposition that saw in his work a flight into a depoliticized, extrasocial aesthetic realm came from a number of sources: his own inner strength, forged steadily from childhood; his constant reading; his recent coming to terms again with the importance of imagination in his life; his acknowledgment of his limitations in facing the pressures of external reality; and, not least, the continued support he felt from the reception of his work in the mid and late thirties. Marianne Moore's and Harriet Monroe's letters urging him to continue writing, for example, and R. P. Blackmur's review of *Ideas of Order,* which appeared in the winter 1937 issue of the *Southern Review*—an analysis of his work which Stevens found "very decent" (*L* 315)—were evidences of how he was appreciated. This kind of support, in addition to his winning the *Nation*'s prize for the 1936 poem "The Men That Are Falling," played a part in helping the poet hammer out the lines of "The Man with the Blue Guitar," so different from those of *Owl's Clover.* This recognition, coupled with the self-exploration that had been necessary for him to compose "The Irrational Element in Poetry," strengthened the poet's commitment to be himself, to follow his Muse once more rather than dawdle behind the "commonplaces of the day," as he had in the poems of *Owl's Clover.*

In collecting a revised and shortened version of *Owl's Clover,* together with "The Men That Are Falling" and "A Thought Revolved" (*CP* 184–86), to be published in the volume titled by "The Man with the Blue Guitar," Stevens offered a mapping of his attempts to face the pressures of the external world in one of its most difficult moments. He wrote in a letter to Latimer in September 1937, a month before the volume's appearance, "all that I care to preserve from what I have done during the last two years is contained in this book" (*L* 326). It was as important for Stevens to leave a record of his imagination's struggle with things as they were—his description of the effect of "Owl's Clover" on the dust jacket of *The Man with the Blue Guitar* volume—as it was to illustrate what he meant by poetry as a subject of the first importance to the spirit, his description of "The Man with the Blue Guitar" on the same dust jacket. Though he found *Owl's Clover* "boring" in some of its aspects, Stevens felt it was necessary to leave behind an account of what occurred when the "commonplaces of the day" preempted the spirit's deeper needs and concerns. These more intimate needs, as he showed in *The Man with the Blue Guitar,* were attached to nature, to the human being's knowledge of himself or herself as "an animal." This animal was "native in this world," unlike the "person" who was a "native of a mind" (*CP* 180) imprisoned in a "mould" (*CP* 174). The mind created artificial structures that led to categories, separation, and eventually the kind of nationalism that bred wars. The difference between *Owl's Clover* and *The Man with the Blue Guitar* illustrated the difference in power between poems that focused on the commonplaces and poems that dealt with the very elements of what it means to be human.

As Stevens stated in "The Irrational Element in Poetry," for him literature was the "better part of life." As such it provided a model for dealing with feeling and reality; this model could be imitated in life. At the same time as

Stevens was putting this perception into practice (the period when he was composing the stanzas for "The Man with the Blue Guitar"), he began to face a family situation that raised difficult feelings from the past. He dealt with this situation gracefully. His older brother, Garrett, Jr., his father's favorite—on whose part Garrett, Sr., had interceded often when Stevens was still a young man, urging him to take on the protective role he knew he himself could no longer sustain—developed a series of symptoms that prevented his continuing work. As a result of an illness twelve years before, his lungs, already weak, failed as his heart enlarged. Consequently, he suffered from incapacitating asthma, bronchitis, and edema. In the early fall of 1936 Stevens and his younger brother, John, began sending monthly stipends to support their older brother and his wife. This support continued until Garrett's death well over a year later. After this Stevens kept on sending money to his widow, usually in the form of holiday gifts. It was not remarkable that Stevens helped his brother financially, but it is surprising that his manner in responding to Garrett's way of asking for help was consistently gracious and generous. At no point did Stevens express either a negative judgment—even when advising Garrett how to budget what he was now receiving—or impatience at the regular, fawning reports of woe that his brother sent as simultaneous acknowledgments of having received the last check and accounts of why he could not go back to work.

This situation was problematic for Stevens not only because it raised the unresolved conflicts of his childhood and youth in relationship to the garrulous, good-looking, "smart," well-loved brother who had squandered his talents but also because it presented him with monthly reminders of an emotional instability that seemed to run in the family or at least in his two closest elders, Garrett, Sr., and Garrett, Jr. Unable to cope with his failure during the economic crises of the end of the last century, Garrett, Sr., had suffered a nervous breakdown. Garrett, Jr., unable to deal with the actuality of what a soldier's life meant, had been discharged from the service because of hysterical epilepsy. And now, under the pressure of the economic decline of the thirties, he developed the symptoms that made him dependent on his two brothers. It was no wonder that Stevens became so aware of the threat posed by what went on in the external world. Knowing his own extreme mood swings from the time that he had first begun to live on his own and support himself, Stevens felt all the greater need to find ways of maintaining his equilibrium when pelted this way and that by the hard facts of life. Reason was the instrument he used in life, just as he used it in his poems, to find the terms—words, phrases, and rhythms—to make his way through reality's storms.

Had he not used reason to work with the irrational feelings called up in response to his brother's obsequious expressions of need, he would either have ignored the requests—and maintained the distance that had characterized their relationship for the last thirty years or more—or have sent money but, at the same time, reacted to his brother's wheedling tone and manner with curt and pointed notes directed at making Garrett somehow aware that he understood he was being manipulated. Instead, he was courteous and kind. There was not even a hint of grudgingness at having now to do for Garrett what his father had wanted him to do more than thirty years before. In this situation, as in all others, Stevens acted in the model fashion that we would want everyone to act, even though we realize that not even one other might follow. Not even during periods when Garrett's moaning letters increased in frequency—usually at times when he seemed to be improving enough to go back to work—or when they were followed up by others he got his doctor and wife to write did Stevens lose his equanimity. On one occasion, over three days, Stevens received from Sarah, Garrett's wife, two almost word-for-word tearful descriptions of her husband's condition, with a reiteration of how bad the doctor had said he was; within the same three-day period he also received the doctor's forced account. Stevens simply responded warmly and sent another check. He continued his regular support although it came to mean that he had to deprive himself and his family of a summer holiday (during the summer of 1937) and himself of one more short trip to Florida the following winter. He also could not do one of the things he thought the "most important obligation" he had during these uncertain times: to save money, as he put it to James Powers in a letter of June 1937. (Since he had remained ineligible for life insurance, Stevens regularly set money aside for his wife and daughter.)

In this same letter to Powers he also expressed how happy he was at the news that he and Margaret were going to have their second child. About his own feeling on this, he sadly added, "There is nothing that I should have liked more, but I was afraid of it" (*L* 321). Here Stevens revealed a subtle yearning still alive well past mid-life. He would have wanted another child. But why? He had always been uneasy about security in relationship to a child. Yet another child would have meant that he would have been in one more way like his father. This came through in his imagining that the Powerses' expected child would be a boy and, more, would be called Jim, Jr. The naming paralleled his father's naming Garrett, Jr., whom the poet was now caring for the way a father would. This association played its part in Stevens's fantasy about the Powerses' child.

He imagined Powers' "knocking about" with his son. While Stevens had swung Holly high on park swings and recited Robert Louis Stevenson, taken her to Elizabeth Park to ice skate and entertained her with his own figure eights, taken her with a friend to a nearby amusement park, taught her how to feed horses sugar, and even taken her fishing often when they were on holiday,[20] he had fears that he could not devote enough attention to a second child. He must have considered his age and the increased demands on his energy made by the pressure of external events.

Moreover, Stevens could not trust that Elsie, so confused about motherhood, could have managed the strain of a second child. This would have been especially true if they would have had a boy, with whose rearing she naturally would have had a great deal more difficulty. With a girl, at least, she could teach her what she knew about sewing and cooking, share the child's interest in dressing dolls, weaving, and other feminine activities. Approaching forty, she would not have been in a position to stretch herself to learn and imagine what would have been necessary for a boy. Stevens's fear was sadly reinforced by Elsie's emotional frailty. While things on the surface of their common life ran regularly, according to the rhythms they jointly established, there were tensions beneath that surface that had never changed. These tensions revolved around their deep insecurities about themselves as a man and as a woman. His insecurity made Stevens afraid to attempt something he could not have liked more.

Stevens's insecurity mirrored a change that had come about after he passed into middle age. The poet regarded the passage into old age as a relief from the pressure of attempting to resolve the problems inherent in his marital situation. It was not accidental that Elsie took on the characteristics of an old woman long before she became one, or that Stevens became happier and more peaceful as he approached sixty, or that both of them established habits while still in their primes that were like those other couples begin to cultivate in retirement. For Stevens and Elsie learning the names of exotic species of roses and irises they planted, having conversations about what kinds of preserved fruits it would be best to stock for their pleasure and health took the place of direct contact. This made sense. Here was a man who had never felt himself the "virile poet." Simply imagining such a figure made Stevens's hand tremble when he penciled these words on the title page of his lecture about this idealized being.[21] When he actually felt that with age he was becoming a "thinking stone" (*CP* 13), it was something to celebrate rather than something to mourn. Though there continued to be occasional outbursts when he carried on as he had as a young man in Cambridge when "more than half lit," they were fewer and farther between. Whenever they did occur, he was as full of remorse as he had been in his youth. In place of chastising himself in his journal as he did then, he now apologized to his host or hostess the next day for doing or saying things they had thought charming.

Just as the regular, easy rhythm of "The Man with the Blue Guitar" neutralized its tragic and brutal perceptions—"Things as they are have been destroyed./. . . Am I a man that is dead"; The earth is not earth but a stone,/ Not the mother that held men as they fell// But stone . . .// An oppressor that grudges them their death" (*CP* 173); "That generation's dream, aviled/ In the mud . . ." (*CP* 183)—the regular, easy rhythms of Stevens's life moved him peacefully toward the time when he would no longer have to do battle with himself, no longer have to "reduce the monster" (*CP* 175). There was conscious design behind both these disjunctive impositions of order on disorder, of forcing ease out of *dis*-ease.

By the late thirties Stevens had made his early wish to be monklike a reality. He established spheres of order in which he moved in the way monks move through their days, weeks, and months, following canonical hours, regular mealtimes, sleeping and waking hours. Within this slow procession whatever breaks came were not interruptions since they, too, were expected:

They came from the demands of work at the office or from editors requesting poems. Though his answers to these requests could not be perfectly regular, his writing of poetry was. His poems were like devotions, composed in the mornings in rhythm to his breath and step as he walked to the office. He made this association explicit in one of his "Adagia": ". . . poetry is like prayer in that it is most effective in solitude and in the times of solitude as, for example, in the earliest morning" (*OP* 163). At the office his secretary, Marguerite Flynn,[22] deciphered his lines from the scraps of paper on which he had written them down during his walk. She gave him back typed copies. In the evening, alone again in his room, Stevens looked over the machine-printed text. He corrected, expanded, and meditated on his lines before falling asleep as he looked out his window at the darkening western sky.

Like a good monk, he came to live more and more with the light. He arranged his room so that from his bed he saw only treetops and sky. His eyes closed with night and opened with morning's cool hues. He seasonally coordinated his sleeping hours to be in harmony with this, in autumn, for example, being in his bedroom by eight to watch the dying of the light. He imagined himself part of the forces of wind and weather. Moving in time with nature, he stopped trying to write poetry in winter when it was too cold or too slippery to walk to and from the office and he took the bus or was picked up by a fellow employee being driven by his wife. The morning and evening devotional hours were then given to reading, and what he read and imagined constituted his "interest in life."

Within this fine-tuned movement, during moments when his attention was not occupied in one of its regular spheres, he gave himself to cataloging items in a variety of lists. These lists constituted the most random aspect of his life. Just as when younger in his letters to Elsie he had put together lists of "Pleasant Things" rather than thread out the implications of observations he made about himself or their future, so now he compiled continuing lists rather than leave himself free to contemplate the deeper sources and consequences of things he might observe about himself, Elsie, and their child. This represented no longer an unconscious escape but a conscious choice. He had come to accept his limits and no longer pressed. He had passed the age when change could have meant a difference—at least in his mind. He turned his attention to his new lists. Some were like the earlier ones: naming exotic species of roses or exquisite blends of tea. Others were collections of matters he could not deal with rationally. These reflected some of the most important aspects of his being and his work: There were lists of titles to be used; notebooks filled with adages about his relationship with the world, the material out of which poems grew. Appropriately he titled these latter notebooks "Materia Poetica." There were also notebooks filled with passages he copied from the things he read, commonplace books. These were not nicely bound volumes, as might be expected, but rather a series of paper pamphlets like examination blue books or other such loosely bound pieces of paper in which things were penciled quickly, without concern for appearance. These documents became invaluable sources for him—not to speak of the future scholars who would search out the "pip[s] of life amid the mort" (*CP* 82) of tales that circulated about his life.

There was a characteristic difference about these lists, and it reflected the disparity between the light rhythms and "gaiety of language" (*OP* 174), and the seriousness of the matters these forms contained. Reading through his lists of titles gives the impression of Stevens's playfulness, as does, to a lesser extent, reading through the titles of *The Collected Poems.* A good number of the extremely humorous titles were never used: "Pretty Hot Weather for Dead Horses," "Preparing a Child to Eat Eclairs," "Sparkling Harness [*sic* singular] of Rich Horses," "Naked and Playing the Harp," "All the Vices of a Chambermaid," "We Are All Indians," "Why Flies Don't Fight," "Still Life with Aspirin" (WAS 71). Early in the thirties, in a letter to Latimer, Stevens had expressed how important titles were for him. He used them as a kind of shorthand to remind him of a poem he wanted to build later from the perception that had generated the title. He also used them to intrigue his imagined ideal reader into solving the puzzle the poem presented. This way his reader, if persistent, would become like Oedipus: solve the riddle of the Sphinx; take possession of the kingdom of the unconscious, the irrational element, the language of the id; ultimately find him or herself "more truly and more strange," with *in*sight, but without blindness. Enacting this ritual on a comic plane—within the game of the poem—obviated the tragic need for punishment still necessary in a god-haunted world. Heaven had been emptied of its gods in the imagined universe where Stevens lived, and so there was no need for punishment.

On the other hand, this did not mean that there were no serious matters to be considered. Stevens's lists of adages and excerpts from things he read reflected a profound concern with the problems confronted by those who attempted to transform what the common man and woman understood of reality. If we look at both sets of notebooks together, it is easy to see the process by and through which Stevens took in and changed perceptions and observations from his reading later to abstract from them notions around which he wove his poems and many of the "Adagia." These notebooks are singularly revealing of Stevens's inner life and of the external habits that were its everyday manifestations.

The first notebook, titled "Sur Plusieurs Beaux Sujets"—the following had the same title with "II" added[23]—has passages taken from his reading between 1919 and 1940, though the earlier items were not entered until this period in the mid to late thirties, when Stevens had again given himself to poetry and taken on his monklike habits. In his room after dinner, in winter's early darkness, he sat and copied from small pieces of paper that it had been his habit to keep in his pockets since his youth—like the personal index on the back dust jacket flaps or endpapers of books, one of the good scholar's habits learned while at Harvard—sentences and paragraphs that had impressed him while reading. Going through these, as he also periodically went through his early journals and letters, he sifted out those that still "mattered" (in the same sense that Marianne Moore was for him a poet who "mattered," as indicated by his title of the review of her volume discussed earlier) and entered them, often adding his comments and modifications of the views presented. It was not important that they were arranged in chronological sequence; entries from 1919, for example, appear on a page facing one on which 1935 entries appear.

In putting these down, Stevens exhibited the same Puritan thrift that he practiced in saving burned-out light bulbs to return to the electric company for their five-cent-apiece reduction on his bill or in using for the small pieces of paper that he kept in his pockets the backs of laundry bills and other odd leftovers, cut into two-by-four-inch size. Just as in his everyday life there was not a moment wasted, so there was nothing thrown away that could in some way be recycled. Only one generation removed from his farming roots, he adapted the good husbandman's attention to conservation. This was not a blanket conservatism but an expedient one that operated selectively.

He did not, for example, save the scraps of paper on which he penciled the first drafts of poems. What mattered to him was the finished, composed piece. Once his scribblings had been deciphered and transcribed onto a typed page, he had no more use for his first drafts. Into the wastebasket they went—something that at first seems inconsistent with his having preserved early letters and journals. This inconsistency appears to be a residue of his early ambivalence about "indulging in poetry," what his father had called his "afflatus." On the one hand, he spent as much as was necessary for fine papers and exquisite bindings for private copies of his own volumes, with an eye to how many hundreds of years these fine materials would preserve the beautiful objects that these specially printed and bound volumes were. On the other hand, writing on scraps of low-quality paper for the initial composition deflated the "afflatus." Since for his letter writing he also chose the highest-quality papers and was keenly attentive, until his death, to the appearance of his handwriting on the page, apologizing to his correspondents if his hand seemed shaky or awkward on a particular day or if he made an error that he crossed out, it appears that his ambivalence about his eventual literary remains was attached solely to these first drafts. One might want to argue that this trait revealed an unwillingness to leave behind evidences of the composing process. But this is contradicted by the fact that the drafts of early poems—before his habit of putting things together while walking to the office—were not destroyed, and they do evidence the steps by which he transformed first ideas into finished poems. And later in his career, when asked by librarians or editors for manuscript contributions, he went out of his way to find and send whatever first-draft versions he could.

That he did not want to hide what went into the shaping of his thought and work also makes itself clear in the "Sur Plusieurs Beaux Sujets" notebooks. Examples of some of the entries, the comments he made on them, and the care he took in citing precise references all attest to this. Quoting the following passage from Richard Storrs's *Divine Origin of Christianity,* he added a personal elaboration in which one of the centrally mysterious figures of his poetry—his "interior paramour," the "ultimate inamorata"—appeared in a context that disclosed her identity for the poet: "The philosopher could not love the indefinite and impersonal principle of order pervading the universe any more than he could love atmosphere and oceans. Storrs." Stevens's gloss: "For myself the indefinite, the impersonal, atmosphere and oceans, and all the principles of order are precisely what I love; and I don't see why, for a philosopher, they should not be the ultimate inamorata. The premise to Storrs is that the universe is explicable only in terms of humanity."

Or commenting on a Latin passage he had copied, he connected it to the "instinct for joy" he had noted in relation to Vincent Van Gogh's paintings in a letter written in November 1935 to Latimer (*L* 296). In his notebook the following directions to himself appeared: "Ex Divina Pulchritudine esse omnium Derivatur, and above all poetry. And in reflecting on this think of it in connection with the association of poetry and pleasure and also in connection with l'instinct du bonheur. If happiness is in ourselves, divine pulchritude is in our selves [*sic*] and poetry is a revelation or a contact."

A sample of the sources of entries and one quotation on two facing pages in the first notebook give a sense of how eclectic Stevens's reading and learning were and also provide an intimation of how associative bridges were formed between the various sources so that, for example, the above illumination on the Latin passage reflects in its few lines the poet's having read Mario Rossi, Freud, Charles Mauron, and some of Van Gogh's letters. The sources of excerpts on these two facing pages are as follows and appear in the same order: *Nouvelle Revue Française* (July 1, 1919); George Chapman; Daphne du Maurier's *Gerald;* Bertrand Russell in the *New Statesman* (January 1935); E. M. Forster's *Liberty in England;* quotations from Robert Bresson and Jean Giraudoux in *Le Figaro,* November 21, 1938; and, finally, an observation of Arnold Schönberg's from the *Musical Observer* for January 1936 on the state of modern music that Stevens noted for the parallel he perceived between the composer's understanding of his work and his own: ". . . modern music is a prophecy—an art still suffering from growing pains."

Out of the many different observations he noted from these and many other sources (*Le Temps,* the *London Mercury, Hebdomadaire, Apollo,* Jean Racine's preface to *Bérénice,* the correspondence of Jules Renard were some that in the same way reflected the breadth of Stevens's range of "interest in life") suddenly burst out a perception that eventually found its way to the "Materia Poetica" notebook that later became the "Adagia." Just above a sentence Stevens copied, phrased by an art critic writing in *Apollo* (October 1936)[24] about the Eumorfopoulos Collection of Oriental Art—"It would be truer to say that Chinese painting is a branch of poetry and that calligraphy is the medium of both"—the poet added the following comment in which he played with the pictorial definition of "plane" to illustrate his own feeling about the identity between poetry and painting: "Poetry creates a fictitious existence on an exquisite plane. This definition must vary as the plane varies, an exquisite plane being merely illustrative." Here in raw form was one of the key perceptions developed in "The Irrational Element in Poetry," expanded further years later in "The Relations Between Poetry and Painting" as well as in the adage that closed his "Adagia" (*OP* 180). The permutation of this understanding was itself an illustration of what it described as the plane; the context in which it appeared changed and so modified its meaning.

It is important to see in this, as in the other aspects of Stevens's behavior and habits, how remarkably consistent he was in his life and in what and how he wrote. There is no observation in the poems, prose, or "Adagia" that was not also reflected in some practical application. That this was so underlines how very seriously Stevens took and used his words. His involvement with poetry was to learn "how to live, what to do." Aware of this himself, in the "Sur Plusieurs Beaux Sujets" notebooks—disclosingly titled using French, in the same way that the French lines in "Sea Surface Full of Clouds" revealed the deepest parts of his states of being—he made numerous transcriptions of passages having to do with what constituted "honesty" or "truth" in art and in life. One such was the poet's opposing a quotation from Renard to Keats's "Beauty is truth, truth beauty": "La vérité n'est pas toujours l'art; l'art n'est pas toujours la vérité, mais la vérité et l'art ont des points de contact: je les cherché [*sic*]."* Stevens added: "The aim of the artist should be not to create as beautifully as possible but to tell as much of the truth as is compatible with creating beautifully. The result of this will be a far more pressé littérature, a littérature contre la littérature in which fancy no longer plays a dominant part. It needs more imagination to see and interpret the world as it is."

A few pages farther on in the notebook Stevens copied out another passage, this one from François Mauriac's preface to a first novel by a young writer who never made it to the fore but whom Stevens had read: "La vertue essentielle de l'écrivain rende, à nos yeux, dans une certaine attitude devant le réel, faite d'honnêteté de scrupule et de candeur, dans l'acharnement à creuser le roc d'un être jusqu'à la nappe d'eau, jusqu'à la source profonde."† For Stevens the task of the artist was to memorialize the moments of privileged, heightened contact with the world. The assumption behind this was that the more exposure the individuals in a society had to beauty, the less the possibility of brutality. Stevens, of course, nursed this Paterian idea before the horrors of Hitler's Germany bellowed their contradictions.

Nonetheless, on the basis of this view of the artist's purpose, Stevens negatively criticized the work of Henry Miller, which, though he knew cursorily, he did not want to get to know better. In the beginning of his correspondence with Henry Church early in 1939, a correspondence that took the place of and expanded that which he had had until recently with Latimer,

* "Truth is not always art; art is not always truth, but truth and art have points of contact: I search for them."

† "The essential virtue of the writer lies, in our view, in a certain attitude toward the real, an attitude forged from honesty to scruples and candor, in the eagerness to excavate the rock of an individual until reaching the water-table, the deepest source."

Church had asked him for his observations on Miller, who was in Church's eyes like Stevens, another of the major avant-garde figures in American writing whom he wanted to represent in *Mesures,* the journal he had founded and coedited with Jean Paulhan. Stevens's only comment was that the objection he had to obscenity was that so little of it was "really obscen[e]: that most of it [was] just no good" (*L* 338). Fifteen years later his feelings had not changed, though he had by then, in fairness, read some of Miller's work. He observed in 1953 to Barbara Church that though he knew Miller was made much of in London circles, what he read "meant nothing at all" to him. He added that "possibly [Miller] was simply a character about whom a literary mythology [had] collected itself" (*L* 772). For Stevens, though the "determining personality" of the artist was all-important, something, as he put it, without which "no amount of other things matter much,"[25] if that personality was not involved in making the lotus bloom out of the mud of experience, the creation of a mythology around it did not make it valuable.

Similarly, even Picasso, whom Stevens in many ways admired because of his energetic commitment to shaping forms that reflected the present's quick-changing aspects, was now also criticized by him. He agreed with a perception about Picasso that though he was a "magnificent draftsman," he was an "over-intellectual designer who moves one to thought but not to feeling." Stevens had found this judgment of the painter, whose *Guernica* had recently been exhibited, to be a "just placing."[26] Because Picasso's slogan had been "Away from nature," he had no "common denominator with the public." His primary concern was "abstract, formal design" based on "cool and calculated explorations."

Stevens made this observation and that about Miller as the world was moving closer to World War II. Under the increased pressure of reality, Stevens became more demanding. Only a year or two earlier he had implicitly compared himself to Picasso and had incorporated a phrase of his into "The Man with the Blue Guitar" as an acknowledgment of the parallels he felt to exist between what Picasso attempted in *Guernica* and what he attempted in "The Man with the Blue Guitar": the murdering of all illusions while preserving imagination's function to work with reason to transform things as they were. Stevens repeated again in 1951, in "The Relations Between Poetry and Painting," that for Picasso a picture was a "horde of destructions," while for him the poem was (*NA* 161). But in the face of the terrible facts of the time Stevens came to believe that Picasso was overly concerned with form. This made him "a leader," as Stevens put it, in terms of the painters who followed him and for whom he set the standard, but the way in which his perception was expressed provided neither a common denominator of understanding nor an access to renewed contact with nature, which, for Stevens, spelled transcendence.

The dated passages in Stevens's notebooks as well as many of the letters he wrote during the late spring and summer of 1939 show that the greater the "horror" (*L* 342) he felt about the war, the more explicit he became about the guiding role of the artist: "My own way toward the future involves a confidence in the spiritual role of the poet who will somehow have to assist the painter, etc. (any artist, to tell the truth) in restoring to the imagination what it is losing at such a catastrophic pace, and in supporting what it has gained" (*L* 340). He wrote this on June 1, 1939.

Echoing this sentiment and his concern with powerful, spiritual acts, one passage copied into his notebook and dated July 1939 from the *Musical Quarterly* had to do with something Charles Gounod observed of Gustave Charpentier that also resonated with the associations Stevens began working with almost twenty years earlier, when he had composed "The Comedian as the Letter C": "At last, a true musician: He composes in C natural and no one but the Almighty could do that." Following this, he transcribed a passage from Ernest Renan's *Souvenirs d'Enfance et de Jeunesse* about the purpose of keeping journals, an activity that Stevens had translated into writing poems and into keeping the kinds of notebooks in which he transcribed this and other excerpts: "On écrit de telles choses pour transmettre aux autres la théorie de l'univers qu'on porte en soi."* In the "Adagia" Stevens incorporated this into his definition of poetry as "the statement of the relation between a man and the world" (*OP* 172). What mattered was to learn how to perceive that relation and out of it to create a personal universe in which to survive "the wild, the ruinous waste."

Paralleling his concentration on the spiritual in art, the greater reality the war assumed, the greater Stevens's attention to the particulars of nature and to everyday details. The poems, the "Adagia" he now composed, and the letters he wrote reflected a conscious attempt to fix on facts of experience that belonged to the ongoing cycles of life. This involvement was constant. From the time of the publication of *The Man with the Blue Guitar and Other Poems* in the fall of 1937 until the spring of 1942, there was hardly a month in which one or a group of poems did not appear in periodicals and journals ranging from *Poetry* and the *Partisan Review* to the newest ventures like *Fantasy, Accent,* and *Furioso* and extending to the *New York Times* and journals in England as well. These contributions he eventually collected for his next volume, *Parts of a World,* which appeared in 1942.

By this time acknowledged as one of the major poets of his generation, Stevens regularly received requests for his work, and he responded to each. In the seasons when poetry came to him, he wrote every day that he could so as to have material to send out in winter, when meeting the continuing demand would have meant forcing himself to produce had he not, like a good farmer, husbanded his harvest and stored for the cold. At the office, between business matters, he wrote long letters to his new correspondents. Besides Henry Church, there were Leonard van Geyzel in Ceylon (with whom he came into contact through Anthony Sigmans, one of the junior members of the Hart-

*"One writes such things in order to transmit to others the theory of the universe that one carries inside oneself."

ford), and Hi Simons, a publisher of medical textbooks and longtime admirer of Stevens's work, who was compiling a bibliography of all that had so far appeared by or about the poet. Interspersed with these were letters to old business-connected correspondents who had become younger friends of "Mr. Stevens": James Powers, C. L. Daughtry, Philip May. And there was also the periodic correspondence with Garrett, Jr., until he died in November 1937. After this Stevens continued exchanging letters with his widow.

Just as the "Adagia" reflected his involvement with what he read, so the poems reflected concrete details of his everyday life. Chronologically following what he wrote between 1937 and 1942 gives a clear sense of this. Through the poems' images we see his repeated movement through the seasons of poetry writing: details from letters he wrote or received; reports of the news and weather; stray lines from popular songs (as he noted years later to Renato Poggioli in connection with Section XV of "The Man with the Blue Guitar," its "Good-bye, harvest moon" line had the song of this title as its source ([*L* 783]). Examples of these overlays are numerous.

In May 1937, for example, in a letter to Latimer, he described how he had rearranged his room: "On one side of my bed there is nothing but windows; when I lie in bed I can see nothing but trees"; he also reported that this change made him more attentive to the sounds of a rabbit that in the mornings delighted in digging out the bulbs he and Elsie had carefully planted (*L* 321). A few months later "A Rabbit as King of the Ghosts" appeared in the October 1937 issue of *Poetry.* His worrying about the rabbit, which had assumed monumental proportions, was echoed by the way the rabbit in the poem took on gigantic proportions and grew "higher and higher, black as stone" (*CP* 210). Contributing to this as well was the memory of his reaction years earlier, in 1916, to hearing Easter hymns. He had expressed then in a letter to his wife his belief that Easter carols represented a "perversion of the activity of Spring in the blood" that went together with the bishops' even having adopted the poor rabbit as one of their symbols (*L* 192–93).

At around the same time he composed this poem Stevens reiterated his feelings about Christianity in the "Materia Poetica" notebook. "Loss of faith is growth," he wrote (and later included as one of his "Adagia" [*OP* 172]), and followed it, after another four or five entries, with "Christianity is an exhausted culture." This was cramped in two lines written in one space beside a seemingly unrelated entry: "The theory of poetry is the life of poetry." The antithetical connection between "life" and "exhausted" seems to have prompted this linking, which had all to do with Stevens's attempt to establish with his poetry a new canon to replace the outworn religious faith that loomed like a ghost, like the ghost of the rabbit, the bishops' symbolic pawn, which, nibbling away at his bulbs, disturbed his sleep. Significantly, a group of poems entitled "Canonica" appeared in the autumn 1938 issue of the *Southern Review;* these became the first twelve poems of the *Parts of a World.*

Illustrating how another fact of his experience was worked into poetry, "A Weak Mind in the Mountains" (*CP* 212), which appeared originally titled

"Force of Illusions" in the July 10, 1938, issue of the *New York Times*, elaborated on the powerful hold the idea of Ceylon had recently taken on the poet's imagination. Stevens's relationship with Ceylon began with a request he made of Leonard van Geyzel to purchase necklaces or carved boxes for Elsie and Holly and some tea for himself to arrive in time for Christmas 1937. Stevens's interest grew as Van Geyzel became a worthy correspondent to whom the poet in turn sent books and subscriptions to the *New Yorker* and other "odds and ends" (*L* 332). Van Geyzel not only continued to send long descriptive letters about all aspects of life in Ceylon, sharing with Stevens his strong socialist commitment as the years passed into war, but also continued to send things that delighted Stevens, Elsie, and Holly: saris in varieties of brilliant colors; broad-brimmed sun hats; jellies; volumes of Singhalese poetry and other books about Ceylon; collections of photographs that particularly fascinated Stevens;[27] and figures of Buddha in different positions. These last Stevens prized. After choosing for his own out of the first Christmas 1937 box one Buddha, "so simple and explicit that [he had] to have it in his room" (*L* 328), he wanted others: one seated and one reclining. He was willing to incur "any reasonable expense" (*L* 333) to have them. His desire for these figures was so pressing that he repeated his request to Van Geyzel in the form of reminders well into the spring of 1939: "I shall be most grateful to you if you will continue to bear the Buddha in mind. Somehow or other, with so much of Hitler and Mussolini so drastically on one's nerves, constantly, it is hard to get round to Buddha" (*L* 337). He reiterated that Van Geyzel should not hesitate about the expense and that he would reimburse him promptly.

The situation Stevens symbolically pointed to in "A Weak Mind in the Mountains," with the "wind of Iceland" (*CP* 212) gripping his mind and grappling with the metaphorical black wind of Ceylon, was one he imagined his Buddha experiencing as he sat on the windowsill in his room: "At night, when my windows are open and the air is like ice, this particular Buddha must wish that I put a postage stamp on him and sent him back to Colombo" (*L* 328). Both the Buddha and the details of life in Ceylon that he received from Van Geyzel, details that he wanted about other places in the East as well (he asked his correspondent-friend if he knew of others in Java, Hong Kong, or Siam who would write to him in the same spirit), provided Stevens with strong imaginative centers that functioned antithetically to the world in which he actually lived and to the religion with which he had been bred. The oppositions he set up echoed the structure he became conscious of imposing while writing the poems of *Ideas of Order*. Projecting himself into the figure of the Buddha sitting on his windowsill, he imagined himself in Ceylon and the East because the Orient seemed to hold the possibility of a different kind of life. As events in the West became more violent, his early interest in the East became keener and less purely aesthetic. Meditating over the years on Buddha and the attitudes he represented, Stevens slowly assumed the Buddha-like smile that characterizes one of his favorite photographs of himself. This one he eventually chose for the dust jacket of *The Collected Poems*.

❧

Stevens was in Virginia when the "unbelievable catastrophe," as he referred to World War II, broke out in September 1939. It was the end of a summer unusually full of travel and unusual, too, in that the whole family spent their time together, moving from place to place. They were at home only for a week or two in the beginning of August. (Not only was this summer holiday spent together, but during the next winter the whole family went to Key West; with the fuel scarcity because of the war, it was impossible to keep the Hartford house warm enough, and so the experience of the summer was repeated.[28]) In June—as Stevens noted to Pitts Sanborn, who had written late in the month asking that his old friend stop to see him sometime when he was in New York—they had been in the city for four days seeing the World's Fair. (Stevens loved the fair and later that fall had one of the Hartford drivers take him down just for the day.[29]) They had spent so much time there that, as Stevens put it, he could "describe it in the dark." As usual on family excursions to New York, they stayed at the Hotel New Weston at Fiftieth Street and Madison Avenue in the two-bedroom–living room suite Stevens referred to, as he did to other places where he stayed repeatedly, as "home." He did not like to sleep away from "home."[30] In the evenings they took in as much theater as possible, Holly having developed a taste for "going" that surpassed even her father's and surprised him. In the same letter in which he reported these details to Sanborn, he noted that generally, these days, he was in New York much less often than he used to be and that when he was, he usually had very little time for himself. When he was in New York on his own, he didn't stay at "home," at the New Weston. His own "home" was the Commodore, where he would have younger business associates meet him for "stiff drinks" before a night out on the town, for dinner and the theater and earlier, during Prohibition, visits to "speak-easies."[31] In closing his note to Sanborn, he expressed the wish that they could see more of each other. He added that he comforted himself by periodically rereading Sanborn's pamphlet on Beethoven: "I take it up just to hear you talk; it is naturally full of your intonations" (*L* 342).

Toward the middle of July the Stevens family left for Maine to stay for a few weeks at Christmas Cove in a hotel, the Holly Inn, managed for that season by Peter Schutt, who had been manager of the Casa Marina Hotel in Key West, where Stevens and Powell had stayed on their many later visits. During this summer aspects of the Stevenses' lives that they had kept separate from one another were exposed simultaneously. Elsie had not witnessed a side of her husband that Schutt knew well, the boisterous behavior of winter holidays spent with Powell and others, while Schutt had not seen Stevens as the sedate family man. Here was Stevens, then, approaching sixty and finally presenting a unified self that he had shaped over years of moving up and down between two elements. A great deal had contributed to bringing this about: his advancing age and the concomitant weakening of his appetites and desires; his daughter, now in mid-adolescence, to whom he wanted to offer a complete sense of himself; his having gradually learned, through the various stages of his relationship with Elsie, to accept the perceptions, feelings, and expectations of others and to integrate these into his own being.

As described earlier, in the recent past he had extended this sensitivity to imagining the life of whatever individual, group, or place caught his attention: Buddha; "The Men That [Were] Falling" in the Spanish Civil War (*L* 798); Ceylon. A poem he wrote probably sometime in the spring of 1939, "On an Old Horn"—one he "particularly like[d]" (*L* 403)—elaborated on what this kind of sensitivity entailed. Appearing in the September 30, 1939, issue of the *Nation,* it must have seemed to those who wanted the poet to be specifically involved in the social and political issues of the day to reconfirm their idea that Stevens did indeed live in an ivory tower from which he disdained a concern with "reality." Yet this poem expressed precisely what was most important to consider ethically, socially, and politically if one was to survive the steadily increasing, deadening effects of national and world events. As he expressed about three years later to Hi Simons, responding to his request to explain this poem, with which Simons had had difficulty in spite of understanding "the body of the work," as he put it, the point was to illustrate that it was only by giving voice to one's imagined vision of reality that one could go on. Stevens called this creating a "benign illusion," as opposed to an "elusion" which resulted from a desire "to escape." The poet had begun the movement toward "Notes Toward a Supreme Fiction," which he would write within the next three years and which would articulate this idea most fully.

The "idea of God" was another—for Stevens, earlier—instance of "benign illusion." Finally paraphrasing the poem for Simons, after gently chiding him for not having figured it out on his own, the poet made his point pellucidly clear:

> Sometimes when I am writing a thing, it is complete in my own mind; I write it in my own way and don't care what happens. I don't mean to say that I am deliberately obscure, but I do mean to say that, when the thing has been put down and is complete to my own way of thinking, I let it go. After all, if the thing is really there, the reader gets it. He may not get it at once, but, if he is sufficiently interested, he invariably gets it. A man who wrote with the idea of being deliberately obscure would be an impostor. . . .[32]
>
> . . . But the things of which birds sing [in the poem Stevens had imagined birds that "had once been men"] are probably subject to change, like the things of which men think, so that, whether bird or man, one has, after all, only one's own horn on which to toot, one's own synthesis on which to rely; one's own fortitude of spirit is the only "fester Burg"; without that fortitude one lives in chaos. . . . Suppose now, we try the thing out, let the imagination create chaos by conceiving it. The stars leave their places and move about aimlessly, like insects on a summer night. Now, a final toot on

> the horn. That is all that matters. The order of the spirit is the only music of the spheres: or, rather, the only music. (*L* 403)

Confirming that imagination provided the self-sufficiency and unity to withstand external change, the poem itself, like almost all the poems after *Harmonium,* echoed an image from an earlier poem. "On an Old Horn" contained, in precise phrasing but with changed terms and a displaced verb, parts of two lines from "Le Monocle de Mon Oncle": ". . . while a frog/ Boomed from his very belly . . ." (*CP* 17). In the new poem this perception was rephrased as ". . . then the bird from his ruddy belly . . ./ boomed" (*CP* 230). This kind of variation, formally adopted from music, gave a unity to the body of Stevens's work unparalleled in poetry since the Middle Ages, when a combination of strict rhyme schemes, alliteration, assonance, metrical patterning, as well as the repetition of certain key phrases, accomplished this end. But just as the gradual breakdown of these tight forms mirrored the decay of a hierarchically ordered religious world view, so Stevens's fluid adaptations, as illustrated in the way an earlier line was echoed by a later, mirrored the way imagination expanded and varied ideas of things as they were.

Stevens would not have been able to come to this understanding and to use it the way he did had he not, in his life, expanded and varied his own apprehension of and relation to the world. As he also expressed in the same letter to Simons in which he gave his *explication de texte* of "On an Old Horn"—this way of reading, part of Stevens's romance with French, he felt to be the only valid one—this kind of involvement with poetry reflected his ongoing exercise over the past several years of making "his imagination the imagination of other people." Translated into composing poetry, this meant reciprocally, then, "making them see the world through his eyes." After, that is, he was secure in feeling his identification with others, he was free to assume that the products of his imagination were valid and worthy objects of contemplation for others. This perception was the basis for his feeling that his poetry was not escapist.

From the summer of 1939 in Maine and before—the few weeks back in Hartford between the visit to the New York World's Fair and the departure for Christmas Cove—Stevens sent out and later collected two poems, "Bouquet of Belle Scavoir" and "Variations on a Summer Day." These, together with the following four as they appear in *The Collected Poems*—"Yellow Afternoon," "Martial Cadenza," "Man and Bottle," and "Of Modern Poetry" (*CP* 236–40)—reflected the operation of Stevens's imagination on reality over the summer into fall and winter of 1939–1940. This sequence is important both because it covered a particularly significant moment in history and because it illustrates again that Stevens did indeed write poems the way he had once written entries in his journal. They were records of his movement through the days and seasons of his life.

In each of these poems Stevens was careful to place either a spatial or a temporal marker that allows, when it is noted in the context of other poems and of details reported in letters, his passage through time to be perceived. This device seems to reflect at least a surface understanding of the basic law of quantum mechanics, the Heisenberg uncertainty principle: If the speed of an electron is known, its location is not, while if its location is known, its speed is not. Since Stevens read in physics, it is not unsafe to suggest that he wanted to integrate an application of this revolutionary concept into his work (just as John Donne had incorporated into his poetry an understanding of the scientific discoveries of his day). In poems in which a specific location was indicated, time was not; conversely, in poems in which time was indicated, location was either generalized or not indicated. This was in marked contrast with a poem like "Sea Surface Full of Clouds," for example, in which both time and place were indicated: "In that November off Tehuantepec." This is not surprising since the earlier poems were, in terms of how Stevens apprehended the physical world, transitional. They reflected his ties to a Newtonian universe where apples fell predictably and obediently, like everything else, and "serve[d] as well as any skull/ To be the book in which to read a round" (*CP* 14). In the poems of this later period in which *both* time and place *seemed* to be specified, the reality described was wholly imaginary, as in "Forces, the Will & the Weather," where "It was at the time, the place, of nougats" (*CP* 228), candies he conjured from the ever-changing colors of the dogwoods.

The group of six poems beginning with "Bouquet of Belle Scavoir" illustrates what was described above. In "Bouquet of Belle Scavoir" no time or season was mentioned, but it is clear that the place was Stevens's home and the bouquet, from the garden, was arranged by Elsie with one perplexing dark rose that focused her husband's attention. Perhaps prompted by an association to William Blake's "rose," sick from being gnawed at by "The invisible worm/ That flies in the night," that with "his *dark* secret love" (italics mine) destroyed life, Stevens found himself musing on the changes that light and time (evidenced by "dew" in his poem) brought to the bouquet. He presented himself with this protective consideration before confronting the pain he felt in facing what time's passage had meant to Elsie and to their relationship:

I

It is she alone that matters.
She made it. It is easy to say
The figures of speech, as why she chose
This dark, particular rose.

II

Everything in it is herself.
Yet the freshness of the leaves, the burn

Of the colors, are tinsel changes,
Out of the changes of both light and dew

III

How often he had walked
Beneath summer and the sky
To receive her shadow into his mind . . .
Miserable that it was not she.

IV

The sky is too blue, the earth too wide.
The thought of her takes her away.
The form of her in something else
Is not enough.

V

The reflection of her here, and then there,
Is another shadow, another evasion,
Another denial. If she is everywhere,
She is nowhere, to him.

VI

But this she has made. If it is
Another image, it is one she has made.
It is she that he wants, to look at directly,
Someone before him to see and to know.
(*CP* 231–32)

Out of the play with "figures of speech"—here centered on making the pronoun "it" as ambiguous as possible—the poem transcended the limits of the personal and moved into exploring the difference between substance and shadow, reality and image, out of which the artistic impulse grew. The "she" then stretched from the immediate Elsie to the abstract Muse and included, in that extension, the full range of intermediate possibilities, associations, so that at the formal level the poem opened the linguistic and philosophical questions concerning the difference between subject, "she," and object, "it." Without consideration of the personal level of meaning in reading the poem, however, something that an adequate *explication de texte* never omits, the emotional basis of the problem and its manifestations would be neglected, thus reinforcing the Cartesian mind-body split that Stevens wanted so much to repair.

This poem, in which place is given but time must be interpolated from its suggestion in the sequential context, presented a problem that the poet had been facing for at least twenty years. It had first been dealt with in "Le Monocle de Mon Oncle" and "Peter Quince at the Clavier." In contrast, the next poem of this new series, "Variations on a Summer Day" (*CP* 232–36) had time specified: It was a summer day, and the variations reflected the passage of longer and shorter moments in the poet's consciousness. Here the place was generalized. That it was Maine is known from particular references to Monhegan and Pemaquid, but it is impossible to locate a fixed position from which the poet observed reality. One moment he could see Monhegan; another, the "last island"; another, Pemaquid; another, "everywhere" around where there were "spruce trees." Close attention to what seem at first to be imagistically connected improvisations, however, reveals that there was a precise movement mapped: Stevens's approach to Christmas Cove in a ferry.[33]

In Section I the real facts around which his imagination built were the gulls following the ferry still at sea; in II, the distant rocks, appearing small, like letters fringed by waves; in III, closer, the rocks' attachment to the cliffs now seen in enough detail to resemble the heads of dogs; in IV, the evening star rising over Monhegan; in V, the trees onshore, at this point close enough to be seen, that prompted the waves as leaves metaphor; in VI, the shore, even closer so that the stones at its base could be particularized; in VII, the sparrow on land closing in, now detectable, and a gull on chimney tops; in VIII, a last look back at the sea—a *reflex*-ion—that produced the reflection that he was engaged in an "exercise in viewing the world"; in IX, clouds gathering over land—the "world"—in the weakening daylight; in X, the "natures" of things and people seen around; in XI, the "timothy at Pemaquid" very close by, "silver-tipped" as the moon rose; in XII, the place where Hugh March was killed, one of the facts gathered from the history he had read concerning the place he was visiting; in XIII, another view of the open sea, Pemaquid passed, now rose-colored in the sunset; in XIV, the "mica" and "dithering of grass" of another island passing; in XV, the "last island" passed before the ferry's return to Christmas Cove and the Stevens family disembarked; in XVI, the bell buoy marking the harbor entrance, through portals of pines on the shore in XVII; in XVIII, low tide perceivable in the harbor, its flat water unruffled by waves in its protected haven; in XIX, a boy swimming under an old "tub" and another sitting on top, greeting the "man-boat" that carried the "man-poet"; in XX, the brass on a sailing ship, very close by now as the ferry approached its berth, the poet having to look up to see the top of her mast taper to nothing (like the tops of distant steeples that had once helped him find his way through the streets of New York). In this record of movement through time, from midafternoon, when the air was "light blue," until early evening, each moment was particularized by its perception. The subject was the process of perception itself. There was no time for considering a problem. Here what was known was the shape and speed of the movement, not the position or stance of the poet in relationship to a situation.

The difference between these two poems represented another level of development of the connecting structures Stevens had begun consciously working with in *Ideas of Order:* that one poem have an antithetical relation to another so that the volume would be built out of a system of contrasts. Looking at the subject matter and the background information together provides another "practical" fact accounting for the difference between these two later poems. "Bouquet of Belle Scavoir" was written at home. Even if it was not transcribed until the next morning on his way to the office, it is clear that both the "occasion" and its accompanying "cry"—"The poem is the cry of its occasion" (*CP* 473)—belonged to a moment of domestic stillness. "Variations on a Summer Day," on the other hand, was conceived while the poet was in motion, like "Sea Surface Full of Clouds," to which it can easily be compared, recording a similar passage through changes of time and light. In the same way, through attention to details of time and place and equal attention to the overall chronological sequence, it is possible to derive, as one would for the path of an electron, a generalized yet accurate sense of the poet's trajectory.

Picking up on this sequence was the next poem, "Yellow Afternoon" (*CP* 236–37). Stevens again provided a sense of time. It was a period of repose "alike in springtime/ And, arbored and bronzed, in autumn." Since the title specified that it was a "yellow afternoon," that the light was bronze-colored; since he also used as the anchor of the central stanza the metaphor "As the life of the fatal unity of war"; and since the poem followed the "Variations" pieces written in Maine during the summer of 1939, it is possible to locate the time of this poem's composition in the autumn of 1939 after the outbreak of World War II. This is confirmed by the next poem, "Martial Cadenza" (*CP* 237–38), announcing its reference to the war and the poet's passage, with the season, into the "beginning of winter . . . full// Of the silence before the armies. . . ." Here the evening star became a symbol for the poet's work as he had described it to Latimer. In the face of the chaos—of "blank skies over England, over France/ And above the German camps"—the only sustaining force that could bring renewal, return, like the return of the opening lines at the poem's end, was careful attention to the "present close" out of which the poem, the "present realized," was made.

The last two poems of the sequence—"Man and Bottle" (*CP* 238–39) and "Of Modern Poetry" (*CP* 239–40)—were products of deep winter. In the first Stevens made the references clear, while the second was a reflection on and continuation of the first. The poet's imagination in this dead season was hard put to find an external subject around which to weave its "Arachne integument" (*CP* 234), its web of words. In winter, as he described in "Man and Bottle," his mind—"the terriblest force in the world" (*CP* 436)—was separated from its life-giving connection with nature and the august activity of the imagination, its Persephone. His mind of winter attempted to destroy the "benign illusions" (here the "tenements of rose and ice") so meticulously constructed in earlier seasons. This force, "More than the man," was, for Stevens, negative because one of the things that it attempted was "to persuade that war [was] part of itself."

In this poem the reference to earlier poems of *Harmonium* was indicated by "an old affair with the sun." Around twenty years before, in "The Misery of Don Joost," the poet had recorded that he had finished "his battle with the sun," while in "Sunday Morning" he had observed that the earth and human life were the issue of "an affair of sun and moon." He had in those poems established the affair as the basic situation, the ineluctable process of life. Here he showed how the mind threatened to destroy this primary situation by annihilating the terms by which human beings understood the world. Against this attempted destruction, the poet had to "lash out," so that now, even in deep winter, when it was most difficult for him to write, he did. He would apply the poetic process to mind itself, use the same power of imagination to put himself in it and understand it, as he had done for years with nature, with his "studious ghosts" and, most recently, with others.

It is very important to realize exactly under what conditions this occurred. In "Of Modern Poetry," Stevens made this explicit:

> The poem of the mind in the act of finding
> What will suffice. It has not always had
> To find: the scene was set; it repeated what
> Was in the script.
> Then the theatre was changed
> To something else. Its past was a souvenir.
> It has to be living, to learn the speech of the place.
> It has to face the men of the time and to meet
> The women of the time. It has to think about war
> And it has to find what will suffice. It has
> To construct a new stage. It has to be on that stage
> And, like an insatiable actor, slowly and
> With meditation, speak words that in the ear,
> In the delicatest ear of the mind, repeat,
> Exactly, that which it wants to hear, at the sound
> Of which, an invisible audience listens,
> Not to the play, but to itself, expressed
> In an emotion as of two people, as of two
> Emotions becoming one. The actor is
> A metaphysician in the dark, twanging
> An instrument, twanging a wiry string that gives
> Sounds passing through sudden rightnesses, wholly
> Containing the mind, below which it cannot descend,
> Beyond which it has no will to rise.
> It must
> Be the finding of a satisfaction, and may
> Be of a man skating, a woman dancing, a woman
> Combing. The poem of the act of the mind.
> (*CP* 239–40)

Stevens also pointed out here that this focus on the process of mind was transitional, useful to consider for as long as it took to realize that the mind could *act* to find "a satisfaction," something even as seemingly trivial as "a man skating, a woman dancing, a woman/ Combing." Giving full attention to something like this in the "present close" was a step in "constructing a new stage." Stevens's subject was the "real" rather than "reality"; the "real" was made of facts.[34] These facts, rather than the idea of some ever-receding future, would sate the hunger for completion in reality, in the imperfect that is our paradise. "The purpose of poetry is to make life complete in itself" (*OP* 162), to give "a momentary existence on an exquisite plane" (*NA* 32).

In light of the way his purpose was misunderstood by the many who, in spite of appreciating his rare talent, criticized him for his "escapism" and lack of social conscience, Stevens's commitment to providing—even in the face of the war's brutality—a sense of the beauty of being reflected the nobility and courage associated with fighting for a cause. At no point in his career did he reshape his work in an attempt to accommodate his strong-voiced critics. Nor did he dismiss them. Rather, he respected the provenance of their desire for social change and expressed in letters and personal interchange his wholehearted agreement with them in principle. It was their method and rhetorical strategy he found wanting.

Stevens was, after all, a master of rhetoric. From his early days at school through his years as an attorney, it was for his persuasive skills that he won prizes and material success. His gift for painting pictures in words, combined with keen intelligence and sensitivity to others' points of view that made him the Hartford's most valued "word merchant," provided the foundation of his poetry. With these gifts, he set himself to proselytize, as subtly and effectively as the Augustine he once wished to be, his new faith. This was not, like Augustine's, a blind faith in some unseeable, unknowable future life. On the contrary, Stevens's faith was in the fact of feeling pleasure in the here and now; this was connected at the most primary level with nature and the satisfaction of the senses in nature—whatever form this satisfaction took. His love of nature, tempered and channeled by the ascetic bent bred into him by his religious training, allowed him to understand by mid-life that it was only from concentrated attention to the ever-repeating unending facts of the natural world, including the movements of individuals in that world, that a sense of peace could come. Focusing on what was accidental and disruptive to the natural cycle—what, if not for history books would be forgotten, products of mind or reason alone—could not stimulate the "instinct of joy" on which life depended. Fastening on these "accidents" could only confuse things as they were even more, remove attention one step farther from what really mattered. Stevens used all his rhetorical skills, beginning with Horace's simple dictum of sweetening lessons with sugar, to construct in his work an argument as meticulously contrived as those he devised to settle claims against the Hartford. This argument would stand its ground against any conceived by the church fathers.

Stevens weathered the late seasons of 1939 that brought the world into conflict once again with the equanimity won from practicing his faith. It was the faith of the "anti-master man, floribund ascetic," who "brushed away the thunder, then the clouds,/ Then the colossal illusion of heaven" (*CP* 241). To preach his new creed he conceived new words—"floribund," for example—made out of his affections (for "Florida," "florid" elements, flowers) and the nature of his time, "moribund." "Poetry is the statement of a relation between a man and the world." Traveling through the South (the Stevens family ended up in Miami before flying back, by way of Washington, to Connecticut) as the war erupted, he focused on the human influences that had made the region what it was:

> When the war broke out I was in Virginia and in a part of it where the influence of the English on both houses and landscape still persists. The influence on the houses, which are as a rule modest affairs, is shown in this fact, that so few of them are really matter-of-fact houses. The people who live in them have some sense of style about living. The influence on the landscape is shown in a resemblance to an 18th Century park. Where I was there was very little of the ordinary fields of other parts of the country, which at this time of year, when all the crops have been gathered except corn, have a definiteness which makes the whole country look like a huge prosperous farm. (*L* 342)

It was especially important now for Stevens to concentrate on whatever was nurturing, whatever had allowed life to be experienced in its full complexity, whether the eighteenth-century "style about living" or his present way—learned from Oriental masters, also "floribund ascetic[s]"—of immersing himself in the pristine beauty of moments as they passed.

It was not only in Virginia that Stevens looked for the roots of what had been planted to sustain the human spirit. On the same trip the Stevens family also went to Reading—Stevens made a point of staying in hotels rather than with relatives, however. The purpose of the trip was to uncover for himself—from the perspective of almost sixty years—and for Holly, now fifteen, the sources of health and strength from which he had drawn when young. He expressed this lightly in a card thanking Wilson Taylor, another of his younger insurance company-connected "friends," for getting the train tickets to Reading for them: "Muchas gracias. We are going back to the natal soil to correct our spirits" (WAS 207).

While Stevens nosed out these roots, Elsie was taken by things of quite a different order. On one postcard she sent to her mother, about a place where they had stopped to eat somewhere on the way from Reading to Virginia (they went by taxi), her enthusiasm centered on the fact that the fighter Gene Tunney had eaten there. On the very next day she seemed to transfer the effect of notoriety to herself. As she expressed in another postcard to Mrs. Moll, a local guide they had just met, named Kachel (the name of Elsie's father), had told her that the name had originated in the Rhine Valley and was German. Shortly after, Elsie began searching out her own background. She first asked her mother. Mrs. Moll related that church records showed Elsie to have been christened on the day of her father's funeral, June 3, 1887, just two days before she was a year old (WAS 4033). At around the same time Elsie also applied for membership as a Daughter of the American Revolution,[35] following in her late middle age an impulse that Stevens as a young man had seen as pretentious on his mother's part. After this Elsie pursued her interest in her own past more actively, trying finally to establish an identity through words on paper. Stevens followed her in her new pursuit. This might, at first, have been only because he was eager to help her develop an interest that truly pleased her. But after the death of his younger brother, John, in July 1940, and then Holly's leaving home for college in the fall of 1941, Stevens's desire to feel his own "bond to all that dust" became quite strong. In addition, as he put it later, becoming involved in genealogy was the best way he knew to learn about American history, something that had begun to be important to him during the summer of 1939.

In October 1939, just two weeks after the war had begun, Stevens celebrated his sixtieth birthday. Hi Simons, expressing his homage to the man to whom he was devoting his "life's work," as he once remarked (January 1, 1940), sent him an appropriately phrased telegram: "Today's quite some birthday, isn't it?" Stevens acknowledged the salutation with humor, noting that "a poet should be 30 not 60. It is incredible to me that I am 60. However, my stenographer was 60 long ago, and doesn't seem to care" (*L* 343). Behind Stevens's playful comment that the "poet should be 30" was a feeling of how demanding the kind of task he had set for himself was. His imaginings of the "virile poet" and his conceiving of the figure suitable to assume the chair of poetry at Harvard as "potent" (like the future critic of the irrational he described in "The Irrational Element in Poetry") expressed the same feeling. What required such vigor was the purpose, the "cause" he wanted poetry to further. In another letter to Simons early in 1940, Stevens laid out the project as "thinking of some substitute for religion." He added, "I don't necessarily mean some substitute for the church, because no one believes in the church as an institution more than I do. My trouble, and the trouble of a great many people, is the loss of belief in the sort of God in Whom we were all brought up to believe" (*L* 348). This sort of "God" he particularized farther on in the same letter: "An anthropomorphic god is simply a projection of itself by a race of egotists, which it is natural for them to treat as sacred." In closing the letter, he commented: "What keeps one alive is the fury of the desire to get somewhere with all this, in the midst of all the other things one has to do."

In order to believe that he could "get somewhere with all this," Stevens had to have had tremendous confidence in the validity of what he was preaching. This certainty grew out of his having applied to himself the principles he espoused and in having found that in spite of whatever might go on in the world around him, he was indeed happier than he had ever been. He might have been deceived in thinking that this state was a result of what he practiced. It could have been simply a consequence of his having arrived at the age when he was no longer driven by passions for anything more than pastries, new wines, or paintings that satisfied his need to puzzle out mysterious forms. In any case, by the end of the thirties he had developed a zeal in connection with what he thought poetry could and should do and with what the spiritual role of the poet should be that fired with majesterial authority whatever he wrote about these subjects. His tone belonged to one who, like Moses or St. John, had received the word. But as though unconsciously aware that this attitude was inimical to what he expressed about not believing in heroes, he also continued to deflate himself humorously and to be uneasy about public appearances where he would actually have *to voice* what he believed. The same contradiction was apparent in his physical being: As Arthur Ficke had described years before, he was a giant, but with a voice that seemed to be on tiptoe at dawn. It was still true that he only felt like the "warrior" when he was able to "declare" and "command [him]self on paper," as he had noted almost forty years earlier to Elsie.

In spite of Stevens's conscious commitment to his "new" faith, founded on, as he put it in the letter to Simons quoted above, "feasting" rather than "fasting," there were still murmurings of his Christian spirit that seem to have colored—if only slightly at this point—his attitude toward himself and his success in the world. His having mentioned to Taylor that he was going back to Reading to "correct" his spirit was an illustration of this. And in a 1939 Christmas note to James Powers—which he began with a wonderfully playful locution evocative of the Germanic roots he had again tapped in his hometown, "Wotthehellsthematter, hein? I like to hear from you now and then"—he observed that he continued "to save a few dollars a year and to put on a few pounds weight, and to grow a little older and more poisonous." He closed the short letter commenting that none of them (he, Elsie, or Holly) had been ill since Powers had last seen them. Between the lines there appears to have been a sense of guilt at his material "fatness" and a hidden expectation that the proper punishment would be illness of some sort. Had he remained the "good Puritan" he had been reared to be, his success would have been a sign of his election. But he had turned away to preach the "opposing law."

He lived as "a man of fortune greeting heirs" (*CP* 13). He continued to indulge his taste for the finer things in life and did not hesitate to enlist the aid of old friends and new to help him get what he wanted. On his way back to Hartford from his trip to Reading and the South, for example, he stopped in New York to see his old friend Walter Pach and his wife, Magda. He wanted Pach to advise him about respectable art dealers in Paris. Stevens had already begun his collection with a Camille Pissarro engraving and one or two other pieces he had acquired through Anatole Vidal, his Paris bookseller. But he wanted better contacts. Pursuing his aims, he came finally to correspond with someone connected with the Louvre. The war might rage, but there was still Beauty. From Magda Pach, he also got a recipe for the gluhwein he had so enjoyed at their apartment.

Similarly, Stevens noted to Henry Church in November 1939 (after the outbreak of the war Church had decided to remain in America, indefinitely extending what was initially to have been only a visit) that one of the reasons he looked forward to meeting him was to consult with him about art dealers (*L* 343). Church obliged, calling on his wife, Barbara, to help. Church was as impressed with Stevens as Stevens was with him. The poet expressed his attraction to Church most directly: "I love to hear from you. You have so thoroughly lived the life I should have been glad to live, and you are so much more intricate a personality than any half dozen people that I can think of put together . . ." (*L* 401). Because of their mutual admiration, both were eager to help the other satisfy what each expressed as his desires. Stevens took every opportunity of availing himself of the possibilities Church offered and was especially keen because he felt that his new friend would help him lay the actual foundation for his faith. Church wanted to establish a trust that would foster the "pure good" of poetry, and Stevens seized the chance. Together they would set up the chair of poetry at Harvard. Stevens broached this idea to Church within six months of their meeting. Within another few months he had drawn up the plans, which, like a master builder, he devised as carefully as the argument for his new faith.

In the plans Stevens spelled out even more specifically than he had for Simons the nature of his project:

> The major poetic idea in the world is and always has been the idea of God. One of the visible movements of the modern imagination is the movement away from the idea of God. The poetry that created the idea of God will either adapt it to our different intelligence, or create a substitute for it, or make it unnecessary. These alternatives probably mean the same thing, but the intention is not to foster a cult. The knowledge of poetry is a part of philosophy, and a part of science; the import of poetry is the import of the spirit. The figures of the essential poets should be spiritual figures. The comedy of life or the tragedy of life as the material of an art and the mold of life as the object of its creation are contemplated.
>
> The delicacy and significance of all this disclose that there is nothing of the sort in existence, and that to establish it would require the collaboration of a small group to prepare the course. Or if a potent enough man could be found, the course could be developed over a period of years starting under such a man, who, as he found his way, would be finding what was needed. The holder of the Chair would necessarily have to be a man of dynamic mind and, in his field, something of a scholar and very much of an original force. A man like Dr. Santayana illustrates the character, although in him the religious and the philosophic are too dominant. He is merely cited as an illustration. It is possible that a man like T. S. Eliot illustrates the character, except that I regard him as a negative rather than a positive force. I don't think that it would be difficult to find the really serious man that is required. (*L* 378)

Church was a man committed to furthering causes that had to do with the changes in ethical outlook necessary for the century that had not yet recovered from the impact of Darwin's and Freud's discoveries and Nietzsche's haunting prophecies. He supported the French resistance, did what he could to help the Jews, and saw in Stevens's ideas a way to neutralize at least the religious sources of demagoguery and fascism. If they were successful in establishing a chair that would, indeed, propagate the notion of poetry's replacing God in America's oldest university a major battle in the revolution in thought in twentieth-century America would have been won.

Except for the period of the family trip to Key West for several weeks beginning in February 1940, Stevens gave whatever time was not taken by the office or writing poetry to threading out the implications of what he proposed. He did this in regular letters to and meetings with Church and in the letters he continued to write almost weekly—at times daily—to Hi Simons. There was nothing about what he felt poetry could and should do that he did not make explicit in these letters. The occasional letters from Van Geyzel in Ceylon or from editors offered only slight relief from the intense concentration he gave to elucidating his ideas. But even in his responses to Van Geyzel, to whom he generally expressed perceptions about literature in a fairly broad way, he found himself slipping into unfolding certain details about poetics and humanism or describing one of the aspects of the ideal poet. This was the case, when in speaking about Delmore Schwartz, whose translation of Rimbaud's *Season in Hell* he was sending to Van Geyzel, as someone who had in this work captured "things that matter," he added that perhaps Schwartz was too philosophic, too "keen" and that "after all, a poet has got to preserve feeling and, say what you will, thinking has a way of clearing up things from which feeling commonly arises: there is an antipathy between thinking and feeling. In the last analysis, a thinker no longer feels, just as, in the last analysis, a man of feeling no longer thinks" (*L* 356). Farther on in the same letter, dated May 1940, another of his preoccupations—the idea of virility, potency, vigor in relation to the poet or man of letters—showed itself in connection with George Keyt, translator of one of the volumes of Singhalese poetry that Van Geyzel had sent Stevens: "Is he personally a man of vigor?" Stevens asked, and then added an observation that had all to do with his ideal of the poet: "After all, it takes an unbelievable vigor to attach oneself to the things that smack one in the eye."

Stevens's word choice in linking "vigor" to dealing with "things that smack one in the eye" may have been associated with an incident of which he had recently been reminded. This February 1940 trip was the last that Stevens ever made to Key West. One of the reasons he did not want to return was, as he reported to Hi Simons about two months after he had come back, that he had "found the place too furiously literary" (*L* 355). Among the literary types Stevens knew who gathered around the palm trees for cocktails that winter were Robert Frost, Lawrance Thompson (editor of Frost's *Selected Letters*), and Ernest Hemingway. Though during this season Stevens's contact with Hemingway was limited to looking in, with Holly, from a distance at one of the parties "Papa" gave,[36] it was not too long before that Stevens and Hemingway had had the meeting that had resulted in the poet-executive's getting the novelist-hunter's fist "smack in the eye."

The problem of "Poetry and Manhood" that had begun to occupy Stevens's attention more than forty years before while he was at Harvard had not been solved. His dwelling on "potency," "virility," "vigor," no less than his desire to create a substitute for God—worthy an aim as it might have been—reflected that the deep insecurity about his maleness was still there. If he expressed ambivalence about or hostility toward Hemingway, it was not surprising. Hemingway, on the surface at least, lived consistently the way Stevens could afford only in snatches. It was as though Hemingway actually repeated over and over the experience that Stevens only dreamed of repeating, the camping trip to British Columbia when he was still a young man, the trip he remembered over and over as he lay dying. In the life he had shaped, the only experiences that came near this had been the winter holidays in Key West—before he began staying at Casa Marina—when he, Powell, and the rest of the "boys" roughed it at the Long Key Fishing Club. The facilities were primitive, with washbasin and bowl outside the door. The days were full of fishing and the nights of fishing tales. In contrast, when Hemingway wasn't out fishing or big-game hunting, he was writing "hard" chiseled prose or "living hard," carrying on in hotels, nightclubs, bars, and cafés around the world without even worrying about the "tab." Stevens could manage only rare weekends in New York or elsewhere—with junior associates he asked to join him and for whom he picked up the "tab."

Stevens didn't see that Hemingway's external displays of manhood, his concern with what was "hard" and "true" were indications of precisely the same insecurity he himself experienced. For both of them the problem involved what it meant to be a writer, to use words in a time when all words were inadequate. None of the developments of the twentieth century could be comprehensively described in anything resembling familiar language. While for nearly 5,000 years it had been the idea of God which could not be captured through words or images, slowly it had come about that nothing essential about reality could be satisfactorily adumbrated.

Stevens also admired Hemingway, in spite of whether he had in fact spoken badly of him at that cocktail party. Quite possibly, because of his having drunk quite a bit, he did. While José Rodríguez Feo, one of Stevens's correspondents during the forties and fifties, remembered the poet's saying he did not like Hemingway,[37] in a letter to Rodríguez Feo, as well as in letters to others, Stevens gave a very different impression. In his mind, Stevens probably separated Hemingway the man from Hemingway the figure of the virile youth as poet. As such Hemingway in some sense would have represented the kind of potent figure Stevens called for as necessary. This sense is supported by what he wrote to Henry Church about Hemingway. Church had asked Stevens to recommend someone to speak on "poetry and actuality" as one of a series of lectures to be given during 1942 at Princeton (near which Church came to live for a while and to which he became quite attached through people like Christian Gauss[38] and Allen Tate). Stevens pointed strongly to Hemingway as "the best man [he could] think of for the job." He went on: "Most people don't think of Hemingway as a poet, but obviously he is a poet and I should say, offhand, the most significant of living poets, so far as the subject of EXTRAORDINARY ACTUALITY is concerned" (*L* 411–12).

Though he seemed to qualify his absolute praise by adding "so far as the subject of EXTRAORDINARY ACTUALITY is concerned," this was not really the case. Quite the contrary. That Hemingway was such a poet made him assume even greater proportions in Stevens's mind. This is clear from what he wrote about the "POETRY OF AN EXTRAORDINARY ACTUALITY" just a bit earlier in the same letter:

> Given an actuality extraordinary enough, it has a vitality all its own which makes it independent of any conjunction with the imagination. The perception of the POETRY OF EXTRAORDINARY ACTUALITY is, for that very reason, a job for a man capable of going his own way. Your subject is not really POETRY AND ACTUALITY, but POETRY AND THE EXTRAORDINARY ACTUALITY OF OUR TIME, or, if that seems a bit too much like Maurois for you, then POETRY AND EXTRAORDINARY ACTUALITY.
>
> There is no point of trying to analyse the thing in a letter. What I am trying to lead up to is the idea that the anti-poet may be the right man to discuss EXTRAORDINARY ACTUALITY, and by discussing it in his own way reveal the poetry of the thing. Such a man would bring us round to recognizing that the mere delineation of an EXTRAORDINARY ACTUALITY is the natural poetry of the subject. It is not a subject that requires conjunction with the imagination.

In describing this figure as the "anti-poet," Stevens revealed that he saw Hemingway in the same way as he did William Carlos Williams, whom he had described as "anti-poetic" years earlier, much to Williams's consternation. What the doctor-poet did not understand was that in Stevens's vocabulary the "anti-poet," like the "anti-master man, floribund ascetic," was the apotheosis of the figure of the poet in the twentieth century. This was the figure Stevens himself wanted to be at the same time that he knew that this "anti-poetic" creator had to work in a dynamic and dialectical relationship with the "poetic." These "anti" figures were the inverse of the anthropomorphic God who was the proper deity for a race of egotists. This notion of the antipoet was a very complex one for Stevens, loaded with his own still-unsatisfied longing for completion, as well as with all he had internalized about "no-mind," the value of negativity (as negative space in painting), derived from his reading in the literature of the East. That he attached it late in his life to Williams and Hemingway, both of whom he saw as involved with "actuality" in a way he was not, said a great deal about what he felt about his success. While in some ways he thought Williams had gone the wrong way—that he was not at all in the same category as Marianne Moore, for example—in spite of all Stevens intended and what he would have liked to accomplish with his own poetry, he feared he had failed in the areas Williams and Hemingway had addressed. Williams called this reaching the masses; Hemingway simply called it being "true."

A further indication that Stevens recognized the positive value of Hemingway's kind of involvement with reality came in a letter written to Leonard van Geyzel a few years later, after he had heard from Rodríguez Feo that Hemingway had begun to write poetry:

> If poetry is limited to the vaticination of the imagination, it soon becomes worthless. The cognitive element invokes the consciousness of reality. Someone told me the other day that Ernest Hemingway was writing poetry. I think it likely that he will write a kind of poetry in which the consciousness of reality will produce the extraordinary effect. It may be that he will limit himself to the mere sensation. No one seems to be more addicted to the *épatant* (but it is not in any meretricious sense). . . . I have no doubt that supreme poetry can be produced only on the highest level of the cognitive. (*L* 500)

In Stevens's mind, following the equation of cognitive element = consciousness of reality with the product of supreme poetry, Hemingway was someone to be contended with. If at any moment Stevens was unsure that he was dealing with "the highest possible level of the cognitive," the full "consciousness of reality," he might have wanted to flatten the man who, he felt, did succeed. Uncertain whether he himself was capable of succeeding, whether he had succeeded at all, Stevens planned a chair of poetry for someone who could do what he couldn't and thought about "Notes Toward a Supreme Fiction," rather than be so presumptuous as to write about the "supreme fiction" itself.

❧

Perhaps it was because of the feelings surrounding Hemingway and himself in Key West that winter of 1940 that Stevens did not write while he was away. Judge Powell was there—with his wife as well. The Stevenses spent time with the Powells. Robert Frost succeeded in "pulling one off" on "old Wally" by taking Holly to a cocktail party without her parents' discovering it. She had been upset at being treated like a child and had resented having to come to Florida at all during a time when things were socially exciting for her at home. She resented even more being excluded from adult activities like cocktail parties. Frost playfully tried to lighten the situation.

It hadn't been the best of vacations. There had been bad omens from the outset. Just before they had left, Stevens had had to correct Hi Simons—who, he had thought, understood him—from misperceiving him as belonging to the "right" (*L* 351). Elsie, who had wanted very much to fly down to Florida, a journey then requiring many stops and changes, was airsick most of the way.

Holly was disgruntled. Once arrived, Elsie seems to have become rather obsessive about the different kinds of palms; she sent a series of postcards to her mother describing varieties and correcting and qualifying earlier reports. Though old friends like Powell and Edwin ("Ed") de Turck Bechtel with their wives were there for company, Key West had become otherwise too "furiously literary." By the time Stevens returned to Hartford he had developed a bothersome case of hemorrhoids—not exactly the kind of ailment that could help him maintain his self-image against that he conjured as Hemingway's. The time away from the everyday world had been filled with disturbances that bubbled beneath his surface.

Once home, he addressed them with renewed vigor, however. As he wrote to Henry Church on April 17, he produced a number of poems: "Since coming back, I must have written a good many things. The truth is that I am at one of those stages at which it is hard to get away from one's thoughts. The difficulty with such a stage is that there is so much push that one is not willing to stop to make things perfect; the desire is to get them down as they come" (WAS 3473). "Arrival at the Waldorf," "Landscape with Boat," "Extracts from Addresses to the Academy of Fine Ideas," "Of Bright & Blue Birds & the Gala Sun," "Mrs. Alfred Uruguay," and "Asides on the Oboe" (*CP* 240–52) are the candidates for these "imperfect" things that he got down as they came. Certainly, "Extracts" and "Asides" were written before the summer of 1940 (on the basis of references made in letters before that time), and both reflected his deep concern with the place of poetry in life that had been with him strongly since the early thirties. Over the decade Stevens had been refining his ideas on this, for him, all-important theme. The poems he wrote now and his fiery interest in persuading Henry Church to establish the poetry chair at Harvard mirrored his own experience of moving through the disillusionments of the thirties as much as his reading—all through the period—of what others believed salutary in such troubled times. He read his contemporaries in the various journals and special editions to which he subscribed. He gleaned ideas from Virginia Woolf and Stephen Spender on the effects of the current political situation on poetry and art in general.[39] He extolled Edmund Wilson for his incisive analysis of both political and literary issues (*L* 357). He praised Philip Rahv for his lucid explication of why the poet had to be seen, in a Hegelian sense, as "the exponent of his time" (*L* 384). He found G. A. Borgese and Edouard Roditi, as heirs of Croce, to be notably involved, as he himself had been for a while, in the psychology of the poet (*L* 384–85). He also ordered and read books by contemporary figures whose thoughts, with which he had first become familiar in journals or through others' references, had stimulated or paralleled his own: Julian Huxley's *Religion Without Revelation,* Frank Kenyon's *The Myth of the Mind,* Bertrand Russell's *Let the People Think: A Selection of Essays,* Julian Symons's *Confusions About X,* and Leonard Woolf's *A Village in the Jungle.*[40]

Moreover, he went back to many of the sources pointed to by some of these writers. From 1933 to 1942 Stevens read and carefully marked new editions of Aristotle's *Art of Poetry* and a special edition entitled *On Friendship* (excerpted from the *Nicomachean Ethics*), Croce's *Defense of Poetry,* as well as critical works on Descartes's *Discourse on Method,* Giambattista Vico's *New Science,* and Milton.[41] Marking passages central to him in the margins of his copies and transcribing words and phrases on his back-flap indexes or on separate laid-in sheets, Stevens braided his perceptions with these and with other historical and interpretive appraisals that he found. These latter included F. W. Bateson's *English Poetry and the English Language: An Experiment in Literary History,* G. G. Coulton's *Europe's Apprenticeship: A Survey of Medieval Latin,* F. C. Green's *Stendhal,* F. L. Lucas's *Criticism of Poetry,* and I. A. Richards's *Coleridge on Imagination.*[42]

Then, too, there were volumes of history, of proverbs and poetry,[43] many sent by acquaintances or admirers, as well as other odd things done by friends, like Walter Pach's translation of Delacroix's *Journal.* Certain affinities he found in these prompted further branchings, so that Stevens read Van Gogh's *Letters to Emile Bernard,* and Rilke's *Letters to a Young Poet* as well as a critical work on this poet who had worked for Rodin. There were numerous other important sources Stevens read during these years that cannot be named because he referred to them only generally and in passing and they have not remained in what is left of his library. In this category, for example, is the book on Hegel that he read in—as was his habit with philosophy, before breakfast—and referred to in a letter of June 1941 (*L* 390–91). He quoted from this book a passage that wonderfully reinforced his own sense of the complementary function of poetry in life: "If all the world was to be conceived as poetic . . . our poetry must find room for much which, to the uneducated eye of the imagination is unpoetic . . . Unreason itself must find a place. . . ."

In all this reading the most common and prominent feature was a stress on the salutary function of poetry. This combined with praise for the poet as the stalwart protector of nobility, love, and virtue in society. From Vico's historical tracing of the kinds of poetry that reflected the soul of a people to F. L. Lucas's pointing out that for the Greeks it was the poet who showed "How to plough, how to fight, how to live, how to die"—the passage from which this is taken will be noted later—each of these figures in some way reaffirmed Stevens's faith in the high seriousness of what he saw as his mission: to become "a priest of the invisible" (*OP* 169) and preserve a sense of the sacred, the mysterious, in the face of the monumental destruction of his time. From individual authors he borrowed particular perceptions. From all he derived a sense of what "must" be for poetry. Within a year he had formulated the rules for his canon: "It Must Be Abstract," "It Must Change," "It Must Give Pleasure."

If the evidence of a continuing dialogue with one of his "studious ghosts" is any indication of the importance of a figure for Stevens, among the most stimulating thinkers the poet imaginatively engaged was Vico. In "Extracts from Addresses to the Academy of Fine Ideas," "Of Bright & Blue Birds & the Gala Sun," and "Mrs. Alfred Uruguay" the poet graciously tipped his hand

and tipped off his readers to listen in on the conversation he held with the Italian master. In "Of Bright & Blue Birds" the clue is the word *"scienza"* (*CP* 248); in "Mrs. Alfred Uruguay," it is the image of the "horse all will," a figure of "capable imagination" (*CP* 249), that in Vico was identified with Pegasus, as the symbol of the father or hero who had the right of divination; in "Extracts" the clue is his address to "Ercole" in Section VI (*CP* 256), "Hercules" in Italian, a figure used by Vico to illustrate a major point about how the notion of a hero functioned for the poets and people of a primitive age. In elucidating these as metaphors, Vico brilliantly showed how they operated as complete sentences in the minds of early men. What allowed these symbols to contain and explain reality was the implicit recognition of the power of imagination. Stevens, in each of these poems, continued the exploration into this primary human force. At the same time he delighted in discovering that for Vico, too, Francis Bacon had been an antecedent, as indicated by H. P. Adams, the author of the volume about Vico which Stevens read.[44] From Adams's explication Stevens gained authority for his own stress on the inextricable tie between the imagination of a people and their language. He marked passages describing how individual minds were shaped by their language, not vice versa, and how important a part in this the poet's imagination played, for example "replacing a merely denotative expression like 'thunderbolt' by an explanatory one like 'fire struck from the clouds,' or 'night' by 'earth's shadow'" (p. 90).

Stevens's musing on "evil" in "Extracts" similarly expanded a thought of Vico's, as pointed out by Adams: The absence of good defines evil (p. 121), for which human beings are wholly responsible. In addition to these ideas of Vico that Stevens dealt with here and in the other two poems he wrote during this period was another germinal notion of the Italian historiographer-psychologist that the poet elaborated a short time later in "Notes Toward a Supreme Fiction": the poet as fiction maker, "supreme phantast," in Adams's paraphrase of Vico's words. Stevens began exploring this idea now in "Asides on the Oboe," which has, as part of its opening, ". . . say that the final belief/ Must be in a fiction" (*CP* 250). The modern poet could fulfill this "supreme" role by ignoring the "truth of science" and its concomitant language of pure reason and restoring through imagination (p. 126) what it was to be a man who, in Emerson's sense, stood erect before nature:

> But, for this, we must again create it in ourselves, must divest ourselves of our rational nature so far as to embody with our imagination the conditions of the men immersed in sense; yet we must retain our rational nature in order to see this knowledge in its causes and in relation to the whole life of mind in history. But since it is not knowledge of a purely rational subject-matter, we require for it not merely reasons but the study of fact, of authority, of what has happened. This, too, is a condition for the possibility of a philosophy of history; for if history could be evolved from our rational

> nature alone, its philosophy would be identical with the philosophy of reason. (p. 215)

Here was another element that contributed to Stevens's developing conception of "fact." It was also a prompt to pay attention to what had happened—in other words, to history. Stevens began with his own family records and then extended his reading in order to understand as fully as possible what the American experience meant, from the time of the European religious wars of the sixteenth century, which led to the movements of populations that included his forebears. It was not enough that he could outline these facts. He wanted to imagine them and re-create in the images of his poems "a knowledge of humanity immersed in sense . . . in concrete . . . symbolic fashion." America was still in its infancy, just emerging from its "early," "heroic age," in Vico's terms, "immersed . . . in the senses, ruled by traditions arising out of a religion of fear, by rigid customs and the letter of a harsh law, . . . not a rational knowledge by causes, consciously arising from rational creation of that which is known because created by the knower" (p. 214).

To create an instrument to express this knowledge would be to contribute to what Vico called—and Stevens copied and underlined on a piece of paper laid in Adams's volume—"the true history of the human race . . . a history of its progressive mental states" (p. 152). Moreover, since the poet's instrument is language—"Words are the only melodeon," Stevens noted in his "Adagia" (*OP* 171)—he would be contributing to what Vico conceived as "the Idea of a Dictionary of mental expressions (*voci mentali*) common to all the nations" (p. 170). As Stevens phrased it toward the end of "Extracts":

> . . . Thence come the final chants, the chants
> Of the brooder seeking the acutest end
> Of speech: to pierce the heart's residuum
> And there to find music for a single line,
> Equal to memory, one line in which
> The vital music formulates the words.
>
> (*CP* 259)

There are many more parallels in the lines of this poem, in "Of Bright & Blue Birds," and in "Mrs. Alfred Uruguay" between particular elements dealt with by Vico—"chaos," the sky as king of thunder (in "Extracts," *"un roi tonnerre"* [*CP* 254]), "nakedness," for example—and it is not necessary to focus on them here. But what is central to remember is that the dialogue Stevens held with Vico gave him further authority for a conviction that "the creative mind which produces the world of institutions is the mind of man" (Adams, p. 181). This encounter brought him closer to the problem he had been attempting to resolve from his years at Harvard: how to educe the will to believe in a world from which God had disappeared. His conversation with Vico both reminded him of all he had learned from Francis Bacon and opened up further explorations into the study of psychology and the value and limits of reason. From Vico, whom Adams had regarded in relationship to Descartes, Stevens went back to the *Discourse on Method* and sifted more ideas that he would meditatively discuss with that French thinker. It was no wonder his thoughts were so simmering that he couldn't get them down quickly enough, as he wrote to Church in April.

In Leon Roth's analysis of Descartes, Stevens found additional elements that he spun into his web of words, and here, too, he came across more reminders of his debt to Francis Bacon, which he would use to temper imagination. Most notably Roth quoted and elaborated on a passage from Bacon that had contributed to Stevens's repeated use of "machine" as a metaphor: "The entire work of the understanding must be commenced afresh, and the mind itself be, from the very outset, not left to take its own course but guided at every step, and the business done *as if by machinery* (*Novum Organum,* Preface)."[45] Roth went on to point out that the purpose of Bacon's "logical calculus" was "to *discipline* the mind, not to 'supply it with wings' but to 'hang it with weights' (*Nov. Org.,* i, p. 104)." Bacon's "organon" was "to be indeed an instrument, a piece of machinery indifferent to the use made of it" (Roth, p. 57) simply a flexible and certainly *"by no means final"* (p. 58) method of perceiving as accurately as possible our connection to the natural world. Stevens had clearly learned a great deal from Bacon in designing his instrument, "The Whole of Harmonium." His mind having been refreshed now, in the context of learning more about Descartes, he acknowledged his debt to his old masters in certain lines of the poems he wrote, as in "Extracts," in which he seemed to address Descartes directly:

> He, that one, wanted to think his way to life,
> To be happy because people were thinking to be.
> They had to think it to be.
>
> (*CP* 257)

His appreciation and integration of Bacon's method went into his own new project, "Notes Toward a Supreme Fiction"—"by no means [a] final" approach. This method would allow "progressive stages of certainty," following a passage Stevens underlined in Roth's text: "The prejudices he [Bacon] would rid us of are not those of the senses but of the intellect, and between the true and the false he would recognize the probable and its degrees" (p. 67). This Stevens translated into the figure he adumbrated in "Asides on the Oboe": "The impossible possible philosophers' man" (*CP* 250).

One more central notion from Bacon that Stevens rediscovered in reading Roth's book on Descartes was that which he now incorporated specifically in two of the poems he wrote in 1940 and 1941. In the first chapter of the *Novum Organum* Bacon described the mind: "The human understanding is unquiet; it cannot stop or rest . . ." (i, 65). In "Extracts," Stevens began exploring this idea:

> And, talking of happiness, know what it means
> That the mind is the end and must be satisfied.
> (*CP* 257)

By the following year he had come to agree with Bacon and closed "The Well Dressed Man with a Beard," with "It can never be satisfied, the mind, never" (*CP* 247).

In the interim, in his day-to-day life, Stevens had gathered more experience that attested to the impossibility of arriving at a resting place for his spirit. From the evidence of political events it grew clearer that the United States would enter the war that had already meant the devastation of whatever had remained, after the First World War, of ideas of nobility. Stevens implicitly agreed with Leonard van Geyzel, however, that the United States' entrance would not mean any improvement if, as his correspondent put it, "Wall Street" won (June 6, 1941). There had to be a fundamental change in the values that had determined the development of the West. And in his mind he agreed with Croce: Poetry could offer the cure for war.[46] In "The Figure of the Youth as Virile Poet" Stevens would elaborate Croce's notion that it was by following the "path of poetry, by which [we] may reach one of the unfailing fountains of perennial youth" (Croce, p. 29). Now he expanded his own notion of poetry as personal cure to restore to it the function it had for the Greeks, who saw in Apollo the source of both poetry and the health of a society.[47]

With all these ideas about the importance of poetry now deeply rooted, Stevens established his friendship with Henry Church. To this, and to elucidating earlier work to Hi Simons, Stevens continued to dedicate himself with extraordinary energy through 1940 and 1941. It was as important that his poetry be understood properly as it was that the foundation of his new faith be firmly laid.

Henry Church was a curious character. Heir to a fortune made primarily from one of his forebears' invention of bicarbonate of soda, he was a member of the board of directors of Church and Dwight, the firm that continued to manufacture it. The income from the family business had allowed him to live for forty years in Europe as a patron of the arts (*L* 376). Church was as personally haphazard and secure in his eccentricities as Stevens was meticulously disciplined and uncomfortable with any manifestations of his spirit's disorder. This difference between the two men was most apparent in the contrast between the letters Church sent to Stevens and those Stevens sent to him. Perfectly illustrating the habits of a capricious millionaire, Church's notes and letters sprawled chaotically over the pages, his thoughts randomly associated; when he attempted to use a typewriter, the results were even more bizarre than when he used a pen. Stevens often commented humorously on these traits in his replies to Church, while always communicating each of his own thoughts and distinctions with the precision of a mind that worked as efficiently as a machine. Whether he was explaining details about Church's will that he had generously had researched—by one of his younger business-connected "friends"—or outlining additional characteristics for the poetry chair, or simply discussing something he had read, Stevens presented his ideas with the same attention that he exercised in his capacity as a lawyer. The only feature common to both men's styles was that for the duration of their relationship, they addressed each other in person and in letters as "Mr. Church" and "Mr. Stevens." In the American supreme court of poetry they jointly conjured, the rules of courtesy were to be maintained.

Stevens's manner of address in letters to Church and others whom he came to know well over a period of years was a significant indicator of differences he wanted to preserve in his relationships. There were very few with whom he came to have mutual first-name intimacy in his correspondence; these included William Carlos Williams (only quite late, however), Pitts Sanborn, and José Rodríguez Feo (unusually, since Rodríguez Feo was much his junior). With Marianne Moore only after almost twenty years of correspondence and later acquaintanceship that evolved into mutually admiring personal friendship (they had always respected each other's work) did Stevens break the ice, opening a letter dated November 30, 1951, with the usual "Dear Miss Moore" but following it with "Marianne at parties" in parentheses. Curiously, after her response, noting, "Why not Marianne all the time[?]" (December 19, 1951), to which he replied by sending his next letter to "Dear Marianne" (December 26, 1951), she maintained her formal salutation to "Mr. Stevens."

With all his business-connected contacts, he maintained another order of formality, one which no doubt reflected a noncodified yet clearly established pecking order. Stevens's superiors in the insurance world addressed him as "Dear Stevens" in correspondence, and he addressed them as "Dear Mr. X." Similarly, Stevens addressed all his junior "friends" by their last names, while they always addressed him as "Mr. Stevens." With those he considered both equal and friends, on the other hand, like Arthur Powell, both parties usually addressed each other by their last names alone and sometimes by first names. This kind of intimacy spilled over into some of Stevens's poetic friendships as well, like those with Allen Tate and Richard Eberhart.

It was curious that with Henry and Barbara Church, with whom Stevens came to spend more and more afternoons and evenings over the years, eating, drinking, and talking for hours, the form of "Mr. Church" and "Mr. Stevens"—and, after Church's death, extended to "Mrs. Church"—never loosened to "Church" and "Stevens" or "Henry" (or "Harry," as he was known) and "Wallace." It is impossible to know which of the two men set and kept the tone of their relationship. But from the evidence of Church's queries about when he might expect to be given Stevens's home address—to which the poet responded that he preferred to receive all his correspondence at the office—and when he would meet Mrs. Stevens and Holly, it seems that Church would have been happy to feel he had established some kind of intimacy with the poet he so admired. Stevens might have felt that Church, so much the man of the world, belonged to a different class and because of that the poet maintained a strict social order. Or perhaps Stevens did not believe he could establish a relationship of true equality with this man who had the careless habits of a child. In this case it was better to maintain some distance, even though he would continue to delight in the company of the circle that Church gathered around him. Or perhaps he wanted, in a benign way, to humor this millionaire, continue to show his respect for "Mr. Church," the man who would found the majestic chair for the study of the "supreme fiction."

Or perhaps, in view of the fact that both Mr. and Mrs. Church did come to know Mrs. Stevens at occasional luncheons, teas, and dinners when she had accompanied her husband to New York for weekends of shopping and theater, he wanted to preserve a discretionary distance that would keep these new friends from asking the kinds of questions that would have been much too difficult to answer. As long as they all remained "Mr." and "Mrs.," it was unlikely that any eccentricities of Elsie's would be referred to when over another lunch, in her absence, "Mr. Stevens" was asked about "Mrs. Stevens." In all likelihood it was a combination of some or all of these possibilities that prompted Stevens to keep his courtier's costume in good repair. And since in the Church court, others who were regular participants were referred to by Mrs. Church in letters to "Mr. Stevens" by their first names—"Marianne" (Moore), "Jean" (Paulhan), "Jean Wahl" (to distinguish him from Paulhan, but not "Monsieur Wahl")—it seems that it was Stevens who set the boundaries of the relationship.

It was fortunate that Stevens's friendship with Church began when it did. A few months after he had first proposed the idea of the poetry chair, both the poet's younger brother, John (who had reached local prominence as an ex-judge and Democratic party boss in Berks County), and his mother-in-law, for whom he had affection, died (she, suddenly, in an automobile accident). This was the summer of 1940. "This sort of thing, and the demnition news, added to the demnition grind at the office, makes me feel pretty much as a man must feel in a shelter waiting for bombing to start" (*L* 365). Just as years earlier the death of his sister Katharine had undone him, loosening his ties of restraint so that he unusually communicated his feelings to Elsie directly, so now these deaths—especially that of John—brought about a radical change in behavior. Stevens not only went back to Reading for the funeral but almost immediately began to reestablish lasting relationships with the remaining members of his family. As his niece Jane MacFarland Wilson (daughter of his sister Elizabeth) related,[48] right after the funeral, which her mother, having just undergone minor surgery, was unable to attend, he accompanied her (they had met at the funeral for the first time) back to Germantown, Pennsylvania, to see Elizabeth, discharged from the hospital that day. Jane noted that Stevens was warm with her from the first (she also noted that the other members of the Stevens family, except her mother, were rather cold and distant) and that he was spontaneously and humorously affectionate with his sister, whom he had not seen for years. After this Stevens maintained this attitude consistently with the remaining members of his family, especially with Jane, helping her through all difficulties, including making a point of cheering her on the day of her mother's funeral two and a half years later in February 1943. But then when Jane divorced, her uncle refused to communicate with her for at least a year (this will be dealt with in the next chapter). Confronting these personal losses against the background of the mass losses of the war—another echoing of the situation surrounding Katharine's death during World War I—spurred Stevens into renewing contact with what was most important, what would suffice.

There was yet another loss in spring of 1941. His old friend Pitts Sanborn was found dead in his apartment in New York shortly after retrieving, with Stevens's help, a letter from his old paramour, Willa Cather; the letter was offered for sale by a bookseller. Life was precarious not only on the battle-ground of war. Thinking about things that reflected his spirit but that would survive for generations was salutary for Stevens: the poetry chair and his work. In explicating his poems and himself to Hi Simons, he revealed his involvement with these feelings, noting that he sensed himself like Dr. Johnson talking to Boswell (August 30, 1940). Simons recognized the poet's meaning and thanked him for showing him how to treat a poem as an expression of a man's reality in the world rather than as an intellectual exercise (September 8, 1940).

In turning his attention to posterity, Stevens was concerned not just with himself. All through this period, beginning in the late summer of 1940 and extending through to the end of his life, the poet did whatever he could to make places on the front bench of poetry's supreme court for those in whom he believed. Some of the works and figures he named as among the very best at first seem surprising. To Leonard van Geyzel, who wanted to be kept abreast of the current "goods" in America and who was committed to a socialist ideal, Stevens sent Willa Cather's *Sapphira and the Slave Girl* in December 1940, commenting: "We have nothing better than she is" (*L* 381). The poet especially appreciated the pains she took to conceal the sophistication of her perceptions. The poet included her in his "pantheon" as someone equally involved as he with the language of the American soil and with the differences the dialects of the language bespoke. Only by making the American public sensitive to the views of minority populations could change come about.

A few weeks later in a letter to Church, approving of his and Allen Tate's selection of Philip Wheelwright and Delmore Schwartz to give lectures on poetry at Princeton in the same series to which Stevens was also invited (where he would deliver "The Noble Rider and the Sound of Words" in May 1941), the poet added, ". . . there is no one in whom I believe as much as I believe in Delmore Schwartz" (*L* 382). This unqualified praise instanced more than an appreciation of Schwartz's work. Though Stevens came to admire both his manner and his content, he had originally had reservations about the dominance of intellect over feeling in his poetry (*L* 356). But what he had no reservations about and recognized as truly essential for the future of American thought was Schwartz's commitment to the left, even though Stevens maintained, as he made explicit in a later letter to him (*L* 589–91), that it was not necessary for the poet to write about politics in order to have a political impact. Never wavering in his support of Schwartz's endeavor, a few months before he died, Stevens reiterated his firm belief in the younger poet, naming him as the "most gifted" among the candidates for the current Harriet Monroe Poetry Award; the others were Randall Jarrell, Richard Eberhart, and Howard Nemerov (*L* 875). This was eleven years before Schwartz's sordid death in a decrepit New York hotel room, after which his body lay unidentified and unclaimed in the Bellevue morgue.

As Alfred Kazin points out in his thumbnail sketch of Schwartz in *New York Jew,*[49] to this poet and the group to which he belonged—the intelligentsia of the thirties gathered around the *Partisan Review*—"Europe [was] . . . the biggest thing in America," and their primary commitment was to the "common man." At the same time they furiously opposed the idea of "the Soviet-American alliance as a progressive war, a people's war" (Kazin, p. 34). Stevens, who never forgot his lessons in rhetoric and continued to persuade with "sweetness and light" rather than with the bitterness and darkness of Schwartz and his compeers, nevertheless shared the same political viewpoint. Like Schwartz, he believed in the "authority of culture, the logic of tradition" but refused to become "the poet on the cross of culture" (Kazin, p. 35). It was not by virtue of a superior moral stance that this was so, but rather, it seems, the result of an accidental, constitutional difference in personalities. Perhaps this was connected to the difference between their generations, perhaps to the difference in ethnic experience; Stevens had a sense of rootedness in the American soil, even if it extended back only a few hundred years, while Schwartz truly belonged to the Diaspora. Schwartz and his contemporaries felt with a renewed sting the contradictions inherent in the American strain that Stevens had first become aware of as a student of the heirs of Henry Adams at Harvard. Stevens recognized Schwartz's attempt to deal with this old "up and down between two elements." But while it drove Schwartz to ultimate despair, Stevens—in spite of his depressions and the periodic return of feeling that he had failed in his task—seemed invulnerable to the absolute despair that perhaps belongs only to those who feel themselves essentially disinherited. Stevens would have been deeply troubled by the nature of Schwartz's end. Like him, Schwartz had put all his "zeal for social revolution into the purer and perhaps more lasting revolution of modern literature and art" (Kazin, p. 66). He seemed to Stevens the "noble rider," the "figure of the youth as virile poet." But he failed in the primary task of completing his life with poetry.

It was in these years beginning with the Second World War that Stevens understood his commitment to the left. This affiliation was strengthened by his relationship with Henry Church and his friends, for whom, in every aspect, "Europe [was] . . . the biggest thing in America." Beneath the surface of his privileged life—some might say that because of it, his commitment was a facile one—Church worked closely with those who fought notions of social hierarchy. Through his involvement with Jean Paulhan and Jean Wahl, he actively supported the French resistance. Through *Mesures,* he had made sure that the same heroes celebrated by Schwartz and his group received the attention they deserved. Kafka, Babel, Joyce, Picasso, Malraux, Sartre, Svevo, Stravinsky, Schönberg were the gods of both these circles of intellectuals.

In light of his role in propagating a better world through literature and art, it is tempting to muse on the significance of the logo of Church's family's product, Arm and Hammer baking soda. It would seem that Church was, in actuality, the enlightened capitalist, "in Filene's sense," in whom Stevens had voiced his belief years earlier to Ronald Lane Latimer (who, by this time, had become a Buddhist). If this perception is accurate, it would secure as sincere Stevens's deep devotion to Church, to whom he dedicated what is perhaps his greatest poem, "Notes Toward a Supreme Fiction."

In translating the ethic of the economic survival of the fittest—the ethic by which Garrett Stevens, Sr., had lived and died—into establishing foundations (*Mesures,* the poetry chair at Harvard) for what were in the end, and in spite of implicit or explicit social aims, the "indulgences of imagination," Church resolved the tension Stevens had experienced all his life. It is not surprising that Stevens went out of his way to help Church in whatever ways he could. In addition to the work on his will and the setting up of the poetry chair, Stevens put Church in contact with those who could help him establish the equivalent of *Mesures* in America when the time came; he made the necessary contacts to find positions for Jean Paulhan (who, besides coediting *Mesures,* had been the editor of the *Nouvelle Revue Française*) and Jean Wahl; he fulfilled Church's wish that he lecture on poetry at Princeton, overcoming his extreme reticence to speak in public ("I am very definitely not a public speaker; in fact, hardly a private one" [*L* 382]); he reported on whatever questions Church had about particular literary figures or works that he considered for various purposes; he encouraged him to write. In some curious way Stevens became like a dutiful son for Church, and Church, unlike Garrett, Sr., was a wholly approving father. At the same time, because Church was himself respectful of Stevens, the poet could reverse the roles and guide him like a son as well. Within the delicate harmony of their relationship it was most fitting that they remain "Mr. Church" and "Mr. Stevens."

As the United States moved close to entering the war, though Stevens believed until late 1940 that America would remain isolated (*L* 364–65), and as the poet attempted to reestablish a connection with his family and a sense of the past after his brother's death and before the separation from his daughter (whom he hoped would be in college in the fall of 1941), he set himself to composing "The Noble Rider and the Sound of Words." This lecture was a compendium of references to the texts that had touched him most in the last ten years;[50] it was at the same time a lecture so "illogically complicate[d]" (*NA* 15) that it evaded and evades any definition. In it Stevens communicated his and the time's feeling of being at sea, while he transformed prose into the poetry that could provide the only sustenance, an imagined anchorage of nobility in the impossible depths of worldwide despair. In this lecture the poet asserted himself as the "potent" figure he desired to be. He spoke of writing not for "a drab but for a woman with the hair of a pythoness"; the allusions were both triumphantly sexual and universal, mythic. The message was that he had found himself, and the utterance was appropriately biblical and prophetic. In the face of the disastrous "pressure of reality" only the poet, the man of true imagination, *he,* could offer a solution. It was no wonder that with the full recognition of his power, Stevens was hesitant about his ability to speak in public. In the tradition in which he had been reared, this was an instance of hubris, of satanic pride. Though he cloaked his argument in evasive and oxymoronic terms, it proceeded with the inexorable logic of certainty and the rhetoric of revelation. In calling attention to the "sound of words," he approached the mystical realistically, calling on his reading in modern physics. A text that he did not name but that he also seemed to recall was Edgar Allan Poe's *Eureka,* in which Pascal's thought experiment of conjuring the movement of one stone on the sea floor that affects the universe with the waves it generates was translated into the effect that every word uttered has the power of transforming the shape of all things. Stevens had long before embarked on his voyage through what others considered "goblinry." He had earned his authority and now voiced it, albeit covertly, as was appropriate to the descendant of "good Puritans."

The United States entered the Second World War on December 7. The event went unremarked by the poet. The important thing was nobility, and the war was not noble. The sense of the past, however, was. He had begun his genealogical researches a month before, shortly after his daughter's departure for Vassar. His commitment to the real was there, in celebrating whatever had conspired to make him who he was, a being who was capable of creating "the world to which we turn incessantly and without knowing it," a being who could give "to life the supreme fictions without which we are unable to conceive of it" (*NA* 31).

Mrs. Stevens and Holly were unable to attend the lecture at Princeton at which the poet revealed himself so forcefully. It was at the same time that Holly was graduating from her twelve years at Oxford School. As her father presented himself in his words, she won the poetry prize for her class. It was fitting. The year ended. She began as a college student at Vassar. Her father read more of Buddha and his teachings; Leonard van Geyzel had picked up on and fostered his interest.[51] Much had gone into Stevens's stance. The period that opened with 1942 would see him coming into his own as the man he had envisaged for himself in 1900, when he wanted to leave Harvard and become a poet.

III

IT MUST BE ABSTRACT

1942–1947

I own myself able to abstract in one sense.

—Bishop George Berkeley

I heard another man say: "I've seen enough of life." This idea of life in the abstract is a curious one and deserves some reflection.

—From a journal entry,
November 1900, *Souvenirs and Prophecies* (p. 90)

As 1942 opened, Stevens was sixty-two, many years away from being the "figure of the youth as virile poet." And yet he had only just begun to discover his potency. This was as ironic as almost everything else in his life had been, a peculiar inversion produced by the mirror he held up to himself. He had abstracted from each aspect of his experience all the essential contours for mapping his supreme fiction. His awareness of it as a primary feature of both imagination and intellect had begun while he was still a boy and had learned from his father not to "look at facts, but *through* them." His perception of it as a necessary analytical tool had been sharpened at Harvard, not only theoretically but practically, as instructors guided their students to outline texts in the margins and create their personal back-flap indexes. Then came law school, where the most central lesson to be learned was how to abstract from numbers of cases and decisions a persuasive argument to "prove the truth" of one's position. With this well-honed instrument of thought, Stevens had, like a master surgeon, carefully examined and operated on his experience. He "drew off," "ab-stracted," each of the excesses of his spirit as if they were elements of improperly balanced humors. Poetry, indeed, was "a health," and being a comedian meant being in good humor, having restored the desired equilibrium of vital fluids through words shaped into "completion[s] of life." By 1942 Stevens had fully understood himself as a man of his time and place, and so, when he performed his surgical tasks, like a good, early barber-comedian, he attempted to alleviate the ills of his society as well.

In addition to the internal development of Stevens's idea of abstract, which, over his formative years, had been reinforced by the uses and understandings of it by particular authors whom the young poet read (each that I have found has been noted in earlier discussions; see Index under "Abstract"), it seemed that external events had conspired to make the "abstract" the most powerful "abstraction" of the century. The flights of the Wright brothers, Blériot, and, later, Charles Lindbergh had a profound impact on how reality was perceived in America and abroad. But it was not until the thirties, when air travel began replacing rail that this was understood. The first nonobjective abstractionists imagined themselves flying or had, in many cases, flown. It was literally from a bird's-eye view that they attempted to describe the intersections of earth and sky, the irregular layers of clouds. They did not look at the phenomenon of flight but immersed themselves in it. Wassily Kandinsky's movement into abstraction serves as the almost ideal illustration. Between 1910 and 1915 his rounded mountains and well-placed, sweet colored huts began to stretch out of their confines; they seemed to speed up across his canvases until they disappeared into suggestive, remembered contours of their original shapes. This change in style mirrored what had happened to consciousness as the twentieth century became the "culture of time and space."[1]

Paralleling the fascination with flight was the appreciation of the primitive, of the geometric abstractions of both African and Indian cultures. It was as though with the perspectives allowed by aerial viewing, people realized how correctly and with what extraordinary power of abstraction Indians, for instance, had mapped their territories. In places where viewing from mountaintops was not possible and did not permit a broad vista, it was from memorially imagining the sinewing path of a river and being able to translate that direct and linear experience in three dimensions into an organic, conceptual rendering in two that a map was produced. This was not different from the chart- and mapmaking activities of Europeans over the centuries. But it had not been expected that cultures without writing and without Western technology could limn the shape of reality as it was now being seen from above. With the conquest of the air people in the West, like Crispin in 1922, began to see how much of what they had always seen they had never seen before.

None of this was explicit. It was simply another part of the pantomime mimicking the spirit of the age. Yet as the century progressed and increasing numbers of people experienced seeing the world from thousands of feet above it, abstraction became more natural, an understandable language. The forms of representing reality changed. By the time Stevens wrote "Notes Toward a Supreme Fiction" and made the first requirement that "It Must Be Abstract," no serious person would have quarreled with why the poet set this rule. Most, however, would have missed—and continue to miss—the inextricable connection between abstract and concrete that Stevens intended and that Indians and European chartmakers knew when they laid down their line and color diagrams of reality and understood that using them, they could safely find their way through dark forests or along dangerous shores.

It was because Stevens understood "abstract" in this way that he wrote so much about the value of real, particular facts. Everything, for him, had to begin with the actual. Abstraction was not an evasion, a way to distance himself from the real, but a necessary tool to find a way through it. Moreover, in order to be able to translate the experience of the concrete particular into its abstracted form, one had to imagine in such a way—rise above oneself and reality, so to speak—that one became spirit, air, the unimaginable. In this experience one felt what it was/is to see with the eyes of a god.

In some ways being able to abstract came naturally to Stevens by virtue of a number of accidents. He had grown up in a place crowned by a mount; right in the middle of Reading rose Mount Penn, constantly inviting residents to survey familiar streets and search for rooftops from above. Even before he ever began walking alone or with friends through the surrounding countryside and up and down hills and small mountains, Mount Penn offered itself to him and the other children brought to it for Sunday outings or afternoon adventures by caring parents.

Then, too, Stevens grew to be quite tall and shared the feeling of all who are like giants among men and women—"You ten-foot poet among inchlings" (*CP* 76). He was at the same time part of the mass yet above it as he walked down crowded city avenues and saw a sea of heads bobbing like regular, irregular molecules. This couldn't but prompt an attitude of considering the individual as part of a larger mass, the mass so much like just another force of nature—a colony of ants, a flock of birds, the movement of atomic particles—regular in numbers, irregular when one was regarded in isolation.

It is impossible to know how conscious Stevens was of the connections between aspects of his disposition and his major elaboration of the abstract. But it is fairly safe to suggest that he must have been aware, at least, of the two above-mentioned "accidents." He did point out in "The Figure of the Youth as Virile Poet" the identity between an artist's choice of images and his temperament (*NA* 48). That "His soil is man's intelligence" was not at all an abstraction for him, but a description born out of the extraordinary introspection that he coupled with his meticulous inspection of expanding vistas. From this fine-tuned attention to all aspects of his experience Stevens observed, too, for example, in speaking specifically of "The Westwardness of Everything" (*CP* 455) that he had always been sensitive to this movement—perhaps the subtlest of the planet's phantasmagoria—because his bedroom as a boy had faced west and since then he had always wanted bedrooms that faced west. When they didn't, as he noted, he always felt he had somehow to turn things around to align them to his most familiar setting. It would be most unusual if the poet so attuned to these features of his disposition did not find himself also musing the obscure associations stirred in him by the "abstract."

It was in 1942 that Stevens named the "abstract" as a necessary aspect of his imagination's residence. The pressure of events surrounding the Second World War, of which he spoke and wrote so much, was largely responsible for this realization. His feelings had begun to be sharpened earlier, during the Spanish Civil War. When he wrote "The Men That Are Falling" (*CP* 187), he was aware of how much the "pathos" of the situation he mentally constructed as existing in Spain made his eyes turn toward something adjacent while they sought some solace, as had happened often when he was a young man. From an abstract perspective the adjacent always showed itself. It was no wonder that during this period from 1942 to 1947, when Stevens became aware of how the abstract had functioned for him in this distracting way, he set out to write, finally, "without evasion by a single metaphor." During the worst atrocities of the Spanish Civil War and the beginnings of World War II he could not look at things directly, as they were. Consequently, he felt somewhat guilty. But finding that it was possible to use the abstract as a grounding constructive principle meant that he could look at things and deal with the "difficulty of what it [was] to be" in those days of the greatest social upheaval that the world had yet known.

At the same time there was something else about cultivating the abstract in the years between the United States' entry into the war and its end that made the notion an appropriate device. The poems that Stevens wrote between 1942 and 1947, those eventually published as *Transport to Summer,* were the most difficult that he had ever forged, and they were and are the most abstract. With a few exceptions their lines offered no immediate delight, no suspension in the pure good of sound, no dispensation in soothing rhythms that overrode their meaning. This was intentional. Stevens created poems during this time that were as resistant to understanding as the events in the world around him. In spite of its title promising desired relief, *Transport to Summer* presented the most impenetrable of the poet's poems. They were mimicking, in the difficulty of their being, what it was to be in those years. The experience of reading this volume, trying simultaneously to feel the essential weight behind the poems and to understand their subtle arguments is as demanding, in its way, as facing actual battle. Nothing at first seems to make sense, yet reality is there and pressing and must be dealt with—if the mind is to find a temporary resting place.

Before writing any of these difficult poems, Stevens spent months simply playing with the *idea* of the abstract. Around this the first notes for his "Supreme Fiction" arranged themselves. In finally setting this poem—actually written before any of the others of *Transport to Summer*—at the volume's end, he made it seem a container for the rest. He was illustrating, through his deceptive placing, his understanding of how out of individual concrete instances of abstract perception—each of the poems themselves—the idea was born. In this way even the notion of "idea" itself, as "something once seen," would be communicated. Nonetheless, in his own and public reality "Notes Toward a Supreme Fiction" appeared first as a separate volume published in 1942 by the Cummington Press. Stevens had the highest regard for the press. It was attached to the Cummington School, which the poet saw as akin in spirit to Byrdcliffe in Woodstock, where he and Elsie had spent time in summers years before. Stevens was delighted that young people at the school were making books in the finest tradition. Apropos of the press's doing this and later volumes as well—*Esthétique du Mal* and *Three Academic Pieces*—the poet gently argued with Alfred Knopf, who voiced dissatisfaction at various points over these "betrayals." The poet pointed out what a noble effort the Cummington Press was—at one point he even sent Knopf a photograph of the school's students at work, printing (*L* 502)—and persuaded him that in the long run these smaller editions would only enhance Knopf's larger undertakings.

In Stevens's mind, his preoccupation with the abstract as well as with the other categories of the "Supreme Fiction"—change and pleasure—was tied into his relationship to Henry Church, who shared his vision of the place of poetry in twentieth-century life. Giving his lecture at Princeton on "The Noble Rider and the Sound of Words" at Church's request seems to have been the catalyst in the process of conceiving the broad outlines for what he felt the "Supreme Fiction" must do. But there was something else about that late spring day at Princeton that predisposed the poet to abstract himself in thoughts about the pure good of theory.

For more than six months after delivering the lecture, Stevens nursed the terrible fear that he had done something at the Churches' dinner party that evening that had offended either his host or hostess or some of the others present. For these months Church had not written to him. This, together with the poet's reflecting on his behavior with the group, indicated to the man still uncertain of himself, except "on paper," that he had lost the friendship of this most valued individual. What had he done? On his way back to Hartford from Princeton Stevens stopped in New York and had dinner with Wilson Taylor, one of his younger lawyer friends connected with the Hartford. He laughingly related to Taylor that he had insulted everybody on campus and closed noting, "I'll never be invited back there again."[2]

When, in late January 1942, Stevens finally received a letter from Henry Church, now living temporarily in Tucson, Arizona, he responded with relief and a more detailed description of what he thought his offenses had been:

> Is it possible that you have been waiting for me to write to you? If so, you will be very much surprised to hear that I felt that I must have done something in Princeton that had offended you or Mrs. Church, and that you had x-ed me out. I cannot tell you how humiliated I was by the thought. While I know that I had made a very bad job of reading my poetry, I took it for granted that both of you knew how difficult that was for me to do, and, that I only did it because Mrs. Church particularly wanted me to do so.
>
> I have so often wanted to have you here: that is to say, to visit us in Hartford, but, if that were possible, I should have asked you long ago. Had it been possible, I dare say things would have gone better. It was because of my sense that I had done something that you very much disliked, and because of the difficulty of doing anything about it, not knowing what it was, that I finally came to think that there was nothing at all to do about it. And, suddenly, your letter turns up.
>
> What I have said will, I hope, explain what has happened. There are so many things that might have been the trouble: For instance, asking Mr. Tate to change places at the table, which was a perfectly innocent thing, because Mrs. Gauss happened to know people that I knew, about whom I wanted to talk to her. Then too, Roger Sessions worried me to death. I thought that possibly my bearing toward him had not been what it should. You see how I have been troubled by things about which I wouldn't ordinarily have given a second thought. . . .

> Please remember me to Mrs. Church. I was particularly on edge about her, because she is so buoyant that I felt that, if I had done something wrong in that direction, it must have been pretty bad, whatever it was. It is not the easiest thing for a man to drop into an academic atmosphere and to fit perfectly. . . . (*L* 400–01)

A further clarification of what "worried [him] to death" about Roger Sessions came in Church's reply to this letter: "No there is absolutely no need to have anything on your conscience. . . . I'm sure of Sessions you made a real friend for you made him sit down at the piano and play again his own composition—that rarely happens to him—that was just before the evening broke up—I dont [*sic*] know what else you could have done to him—I am deeply grieved that you have had so much *mental torture*. . . ."[3]

A strange perception of himself had operated here, as it did on almost all occasions when Stevens showed himself among a group of new people and even sometimes among acquaintances or friends of long standing. While the fear that he had offended someone could have been connected to his having drunk a bit too much and not quite remembering the next day what he had done, there was another side to this behavior that was curiously bound up with that other being, Elsie, the "second self" with whom he spent his life.

From numerous accounts and from comments that Stevens made to some who in filially distanced ways became his intimates—his assistants at the company and, later, Holly—it is clear that it was because Stevens was always afraid that Elsie might insult those he asked to their home that he did not, except in rare instances, extend such invitations. Only those to whom he came at some point to explain Elsie's eccentricities and his fear, and whom he could trust to understand and not be offended, could enjoy their hospitality and her exquisite talents as cook and homemaker. Eventually the Churches were to join this group, which included a chosen few of the couples Stevens knew from the Hartford. Late in his life Stevens seems to have trusted that William Carlos Williams understood as well, for he warmly asked him to visit on his way back to Rutherford, New Jersey, from New England. Frost, however, on his visit years before had been insulted in a way that Stevens must have been sure meant he would never return.[4] It was no wonder that about Carl Sandburg's visit to Hartford Stevens had been so vague when he related the fact to Harriet Monroe (see p. 489, Volume I).

In his letter to Church now Stevens skirted the problem at home: "I have so often wanted to have you here: that is to say, to visit us in Hartford, but, if that were possible, I should have asked you long ago." Yet when he was away from home, it was he, he felt, who did what Elsie did. There was a mystery here, one deepened by an account given by Manning Heard, Stevens's assistant at the Hartford from 1933 to 1937. (Heard and his wife were one of the couples who had been invited—though only once, it seems—to the Stevens's inner sanctum for dinner; it was a "very fine evening," as Heard remembered it, with everything meticulously prepared and served.) Heard recalled Elsie as "shy, very shy" while her husband was alive, but he noted, ". . . after Mr. Stevens died, I went to see her, and I can't remember a more charming lady, and we had such a perfectly normal, interesting conversation." Heard went on to say that he thought Stevens "completely subdued her." He thought the poet "was a little jealous of her . . . because he was very protective of her, very protective, and he never took her anywhere. As a matter of fact, Mr. Stevens would go to a [company] party but never with Mrs. Stevens." He and the other Hartford people "often wonder[ed] why." Elsie told Heard, after Stevens died, "that for some reason or other he just didn't want her exposed. She said, 'I would have loved to have come, but Wallace didn't want me to. He didn't want me to go, and I didn't go, naturally.' But she was a lovely, lovely person," Heard added in closing his memory of Elsie.[5]

Since other accounts of Elsie's behavior after her husband's death point to her being, in fact, as insulting or cutting as Stevens feared she would be, it is more than likely that Heard happened to visit Elsie on a day or during an hour when she was "in possession of herself." This last phrase seems to contain a partial answer to the mystery that surrounded Elsie and the nature of her marriage to the man whose poetic gift was attached to an extraordinary sensitivity to things outside himself, an empathy that no doubt entailed a blurring of the boundaries of selfhood in the world. Stevens's early and repeated perceptions of only being able "to command" himself on paper, his discomfort with superiors and peers that ensued in his having as friends only those with whom he communicated primarily "on paper" were also parts of this mystery. His involvement with the abstract later in his life was no less an expression of his own extreme inability to remain "in possession" of his self when confronted by the real—whatever form it took. This was both a blessing and a curse. In terms of his relationship with Elsie, it was the key to what others perceived as bizarre.

There is no doubt that Stevens felt strong devotion to Elsie throughout his life and that this devotion was not simply one of obligation, a kind of moral right-doing toward the being whom he had had a large part in shaping. The fact was that he had, to a great degree, made her in his own image. She did become his "second self," the self that Stevens knew existed and enjoyed fully but of whom he was ashamed. This was a self not in keeping with the image he projected. This imaged self, originally patterned on his patrician peers at Harvard like Walter Arensberg and later on W. G. Peckham, wanted, more than anything, to be like Henry Church, someone who moved with grace among "the best and the brightest," someone who completely fulfilled the dreams Stevens's father had had for him of making a place for himself "on the front bench." The other self he shared with Elsie showed itself when he let himself go, during evenings or days with young associates in groups, alone, or with their wives, when he indulged his taste for coarse German sausages and sauerkraut, when he reveled unafraid of showing his peasant roots, celebrating the robustness of "that monster, the body." How many people, he worried, would accept this part of him, his spontaneous yielding to dance rhythms and ribald stories? He kept his contacts separated. He showed only parts of his world to different individuals. The alternate title he contemplated for the appropriately titled last volume, *Parts of a World,* "The Man, That's All One Knows," ironically revealed the abstraction of his being.

It was not so much that Stevens wanted to keep Elsie from exposing herself as that he wanted to keep parts of his own being from being exposed. Unfortunately Elsie could not have begun to understand the complexity of the mechanism at work here. Her only recourse was fearful confusion. Being shy was not the issue; she was simply unsure of how her husband would react if she showed herself—his "second self." The sad end was that he could never trust her not to reveal this, their intimate aspect. And when she was not around, he could never trust himself—when "half-lit"—not to do the same.

Still, Stevens was not the sole cause of what was perceived as Elsie's imbalance. There is no doubt that the accidents of her childhood and adolescence had left their marks and that her husband's influence notwithstanding, she had a particular set of disturbances to her personality. Stevens could not have been unaware of this. In spite of his reticence about her in public, it is quite likely that Stevens appreciated the turns of Elsie's mind. While he always valued her superlative gifts as the keeper of his domain, there was something much deeper that bound Stevens to her. Something about Elsie was indeed part of the intelligence of their soil. She dug in the garden and devoted herself to satisfying the primary instincts for food and shelter; she became intensely involved in digging out natal roots as well. Stevens must also have been intrigued by her madness. He must have tried to figure her out, follow the associative links in her mind like some elaborate puzzle—a puzzle he had an edge on solving since he had contributed complexities to its being. Seen in the best light, living with her must have been something like living with Gracie Allen. An avid admirer of Groucho Marx, Jack Benny, George Burns, and Bob Hope, Stevens must have chuckled to himself quite often. Perhaps she even cast part of "the shadow of his e*quip*age [italics mine]" (*CP* 94), his verbal baggage, spontaneously providing him with phrases or odd perceptions that he turned into some of his curious titles or conceits. It had been Elsie, we remember, who "that November off Tehuantepec" began commenting on how the surface of the sea appeared one morning (*L* 241).

One of Stevens's most direct expressions of his valuing his wife came in a letter he wrote to Holly during the time when she was most vociferous in her complaints about her parents and the way she had been raised. (This was the fall of 1942, shortly after she had first announced that she did not want to continue at Vassar following her first year there; this period will be looked at shortly.) In defending Elsie against her daughter's verbal attacks, Stevens noted, "That your parents—any one's parents—have their imperfections is nothing to brood on. They also have their perfections. Yr [*sic*] mother has them to an exquisite degree, tough as she is" (*L* 422). Had the poet not both perceived and appreciated Elsie's perfections, it is very unlikely that in addition to being the dutiful husband he was—Stevens helped Elsie around the house a great deal, regularly washing dishes after dinner, scrubbing the kitchen floor when they no longer had household help (largely because of the difficulty of Elsie's personality[6])—he would have indulged her whims in the ways he did. He never failed to take her shopping to New York for a new spring hat or whatever else she wanted; he took her to the kinds of musicals and theater offerings she enjoyed. And as has been remarked earlier, even in their later middle age, he bought her necklaces and kimonos and other such precious additions to the beauty she once was. These were not the gestures of a man who acted only out of moral responsibility.

This leaves the question of what her "perfections" were. Since Stevens was not a man who used language lightly, it is important to give this word its full weight in his own vocabulary and to remember that he felt Elsie to have them "to an exquisite degree." For Stevens harmony came from balancing imagination and reality. "Perfection" was the "health," the "completion of life" that poetry afforded him in its endless variations on the theme of life. In the same way Elsie also provided completion and health. Elsie conformed to as many of the models Stevens had set up for her early in their relationship as she could. She played both the roles of "little girl" and, as spiritual guide, mother. Though she didn't garden when they first married, she eventually became a perfect gardener and a perfect cook. She enrolled in the program in euthenics at Vassar in 1931, trying to learn, in spite of her ambivalences about motherhood, how to rear their child well. As a result of consistently following her husband's wishes, however, she remained dependent and grew more irrational as she shifted between being both child and parent. Rather than develop into a mature beauty as she grew older, she became shriveled and eccentric, a wizened version of the "country girl." Of course, what must be considered here is how Stevens would have felt had she blossomed in her womanhood and remained as attractive into later life as she was when her beauty was stamped on coins that flooded the country.

At this point it is important to speculate on one of the most delicate aspects of Stevens's health. As Dr. Herrick had reported after first examining him, the poet was an acromegalic type. Though the symptoms of the gradual overdevelopment of the thorax, head, hands, and feet connected with this pituitary disturbance do not begin to show themselves in any noticeable way until middle age, there are other effects of the condition that operate earlier. One of them is a reduced sexual drive.[7] It is impossible to know whether Dr. Herrick ever explained to Stevens the full nature of what it meant to be an acromegalic type. If he did, there is no doubt that there would have been relief on Stevens's part to know that there was a physical explanation for something that could not but have disturbed him, at least on occasion. If the physician did not detail or ask questions about his sexual life, Stevens's reduced sexual urge and performance had to have remained something that at the very deepest level troubled him. In either case it seems reasonable to suggest that in part, at least, Stevens's appreciation of and devotion to Elsie had to do with her not asking for what she could not get. Considering the time and atmosphere in which she was bred, this may have suited her quite well. Nonetheless, it is not farfetched to think that to some degree the details of Stevens's intimate life played their part in Elsie's becoming who she did and that Stevens was aware of this and thus valued all the more her attempts to make a common life around dinners, roses, irises, preserved fruit from California and Florida, and occasional trips to New York.

And since, given his natural taciturnity, Stevens probably never openly addressed what was at issue, it was understandable that Elsie resent his withdrawal into his room alone to think about and write poetry. It was perhaps because of this that most of her insults to others seemed to be addressed to those connected with Stevens the poet, the man abstracted from her. Manning Heard and his wife were not parts of this world.

Yet another side of what Stevens appreciated about Elsie's "perfections" had to do with his perception—once again revealingly penned in French—that "Il faut être paysan d'être poète"* (*L* 461). Though at first it might seem inconsistent that the poet voice this at the same time as he attempted to place himself among the most elite of Americans, the Holland Society, the discrepancy is in some ways illusive. While there is no doubt that Stevens wanted to figure himself among the best few not only of the country but in history, he also felt very strongly about the positive qualities of people tied to primary activities. As he expressed about midway in his genealogical searches to one of those whose help he enlisted, though one of the researchers he had employed seemed determined to ferret out coats of arms and escutcheons for his forebears, he was equally content to imagine them as butchers or carpenters or one of his great-grandmothers as a woman who had borne eleven children and who had woven all their clothes. Even in his admiration of Henry Church this appreciation for basic concerns was central. As he said in a letter to Rodríguez Feo, Church, the "richest man I know seems not to be conscious of the fact that he has any money at all and luxury is repulsive to him" (*L* 514). Stevens knew that nobility came from action, not from class, even though his own uncertainty of self made him aspire to only the better things of life and made him reticent to show his homely roots.

Sharing these roots with Elsie was another aspect of her "perfection." With her he could enjoy some of the most direct pleasures of life to an exquisite degree. Unfortunately for the possibilities of their joint life, she had never acquired the "piano-polished" surface that allowed him to move, even without the greatest of ease, in the most cultivated circles. She would always do or say what he only perhaps felt among a stiffly mannered group commenting on the latest piece of such and such by so-and-so. In business-connected situations, however, Stevens himself was known for acid comments aimed at the core of deceptiveness that someone was trying to cloak. One such retort was related by Wilson Taylor:

*"One must be a peasant to be a poet."

> Stevens was at a football game at Yale one Saturday and ran into an officer from the home office of the Aetna [Life and Casualty Company, also in Hartford]. So Stevens and the home-office man greeted one another. Then Mr.——said, "Stevens, you know Mr.——from our New York office." It was a mystery how Aetna put up with him for so long; he used to pull some of the most crooked things. And Stevens said, "Oh, yes. I've heard that Sing Sing lost its quarterback!" Whammo! It's just this type of thing he'd say. . . .[8]

Stevens and his wife, then, did share common values, but he had an additional set, with which she remained largely unfamiliar, that he wanted to protect. Their common values were so strong, in fact, that without her and when not quite in possession of himself, he feared that the peasant in him, the rude descendant of farmers, would have shown himself and offended one of those not similarly immersed in the "real."

Luckily for Stevens, the greater part of his life, outside of the daily routine of home and office, was conducted on paper. The self that he continued to show there remained into his old age the "vigorous warrior" he had described himself to be in writing in a letter to Elsie when he was still courting her. When, for example, William Carlos Williams wrote to greet him for the New Year of 1942, while Stevens was still preoccupied with his imagined offenses to the Churches or their guests the previous May, Stevens responded with a note indicating anything but uncertainty, in spite of the different forms he chose for address and signature:

> Dear Bill:
>
> Thanks for your postcard. I am just getting under way. Twenty or thirty years from now I expect to be really well-oiled. Don't worry about my gray hair. Whenever I ring for a stenographer she comes in with a pistol strapped around her belt.
>
> Best regards young feller and best wishes,
>
> Wallace Stevens
>
> (*L* 400)

The playful assertion here of his being still a vigorous man, in view of both his age and the complications of his health, is touching evidence of Stevens's command of himself through his veils of words. Within a few days of this note he received the letter from Church, which he answered with his explanations and with the news of his other verbal achievements and plans. He was sending off the typescript of *Parts of a World* and had begun planning the shape of "Notes Toward a Supreme Fiction."

A few days later Stevens heard from Allen Tate that Church had been having trouble with his heart so he sent off another letter, humorously encouraging Church with an anecdote about the only other man he had ever known with angina who "bought himself a houseboat and proceeded to live in the boat a life that would have exhausted a Roman gladiator" (*L* 402). The relationship seemed intact. This was fully confirmed for him within another week, when Barbara Church wrote to him echoing her husband's reassurances about the evening in Princeton and sending him, as she would to a member of the family, photographs of the house where they were living in Tucson. Stevens responded graciously with a letter in which he created an imaginary dialogue between her and himself about the study of poetry. He observed that it was, for him, "the medium of a particular *joie de vivre*" (*L* 404). He included her in his paper intimacy. It was she who had, on that day at Princeton, persuaded him to read—in addition to the lecture he delivered—some of his poems. He feared he had done it badly. She made certain to stress he had not. They were now friends in their own right, beyond the relationship with Mr. Church. He closed noting that things were covered with frost in these "early war mornings." It was the end of February.

Within the next two and a half months Stevens had settled on the name of *Parts of a World* for his last volume, had completed the 420 lines of the first two sections of "Notes"—"It Must Be Abstract" and "It Must Change"—and had begun the final section, "It Must Give Pleasure." He wrote to the Cummington Press on May 14 advising of this progress. By May 19 he wrote again, to Katharine Frazier, director of the press; he noted that he had only the last poem, 21 lines, left to finish and expected to do this and the epilogue within the next week. He promised to send her a copy of one of the poems as soon as he was done, but not before going over the whole thing, which he did not like to do until he set the final period (*L* 406–07). The poet had clearly been deeply immersed in his "flüent mundo." The 630 lines—excluding the 21-line epilogue and 8-line prologue—commemorating his sixty-three years had been written in fewer than ninety days. The product was "one of the consequences of concentration," as he described a poem that captured "a peculiarity," the "momentary complete idiom of that which prompt[ed] it, even if that which prompt[ed] it [was] the vaguest emotion" (*L* 500).

For this major effort in a time of one of the world's major efforts, Stevens saw fit to make the emotion that prompted the long breath of "Notes" unusually clear. The epilogue he appended addressed the occasion of his cry as specifically as he ever had. He wanted its first lines on the back outside cover of the volume "to state the idea" (*L* 408):

> Soldier, there is a war between the mind
> And sky, between thought and day and night. It is
> For that the poet is always in the sun,
>
> Patches the moon together in his room
> To his Virgilian cadences, up down,
> Up down. It is a war that never ends.
>
> Yet it depends on yours. The two are one.
> They are a plural, a right and left, a pair,
> Two parallels that meet if only in

> The meeting of their shadows or that meet
> In a book in a barrack, a letter from Malay.
> But your war ends. And after it you return
>
> With six meats and twelve wines or else without
> To walk another room . . . Monsieur and comrade,
> The soldier is poor without the poet's lines,
>
> His petty syllabi, the sounds that stick,
> Inevitably modulating, in the blood.
> And war for war, each has its gallant kind.
>
> How simply the fictive hero becomes the real;
> How gladly with proper words the soldier dies,
> If he must, or lives on the bread of faithful speech.
> (*CP* 407–08)

The "Notes" were to constitute the missal in the mud promised in "The Man with the Blue Guitar": "The poem {went} from the poet's gibberish to/ The gibberish of the vulgate and back again" (*CP* 396). Sitting in his room that spring, watching "Weather by Franz Hals" (*CP* 385), the poet wanted to make explicit that his "struggle with the inaccessibility of the abstract," as intense as that of "the theologian with God," was inextricably bound with the struggle in which the soldier was involved. Were there no ideas, no ideals, neither he nor the soldier would have "borne his labor" (*CP* 393). He was not "An unaffected man in a negative light" (*CP* 393). In these codifying lines Stevens extended his major theme—the "up and down between two elements," the movement of imagination against reality—to the soldier marching "up down," "right and left." He wanted the soldier to be enriched by his (the poet's) "petty syllabi" that nonetheless could provide transcendence, meaning, "Sounds that stick"—an explanation of why he would risk his life to defend anything at all. Perhaps there never had been or could be again another war for which any explanation could hold. But this one, in which a madman exterminated a population on the basis of words loaded with myth, had to be fought by other words even more strongly weighted with the myth that no myths were valid:

> Begin, ephebe, by perceiving the idea
> Of this invention, this invented world,
> The inconceivable idea of the sun.
>
> You must become an ignorant man again
> And see the sun again with an ignorant eye
> And see it clearly in the idea of it.
>
> Never suppose an inventing mind as source
> Of this idea nor for that mind compose
> A voluminous master folded in his fire.

How clean the sun when seen in its idea,
Washed in the remotest cleanliness of a heaven
That has expelled us and our images . . .

The death of one god is the death of all.
Let purple Phoebus lie in umber harvest,
Let Phoebus slumber and die in autumn umber,

Phoebus is dead, ephebe. But Phoebus was
A name for something that never could be named.
There was a project for the sun and is.

There is a project for the sun. The sun
Must bear no name, gold flourisher, but be
In the difficulty of what it is to be.

(*CP* 380–81)

Stevens was fiercely serious about this "project." He was fighting no less intensely than the soldier, and as he well knew, his battle was intrinsically connected to the old argument he had had with "A High-Toned Old Christian Woman." His illustration to her, "And palm for palm,/ Madame," he translated now into "And war for war." The stakes had changed, but the game was still to win against monotheistic religion or, indeed, any ideology that cloaked our "bond to all that dust" in robes of named anthropomorphic majesties. The "will to believe" was there, yes; he agreed with William James but also followed the thread of his last argument in *The Varieties of Religious Experience:*

> All that the facts require is that the power be both other and larger than our conscious selves. Anything larger will do, if only it be large enough to trust for the next step. It need not be infinite, it need not be solitary. It might conceivably even be only a larger and more godlike self, of which the present self would then be but the mutilated expression, and the universe might conceivably be a collection of such selves, of different degrees of inclusiveness, with no absolute unity realized in it at all. Thus would a sort of polytheism return upon us. . . .
>
> Upholders of the monistic view will say to such a polytheism (which, by the way, has always been the real religion of common people, and is so still today) that unless there be one all-inclusive God, our guarantee of security is left imperfect. In the Absolute and in the Absolute only, *all* is saved. If there be different gods, each caring for his part, some portion of some of us might not be covered with divine protection, and our religious consolation would thus fail to be complete. . . . Common sense is less sweeping in its demands than philosophy or mysticism have been wont to be, and can suffer the notion of this world being partly saved and partly lost. The ordinary moralistic state of mind makes the salvation of the world conditional upon the success with which each unit does its part. Partial and conditional salva-

> tion is in fact a most familiar notion when taken in the abstract, the only difficulty being to determine the details. Some men are even disinterested enough to be willing to be in the unsaved remnant as far as their persons go, if only they can be persuaded that their cause will prevail—all of us are willing, whenever our activity-excitement rises sufficiently high. I think, in fact, that a final philosophy of religion will have to consider the pluralistic hypothesis more seriously than it has hitherto been willing to consider it. . . .[9]

The consequence of not entertaining this hypothesis was the war now being waged, the "war between mind and sky." As long as human beings continued to see themselves as separate from the rest of nature and, worse, as different from one another as a result of identifying with invented names—gods, goddesses—for forces they could not otherwise understand, there would be no end to the possibilities of Hitlers. "You must become an ignorant man again," know that you don't know, can never know beyond the "final no"—this was Stevens's position. On the foundation of this "no faith," the purpose of building the "Supreme Fiction" was precisely to show it to be a fiction, to create in the progress of its lines an edifice that could not be penetrated so that one could become comfortable with not understanding, though the surface brilliantly delighted—like the glory of "blazoned days" themselves, if only perceived in their transient unmeaning.

One could spend, and many have spent, countless hours and pages explicating "Notes Toward a Supreme Fiction," trying to pin its words like exquisite butterflies to walls of meaning. It is a noble exercise, though it never really goes anywhere, and that is precisely the point. The involvement yields an awareness of "the difficulty of what it is to be." Echoes of earlier lines and influences are heard, just as every moment of consciousness when attended to is thundering with echoes, memories, associations of things that have gone before, been seen before—"ideas." The movement is the thing:

> They will get it straight one day at the Sorbonne.
> We shall return at twilight from the lecture
> Pleased that the irrational is rational,
>
> Until flicked by feeling, in a gildered street,
> I call you by name, my green, my fluent mundo.
> You will have stopped revolving except in crystal.
> (*CP* 406–07)

As soon as a name is fixed, a meaning pinned, the world stops moving. That is the illusion: that it is stopped. To be alive without illusion is to be immersed in the observation of endless change. Heraclitus, Buddha, Hegel—the notion was not new with Stevens; he had learned well. His words, simply continual permutations. To understand them was and is to understand our condition. The "poet's gibberish" was a new "vulgate." Just as once Genesis provided the fiction through which a people fearful of a punishing god could explain their condition, so Stevens's poetry provides the fiction through which a people fearful of the "Nothing that is not there and the nothing that is" can accept theirs.

❧

The record of Stevens's movement toward this realization is the record of this book. Because he quizzed "all sounds, all thoughts, all everything/ For the music and manner of the paladins/ To make oblation fit" (*CP* 16), we follow. The thickness of allusions hanging in earlier chapters were illusions—his, mine—not in the end necessary, though necessary to have been there to be stripped away. The feeling of passing through the pages is the feeling of passing through the century, a time overburdened with words, images, increasingly speeding up to become a blur, an abstraction—*but* an abstraction blooded by the thought of the man who intensely sensed his time—the beats of its measures, and who slowed himself to listen, look.

This biography should, perhaps, end here. Is what precedes or follows a fiction or "The exquisite environment of fact . . . but fact not realized before" (*OP* 164)? Who am I who knows what Stevens did on a certain crisp October morning in his eighteenth year but don't know this about myself? Men and women made out of words.

❧

One day sometime in the forties or early fifties Stevens called in Herbert Schoen, another of his assistants at the Hartford at the time, and asked him what "ellipse" meant to him.[10] Schoen answered. Stevens reimmersed himself in his mind and papers. A poem was brewing. Schoen took himself to the law library across the hall and went directly to the *Webster's* to which Stevens had so often referred, either going himself or sending another underling to peruse its columns. Central to this anecdote is the poet's interest not only in the meaning a word had for him or in the registered dictionary definition but in the meaning attached to it by someone else, an everyman. Stevens paid attention to these nuances. He gathered them not only from those around him but from the way words were used in all forms—news reports on the radio and in papers, phrases caught in passing on planes and trains and on city streets at corners where people stopped for traffic lights. This engagement was not essentially different from the way he heeded connotations when he read or from how he translated the sound of the winter wind or summer sea into the whirrings and hissings of his alliterations and assonances. Stevens tried

> . . . by a peculiar speech to speak
>
> The peculiar potency of the general,
> To compound the imagination's Latin with
> The lingua franca et jocundissima.
>
> (*CP* 397)

He wanted "To be crested and wear the mane of a multitude/ And so, as part, to exult with its great throat" (*CP* 398).

The "project" was to create "the final poem of fact in the language of fact"—Stevens's response to William James's call for a "final philosophy of religion." That in his last years the poet became involved with Harvard and its poetry chair was fitting since it had been what he had been exposed to at the university that had left him perplexed with the "will to believe," what he called the greatest problem of the age (*L* 443). He wanted to be a new, secular St. Jerome, and he placed him centrally in "Notes," subtly suggesting his purpose. It was not accidental that one of Stevens's early idols was Thomas More, as he noted to Henry Church in June 1942 (*L* 409). The poet, too, had a vision of a utopia; "Oxidia" he named it (*CP* 182), a "banal suburb" of the imperfect world, built (as its derivation from the Greek, 'οζύς, suggests) out of bitterness by men of sharp wits and senses, skilled shearsmen, like "The Man with the Blue Guitar," who cut out and shaped from the cloth of reality a patchwork of hope.

Given his own spirit of rebellion, Stevens should not have been surprised by that of his daughter, who began to act on it during the summer of 1942. Amid the satisfactions of his poetic endeavors in those months (*Parts of a World* was going to press at Knopf, *Notes Toward a Supreme Fiction* at Cummington, and he was deeply satisfied with both efforts; he delighted in having both his personal volumes bound in "dignified," not "foppish" style; his fame had spread even to *Harper's Bazaar*) a storm was brewing at home. Holly, it seemed to her father, was bored being in Hartford that summer and found relief only in the company of friends who were not the best influences. Though he believed she had always been given the greatest freedom, symbolized by the red convertible she had been given for her sixteenth birthday, Holly felt more than a little constrained. On the one hand, though she was nominally free to come and go as she pleased, Elsie erratically blew up—when, for example, Holly did not come home at the hour Elsie expected. Her father, too, wanted Holly to be at home with her mother on the occasions when he had to be in New York for business or for a meeting with Henry Church, now back from Arizona. In addition, her father had been the one who had wanted her to go to Vassar while she had wanted to go to a college less prestigious, farther away, untrimmed by "ivy." He had allowed her to apply only to Vassar and to another small girls' college. Now, after her first year in the hothouse atmosphere of Vassar, she was doubly perturbed—especially since the outbreak of the war. Her father's plans for her future did not make sense to her, given the future the war portended. She preferred to leave school and get a job. All these feelings stirred beneath the surface as Stevens walked back and forth from the office where he continued with his correspondence and his work for the company.

To Harvey Breit of *Harper's Bazaar,* who had taken up a cue from William Carlos Williams to include Stevens in an article about poets as "ordinary," working men, the poet expressed negative feelings. Was Stevens simply generally disgruntled because of Holly's attitude, or was he wary because of the result of an interview he had had with Charles Henri Ford two years before that had resulted in "Verlaine in Hartford" which had appeared in *View* in September 1940? He had not liked that piece and found Ford and the magazine, after its appearance, meretricious in the worst sense. (His reaction notwithstanding, however, he subsequently fulfilled a promise for a poem for a future issue which he had made before "Verlaine in Hartford" appeared.) Stevens's first response to Breit's request was: "What is so unusual about being a lawyer and a poet?" He cited Francis Bacon, thus revealing his ties to the central figure of the Arensberg circle. In a second letter to Breit, who persisted, he voiced that he did both poetry and law with his "whole mind" and denigrated poets who flaunted the poetic stance, like Whitman, as "poseurs" who, for him, belonged "in the same category of eccentrics to which queer looking actors belong[ed]" (*L* 414). Echoing lines from "Notes," Stevens added that he wanted to be seen *as he was,* "in terms of . . . ordinary men and women." He went on to refuse "an interview and photographs and that sort of thing" but welcomed Breit to quote from or use parts of this letter if he so wished. Breit took the bait. The article, "Poets with Hands," with Williams and Stevens as the examples, appeared in December 1942. Stevens's last letter to Breit, acknowledging the editor's decision to follow what the poet had written in his previous letter, cited an article about Spinoza: "Indeed when Spinoza's great logic went searching for God it found Him in a predicate of substance." Stevens commented that this same desire to understand the "predicate of substance" was his pursuit and "that lawyers very often make use of their particular faculties to satisfy their particular desires" (*L* 415–16).

It was appropriate, in terms of Stevens's desire to secularize poetry—to make it part of the vulgate of experience—that in spite of his initial hesitation, a piece like Breit's came out in a magazine like *Harper's Bazaar.* Though there is no mention of his reaction to its appearance in the letters that remain, one may assume that he was pleased both because Breit observed the spirit of his law and because through such a mass medium Stevens was, in some ways, reaching a broader audience. (The article included his "God Is Good. It Is a Beautiful Night" [*CP* 285].) At least since the time of Stanley Burnshaw's review of *Ideas of Order* in *New Masses,* which, if for no other reason, pleased Stevens because it put him in the middle of a central public issue, he had long been preparing to be a voice in the arena. This wish had become sharpened to the purpose behind his address to the "Soldier" on the cover of *Notes* by his careful reading, through the late thirties and into the forties, of everything he could get his hands on of the French philosopher known as Alain.

Stevens's book orders to Anatole Vidal before the war had followed each of Alain's volumes. One of the first communications he had with Paule Vidal, Anatole's daughter who took over the business after her father's death in the last months of the war, concerned a late volume of Alain's that had been sent to the binder's (Aussourd) by Vidal just before it became impossible to get parcels from France to America. Stevens finally received it in 1946. The poet had each of this philosopher's volumes bound not simply expediently but with melodiously colored calf and morocco leathers and the expense was not considerably less than that which he laid out for his own volumes. Stevens did not do this for all the books he acquired from the Vidals, though he had certain volumes of Stendhal so bound, but not those of Flaubert, for example.[11]

From this information a speculation can be made. Perhaps Stevens wanted to leave behind a library of things he thought should comprise the core of reading for an American interested, as much as he, in how to live, what to do. It was not necessary to bind for posterity things that were already parts of the canon. But how many had heard—or still, today, have heard—of Alain? Unfortunately Stevens's library was sold off without, in some instances, a record's being kept of individual titles. Though it is possible to reconstruct from the orders to the Vidals and connected bills paid to Aussourd many of the works that the poet might have intended for a library greater than his own, much has been lost.

But to get back to Alain and what Stevens learned from or, better, perhaps, shared with him:

Alain was the pen name of Émile Auguste Chartier, born in Normandy in 1868, son of a veterinarian and grandson of a farmer. His husbandman's roots were not all he had in common with Stevens, though unlike the poet, Chartier followed only his natural proclivities for the "impractical" in the university, taking a degree in philosophy, which he completed in 1892. He taught for a year in Pontivy, then went on to Lorient, where he spent the next seven years in intense political and intellectual activity. "He joined the Socialist movement, took part in electoral campaigns and ran for office himself. He also collaborated in the founding of a radical newspaper and of a free night university for workmen."[12] During the same period he also began his curious serious work, writing philosophical essays in a journalistic mode. His first pen name then was Criton.

In 1900 he moved on to Rouen and a teaching position; he continued his active support of the left in his newspaper writing and in public speeches. In 1913 he went to Paris, where he remained, with a wartime interruption, until 1917, when he bought a small house in a village near the capital. From then on he divided his time between his home and Brittany, where he spent the summers. Shortly after his arrival in Paris, where he taught at various institutions, he, together with others, founded the *Dépêche de Rouen,* another radical newspaper, in which he published, first weekly, then daily, and later as monthly collections, his *propos*—his "conversations," "talks"—on subjects ranging from "Irritation" to "A Hymn to Milk" (a title that must have tickled Stevens with his bent for unexpected, intriguing titles) to "The Smile" to "Happy Farmers," all treated with the same precise, philosophical manner as the more explicitly titled "Aristotle," "Plato as Doctor," and "On Passions." Between 1903 and 1936 he wrote more than 5,000 such brief essays (an average of one every two and a half days), for which he set himself unusually stringent formal constraints:

> . . . to fill two pages, at one sitting, with no revisions . . . not erase a sentence once it was put down, [to] make . . . thought follow . . . words. In a note written in 1908, he compared the *propos* to the *stretto* in a fugue, the abbreviated repetition of the subjects, which came together "as if they were passing through a ring, the material crowds in, and it has to line up, and pass through, and be quick. That is my acrobatic stunt, as well as I can describe it; I have succeeded perhaps one time in six, which is a lot . . ." In the same note, he [wrote], "It is not the desire for fame that makes me write, but rather a lively political passion. . . ."[13]

The products of his effort are models of concision and concentration, in which images and thoughts follow one another with intricacy, but an intricacy that can be appreciated only by one's paying close attention to the same kind of elliptical associations that Stevens mastered so well in his own carefully reasoned poetic style. It was with the knowledge of his parallel purpose that Stevens, too, saw himself as a juggler, a jongleur, an acrobat of words. It is uncertain how Stevens first came to Alain, but it was probably through a reference to his work in one of the many French weeklies he had avidly devoured from the time he was a young man. What is certain is that when he did find this magician of thought, he followed and delighted in his conjurings and through him learned how best to shape some of the attitudes he took on during the thirties that became fixed forms by the end of his life.

Alain, too, was an iconoclast, as subtle as Stevens, though less covert. His socialism was not a historical one like Marx's but, "as he would have said, physiological."[14] He believed change had to occur in "individuals," not only in "classes," and, through his writing, devoted himself to elaborating the kinds of perceptions that, once read, could not leave a reader spiritually unaltered. His address was direct, even when he dealt with the most complex ideas. One of his major preoccupations was the atrocity of war. Though he enlisted at forty-six as a private in the heavy artillery, he continued to voice opposition to any policy of war. After the publication in 1915 of his *Twenty-one Propos for the Use of Non-Combatants,* which was issued without the approval of the censors, he was forced to keep silent until the war's end. The attitude Stevens began voicing in the thirties Alain had begun phrasing twenty years earlier: ". . . people who are constantly at war, whose peacetime life is also a kind of war, will lose the art of storytelling [on which, he believed, culture fully depended] and will find themselves speaking a language of migratory ciphers."[15] After the war Alain was unable to renew the relationship he had had with the *Dépêche de Rouen* from 1903 to 1914. Consequently, another periodical was founded: *Libres Propos,* in which Alain's pieces appeared, together with others by younger writers like Simone Weil and Jean Prévost, who were once his students. (It was probably through this connection that Stevens later came to read and admire the work of Simone Weil.)

Beyond the commitment to the left and to peace, Stevens shared with Alain an uncanny similarity of images with which to express the nature of imagination, that all-important function. In his introduction to *The Gods*—which Stevens could not have come to before 1934, when it was first published in France—Alain used metaphors in his opening two paragraphs that the poet had begun using as central images in some of the major poems of *Harmonium:*

> A man who takes philosophy in the right way, that is, for his own salvation, once described to me his experience of a vision, which, he said, had shown him the possible truth in what he had always thought of as a long series of errors. One day he was riding on a train, letting his eyes wander over a hilly landscape, when he saw a monster with a huge head, powerful wings, and several pairs of legs, climbing up one of the hills toward a village; a terrifying sight. It was only a fly on the window. This short moment of error and belief delighted him. The truth, he said, deceives us about ourselves; error is far more instructive. To his mind all the visions in history could be explained by this simple example, and by the luck of having surprised consciousness in its most primitive state. That was a hasty conclusion. On the contrary, I plan to move very slowly into this formidable subject. But since the method I intend to follow is rarely used, it will not be wrong of me to anticipate somewhat and present to the reader, at first in abstract form, the guiding idea of the present study.
>
> Our knowledge of things often comes to us through a pane of glass; and the fly is not really necessary. With the slightest movement, the irregularities of the glass roll across our view like waves, rippling and twisting the images; from which I draw this first warning: that we always see through something like a pane of glass, and the glass is in motion. But setting aside this important idea, which reveals the truth of so many well-known distortions, for example the stick that seems broken in a glass of water, what I want to look for here is the imagination; by here I mean in the pane of glass that distorts one thing and another as I move; and I find that the imagination is precisely that movement. I understand then that I not only see all things as if through another pane of glass, which is myself, but that, moreover, the various movements I make, be it intentionally, if I act, or emotionally, if I am afraid, or simply through the continual transports of respiration and circulation which sustain life, never cease to distort what I see, what I hear, what I taste, what I smell, what I touch. I might think that this time I have got hold of error properly speaking; and at bottom it is because of the uncontrollable impulses within him that a madman no longer knows where he is, or what he sees, or what he is doing. It is clear that we are all a bit mad in this sense, and that wisdom consists in eliminating as much as one can that portion of oneself in what one knows. That this can be achieved, the various sciences show; but it cannot be achieved without difficulty, which makes us understand that order we are forced to follow from the abstract to the concrete, selecting out of the mass of our continual astonishment, first numbers and distances, then types of motion, then the

> effects of shock and encounter, then the intimate combinations which are called chemical; which leads us, by an arduous path, to some understanding of the movements of life and brings us finally face to face with our own passions; demonstrating that the cause of our errors was at first eliminated only provisionally, and that the disturbances of the knowing subject must finally take their place among positive truths. We know enough about this process to affirm that everything would be true, even a madman's extravagances, if we could know everything.[16]

Stevens's eleventh way of looking at a blackbird was the following:

> He rode over Connecticut
> In a glass coach.
> Once, a fear pierced him,
> In that he mistook
> The shadow of his equipage
> For blackbirds.
> (*CP* 94)

The poet also realized that the "blackbirds" were not really necessary. "Le Monocle de Mon Oncle" explored all aspects of how the world seemed when seen through the glass of imagination and how one had to make a "new mind"—with distortions eliminated—before coming again to know that the "disturbances of the knowing subject must finally take their place among positive truths." This was Stevens's "more than rational distortion," as expressed later in "Notes" (when he could have been recalling Alain's words): knowing "that the irrational is rational" (*CP* 406).

Curiously, in the next paragraph of his Introduction, Alain went on to entertain the same "pluralistic hypothesis" that William James had suspended in America's turn-of-the-century air and that tantalized Stevens all his life:

> Spinoza says that there is nothing positive in error, which means that in God man's imagination is entirely true. I doubt my own ability to form, in the style of this abstruse master, an intuition of that wisdom of the prophets and soothsayers that should be one with the meditation of the sage. Nevertheless this great idea cannot be avoided, even if, to my mind, it is wise to delay its arrival; which means that we promise a doctrine according to which all religions are true, and at the same time we put it off as long as we can. If I could think of the gods in god and as god, all gods would be true; but it is the human condition to question one god after another, one appearance after another, or better, one apparition after another, always pursuing the truth of the imagination, which is not the same as the truth of appearance. I perceive the stick in the water as broken, but I certainly do not try to straighten it; on the contrary, I measure the distortion, I draw knowledge from it about the properties of water and light. The rainbow is likewise a vision only for

> someone who does not understand, here as in other cases, the refraction of colors. These illusions are not denied but confirmed.[17]

The spiritual ties between Stevens and Alain were strong. Alain, in true Socratic fashion, though he loved teaching, calling it his métier, disliked "professors as a type." Like Stevens, who early mocked "Rationalists, wearing square hats" (*CP* 75), and later ironically noted that "They {would} get it straight one day at the Sorbonne" (*CP* 406), Alain often satirized the *docteurs* and *Sorbonnagres,* "who give themselves titles and an air of majesty simply because they know a few languages and can recite tables of contents," whose "pretended discussions consist in an exchange of compliments."[18] Was Stevens's discomfort among the academics at the Churches' in Princeton that May 1941 perhaps another result of rubbing against Alain? If so, luckily, through coming to know Allen Tate and other men of similar spirit inside the Church circle and others outside, like Richard Eberhart and Samuel French Morse, the poet was reminded of the best people in the American educational system, some of whom he had known, too, at Harvard.

So as Alain stressed the importance of a public posture in making sure, through his journalistic *propos,* that his perceptions would reach a broad audience, Stevens appeared as a new model for the twentieth-century poet in *Harper's Bazaar.* Yet another instance that fall of 1942 that showed he was pleased about this kind of involvement came in the form of an invitation to visit him at home which he extended to Frank Jones, who reviewed *Parts of a World* for the *Nation.* (The review appeared in the November 7, 1942, issue.) In Hartford one day Jones took the chance of phoning the poet, who spontaneously asked him to stop over. Either Elsie was in a particularly friendly state of mind, or Stevens took the risk that he could explain any insult she might express to this Yale classics instructor. As it was, Jones seemed to catch only a passing glimpse of her. It worked out well. Stevens reported to Henry Church that Jones came "to the house and {they} had a good time, never mentioning the book" (*L* 415).

From his recollection of the visit[19] this seems to have been one of the days when Stevens's life arranged itself into a poem into which the younger man easily fitted. Light streamed in as the two sat in the downstairs sun-room on chairs covered with printed flowers surrounded by plants and fresh-cut blooms. The poet seemed "cherubic," Jones noted, even in his country-squirish tweed jacket. They flitted from one subject to another in a manner that seemed very "English" to Jones, without ever touching on the book or the review, as he corroborated. The poet was both ironic—describing himself as a poor letter writer—and revealing. He spoke touchingly about how he hated witnessing the quick deaths of new little magazines in a time when the only decent thing, to him, was the *Partisan Review,* which, he added, he *always* read, as he did the "English *Nation*" (*New Statesman and . . .*). He also noted that he kept up with new poetry, often making suggestions to the poets who sent him their work, but too often, he felt, to their egotistic consternation. His smile broke into one of his deep chuckles. He showed Jones his beautifully bound copies of his own volumes, remarking how much he liked the "dithering" quality of the silver-striped endleaves of *The Man with the Blue Guitar;* they mimicked his musician's imagined strings in their trembling movement. He tenderly observed, too, apropos of Anatole Vidal, who had sent so many other things to be bound for him, that he had wanted so much to know what the man looked like that he had had a portrait of him commissioned. His imaginings always needed their factual anchorages. He beamed on his collection of bindings, adding that he often ordered things because they had certain bindings (an eighteenth-century sample was a special prize) not because he read or wanted to read the volumes. Jones left Westerly Terrace with a wonderful impression of Stevens and of his "very good-looking daughter," two of whose photographs he had noticed. Things were going well for the poet and man of letters.

But while success in the public domain continued, the situation concerning Holly did not improve. Early in October Stevens wrote his sister Elizabeth in regard to her daughter Jane's marriage. He thought this a good thing, he noted, if the young man was of fine character, in spite of the fact that he would be leaving shortly after the wedding to serve in the armed forces overseas. He added that Holly, unlike Jane, did not care at all about the family and seemed to be drifting away even from Elsie. He quietly suggested that she had already drifted away from him, for he had heard of Jane's impending nuptials from Elsie, who had heard it from Holly, who was in contact with Jane. (In spite of hearing of Jane's plans indirectly, when the time came a few months later, Stevens sent his sister money to buy Jane's gown. He was not losing a daughter; he was gaining a niece who would act as another.)

To ease the pain his daughter's coolness caused him, Stevens recalled that he, too, had not been concerned at her age with the family (*L* 421). He was doing his utmost to maintain his sense that things as they were—no matter what might obtain in the world around him—were as they should be. Reaffirming this, he noted in another letter to Elizabeth a few days later that in spite of being spoken of "as though [he] might well be an old man" by one of their family acquaintances, he did not feel "a day older than [he] was when [he] left Reading" (October 6, 1942).

The next day he wrote Holly the letter in which he extolled her mother's "perfections." He added an explanation of the qualities that perhaps prevented Holly from seeing his own; it echoed one of the early explanations he had given to Elsie of the peculiarities of his character: "My own stubbornnesses and taciturn eras are straight out of Holland and I cannot change any more than I can take off my skin. But I never hesitate to seek to undo any damage I may have done . . . (*L* 422). The occasion of this letter, it seems (from another he wrote on October 23 [*L* 423–24] to Ruth Wheeler, who was a member of the Vassar faculty and had been director of the Institute of Euthenics, which Holly and Elsie had attended in the summer of 1931), had been a visit home that Holly made on October 4 or 5, during which she announced that she wanted to leave school or at least to take off the balance of the school year. Stevens expressed to Wheeler that this came as "a great shock" to both him and Elsie but to him in particular. He noted that in spite of his explaining to Holly that he did not care what subjects she studied and that "the essential consideration was that she was at least using her mind," she preferred to do anything else but continue. She wanted to "get a job as a copy boy on one of the local newspapers." Stevens persuaded Holly to return to Vassar, "against her will," he imagined, since she left "saying that when she came home at Christmas she would want to discuss it again" (*L* 424).

Though he stated that Holly's unhappiness at Vassar had come as "a great shock," this could not have been entirely true. From the evidence of a letter that Holly sent to him on September 30, it is clear that the friction between her and her parents was already in the open. She began the letter with a birthday wish—in a cynical tone not uncommon to rebellious adolescents:

> Dear Dad,
>
> Best wishes and all that sort of stuff on your natal day. Enjoy yourself.

She thanked him for the "little bit more" he had sent for her expenses and went on to detail the kinds of incidents that had occurred while she had been at home that had made her feel she was still a child rather than the adult that "thirty-six of the forty-eight states" recognized her to be, though Connecticut was not one of them. She pointed out that she was not arguing with her father now but that the next time he "outrageously" said, "Don't argue with me," she certainly would. She added that if he showed this letter to Elsie and an argument ensued, she would not want to hear from either of them on the subject for several weeks, but that if they could discuss it "with calmness and understanding," she looked forward to hearing both their "sides of the story" soon. She closed with sentences reasoned as elegantly and jesuitically as any her father constructed, thus proving herself a worthy daughter and opponent:

> This letter, in a nutshell, demands independence and freedom from criticism, but with a more understanding attitude on your parts my independence will not be so demanding, and I will become the critic of my own freedom. For as yet I have not felt freedom in being with either of you, and my independence has had to be formed elsewhere. For the liberty I seek is not a freedom from things and people—but independence with people and things.

Stevens could not but have been moved by the eloquence with which Holly voiced her need. In some part of himself he had to have recognized the true maturity and legitimacy of her complaint. An undated postcard, penned sometime after in October, may have been his response:

HOLLY:
I am sorry,

Love,
WALLACE
(WAS 2251)

In signing himself with his name rather than as "Dad," he implicitly acknowledged her as his equal. Yet after her visit home a few days after her letter, he could not restrain himself from writing his letter to Ruth Wheeler on October 23, explaining the situation, describing Holly like "all other children" who "hated to go to school," and asking that she attempt to persuade Holly to remain at Vassar without letting on that he had written to her. He commented to Wheeler that he had told Holly he would write to her directly to describe in more detail and calm than he had been able to while she was at home why he felt her education was important. But, he added, he realized that this would be "a very inadequate way of handling the situation" (*L* 424). Holly had shed both her baby fat and her docile manner, and her father did not quite know how to handle his truly "good-looking" young woman.

Nonetheless, within three days he did write to Holly, enclosing a check for her allowance and for an extra typing course she had enrolled in to prepare herself for the job market. In his letter the urgent voicing that she continue with her studies was as sincere and direct as his detailing of the reasons for his feeling:

> Please don't allow yourself to come to a final decision about college and I *beg* you not to do this. It is difficult for me to write. But you cannot possibly know what you are doing, without any experience of life, however sure you may be otherwise. The uncertainty you feel should be dismissed from your mind . . . confronted by himself and by the enormous complication of the world; and, if this is so in ordinary times, it is all the more so in the very centre of the huge struggle for survival that is now going on. But you don't find yourself or your way through life by getting a job, except for a very brief period of time. I think you may have been influenced by the friends you have here, even unconsciously. We have not tried to influence you respecting your friends. But take my word for it that making your living is a waste of time. None of the great things in life have anything to do with making your living; and I had hoped that little by little, without being able to say how, you would find the true field for your intelligence and imagination in something that was at least a part of one of the great things of life. Study at college, a period of leisure and study and reflection at a sensitive period, is the readiest instrument by which to find yourself and your work. Perhaps your fundamental difficulty is that you have never formed the habit of hard study, a habit which soon becomes a source of unfailing happiness. The station of most of your friends will never change. They will get chance jobs, without plans and without ambition, and will hold onto them and go on merely holding on to them.

> Hold on where you are above everything else. Learn to live the good in your heart, although you may never speak of it, and devote your life to it. The very agitation around you, the social and political agitation, acquires all its force, all its sanction, from one thing only and that is the love of good. To turn your back on that and simply get a job, when it is so unnecessary, is simply crawling into a hole and hiding. How can you lead without courage?
>
> With love,
>
> DAD
>
> (*L* 425–26)

Holly could not have known it, but her father was expressing his strongest wish for her real freedom. Moreover, he was doing it by countering the very advice his own father had given him, though he, too, expected his child "to lead" and "with courage." Rather than persuade her to prepare herself for something practical, he wanted her to ignore "anything to do with making [a] living." While it could be argued that his counsel might have been entirely different and that he would have echoed Garrett, Sr., had Holly been a male, I would suggest that at this point in his life this would not have made a difference to Stevens. In spite of his repeated voicings to various individuals that he fully enjoyed his work as a lawyer and that he would not have had the shape of his life be otherwise, it was also true that he looked forward to a time when to be a poet or any kind of artist would carry adequate social sanction and reward. In this light, it is not unreasonable to propose that the library that he was building and the hopes he had for the future poet were quietly intertwined with his wishes for his daughter as he urged her to pursue habits that would become "a source of unfailing happiness" in a life circling "the love of good."

In the troubled days between Holly's visit home and his letters to her and Wheeler, the poet continued his own work for the greatest good. Even though he had not been able to write poetry at all during this summer of 1942 because of the emotional disturbance the situation with Holly caused, he acted as a kind of midwife for others whom he believed to be as committed as he. To Anaïs Nin, who wrote offering to print one of his volumes, he responded that this was not necessary but that he would lend her a hand without this. To Robert Frost, who, in spite of Elsie's insult years before, did see both of them again—they all had lunch in Hartford's Blue Plate Tea Room—he sent a copy of the newly printed *Notes Toward a Supreme Fiction* and extended an invitation that he visit them again in Hartford in "spring, summer or autumn, but not winter. We can only show you seed catalogues in winter," he humorously added before closing with a wish that compensated for the horror of the political situation: "How nice it would be to sit in the garden and imagine that we were living in a world in which everything was as it ought to be" (*L* 422–23). To John Crowe Ransom and Allen Tate, who wrote asking for contributions to their respective journals, Stevens promised poems as soon as he could get around to them; he added to Tate that he was sending a copy of *Notes*. To

Henry Church, who had already received and read *Notes* by the end of October, the poet sent the beginnings of his explications of certain images and figures about which his friend had queried him (*L* 426–27).

By November Stevens had visited Holly in Poughkeepsie and she had absolutely refused to remain in college. He said to Church in a letter of that date that the situation was interfering with his social commitments and further postponing his ability to concentrate on writing more poetry. As he put it, maintaining his humor even now, his concern with Holly involved "a good many adjustments that [could] be made more easily with [his] nose in his navel than in the Persian Room," where he was to have met Church the following Saturday (*L* 427). But illustrating his stalwartness in focusing on the *summum bonum* under the greatest of pressures, he concentrated on what he could. Again, he stressed the importance of the poetry chair and continued in his elucidation of *Notes* by clarifying for Church that his intention had not been at all mystical, in spite of an advertisement for the volume in a journal he had just received (*Chimera* [winter 1943], published at Princeton) which compared the eccentricities of its author to those of Giotto, Duns Scotus, and St. Augustine. The young man who would have given "a great deal to be like St. Augustine" had grown to realize that what was necessary for his time was to describe a "City of Man" rather than a "City of God" and that for this the mystical had to be eliminated.

Maintaining his stiff upper lip in the face of his personal adversities, a few days later Stevens wrote to Lila James Roney, his chief genealogist of the time, with the same kind of humor he exhibited in his aside to Church about the Persian Room. She was hot on the scent of the first of the Stevens line in America (*L* 429). Within another few days he was in New York boosting his spirits with a visit to the Wildenstein Gallery to see a Corot exhibit. It pleased him thoroughly; on his return he wrote immediately to Church and recommended it. Five days later encouragement came in a different form. Allen Tate wrote to praise "Notes" as the best thing Stevens had done since *Harmonium;* he especially liked the sections about the "blue woman" and "General Du Puy." He also observed something that must have delighted Stevens with his secret wish to be the Dante of his time: "What would a series of poems by Stevens accomplish if they were written in strict terza rima?" (November 23, 1942).

But by December 8 there were also discouragements for Stevens beyond those of the family circle. Most of the reviews of *Parts of a World* had already appeared, the last in the *New York Times Book Review* of Sunday, November 29, following that in the *New York Herald Tribune* of November 8 by Ruth Lechlitner, who years earlier had not done justice to *Ideas of Order.* In spite of Hi Simons's review in November's *Poetry,* which was sensitive to the poet's purpose, Stevens voiced an overall complaint to Henry Church that in none of the reviews of *Parts of a World* "was there even so much as a suggestion that the book gave the man [he did not mention the woman] who read it any pleasure" (*L* 430). Because of this, he was particularly gratified that Jean

Wahl, the French philosopher and friend of Church's for whom Stevens had helped find at least a temporary position in America, had derived pleasure from "Notes." He commented: "I am most *content,* in the French sense of the word, to have pleased Jean Wahl." Stevens went on in the same letter to reveal to Church something about the process of composing "Notes" and observed that Wahl had correctly intuited that he had attempted at first to follow a scheme. He also expanded on how much this poem had to do with the "will to believe":

> There are things with respect to which we willingly suspend disbelief; if there is instinctive in us a will to believe, or if there is a will to believe, whether or not it is instinctive, it seems to me that we can suspend disbelief with reference to a fiction as easily as we can suspend it with reference to anything else. There are fictions that are extensions of reality. There are plenty of people who believe in Heaven as definitely as your New England ancestors and my Dutch ancestors believed in it. But Heaven is an extension of reality.
>
> I have no idea of the form that a supreme fiction would take. The *Notes* start out with the idea that it would not take any form: that it would be abstract. Of course, in the long run poetry would be the supreme fiction; the essence of poetry is change and the essence of change is that it gives pleasure. (*L* 430)

He also described how the notion of the "supreme fiction" had recently obsessed him, observing that because of his taste for the better things in life, he had to interrupt his obsession with his work at the office:

> I have a genealogist in New York working on my family of Dutch farmers. This morning I received a letter from her written in a state of great excitement because she had just made another discovery. It is the same thing with an idea like the idea of the supreme fiction. When I get up at 6 o'clock in the morning (a time at which you are just closing your novel, pulling the chain on the lamp at your bedside) the thing crawls all over me; it is in my hair when I shave and I think of it in the bathtub. Then I come down here to the office and, except for an occasional letter like this, have to put it to one side. After all, I like Rhine wine, blue grapes, good cheese, endive and lots of books, etc., etc., etc., as much as I like supreme fiction. (*L* 431)

In closing his letter, he mentioned that he was still pursuing an edition of Nietzsche, following up on Church's preoccupation, even though he thought the German philosopher's mind one that distorted the world a bit too much. But, he added, "Of course, the answer to all this is that it is either his kind of a mind or pretty much none." About an article he had just read in the *Gazette des Beaux Arts* by Lionello Venturi on "The Idea of the Renaissance," he concluded to Church that the author's position in the end was "one more proof that the [political] right always comes to nothing" (*L* 432).

The coming of the new year did not bring relief. As Stevens reported on January 4 to Louise Seaman Bechtel, wife of his old friend Ned Bechtel, who soon would become the lawyer for Church's will, through Stevens's recommendation, he was still disturbed about Holly. After her return home in mid-November, she had gotten a job as a clerk with the Aetna Life Insurance Company, probably through her father's connections (she had been all set to go to work in a factory). He had arranged with the dean at Vassar that Holly could go back in the autumn. For the present he had no hope since her mind was made up. Moreover, he reiterated his disappointment about the reception of *Parts of a World.* Only Hi Simons's review, he noted to Mrs. Bechtel, had done anything to help get the book "accepted." He added: "By being accepted, I mean the sort of thing that is meant when you ask for a book by so-and-so. That this element is lacking in my own case is demonstrated by the fact that no one seems to enjoy the poems." He chidingly included her in this category and stressed that he had intended the opposite of what she had perceived: "Apparently you feel that I am satirical, but I am not. No one could be more sincere than I am about poetry" (*L* 433).

To relieve his burden somewhat, Stevens wrote to Simons about a week later (*L* 433–36). In his letter he offered himself and his explications of "Notes" generously to this critic, who had become his comfort. Amid the detailed descriptions of sources and associations to images and sections, the poet stated his intention clearly: He was "trying to create something as valid as the idea of God has been." He gently explained to Simons whatever might seem elliptical in this long elucidation: ". . . as soon as I start to rationalize I lose the poetry of the idea." But he also offered a rationalization of why the other reviewers had missed his point: ". . . people can't stop to put one man under the microscope." The metaphor he had once used in explaining himself to Elsie in the early years of their relationship—"I don't believe in holding the microscope up to myself . . ."—now turned and bit its own tail, his own tail. A few years later, in 1946, the same metaphor reappeared, almost as a hidden wish that he had so examined himself, as suggested by "one of the greatest figures in the world": "Freud's eye was the microscope of potency" (*CP* 368). Stevens's tensive relationship to himself, which had kept him ever wary of "indulging personality," was revealing itself.

On January 25, following up on his commitment to do whatever he could to foster the pure good of poetry, even if it was not his own, Stevens wrote to Henry Church that he was going to do an introduction (reprinted in *OP* 266–68) to a volume of poems by Samuel French Morse, *Time of Year,* to be published by the Cummington Press. He expressed to Church the belief that "This young poet [wrote] very awkwardly" but that he found, nonetheless, especially in one poem he described, "a rectitude about him that [made] his book precious . . ." (*L* 437). Keeping to the letter of his law, in the Introduction itself, Stevens voiced precisely the same sentiments. Because it was he who was providing the Introduction or because of an artificial position that an introduction should unqualifiedly praise volume and author, he did not dissemble. Instead, he sensitively explained the reasons why a first volume might seem "obstinate" to readers and revealed that he himself had understood Alain's perceptions about the particularity of each individual's imagination. In terms of how he used material he had just read, he cited a perception of Mr. Venturi's about Cézanne in the article from the *Gazette des Beaux Arts* that he had recently mentioned in his letter to Church. In a similar yet closer vein, he noted in his Introduction the same poem he had described to Church as having specially moved him and used the same word, "rectitude," to set the stage for readers' responses to Morse's value. One cannot help remarking at the fidelity of Stevens's informal to his formal statements. The man and the poet had become one.

In a note to Morse the following day (*L* 437) Stevens again used "rectitude" to express his feeling about the poems. But tenderly sensing the uncertainties of a poet who had just completed his first volume, he did not, in this case, voice any of his hesitations. Rather, he acknowledged an identification with those who, like himself, used iambics: "I feel . . . that the insistent use of iambics must be deliberate, as a contribution to the New England effect. . . ." And exercising his more experienced professional judgment, though it would mean that he would not be openly credited with being the inspiration he obviously was to the younger poet, Stevens advised the following: "The poem that you have inscribed to me is one of the best in the group, and I shall be happy to allow the inscription to stand. However, I don't think that it would do both for me to introduce the book and to have this inscription. Perhaps it would be better to sacrifice the inscription, which might involve a change of title . . ." (*L* 437).

Besides the satisfaction that Morse's intended inscription to him offered, there were other small pleasures that very cold winter. Wilson Taylor sent yet another crate of oranges from Florida. Stevens, as usual, was humorously appreciative. He also shared with this younger associate more news about "His Eminence," the archbishop of the Greek Orthodox Archdiocese of North and South America who seems to have been involved in rather Byzantine machinations over a bit of real estate on New York's fashionable Upper East Side. Stevens verbally chuckled as he composed his note, in spite of his spiritual disappointments around reviews, being "accepted," and his daughter.

As though sensing in himself, too, finally, that the man and the poet were one, Stevens began a letter to Hi Simons on January 28 in a form that evoked the opening of a poem he had written in 1923 ("Two Figures in Dense Violet Night" [*CP* 85]): "*I had as lief* [italics mine] answer letters at once as put off doing so . . . (*L* 438). He went on to provide more details explaining the complexities of Section II of "Notes"—"It Must Change"—making it very clear that at least part of the inspiration of the poem had come directly from his experience of change in his garden at home (*L* 438).[20]

In addition to the bitter climate of that winter, on February 19, 1943,

Stevens was wired by his niece Jane that her mother, the last of his siblings, was critically ill. Later that day Jane called to say that her mother had died, succumbing to encephalitis. Stevens went to Philadelphia immediately to be with Jane and to take care of the necessary arrangements for the funeral and cremation. (Jane's parents had been divorced when she was a child; she did not have contact with her father, who, in any case, had already died.) On the day of the funeral Stevens took the next steps in informally adopting Jane, guiding her out to take a long walk around the crisply sunlit City of Brotherly Love, where he had promenaded Elsie on the Memorial Day weekend three and a half months before their marriage. He turned his niece's eyes to look at what was still bristling with life in the face of death. That weekend long ago he had made a point of buying Elsie sweets and candies, and now he walked Jane past one of his favorite bakeries. Unfortunately it was closed, but he saw a whiskey cake in the window. Making sure she would have something life-affirming to do the next day when he would be gone, he directed her to go back to the shop and have one of the cakes sent to him. When he left, he reassured her, "Now you're not alone. You've got me." The niece he had responded to immediately at his brother's funeral two and a half years before as a real Stevens woman had won a place in his heart.[21]

Four days later, after sending the cake, Jane wrote, thanking her uncle profusely for his emotional support and his generosity in covering all the expenses. On the day following Jane's appreciative note, Stevens received from his sister-in-law Sarah (Garrett Jr.'s widow, still in Cleveland; she had not attended the funeral) news that she had heard from their nephew John, who has also been at the funeral, that Jane had said her mother appeared peaceful in death: ". . . it looked as if she might open her eyes any minute" (February 24, 1943). The poet must have thought of his mother, "sleeplessly waiting."

By the beginning of March there was still no sign of spring—either externally or internally. In this weather, as the poet wrote to Henry Church, even New York, where he had been on business last Saturday, seemed dull (*L* 411). On the brighter side, Stevens was pleased that Allen Tate, "as sincerely interested as it is possible for a man to be," would be giving the lectures on "The Language of Poetry" later in spring, and more immediately the poet looked forward to meeting Church again in New York on March 18. Anticipating new buds of thought, Stevens noted that he intended to apply himself to reading particularly attentively. He stated in his March 8 letter to Church:

> This last weekend I had meant to read with more care the last number of *The Partisan Review,* which I have gone through once, but without quite making everything in it my own. There is an article by John Dewey on Philosophic Naturalism which strikes me as being valuable. The article that precedes it, by Sidney Hook, ought to be good, but somehow isn't, or so it seems to me. He tries to deal with too much, without first having reduced many thoughts to one or two. Then I have a number of things by Harold Laski that I should really like to get at. Laski is important without seeming to be so. The truth

> is that he reads like a casual commentator: he is the last man in the world to be described as casual and as a commentator. If there is any man who has in his head a complete synthesis of what is going on, it is Laski. (*L* 441)[22]

But instead of reimmersing himself in others' words, he found himself contemplating the snow still covering his native landscape. Poems seemed to be about to show their heads. The dry season was over.

Properly heralding renewal, Stevens took Elsie with him to New York that Saturday, March 18, to buy a new spring hat. They met Church at the Plaza Hotel at twelve-fifteen and had a superb lunch. If Elsie, for any reason, did not express her enthusiasm about the excursion, Jane—to whom Stevens wrote a few days earlier offering to pay her moving expenses and noting that he and Elsie were to be in New York, where she would look for a bonnet—did. In a reply thanking him once more for his generosity, she added: "Did Aunt Elsie get her spring hat? What few go to New York for a new hat! Of course, I realize that this was not what you went for, but it was probably a very important part of the trip!" (March 21, 1943).

On the first day of spring Stevens sent Gilbert Montague, his classmate at Harvard and friend of long standing, a letter in which he made explicit, for him, too, the intention behind "Notes" (*L* 443). He sent this letter along with another short note indicating that he was enclosing the other so that Montague could lay it in his own copy of *Notes* if he so desired. The poet seemed to assume that one who had also been preoccupied with the problem of the "will to believe" while they were in college would similarly share his delight in placing letters from authors in copies of their volumes. It was a touching consideration.

Five days later, still musing on his desire to produce in "Notes" an idea as valid as that of God had been, Stevens wrote to Hi Simons. He went deeper into making the meanings of his lines and allusions clear. Apropos of Section IV of "It Must Be Abstract," where he expanded on the notion that "we live in a place/ That is not our own" (*CP* 383), Stevens added: "It is not the individual alone that indulges himself in the pathetic fallacy. It is the race. God is the center of the pathetic fallacy" (*L* 444). He observed, too, that this understanding, as well as that of the abstract itself, was "accessible to poets," a special breed. His early feeling of not fitting in, not belonging, had been transformed into a secular version of being one of the elect.

The next day he received a letter from Jane concerning the setting of her mother's gravestone. Stevens responded that he could not make it to Reading on the date she proposed, April 24, and suggested May 2 instead. He also wanted to be sure that the transport used for the ceremony and the rest of the arrangements would be handled in a most "dignified way." The poet who as a younger man had conjured the everyday, almost tawdry details for the funeral of the woman with horny feet in "The Emperor of Ice-Cream" now, himself approaching old age, wanted proper pomp surrounding "death . . . the mother of beauty."

❧

Again, as though imitating the forms he created in his work, as he had done in middle age, when he consciously became the "comedian" he had projected as Crispin, Stevens now followed the central dictum of "Notes": that "It Must Change." Aside from the change in his attitude toward death, he went to work to change the nature of his social relations. On March 30 he made a point of inviting Henry Church to come stay at home with him and Elsie in Hartford. Although he explained that they were "not organized . . . for visitors" except those who lived "pretty much the same sort of lives that [he and Elsie] did," he wanted the Churches to visit them. He felt safe in extending hospitality in this way now because a recent letter from Church that he took home and read to Elsie made her "very happy."

He went on in the same letter to specify additional qualities for the poetry chair, distinguishing what he envisioned from what the Charles Eliot Norton Chair at Harvard had come to be: a host for miscellany. He couched his aspirations in an expression about the passionate seriousness of poetry: "The belief in poetry is a magnificent fury, or it is nothing. If it is a magnificent fury, it does not lead to an insipid miscellany" (*L* 446). He closed the letter stressing how nice it would be when they (the Churches, he, and Elsie) all could be together again.

Another change that the poet apparently enforced on himself was revealed nine days later in a letter to Jean Wahl. Apropos of the series of talks the philosopher proposed for the following summer at Mount Holyoke College, Les Entretiens de Pontigny,[23] Stevens voiced no hesitation about presenting a paper. Whatever reservations he had about showing himself, speaking in public, he conquered so as to be able to further the cause in which he believed. This cause was, as he described to Wahl, the "philosophy of poetry." In connecting this cause to the proposed poetry chair he wrote, "There is no point to a chair of poetry unless poetry is a permanent value" (*L* 447).

On April 16 Stevens wrote to Church that he had accepted the invitation for Les Entretiens de Pontigny. He observed that working on his paper and participating in the conference would give him "an opportunity to gather together [his] ideas about the status of poetry as something to teach . . . to study." After first having thought he would title his paper simply "Project for Poetry" and then changing to the more allusive "The Hovering Fly," the poet decided against both. The first was, perhaps, too dry. The second he "expelled [as] cynicism," adding, "There are few things that one loves intensely; the least one can do is to keep the flies off" (*L* 447). He settled finally on "The Figure of the Youth as Virile Poet." This intriguing title communicated all the poet had come to understand about the subtle intricacies of "Poetry and Manhood" that he had first attempted to unravel as an undergraduate when he followed the lines of the "man-poets" he had placed in his imaginary pantheon.

Perhaps the only constant during these days of change was the poet's continued preoccupation with his family history. The searches went on. His father's line had been completed, but there was still much to be learned about his mother's. Still, even in this study of what seemed to be hard facts, ideas became shimmerings. As the poet noted to Church on May 18 after spending the previous Saturday in the library in New York and feeling "a bit blue" because of the weather, "It is a hard job for me to form an acceptable realization of the past, and the more lithographs, maps and portraits I see, and the more old letters, etc. [*sic*] I read, the harder the job becomes" (*L* 448).

That a change in the weather at home had come about, too, was revealed in an exchange of letters between Church and Stevens around the long Memorial Day weekend. After noting to the poet that he was surprised that both Ransom and Tate found themselves "aghast" at his suggestion that they contribute portions of their salaries to the journals they each represented, Church expressed the hope that Stevens had fully enjoyed his "holiday" with the usual bottle of Rhine wine and cheese. Elsie seems to have relaxed her strictures. Church added that he thought the poet "moderate" since Goethe had been a "six-bottle a day drinker" (May 31, 1943). The flattering comparison of himself to the great German no doubt pleased Stevens. He picked up on the reference in his return letter to Church and gave him a little background on his relationship to Goethe and wine, referring indirectly to Livingood, the friend of his youth in Reading. He also detailed his "holiday":

> Yes, we had an unusually agreeable weekend. I read two or three things. What bores me purple is that after a holiday I have to go back to the office. When I come home after the office a book that seemed one thing when I had time seems something quite different read while waiting for dinner. There is too little time left to do anything. Later, last evening, in the course of two or three hours, I read Cézanne's letters, in which there is quite nothing at all except his sharp definitions, and the stubbornness of his will.
>
> And it is true too that we had lunch outdoors several times. I [had] two or three cheeses left and worked on them and feel like throwing away what is left because it is now time to switch to something better. And I had a very good bottle of Alsace white wine (don't pout), and a bottle of so-so claret.
>
> It is curious how you put Goethe and this sort of thing together. When I was about as old as you were when you went to Europe, the friend that I saw the most of was a fanatic on Goethe, and also on the country wine at home. He read the whole of Goethe's 60 volumes in the original, and after he had a bottle or so of what was simply called red wine Goethe really got somewhere. (*L* 451)

And concerning Church's shock about Ransom's and Tate's stinginess, Stevens commented that this was a very "common experience." He went on: "I used to know Amy Lowell very slightly. She was rich and, as a result, was a mark for panhandlers. The trouble with all this is that people never let go. Moreover, they don't realize that a man who is interested at all is likely to be interested in things of his own choice." He added that he himself did not think the *Kenyon Review* of "great value" and that there were other things he would rather help.[24] "It is a case of making one's own choice and resisting pressure."

Feeling intensely that there was "too little time left to do anything," as the date for the Pontigny conference drew near, Stevens found he had to stay away from the office for a few days to complete "The Figure of the Youth as Virile Poet." By June 28 he had finished, as he wrote to Church, but still did not know precisely when he was to deliver it. He was slightly irritated that the arrangements had not been made as carefully as he would have had them. Nonetheless, whatever the dates were to be, he repeated to Church that he expected him and Mrs. Church to return with him to Hartford after the conference and to stay overnight. He humorously promised that they would be able to see their "magnificent" Japanese beetles by then (*L* 452).

Yet another and very important change seemed to be going on in the Stevens home, one that prefigured the warm and rewarding relationship that eventually developed between the poet and his daughter. Though he had planned originally to travel to and from Mount Holyoke by train, at a certain point Holly decided to drive her father. Stevens might have hoped this meant that she would also want to attend the conference that held so much significance for him though he was probably also uneasy about having someone so close to him in the audience. Between the time of this pleasant change of plans and August 11, the date of the conference, Stevens clarified how he was to present his paper. The restatement of his position came about in relation to just having read Jacob Burckhardt (*Reflections on History,* tr. M.D.H. [London: Allen & Unwin, 1943]; at Amherst). As he noted on July 29 to Henry Church:

> When we talked about my paper, I said that this might be an occasion to provoke a discussion of poetry as an academic subject. I have scrapped that after seeing what Jacob Burckhardt (who was a friend of Nietzsche's at Basel) made of it. I was thinking of poetry in the sense of poetry, if I may say so, and not as an aspect of history, which is what Burckhardt made of it. Generally speaking, it is treated as a phase of literature, but that is not to be treated as, for instance, one treats painting when one is painting. (*L* 452–53)

Also within the same period, Stevens heard that Allen Tate had been appointed Librarian of Congress. He was delighted that this southern agrarian poet-critic who shared his newly articulated antiacademic stance had been so recognized. The choice "couldn't be better," he wrote in congratulating Tate, who had just sent Stevens the *Revista de Avance* in which his "Academic Discourse at Havana," an ironically antiacademic piece, had appeared in Spanish translation (July 6, 1943).

The date of Les Entretiens de Pontigny arrived, Stevens spent the night before in the Lord Jeffery Inn in nearby Amherst, a distinguished hotel serving excellent food. (Inasmuch as Stevens reserved only one single room, it seems that Holly did not stay to attend the conference.) Stevens's lecture was a tremendous success; John Peale Bishop reported to him a short time later that his talk was clearly the best. The poet himself was pleased. He had finally met Marianne Moore and found James Rorty, one of the other speakers, to be "agreeable" (*L* 457). But he did have criticisms of the other presenters: "I thought that the politicians in the afternoon were rather a nuisance and this includes even Professor Cohen, with his idea of a Republic of the Rhine" (August 25, 1943). There were other details about the conference that he thought could have been improved. As he related to Henry Church on August 27, he felt the tone for the Entretiens in the future could be better set by "soup jellies, artichokes, soufflés, etc." than by rye bread and lettuce. "There is nothing French about lettuce and rye bread. The mere language is not enough; obviously, people look to Paris for more than clothes" (*L* 453).

In the same letter to Church Stevens obliquely referred in his opening to how they had spent their time together during his and Mrs. Church's overnight stay:

> Item one Being, as I think of it, is not a science but merely eating duck, or doing some such thing. And I am not really a tyrant; after all, it took me till after one o'clock the night you were with us to get things straightened out, so that I still think that such things are impossible. It is precisely the care with which she does things that makes Mrs. Stevens unwilling to let anyone else do them for her. Of course, it has its advantages: vegetables appear on the table in their own vivid colors, etc., and moderately high living of that sort goes well with an effort to think plainly and is incomparably better than the old plain living and high thinking. (*L* 453)

"Item Two" had nothing more to do with the domestic scene but was a sharp remark intended, it seems, to make Church aware that the poet never said anything lightly: "I don't profess to be erudite. My whole point is that, if I refer to a book as if I had read it, I have in fact read it." Stevens seemed intent on his friend's having no misunderstandings of his character. Such straightforward assertions of personality were indications of the deeper changes that had developed in him over the last years.

A more personal reflection of this deliberate turnaround showed itself in a letter the poet wrote about a month later to his niece Jane (*L* 454–55). Apropos of a photo of his father that she had recently found and sent him, he voiced appreciation especially because unlike the one "the people in Reading" had, this one (reproduced in *L*) showed Garrett, Sr., in the way Stevens wanted to remember him. After revealing to Jane some of the details surrounding his father's breakdown, he noted: "Personally, I intend to forget all that because I think we have to take him as he wanted to be. . . . The photograph that you have sent me shows him at a time when he was looking forward to everything." Though, as the poet commented to Jane, his father, because of the difficulties of his personality which made his children afraid to approach him, had "lived alone," Stevens chose now to ignore, to forget all this. In a similar way he was choosing to forget the eccentricities of his own past behavior that had contributed to the various problems he experienced with Elsie and Holly. The important thing now was to change, and he was trying. If Erik Erikson was accurate in his mapping of the steps an individual takes in working through an identity, then Stevens, in his mid-sixties, was resolving the crisis of old age. Just as in mid-life he had "celebrate[d] the faith of forty" with a commitment to live from that point on as a comedian, so he was now reaffirming this decision and extending it to effect practical changes in the remaining days of his life. This seems to have meant setting aside completely the determinants of the past and engaging life as though he himself were "looking forward to everything."

This change was connected in Stevens's own mind with what the war portended, more specifically, with the United States' entry into it. It was as though this event had pulled a mental trigger meaning there was little time left. As he wrote to Nicholas Moore (son of G. E. Moore and editor of the English journal *New Poetry*) in mid-September 1943 in response to a request for a poem for an anthology he planned to publish, "The reason for all this activity last year [*Parts of a World* and *Notes Toward a Supreme Fiction*] was that I was afraid it would become difficult to publish anything after we really got under way in the war. Moreover, I felt that it was likely to be a good deal more long-drawn-out than people commonly expect, so I took time by the forelock" (September 18, 1943). He told Moore that he could take anything he liked from *Notes* because it was not published by Knopf and had no copyright restrictions, as did *Parts of a World.*

As Stevens became more conscious of the precariousness of the world situation, he became more sensitive to the individual's place in time. He was attuned to this because of his long involvement with his family history. It was as though he had begun to see himself like other great figures, one of the identifiable particles in the wave of history. He made this obvious in a note he wrote to Hi Simons, responding to Simons's birthday greeting to the poet he saw as having the stature of Goethe: "The other day, for instance, I happened to be saying something with respect to one of my grandfathers when I noticed that he was born in 1809. I thought automatically Goethe was still alive" (*L* 457).

The filtering process applied to his personal past combined with the attention he gave to the greater movement of history was an abstracting activity. The end product—a sense of his life in which things as they were changed as though on the blue guitar or as though seen through Mr. Lomax's magical blue spectacles—gave pleasure. Stevens was practicing what he preached, arranging the past into a supreme fiction in which he chose to believe, knowing it to be a fiction.

It was perhaps this sense of not seeing things quite as they were that disturbed his nephew John, who wrote to Stevens in February 1944 (WAS

2296) that his uncle was correct in thinking that he felt there was something "snobbish" in all his interest in genealogy. John trusted, however, that his uncle's interest went beyond this and was particularly pleased with the news that one of their forebears had been a ship's carpenter. He also expressed gratitude for himself and the rest of the family that Stevens was gathering all this information for them. It was true that this formed a great part of the poet's interest now in selecting photos, having albums beautifully made and bound, preserving the family Bible. It appears that as Stevens felt he had failed as a father with Holly, he took on the role of patriarch. He expressed, again to Jane, that his being "hepped upon on family ties . . . [was] one of the sources of strength in life" (August 7, 1943). Though he now recognized Holly's "unusual behavior" as an indication of the "independence" of the Stevens line (August 26, 1943), he had nonetheless been undone by the dashing of his hopes for his child. In this state of mind he preferred looking at larger patterns and trying to make sense out of them to examining the intricacies of the various failures he had witnessed and experienced in life.

Stevens wrote to Simons in the letter quoted above, that he wanted to "realize the past as it was." He described being moved by how much one could come to understand this through what at first seemed so little (he was reading a history of the early American settlements that re-created the political tensions and business activity of the seventeenth century). He had no problem imagining ancestors many generations removed reacting to the religious wars in France during the sixteenth century (December 3, 1943), but he could not come to terms with closer conflicts and crises. This was apparent in what he observed to his niece Jane about three weeks after his letter to Simons:

> I am returning today the album, with everything in it. I have had copies made of the picture of my father as a boy, also of the picture of him with a beard and, finally, I have had a copy made of one of the pictures of my mother. These are all that I care to have for my own purposes. Many of these pictures I know as well as I know my own hands and I must say that it gives me no particular pleasure to see them. Looking at them is somewhat the reverse of looking at the picture of my father taken in April, 1910, which was, I believe, only a few months before his death. When I look at the pictures of the children and then consider that I am able to think of their lives as wholes, the thing becomes disturbing. It is like standing by and watching people come into the world, live for a while and then go out of it again. It isn't that it makes me feel old, because I don't feel old; I feel young. And it isn't that I think of all these lives as having ended before they had really matured. It just upsets me; I have not thought about it long enough to know why. But obviously one reason for returning the album to you is that I expect to be happier with this selection that I have made than if I had all of these pictures constantly before me. I mean to think well of everyone in my family and if there are any of them that were not as fortunate as the others or, say, as they might have been, I mean to forget that. When I think of my father's pride and of all the anxiety that he

> must have felt, and then look at this last picture of him in which he seems so completely defeated, the feeling isn't anything I want to renew. I very much prefer to look at him and think of him in his prime. The truth is that I rather think that, seeing him as a whole, I understand him better perhaps than he understood himself, and that I can really look into his heart in which he must have concealed so many things. I say this because he was one of the most uncommunicative of men. Had he been more selfish than he was, everything would have been different for him, so that I am bound to think well of him. (*L* 457–58)

Stevens had never learned how to deal with the pathos of human situations.

Yet, he had gotten closer to his family since the deaths of his brother and sister. His nieces and nephews especially appreciated his interest in them and the family history. Their reaction to him during his recent visits back to Reading for the funeral of John and the interment of Elizabeth (in May 1943), warmed him but did not compensate for the growing sense of loss he experienced as he, too, neared the end of his years. In early August 1943 he received a "round-robin" letter from the various young people of the family (it arrived at his office in an envelope marked "S.W.A.K."); they had been sitting around of an evening over drinks, thinking of "Uncle Wallace," and wrote to let him know what they had been thinking and that they missed him. Stevens responded with a "round-letter" of his own, a short paragraph addressed to each of them.[25] He sweetly addressed the particulars they had mentioned in what was a kind of family prose poem. "The 'round-robin' stirred me up considerably," he noted to them (WAS 2763).

But as the winter of 1943–1944 came and deepened, Stevens had still not managed to get back into the spirit of writing. Though a few poems came, part of the resistance he felt about not looking too closely at what had been the reality of his own and his immediate family's pasts transferred itself onto the way his imagination functioned. The poems he did write—"The Motive for Metaphor," "Chorcorua to Its Neighbor," "So-and-So Reclining on Her Couch," "No Possum, No Sop, No Taters," "The Lack of Repose," and "Somnambulisma" (*CP* 288 and 293–304)—were the first of his most abstract ones. The suggestive first line of "The Motive for Metaphor" was a tip-off: "You like it under the trees in autumn" (*CP* 288). The ambiguity and elusiveness of "it" had troubled him all his life. "No Possum," an attempt from the beginning of January 1943, when he was still almost completely preoccupied with Holly's situation, was a hearkening back to experiences he had when he was about his daughter's age and first experienced deep disillusionment. "Chorcorua to Its Neighbor" could just as easily have been a comment on Henry James's *American Scene*[26] as about Stevens's own projection onto the New England landscape. "So-and-So Reclining on Her Couch" seemed a comment on one of the paintings he had seen at a New York exhibit rather than a product of more direct experience. The poet was evading. "X" appeared as the most impenetrable of his personae. That these were the first poems of the volume to be entitled *Transport to Summer* was almost too bitterly comic. The comment made by this opposition was like a snickering dramatic aside; this tone paralleled, the first step of abstraction: the distancing from a subject that brought into focus what was "aside" it, adjacent.

The pressure of reality was now too great. Stevens wanted "to seize the whole mass of everything and squeeze it, and make it [his] own" (*L* 459), but things as they were would not yield. The poet articulated this desire early in November, a few days after his last letter to Jane in which he had expressed his sense of powerlessness before the harsher facts of life. He had gone to New York for the weekend with Elsie; one of the reasons for the visit was so that he could see the Van Gogh exhibit at the Wildenstein, just up the block from the Mayfair House at Sixty-fifth and Park, the Stevenses' most recent home away from home—"the very center of inactivity, and therefore much to be desired." He came away from the exhibit wholly taken by what he called Van Gogh's "*maniement,*" not "a mania of manner, but . . . the total subjection of reality." He was excited by the way Van Gogh "mastered" reality. It did not matter to Stevens how the painter had effected this. The suggestion was that perhaps even temporary madness was to be welcomed if it allowed one to transform things as they were into illuminations of things as they seemed.

Sitting in his hotel room, looking again through the listings of events in the current *New Yorker* (Stevens kept abreast of cultural events with this magazine, which charmed him with the humor of its cartoons, close in spirit to his own wit; he always read it on the train going down to New York), the poet had not found anything else of particular interest, and so after the Wildenstein he went down to one of his favorite haunts, the Pierpont Morgan Library. He appreciated the spirit of the man who had surrounded himself with the treasures he amassed as much as he appreciated the treasures themselves. On his return to Hartford he made a point of communicating this to Henry Church and strongly urged him to visit what he called Morgan's "*soledad*" ("solitude") (*L* 459).

As though trying to rekindle his imagination, Stevens became more attentive over the next month to what was being shown in New York galleries. He returned to the city as shows changed. In the beginning of December he went down to see two more exhibits. At the same time he refused a suggestion made by Henry Church, to whom it was communicated by Monroe Wheeler of the Museum of Modern Art, that he read from his poetry there. As Stevens wrote to Church, he had just recently said no to another similar request: "I am not a troubadour and I think the public reading of poetry is something particularly ghastly" (December 3, 1943). In the same letter he noted that he had gone to see the Blumenthal show and what was at Knoedler's and had also wanted to be in New York to get new suspenders and gloves. He returned again to his negative feeling about reading at the museum and commented that it would be "quite a complication apart from the mingled problems of obesity and minstrelsy." He was uncomfortable with himself, insecure in the old ways, and thought himself physically grotesque. He had a short time before been insulted by "young Ford" (Charles Henri, editor of *View*), who had disparaged the poet's collection of paintings, saying they constituted "a mere handful of nothing at all and these things relics of nobodies" (WAS 3529). According to Stevens, Ford had reported this in the context of noting that the poet's assessment of the personal collection of James Thrall Soby as "a typical collection of modern French pictures" was demeaning to Soby, who was now director of the museum. Stevens wrote to Soby to clarify the matter but still felt the "complication" of the situation.

Stevens added to Church, in closing his letter, that he was attempting at least to get back a sense of physical vigor by skipping lunches and walking instead. Lightening the general tone of his letter, he humorously suggested that his friend do the same: "What is the point of living on the edge of the Park, unless you drop into it and growl at the tigers? It takes three hours to walk round the Park. See if you can do it in less time, and I shall present you with a sweat shirt. If you can get it down to two hours and a half, I shall present you with a medal."

Reflecting the difficulty of being that he was experiencing, the two new poems that Stevens forced out that late winter (given the family disturbances that had prevented his writing during summer, the poet had changed from his old seasonal habits of composition) were equally difficult. "Repetitions of a Young Captain" and "The Creations of Sound" (*CP* 306–11), apparently contributions promised months before to the two journals in which they were first published (*Quarterly Review of Literature* and *Maryland Quarterly*) were masterpieces of inversion and ellipticality. "Repetitions," as its title suggested, echoed earlier works: the epilogue of "Notes"; the scene of the cathedral in "The Comedian"; the setting in "Of Modern Poetry"; a part of the action of *Carlos Among the Candles;* "Metaphors of a Magnifico"; the phrasing, at one point, of "A High-Toned Old Christian Woman," at another of "The Emperor of Ice-Cream." The poet seemed to be remembering these traces of his past voices as the figured young captain hauntingly "remembered overseas. . . . something overseas" (*CP* 306). Stevens was again asserting his identification with the soldier, and through this his spiritual participation in the war, as he had done in closing "Notes." Here the announcement was even clearer:

> His route lies through an image in his mind:
>
> My route lies through an image in my mind.
> (*CP* 307)

Against the awful pressure of the war, the event that left him feeling powerless, it was only "On a few words of what [was] real in the world" that he nourished himself. When e. e. cummings read the poem on its appearance in the *Quarterly Review,* he noted to Stevens that he felt equally nourished. He had been "sick," but "after reading 'Repititions [*sic*] of a Young Captain,'" he wrote, "I feel whole" (July 2, 1944).

In "The Creations of Sound" (*CP* 310) the poet lost himself completely. "X" again appeared in his stead, the central figure in a tortuous hypothetical argument that failed to convince because of its overqualifications—confusions that posed as clarifications, perfect defenses against revelation. But what did show itself in this poem was Stevens's temporary lack of faith in himself, the loss of vigor that he had communicated in his last letter to Henry Church. He felt that his words were "silence made still dirtier," that he lacked the "venerable complication," and that "His poems [were] not of the second part of life." Though both these poems obviously have layers of meaning beyond the literal grounding pointed out here, it is important to recognize the more or less direct utterance as well.

About this time the poet seemed preoccupied with things German. He voiced this humorously just before the end of 1943 in a note to Wilson Taylor apropos of a volume of poems recently sent him by Frederick Mortimer Clapp of the Frick Museum. He found Clapp's lines wanting: ". . . what they seem[ed] to need," he commented, was "Wein, Weib und Gesang (Nazi for whoopee)" (*L* 460). Three months later he wrote to Henry Church that he had just read the first volume of Nietzsche's *Human, All Too Human* in German and, though he did not think of it what his friend did, he enjoyed "all of the sharp edges and intensity of speech" of the original language, which he felt properly reflected the philosopher's spirit. A few days after reading Nietzsche, Stevens took his watch downtown to be repaired. While waiting, he began a conversation with one of the employees who, appropriately, knew a great deal about Switzerland. The poet asked about Basel, about Nietzsche, and about Germans. The first, he was told, was lonely; the second, crazy; and, about the Germans, the watchmaker said they "had not changed since Tacitus described them" (*L* 462). The poet, like his imagined young captain, was haunted by "something overseas." He wanted to understand the spirit that informed the collective madness of a nation. Perhaps there was something in their language. . . . Stevens's intense involvement with Vico a few years before would have predisposed him to muse on this.

❧

As spring approached, something in Stevens seems to have come to life again. A number of facts accounted for this. On one side, the poet again became involved in conjuring the classical world, one of his dearest loves. In late December or early January he had thumbed through Allen Tate's new translation of *Pervigilium Veneris,* which he had gone through most carefully about a year before; he loved both Tate's translation and the book as object, another product of the Cummington Press. About two months later he received John Burnet's *Early Greek Philosophy* from Blackwell's. This was another of Church's recommendations. The poet looked forward to going through it but for the present held himself off. He felt he had been reading too much—perhaps stifling his imagination. It would be preferable for a while just to recall his idea of Greece before yielding to another's perception.

Other elements contributing to Stevens's sense of renewal were his rediscovery of the peasant in himself, as he voiced to Church (*L* 461), and the knowledge that his reputation was spreading abroad. When Henry Church asked Stevens if he would mind if he sent *Notes* to André Gide, the poet responded enthusiastically and added that he, in turn, would like to go through Gide's journals now that they had "taken the place of Flaubert's Letters" (*L* 461). And in spite of Stevens's feeling that he had not been "accepted" publicly here in America, Alfred Knopf wrote in mid-April that he would like to do another volume. The news "knock[ed] [Stevens] cold," but he was delighted (April 28, 1944).

The poet's refound strength showed itself in both his behavior and his work. When, during early spring, he received a letter from Theodore Weiss querying him about his reactions to Yvor Winters's recent essay, "Wallace Stevens or the Hedonist's Progress,"[27] the poet refused to enter the arena; he held his own ground. Rather than begin to cavil about terminology, definitions, or the moral attitudes of someone like Winters, who, in large part, added to the "unacceptability" of Stevens,[28] the poet simply stopped reading Weiss's letter after the first paragraph, as he noted to him in his return letter. He graciously added that at bottom Mr. Winters and he were probably after the same thing, though the critic had obviously misunderstood his purpose as hedonistic (*L* 463).

And as though announcing the return of his vigor, Stevens composed "Holiday in Reality." While this poem followed the rule that "It Must Be Abstract" in Part I, it changed, retransformed the abstract into the concrete in Part II, and ended by giving the same kind of pleasure as the strongest poems of *Harmonium*—a sublimated sexual pleasure that would "make widows wince":

I

It was something to see that their white was different,
Sharp as white paint in the January sun;

Something to feel that they needed another yellow,
Less Aix than Stockholm, hardly yellow at all,

A vibrancy not to be taken for granted, from
A sun in an almost colorless, cold heaven.

They had known that there was not even a common
  speech,
Palabra of a common man who did not exist.

Why should they not know they had everything of
  their own
As each had a particular woman and her touch?

After all, they knew that to be real each had
To find for himself his earth, his sky, his sea.

And the words for them and the colors that they possessed.
It was impossible to breathe at Durand-Ruel's.[29]

II

The flowering Judas grows from the belly or not at all.
The breast is covered with violets. It is a green leaf.

Spring is umbilical or else it is not spring.
Spring is the truth of spring or nothing, a waste, a fake.

These trees and their argentines, their dark-spiced branches,
Grow out of the spirit or they are fantastic dust.

The bud of the apple is desire, the down-falling gold,
The catbird's gobble in the morning half-awake—

These are real only if I make them so. Whistle
For me, grow green for me and, as you whistle and grow
green,

Intangible arrows quiver and stick in the skin
And I taste at the root of the tongue the unreal of what
is real.

(*CP* 312–13)

The lines revealed that the poet was again looking at reality, but a greater reality than the political or personal one; it was the reality of nature in which he reimmersed himself. Doing this was like a "holiday" because it allowed him to get beyond mundane aspects. This was the inverse of the "Banal Sojourn" about which he had written years earlier, when he was attempting to do just the opposite of what he did now—that is, make the events of the day the subject matter of poetry. From a letter to Hi Simons—another detailing of earlier work that the critic had asked him about (*L* 463–65)—it is clear that Stevens's focus on the yellow in the light of Part I of "Holiday" derived from his experience of the New England spring that year: "Here, in New England spring is always yellow before it is green and that is unexpected because spring with us comes from Labrador or often seems to do so." With this observation the mysterious "their" and "they" in "Holiday" disclose themselves as referring to himself and the other inhabitants of his region. The poet was again feeling himself part of his world, his soil and weather, his intelligence and imagination.

Yet one more sign that he was feeling stronger the spring of 1944 was his having come to accept, if only temporarily, Holly's state. On hearing from Jane in early March that Holly wanted to find a job in New York, something that would make her independence even clearer than before, he did not seem to react; if he did, he at least did not dwell on it as he had in the past. Quite the contrary. He focused on his life rather than hers, kept up his monthly visits to New York, read, spent as much time as he could digging and musing in his garden, and by the end of May had planned to give his summer entirely to poetry. This he wrote to Henry Church, at the same time explaining that because of his desire to give his full time again to the Muse, he would not consider preparing another paper for this year's Pontigny conference. About traveling, the answer was no as well. Though he would have liked to go to Pennsylvania, he wrote, there was no place to stay that was acceptable to both him and Elsie; Elsie did not like to "knock around a great deal" and he was "too old to do the amount of walking . . . required" (*L* 467).

Stevens's turning his attention away from family concerns for the while and toward work alone had perhaps to do, too, with his learning in the last days of April from Jane that she planned to divorce her husband, still overseas in the service. Stevens's reaction was stony silence, which he maintained for six months, in spite of Jane's monthly letters pleading for some kind of contact. His "adopted" daughter was now causing him the pain of disappointed expectations that he had just managed to neutralize in relation to Holly. He had to turn away, it seems, from the quiet resentment he must have felt at the apparent ease with which the younger generation broke through the life of forms to follow feelings.

The idea that his imagination now seized on was one that he had had most difficulty with his whole life: pain. The immediate suggestion, he reported, came from his reading a letter concerning "the relation between poetry and pain" sent to the *Kenyon Review* and quoted by Ransom in his article in the journal's last issue.[30] For days after, Stevens could not get the subject out of his mind, as he wrote to Ransom on June 17. It seemed to loom larger than the reality of D-Day, an event of a few days earlier.[31] He became preoccupied with doing what he called in the same letter to Ransom an "esthetique [*sic* no accent] du mal" (*L* 468). He worked with and around this idea for more than a month, shaping it into one of the major poems of his later career. The piece he had promised Ransom for his journal became this one; by July 28 he had completed and sent it in. It was perhaps because Ransom had been so full of praise for "Notes" in his last letter, when he asked the older poet for a contribution, that Stevens offered him this undertaking, even though, as he wrote just a month or so before to Church, he did not think much of the *Kenyon Review*. There was nobody better than Stevens, Ransom wrote, commenting that he had come to this conclusion on his recent rereading of "Notes" (June 15, 1944).

When Stevens sent in "Esthétique du Mal" to Ransom, he noted that the title was "not quite right in the sense that anything of that sort seem[ed] to be not quite right now-a-days." He added, however, that he meant "aesthetics as the equivalent of apérçus, which seems to have been the original meaning." He also commented that though the "last poem ought to end with an interrogation mark . . . [he had] punctuated it in such a way as to indicate an abandonment of the question, because [he could] not bring himself to end the thing with an interrogation mark" (*L* 469). This was more than a formal reticence. The question ending the poem, if taken as more than rhetorical—

> And out of what one sees and hears and out
> Of what one feels, who could have thought to make
> So many selves, so many sensuous worlds,
> As if the air, the mid-day air, was swarming
> With the metaphysical changes that occur,
> Merely in living as and where we live.
>
> (*CP* 326)—

expressed the poet's sense of awe, an awe bordering on bewilderment, before the mystery of consciousness. He was again dealing with the irrational element, that which continually eluded the grasp of the ever-hungry intellect, the bird with the coppery keen claws. If he had ended the poem with a question mark, he would have been admitting too openly his feeling of impotence even in the very power of having conceived "so many selves, so many sensuous worlds." Unfortunately evil was just as elusive, a manifestation of consciousness unable to deal with its own pain. The "apérçus" of the poem had been, in part, illustrations of this. The various juxtapositions—such as

> It was almost time for lunch. Pain is human.
> There were roses in the cool café.
>
> (*CP* 314)—

were instances of the way a sensuous world was conceived; its birth displaced a painful perception. The problem with creating a "fluent mundo" in which to reside while the world or one's spirit warred was, as the poet made clear in the opening of the last poem of the sequence, that:

> The greatest poverty is not to live
> In a physical world, to feel that one's desire
> Is too difficult to tell from despair.
>
> (*CP* 325)

In composing "Esthétique du Mal," Stevens came to terms, more directly than he had ever done before, with the limits of his being. Throughout the fifteen poems making up the whole, echoes of his earlier "selves" and images of the "sensuous worlds" he had created swarmed around him like flies, his Erinyes, reminding him that in giving his attention to beautiful objects and ideas he had been avoiding the pain that truly living in a physical world means. Stevens came to understand that the greatest sin was not to live in the fullness of what it means to be a human being, a "rational animal," with equal weight given to both terms.

This was not a different perception from what Ernest Becker later described in *The Denial of Death:* Human beings, especially after Darwin, would go to almost any lengths to deny their "creatureliness." They ignored or repressed impulses that would draw them to individuals and experiences they could not rationally understand because to acknowledge and follow them would mean opening to what Stevens called the "verve of earth" (*CP* 14), the feeling of dissolving into the movement of waves and particles of light flashing, a loss of self. Stevens's oblique references, through his title and the evocations of "Fleurs" in his "Esthétique," to Charles Baudelaire and his *Fleurs du Mal* hinted appropriately at the connections between sexuality, love, perversion, and death—all issues brought to the surface by the news of Jane's divorce.

In a secular way the theme Stevens was exploring in "Esthétique du Mal" was the basic Christian premise: Evil was the opposite or the absence of love, the ultimate good. "The death of Satan was a tragedy/ For the imagination" (*CP* 319) because now human beings could no longer blame an external force for their own lack of courage to be good: to love, to show themselves and to trust in all their vulnerability. Stevens elliptically described in Section X how in his own life he had substituted a yearning for the past for the grappling with a real other in a present that would have forced him to face his creatureliness. Consequently, he, too, suffered and propagated evil in attempting to avoid "That he might suffer or that/ He might die." On the other hand, to acknowledge this was to know good, the "innocence of living":

> He had studied the nostalgias. In these
> He sought the most grossly maternal, the creature
> Who most fecundly assuaged him, the softest
> Woman with a vague moustache and not the mauve
> *Maman.* His anima liked its animal
> And liked it unsubjugated, so that home
> Was a return to birth, a being born
> Again in the savagest severity,
> Desiring fiercely, the child of a mother fierce
> In his body, fiercer in his mind, merciless
> To accomplish the truth in his intelligence.
> It is true there were other mothers, singular
> In form, lovers of heaven and earth, she-wolves
> And forest tigresses and women mixed
> With the sea. These were fantastic. There were
> homes
> Like things submerged with their englutted sounds,
> That were never wholly still. The softest woman,
> Because she is as she was, reality,
> The gross, the fecund, proved him against the touch
> Of impersonal pain. Reality explained.

> It was the last nostalgia: that he
> Should understand. That he might suffer or that
> He might die was the innocence of living, if life
> Itself was innocent. To say that it was
> Disentangled him from sleek ensolacings.
> (*CP* 321–22)

Yet beyond what he had not lived that left him perceiving "Life [as] a bitter aspic" (*CP* 322), he had come to these realizations in words. Once again he found himself "on paper," faced himself there. What would come of this knowledge? Was this knowledge at all?

While he had been immersed in working through these major concerns in "Esthétique du Mal," life seemed to go on as usual. There were the ongoing exchanges with his chief genealogist, meetings with Henry Church, another invitation from Kimon Friar to read his poetry at the YMHA in Manhattan, which the poet refused, though he was happy to have Friar use some of his poems for the *Borzoi Book of Modern Verse.* He continued to receive praise for his work. William Carlos Williams wrote on July 21, enthusiastic about Stevens's preface to Samuel French Morse's volume. Stevens responded with a very warm note. He called his fellow poet "Bill" for the first time, thanked him for his words about his work, and took the opportunity to extend the invitation that Williams stop in Hartford to spend time with him if the good doctor still passed through Connecticut, as he used to on his vacations years ago. Stevens was also honored by being asked to become a trustee of the Cummington School by Harry Duncan (Katharine Frazier had recently died). The poet refused, however, both because he felt he was already overcommitted and because he was not in a position to make up financial deficits, one of the functions of a trustee. There was, too, reading that continued to delight him. He was particularly moved by Friar's latest piece in *Poetry* and noted to him that he had gone over it several times "because it really meant something" (June 1944). And there was work at the office. He did not take a holiday that summer. But just as he finished "Esthétique," something happened to test all his newfound strength.

Holly stopped by the office one afternoon with the man she announced she intended to marry. Stevens bellowed his angry disapproval. The stately halls of the Hartford echoed his outrage so that all were witness to a feeling that he did not even think of attempting to hide. Though Holly had known John Hanchak for almost the year and a half since she had been working at the Aetna (he was a repairman of business machines who periodically visited this and other offices in the area), her father had not wanted him in the house from the time they began dating. This situation had no doubt contributed about a year before to her having taken a room in a local boardinghouse and to her having temporarily broken with Hanchak—or at least telling Stevens that she had. (He wrote to Jane on August 26, 1943, that Holly had "broken off with the Pole, thank goodness.") Whether he knew that their relationship had resumed—or had never been interrupted—he was clearly not prepared for their visit to his office this midsummer of 1944. Ironically, his reaction to her rebellious choice mirrored his own father's to his own thirty-five years before. To Jane (who maintained a correspondence with Holly) and other family members it appeared that the poet had disowned his daughter. After her marriage on August 5, 1944, the couple left for Canada on their honeymoon. On their return Holly visited the house on Westerly Terrace only when her father was at the office.

But quite the opposite to what he felt and expressed about Holly, her choice, and her future, Elsie—no doubt much to her husband's consternation—expressed her feeling that she was "very glad for Holly's happiness." This she wrote to her half sister, La Rue, just over a month after the wedding. The letter in its entirety reflected a blithe, almost naïve acceptance of what Holly must have told her about her husband and his background. Moreover, in its fragmentary leaps from one subject to another, it reflected the nature of Elsie's consciousness. Although Elsie's acceptance must have helped Holly get through a very difficult period, the sense of Elsie's personality that comes through this letter suggests that beyond Holly's late adolescent rebellion's being a major reason for her marriage, the strain of negotiating between the elliptical nature of her mother's character and the rigor of her father's must have made her long to live in a climate of her own with someone attentive and sympathetic to her need to be seen as a woman. Stevens, beneath his fulminations, could not have been insensitive to these elements of his daughter's reality.

Just as he had come to realize his difficulty in dealing with pain by beginning to come to terms with it "on paper," so he had to face what was one of his greatest disappointments. The reality of this pain fractured his imagination. But on the surface, after his initial explosion, he did not quail. He did not mention Holly's wedding; he maintained his sense of humor with correspondents. He was particularly cajoling with Lila James Roney, his chief genealogist, who had a rather eccentric, worrisome nature. He went on with his "family" work. In addition to putting together the histories, photos, and documents, he now became active in seeing to it that family gravesites were properly maintained. Beyond the practical aim of his genealogical researchers over the past few years—that is, of verifying that he was "descended from the first white child born in New Netherland," as he exaggeratedly put it, so that he could become a member of the Holland Society and have "people who wouldn't believe . . . otherwise" that he had this pedigree "believe it" (*L* 472)—Stevens took very seriously the role of being the preserver of the past.

Nonetheless, there were moments that late summer when Stevens's feelings showed through his façade. The indications were sometimes subtle but at other times surprisingly direct. At the end of August, for example, writing to Henry Church about having finished and sent off "Esthétique," the poet expressed doubts about the poem that sounded more like doubts about how he had dealt with Holly: "Every now and then as I walk along the street I think of something that I said in the course of it that I wish I hadn't said, but it doesn't matter" (*L* 472). He then added, perhaps by way of consolation of sorts, "I got Mrs. Church's paratroopers in" (in Section XI, lines 3–4). Mrs. Church sometimes related her dreams to Mr. Stevens (*L* 516–17), and in this case it appears that Morpheus had brought her images of paratroopers who, as they fell, mowed the lawn.

In contrast with this voicing of uncertainty was an unusually straightforward expression of need Stevens made to his cousin Emma Stevens Jobbins almost two weeks later: "It is such a pleasure to hear from you. In the autumn I badly need my mother, or something. This has always been the toughest time of the year for me: I want to migrate; I want to give the office a kick in the slats" (*L* 473). He added that he had, like a caring mother himself, spent the last two weekends bringing his tenderest plants indoors so that his room looked like a begonia farm, and in the rest of the house, upstairs and down, there were "plants all over the place" (*L* 474). Within this same period he had also written to Hi Simons, describing his equally tender feeling for his poems, still connected by the invisible thread of the past to his mother and her characteristic piety: "I write poetry because for me it is part of my piety: because for me it is the good of life . . ." (*L* 473). This direct utterance was made, in part, because Stevens wanted to explain to Simons why he did not feel he could exert his influence with the Cummington Press to publish the critic's monograph on him ("Wallace Stevens and Mallarmé," which finally appeared after Simons's death in *Modern Philology:* "I don't intend to lift a finger to advance my interest, because I don't want to think of poetry that way." Quite apart from anything Stevens might have done to further Simons's interest, Harry Duncan, now directing the Cummington Press, noted to the poet that he felt the critic's work did not treat Stevens with enough humor. Stevens must have been touched by Duncan's recognition of his comic intent, though he no doubt regretted his rejection of Simons's typescript.

As the autumn reddened and his senses paled, Stevens went on doing what he had to do for his poems and finally softened in his feelings for Jane. In late October he wrote to Jane and to his nephew John (the poet's brother John's son): "Everyone in the family is precious to me and it is the easiest thing in the world for us to drift apart instead of clinging to each other as we should. . . .

"I regret more than I can tell you not having been able to visit Reading this summer. I want so much to see so many things and most of all those ponderous twins [the newest additions to the Stevens line]" (October 25, 1944).

To Nicholas Moore, who wanted to publish a selection of the poet's work in England, Stevens wrote urging him to make the choices for the volume himself, commenting only that he felt the best things he had done were in his last two books, *Parts of a World* and *Notes Toward a Supreme Fiction* (*L* 475). To Theodore Weiss, who wrote asking about the poet's philosophical predispositions, Stevens observed that he thought that Alfred North Whitehead, like most modern philosophers, was too "purely academic," but that his own liking for Bergson and James had been criticized by an academic philosopher, Paul Weiss (who taught at Bryn Mawr). The poet, humbly and honestly, even shared with Theodore Weiss the other Professor Weiss's complaint that Stevens had not tackled "full-sized philosophers" (*L* 476). Either Stevens was secure that in having dealt with his "man-poets," he had gone beyond what "full-sized philosophers" engaged, or he was admitting limitations, falling back into one of the postures of his youth, when he felt he did not have "brains" enough. Perhaps the poet himself did not know which was the case; all he did know was that he could only be himself, as he had learned he had to let Jane be herself.

Yet there were always evidences of his mastery of thought in his work as a lawyer. This important fact should not be underestimated in evaluating Stevens's mental economy. His continued success in negotiating claims provided Stevens with a constant measure of his powers, no matter what else might be going on in his life. This sense of grounding was reinforced in late November 1944, when Henry Church, familiar with his skills as an attorney, entrusted Stevens with the task of acting under his will. Stevens was pleased by this recognition, as he expressed in a letter to Church on November 20 (*L* 477). After accepting, he immediately responded in his new capacity and explained to Church why a certain vagueness was appropriate in his will. Stevens understood that it was not solely in poetry that this quality had value. In the same letter, moving easily back into the role of the man of letters, Stevens critiqued a book Church had asked him about and that he had just looked over the previous weekend, Georges Duthuit's *Chinese Mysticism and Modern Painting* (1936). He also commented on the latest Delacroix show at the Wildenstein, expanding on the "romantic," a longtime favored subject. In responding to Church's trust in his authority, Stevens again felt himself "put on his knowledge with his power."[32] This did him good, as did the first letter from José Rodríguez Feo a few days later. After listing his credentials as editor of the Cuban journal *Origenes* and noting that he had graduated from Harvard in 1943, Rodríguez Feo asked if he could translate "Esthétique" for his publication. This was to be the beginning of another nourishing relationship through correspondence for the poet who felt so much the master "on paper."

Reinvigorated by these boosts to his morale, Stevens responded to Oscar Williams in early December (Williams had written to ask the poet to do a prose commentary on war and poetry) with the following, which he had voiced in almost the same words to Allen Tate on the same day (*L* 479 n.):

> A prose commentary on War and Poetry is out of the question. I wonder if the war has not ceased to affect us except as a part of necessity, as something that must be carried on and finished, with no end to the sacrifice involved. But I think that even the men in the Army etc. feel that it is no longer anything except an overwhelming grind. The big thing in the world today, the thing that really involves the future, is not the war, but the leftist

> movement. Just at the moment it seems clear that the proletarian politics of the New Deal and its efforts to improve the condition of labor, have created in the labor movement a force quite as great as the force of war, which will survive the war, so that, in that sense, it is definitely the great thing in the world today, or so it seems to me.
>
> (*L* 479–80)

The poet brilliantly evaded stating what he felt about the "great thing" he saw the "labor movement" to be in the same way that he had refused to take a fixed political position ten years earlier, when queried by Ronald Lane Latimer and others. This was part of a strategic tactic. As long as he did not allow himself to be pinned by a label, he could continue to speak, to write with the expectation that readers would—as he himself had done with the figures he had felt to be important in his development—"quiz all sounds, all thoughts, all everything." And as long as this questioning continued, the querying minds of his readers would go on proposing solutions. Out of this engagement came growth. This was what made change possible. With the skill of a talmudic scholar, a "rose rabbi," Stevens continued to negotiate his way through his troubled times. As he wrote early in January 1945, to Rodríguez Feo, the "greatest subject" was *"felicidad"* (*L* 481), happiness. To address this, one had to be as simultaneously slippery and dogged in presenting enigmas to the mind as Socrates, the West's first seeker of happiness, had been.

Pursuing happiness, Stevens had once more gone back to Reading for the Christmas 1944 holiday. There was a huge celebration given for his nephew John, Jr., home on furlough from the war that would soon end. He went without Elsie and really celebrated. According to John Sauer (married to Eleanor, sister of John, Jr.), who threw the party, after the poet had downed the first three of the martinis he continued to drink throughout the evening, he, one of the few older people at the gathering, became the proverbial "life of the party." John, Eleanor, and another friend accompanied Stevens back to his hotel much later, marveling that he seemed to show no effects from the amount of alcohol he had consumed. He then kept them up even longer, reminiscing and telling wonderful stories. In parting, he said, "I [haven't] let my hair down like this in many years. I just had one hell of a good time!"[33]

❧

Stevens opened the year that would explode with the dropping of the bombs on Hiroshima and Nagasaki with a commitment to happiness as the greatest good. He, no less than Einstein (who, after the catastrophe, voiced that had he known what his contribution to the work on atomic theory would produce, he would have become a shoemaker), could not have foreseen what an end to even considerations of happiness the year would bring. The poet and the scientist shared exactly the same life span, 1879–1955. The gently mannered world into which they had been born could not have prepared them to expect the devastation that human beings inflicted on one another in the century of "progress." Both men had been properly reared to attend primarily to their work, to pursue truth through the alleyways of confusion, to concentrate on their tasks, so that even in the months before the cataclysm, they continued in their chosen pieties. How could they have known that it was not, as it appeared, that during the period of increased attack on the Pacific front Hiroshima had been spared not because it was a Buddhist center, but because the Army Corps of Engineers had wanted to preserve a pristine place so that when it tested its weapon, its effects could be observed unspoiled?[34]

Nonetheless, in spite of his desire to focus on happiness and in spite of having properly celebrated the close of 1944 on yet another occasion with the other members of the St. Nicholas Society at their annual bash in New York, Stevens was uneasy about things as they were. After commenting to Henry Church in mid-January that the last two issues of the *Sewanee Review* were a "miscellany" and adding that it must have been difficult for Tate "to find people to do things now-a-days," he went on:

> The place to edit a review is Paris, or Vatican City or Moscow, or up an alley full of cats alive and dead. If you do it in Shanghai, you get articles on floating participles in Sung Poetry, and if you do it in Ethiopia you get communications from Kenneth Burke. Here we are all in the fever of contemporary life, with everything that is fundamental turned upside down and in course of re-examination. That alone and without reference to the profound misery in Europe, should exact from the right people the best they have. I say this because I don't believe that Tate is going to be content with the sort of thing that he has had in his last two numbers. I feel sure of the contrary. But he is going to have to break with a lot of things before he really gets going, and I rather think that he will be the man to do it. At the moment, the past is terribly tepid, and I don't think that Tate is going to be content there in the face of what might be called the rising fury of the future, which is rather an elaborate way of putting it. (*L* 483)

The humor of this analysis—for the "sublimity" of which Church later congratulated him (April 24, 1945)—covered Stevens's deep concern with the *dis-ease* of his time. In the face of it, again, his only solace was in nature. As he observed to Church in closing his letter, accounting for why he would not be coming down to New York "just yet," besides his "shopping list" not being "quite long enough," "with all the snow that we have been having, it is pleasant to be right where I am. Last Sunday's storm did me more good than I can tell you. . . ."

The man for whom snow was "like eyesight falling to earth" fell with it, dissolving into observing particles, freezing in beautiful images what others could not see. The only way to ease the tension he felt as part of the world in which he lived was to draw out of himself exquisite crystals of perception that at least would cover the earth for a while before melting. Stevens was back to writing poems. The winter did not matter.

Reading this letter seems to have reminded Church of another of his friends who had created out of the decay of an empire another monument to beauty. In his return letter (WAS 3452) Church asked Stevens if he knew the work of Robert Musil, author of *The Man Without Qualities,* someone else who dissolved himself in describing "the relation between a man and his world." Stevens, who had read Church's *Mesures* from its first number, obviously did know of Musil, some of whose work had appeared in the journal; he recommended possible translators (May 2, 1945).

With the collapse of time and space signaled in a practical way early in the century by the wireless telegraph,[35] still moments, moments of repose when one could reflect on one's qualities, and those of others seemed increasingly unavailable. Henry James was among the last who enjoyed the activity of carefully observing people in settings that did not change as one entered them. Now the only possible vision was abstract, as Stevens well knew. As art historian Henri Focillon had pointed out in a text Stevens annotated in his characteristic way sometime during this period,[36] one studied the life of forms rather than the life of individuals, and the form that dominated all others for Stevens, the man of his century, was time—the greatest abstraction.

Stevens's consciousness of time passing in his own life, his long involvement with genealogy and history, and the pressure of the war seem to have combined into his concentrating on time itself as a subject, particularly time as mastered by the poet in the way he measured sounds falling in his lines. Time and its manifestation in sound became focal points for Stevens beginning in the early months of 1945. In a letter of January 26 to Rodríguez Feo, thanking him for some watercolors, especially one of a pineapple, which he hung in his room and which delighted him,[37] Stevens observed that he had always been especially interested in "sounds" and that "many [of his] lines exist[ed] because he enjoy[ed] their clickety-clack in contrast with the more decorous pom-pom-pom that people expect[ed]" (*L* 485). It was as though the dominant transforming force of his particular experience in time—still, in memory, the railroad with its "clickety-clack"—had continued to control the movement of his mind insofar as it was attached to sound. This sensitivity regularized and slowed the other, broader rhythm that came from Stevens's seeing from a bird's-eye perspective, from above—that abstract view of the poet conceiving himself as a planet, circling in an inhuman sphere. In short, Stevens's concern with time as perceived through sound acted as a brake on time as abstracted into spatial shapes and metaphors.

Stevens was aware of this complementary split in his perception. He explored its consequences in one of his strongest sequences of poems, "The Pure Good of Theory" (*CP* 329–33); these were written early in 1945. The four sections of seven tercets—"All the Preludes to Felicity," "Description of a

Platonic Person," "Fire-monsters in the Milky Brain," and "Dry Birds Are Fluttering in Blue Leaves"—illustrated Stevens's major preoccupation with time and revealed his present state of mind:

> It is time that beats in the breast and it is time
> That batters against the mind, silent and proud,
> The mind that knows it is destroyed by time.
> (*CP* 329)

Where the imagination began to create the metaphorical "green glade" of escape, the poet did not allow it to persist:

> But there was one invalid in that green glade
> . . . .
> Ill of a question like a malady,
> Ill of a constant question in his thought,
> Unhappy about the sense of happiness.
> (*CP* 331)

Whenever the conjured "platonic person" attempted to exist in the "pure good of theory"—dreaming only of the "spectacle of the mind"—reminders of sound came clattering to disturb his sleep of reason. "Man" was born not "of air . . . in the solar chariot" but of "woman." Stevens was announcing that he finally had "come down," that he was using "tooth and nail," struggling with his elemental nature. Sound, the reality of sound, reminded him of this. Plato was right in wanting to ban the poets—orderers of sound, makers of their own cosmos where others would prefer to dwell as well, hearing the constant din of their own natures. It was as though the poet were being forced into a confrontation with his "creatureliness" by "Time . . . the hooded enemy" (*CP* 330). For years Stevens had evaded this battle. Though at one point he had entered it, during the period when he wrote most of *Harmonium,* by the time he completed the poems of his first volume, he had abandoned the struggle, thought that he had "finished [his] combat with the sun" and that his "body, the old animal, [knew] nothing more" (*CP* 46). As he removed himself from dealing with "that monster, the body," accepted the limitations of his relationship with Elsie, and consciously chose to become the "comedian," the slashing, succulent sounds that characterized the poetry of his provocative first volume largely disappeared. Though they were heard again in "Owl's Clover" and in "The Man with the Blue Guitar," they were not sustained; they yielded in the other volumes to meditative whispered strains. Now they again began to squiggle out. They seemed to gain power and to reassert themselves in "Holiday in Reality"; and in the last five stanzas of the final section of "The Pure Good of Theory" sounds masterfully mirrored their content:

IV
Dry Birds Are Fluttering in Blue Leaves

It is never the thing but the version of the thing:
The fragrance of the woman not her self,
Her self in her manner not the solid block,

The day in its color not perpending time,
Time in its weather, our most sovereign lord,
The weather in words and words in sounds of sound.

These devastations are the divertissements
Of a destroying spiritual that digs-a-dog,
Whines in its hole for puppies to come see,

Springs outward, being large, and, in the dust
Being small, inscribes ferocious alphabets,
Flies like a bat expanding as it flies,

Until its wings bear off night's middle witch;
And yet remains the same, the beast of light,
Groaning in half-exploited gutturals

The need of its element, the final need
Of final access to its element—
Of access like the page of a wiggy book,

Touched suddenly by the universal flare
For a moment, a moment in which we read and repeat
The eloquences of light's faculties.

(*CP* 332–33)

The message was clear: For Stevens, sounds proclaimed his bond to the actual, and their repetitions had to proclaim vision, the product of "light's faculties." The sense of time passing that Stevens experienced in his aging body had forced him to reenter the battle to assert the perceptions and rhythms of his own being over his "hooded enemy." His masterful and surprising transposition in the last section's title of the adjectives "dry" and "blue" from their *natural* places reflected his "version of the thing," his domination over "things as they are."

The power of this poem came from resolution, out of a long period of "think[ing] things out," and the things that were thought out had to do with the man in relation to his world. Stevens had refused to be preoccupied with the vicissitudes of his reputation, though he continued to be concerned about his work itself. He noted in the same January letter to Rodríguez Feo referred to above that he had not read Yvor Winters's recent criticism of him (the same essay that Theodore Weiss had asked him about) and that he didn't, in general, give much attention to criticism except in the rare cases of men "about whose judgment no question exists" (*L* 484). On the other hand, he was keenly caught up with what had to do with the world political situation, as he related to Leonard van Geyzel at the end of January:

> I have not been doing a great deal of writing, but this is not because I haven't wanted to do so. There is an incessant pressure to think things out, not to speak of one's work. You may remember a man named [Dwight] MacDonald [*sic*] of THE PARTISAN REVIEW. He left it some time ago and started a thing called POLITICS, which is about as far to the left as such a thing can be. MacDonald [*sic*] represents the intelligent man trying to get at the good of socialism and to exploit it. In the number for January, 1945, there is an article by D. S. Savage, an English poet, on Socialism *in Extremis.* This is as extraordinary a piece of thinking and writing as I have seen. If the exponents of socialism were as interested, as keen and as honest generally speaking as Savage is and as MacDonald [*sic*] is, this great force in politics and in life would be more than the mere disruption that it so often seems to be. (*L* 486)

He closed this letter to Van Geyzel commenting that through his new Cuban correspondent he had also become especially interested in Latin American observers of the world scene like Alfonso Reyes[38] and wished that he had enough Spanish to read them. (He later ordered books by Reyes and plodded his way through with his rudimentary Spanish, left over from when he had begun to study it after his 1923 trips to Havana.)

It was during these years, too, that Stevens focused on the idea of "major man." Perhaps more than anything else, this was a figure for someone who could play reality in a "major" key. The poet's many elucidations of the meaning of this metaphor to Rodríguez Feo and others repeatedly stressed that it was to be understood as entirely distinct from any Nietzschean notion of superman. Quite the contrary. The major man was an abstraction of all men,[39] but at the same time not an "everyman." An "everyman" was all too easily the victim of his circumstances, while the "major man" shaped them without, like Nietzsche's superman, going "beyond good and evil," though it was clear that it was necessary to establish a new moral order.[40] While it would have been very much out of character for Stevens to admit that he saw himself as this fictive hero he conjured, in describing him, he described himself, especially as he was now: once more doing battle with the sun. The "major man" was also the "great captain" (see "Notes" and "Paisant Chronicle"), a curious character who seemed to derive part of his identity from the "Great Captain" described by Baldassare Castiglione near the end of Book II of *The Book of the Courtier.*[41] The distinctive feature of the "Great Captain" was his particular humor, using "innocent words to describe something unworthy"; with "innocent and inoffensive words" he was able to sting men badly, make them realize the errors of their ways.

Here was Stevens, again using innocent words to delight, give pleasure, while making his mordant points. It was, in part, because he had seen that *Parts of a World* had not elicited from its readers the pleasure he felt to be a necessary element of poetry that he once more devoted himself to playing with words, with sounds, as he had done abundantly in *Harmonium.* He wrote in midyear to Alfred Knopf, who had wanted him to consider putting out an edition of collected poems, that because of the reception of *Parts of a World,* he wanted "another chance" with a single volume before doing a collection (May 16, 1945; *L* 501). But with things as they were now, it was considerably more difficult to find bravura adequate to the great hymn of being. The pressure of reality resisted him, as he resisted feeling the "pathos" of his aging. The difficulty of the poems he now wrote mirrored these tensions.

❧

One of the most surprising developments of this period was the quickness and ease with which Stevens gave himself to José Rodríguez Feo. Within two months of Rodríguez Feo's first letter, Stevens was imagining dialogues with him beyond those he maintained in the correspondence. One such was recorded in "A Word with José Rodríguez Feo" (*CP* 333), a poem which he sent him after he had already submitted it, together with others, for a special issue of *Voices* devoted to the poet.[42] Perhaps Stevens's immediate sympathy for Rodríguez Feo had to do with his living in the only one of the exotic places that the poet had conjured which he had actually visited. In his first letter to the young Cuban, Stevens, in speaking of his visits to Havana, mistakenly related that five years rather than five months had separated his two sojourns there. As Holly Stevens notes, it could have been because the second stay in Havana in 1923—on the trip when she was conceived—was so different from the first that in his memory what seemed took the place of what had been (*L* 484 n.). He wrote to his Cuban correspondent how on his first trip alone he had "wanted in the wildest way" to learn Spanish and that he had begun. He had wanted to feel a part of this tropically magical place. On his second visit things were completely different. Now, more than twenty years later, it was as though the poet again touched through Rodríguez Feo the excitement of that time when he was alone, like his hero Crispin, in a place alive with the actual sounds he had called forth in "The Comedian," the poem that had strangely prefigured the experience. Perhaps this subtle identification with the young Cuban was also in part responsible for the new eruptions of vital sounds in his latest poems.

Over the next year this identification strengthened. Its aspects echoed the poet's early identification with Elsie as his "second self" in the years of their courtship. He wrote Rodríguez Feo that he wanted to meet him, find out how alike they were (*L* 504) and wanted his photo, which the Cuban sent. Stevens was sorry, he noted, that he could not reciprocate. The poet obviously had many photographs of himself, but it seems either he felt that none was an appropriate portrait, or perhaps he feared the younger man would be somehow disillusioned by what he saw. After all, "on paper" Stevens still seemed the "vigorous warrior." And, Rodríguez Feo had heard none other than Hemingway announce that "he thought Wallace Stevens a great poet" (May 5, 1945). A photograph of the man "tall and of a port in air" (*CP* 76), decorously dressed in his three-piece suit or in shirtsleeves in the garden, displaying his "muzzy bell[y] in parade" (*CP* 59), would shatter this image. Stevens preferred to wait until he could show himself in person, use his voice to express who he was.

As he had done with Elsie, Stevens uncovered parts of himself in his letters to Rodríguez Feo. And since the young man was intellectually complex in a way that Elsie clearly had not been, Stevens's revelations were more involved with the complicated harmony of his spirit. He wrote openly of what he felt to be his strengths, his weaknesses, his habits, his dreams, and as he had guided Elsie, he guided this new friend. He advised him to dedicate himself to "great works" and "lofty aims" in order to mitigate his "Platonism . . . the typical disease of young men of 24 or 25" (Fragment, July 1945). He realized Rodríguez Feo to be someone who devoted himself to reading as much as he himself once had and gently tried to nudge the young man to read less and think more, as he now did:

> . . . the desire to read is an insatiable desire and you must read. Nevertheless, you must also think. Intellectual isolation loses value in an existence of books. I think I sent you some time ago a quotation from Henry James about living in a world of creation [quoted below]. A world of creation is one of the areas, and only one, of the world of thought and there is no passion like the passion of thinking which grows stronger as one grows older, even though one never thinks anything of any particular interest to anyone else. Spend an hour or two a day even if in the beginning you are staggered by the confusion and aimlessness of your thoughts. (*L* 513)

Stevens seems to have found in Rodríguez Feo, whom he came to address affectionately with different names like "Dear Caribbean," the proper "heir"; he could greet him as if he were a "man of fortune." He shared with him the realizations he had come to about the themes that had most seriously preoccupied him through his life: God, Poetry and Manhood, the notion of poetry itself and the way it came and what it had to do with existence on a simple plane:

> The truth is that I have been thinking a bit about the position of the ignorant man in what, for convenience, may be called society and thinking about it from this point of view: that we have made too much of everything in the world and that perhaps the only really happy man, or the only man with any wide range of possible happiness, is the ignorant man. The elaboration of the

> most commonplace ideas as, for example, the idea of God, has been terribly destructive of such ideas. . . . (*L* 512)

> The poem, or poems, that I shall send to you will have to be written during the summer ["Thinking of a Relation Between the Images of Metaphors," "Chaos in Motion and Not in Motion," "The House Was Quiet and the World Was Calm," "Continual Conversation with a Silent Man" (*CP* 356–60)] because I have been busy with something else and, besides, I almost always dislike anything that I do that doesn't fly in the window. Perhaps this has some bearing on what you call "the monotony of elegance." To live in Cuba, to think a little in the morning and afterward to work in the garden for an hour or two, then to have lunch and to read all afternoon and then, with your wife or someone else's wife, fill the house with fresh roses, to play a little Berlioz (this is the current combination at home: Berlioz and roses) might very well create all manner of doubts after a week or two. But when you are a little older, and have your business or your job to look after, and when there is quite enough to worry about all the time, and when you don't have time to think and the weeds grow in the garden a good deal more savagely than you could ever have supposed, and you no longer read because it doesn't seem worth while, but you do at the end of the day play a record or two, that is something quite different. Reality is the great *fond,* and it is because it is that the purely literary amounts to so little. Moreover, in the world of actuality, in spite of all I have just said, one is always living a little out of it. There is a precious sentence in Henry James, for whom everyday life was not much more than the mere business of living, but all the same, he separated himself from it. The sentence is . . .
>
> "To live *in* the world of creation—to get into it and stay in it—to frequent it and haunt it—to *think* intensely and fruitfully—to woo combinations and inspirations into being by a depth and continuity of attention and meditation—this is the only thing."[43] . . . (*L* 505–06)

The poems he promised to write for Rodríguez Feo appeared first in Spanish translation in the winter 1945 issue of *Origenes.* As though composing and presenting himself for his idealized "one reader," Stevens revealed particularities of his being. Elements from his past—"The wood-doves . . . singing along the Perkiomen" (*CP* 356) and memories of the Indians still haunting the countryside in his recollections of Reading—combined with those from his present—the feeling of growing old during a thunderous July storm that made memories tremble surrealistically with what he actually saw and heard—so that it seemed that the whole "theatre" of his life was "spinning round,// Colliding with deaf-mute churches and optical trains" (*CP* 357). The last two figures bespoke his perception of the facts of his experience: "The death of one god is the death of all" (*OP* 165); consequently, churches were deaf-mute. In his memory he saw "optical trains" carrying him back to recollect himself in trains of thought. He expanded on the nature of his present: When his "house was quiet and the world was calm," he could become one with what he read. But the world was not calm, so the statement in this poem that "The truth in a calm world,/ In which there is no other meaning, itself// Is calm, . . ." brilliantly communicated its converse. Yet in "Continual Conversation with a Silent Man" it was possible to arrange a harmonious world, as that poem with its sounds successfully proclaiming in linked rhythms illustrated:

> The old brown hen and the old blue sky,
> Between the two we live and die—
> The broken cartwheel on the hill.
>
> As if, in the presence of the sea,
> We dried our nets and mended sail
> And talked of never-ending things,
>
> Of the never-ending storm of will,
> One will and many wills, and the wind,
> Of many meanings in the leaves,
>
> Brought down to one below the eaves,
> Link, of that tempest, to the farm,
> The chain of the turquoise hen and sky
>
> And the wheel that broke as the cart went by.
> It is not a voice that is under the eaves.
> It is not speech, the sound we hear
>
> In this conversation, but the sound
> Of things and their motion: the other man,
> A turquoise monster moving round.
>
> (*CP* 359–60)

Whatever it was about Rodríguez Feo that allowed Stevens to respond so immediately to him, it was most fortunate that this relationship came about, especially when it did. The two men exchanged letters for the remaining years of the poet's life, and in these letters, as in the occasional meetings they eventually had, Stevens continued to find nourishment and to nurture.

One of the constant themes that began during their first year of correspondence and that lasted until the end was that of Pompilio, a burro belonging to Rodríguez Feo's mother. After one of Rodríguez Feo's early descriptions of Pompilio, Stevens wrote: "I take the greatest pride in knowing Pompilio, who does not have to divest himself of anything to see things as they are. Do please give him a bunch of carrots with my regards. This is much more serious than you are likely to think from the first reading of this letter . . ." (*L* 513). It was, perhaps, Rodríguez Feo's sensitivity in describing the tender elements of his life that secured the bond Stevens felt. Pompilio became a constant figure around which Stevens wove some of his most brilliant perceptions; Pompilio was a pure and natural figure for things as they were against which human beings plotted their more than rational and irrational distortions. A few months before he died, Stevens wrote to Mrs. Church (with whom, as with her husband, who had died years before, he had shared from the onset news of his relationship with his Cuban friend):

> And finally my old José wrote from Havana that Pompilio, his mother's burro, about whose health I always used to ask, is still alive and well and kicking. What blessed news! It means that beneath all this arrogance of politics and taxes and nuclear fission there still remains in Cuba a nice old woman, who loves her burro and asks José to tell me, for Xmas, that Pompilio is well. Saludos, Pompilio. (*L* 865)

There it was, there Pompilio still was, a thing as it was, part of nature, part of us. Beneath all the exchanges about books,[44] observations about poetry and the Greeks (a letter from Rodríguez Feo had sent Stevens back to Burnet on *Early Greek Philosophy* [*L* 495]), about art and the state of the world, Stevens had been sustained by knowing that there was at least one young man he knew who was still attached to the *summum bonum,* part of the intelligence of his soil. To read through the letters to Rodríguez Feo over the years is to glimpse Stevens as preceptor to the seeing, teaching how to live, what to do in a world unpurged.

❧

The period during which Stevens's relationship with Rodríguez Feo was beginning brought other new discoveries and developments. One of these was the poet's delight in the drawings of Paul Wightman Williams, who, through the Cummington Press, had done illustrations for "Esthétique du Mal," which Duncan wanted to publish as an edition with these drawings. Contrary to what might be expected—considering Stevens's predilection for neoimpressionist styles in the paintings he bought—the poet was pleased by these abstract, almost skeletal renditions of what seemed ideas more than things; punning on their "Dorian Gray" aspect he called them "Wilde and weird" (*L* 498). Stevens was especially taken with the quality of the artist's line; he found it even better than the German etchers'. But he remarked on his liking for Williams's work: "I have lived under the New Deal so long I can take Mr. Williams' graphs . . ." (*L* 488). They reflected the analytical posture that the poet had assumed in the face of the pressures of the current reality. More, they suggested the schematics of his own slow disintegration, his approach to death. Stevens was sixty-five, entering his last phase. He found in Williams's style an appropriate medium to concretize what he attempted in his own work. As he noted to Duncan in the letter cited above, "Possibly what Whistler did for his mother Mr. Williams is doing for my poems": making them a symbol of how he felt as an aging being in a time he saw declining as much as he. The Cummington Press edition with the drawings was issued in early

November; there were 340 copies in total. One month after the explosions at Hiroshima and Nagasaki, the poem that had first appeared a year before in the *Kenyon Review* reappeared as though to help at least a few more individuals understand the aesthetics of evil.

Another development, not wholly new but changed, was the reestablishment of Stevens's contact with his Parisian bookseller. As we noted earlier, Paule Vidal had taken over the business after her father's death, and with the war winding down, she took up where Anatole had left off. The volume of Alain, after its long stay at the binder's, would soon be sent. Many other things would follow: books, journals, and the paintings over which she agonized in her selection for the poet she admired so much but would never, to her sadness, meet. Over the next ten years Stevens came to enjoy his exchanges with her in a way he could not have enjoyed those with her father. From the way she addressed him, from her diffident yet protective concern, and from descriptions of how she spoke of him, related by those of the poet's acquaintances, like Barbara Church, who visited her shop in Paris and later reported her questions and comments about him, Stevens knew he had made a conquest of this aging but well-cared-for red-haired spinster. In his letters to her he played tenderly with what he knew while never going beyond the bounds of courtesy. Within them he expressed affection, made perfectly safe by distance. Here was another curious replay of a situation experienced in his youth with Elsie and again neutralized—though in a different way from his relationship with José Rodríguez Feo—by the absolute security that whatever transpired between them would always belong on paper and be guarded by the forms dictated by their roles.

The end of the war meant other renewed contacts as well, such as that with Leonard van Geyzel (their correspondence had been interrupted since 1941) and with Henri Amiot, a Frenchman who had been brought over to work for the Hartford in the twenties at about the same time Stevens hired James Powers (*L* 480 n.). Amiot had returned to Paris after a couple of years. When he wrote to Stevens in late December 1944, the poet was glad to know he had survived his time as a prisoner of war unharmed. In March 1945 Stevens thoughtfully put Amiot back in contact with Powers; in his letter he noted to Amiot that Powers had recently sent him a pair of socks made by the Indians of Vancouver. The poet was obviously touched by the little offerings of gifts that still came from some of his friends. Sharing this warm detail with a man he had not seen in twenty years was a metaphor for the structure of Stevens's inner being: The more distance, the greater the possibility for expressing tenderness.

In early March 1945 there was an occasion of tender recognition of a different kind. Theodore Morrison of Harvard wrote asking Stevens to give the Phi Beta Kappa poem at that year's commencement. The poet readily agreed to return to his "nourishing mother," the institution that had "made an enormous difference in everything." Within a month he settled down to writing "Description Without Place" (*CP* 339). He only just recently repeated to

Henry Church that he did not like to read his poetry in public and had even more recently refused Robert Penn Warren's invitation to read on tape for the Library of Congress archive—telling him that he had also refused a similar invitation made about ten years before for the same reason he gave now: that he felt he didn't read well (March 30, 1945). But April 4 he wrote to Church that he was to read "Description Without Place" as the Phi Beta Kappa poem at Harvard; he added that there was "nothing more helpful to reading a poem than to have someone to read it to, and [that] that particular audience [would] be a good audience" (*L* 494). Was it because he felt an automatic identification with the young men at Harvard that Stevens did such an about-face? Was he aware of how this reaction contradicted his earlier reticences?

Though I have not felt it necessary before now to quote in its entirety any of the other longer poems, there is about "Description Without Place" so much that should not be missed by the reader who does not have the work at hand that I shall:

I

It is possible that to seem—it is to be,
As the sun is something seeming and it is.

The sun is an example. What it seems
It is and in such seeming all things are.

Thus things are like a seeming of the sun
Or like a seeming of the moon or night

Or sleep. It was a queen that made it seem
By the illustrious nothing of her name.

Her green mind made the world around her green.
The queen is an example . . . This green queen

In the seeming of the summer of her sun
By her own seeming made the summer change.

In the golden vacancy she came, and comes,
And seems to be on the saying of her name.

Her time becomes again, as it became,
The crown and week-day coronal of her fame.

II

Such seemings are the actual ones: the way
Things look each day, each morning, or the style

Peculiar to the queen, this queen or that,
The lesser seeming original in the blind

Forward of the eye that, in its backward, sees
The greater seeming of the major mind.

An age is a manner collected from a queen.
An age is green or red. An age believes

Or it denies. An age is solitude
Or a barricade against the singular man

By the incalculably plural. Hence
Its identity is merely a thing that seems,

In the seeming of an original in the eye,
In the major manner of a queen, the green

The red, the blue, the argent queen. If not,
What subtlety would apparition have?

In flat appearance we should be and be,
Except for delicate clinkings not explained.

These are the actual seemings that we see,
Hear, feel and know. We feel and know them so.

III

There are potential seemings, arrogant
To be, as on the youngest poet's page,

Or in the dark musician, listening
To hear more brightly the contriving chords.

There are potential seemings turbulent
In the death of a soldier, like the utmost will,

The more than human commonplace of blood,
The breath that gushes upward and is gone,

And another breath emerging out of death,
That speaks for him such seemings as death gives.

There might be, too, a change immenser than
A poet's metaphors in which being would

Come true, a point in the fire of music where
Dazzle yields to a clarity and we observe,

And observing is completing and we are content,
In a world that shrinks to an immediate whole,

That we do not need to understand, complete
Without secret arrangements of it in the mind.

There might be in the curling-out of spring
A purple-leaping element that forth

Would froth the whole heaven with its seeming-so,
The intentions of a mind as yet unknown,

The spirit of one dwelling in a seed,
Itself that seed's ripe, unpredictable fruit.

Things are as they seemed to Calvin or to Anne
Of England, to Pablo Neruda in Ceylon,

To Nietzsche in Basel, to Lenin by a lake.
But the integrations of the past are like

A *Museo Olimpico,* so much
So little, our affair, which is the affair

Of the possible: seemings that are to be,
Seemings that it is possible may be.

IV

Nietzsche in Basel studied the deep pool
Of these discolorations, mastering

The moving and the moving of their forms
In the much-mottled motion of blank time.

His revery was the deepness of the pool,
The very pool, his thoughts the colored forms,

The eccentric souvenirs of human shapes,
Wrapped in their seemings, crowd on curious crowd,

In a kind of total affluence, all first,
All final, colors subjected in revery

To an innate grandiose, an innate light,
The sun of Nietzsche gildering the pool,

Yes: gildering the swarm-like manias
In perpetual revolution, round and round . . .

Lenin on a bench beside a lake disturbed
The swans. He was not the man for swans.

The slouch of his body and his look were not
In suavest keeping. The shoes, the clothes, the hat

Suited the decadence of those silences,
In which he sat. All chariots were drowned. The
swans

Moved on the buried water where they lay.
Lenin took bread from his pocket, scattered it—

The swans fled outward to remoter reaches,
As if they knew of distant beaches; and were

Dissolved. The distances of space and time
Were one and swans far off were swans to come.

The eye of Lenin kept the far-off shapes.
His mind raised up, down-drowned, the chariots.

And reaches, beaches, tomorrow's regions became
One thinking of apocalyptic legions.

V

If seeming is description without place,
The spirit's universe, then a summer's day,

Even the seeming of a summer's day,
Is description without place. It is a sense

To which we refer experience, a knowledge
Incognito, the column in the desert,

On which the dove alights. Description is
Composed of a sight indifferent to the eye.

It is an expectation, a desire,
A palm that rises up beyond the sea,

A little different from reality:
The difference that we make in what we see

And our memorials of that difference,
Sprinklings of bright particulars from the sky.

The future is description without place,
The categorical predicate, the arc.

It is a wizened starlight growing young,
In which old stars are planets of morning, fresh

In the brilliantest descriptions of new day,
Before it comes, the just anticipation

Of the appropriate creatures, jubilant,
The forms that are attentive in thin air.

VI

Description is revelation. It is not
The thing described, nor false facsimile.

It is an artificial thing that exists,
In its own seeming, plainly visible,

Yet not too closely the double of our lives,
Intenser than any actual life could be,

A text we should be born that we might read,
More explicit than the experience of sun

And moon, the book of reconciliation,
Book of a concept only possible

In description, canon central in itself,
The thesis of the plentifullest John.

VII

Thus the theory of description matters most.
It is the theory of the world for those

For whom the word is the making of the world,
The buzzing world and lisping firmament.

It is a world of words to the end of it,
In which nothing solid is its solid self.

As, men make themselves their speech: the hard
 hidalgo
Lives the mountainous character of his speech;

And in that mountainous mirror Spain acquires
The knowledge of Spain and of the hidalgo's hat—

A seeming of the Spaniard, a style of life,
The invention of a nation in a phrase,

In a description hollowed out of hollow-bright,
The artificer of subjects still half-night.

It matters, because everything we say
Of the past is description without place, a cast

Of the imagination, made in sound;
And because what we say of the future must portend,

Be alive with its own seemings, seeming to be
Like rubies reddened by rubies reddening.

(*CP* 339–46)

Sounds simmered out of his spinning, hissing mind as he set himself the task of writing this poem for the young men who were about to begin the adventure into life that he had begun in 1900. He felt himself both in their position and, as with Rodríguez Feo, "a man of fortune greeting heirs." The images that up-poured from the salty well of memory reflected both sets of feelings. At the very opening he paraphrased the letter he had received during his first term at Harvard from his father, the letter in which Garrett had instructed his son to question appearances by using the example of the difference between what the sun seemed and what it was (see Vol. I, page. 45). This lesson had stayed with Stevens throughout his life, accounting in part for the sun's being the predominant image in his poetry; its most direct and recent manifestation, before this poem, was in "Notes." At the same time the poet now evoked, too, the persona of the "green queen," imagination, still attached in feeling to his mother, aggrandized to the suggested Semiramis, who existed for him "by the illustrious nothing of her name." Earlier, in "Certain Phenomena of Sound" (*CP* 286–87), he had acknowledged himself as "Semiramide," her son. In his verbal play, "half"—*semi*—belonged to that "branch"—*ramus.* He was, as he had felt in his young manhood, "half-dream"—child of his mother—and "half-deed"—child of his father. Expanding his sense of what he felt when he was the age of the young men he imagined before him as he composed his poem, the poet pointed back to the period that had shaped him: That ". . . age [was] a manner collected from a queen." It was the age that was dying as he left Harvard, the age of Victoria, whose funeral he had poetically celebrated in "The Emperor of Ice-Cream." It was up to those of the present generation to describe their age, what they felt now: "An age is green or red" etc. As he had instructed Rodríguez Feo in a letter written on April 6, 1945, while he was writing this poem: "the power of literature is that in describing the world it creates what it describes. Those things that are not described do not exist, so that in putting together a journal like ORIGENES you are really putting together a world" (*L* 495).

Similarly, Stevens was directing these young men to choose carefully their terms, their weapons in the war of life. He suggested that he as the "youngest poet" had been "arrogant," that later he became a "dark musician," until most recently, when he became involved, as he had been most explicitly in "Notes," with the idea of the "death of the soldier."

In this last phase the earlier, still self-involved image captured in "Le Monocle de Mon Oncle" of tears "up-pouring" was transformed here to the "breath that gushes upward and is gone" in the death of a soldier. With this enlarging of the sense of self, other transpositions came. The myth of Venus/Aphrodite as Botticelli's idealized Primavera, evoked in "The Paltry Nude Starts on a Spring Voyage" of 1919, was now changed. The "curling-out of spring" conjured here reinvested the myth with its more primitive sources. The sign of power, the "purple-leaping element that forth// Would froth the whole heaven with its seeming-so," properly called back the brutality of the birth of love; it was out of froth made purple by the blood of Uranus' member when Cronos (Time) castrated him that the goddess of love was born. Stevens's experience of the century now almost half-dead in the blood of its wars had reinforced his earlier perception that it was time to abandon the romantic (in the "perjorative" sense) myths handed down since the Renaissance had apotheosized the classical past as the Golden Age. The Victorian sensibility—in its ferocious attempt to escape the savage source of human origins suggested by Darwin—had triply strengthened this myth, compounding the romantics' distortions. Stevens was attempting to invert the myth, as he inverted the letters of his words to show that we come "forth" from the "froth" of blood. He did not absolve himself, however, from having contributed to the collective myth. He had had his pantheon of "man-poets," but all "the integrations of the past [were] like//A *Museo Olimpico,* so much/ So little. . . ." They were sketches of the possible that had not become actual.

Stevens poetically described for the young men he saw as his "heirs" his perception of Nietzsche, as he had revealed it to Henry Church. The philosophy of the man who had announced the death of God was a maddened distortion but was perhaps the only adequate response to having confronted what this absence meant—at least at first. Lenin's attempt to deal with the practical aspects of what this knowledge entailed transformed Nietzsche's "swarm-like manias" into a theory of "perpetual revolution" that separated man from nature—"disturbed/ The swans." Lenin's carriage, his "look" were not "*sua*vest," had nothing to do with the "*swa*ns." Stevens's brilliant use of language throughout the poem was especially concentrated here. The procession of sounds from "swarms" to "swans" to "suavest" to "suited" to "silences" spelled the gradual constriction of experience that went together with giving up all myths of having been born in solar chariots. Just as the poet himself had felt when in middle age that the wish for "some imperishable bliss" still "up-poured" inside him, so Lenin's mind raised the "down-drowned" chariots. His was a myth, like any other. In a most extraordinary display of mastery, in the last three lines of the section, Stevens prepared his audience to create an image that would perfectly communicate the power of words to create myths that shaped minds. Because of the "chariots" at line end in the penultimate stanza, the "regions" of the next line call forth "legions." The last line unfolding to the "apocalyptic legions" at its end wholly captures the audience's imagination, makes it one with Lenin's and the poet's. Stevens the sleight of hand man had set his trap. The message was clear, "reaches, beaches, tomorrow's regions"—the world of nature—would become only "One thinking of apocalyptic legions" if certain changes were not made in the description of things as they are. In describing the world we create what we describe.

Appropriately, in the next section, the poet guided his audience to regard "a summer's day" as it was, "without evasion." But for one, all of the section's terms of comparison were unevasive, and belonged to the natural world. The only "unnatural" image was the "column in the desert," set there so that the dove could alight. This column was language. The dove, symbol of the spirit, here learned the tongues necessary to spread the "thesis of the plentifullest John" of the next section. The "revelation" was that the "description" we give to things is all we have. Stevens's commitment was to spread the word of "The buzzing world and lisping firmament," a continuously evolving, ever-changing place in "which nothing solid is its solid self." This poem, perhaps more than any other, was Stevens's testament of praise, a "jubilant" paean to the "forms that are attentive in thin air."

Stevens was articulating his planetary consciousness. He had transformed the youthful defense that allowed him to feel a part of the "Jovian atelier" when he did not feel his kinship with those around him. He here reshaped the defense into an instrument that, if properly used, would shatter the walls that human beings constructed to protect themselves from knowing themselves as "merest minuscule[s] in the gale." In closing the poem, Stevens touched, again through verbal play, on one of the subjects that made him feel his own powerlessness most keenly. "In [this] description hollowed out of hollow-bright" was the presence of his daughter, Holly Bright. He was addressing her as well, his actual heir in this poem to heirs. This and everything else mattered. He did not understand her; she was one of "the subjects still half night" that he would attempt to describe to himself as well.

In the last lines of his poem Stevens subtly but strongly proclaimed to his imagined listeners the importance of taking responsibility for the words they used. The words of the past shaped the "cast"—wonderfully suggesting both a mold and an array of characters—that in turn would shape the future. The underlying pattern of the poem, figured also in the inversions of letters, sounds, and images, was an infinity sign. The individual stood at the point where time twisted on itself:

> . . . alive with its own seemings, seeming to be
> Like rubies reddened by rubies reddening.

The suggestion was, too, that the project for the future, "rubies reddening" colored the sense of the past, "rubies reddened." In this superinversion the operative force was what Stevens indicated in the structure and content of his penultimate line. The verb constructions carried their meaning; the conjurings of the possible, what "must . . . be" determined the seeming complacency of the infinitive "seeming to be." With this sense of responsibility Stevens would urge the young men before him to go out and make their supreme fictions.

Another strain that sinewed itself into the shaping of this poem's lines was the unexpected death of Hi Simons. When Stevens learned of it on April 13 he was "horrified" (*L* 496). This had also made him feel his "helplessness." He wrote this to Simons's widow as he expressed the sympathetic identification he had come to experience with her husband:

> DEAR MRS. SIMONS:
>
> I am horrified to hear of your husband's death. The relation between us in the everyday sense was slight but, in the sense of knowing one another, it was—it could not have been closer. . . . We were much alike in many ways. In the beginning I held off. As time passed, and as we grew accustomed to exchange letters, I felt much freer and had it been possible for us to see one another more often [they had met only once or twice (*L* 498)] we should soon have had something much heartier in common. Please keep this letter.
>
> If I can be of any help to you and your daughter, Sylvia, please let me know. All of us are having a special experience of the loss of friends and

All this with many mulctings of the man,
Effective colonizer sharply stopped
In the door-yard by his own capacious bloom.
But that this bloom grown riper, showing nibs
Of its eventual roundness, puerile tints
Of spiced and weathery rouges, should complex
The stopper to indulgent fatalist
Was unforeseen.

THE COMEDIAN AS THE LETTER C

The poet and his daughter cultivating their garden, c. 1935.

The Bed of Old John Zeller

This structure of ideas, these ghostly sequences
Of the mind, result only in disaster. It follows,
Casual poet, that to add your own disorder to disaster

Makes more of it. It is easy to wish for another structure
Of ideas and to say as usual that there must be
Other ghostly sequences and, it would be, luminous

Sequences, thought of among spheres in the old peak of
night:
This is the habit of wishing, as if one's grandfather lay
In one's heart and wished as he had always wished, unable

To sleep in that bed for its disorder, talking of ghostly
Sequences that would be sleep and ting-tang tossing, so
that
He might slowly forget. It is more difficult to evade

That habit of wishing and to accept the structure
Of things as the structure of ideas. It was the structure
Of things at least that was thought of in the old peak of
night.

> relatives to-day, so much so that we shrink from each new one and feel it with an accumulated intensity and feeling of helplessness. The personality which was a part of your own and in which you and Sylvia lived a large part of your own lives will never be really lost. However that may be, death always terrifies one for a time and overwhelms us with its solitude. . . . (*L* 496–97)

Stevens had written his last letter to Simons on the day that Simons suffered his fatal heart attack; the night before, the critic had been hard at work at his desk, threading together additional notes on the poet. It was perhaps in part because of the loss of this friend on whom he had come to depend as one who would ensure that the meaning of his work would be articulated that the poet was as directive as he was in "Description Without Place." In any case Stevens connected the poem with the death of his friend. Within a couple of weeks he wrote to Allen Tate telling him that he wanted to send him the poem so that it could appear in the same issue of the *Sewanee Review* as Simons's article "The Genre of Wallace Stevens,"[45] which Tate had earlier accepted for publication (*L* 497). The loss of Simons might have contributed, too, to the quick intensity with which Stevens's relationship to Rodríguez Feo developed in the months ahead.

A far less important loss, one of an entirely different kind, came just shortly after the news of Simons's death. As Stevens wrote on May 4 to Florence McAleer of the Holland Society (*L* 498), the latest word from one of the genealogists doing research on his family showed that he was ineligible for membership. This was a "disappointment," as he put it to McAleer; it was a blow to the man who had been trying all his life to establish his place, to know himself as part of the world he inhabited. The investigations into his familial past made it seem, as he wrote to Emma Stevens Jobbins on the same day that he wrote to McAleer, that he was "like the advertisement of Corticelli silk in which they used to represent a kitten all snarled up in a spool of thread" (*L* 498). This feeling, too, contributed to how he described himself in his poem; he belonged no place, hence it was a "Description Without Place." In compensation there was the return to the old solace of imagining himself simply as part of nature. As he noted to Leonard van Geyzel twelve days later, in his poetry he expressed his "desire to contain the world wholly within [his] own perception of it . . . within perceptions that include perceptions that [were] pleasant" (*L* 501). "Description Without Place," then, completed his life, served as the necessary "cure of the mind" for the poet now preoccupied with losses as much as with gains.

❧

As the summer of 1945 opened, there were additional renewed contacts with individuals whose connections with Stevens had been interrupted by the war. One of these was James Guthrie, director of a press in England that published fine editions. To him the poet communicated a sense of what the war had meant and continued to mean:

> It is a relief to know that you have pulled through, even though you are that much older; after all, I am that much older too. But what bothers me isn't so much the mere growing old as the sense of general obsolescence. All through the war there have been very few visible signs of it here in Hartford. Occasionally, on the street, one would see a long string of young men on the way to the draft board, but that was all. We were intent on the war, yet it was far away. At first, when someone that we had known was lost, there was an extraordinary shock; later, this became something in the ordinary course of events, terrifying but inevitable. At the moment we are passing through a period of readjustment. The ordinary state of mind seems to be one of suspense. Shortly, when the Japanese war begins to mount in fury, we shall feel differently. I think people here have no interest whatever in the Orient, and the truth about Japan seems to be difficult for most of us to grasp. From our point of view here at home, America has never been on the make, or on the grab, whatever people may have said of us elsewhere. The Japanese war is likely to change all that. This morning one of the people on the radio was talking about the necessity for having fortified outposts throughout the Orient. I think most people would accept that idea quite naturally, and be willing to fight for it.
>
> What all this means is a general change in our ideas respecting other people. I don't think that most of us have realized the extent to which conspiracy and greed and gall dominate the world. America is really a vast countryside: what you call in your letter a "hamlet among elm trees and farms." America is just that on a large scale. And the people in it, whatever people abroad may think of us, are very largely the sort of people who are happy and contented with life "among elm trees and farms." But it almost seems as though that was all over for the present, and for the next generation or two. There is an impression of profound disturbance and of bewilderment as to the outcome, and of intense doubt as to the purposes of the disturbance. . . . (*L* 506–07)

In mid-July the poet repeated to Henry Church his feelings of frustration at what the war meant: "The benumbing effect of the war seems to grow constantly worse." He went on to describe some of the satisfactions of the time he had spent in Cambridge when he read his Phi Beta Kappa poem. This, at least, had been renewing: "The truth is that these occasional returns to Cambridge seem to get at something one vitally needs and that this is all the more true when one meets people there." The poet had met Dr. (I. A.) Richards, Robert Woods Bliss "(the man who gave Dumbarton Oaks)," and one of China's delegates to San Francisco, "who quoted from Confucius one of those sayings that relieve life of all its complexities." The Chinese delegate had also said that "we must struggle a long time to acquire humanity." After seeing, too, his old housemate Arthur Pope, Stevens came away feeling that he had to "struggle to stay among the humans whose humanity [was] necessary to [him]" (*L* 508). Church was clearly in this category, and the poet wrote to him of the inner workings of his spirit. He added that again this summer, though he would have liked to go to Pennsylvania, he was not up to doing the walking that would be necessary if he were to experience "nature" in more than what John Crowe Ransom called the "picnic sense" (*L* 507). He was feeling old, obsolescent, as he had observed to Guthrie.

But there were compensations. Elsie filled the house with roses every day. A young man from New Haven who was interested in Stevens came up one day to have lunch with him. Though the poet was somewhat disturbed by the fact that this "really accomplished youth" seemed to be influenced by "reputations" and had not discovered anything of "novelty" on his own, Stevens still valued the contact and spent a long time talking with him, no doubt guiding him to question the basis of "reputation . . . something in itself [that] lives and dies pretty much without roots . . . produc[ing] growths out of air that have little to do with nature" (*L* 150).

And as usual, there was reading. While still heavily immersed in the history of the Pennsylvania settlers, Stevens looked forward to getting to the four-volume *Journal of Jules Renard* (*L* 510). An anecdote the poet related to Henry Church after going through two volumes of the early German sectarians of Pennsylvania seemed curiously to echo the theme, albeit somewhat transposed, of "Cy Est Pourtraicte, Madame Ste Ursule, et Les Unze Mille Vierges":

> At Ephrata [a town near Reading] one of these groups [of sectarians] built the earliest monastery ever built in this country. One of the sisters, Bernice, described as a young woman of extraordinary beauty, died there. In one of the prayers that was said for her the wish was expressed that, in the garden of the future, she would be affable to her many suitors. In short, she took vows so that, in chastity, she might dream of suitors hereafter. I stopped to think about that last evening. Now that I have heard of the world as Wartesaal ["waiting-room," from Mrs. Church] doesn't it seem, in the light of the spirit of Bernice, as if what we do was merely a crude form of what we shall do hereafter? Is it going to be any better after waiting in New York to wait in Jerusalem the Golden?
>
> The whole story of the early Pennsylvania Pietists is precious. When I was a boy I met one of these sisters in Ephrata. She was then 90 and her father could very well have gone back to the time when the vital characters were still alive. (*L* 511)

The date of the letter in which Stevens related the above anecdote was August 27. July 26 was the date of the previous letter Stevens wrote in the collection as it is. Between these two dates the United States had dropped the bombs on Hiroshima and Nagasaki (on August 6 and 9). Did Stevens remain completely silent about this catastrophe? Were his retreats into yet more reconstructions of the past and his musings about life's being a "waiting-room" for the hereafter distractions from facing the "pathos" of what had happened?

It is impossible to know how the poet was affected. The evidence as it stands indicates that for the present he continued as if nothing had happened. He did not even refer to the war's end.

The fair weather over the long Labor Day weekend brought the summer to a close. In his description of how he spent this short holiday the poet revealed some of the tender details of his relationship to domesticated nature:

> We had a long weekend last week and I spent three afternoons sitting in the garden at home. Everyone seemed to be away. I had lunch there three times in succession, mostly white Burgundy. Someone in the neighborhood keeps pigeons and they come at noon and pick up things from the grass. There is one of them, a black and white, an old friend of mine whom I call Marble Cake. Sitting there, with a little of Kraft's Limburger Spread and a glass or two of a really decent wine, with not a voice in the universe and with those big, fat pigeons moving round, keeping an eye on me and doing queer things to keep me awake, all of these things make the New Republic and its contents (most of the time) of no account [Stevens was referring particularly to an article on Ransom by Jean Wahl in the latest issue; both the poet and Church, to whom this letter was addressed, were disturbed by Wahl's negative criticism]. (*L* 512)

Within a little more than two weeks there was another occasion of a seemingly festive sort. Stevens invited Allen Tate and the Churches to lunch at one of New York's finest French restaurants, the Chambord. In a note to Church confirming time and place, the poet prevailed on his friend to call up for him and in his "best French ask for the best table in the place" (September 6, 1945). The afternoon went very well. After it Tate sent "Dear Mr. Stevens or Dear Mr. Wallace if [he] prefer[red]," a thank-you note in which he added "no more Mr. Tate from you, please," and suggested, too, that the next time they gathered Stevens ask Marianne Moore to join them; "she is one of the *real* people," he commented. He also thanked the older poet for getting Knopf to charge more for his latest volume, *Seasons of the Soul* (October 20, 1945).

On October 18 the poet again wrote to James Guthrie. After commenting on some of the printing details surrounding the Cummington Press's forthcoming edition of *Esthétique du Mal* (one concerned his dislike of colored inks except for illuminated first letters), Stevens again voiced observations about the political scene, but they were empty of any mention of August's catastrophe:

> More than ever there is a feeling that anything not a part of politics, not a part of sociology and not in a general way a phase of mass thinking has any right to exist. What is going on in the world now is an extraordinary manipulation of the masses. The manipulating forces are not apparent. It can hardly be said that the politicians are manipulating forces because, as the great strikes demonstrate, the forces behind the strikes are defiant of the politicians. The mechanism for this sort of thing has been perfected beyond

> belief. I cannot say that it disturbs me very much. One has the feeling, at least over here, that it will come right in the end. We have never exploited the workers as they have been exploited elsewhere; it is still true I think that the man at the very bottom feels that there is a chance for him to be the man at the top. . . . (*L* 515)

Stevens's silence about the bombings, together with the closing comments in the above quotation from his letter, are disturbing. They point to a kind of meliorist attitude associated with a conservative posture that has usually been attached to the poet. In the context of all the other voicings of his sympathy with the left and with socialism, however, assigning him this position is impossible. But perhaps Stevens's disappointment in the "mass of men" prompted him to fall back into a version of the old misanthropic feeling of his youth. As noted earlier, it was at such moments that he was prone to racist remarks. It might be possible that his peculiar expression to Guthrie was of the same nature. It was clear, after all, that Stevens was deeply troubled by the state of affairs in America. As he observed to Harry Duncan on November 8, apropos of how pleased he was by the way the edition of *Esthétique du Mal* had turned out, "At the present time, when everything is in such a funk, this book has done more for my own reconversion than anything else I can think of . . ." (*L* 516).

While a severe critic could find in this statement more evidence for thinking Stevens someone without moral concern, as John Crowe Ransom had described him in connection with "Sea Surface Full of Clouds,"[46] wholly self-involved, an elitist of the first order, this judgment would not gel with the other facts as they appear. It would be more accurate to see Stevens's expression above rather as pointing to one of those occasions when he was so moved by the horror of what he observed that he once more turned his attention to something that could give solace, in this case, the edition of his volume, not particularly as his work, but as a product of the Cummington School students' concern and application in creating an object of beauty.

With his spirits raised out of the "funk" however slightly, the next day Stevens addressed himself to answering a letter from Charles Norman (a member of the staff of *PM* newspaper), who had written asking the poet to contribute a statement on the case of Ezra Pound. The other contributors included e. e. cummings, William Carlos Williams, Karl Shapiro, F. O. Matthiessen, Louis Untermeyer, and Conrad Aiken. The young man who had never gotten on with his peers did not now, in the wisdom of his older age, bend to peer pressure. He refused Norman in a letter characterized both by the skill he used in setting things out as an attorney and by the biting wit he used—as did Castiglione's "Great Captain"—whenever he wanted to criticize unworthy or questionable acts:

> DEAR MR. NORMAN:
>
> I prefer not to take part in your symposium on Pound ["The Case for and

Against Ezra Pound" appeared in *PM* on November 25, 1945] and although I am going to say a word or two about the thing, I don't want to be quoted or referred to in any way.

It seems to me that since Pound's liberty, not to say even his life, may be at stake, he ought to be consulted about this sort of thing. After all, he might shrink from the idea of your doing what you propose to do. Then again, he may be guilty and he may admit it. He is an eccentric person. I don't suppose there is the slightest doubt that he did what he is said to have done. While he may have many excuses, I must say that I don't consider the fact that he is a man of genius as an excuse. Surely, such men are subject to the common disciplines.

There are a number of things that could well be said in his defense. But each one of these things is so very debatable, that one would not care to say them, without having thought them out most carefully. One such possibility is that the acts of propagandists should not entail the same consequences as the acts of a spy or informer because noone attaches really serious importance to propaganda. I still don't smoke Camels, don't eat Wheaties and don't use Sweetheart soap. I don't believe that the law of treason should apply to chatter on the radio when it is so recognizably chatter.

At the same time, that remark illustrates what I said a moment ago, that the things that might be said in Pound's defense are things that ought to be carefully thought out. His motives might be significant. Yet it is entirely possible that Pound deliberately and maliciously undertook to injure this country. Don't you think it worthwhile waiting until you know why he did what he did before rallying to his defense?

I repeat that the question of his distinction seems to me to be completely irrelevant. If his poetry is in point, then so are Tokyo Rose's singing and wise-cracking. If when he comes over, he wants help and shows that he is entitled to it, then I, for one, should be very glad to help him and I mean that in a practical way and [will] do anything possible for him.

I write this way because I think it highly likely that Pound has very good personal friends who will rally around him. They might well resent just this sort of thing that you propose to do, but I know nothing about it. I merely want to keep out of it.

This letter is not to be quoted or used in any way.

Yours very truly,
W. STEVENS
(*L* 516–17)

It should be especially noted that Stevens voiced that he would be very happy to help Pound in whatever ways necessary if Pound were to announce that he wanted help and if he merited it. Stevens's circumspection in dealing with this issue belonged, I think, to the sense he had developed as a lawyer. On the one hand, he knew the binding power of the written word and on the other he was sensitive to the care that had to be exercised in respecting individual rights and wishes. He was also keenly attentive to wanting to get facts firsthand. Propaganda was one thing; reasoned dialogue was another. One could easily extend this observation to Stevens's whole sphere of involvement with politics over the years. As a lawyer he knew how much was at stake in committing to paper even one slip of the tongue. But, then, at what point does prudence yield to equivocation, which can then be misinterpreted? This suggests one of the reasons why Stevens was so easily subject to being misperceived.

As rotting winter rains approached, bringing their misery, Stevens tried to raise his spirits with little treats and anticipations of pleasant events to come. As he wrote to Henry Church on November 20, he had been in New York the previous week and did not stay into the evening as he would have liked because of the rain. But he did stop at Dean's, his favorite bakery, where he bought a plum cake, some of which, together with a glass of milk, he made his dinner back home in his Hartford kitchen. He "went to bed quite happy," he added, like a child who likes nothing more than to dine only on sweets. He noted, too, that he would be back in New York on December 5 for "one of the St. Nicholas blow-outs" that he so enjoyed and looked forward to seeing Church then. As always, he commented on his most recent reading—an article on Kafka in the current *Quarterly Review of Literature,* which he found quite good—and replied to his friend's latest query about whether the poet knew a certain author, this time Henri Pourrat, whose work Stevens did not know but soon would. Stevens then mused about the kind of individual he would like to imagine as existing:

> Every now and then one comes across some really powerful character in an out of the way place. I mean a really powerful character who writes, or paints, or walks up and down and thinks, like some overwhelming animal in a corner of the zoo. Personally, I feel terribly in need of encountering some such character. The other night I sat in my room in the moonlight thinking about the top men in the world today, people like Truman and [British Foreign Minister Ernest] Bevin, for example. That I suppose is the source of one's desire for a few really well developed individuals. What is terribly lacking from life today is the well developed individual, the master of life, or the man who by his mere appearance convinces you that a mastery of life is possible. Very likely the only reason Stalin has been out of sight recently is that he is laughing his head off at the thought of the soft people who are trying to oppose him: to hold him back. He doesn't want everybody to know it. The unfortunate part about that is that in the long run these people will hold him back and, for my own part, I think they should. But they don't make life a particularly agreeable thing to experience. I shall remember Pourrat. Somehow his name makes me think of Aix. A few years ago I bought through Vidal about twenty books from the library of a man who used to live at Aix, Gustave Mouravit. Many of these are exquisite things. I still have all of them. No doubt Mouravit knew everyone in Aix that was

> worth while. He was a lawyer who seems to have had a large practice in the south of France and was intensely interested in local things. He was precisely the sort of tough being that I have been speaking of. . . . (*L* 518)

In describing Mouravit as this kind of man, Stevens was describing himself, who, in addition, had the qualification of being a poet. Could he have been unaware of this comparison that in effect meant he was patting himself on the back? In a later note to Barbara Church in which he again praised Mouravit, he added: "No man could have caressed his books more than this man . . ." (*L* 567)—no one perhaps but himself. There was an ironic underside to this subtle identification. As Stevens also observed to Barbara Church, Mouravit left his entire library to his daughter, who kept it "in austere solitude in a lonely house in Aix." After her death the only one left was a son, who simply sold the library. Stevens's library met a similar fate.

In addition to the coming winter storms, a storm of a different kind arrived at the end of November to dampen the wholehearted pleasure that the Cummington Press edition had given Stevens. On November 23, Alfred Knopf wrote irritatedly: "I do think I have a right to expect you to drop me a line informing me whenever you plan for someone else to publish a book by you, however slight it might be—even fifteen printed pages. The volume of your work has never been great and 'seven or eight sheets' mean much more in your case than so little might where another poet is concerned." Not even the photo of the Cummington students at work soothed the publisher's pique. But, then, the publication of *Esthétique du Mal* had unfortunately coincided with difficulties Knopf had been having over the Fortune Press edition of selected Stevens poems that Nicholas Moore wanted to bring out in England. After exchanging summaries of the files both Knopf and Stevens had kept in regard to this edition, with the poet offering to reimburse Knopf for the cables he had sent to England, the two men eventually ironed out their differences, though not without the poet's becoming extremely sensitive, in the future, to anticipating his publisher's requirements. As Stevens once remarked, Knopf was his "guardian angel" (August 28, 1946), necessary once, to be respected now.

But there were bright notes as the close of the year approached. The Harvard-Yale game at the end of November—this year Stevens attended it with Elsie. There was also a wonderful New Year's wish from Rodríguez Feo. As Stevens wrote back to Rodríguez Feo, though there was not the slightest chance of his "going to Cuba or anywhere else faraway for the present," he would "like to take a trip through the air and go several thousand miles straight up and there explode into no end of stars, which would read, in Spanish, 'regards to Pompilio'" (*L* 520).

The explosions of the bombs over Hiroshima and Nagasaki seem not to have gone unnoticed. The poet could not escape his sympathy with things as they were, and his need to transform them into what could "give pleasure" was as strong as it ever was, perhaps even stronger in the face of the monumental event that had, in effect, brought the war to an end. The result for Stevens was a cosmic fantasy, a wish fulfillment of magnificent proportion. But just as in his youth he had deflated his grandiose ambitions and expressions, he did so now, having the stars spell out greetings to a dumb beast. Nonetheless, this imagining was significant. The image stayed with Stevens and connected with others—those attached to his delight in the aurora borealis,[47] for example. By the time he wrote "The Auroras of Autumn" about two years later, the soothing quality of the positive images allowed him to look at what the explosion of the atom bomb had meant and to counterpoise evocations of it against those of natural phenomena, like the northern lights, to suggest the perversion of the power of nature in the hands of human beings.

Charles Berger has made an admirable contribution to the reading of Stevens in having first pointed out the connections between "The Auroras of Autumn" and the explosion of the atom bomb. The ever-present cloud in the poem had never been adequately explained, nor had lines like the following:

VI

It is a theatre floating through the clouds,
Itself a cloud, although of misted rock
And mountains running like water, wave on wave,

Through waves of light. It is of cloud transformed
To cloud transformed again, idly, the way
A season changes color to no end,

Except the lavishing of itself in change,
As light changes yellow into gold and gold
To its opal elements and fire's delight,

Splashed wide-wise because it likes magnificence
And the solemn pleasures of magnificent space.
The cloud drifts idly through half-thought-of forms.

The theatre is filled with flying birds,
Wild wedges, as of a volcano's smoke, palm-eyed
And vanishing, a web in a corridor

Or massive portico. A capitol,
It may be, is emerging or has just
Collapsed. The denouement has to be postponed . . .

This is nothing until in a single man contained,
Nothing until this named things nameless is
And is destroyed. He opens the door of his house

On flames. The scholar of one candle sees
An Arctic effulgence flaring on the frame
Of everything he is. And he feels afraid.

VII

Is there an imagination that sits enthroned
As grim as it is benevolent, the just
And the unjust, which in the midst of summer stops

To imagine winter? . . .

. . . .

It leaps through us, through all our heavens leaps,
Extinguishing our planets, one by one,
Leaving, of where we were and looked, of where

We knew each other and of each other thought,
A shivering residue, chilled and foregone,
Except for that crown and mystical cabala.

. . . .

IX

. . . .

Shall we be found hanging in the trees next spring?
Of what disaster is this the imminence:
Bare limbs, bare trees and a wind as sharp as salt?

The stars are putting on their glittering belts.
They throw around their shoulders cloaks that flash
Like a great shadow's last embellishment.
(*CP* 416–17 and 419)

"The Auroras of Autumn" was Stevens's final "Farewell to an idea . . . ," the idea of human progress that had been the earmark of the age in which he had been born and come to maturity. The question that had been raised by those who had taken Darwin seriously and which had begun to perplex Stevens as a young man at Harvard seemed to have arrived at its inescapable answer. But there was still some time that passed between the autumn of 1945, when Stevens had his first inklings of his bond to the dust the bombs sent up, and the "final no" that came in 1947.

In spite of how his political position was perceived, in late December 1945 Stevens's peers at the National Institute of Arts and Letters voted to install him as a fellow. This was certainly a fitting honor for the poet who had been struggling throughout his career to articulate what he understood as necessary if words were to play their part in describing the landscape of spirit in a world where God no longer set the rules. In the months between the letter announcing his election and the ceremonies on May 17, 1946, Stevens continued in his attempt to make his speech fluent.

He went on searching throughout the various things he read for signposts and points of recognition. He communicated many of these, as he had done over the years, to Henry Church; others he voiced to José Rodríguez Feo. In response to Church's announcing in mid-January that he had recently been trying to "penetrate Kierkegaard (WAS 3461), the poet wrote that he had come across the following:

> Here is a little note by a Scot on Kierkegaard. I like the conclusion that unless one is abnormal one ceases to exist as part of civilization since civilization is itself abnormal. That is not quite what he says but it is involved. I don't wonder therefore that he winds up with nothing at all since what is "vague and rhetorical" is certainly nothing at all. I send this to you because you mentioned Kierkegaard. For myself, the inaccessible jewel is the normal and all of life, in poetry, is the difficult pursuit of just that. (*L* 521)

He was dogged in his pursuit. In the same letter he mentioned just having read an enchanting review of Morris R. Cohen's *A Preface to Logic* (1944)[48] and another book by Stephen Coburn Pepper, *Aesthetic Quality: A Contextualistic Theory of Beauty* (1937). He had also just read Palinurus (Cyril Connolly), *The Unquiet Grave: A Word Cycle* (1945), some of Henri Pourrat (probably *Vent de Mars*) and a biography of Conrad Weiser, the religious leader who, Stevens thought, had most likely "emigrated, possibly in the same vessel, with [his] own people." Of the last book, Stevens remarked: "He [Weiser] became an Indian interpreter and a local hero in my part of Pennsylvania. It has been like having the past crawl out all over the place. The author has not corrected his spelling. This is pure Pennsylvania German and, while it might bore anyone else to shreds, it has kept me up night after night, wild with interest . . ." (*L* 521).

There appeared to be a large element of distraction from things as they were in what Stevens chose to focus on—again, sounds, in their transformations, indicators of a people's movement. But another aspect of the poet's reading and his long immersion in history, particularly of the sixteenth- and seventeenth-century religious wars in Europe and the consequent events in the New World, could also have accounted, at least in part, for the attitude he had maintained in the face of the war. The U.S. opposition to Germany and Japan represented an ideological, if not an openly religious, confrontation. The late reported facts that the Japanese were willing to fight to the last man in order to defeat the United States easily justified, in the minds of most, Truman's decision to drop the bombs on Hiroshima and Nagasaki. The inhuman horror we associate with these events, with hindsight and the availability of films recording some of the effects, could not have been imagined behind the black letters coolly describing the successful deployment on our enemy of the newest weapon in the American arsenal. While Stevens was, I believe, like

Alain, wholly opposed to war, he, again like his French counterpart, could not separate himself from the battle for what he hoped would stem the aggression of antidemocratic powers. This was precisely the time when America became aware of its role as a global power in preventing the kinds of unprovoked acts that had led to both world wars.[49] The position in which Stevens found himself was, as it was for many, agonizing; he was pulled in opposite directions. The result was, as he had expressed to Church, "benumbing." It was not, as it might have appeared, that he simply took on a stoical posture. Quite the contrary. As he voiced in his poetic address to the young men at Harvard, everything mattered, every sound, every phrase.

Because he felt this way and also realized that his perspective about what mattered most was colored by his limited experience of the war from his stately Connecticut home, Stevens was uneasy about how his most recent work would be received—especially by those closer to what the reality of the war had meant. On February 19, 1946, he wrote to Harry Duncan, first to express how delighted he was about the news that the *Esthétique* edition had been chosen by the American Institute of Graphic Arts as one of the fifty best examples of books for 1946; he then noted that because of the recent difficulties he had had with Alfred Knopf, he was not going to let Nicholas Moore use "Esthétique" or go ahead, for the time, with the Fortune Press edition. He added that beyond wanting to keep his publisher happy—since "it was more important to be published in this country than anywhere else"—he was also

> not at all sure that the sort of book that the English book would be [would be] the right thing to publish in England at present. At best it is difficult for an American poet to make his way in England. With all the realism of their situation over there, my sort of thing might find itself terribly out of place, and, if so, given the freedom with which Englishmen discuss American books, would probably have no chance at all. (*L* 524)

About two weeks later Stevens repeated his reservations to Rodríguez Feo in a more specific manner—at least until the paragraph's last cryptic sentence:

> It is a curious experience to read poems like those that have just appeared in ORIGENES after the lapse of six months or more from the time when they were written. We seem to be experiencing a rather violent change of taste. The misery of Europe, which was greater six months ago than it is now, seems not to have been so real to us then as it is now; and the more real it becomes the more sharply one feels that poetry of this sort is academic and unreal. One is inclined, therefore, to sympathize with one's more unsympathetic critics. It is all well enough to say that, in the long run, what was appropriate once will be appropriate again, but it does not follow; after all, nothing follows. The life of a poet, like the life of a painter, is just as difficult and as unpredictable as the life of a speculator on Wall Street. But if a poet experiences these eras in which what he thinks and writes seems to be

> otiose, he is bound to recognize that, in the same eras, almost everything that other people write, as well as the pictures they paint, and the music they write seems [*sic*] to be equally otiose. Yet to live exclusively in reality is as intolerable as it is incomprehensible, and I can say this even though yesterday, after playing a little Debussy on the gramophone, I thought how exactly he sounded like [Cécile] Chaminade. . . . (*L* 525)

What did that "even though" mean? Did the pleasure he felt mean that art was not "otiose" even when it seemed so if the individuality of the artist lost its distinctiveness and became identical with that of another who shared in the spirit of an age?

In spite of his hesitations about how his work now seemed, Stevens still defended what he had been attempting. This is clear in his response to a question put to him on April 14 by the editor of the *Yale Literary Magazine.* The poet was asked what he considered the greatest problem facing the young writer in America at the time; his answer appeared in the spring number of the magazine:

> Today, in America, all roles yield to that of the politician.
>
> The role of the poet may be fixed by contrasting it to that of the politician. The poet absorbs the general life: the public life. The politician is absorbed by it. The poet is individual. The politician is general. It is the personal in the poet that is the origin of his poetry. If this is true respecting the relation of the poet to the public life and respecting the origin of his poetry, it follows that the first phase of his problem is himself.
>
> This does not mean that he is a private figure. On the other hand, it does mean that he must not allow himself to be absorbed as the politician is absorbed. He must remain individual. As individual he must remain free. The politician expects everyone to be absorbed as he himself is absorbed. This expectation is part of the sabotage of the individual. The second phase of the poet's problem, then, is to maintain his freedom, the only condition in which he can hope to produce significant poetry.
>
> If people are to become dependent on poetry for any of the fundamental satisfactions, poetry must have an increasingly intellectual scope and power. This is a time for the highest poetry. We never understood the world less than we do now nor, as we understand it, liked it less. We never wanted to understand it more or needed to like it more. These are the intense compulsions that challenge the poet as the appreciatory creator of values and beliefs. That, finally, states the problem.
>
> I have not touched on form which, although significant, is not vital today, as substance is. When one is an inherent part of the other, form, too, is vital. (*L* 526)

His statement was a subtle argument. It reflected the skill of lawyer Stevens as much as it did the thought progressions of his best poems. His stressing the importance of maintaining individual freedom in the face of even the greatest pressures at the same time as he emphasized that the poet was not "a private figure" but one who "absorbs the general life" exemplified his mastery of equivocation. The laying out of this casuistic argument also explained the last sentence to Rodríguez Feo above.

But a deeper question arises. Was Stevens presenting a challenge to the youths who might become virile poets? Was he presenting a paradox as a Zen master might, in order to force possible future poets to use all their "intellectual scope and power" to meet the questions facing them? Or was Stevens's response an indication that at sixty-six he had resolved nothing but was still "moving up and down between two elements," unable to take a fixed position because he had never become certain enough of himself? The answer is that both were true. Stevens saw the human personality as "the more than rational distortion." He knew that in accounting for motivation, it is not "either-or" but "both" or "all" that gives the answer.

Stevens knew too that in his century the awareness of this complexity belonged to more than those who in the past had systematically questioned belief. It was true that he had never stopped moving up and down, that he was as uncertain as ever, but he belonged to an age when reason, the same tool that had been consistently unfolding the mysteries of our tie to nature, had also come up against itself in explaining the particularly human aspect of nature. "There are things in a man besides his reason" (*CP* 351). It was not only he who was uncertain. With the disappearance of a 5,000-year-old god certainty itself had been pulled away. Stevens was simply one of those few attuned to how it felt to exist in this vacuum where he still believed that there was "a sense in sounds beyond their meaning" (*CP* 352). The greatest problem of the age was the "will to believe," the desire, born out of Western thought's reasoned progress, to find something that would suffice. It was as Nietzsche expressed in *The Twilight of the Idols,* "I fear we shall never be rid of God, so long as we still believe in grammar."[50] Faced with this dilemma wasn't the best advice to apply oneself to the work of forging the "highest poetry," a new language cleansed of the terms of cause and effect, a new language that at least would not contradict the present experience of uncertainty? Seen in this light, Stevens's statement was not an evasion prompted by the fear of judgment but a straightforward confrontation with and admission of his limitations and an explanation of why he had attempted what he did:

> A text we should be born that we might read
> More explicit than the experience of sun
>
> And moon. . . .
>
> (*CP* 344)

An estimated 35 million had died serving in World War II; 10 million more had been exterminated in Nazi camps. It was April 1946. Henry Church was soon to return to his home in France, Ville-d'Avray, memorialized in the last century by Camille Corot. Stevens imagined that some of the soldiers now dead had probably, in their sequential occupations, left it in a bad state, yet he was happy that his friend was returning and that he planned to come back to New York in the fall.

With his awareness of what could have been seen as the "academic and unreal" aspect of the poems he had been writing, when new requests came in late spring and through the summer,[51] Stevens responded by composing lines around more timely subjects. "A Woman Sings for a Soldier Come Home" (*CP* 360), "Burghers of Petty Death" (*CP* 362), "The Pediment of Appearance" (*CP* 361), "The Good Man Has No Shape" (*CP* 364) touched, in their titles or in their content, the brutal facts or informing causes of what had passed. The remaining poems that eventually made up *Transport to Summer*—"Human Arrangement" (*CP* 363), "The Red Fern" (*CP* 365), "From the Packet of Anacharsis" (*CP* 365), "The Dove in the Belly" (*CP* 366–67), "Mountains Covered with Cats" (*CP* 367), "The Prejudice Against the Past" (*CP* 368), "Extraordinary References" (*CP* 369), "Attempt to Discover Life" (*CP* 370), "A Lot of People Bathing in a Stream" (*CP* 371), "Credences of Summer" (*CP* 372), "A Pastoral Nun" (*CP* 378), and "The Pastor Caballero" (*CP* 379)—reflected in their progress the slow, healing movement away from the pain of things that were. These gradually became "green flauntings of the hours of peace" (*CP* 380) when the poet could again contemplate nature and imagine the sounds of clouds passing, as in "Human Arrangement." Later, with ". . . midsummer come and all fools slaughtered," his mind could [lay] by its trouble and consider once more the "fidgets of remembrance" (*CP* 372). As the pressure of events eased, his personal past could begin to live for another few years in his memory. He recovered moments step by step. Amid the scattered pediments of abstract appearances he placed images redolent of the odors of his childhood. Through the figure of Anacharsis he recollected his grandfather's "farm . . . fat and the land in which it lay" (*CP* 365). The address of the mother to her child in "Extraordinary References," *"This first spring after the war"* (*CP* 369), carried the accent of the Pennsylvania Dutch women he recalled talking with his mother in the marketplace. In "A Lot of People Bathing in a Stream" he re-created his own boyhood joy at "passing a boundary to dive/ Into the sun-filled water" (*CP* 371). "Credences of Summer" circled Reading's tower atop Mount Penn as if it were "the natural tower of all the world" (*CP* 373). The poet was regaining himself as the world returned to what at least seemed peace after the major devastation.

There were other signs of transition, signs of a different sort. The poet wrote to Paule Vidal apropos of not feeling he was in a position to spend 60,000 francs for a painting she had recently described to him in tantalizing words:

> You ask about Truman. He is very much of a politician and, while he seems to be a man of sincerity and of sufficient ability, I think most people who are

> not themselves politicians feel diffident about him. I note that Samedi-Soir has an article in it to the effect that the United States is going to go without hot biscuits in order to feed the world. That is a political statement. Of course it is quite untrue. What is actually happening is that I am paying half my income for taxes and expect to do so for the balance of my life. Europe is having its share of the benefit of that sort of thing. One unspoken reason why I hesitate to pay as much as 60,000 francs for a painting is that I have only half my income at my disposal. When a newspaper says something that indicates that we are merely giving up a crumb this may be good politics. But that sort of thing is why people are diffident about politicians. You and I and most other people have only one foothold in the world and that is the truth. . . . (*L* 528)

In compensation for not being able to afford this piece, he wanted Jean Paulhan's *Clef de Poésie* and additional samples of new French weeklies. These and lesser things would have to do: a watercolor by someone just beginning to be known in the United States, Camille Bombois, if she could get one for between 5,000 and 7,000 francs (the poet added that he wanted to know about the intention of the painter). By August 9, after hearing of two Bombois canvases, the poet wired 50,000 francs to Mlle. Vidal in spite of his earlier reluctance to spend 60,000 on La Patellière's work. Perhaps receiving the Harriet Monroe Poetry Award (together with Marianne Moore, Robert Penn Warren, and Morton Dauwen Zabel) in June had made Stevens feel he could indulge himself.

The renewed activity with Vidal that regularly brought his new weeklies brought the poet back into contact with Europe. This was especially valuable to him now, for it prompted a reassertion of his Americanness, while making him sense, at the same time, how truly the New World was the child of the Old. The reviews he received from Paris whetted his appetite for more. As he noted to Henry Church on August 6, on his last trip to New York a week or two before he made his way to Wittenborn's bookshop, where he spent $14.50 on "a copy of Graphis, Quadrique and one or two others." But he felt that they were "worth it because one never realizes how completely we seem to belong to Europe until we attempt to get along without it" (*L* 531). He then went on to voice his chauvinism, in spite of these ties:

> There is a growing sense here of the increasing strength of the powers at work to promote interests other than our own. Such powers are always at work but they are not always strong and we have been accustomed to take them rather lightly. England is trying to commit us to her welfare. The Jews are trying to commit us to their welfare. It is hard to understand Russia. One English weekly says that we made the loan to England because we were afraid of Russia. That, of course, is a typically English weekly attitude. We are not afraid of Russia. It may be that with her aggressive attitude she is making progress toward her goal a good deal more rapidly

> than we are toward our goal, but, surely, we are not afraid. Nevertheless, we have the sense that Russian antagonism is growing stronger and more widespread and we are bound to meet it everywhere. The world is full of poverty and misfortune and it seems to take little or no effort to convince people that communism means an escape from poverty and a refuge from misfortune. Maybe it does. It is true that there are great masses of poverty and misfortune in the United States itself, but there are great masses of the opposite: there are great masses of happy, hopeful and ambitious people who expect to make something of themselves and of the world in which they live. Why Russia should be so aggressive unless she feels that she cannot maintain herself in competition with our system is more than I can imagine. . . . (*L* 532)

Recollecting parts of his past and feeling the more relaxed pulse of peace nurturing his ties to nature, Stevens made plans to return with Elsie to Pennsylvania for the last weeks of summer. The expressed reticences about his ability to walk long distances that he had used to quell his desire to return for the last years now showed themselves to have been mere excuses. Imaginatively preparing for the trip, in mid-August he wrote of his plans to José Rodríguez Feo and added the following about his feelings for nature:

> It would be interesting to talk to you about our loss of interest in what you call the beauty of Nature, but it would be most interesting to talk to you about the eccentricities that ensue. I wonder whether you are right about outgrowing nature. Perhaps the man who has never had a chance to enjoy life, outgrows it. One of my firm beliefs is that Life and Nature are one. Consequences of boredom are, therefore, practically unknown to me. Perhaps I have been bored at Church, or at the Theatre, or by a book, but certainly, I have never been bored in any general sense and at my ripe age, I am quite sure that I shall never be. The extent to which Nature and Life are the same, is something on which you ought to be able to throw a particular light, because you have the advantage of all your wonderful beaches. . . . (*L* 534)

It was clear that on this trip, back in contact with the "soil" that was his "intelligence," Stevens was as far as he had ever been from being bored. The stay was, for the most part, so enjoyable that he and Elsie extended it to more than three weeks, even though this meant that the poet missed meeting Rodríguez Feo for the first time on September 18, as they had previously arranged. In his note of apology to his "Dear Antillean," he explained by saying that he and Elsie had "had one of the happiest holidays [they had] ever had" (*L* 534–35). They had been mostly in sweet-smelling Hershey, where they met with the Powells, whom they had not seen for years, and they spent the last "several days" in Reading (after having originally planned to go for a few hours, according to a postcard Elsie sent her sister September 7, 1946). But some new phrasing of the old "movement up and down" seems to have occurred since in a later letter to Powell (December 12, 1946),[52] he contradicted what he had written to his Cuban friend: "We left to go down to Reading, intending to stay for three or four days. But we found the place really unbearable and we left almost immediately without seeing a single one of the few relatives of mine who still live there. When one has left home the place naturally changes. What I had not realized is that it keeps changing until a point is reached at which the old familiar life of it is dead and gone." It is impossible to account for what went on here. Had Stevens forgotten "how precious" everyone in the family had seemed to him just two years before? Had the old feeling of revulsion for Reading as the "acme of dullness" suddenly welled up with a recollection of how he had been in his youth when he stood before the mirror, gloatingly remarking, "What a handsome man am I!" much to his mother's dismay?[53] Reading was, after all, his *fons Bandusiae,* the glass in which he saw himself reflected. Did he see in its decaying changes an image of himself from which he had to turn away? But why the conflicting reports to Rodríguez Feo and to Powell? Did he want to preserve for the younger man an image of what he once was, while knowing that his contemporary also understood the effects of the ravages of "Time . . . the enemy"? Or had he lied to Rodríguez Feo because he did not feel like keeping their appointment?

In any case, on this trip Stevens did renew his sense of the countryside around Reading and also got a stronger feeling for the reality behind his genealogical pursuits. The history of the Zeller family, his mother's line, was particularly fresh in his mind as he and Elsie crisscrossed roads filled with memories of their courtship. This, too, must have stung. They stopped to see the places marked by the history of the Zellers, "these people [who] whatever else they were, were fanatics." Their ancestral home was "consecrated to the glory of God." The architectural cartouche which seemed to the poet to indicate this was a "cross with a few palmations" beneath it (*L* 534). In the last years of his age Stevens was approaching the "palm at the end of the mind"; in the mind, at least, he could rest in peace.

Home again on September 24, Stevens slowly prepared for winter as the months passed. Wanting to lay in more food for thought, he wrote to Vidal that he wanted to buy something by Albert Marquet. He liked the drawings of his that he had seen reproduced in an issue of *Le Point* (December 1943) that he had recently gotten to. He noted how his "curiosity" had "a lot to do" with his interest in lesser-known rather than in well-known figures (*L* 535).

He also picked up loose threads left hanging. Answering Allen Tate's note that accompanied a check for Stevens's latest contribution to his journal, the older poet referred to Tate's earlier wish about changing the forms they used to address each other: "Why don't we compromise on just dropping the Mr. so that, like a pair of Liverpool clerks, I can call you Tate and you can call me Stevens? I suggest this as a compromise" (October 31, 1946). Stevens, as was his habit with all journals that paid, also returned the check "by way of lending a hand" (October 25, 1946).

And as though commemorating his visit to his birthplace, Stevens commissioned a bookplate to be designed around the German inscription placed by George Zeller in 1772 which the poet had found on the wall of the Trinity Tulpehocken Church. As part of the exchange with Victor Hammer, who was to print the plate, Stevens learned of the relation between typefaces and the eras in which they appeared. This was "something [he] had not thought of" (*L* 537), and it gave him delight to muse about how the very letters used to print his words would themselves reflect his time.[54]

Something else that had to be attended to in these days was putting together his latest volume. The title, *Transport to Summer,* reflected the poet's latest movement, circling back to his past once again after his years of preoccupation with what he called the pressure of external events. It was not that he thought that things as they were now were as they should be. He wrote to James Guthrie in late fall: "While we are in an agitated condition over here, there come times when politics, economics, socialism, and so on, don't matter in the least and when one realizes that if it is not one thing it is something else, and this, for me, is such a time. It would be so easy to feel completely blue . . ." (*L* 540). Stevens's state was in part a function of the old up and down that showed itself as his seasonal malaise, but there was something more. The "catalogue" of things that had to be attended to was "too commodious." In the face of this, in spite of his recent sense of personal renewal, he could only feel "impotent." "Regard the invalid personality," Stevens directed (*CP* 368). Its usefulness was expired; it was "inválid." And sharing in the spirit of its age, it was an "ínvalid," suffering from the *dis-ease* that was its most singular characteristic. One could transport oneself to a sense of summer, as he had done in the last poems he wrote for his volume, only in imagination. "The imperfect is our paradise."

Feeling the postwar depression added to his own autumnal slump, Stevens wrote to Helen Head Simons in mid-November that he did not expect that there would ever be another who would "follow Mr. Simons in his interest in [his] things," that no one would feel the "same responsiveness." He closed the letter apologizing for his "stiffness and awkwardness" (*L* 539). About a month later he wrote to José Rodríguez Feo that the point of one of his latest poems, the "Attempt to Discover Life" (*CP* 370), was to "question . . . whether the experience of life is in the end worth more than tuppence: dos centavos" (*L* 540).

But as Stevens became aware that he was falling back into one of the darkest of his black moods, he used the device he had perfected over the years to bring himself out; he again put on his comedian's mask. The change was quick. Within a week of his letter to Mrs. Simons, the poet wrote on December 11 to Henry Church (still in France despite his original plans to return in fall), treating lightly even unpleasant things, like the renewed trouble with his vision (which certainly could have contributed to his feeling like the "invalid"). He opened the letter (unusually, it was handwritten, indicating perhaps his spontaneously acting on his will to make things seem better) with a remark most characteristic of his brighter side. He then went on, compensating for every negative with a positive, as though he had just reread Emerson's "Compensation":

> DEAR MR. CHURCH:
>
> I hope that you have not been thrown into some concentration camp of the Communists. Last week one day I had lunch with Allen Tate in New York. He asked after both of you and I said that I had not had any recent letter. He and his wife seem to be together in New York. Since he was in a most cheerful state of mind, it is possible that their collisions are merely too much coffee. I had gone down in part to see my infallible Dr. Mittendorf about blobs in my left eye. Happily these have largely disappeared since then. But I am left with one more eye medicine, in addition to the three that I have been using for the last twenty years. New York seemed threadbare and almost wholly without any of the freshness and variety which I had thought to be indigenous there. The struggle for existence was too revealed and anything at all smart looked like an anachronism, something lacking in social humility; an Indian with diamond ear-rings. Here in Hartford, which goes through so many metamorphoses with admirable distance, things are better. We have been having an exceedingly bright, warm autumn. To-day, there is not a cloud in the sky. Xmas trees are already on sale: one comes with a shock to think that Xmas is only two weeks away. In this clear weather we get none of the dirtiness of New York. On the contrary, when I walk down town in the mornings, everything glitters, including the evergreens that seem to be everywhere. . . . I hope that everything has been going well with you. I wonder about your reactions to French politics and what they mean or suggest respecting the future. France leads us far more than we realize, probably because French political and economic conditions are duplicated here far more truly than English conditions are duplicated. Eh bien! Merry Xmas and a Happy New Year to you and to Mrs. Church. How eagerly one grasps the happiness still secreted in such wishes—or grasps at it. (*L* 542)

Similarly, writing to Rodríguez Feo about a week later, on December 19, Stevens voiced his disappointment with the way New York was those days, culturally isolated as a result of the war. He compared the city now to how it had been during World War I, when again the United States had been cut off from Europe. He observed that of course, things would change. He also related to his young friend how frightened he was about his eye troubles (he had been in New York to see the doctor once more only the day before); he added that what was particularly disturbing was not the problem itself but what it symptomized. The doctor's advice was that in addition to cutting out coffee (which, Stevens noted, he never touched) and anything alcoholic (which, he wrote, he rarely indulged in any longer), he cut down on reading and not read at all at night. This, too, the poet immediately translated into its positive aspect. The lecture that he was preparing to give at Harvard in February (*Three Academic Pieces*, which included "The Realm of Resemblance," "Someone Puts a Pineapple Together," and "Of Ideal Time and Choice") would be a product of his own thought. "I am not going to quote anybody," he commented and added, to soothe whatever fears he felt creeping: "[T]aking a new and rather quackish subject and developing it without the support of others is not quite the easiest thing in the world to do. If, however, I get nowhere with it, I can always abandon it and do something else. It is curious how a subject once chosen grows like a beanstalk until it seems as if there had never been anything else in the world." Two of the three pieces would be poems. His exercise as the comedian seemed to bring back his self-confidence. Responding to Rodríguez Feo's query, Stevens wrote that he knew the work of Elizabeth Bishop and William Carlos Williams. About his old friend Williams he remarked that though he had the "greatest respect" for him, there was "the constant difficulty that he was more interested in the way of saying things that in what he [had] to say. The fact remains that we are always fundamentally interested in what a writer has to say. When we are sure of that, we pay attention to the way in which he says it, not often before." Stevens closed the letter with one of his observations about nature, a sure sign that he was raising his spirits by again raising himself to view things from his bird's-eye perspective: "Merry Christmas and a happy New Year. How do you say that in Spanish? I should be much at home in Caracas [where presumably his friend was to spend the holidays] because I believe that many of the birds that spend their summers in Hartford spend their winters in Caracas" (*L* 544).

The new year opened with Stevens back on an even keel, which he helped maintain by indulging himself in more "things that [he could] not go without," even though it meant, as he wrote to Paule Vidal, "some sacrifice," more pulling on his purse strings. Though he had just received the Bombois, he wanted to look forward to something else and was sending an additional 50,000 francs for a painting "light . . . cheerful . . . and saturated with the feeling and imagination of the artist . . . *something that the artist himself regards as the best thing he has provided we can afford it.*"[55] His comment on the painting just arrived—that "Bomboi . . . [was] a Rousseau who [had] never visited Mexico, that is to say, a Rousseau without imagination" (*L* 545)—revealed the poet to be at his most quizzical. He was toying with what Mlle. Vidal would think he knew about Rousseau. Would she think he believed the story that the painter had gone to Mexico and there found inspiration for his primitive renditions of flora, or would she realize that the poet was using Mexico as a figure for the imagination?

In spite of his initial judgment, however, after Stevens had hung the Bombois, he delighted in it. It seemed to have the quality he valued most highly—that it declared itself slowly; its first "impression of tightness and correctness . . . disappeared." He liked paintings that mimicked his own technique. In the same vein, about a month later, in sending a copy of the now ready *Transport to Summer* to be bound by Gerhard Gerlach (someone who worked in the finest old European tradition), the poet stressed, as was his habit, that he wanted "not birds and flowers but a good masculine decoration . . . something in [Gerlach's] best style" (*L* 547), something correct. In spite of this impression, the finished volume, like Stevens's other personal copies, invited caresses.

Wearing the mask of the comedian with which he greeted the year, Stevens composed the *Three Academic Pieces* (*NA* 69–89) that he would deliver on February 11. (As he did this, Elsie, still trying to complete herself, seemed to follow what her husband had done in attempting to complete himself: She was now gathering her family photos and having them framed [February 2, 1947].) The poet's opening sentence echoed and extended the observation made to him by Victor Hammer about the connection between typefaces and their eras: "The accuracy of accurate letters is an accuracy with respect to the structure of reality." Thinking about this prompted another connection to something Stevens had recently read in one of the periodicals to which he subscribed, *Signature,* a magazine devoted entirely to aspects of printing. And though he had written to Rodríguez Feo that he was not going to quote from anyone in putting together this lecture, he did include one quotation, this sentence: "The business of the [printing] press is to furnish an indefinite public with a potentially indefinite number of identical texts" (*NA* 73). Around these facts of the life of books the comedian wove his most baroque piece of prose. His purpose was to explore the resemblance that a poet's metaphors had to reality. The connection between types and their eras was the concrete particular that anchored his mind and allowed him to swing safely into the various analogies he used to illustrate his meaning. Without the usual anchorage of thought offered by reading other texts, as he had done in the past when preparing lectures, Stevens needed some pivot in the world of fact to ground him; from this he would abstract. The process of composition here was the same as that of his poems. As an unfolding of the process in prose, it was to be a key to understanding his poems. It was, then, "academic." The two poems that followed were two of his most difficult and were to be attended to by keeping the preceding gloss in mind. The *Three Academic Pieces* together represented a study in studying himself. What was there to be learned from Stevens as he developed in prose his thoughts about poetry for the first time without immediate support from others' work?

To elucidate what he meant by "resemblance" and its central function in disclosing human ties to the "structure of reality" Stevens followed Aristotle's analysis of good metaphor. The spirits of the "old Chinese," of Wordsworth, and of Coleridge also breathed life into his lines. Their texts were parts of Stevens's "structure of reality." Revealing his own modification of the structure, Stevens spelled out his perceptions about his time, perceptions that led him to find the particular resemblances he did. He slowly and carefully unfolded his sentences and then folded them up again. His mastery of laying out the points of an argument by the rules of strictest logic was apparent. Yet at crucial moments logic's progression was stopped by brutal intrusions of the cold facts of the reality he observed; then seeming contradictions followed. One such passage, a central one, is this:

> It quite seems as if there is an activity that makes one thing resemble another (possible as a phase of the police power of conformity). What the eye beholds may be the text of life. It is, nevertheless, a text that we do not write. The eye does not beget in resemblance. It sees. But the mind begets in resemblance as the painter begets in representation; that is to say, as the painter makes his world within a world; or as the musician begets in music, in the obvious small pieces having to do with gardens in the rain or the fountains of Rome and in the obvious larger pieces having to do with the sea, Brazilian night or those woods in the neighborhood of Vienna in which the hunter was accustomed to blow his horn and in which, also, yesterday, the birds sang preludes to the atom bomb. It is not difficult, having once predicated such an activity, to attribute it to a desire for resemblance. What a ghastly situation it would be if the world of the dead was [*sic*] actually different from the world of the living and, if as life ends, instead of passing to a former Victorian sphere, we passed into a land in which none of our problems had been solved, after all, and nothing resembled anything we have ever known and nothing resembled anything else in shape, in color, in sound, in look or otherwise. To say farewell to our generation and to look forward to a continuation in a Jerusalem of pure surrealism would account for the taste for oblivion. (*NA* 76–77)

Was the poet being the sleight of hand man, or had he come up against himself? Was he stating that he believed that in death he would pass into "a former Victorian sphere," where, moreover, his problems would have been solved? The mental map he provided earlier in the passage gave a clue. He created an image of himself listening to the enchanting musical strains of Ottorino Respighi (*The Fountains of Rome, Brazilian Impressions*) and of others and then being jolted by the fact of the atom bomb. What had this done? What did this atrocity resemble? The metaphor was used to account for the "taste for oblivion." His choice to remember the past, his "former Victorian sphere," in an attempt to understand, if not solve, his problems, was the creation of his heaven, his poems, the eternity where he would go on living. That he could still do this was, in large part, a function of having experienced a world where "birds sang preludes . . . ," in other words, where nature was present.

But as he indicated in other passages marked by unusually explicit explosions of venom at the way things were, the present world was built of resemblances that could not provide transcendence; the present world was cut off more and more from nature:

> In reality, there is a level of resemblance, which is the level of nature. In metaphor, there is no such level. If there were it would be the level of

> resemblance of the imagination, which has no such level. If, to our surprise, we should meet a monsieur who told us that he was from another world, and if he had in fact all the indicia of divinity, the luminous body, the nimbus, the heraldic stigmata, we should recognize him as above the level of nature but not as above the level of imagination. So, too, if, to our surprise, we should meet one of those morons whose remarks are so conspicuous a part of the folklore of the world of the radio—remarks made without using either the tongue or the brain, spouted much like the spoutings of small whales—we should recognize him as below the level of nature but not as below the level of the imagination. It is not, however, a question of above or below but simply of beyond. Level is an abbreviated form of resemblance. The statement that the imagination has no level of resemblance is not to be taken as a statement that the imagination itself has no limits. The imagination is deceptive in this respect. There is a limit to its power to surpass resemblance and that limit is to be found in nature. (*NA* 73–74)

The present, moreover, was cut off from the personal. Individuality disappeared in the "mass of men"; this was a "phase of the police power of conformity":

> [T]he whole point is that the structure of reality because of the range of resemblances that it contains is measurably an adult make-believe. Perhaps the whole field of connotation is based on resemblance. . . .
>
> What has just been said shows that there are private resemblances. The resemblance of the baby's shoes to the baby, by suggestion, is likely to be a resemblance that exists for one or two alone. A public resemblance, by contrast, like the resemblance of the profile of a mountain to the profile of George Washington, exists for that great class of people who co-exist with the great ferns in public gardens, amplified music and minor education. What our eyes behold may well be the text of life but one's meditations on the text and the disclosures of these meditations are no less a part of the structure of reality. (*NA* 75–76)

What was to be done? His suggestion was to be expected: to do as he had done. The lecture became an explicit *apologia pro vita sua,* the continuation of his "Defense of Poetry" begun years earlier with "The Irrational Element." He was accounting for the kind of poetry he had written; he had wanted to provide at least in "accurate letters," "on paper," a vision of the world as it could be, the only possible heaven. At the same time the vision would bear the lineaments of the world of which it was a part; it had to in order to observe the limits of nature that prescribed the terms for metaphors that revealed the structure of reality. How had Stevens accomplished this?

He gave the answer in his characteristically oblique manner: "Euphuism [that] had its origin in the desire for elegance . . . euphuism that was the reason in the sun for metaphor" (*NA* 78). Stevens remembered the primary lesson from the Victorian sphere of Barrett Wendell: All art was to serve elegance—*ex-lege,* to pick out from the abundance of elements those that were most desirable, those that gave pleasure. Euphuism was the ideal vehicle. It referred particularly to the style John Lyly perfected in his two novels, *Euphues: The Anatomy of Wit* (1578) and *Euphues and His England* (1580), as well as in his comedies. Its manner derived from one who wore the "cap of Spain" referred to by Stevens in his "Comedian"; this figure now suggested itself to be Fray Antonio de Guevara,[56] inquisitor (Crispin, related to him, was the "inquisitorial botanist") and teacher in the court of Charles V. Following the example of Castiglione's *Courtier,* Fray Antonio in his work drew a portrait of the ideal prince; he also discoursed on marriage, women, politics, religion, all in a spirit of reconciling things as they were to things as they should be.[57] The euphuistic style developed by Lyly (various works of Guevara's had gone through twenty-four editions in England before 1578) grew out of a period of crisis in belief. This style was a step in the evolution of prose writing understood as an instrument of artistic expression,[58] capable of communicating both the sharpness and the ambiguity of human experience. This sense was carried by what most characterized euphuism: "the elaborate and persistent use of balance and antithesis both in sound and sense . . . learned allusions, elaborate comparisons and far-fetched metaphors . . . without regard to any canon of verisimilitude. . . . [E]uphuism is a highly analytical style which ceaselessly dissects, catalogues, compares and contrasts: it aspires thereby to represent the polite discourse of urbane and elegant persons."[59]

This style, which had also influenced Sir Philip Sidney in *Arcadia* and Shakespeare,[60] was well suited to Stevens's purpose of teaching how to live, what to do to the archetypal American, who began, like him, as a raw youth, one of the "mute/ And maidenly greenhorns" (*CP* 28) who wanted, nonetheless, to become *erudite*—to get rid of his rudeness—in the ways of the world so that he could participate in the highest court. It is easy to see how Stevens's need to make a seat for himself "on the front bench" of this court was largely responsible for his own cultivation of this style, but it is also central to see something less apparent—that is, the essential way he modified euphuism. Unlike the received version that operated "without regard to any canon of verisimilitude," Stevens repeatedly stressed in practice and theory the necessity of beginning from facts, from the particulars of the natural world. The figure who would evolve from this education would be a courtier of the most desirable female, earth, "Fat girl, terrestrial" (*CP* 406). In perfecting his "fluent speech," the poet repeated the resemblances he found between his nature and nature outside himself; for Stevens, realizing one's connections with things as they were was a "source of the ideal."

The apology for his work, this latest version of his Shelleyan defense of poetry, ran as follows: Since there is resemblance between all things (the premise with which he began), it is necessary that there be at least a few who seek the most beautiful, what gives most pleasure, especially in an age in which the mass of men saw only the resemblances of the least transcendent kind. For if these were the only resemblances that people knew, there could be no aspiring to a better state. Moreover, only those who had found the most exquisite yet distant resemblances, as between the atom bomb and the northern lights, who saw the birds' singing as a prelude to the explosion, could dispel the total despair and the "taste for oblivion" that naturally would follow from regarding the bomb, or the acts of war, or countless other manifestations of horror as having no resemblance to what was held to be human—therefore, natural. In other words, had not the poet made himself elegant by selecting out the most pleasing resemblances, he would have remained among that "great class of people who co-exist with the great ferns in public gardens, amplified music and minor education" and so he would have been blind and deaf to what still remained possible, even in the face of the most heinous facts. Stevens's coming to this perception had to do both with his youthful wish to be like St. Augustine, to whom nothing human was alien, and with his having learned from the teachings of the old Chinese sages, who, following Buddha, taught that demons should be embraced.

This lecture and the two accompanying poems were Stevens's profession of faith in poetry, in himself. This profession belonged to the project of framing an adequate theory of poetry that he had been thinking out for years, most recently in connection with the poetry chair at Harvard. In setting down his beliefs in prose, euphuistic as it was, Stevens resolved the crisis of his old age. The five-year period from 1942 until now had been one of his most difficult for both personal and historical reasons. Since the end of the war he had set himself the task of looking back, reexamining once again what had shaped him, and reflecting on his values. In thinking through the words he would present to his Harvard audience on February 11, he came to terms with himself and was pleased; he placed himself proudly in the celestial pantomime:

> It is as if there were three planets: the sun,
> The moon and the imagination, or, say,
>
> Day, night and man and his endless effigies.
> (*NA* 83)

While in middle age Stevens had resolved his period of crisis by "celebrat[ing] the faith of forty" humorously as a "ward of Cupido," now approaching seventy, he regarded a different kind of faith, the faith that his words could guide those who would follow him. In this spirit Stevens prepared to enter his final phase.

❧

Stevens had presented himself and the *Three Academic Pieces* most seriously, but this did not mean that he had given up the humor with which he had learned to consider himself over the years. In a note to Theodore Spencer, who had invited him to give the talk at Harvard, the poet wrote: "Being followed around like Frank Sinatra was demoralizing, but I enjoyed it. I stayed until Wednesday afternoon walking in the wonderful weather of that particular day and then, when I was quite sure the demoralization was over I came back home" (February 13, 1947). About three weeks later, he refused yet another invitation to record a reading of his poems for the Library of Congress archive, this time to Allen Tate (who had lightly noted that he had taken T. S. Eliot there the previous summer and that Eliot hadn't complained once [March 4, 1947]). Stevens again used a comparison of himself to Frank Sinatra in his very comic reply:

> Mr. Shapiro [the current poetry consultant for the Library of Congress] wrote to me only the other day. I refused to do this up in Cambridge. This is probably because I am voice shy. But I had previously refused to do it for Mr. Warren and also for someone at Columbia. Several years ago they put in a dictaphone system here at the office. In using this system you dictated your letters down a pipe, so to speak, and when you turned the machine so that it read back what you had dictated it sounded very much like a leak somewhere in the house in the middle of the night. Of course, you will say that NBC will fix that all up and I won't be able to tell myself from Frank Sinatra, but you are going to have a tough time talking me into it. And, besides, my contract with Knopf makes it necessary for me to procure his permission. You could leave a blank space at the end of it and say that Mr. Stevens has just completed reading Sunday Morning in deaf and dumb. (March 6, 1947)

But Tate persisted. In a return letter, in which he also acknowledged receiving *Transport to Summer,* he used his best rhetorical strategies. He praised Stevens's "great accomplishment," adding that he was "depressed by [his] own idleness at a time when [Stevens] at [his] age [was] able to do [his] best work." As a final ploy, he wrote: "I don't know what general or specific arguments I can bring to bear upon you that will persuade you to do this, for no proper man is willing to believe that he is as valuable as other people think he is. I might even ask you to do this as a favor to me, but I have no right to ask it . . ." (March 18, 1947). Nothing worked. Stevens sent a note back confirming a luncheon date he had set up with Tate and Rodríguez Feo on April 7 at the Ritz Tower (Park Avenue and Fifty-seventh Street) and closed it, acting the comedian, by saying that he was restating his refusal here so that when they were together, Tate could devote himself wholly to "the life and letters of Havana and Hartford" (*L* 551).

These first few months of 1947 were bringing good weather for Stevens's spirit. As a result of the lecture at Harvard, the poet made contact with another who was to be important to him in the years ahead, Renato Poggioli, who opened their relationship with a request to translate some of his poems for *Inventario,* the Italian journal he edited. Stevens was pleased and directed Poggioli to contact Knopf.

At the end of February Stevens received the first copies of *Transport to Summer;* the volume delighted him. He wrote to Knopf that he thought the edition a "Lollapollooza" and hoped it would bring good luck to all of them, including Herbert Weinstock, who was handling the Stevens material for Alfred Knopf. Though Stevens had never met Weinstock, he sent him a specially inscribed copy of the latest volume. Weinstock replied: "The generosity of your autograph leaves me gasping"; he added that poetry in America would not be what it was without Stevens (WAS 3115). On March 1 another request to do a translation of "Peter Quince at the Clavier" for a German publication came from Edouard Roditi; Stevens wrote back that he was very pleased and again referred his correspondent to write to Knopf for permission.

A few days later an unexpected note of pleasure came from Ebba Dalin, one of the poet's old contacts in Sweden. Mrs. Dalin wrote that she had recently read *Parts of a World* aloud to a friend. "Your ear for tone is certainly very good," she observed (March 5, 1947). Finally the volume Stevens had thought his best was giving pleasure, specifically to someone who had read it *aloud* and had heard what Stevens had heard intoning in his mind's ear as he wrote.

On or around the same date an acknowledgment of a different kind came from Jerome Mellquist, who wrote asking Stevens to contribute something on Paul Rosenfeld for a forthcoming issue of *Mosaic.* Stevens immediately answered that he would and that he would get to it as soon as he could. This piece, "The Shaper," eventually appeared in *Paul Rosenfeld: Voyager in the Arts,* edited by Mellquist and Lucie Wien (1948). But before the poet could sit down to this, there were other matters needing attention.

After another few days came a letter from Harry Duncan that must have touched Stevens especially, because it expressed the printer's recognition of the poet's intention in composing his *Three Academic Pieces:* "It would be foolish for me to try to tell you how much we like these 'pieces' which (if I may be so bold) turn out to resemble an order of devotion, as the book may turn out to resemble a missal" (March 12, 1947). Duncan wanted to print an edition of these pieces. Stevens wisely introduced the proposal to Herbert Weinstock (perhaps the poet feared a quick negative if he were to approach Knopf directly) noting that in any case, the "pieces" would have appeared first in the *Partisan Review* (*L* 549). Knopf agreed, as Stevens happily reported to Duncan on March 21 (*L* 551). It was fitting that these pieces, which opened with a statement about "the accuracy of accurate letters," be printed under the direction of this fine craftsman, whom Stevens had once compared to a Renaissance illuminator.

Again, after a few more days came this note from one of those who mattered most to Stevens. On March 16 Marianne Moore wrote:

> DEAR MR. STEVENS,
>
> The title "Transport to Summer" is in itself a gift, and I thank you for

giving my Swedish cart [see "The Prejudice Against the Past" (*CP* 368)] the savor of poetry.

This use of words—strange but also natural—makes me realize why I used to think I would like to be a writer.

Sincerely yours,
MARIANNE MOORE[61]

Beyond testifying to Moore's appreciation of Stevens's work, this short letter provides one more glimpse of how a poem became for Stevens an instance of dialogue with someone whom he admired. His subtle transformation of Moore into the "Marianna" of his poem indicated, too, in yet another way how carefully protected were his disclosures.

During this same period of fair weather there was the regular letter from Paule Vidal reporting on her latest attempts at purchasing paintings for her "patron." Stevens, in his usual courteous fashion, commended her for her most recent decision not to buy a particular René Renaud, adding that he felt, in any case, that she liked "pretty much the same things" as he. But to sharpen her eye, just to be sure, he went on gently instructing her to make the kinds of distinctions he made:

> While I like Braque, I like him in spite of his modern perversions. There is a siccity and an ascetic quality about his color that is very much to my liking. Some of his greens and browns are almost disciplinary. In his case his modern perversions are not particularly offensive. On the other hand, I find such things particularly offensive in the work of younger men of little or no taste and little or no intelligence. After all, one can be as much ravished by severity as by indulgence. . . . (*L* 548)

He continued to describe which of the paintings in his collection he especially liked and urged her to remember that "[he fed] on these things." He then listed the names of those painters he had become most interested in of late. He also told her to go directly to the artists rather than to dealers, in the interest of getting the best price. He looked forward to the arrival of a new painting as a reward for his latest successes.

Something else that Stevens had been anticipating that was now about to occur was the return of the Churches from France. In mid-February he had written to Barbara Church: "Here even the world that you will find about you is more and more as it ought to be every day" (*L* 546). They arrived back in New York within the month. On Wednesday, March 19, Stevens wrote to Church that he would be in New York the next day (the third Thursday in March was the annual meeting of the Hartford Livestock Insurance Company, of which Stevens was a director) and hoped to be able to see him. In spite of the short notice, Stevens and Church managed to get together. This was fortunate since the meeting was their last. Church died suddenly on Good Friday, April 4. The day of the luncheon Stevens was to have had with Allen Tate and

José Rodríguez Feo saw the poet attending the funeral of his friend at St. Bartholomew's Church (Park Avenue at Fifty-second Street). Though the loss was great, Stevens was consoled by knowing that Church had entrusted him with his wishes to make "a contribution to the ideal welfare of his fellows." The poet's last memory of Church was of a man "greatly changed . . . thinner and tenser," curiously unresponsive to the pleasure of being back in "the warmth and brightness of the early days of Spring" in New York. The evidences of the war had taken their toll. Stevens consoled Barbara Church with the observation that it was better that her husband had died before her since his life was so deeply dependent on hers that he could not have carried on without her (*L* 552).

A chapter in the poet's life had closed. But another opened. Within two weeks there was a new life for the poet to celebrate: Holly gave birth to Peter Reed Hanchak on April 26, 1947. Stevens would call him Peter the Voyant.

IV
IT MUST CHANGE
1947–1954

THE WAY UP AND DOWN IS THE SAME.

—HERACLITUS, Fragment CIII

We cannot look at the past or the future except by means of the imagination but again the imagination of backward glances is one thing and the imagination of looks ahead something else. Even the psychologists concede this present particular, for, with them, memory involves a reproductive power, and looks ahead involve a creative power: the power of our expectations.

—"Imagination as Value,"
The Necessary Angel (p. 144)

All of us want social change when and where it becomes necessary. My only point about all this is that I wish it was taking place when I was not half-plaster. I don't want to be knocked off the shelf and wind up all smithereens.

—From a letter to BARBARA CHURCH,
June 8, 1953, *Letters* (p. 780)

The death of his friend and the birth of his grandson set Stevens moving once more up and down between two elements. He considered the curriculum he had followed and the compass of things still wished for. While he had never resolved the essential tension of his personality, when he looked back now, and in the absence of the friend who had been unequivocally supportive, he again found himself wanting in the scales of possibility he had envisioned for himself. In spite of his obvious success in the worlds of both business and poetry—Stevens's salary, always substantial, continued to increase through the war years and after;[1] the reviews of *Transport to Summer* (published on March 7, 1947), which began to appear almost immediately and ran through the year, were, almost without exception, full of praise for the poet as a master in and of his time—he felt somehow inadequate, specifically to the task he had singled out as most important during the last five-year period of his friendship with Henry Church. This task was to formulate a theory of poetry so that in the future, poetry, the "Supreme Fiction," could take the place of the idea of heaven haunted by hymns. Repeatedly, from mid-1947 on Stevens stated to correspondents that he had not and could not articulate such a theory, that the lectures he had composed and continued, on request, to compose, were unsatisfactory, that they rambled on for an hour's length around only ten minutes' worth of substance. Only very near the end of his career was he persuaded that these pieces were good enough for publication.

When they were finally in book form as *The Necessary Angel,* he was pleased with them as makings of the planet of which he was a part.

Perhaps the poet's seeing how much Church had changed during his return stay in postwar France contributed to the difficulty he had in facing, yet another time, death, the final fact that since his youth had been the ultimate occasion against which his cries rose and "twanged him through and through" (*CP* 433). Though he had until now maintained in his poems and in his life that death was the "mother of beauty" (turning his niece's attention to the day's shimmering sunshine after her mother's funeral, for example), there was something about Church's death that changed this feeling. In "The Owl in the Sarcophagus," the elegy he wrote in the "frame of mind that followed" (*L* 566) his friend's death, the change showed itself:

> And death cries quickly, in a flash of voice,
> Keep you, keep you, I am gone, oh keep you as
> My memory, is the mother of us all,
>
> The earthly mother and the mother of
> The dead . . .
>
> (*CP* 432)

"This [was] the mythology of modern death" (*CP* 435), purged of notions of transcendence. It no longer seemed possible to assert that it was the limitation imposed by life's end that accounted for the human perception of beauty and the establishing of values. Suddenly all that mattered was memory. This poem was empty of life's images and the sense of continuity. It was the inverse of "Sunday Morning" and "The Emperor of Ice-Cream," the lines of which spectrally echoed in these.

What had changed? A whole world, worn by the years of a war that ended without ending, was reflected in the strained lines of Church's face as Stevens last remembered it. Something in Church had broken. The poet knew it, felt it. He experienced a loss of faith at a level more profound than he had ever prepared himself to expect. It was, paradoxically, loss in the faith he had so diligently worked to establish for himself from the time when he first became conscious that "Loss of faith is growth" (*OP* 172). He had consistently denied faith in the myth of an anthropomorphic god who promised redemption and everlasting life. In its stead he offered a myth of nature as life, life as nature—updated paganism. But now he called this, too, into question since in this mythology the only solace was "peace" envisioned as

> . . . that figure stationed at our end,
> Always, in brilliance, fatal, final, formed
> Out of our lives to keep us in our death,

To watch us in the summer of Cyclops
Underground. . . .
(*CP* 434–35)

In this mythology, as in its archaic prototype, peace, death, memory all meant the same thing in the end; only reputation lived on. If one had not lived nobly, there was no knowledge that could bring forgiveness.

What did Stevens, looking back with the notion of nobility in mind, see? A man who had always abstracted himself from things as they were, who continued to search for the "central" while he looked at the peripheral, who turned the pathos of human experience into the streaked and rayed lines of poems. A man who, because of the august activity of imagination, had evaded the essential facts of his life, a man who saw his wife completely dependent on him (as he was careful to note that Henry Church had been on Barbara Church). A man who saw the life of his child—now with her own child—as a failure, a life he wanted to break up.[2] A man who had devoted himself to feasting rather than fasting, as was appropriate to his denial of his forebears' faith, yet who had never managed to escape the sense that in feasting, he sinned so that feasting always had to be followed by fasting as "that monster, the body" continued to rebel against his mind. A man who, in spite of repeated reassurances from friends, acquaintances, and the public, still felt that when he showed his "plain self too plainly," he offended and who into his very last years was still "surprised when people [were] friendly" (*L* 864). How could this man believe that his reputation, his memory, would be honored in death?

It was time for final questions.

And what did he see, looking forward? He could only extrapolate from the past and from the present. The balancing he had attempted until now—sometimes with greater, sometimes with lesser success—had not brought him the sense of nobility he desired. It was time then, to try another tack. But before he could set a new course, he had to determine, as closely as possible, where he was, even if it could now be only by dead reckoning. During the first and well into the second decade of the century it had seemed that it was, indeed, the time, not he, that was out of joint. His fine-tuned spirit had been poised precisely where it should have been to ride the wave of the future. He did not then quail before modernism but saluted its attack on things as they were. Yet now—having in his middle age crested with the wave of the new, playing the melodies of his *Harmonium;* having survived the long calm that followed the wave's breaking; having tried a more moderate course all through the storms of the thirties and the worst of the roaring forties—he hove to. He was out of joint with his time, and he did not know why. From having been the chorister whose "c" preceded the choir, he became a most inappropriate man in a most unpropitious place.

The ideas of both the world he had known and the world he had thought possible were gone. He found modernism as it was understood and practiced now and into the fifties anemic, derivative, meretricious. He found the New Deal to have slowly undone the hope he and those he felt to be of like mind had had for "doing everything possible to improve the condition of the workers . . . [for] education as the source of freedom and power . . . [for] experiment[ing] a little more extensively in public ownership of public utilities" (*L* 351). The man who had, as he reported in 1954, followed his father in being a lawyer, a Presbyterian, and a Democrat,[3] found himself in 1952 unable to support Adlai Stevenson (*L* 765), the "egghead" intellectual whom another "New England manic-depressive," Robert Lowell (who had used the term to include himself), found to be, as did many others who still nursed liberal hopes, so much better than anyone had a right to expect.[4] Was Stevens unwilling to vote for Stevenson because Stevenson advocated an easing of the cold war whereas Stevens, if only playfully, by the time of the campaign had described himself as looking for Communists behind every tree?

Stevens had made it clear from early in the thirties that he opposed Marxism and did so precisely because he felt it would be impossible under a Marxist regime to enjoy the pleasures of merely circulating or the *summum bonum* of red-winged blackbirds or anything else. But he had also made it clear that his sympathies were with the left, and he had done more than simply state his feelings in vagueness. His explicitly voiced support of Philip Rahv, Delmore Schwartz, and the others connected with the *Partisan Review* attested to the sincerity of his position. Yet by the summer of 1947, when he had become familiar enough with the "group" to be having dinner with the *Partisan Review* editors, meeting with individual members for lunch or drinks, and being "really impressed" (letter to Barbara Church, July 17, 1947, edited out of *L* 562), he also seems to have begun having reservations about how openly he would support their purpose in the future. By the middle of October 1948 he expressed this as one of his characteristic equivocations, which he then followed with an appropriate defense, in a letter to Barbara Church, who had almost immediately replaced her husband as the poet's most regular recipient of letters:

> DEAR MRS. CHURCH:
>
> Yesterday I received a letter from Allan Dowling who is at the Hotel Vendome in Paris. He is the man who is putting up the money for the Partisan Review at the present time. I think that he is helping a group well worth helping although I do not share that group's politics. I have a clipping in my desk which says that Socialism is competition without prizes, boredom without hope, war without victory and statistics without end. This destructive thing is what Dowling is actually backing though, in intent, he probably has something quite different in mind.
>
> The Russians who are threatening us with an atom bomb of their own when they are not complaining that we are threatening them with ours know that the freedom of speech and thought that we talk about are not the freedom of speech and thought on which our institutions were originally based; and they act accordingly, by taking advantage of them here and by

> limiting them at home. The total freedom that now endangers us has never existed before, notwithstanding Voltaire, and so on. We might need a police state before long to protect ourselves against Communism. Not that I am not for freedom and against a police state. But the great critical and expository minds that our time so greatly needs do not seem to exist. These are the natural enemies of the abuses of freedom and the sheer imagination of Communism. Allan Dowling is typical: a man of wealth destroying himself. (*L* 620)

The man who in the early thirties thought he was headed more and more to the left changed his course. In the postwar world, with positions becoming dangerously polarized and the first whisperings of what would end up as Senator Joseph R. McCarthy's witch-hunt already being heard, Stevens, by nature prudent, retreated from voicing sympathies. In his poetry he ceased attempting to play "man number one," to provide in his lines words for "a million people on one string." He abandoned the project for a new "vulgate of experience" in favor of a personal book of hours. Whatever was was, but from now on, with few exceptions, his poems would compose "his book unto himself," like that of his "good Emperor" (Marcus Aurelius' *Meditations* bore that inscription). The poet's subject now would be the "auroras of autumn," the sense of life flickering on the borders of death before coming to final stillness as nothing more than part of the "rock" of earth. The man who at forty had wished to be a thinking stone shrank into the compass and curriculum of his mind alone. And how did he conceive the mind now?

> It is a child that sings itself to sleep,
> The mind, among the creatures that it makes,
> The people, those by which it lives and dies.
> (*CP* 436)

Not surprisingly, as Stevens entered this last stage of his crisis of faith, a period of complete disillusionment with the world, its beliefs, himself and his beliefs, it was apparent, both to him and at least to some of those close to him that he was experiencing the difficulty of what it was to be. Stevens made this clear in a comment he made almost as an aside to James Powers in a letter he wrote years after the time of intense pain had passed: ". . . you are one of the people I am most grateful to for all you did in my dark year of 1947. It was good at that time to feel that friends around me tried to understand what I could not grasp about myself" (edited out from letter of December 21, 1953 [*L* 805]). Since Stevens felt that he had been unable himself to understand what was causing his "dark year," Powers could only have gotten a sense of his friend's troubles from snatches of conversation and passing expressions. Some of the comments Stevens made in letters of this period were like motifs announcing that he had fallen back into one of the familiar patterns of his youth, when to block pain or a sense of inadequacy, he had indulged in one of his passions, which, in turn, prompted feelings of guilt—the "dark moods" he characteristically vented on the most available cultural scapegoat.

These comments and what they point to simply confirm that Stevens had again been deeply unsettled by a death. As in the case of his sister Katharine's death in relationship to World War I, Church's death appears to have represented the death of a world. Beyond whatever sense of personal inadequacy Stevens felt as he once again weighed himself and found himself wanting, he also became acutely aware of the inanity of political systems that imitated the worst fact of nature rather than the best. That is, in having control of a weapon capable of totally destroying human life, government was taking on the role of an arbitrary and irrational god before whom all—not only its own citizens—could not help feeling wholly helpless. With this "god" one could not even begin to negotiate. It was impossible to make a new covenant with a god who spoke only "propaganda," as Stevens was careful to point out. Venting his present "dark mood" on the current group to bear blame, he attacked only "Communists," "Russians," as open purveyors of the newest political commodity: "It will be nice when we have something besides the weather and the Communists to think of, something besides Russia, and when, while we may be living once more in an illusion, it won't be the—or an—appal[l]ing illusion of propaganda. I am sick of propaganda down to the soles of my feet" (*L* 569).

It was, of course, true that the Russians would take the next major step in escalating political tensions by exploding their first atomic bomb in 1949. Unlike the explosions at Hiroshima and Nagasaki, this did not even have as its occasion the excuse of ending a war. Perhaps Stevens was exhibiting reasoned foresight in his repeated singling out of the Communists as culprits. In any case, Stevens was angry about the situation in which the culture found itself: facing death at what could be any moment. Rather than arrange systems that would in some measure protect individuals from being constantly aware of their helplessness and the absurd and precarious nature of existence—a system, say, of elaborate rituals designed to produce and share as much food as possible with as many different nations and groups as possible, with elaborate rewards given to the most successful—the major world powers had managed to intensify the threat. Seeing what had come about in the world led Stevens to extreme skepticism: "As skepticism becomes both complete and profound, we face either a true civilization or a blank; and literature ought to be one of the factors to determine the choice. Certainly if civilization is to consist only of man himself, and it is, the arts must take the place of divinity, at least as a stage in whatever general principle or progress is involved" (*L* 564). While in youth his skepticism had been limited to religious positions, it now extended to all realms of experience—except art, the still-sacred grove. Unfortunately, however, Stevens had by this time lost faith in his possibility of contributing to art any more than he already had. And what he had contributed had not, as far as he could see, been a determinant in the choice of anything but "a blank." There didn't seem to be any "true civilization" waiting in the wings of the theaters of war.

So, in spite of his being invited in late April 1947 by Wesleyan University to receive an honorary degree of Doctor of Letters (conferred on June 15), being told by John Crowe Ransom that he "covet[ed] the chance" of publishing more of his work in the *Kenyon Review* (June 20, 1947), being asked in early December by Norman Holmes Pearson for the Bergen Foundation at Yale to give a paper (which Stevens, pleased at being himself a member of the Bergen family, agreed to do, delivering "Effects of Analogy" [*NA* 105–30] on March 18, 1948)—in spite of all these loud trumpetings of recognition, the poet felt, in the face of the world situation and what it portended, the way he had described his comic hero Crispin's feeling in the face of nature's indifferent vastness: the "merest minuscule in the gales" (*CP* 29).

To alleviate some of the pain he experienced—grief and fear prompted by Church's death, frustration and impotence at not contributing a determining factor in the choices being made that directly affected his life and would certainly affect the life of his newborn grandson—Stevens did what he usually did: distracted himself with indulgences. As he noted to more than one correspondent through the last eight months of 1947, he had become almost manic about food. Not unexpectedly, these glimpses of self-disclosure, like almost all the comments about the Communists, while describing something he realized to be serious, were couched in humor. The comedian was at work cutting away at what symbolized threat, whether to health or to the possibility of work, as he expressed at the end of June to Harry Duncan:

> There are many things that I should like to be able to do and usually summer is a good time to do them, but this summer has been anything but. Not long ago a French baker opened a shop in West Hartford and this has set me back terribly. His brioches are as good as any. His *croissants* are not quite so good because he doesn't use butter, but some queer substitute. Nevertheless, to start the day so full of these things that every time one breathes one whistles does not help to get things done. Over this last week-end I neither read nor wrote a single line. In part, this was due to the fact that two friends of mine who like to grow strawberries brought huge platters of freshly picked berries to the house. One man even went to the extent of laying his out on mint leaves. Why should I struggle under such circumstances? (*L* 561).

The only thing that seems to have stopped the "Giant" from continuing to stuff himself was the inconvenience and expense that would certainly follow if he went on feasting and then had to have a new wardrobe made. This he indicated in the following delightful description, which he presented to Wilson Taylor toward the end of August:

> Dear Mr. Taylor:
>
> Thanks for your letter of August 13th and for the cocoanut syrup. The syrup tastes like old-fashioned cocoanut caramels which are back on sale

again on Main Street here in Hartford. While the stuff is great stuff, it is very sweet and I have now reached a point at which the tailor tells me that my clothes cannot possibly be extended farther. The other day I wrote to a couple of ladies in the country in New York for some mayonnaise, salad dressing, and things of that sort. Last Saturday I had one of the season's apples together with a pile of mayonnaise about the same size as the apple and I was just beginning to open my eyes when your cocoanut syrup came along. God help me, I am a miserable sinner and love being so.

In addition to your interest in old fashioned syrups I notice that you are also interested in fuchsias. Curiously, these are another one of my weaknesses. Next to the passion flower I love fuchsias, and no kidding. I used to include water lilies. The trouble with water lilies is that once they shut it is impossible to get them open again. In the case of passion flowers the trick is to stick them in the icebox. They are so astonished by the various things they find there that they are afraid to shut. With fuchsias it is not a question of shutting. Down among Pennsylvania Germans there was a race of young men, perhaps there still is, who carved willow fans. These men would take a bit of willow stick about a foot long, peel it and with nothing more than a jackknife carve it into something that looked like a souvenir of Queen Anne's lingerie. The trouble that someone took to invent fuchsias always makes me think of these willow fans.

However it is a dark and dreary day today and who am I to be frivolous under such circumstances.

Sincerely yours,
WALLACE STEVENS
(*L* 564–65)

Here was Stevens playfully acknowledging God and perceiving himself to be both a "miserable sinner" and "frivolous," very much like the characters in Boccaccio's *Decameron,* indulging themselves, simultaneously sinning and delighting while composing descriptions around the *carpe diem* tactics they devised in the face of their possible imminent deaths to the spreading plague. The plague now was of words, words emptied of meaning, infecting minds with poisonous thoughts that would mean death if believed. It was almost as if Stevens had become painfully sensitized to the consequences of the sin of his forefathers—or of any who used rhetoric unattached to the real, to fact. The Puritans, in using words to describe having found the New Jerusalem while all too often acting in ways the savages they attempted to civilize could not have begun to conceive, were like inverted mirror images of the "Communists" the poet angrily derided. They, too, had substituted an image of the world as it could be for what was. And so the poet mocked in magnificent measure, but was it that he mocked himself alone? The sins of the fathers are visited on their children.

Perhaps one of the reasons that the poet, together with most of the population, fixed doggedly on the Communists was that it was impossible for the children of the "elect" to acknowledge that they, too, were guilty. Admitting guilt or inadequacy is especially difficult for those without secure senses of personal identity. There was something very American in this. Because America did not have a long and coherent cultural identity, ideological rhetoric became all the more important in providing a unifying force. Notably, at precisely the time when the cold war began and rhetoric/propaganda strained this factitious identity to the utmost, Stevens himself equated virtue with devotion to the spirit of one's nation. As he wrote to Barbara Church, apropos of one of the latest additions to his long list of reading in American history—François Jean de Chastellux, *Travels in North America, in the Years 1780–81–82* (1787)—"It is a curious thing that virtue should show itself in love of one's country. But it does" (*L* 568).

Stevens was also preoccupied with the idea of his own impending death, beyond the more abstract idea of the death of civilization. This showed itself in certain observations he made in letters he wrote to friends. In these communications recollections of his childhood and youth punctuated his comments about the weather, the state of the arts, or the world. After writing about "complete and profound skepticism" to Barbara Church, for example, he noted that he had that morning walked in Elizabeth Park and there "inhaled the deep woods coolness as [he] used to at home" (*L* 564). About a month earlier, on July 17, 1947, again to Barbara Church, he recalled how restorative it had felt for him to go back to Reading from New York when he was a young man; as he put it, it was "a way of going back to an earth which always filled [him] with whatever [he] really needed at the time" (*L* 563). These evocations of the past, fixed in memories of the landscapes at home, recurred like refrains over the last eight years of Stevens's life. It was almost as if his intelligence were gradually narrowing its scope to become, once again, simply part of his soil.

Balancing this centripetal movement was an equally strong centrifugal one that revealed itself in another form of indulgence during this same period. Stevens hungered for paintings, "new" things to stimulate him. Writing to Paule Vidal near the end of June 1947, he attributed his "wild impatience" to have something to the long spell of bad weather during the spring that had afforded him only "occasional brilliant days" (*L* 561). Deprived of regular walking during one of the seasons (the other was autumn) when because of the contact with nature—even in the limited space of Elizabeth Park—he usually wrote poetry, a painting would serve as the book in which his imagination read its rounds and attended to some subtle transformation of line or color, change. What Stevens craved was change. The combination of a period of bad weather and news of a death had almost fifty years earlier sent the poet into one of his darkest periods. The month of rainy Sundays during his first year in New York had contributed to the early stage of Stevens's crisis of faith. Now the final stage would come out of this spell of bad weather and Church's death.

Unusually, as though mimicking the return of the past, the kind of painting Stevens now wanted was something old, not "broken down," but something "really desirable, touching, of almost any school" (*L* 560). His feeling for the past was invading his delight in the experimental uses of color and line that he appreciated in the impressionistic style. But it would prove to be difficult for Mlle. Vidal to locate a reasonably priced "French primitive" or example from the "Italian school," even in the postwar marketplace, so the appetite of the "Giant" had to be satisfied for the time being with two more canvases by one of the lesser-known contemporary painters—Roland Oudot. Though, as often happened, Stevens was eager to have these after reading Vidal's tantalizing descriptions of them—she was "killing [him] with curiosity," he noted to her (*L* 559)—when the works arrived, he was disappointed. They were not exactly suited to his palate. As he wrote to Vidal after the long-awaited arrival of the paintings in mid-November (prewar efficiency had not begun to be regained, much to Stevens's chagrin), Oudot seemed to limit himself to "esthetic truth instead of attempting to realize the object and figures in his picture" (*L* 569). Not sated by these acquisitions, the poet was soon asking again for something "new" for "stimulation."

Henry Church's spirit was an almost constant companion of the poet's through the end of the year. Feeling this presence no doubt contributed to keeping alive the sense of death as he wrote about it in "The Owl in the Sarcophagus"—that is, as memory and reputation. Stevens had Barbara Church send him all that her husband had ever written. She happily obliged, even offering her American poet friend Church's French correspondence with Jean Paulhan. Stevens discovered a great deal he had not known—for example, that Church had written poetry. After seeing the first samples that Mrs. Church sent, Stevens wanted to see all of it. By the end of November he had gone through published and unpublished material and had, in addition, written a description of Church that was to be translated into French and issued in a special number of *Mesures* sometime during the next year. Thus, though Stevens reported to Paule Vidal that he had not been ordering journals and books lately because he had no time to read, he had actually read quite a bit more than Chastellux's description of his experience in Revolutionary America. In light of what Church seems to have come to represent for the poet, the feature around which he built Church's portrait was the one that most characterized himself: "the existence in him of . . . opposites." So strong was the identification that Stevens's first eight sentences—with the exception of the second reference to Paris—could serve as a perfect thumbnail self-portrait:

> As I saw him in New York, although he was withdrawn, he was eager to make friends and it was clear that his friendships were precious to him. This sort of duality: being withdrawn and at the same time being eager to make friends, was characteristic of him. Thus, in New York, he seemed to be essentially of Paris and, very likely, in Paris, he seemed to be essentially of New York. He was a simple man who had little interest in things that were not complex. He was a plain man who lived in a certain luxury which he ignored. He was most literate yet had only a few books on his table. He had

read philosophy for forty years but it seemed to be, for him, pretty much a substitute for fiction. Ideas were the bread of life to him, but, although I saw him frequently, what he actually enjoyed was not the discussion of ideas, but casual conversations. (*L* 570)

It is impossible to know if Stevens was aware of how closely he himself fitted this description, though it is very likely that he was. He had noted the tendency to opposites in himself from the time he was a young man, and it was the characteristic feature of his autobiographical mock epic hero. What was unusual was that he had found someone so essentially like him that his loss must have figured as a loss of part of himself. It was almost as though in composing his memorial pieces for Church, he were mourning himself. The words he found for his friend he wished for himself.

As the dark year of 1947 ended, Stevens spiritually retreated more than he usually did during the Christmas season. He reported to José Rodríguez Feo (now at Princeton) that he had been telling people he and Elsie expected to be away over the holidays, even though they planned to stay in Hartford. But through all the black moodiness the poet managed, as he always had, to maintain his sense of humor. His Christmas letter to Barbara Church, concerning practical details of her new Park Avenue apartment, pointing another comedic gibe at the Communists, and closing with an evasive but revealing comment about the season now upon him, communicated the tenor of the year past. The year 1948 would open with more orders to Mlle. Vidal drawn from the catalogs of pictures and books, "not automobiles," he teasingly told her as he sent his holiday greetings.

❧

From the time of Henry Church's death until his own, Stevens attempted to fill his moments with more activity than he ever had. He wrote the greater part of his remaining letters, apart from the business letters he had always composed as regular parts of his workdays and the hundreds of letters related to his genealogical searches; he read seasonally, as usual, whenever his eyes allowed; he composed the poems of *The Auroras of Autumn* and "The Rock," each new short poem being something that he had to prepare himself for freshly, a repeated process that was much more demanding, he reported, than working on a long poem over a period of time; he composed more lectures, in spite of his resistance that had to be overcome with each new request. Whatever time was not filled with words "on paper," Stevens gave to musing on paintings and painters, one of the strongest interests of his last years. He bought many more canvases, went to museum exhibitions and galleries with renewed vigor, and bought a number of art books. He was particularly interested in figures who were roughly his contemporaries. It was as if he were looking at his time through others' eyes and a different medium and recording the parallels he found. Eventually these musings were beautifully shaped into "The Relations Between Poetry and Painting" (*NA* 157–76), a lecture he delivered at the Museum of Modern Art in 1951. About this lecture, for which there was immediate and enthusiastic praise, Stevens surprisingly had no reservations.

The poet's increased activity during this last phase echoed the period of intense activity that had followed his sister Katharine's death with its close associations to the Great War, the period in which he had produced the poems of *Harmonium.* It was then that Stevens had been told that he might not live beyond the age of forty. Now he *knew,* not only feared, that there was little time left. It is difficult to know the nature of the pressure Stevens felt in the face of death. Did he want to take in as much as he could so that in composing his lines, he could leave behind as full a picture of things as they had been during his lifetime? Or were moments of being without evasion by a single metaphor or without the distraction offered by giving attention to a new painting, a piece of music, a business letter, or a new journal simply too painful to withstand?

In connection with this it is important to recognize how much Stevens appreciated what he called the "routine" of the office. Even though he often complained about the amount of work he had piled up on his desk and though he sometimes resented having to put off an editor requesting a new piece, as the year of retirement came and passed, Stevens devoted more time to the office than he ever had. He worked through the summer and took as holidays only those when the Hartford was closed. With each year that went by he repeated with increasing emphasis, usually in letters to Barbara Church, his gratitude for the regularity the "routine" established in his life. How essential the poet believed this to be was indicated by his declining the honor of the Charles Eliot Norton lectureship at Harvard for 1955–1956. As he explained in a letter to Archibald MacLeish, accepting the appointment would have meant that he would have had to be away from the office for a year, and he was uncertain whether after such a long absence he would be able to return to the company, which might have chosen the occasion to retire him. Here was a chance for the poet to attempt to put into practice what he was convinced was so important for the future of poetry, if it was to assume what he believed to be its proper place as a discipline for shaping young spirits. But he refused it. As noted earlier, Stevens had lost faith in himself as someone capable of articulating the theory of poetry. He also knew how difficult it was for him to speak in public. The thought of giving a series of lectures to the same group of students, whom, if he were to embarrass himself, as he always feared he would, he would have to face again and again for a year, no doubt made him shrink. But even if these reactions could have been overcome, leaving the order that work at the Hartford enforced was something Stevens could not have begun to contemplate.

There were, I think, two central and interconnected reasons for Stevens's extreme dependence on this "routine." Having given at least half his attention throughout his adult life to being a "money-making lawyer" meant that he had never had to face what could have been had he followed the "literary life" he had longed for as a young man when he did not want to be "half dream, half deed." Ironically, this fear became his reality, only because there was another fear behind it: that he might have broken like his father and older brother had he truly followed his own way. Each day that he fulfilled his obligation to the Hartford was yet another confirmation that he was not like them. At the same time his work at the company provided him with thousands of details to distract him from applying the microscope to himself. Stevens worked hardest whenever he felt the "encroachment of that old catastrophe," the return of the "black mood" that had followed him from his youth.

While becoming the successful lawyer satisfied the very American needs bred into Stevens and won him the approval from his father's ghost, if there were not more to his involvement with this side of his life than these fulfillments, then he would have been able to accept the opportunity Harvard offered him. That Stevens refused this offer in fear that it would mean the end of his life at the Hartford points to how he used this half of his experience to shield him from ever having to attempt fully what he had desired so intensely "on paper," to become "man number one" in his own terms, take the risks, cut loose, and give himself wholly to the Muse, even for just a year.

If he had, what was he afraid that he would find—that he could not whip from himself a jovial hullabaloo, write the final poem of fact in the language of fact, but fact not realized before, that he would go mad? It is not surprising that though he continued to win honors and awards and though he was consistently happy and proud about them, not ever having proved himself in his own terms, never having found out what could have come had he given his full time to poetry, he remained as uncertain of himself as he had ever been in his youth. In his own eyes he was still the young man who had not had the confidence to believe anything but what his father had said, that "the afflatus [was] not serious." As a result of his not having had the courage of his convictions, a situation no doubt compounded by the misfortune of his father's breakdown during the period when Stevens was first testing his wings of words as a journalist, so many other "choices" had been made. If he had not had the "routine" at the Hartford that gradually came to tire him out so much that he had all he could do to get through the evening newspaper at home before falling asleep, how many "what ifs" might have presented themselves? And when he was not too tired out by "routine" or not occupied with one of the "new things" he surrounded himself with to "give pleasure," distract him, he parried whatever "what ifs" might crop up with "as ifs" and around them composed his poems.

Through these years of almost superhuman effort, Stevens did feel himself aging. But while his senses weakened, instead of complaining or mourning, he compensated. When his eyes dimmed so that he could not read as he used to, he studied painting more closely. When the length and frequency of his walks diminished, as they did especially after a fall in the winter of 1950 that caused an ankle injury from which Stevens never quite recovered, he became more attentive to certain favorite spots in Elizabeth Park where he would stop to rest; there he made sequential mental notes on other "regulars" and on the smallest changes in the flower beds. He spent more time in—and, when the weather was not congenial, watching—his garden; he recorded the dates each year on which the first snowdrops pushed out beneath the heavy spruce trees. The "imperative haw of hum" became an "inquisitorial botanist"; lines he had written thirty years before still held him. He had composed the script for his old age even before he had set out on his voyaging, so that now, as he began to experience its effects—expressing to friends and family in letters that he no longer felt as though he were twenty-eight—he did not voice suffering or complaint. He simply set himself to his tasks with good humor.

The task that occupied him for the first three months of 1948 was composing "Effects of Analogy." He declined an invitation to Barbara Church's spring cocktail party; he again set aside all reading and put off requests from editors for new poems until he had set down this latest installment of his defense of poetry. His involvement was so demanding that by the end of the time of working on it, a period of "intense choosing" (*NA* 130) of the right words, he wished that he could go away for a whole month and "forget the whole thing" (March 15, 1948). In his characteristically self-mocking manner with José Rodríguez Feo, he described his work habits:

> . . . at the moment have suspended all reading until I am able to dispose of something else. After I have walked home when I would ordinarily have a glass of water and a few cookies and sit down in an easy chair with the evening paper, I go upstairs nowadays and work over my chore like one of the holy fathers working over his prayers. In fact, this morning I was up at five o'clock under the impression that it was six and did not discover my mistake until I had finished my bath and was half dressed, when it was too late to go back to bed. I thought that the darkness was due to the mist when in fact it was not due to anything: it was just dark. (*L* 579–80)

He humorously compared himself to one of the "holy fathers working over his prayers." Even though he had been spiritually weakened in his profession of faith by the death of Henry Church, Stevens had not lost the sense that his involvement with poetry, however imperfect it might be, was a sacred occupation. The offhand lightness of his metaphors only attested to the seriousness of his intent; it was a manifestation of the same mechanism that had informed the style of *Harmonium* years before: "[A]ngelic hilarity" was the attitude Stevens wanted to cultivate before the harsher facts of life. Yet when others also laughed as he laughed at himself, the poet crumbled. This was sadly illustrated by a curious situation surrounding the delivery of "Effects of Analogy" on March 18.

Unlike the *Three Academic Pieces* and "The Figure of the Youth as Virile Poet," which shivered with complication, this lecture was direct, straightforward. It was as though, having lost confidence that he could articulate *the* theory of poetry, Stevens set himself simply to elucidate the theory of *his* poetry. In this sense, "Effects of Analogy" picked up where the poet had left off after writing "A Poet That Matters" thirteen years before, when he used the occasion of introducing Marianne Moore's poems to point out precisely the elements of strong poetry that should be looked for in his own work as well. He also picked up on what he had laid out in "The Irrational Element in Poetry" written not long after his Moore piece, when he described the essential interaction between the "true subject" and the "poetry of the subject" that had to be understood if the relation between a man and his world was to be grasped.

In "Effects of Analogy" Stevens returned to the central points he had foregrounded in those earlier pieces and made them more explicit. He outlined in measured and numbered "lessons" the necessary keys to read his poems and understand his purpose. He focused attention once again on the interaction between the true subject and the poetry of the subject and described the kind of reader who would be sensitive to it: "But there is a third reader, one for whom the story and the other meaning should come together like two aspects that combine to produce a third or, if they do not combine, inter-act, so that one influences the other and produces an effect similar in kind to the prismatic formations that occur about us in nature in the case of reflections and refractions" (*NA* 109). This kind of reader would apprehend the poem as one apprehended facts "in nature": "A poem is part of the res itself and not about it." The subject of the next lesson—Stevens divided the lecture into five sections—was image. He directed his audience to recognize that the choice of images reflected the poet's emotions; the reader who derived this "effect of analogy" would feel the "effect of consummation" (*NA* 114). Stevens's ambiguously religious/sexual term was weighted with all his desire. "There was a mystic marriage . . ." (*CP* 401) that he continued to imagine between his spirit and that of "a woman with the hair of a pythoness" (*NA* 29)—the image around which he had six years before built his argument for aspiring to a "noble" purpose in "The Noble Rider and the Sound of Words."

The poet's third lesson was a clarification. He distinguished himself as one who had sought two things: the "marginal, subliminal" and the "very center of consciousness" (*NA* 115). When during the thirties and early forties he had attempted "to feel that his imagination [was] not wholly his own but . . . part of a much larger, much more potent imagination, which it [was] his affair to try to get at" (*NA* 115), he, like Paul Valéry, whom he singled out in comparison, was working "on the verge of consciousness." The clearest expressions of this had been "The Man with the Blue Guitar" and *Parts of a World*. Now, disillusioned with the practical results of what he had tried (we remember that the poet had been terribly disappointed with the reception of the work of his late middle period), realizing that his work had not contributed to determining any of the choices that were being made in his world, Stevens concerned himself with "imagination as a power within him to have such insights into reality as [would] make it possible for him to be sufficient as a poet in the very center of consciousness." This was a return to a purely Emersonian stance. Stevens hoped that in his last devotions to the "central" he would express what he quoted "Dr. Whitehead" naming as "that ultimate good sense which we term civilization" (*NA* 115). In illustrating what kind of poetry this would produce, the poet compared himself to St. Matthew and to Leonidas of Tarentum, one of the poets of *The Greek Anthology*. Stevens was returning to the sources from which he had drawn nourishment as a young man about to begin his poetic search for what would suffice.

The fourth lesson centered on "subject," the "particularity" he had named years earlier in connection to Marianne Moore's special talent. In this section Stevens expanded on the importance of "personality" or "temperament" that he had begun to explain in "The Figure of the Youth as Virile Poet." Just as he then had used the example of Picasso to illustrate what he meant by an artist who was not afraid to reveal his temperament in his work and was, therefore, a "leader," he did so again now. He directed his listeners to look carefully at his own "choice of subject," explaining that "For each man . . . certain subjects are congenital" (*NA* 120). He disclosed himself as openly as he ever had or would again, noting: "It is often said of a man that his work is autobiographical in spite of every subterfuge. It cannot be otherwise" (*NA* 121).

Lastly, Stevens drew attention to what was to be understood as the "music of poetry" in his time. He made a point of finding the exact words to ensure that his audience would comprehend that "music was a communication of emotion," that each subtle variation was an indication of a man's being "disturbed by his feeling for what he says" (*NA* 125–26). The experience of attending to the music of poetry this way would be like having directly "participated in what took place" (*NA* 126). Here was the man uneasy about revealing himself giving directions about reading his poems so that the reader who followed them precisely would, in effect, become him. "Bethou, bethou, bethou me . . ." (*CP* 394).

Stevens wanted to consummate a "mystic marriage" between his spirit and that of his imagined ideal reader. Unlike Eliot's voice crying in the desert of twentieth-century civilization for the finding of another way, Stevens's voice cried for the recognition of his essential loneliness as much as it did for the recognition that there could be another way. This ambiguity of expression accounts, in part, for the difficulty of Stevens's work. The poet himself pointed to his difference from Eliot: "Eliot and I are dead opposites and I have been doing about everything he would not be likely to do" (*L* 676). Eliot's immersion in the lessons of the East truly did make possible his modification of his Western tradition. Stevens, on the other hand, in spite of continued attempts to transcend his preoccupation with self, did not succeed at this, so that in the end one can't escape a sense of tragedy—the fall of a hero. Through the stoic intoning of Stevens's last poems we can still hear the mournful lowing of the human animal being carried to his death without ever having known what it was to have lived beyond the edge of his fate, beyond the limits set for him by his past.

Stevens carried this tragic sense, in spite of his comedian's posture. It was probably because the feeling of absence, of loss, had always occupied such a prominent place in his consciousness that he was so quick to put on the comic mask early in his career. Now, late in his life, facing the final loss of breath, Stevens could no longer restrain the sounds of sorrow.

In "Effects of Analogy" he prepared his audience and future readers to hear them. It was not accidental that the central example—"subject"—he chose was Leonidas' epigram: "Even as a vine on her dry pole I support myself now on a staff and death calls me to Hades." Nor was it accidental that in addition to a few examples from contemporary figures such as Allen Tate and Kenneth Burke, the lecture was filled with references to other things Stevens had read in his youth besides *The Greek Anthology* and the Bible. He cited John Bunyan's *Pilgrim's Progress,* a fable from Jean de La Fontaine, Edmund Spenser's *Faerie Queene*—which he had gone through meticulously in his early years, gently marking in pencil special passages throughout his fine, old illustrated volumes—Virgil's *Georgics,* Walt Whitman. Even David Gray appeared; though he was not mentioned by name, his "edge of night" metaphor echoed in Stevens's mind as he made Leonidas' image of old age even more powerful by conjuring his "old man" before death "wandering on the edge of night" (*NA* 114). These last whisperings of the "studious ghosts" who had inhabited him all his life were like the periodic refrains from the past in the letters he now wrote—evidences of the strong pull back to the center from which he had sprung.

The poet made it clear that he was not himself unaware that in composing "Effects of Analogy," he was laying himself bare, exposing as directly as he could how he felt about being on the brink of death. He was like Leonidas' figure, "an old man at that point at which antiquity begins to resume what everything else has left behind" (*NA* 124). He was careful to note, too, that if a feeling of "despair" came through the lines describing the world experienced by such an old man, "it was not within the poet's power to suppress" that feeling.

Writing this lecture seems to have functioned in the way that writing "The Irrational Element in Poetry" had functioned about ten years before. The earlier lecture/essay served as a bridge between the poetry he had been writing through more than half the thirties, when he had tried to attach his imagination to the common reality, as he had expressed he had done in *Ideas of Order,* and the poetry of "The Man with the Blue Guitar," the "duet with the undertaker," when he spelled out what he had attempted: the sense that he had failed and the announcement of his return to a more personal voice. But through the forties he had again tried to play "man number one," even addressing the "Soldier" at the end of "Notes." Again, he felt he had failed, so now there was this lecture, laying out in plain terms how he felt he should be read and why he was again turning to the "central." As he explained indirectly, he had realized, finally, that to "create a poetry of the present [was] an incalculable difficulty, which rarely is achieved, fully and robustly, by anyone" (*NA* 116). He had tried more than once and would not try again. The poetry that followed from this point on would not attempt to be anything more than an expression of his "temperament." No doubt realizing that this might leave him open to an attack by some astute critic who would see that, in the end, for Stevens the "central" meant his "self," the poet defensively added, in explaining that it was justifiable simply to render "his sense of the world," that "There is nothing of selfishness in this" (*NA* 121). He knew that he was a man made out of words and that his self was no less and no more than a container of many voices that he had been arranging and orchestrating all his life. Thus armed, Stevens crossed the bridge leading to the last phase of his career.

But crossing the bridge would be difficult.

As a result of his extreme overindulgence during the months before, when Stevens entered the hall where he was to speak on March 18, he felt that he must have appeared "more like an elephant at every step" (*L* 583). Once on the platform, noticing that the lectern was too low, he asked that it be raised. For some reason, the raising of the reading desk's pedestal made the audience laugh. Stevens understood the laughter to have been directed at him, a comment on the grotesque figure he believed he presented. In consequence, the poet was even more uneasy than usual as he read. How painfully ambivalent he had to have felt after this as he uttered the lines of the poem he had chosen to follow his lecture, "A Primitive Like an Orb," in which "A giant, on the horizon, glistening," was conjured. How nearly impossible it must have been for him, unable to escape the embarrassment he felt about "that monster, [his] body," to get through the last two stanzas—after he had offered in the sixth his essential metaphor of "mating," in which the idealized figure of the poet "espoused" the earth:

XI

Here, then, is an abstraction given head,
A giant on the horizon, given arms,
A massive body and long legs, stretched out,
A definition with an illustration, not
Too exactly labelled, a large among the smalls
Of it, a close, parental magnitude,
At the centre on the horizon, concentrum, grave
And prodigious person, patron of origins.

XII

That's it. The lover writes, the believer hears,
The poet mumbles and the painter sees,
Each one, his fated eccentricity,
As a part, but part, but tenacious particle,
Of the skeleton of the ether, the total
Of letters, prophecies, perceptions, clods

Of color, the giant of nothingness, each one
And the giant ever changing, living in change.
(*CP* 443)

As Louis Martz, the faculty host for the occasion, recalled, Stevens read so badly, so quietly that at one point a woman in the audience raised her hand and asked that he speak more loudly. He replied, "I'll try, lady. I'll try," but his voice then dropped even lower.[5] To ease some of the discomfort he had experienced, at the dinner party following the lecture Stevens "rather let go," as he put it in a note to Norman Holmes Pearson the following day, "on the cocktails and Benedictines" (March 19, 1948). Though the others around him seemed "very friendly," as the poet also remarked in the same note, he had needed the fortification alcohol provided. Expectedly, with the loosening that a few drinks allowed, Stevens came away from the party feeling that he had somehow terribly offended Cleanth Brooks and his wife by arguing insistently that Louisiana was not a part of the United States at the time of the Revolution.[6] The poet was so mortified by his imagined rudeness that for three years he kept alive the fear that Brooks must have hated him. Finally, in 1951, Stevens wrote a note of apology to Brooks for what had happened in 1948. Needless to say, Brooks was "bowled over," as he put in January 18, 1951, to receive this penitent expression from the poet whom he and his wife warmly remembered as having simply been relaxed enough with them on their first meeting to be himself. (Perceptively Brooks added in his reminiscence of the incident that Stevens's living in the imagining of what had occurred rather than in the reality of it marked him as a true poet.)[7]

On this same evening, after Stevens had delivered the lecture in which he revealed his "plain self" as "plainly" as he ever had, there was another incident around the dinner table that was perceived to be embarrassingly sharp by Louis Martz and clearly by the two others who were directly involved. It seems that the poet openly questioned Dudley Fitts about why he was spending all his time, "energy," and "best thoughts" teaching (at Phillips Academy in Andover, Massachusetts) instead of devoting himself fully to writing his poetry as he "ought." Fitts replied that he had to make a living, to which his wife added that they had two children to support. Stevens, very aware that he had touched one of the couple's raw nerves, replied, "Oh, I apologize. Never should come between a man and his wife. Never. Never. I won't say anymore."[8]

Martz observed that Stevens's advice, disguised as a question to Fitts, was "a funny thing" for him to say. Yet, seen in the context of the final stage of the poet's coming to terms with himself, it fits right into place as one of the "what ifs" that he usually managed to distract himself from or transform into an "as if" when he was fully in possession of himself, as he clearly was not when he drank. In addressing Fitts the way he did, Stevens was expressing a wish he had spent a life suppressing, a risk he had never taken. Rather than see that it was not Mrs. Fitts who—as the story was reported in any case—

alone voiced her opposition to "taking off for the wilderness" so that her husband could write his poems, but that she only reinforced what her husband had already said, Stevens apologized for "coming between" them, as though he had taken the part of the poet who felt constrained by marital obligations from fulfilling himself and so becoming more than just "half dream, half deed." Echoing the poet's identification with Fitts, his thrice-repeated "Never"—if recalled correctly by Martz—seemed to escape from the line of powerful negatives in "Le Monocle de Mon Oncle," which bespoke the poet's frustration at having been denied and denying himself the satisfactions he craved.

Another expected consequence of Stevens's experience at Yale was that it reinforced his diffidence about the possibility he felt about articulating the theory of poetry in any adequate way. On being asked after the lecture to publish the piece in the *Yale Review,* he expressed his fear that no one would care to read it and noted, as he had about his earlier lectures as well, that "Effects of Analogy" had been drawn out to fill an hour's time. On being pressed, he agreed but asked that the editors themselves do whatever they thought necessary to make it presentable. And on being asked within the next few weeks by Allen Tate to participate in a poetry festival, he flatly refused; "not on your life," he remarked, describing his embarrassment at having felt like an "elephant" (*L* 583). During the same week he noted to Barbara Church, apropos of how much he would like to be able to get to know one of the young men he had just met at her apartment, where he had stopped on one of his afternoons in New York, that the "difficulty in seeing people [was growing] greater not less." Though he based his inability "to do more than tell him [Fernand Auberjonois, son of one of the French painters of the Churches' acquaintance] how good grated cheese is on soft-boiled eggs" on the fact that he had wanted to catch the 5:25 train back to Hartford (*L* 582), it was apparent that Stevens was feeling more keenly than he ever had the disjunction between the "vigorous warrior" he presented "on paper" and his "plain self." This, too, would play its part in his turning the mirror to the "central," the "self alone" for his last years. Perhaps he hoped to transcend his fears by doing this.

❧

While Stevens completed the draft of the "Effects of Analogy," he sent Paule Vidal new requests for things to read and look at: a subscription to the *Bulletin des Musées de France* (March 8, 1948), the latest numbers of *Quadrique,* a fine old edition of Villon, a critical monograph on Juan Gris, Malraux's recently published *Psychologie d'Art,* a book of Poussin reproductions with an introduction by Gide, and another painting, this one by Pierre Tal Coat (*L* 581–82). If the poet was afraid that he might not be sufficiently distracted without these additions, he was mistaken. No sooner was he back in Hartford from New Haven than a letter arrived from Delmore Schwartz requesting that Stevens respond to a questionnaire on the current state of American writing to be published in the *Partisan Review.* Stevens complied, with three and a half double-spaced typed sheets (*L* 589–90) but not without limiting his responses only to the questions he wanted to address. Ignoring those that would lead him to name other figures or to voice anything that might begin to suggest a political affiliation, Stevens concentrated on the features of his newest hobbyhorse, the "central," incorporating into it what was valid "experiment," as opposed to "trivialities" like calligraphic shapes, and making a case for his latest decision to focus on "remaining himself." He closed his "answers" with an implicit apology for his "evasion," though he wanted to make it appear that this very evasion was contact with "reality":

> You may not regard these answers as responsive to questions that contemplate literary tendencies, literary atmosphere, literary interest, literary criticism, and so on. From this point of view it is easy to say that the basic meaning of literary effort, and, therefore, of poetry, is with reference to life and reality and not with reference to politics. The basic meaning of the effort of any man to record his experience as poet is to produce poetry, not politics. The poet must stand or fall by poetry. In the conflict between the poet and the politician the chief honor the poet can hope for is that of remaining himself. Life and reality, on the one hand, and politics, on the other, notwithstanding the activity of politics, are not interchangeable terms. They are not the same thing, whatever the Russians may pretend.

Within the next two weeks there were additional requests for responses of different kinds. Robert Lowell, the latest recruit in the effort to get Stevens to read for the Library of Congress tapes, wrote what he no doubt thought a most persuasive note, pointing out that Stevens was the only "important American poet"—with the exception of Pound, because the government would not "let him out of St. Lizzie's"—not recorded (April 6, 1948). Stevens charmingly refused, commenting, "You put me in the class of the only Esquimo in the arctic circle that does not like snow" (April 9, 1948). During the same week Sister Mary Bernetta Quinn wrote her first letter to the poet, explaining that she had been introduced to his work through Yvor Winters; she enclosed one of her interpretations of his poetry. Stevens began his return correspondence with her by observing that he felt she shared a mind like his own, one that constantly sought the "centre" of things (*L* 584). William Van O'Connor, one of the worthy younger men Stevens remembered meeting in the last few years, also wrote, asking the poet whether he could include his yet unpublished prose pieces in an anthology devoted to the theory of poetry. Stevens responded that he would like nothing more than to contribute to the theory of poetry but that his "prose [was] not what it ought to be" (*L* 585).

Another two weeks passed and Stevens received his first letter from Thomas McGreevy, who presumed on the common contact they both had with the Churches to open a correspondence with him. Stevens's return letter to the Irish art historian and poet, who had mentioned his connection to Jack Yeats, the painter, was to ask for McGreevy's book on his friend with, if possible, a sketch of McGreevy done on the flyleaf (*L* 586–87). Stevens wanted to add his portrait to the gallery that already included Anatole Vidal's portrait and José Rodríguez Feo's photograph. He had never asked Paule Vidal, nor would he have dared to ask Sister Mary Bernetta, even though the likelihood that he would ever meet these regular and worthy correspondents was as remote as the likelihood that he would ever meet their male counterparts, (in fact, he did come to know both Rodríguez Feo and, eventually, McGreevy in person). It seems that the boy who did not know any of the girls in his class, the young man who had felt uncomfortable with young women did not feel, as an old man, any freer with the fair sex, even if one of their number happened to be habited and to inhabit a similar mind.

The regular correspondence with Rodríguez Feo continued. Of Stevens's latest letter written toward the end of March, when the poet's secretary was on holiday, his friend complained to his "Dear Wallacio" that though his handwriting—like his poems, it might be added—appeared so beautiful, it was "cryptic," and he looked forward to Miss Flynn's return (April 9, 1948). Eerily echoing the poet's feelings over the last year, Rodríguez Feo, still a young man, added that he had a "strong feeling" that he was not going "to live very long," that he was simply waiting for his mother to die. Stevens did not pick up on his fear or attempt to reassure him.

By the end of April Stevens seems to have recovered somewhat from the effects of having again exposed himself in public a month before. In the interim there had been sufficient occasions for him to recompose himself "on paper," and so when Theodore Weiss wrote asking the poet to recommend worthy young poets, he responded that the present was not a "creative period" and that though he felt certain that there must be somewhere in the country "hermits" who devoted themselves as they should exclusively to poetry, he did not know any. In recompense, he would send some of his own work. He added: "I have now reached an age at which I think about everything and this is a great impediment. But I could not let spring and summer go by without poetry of my own and I shall send you what I can when I can" (*L* 587).

Here was another evocation of the poet Stevens wished he had become when as a young man he often playfully described himself as a "hermit" devoted to a sacred task—the same message he had recently tried to communicate to Dudley Fitts. In bemoaning the fact that there were no such figures of youths as virile poets, Stevens was at the same time expressing, though again indirectly, his regret at never having so applied himself and—in offering his work in place of being able to recommend the work of such a "potent figure"—gloating quietly over the fact that no one else had yet managed to do what he thought necessary. It was not difficult to be a man of fortune greeting heirs who, in their absence, posed no threat.

Another day or two passed, and Stevens learned of William Carlos Williams's winning the current Russell Loines Poetry Award at the annual ceremonial of the American Academy and National Institute of Arts and Letters. Here was a contemporary who had also not been able to manage becoming the full-time hermit Stevens was now extolling as the perfect embodiment of the poet. Perhaps feeling that his old friend would think this award a secondary one, Stevens went out of his way to indicate how devoted Loines had been to the best idea of poetry and that Williams should, accordingly, value this award very highly (*L* 588–89). Three days later Stevens reiterated his feeling in another short note comparing Loines to Marianne Moore in his commitment to poetry. Stevens also tenderly responded to Williams's request about how he should dress. He should "wear what he wore every day," he wrote. Lines from "The Emperor of Ice-Cream" suggested themselves now, it seems, around the theme of "new clothes" and "emperors" who won awards. Beyond his congratulations and his stress on the significance of the prize, a note of satisfaction that this was not the Pulitzer or the Nobel sounded. When in the same year W. H. Auden won the Pulitzer and T. S. Eliot the Nobel, Stevens could at least comfort himself with the fact that neither of these poets was a rival known "in person," someone who had frequented the same "literary" circles as he years before. More, in the case of Auden at least, there was the rationale that unlike Stevens, this poet had spent all his poetic energies in subjection to politics. In the case of Eliot, perhaps there was no rationale; Stevens knew only that they were "dead opposites."

On the same day that Stevens wrote his second note to Williams he wrote to Barbara Church. He had just received a copy of the "Hommage à Henry Church" issue of *Mesures* (Paris, April 15, 1948). He observed what it made him feel—". . . the experience of these images is an experience of how unreal we are and also of the pathos of looking back. We lose not only the personality of one person but part of the personality of our whole world. And yet *the* world as distinguished from our world goes on and carries us with it and we are bound to say that it is good under such circumstances" (*L* 592). He suggested what he foresaw the effects of his own death would be in images that would reappear in some of his last poems. He went on to report on having received and having replied to Thomas McGreevy's first letter, on Philip Rahv's comment to him that "he thought all poets were crazy," on Roger Caillois, whom Stevens placed in that category, and on the news that Williams, to whom he referred without naming him, had won a "substantial prize." In expanding on this, Stevens set down a sentence that had no clear referent; it appeared to describe Williams's reaction to the prize but at the same time could have referred to his own "reply" to him: "Such a queer reply—the reply of a man somehow disturbed at the core and making all sorts of gestures and using all sorts of figures to conceal it from himself?" (*L* 592). He then continued to contrast the kind of person who responded in this way with Henri Pourrat, the Swiss regional writer whom the Churches had recommended to Stevens a few years before and whose work the poet had since come to know and appreciate: "How right both of you were to like Henri Pourrat. He is just the opposite of this sort of thing. . . . Pourrat . . . from a literary point of view is probably too good and, anyhow, one is good only in villages. Every man of any sense knows that in literature goodness is finished. . . ."

Stevens closed his letter with one of his characteristic codas about the weather, commenting about the "resplendent exhibition . . . and brilliance" of the last few days: "One wants to be sure that it is right to be made happy by these things. They do make one happy and I am not sure that it is not right that they should. But how nice it would be if I was sure that it was right in the sense that *Wirklichkeit* in general would no longer find it necessary to justify its effects. Spring always comes so near to justifying not only itself but everything" (*L* 593).

There were more than a few curiosities ambling around in Stevens's consciousness as he revealed it here. The ambiguous "man somehow disturbed at the core . . . and concealing it from himself" coupled with the poet's expressed uncertainty about whether it was right "to be made happy" by spring, which through his youth and early middle age had so troubled him, reflected the present dissolution of his personality in its last crisis. This crisis was connected to thoughts of final disappearance prompted by the "pathos" (the return of this word signaled the importance of what Stevens was experiencing) of Church's death. At the same time, if we assume that the equivocal sentences did refer to Williams, the poet here revealed that he still measured himself against his rival and covertly aggrandized himself by finding Williams wanting in comparison to Pourrat. Perhaps it was because he was aware of the quiet mean-spiritedness of his judgment of the man he had just so enthusiastically congratulated that he felt unsure about whether it was "right" to be happy about the spring. Or perhaps, having been for so many years depressed during this season of renewal and now being in a period when he deliberately recalled feelings from the past, he simply found it strange to be feeling the opposite way. Whichever the case, it is apparent that the poet was at one of his in-between stages. He had slithered out of an old skin and had not yet grown a new one. The emperor wore no clothes.

Within another few days Stevens received a second letter from McGreevy in which he expanded in a very Catholic manner on the equation of "self-will" with "original sin," "self-will" being what prevented one person, or one poet, from understanding another. McGreevy was sure that Stevens did not bear the strain of this sin since he had "understood" his poetry. Stevens must have been both amused and slightly disturbed by this observation since he had just reported to Barbara Church that he did not remember McGreevy's poetry though he had read it, on the recommendation of her husband, during the last few years. McGreevy's religious, mystical kind of perceptiveness, which showed itself in various ways in the letters he wrote to his American poet friend, would have its effect on Stevens. As he stated repeatedly over the next seven years to Barbara Church, it was always difficult to gather himself and reply to McGreevy's letters. Ironically, in his last years Stevens had found a correspondent who spontaneously expressed the voice of conscience with which Stevens had imaginatively invested Elsie so long before. Without knowing it, McGreevy consistently addressed the poet's dark side. This, too, was to play its part in how Stevens came to terms with himself in the time left to him.

While the *Mesures* issue gave homage to the spirit of his dead friend, Stevens continued to receive homage as he lived. Often these offerings came from individuals whom Stevens had praised. At the beginning of May the poet received two line drawings—reminiscent of Arp-like shapes—from Raymond Larrson, whose work the poet had seen and very much liked in a recent journal. Stevens's appreciation of Larrson's elusive, spectral style seemed to be a development of his attraction to the spidery lines of Paul Wightman Williams, whose "Wilde and weird" manner echoed his own feeling for the "abstract." Stevens's liking for these more absent than present renderings is somehow surprising. It does not seem that the man who surrounded himself with paintings derived from the impressionist school would also see something in such an opposing style. Yet considered from our own abstract perspective, this taste for both the sensuous delight of colorful impressionistic canvases and the edgy emptiness of abstract line drawings perfectly reflects Stevens's movement up and down between two elements. These pictorial examples of the poles to which Stevens's imagination attached itself serve as a mirror of his spirit. Seen in this way, his being particularly drawn to the work of Paul Klee and Georges Braque is illuminating in that both these painters balanced these two elements almost ideally, their pastel and muted colorations counterpointing their strenuous lines in the same way that the poet managed to complete his life, bring his two parts into harmony by composing poems in which the poetry of the subject's lapidary brilliance was spun around the true subject's dark center.

Another expression of respect and gratitude came from John Berryman, who had earlier sent Stevens two of his poems and asked for comments. The older poet had liked what he saw and indicated as much in his return note. Acknowledging how much he appreciated Stevens's interest, Berryman also expressed a wish that Stevens understood very well—"If only a few readers *would hear* them slowly . . ." (May 4, 1948). Stevens must have been touched by this, feeling sympathy for another who also realized the significance and weight of sounds and silences in reading poetry.

But here there rises a question in connection with Stevens's positive reaction to Berryman's work as well as in connection with similar evaluations of Randall Jarrell and Delmore Schwartz. Since he had given approving indications about the work of these poets to them directly or to others, why, when asked recently by Theodore Weiss to name some worthy younger poets, did Stevens report that there were none? In part it could have been because the poet was just coming out of one of the periods when he had been most insecure. But perhaps, too, his reticence to name individuals—which had just shown itself as well in his craftily dodging reply to Delmore Schwartz's *Partisan Review* questionnaire—had to do with fears about being taken as someone with the wrong political leanings. How could he, for example, know how Berryman was perceived? If he publicly recommended him and it happened that the younger poet was thought to be of or tending to the Communist persuasion, the results, Stevens might have been afraid, would be dangerous for him personally. The witch-hunt had begun. It would only be a few more months before eleven U.S. Communists were found guilty of conspiracy to overthrow the government.[9] The crucible was being prepared just as Stevens faced what would be an additional and weighty financial responsibility.

Holly had come to realize her marriage had been a mistake and was to begin divorce proceedings within the next month or two. Though her father had finally gotten something he wished for, it meant that he had to be absolutely certain that there could be nothing that might endanger his security since he knew that his daughter could not support herself and her infant child and that her soon-to-be ex-husband, who did not want the divorce, would not, in any case, be able to provide more than minimal payments to her. Stevens was not being overly cautious in his thoughts respecting what the Hartford would and would not approve in terms of the political affiliations of its employees; the company and the city of Hartford itself, insurance capitals of the world, were bastions of conservativism. It was no wonder that Stevens took almost every opportunity to take a swipe at the Communists lurking behind trees and competing with burglars and that he came to eschew publicly even the mention of politics in connection with his poetry, especially now, as he received wider and wider recognition.

Stevens could not help being sensitive to the sidestepping he had to learn in order to maneuver gracefully through his moral dilemma. Perhaps because of his self-knowledge, he was also more aware than most of the signs of evasion around him. His opinions concerning current abstract painting seemed to grow out of this, as he wrote to Rodríguez Feo on May 4 after noting that he paid just as much attention to painters as to writers because their problems were essentially the same:

> I think that all this abstract painting that is going on nowadays is just so much frustration and evasion. Eventually it will lead to a new reality. When a thing has been blurred by the obscurity of metaphysics and eventually emerges from that blur, it has all the characteristics of a brilliantly clear day after a month of mist and rain. No-one can predict what that new reality is going to be because it will be developed in the mind and spirit and by the hand of a single artist or group of artists strong enough to conceive of what they want and to produce it. I am saying that particularly with reference to painting. It is certainly no less true with reference to poetry and even to politics. (*L* 593–94)

On the same day Stevens wrote to Paule Vidal and voiced the same perception more explicitly in reference to the Tal Coat that he was considering:

> Cogniat [a French writer] says that Tal Coat is one of the few young painters from whom it seems possible to expect a new reality. A painter finding his way through a period of abstract painting is likely to pick up a certain

> amount of the metaphysical vision of his day. As a matter of fact, the physical never seems newer than when it is emerging from the metaphysical. I don't object to painting that is modern in sense. To illustrate: I have the greatest liking for Klee. No-one is more interested in modern painting if it is really modern; that is to say if it is really the work of a man of intelligence sincerely seeking to satisfy the needs of his sensibility. But the so-called metaphysical vision has been intolerably exploited by men without intelligence. In short, I should not object to a picture of Tal Coat exemplifying some theory of his own. But I should want you to like the picture and I should want you to feel after talking to Tal Coat about it that he knew what he was doing. (*L* 595)

The important thing, he stressed, was that the maker "knew what he was doing," as he knew what he was doing by concentrating now in his own "abstract" way on the "central" in his poetry. The "central" was an abstraction of the "self," and Stevens knew it; as long as he knew it, what he did was not evasive. "I am an erratic inconsequential thinker, at best," Stevens once wrote in his characteristically self-deprecatory manner. Was he aware of his disingenuousness, or did he discount the kind of slippery distinctions he used almost every day in settling claims and obviously used in rationalizing about himself as something different from thinking?

With the chore of the "Effects of Analogy" out of the way and before the arrival of summer, when he wanted to give himself as completely as possible once more to the Muse, Stevens devoted himself to clearing away all the reading that had piled up on his tables and footstools in the past months. He wrote of this to Rodríguez Feo in the same May 4 letter, using terms of perfect equivocation that announced that he had come out of the year of depression following Church's death but that he had not yet secured himself in his craft for the final voyage out of goblinry:

> If things go well this summer, I hope to accomplish more or less. During the last several months I have been busy clearing up a tremendous accumulation at home of things to read. Now at last I have reached a point at which when I go home in the evening there is nothing for me to do after I have read the Hartford Times and have had a glass of orange juice except to enjoy life: to try to get the feel of it and to think about it and to work on it. This is an intense pleasure but it requires almost total leisure. I have promised a good many poems to people. These come very easy or not at all and I hope soon, with this new freedom and wider margin, to reach a point at which I may be able to do enough to send something to everyone. Are you writing? I had thought that in the absence of anything from Germany and with the dilution of interest that everyone must feel in what is coming to us from France and again in the absence of anything, or almost anything, from England I was going to have an opportunity to think about many things that had originated in one or the other of those places. But suddenly, I began to

> think about Switzerland. There is a great deal coming from Switzerland. Then, too, Switzerland is something that one ought to think about in the summertime. It is so much more agreeable to think about Lake Geneva at this time of year than it is to think about the rue de Babylone, nicht wahr? (*L* 594)

He hoped to accomplish "more or less"; the poems would "come very easy or not at all"; Switzerland was "something one ought to think about in summertime." Would the old movement up and down never stop? And why Switzerland? Because it was, like Sweden, a place where his imagination could take up residence in neutrality? Or was it because Elsie, having learned she had Swiss forebears, had been preoccupied with it, clipping from newspapers every last reference she found about Switzerland or the Swiss? Or was it because, as he reported to one of his current correspondents, Switzerland was one of the places where his forebears as well had lived part of their history and he preferred roaming freely again in some conjured collective memory of his familial past to contemplating the reality of his present? It was probably a combination of all these reasons and others as well—thinking of Henri Pourrat, for instance—that accounted for Stevens's latest obsession. Then, too, Switzerland was a symbolic version of the poet himself as he carefully scaled the cold, lofty peaks of his old age—an extremely ordered and highly civilized country for an extremely ordered and highly civilized man to dream about.

In addition to Switzerland where he chose to go spiritually traveling, Ireland accidentally found its way onto Stevens's itinerary through his contact with Thomas McGreevy. In his eagerness to establish a strong bond with the Churches' highly esteemed American poet, McGreevy was quick to respond to Stevens's first return letter and each following one. As noted earlier, it was unusually hard for Stevens to compose and present himself, even "on paper," to this expressively sincere and devout Irishman. His responses reflected the difficulty he experienced. He fended off the kind of mystical intimacy that McGreevy immediately suggested while he tied his craft up securely to his new friend's. While the greater parts of his letters to McGreevy were filled with comments about recent reading, common acquaintances, how Dublin and Ireland were becoming familiar to him, there were also sentences slipped in shyly that whispered the budding identification Stevens felt. Now that Henry Church was gone, he conjured McGreevy as another with whom he could share the communion of spirit. In his second letter of May 6, for example, after thanking him for the Jack Yeats volume and for McGreevy's own *Poems* (1934) and commenting praisefully about both, as well as about a chapter on Friedrich Hölderlin by Bernhard Groethuysen (another darling of the Church circle) Stevens noted: "These poems [McGreevy's] are memorabilia of someone I might have known and they create for me something of his world and of himself. It is possible to see that you were (and I hope are) a young man eager to be at the heart of his time" (*L* 596).

The terms Stevens used to describe McGreevy's work, now that he had reread it, were those he used to describe his own: "Poetry is the statement of a relation between a man and the world" (*OP* 172); he "was glad he had written his poems.// . . . What mattered was that they should bear/ Some lineament or character// . . . Of the planet of which they were part" (*CP* 532–33). More, he imagined him as "a young man," a version of the figure of the poet as virile youth. Another "second self" was being shaped by the poet. The need to establish intimacy—however covertly, so much so that he was probably unaware of the parallels between the identification he was making now and that he had made over forty years earlier in his letters to Elsie—"on paper" was still with him. In closing this letter, Stevens mentioned how profound an impact reading the "Hommage" issue had made on him, as though pointing out how the loss of Church in his spirit's economy was being compensated for by the gain of McGreevy.

A few days later Stevens wrote again to McGreevy. He commented that the play between reality and metaphysics that McGreevy pointed out in relationship to Jack Yeats's work made him realize that just as for the Irish, God was a member of the family, so for Mr. Yeats, "reality was a member of the family." Stevens found Yeats's imagination to be like his own. Farther on in the same letter he hinted at one of the possible causes for his need to project, identify. He had sent McGreevy volumes of his own poetry and seemed to be uneasy about how they would be judged, but covering himself as usual, he generalized the fear: "The truth is that American poetry is at its worst in England and, possibly, in Ireland as in any other land where English is spoken and where inhabitants feel that somehow our English is a vulgar imitation" (*L* 597). Stevens's early feelings about being judged still operated, and when they did, the old devices of seeking another, mirroring self were also resumed. Though the years had changed his appearance, things as they were remained the same in the core of his being.

By the beginning of June Stevens seems to have regained some confidence. At least he felt secure enough to accept an invitation extended by Louis Martz to speak at the Connecticut Academy of Arts and Sciences sometime during the fall of the following year. Perhaps he planned to lose by then some of the weight that had made him feel like "an elephant" at his last public appearance. Or perhaps he was tempted by the idea of composing "a poem as poem" (July 6, 1948) to deliver to scientists as well as humanists and liked, too, that Paul Hindemith would be performing a piece that he would have specially written for the occasion. Or perhaps his recent burst of reading, which had finished up with some of the poems of Léon Paul Fargue[10] that he found to be unsatisfying, had distracted him enough so that he could now begin to direct his attention once more to cultivating the seeds that would develop into poems. Or perhaps it was the proffering of another little offering—two delightful "rainbow hats" from Ceylon, one of which Elsie found perfectly suited for her almost constant work in the garden—from his old correspondent-friend Leonard van Geyzel that made the poet see himself again as a powerful rather than grotesque giant. In any case, by the middle of June and into July Stevens found himself in fine form, evidenced by a sequence of letters to his various friends that as a group are remarkable for the turns of mind they reflect, for their quietly comic manner, and for their containing in raw form ideas that he shaped into poems over the next few months. Stevens was resolving his last crisis. As the consummate entertainer, he began to stride majestically onto the stage where his imagination had performed for so long. His voice, captured in the curious black shapes of silent letters, had never been more certain.

Announcing this swing into the completing arc of his career, Stevens wrote to José Rodríguez Feo on June 14:

> Dear José:
>
> It has been prodigiously dull up here. The almost continual rain has been bad enough, but it has been cold and gray or hot and gray or just gray. And I have not been able to get away from it by flying to Switzerland, say, or by attending King Michael's wedding. In recent years it has meant at least a little something to me to go to New York for a day: to buy a raincoat, to choose wall paper, to look at books from Europe, to walk through the streets. But all this bad weather has brought it about that I say that I already have a raincoat, that the present wall paper is good enough, that it is hopeless to get anywhere by reading, that the streets are all dug up anyway and, in general, the hell with it.
>
> Perhaps I am beginning to think permanently, and without regard to the weather, that one gets nowhere by reading. Nowadays it is common-place to speak of the role of the writer in the world of today. But why not think and speak of the role of the reader in the world of today: the role of the reader of *Origenes,* the role of the reader of any poetry, say, in the midst of the contemporary conspiracy and in the midst of the contemporary conspirators. Would not one's time be better spent seated in an excellent restaurant on the shore of Lac de Genève (Genfersee to students of German) listening to a sacred concert of a beautiful Sunday evening and meditating? Is not a meditation after soup of more consequence than reading a chapter of a novel before dinner? We do not spend enough time in thought and again when we think we usually do it on an empty stomach. I cannot believe that the world would not be a better world if we reflected on it after a really advantageous dinner. How much misery the aphorisms of empty people have caused!
>
> Well, however that may be, I have a new correspondent, a citizen of Dublin, a fellow of great piety but otherwise of impeccable taste. It seems that troupes of singers of operas fly from Paris to Dublin, fill the night air with Mélisande, then go to a party and fly back to Paris, all in a single circuit of the clock. What a dazzling diversion. And I am sure that even without such things one is never bored in Dublin because with all the saints they know, and know of, there, there is always company of a kind and in Dublin saints are the best company in the world. There are no saints at all in Hartford. Very likely they exist at Veradero Beach, walking by the turquoise water and putting ideas into one's head, with nothing to do except to water

the geraniums on the window sill (and, I hope, write an occasional letter to Hartford). All the time one would be finding out about life. It would come to one without trouble like a revelation and it would ripen and take on color. I am speaking of Lebensweisheit, which is what one particularly picks up on beaches and in the presence of one-piece bathing suits.

We have on a table in the dining room at home several Hayden mangoes. What healthy looking things they are. A friend who has been to Munich this summer wrote to me the other day of the extent of the destruction of "blue and white Munich." It is like changing records on a gramophone to speak of the red and the almost artificial green of mango skins and then speak of blue and white Munich. But unless we do these things to reality, the damn thing closes in on us, walls us up and buries us alive. After all, as you spend your summer getting well again [he had had a benign rectal tumor removed], aren't you in an extraordinary position to carry on the struggle with and against reality and against the fifth column of reality that keeps whispering with the hard superiority of the sane that reality is all we have, that it is that or nothing. Reality is the footing form which we leap after what we do not have and on which everything depends. It is nice to be able to think of José combatting the actual in Cuba, grasping great masses of it and making out of those masses a gayety of the mind.

What makes life difficult here or anywhere else is not the material of which it is made but the failure to use it. I could argue that against all the rabbis in the world. But then the rabbis would not argue against it. The things that we build or grow or do are so little when compared to the things that we suggest or believe or desire. (*L* 598–600)

Stevens was feeling strong again; he accepted himself as he was; he praised indulgence and the satisfaction of using his imagination to complete life. The notion of things coming as bits of revelation, encoded in his German word, he would eventually spin into "Lebensweisheitspielerei" (*CP* 504). "Reality," figured as the "footing from which we leap after what we do not have and on which everything depends," became "the rock," the central metaphor for his last poems. The perception almost precisely as it was expressed here was modeled into some of the most haunting lines of the poem that gave its name to his last collection:

> The rock is the gray particular of man's life,
> The stone from which he rises, up—and—ho,
> The step to the bleaker depths of his descents. . . .
> (*CP* 528)

Echoes of William James's definition of facts also whispered here in the poem that seemed to memorialize the feeling Stevens expressed in closing his letter to his Cuban friend. In his own words, what else was he saying but that all that mattered was the "will to believe"? The poet was in the process of finally satisfying what he had—recognizing James's centrality for his time—named a few years before as the "greatest need of [his] age."

The next day Stevens wrote another letter to McGreevy. Responding to his Irish correspondent's latest comments about Giorgione, Stevens noted that he would put off writing to him at length on the subject until he "came to terms" with this painter. He would begin by looking for an old photograph of one of the artist's portraits of a young man that Elsie had "hanging around the house somewhere" and by rustling out of the attic Walter Pater's essay on him. And asserting his rediscovered faith in himself, he responded to McGreevy's question "about the audience for whom [he] wrote." Asking him this, he commented, was "very much like the question that was asked of a man as to whether he had stopped beating his wife." He answered: "[A]s it happens, I know exactly why I write poetry and it is not for an audience. I write because for me it is one of the sanctions of life" (*L* 600).

In his present frame of mind Stevens felt secure about voicing his judgments. He had commented to Rodríguez Feo that it didn't seem worthwhile to read now. There was such a paucity of what was good; what was being published was not "abstract," nor did it "change" or "give pleasure." Similarly, in a letter to Barbara Church within the next few days, Stevens continued his criticisms of things as they were by extending his sharp judgments to painting, religion, and the world as it was. He burned through the various false surfaces he perceived with his acid wit and offered, in contrast, his understanding of what it was that prompted at least "a very slight sensation" of the real:

> DEAR MRS. CHURCH:
>
> I intend to be virtuous on a gigantic scale and not to talk about either the weather or politics. This ought to make of me a figure equal in merit to a friend of mine. He was told that he would have to stay in bed in order to recover from an operation. Instead, he put on a pink shirt and a flaming red tie and went downtown: it was more cheerful.
>
> Anyhow, these bad periods are precisely the ones in which to write letters, particularly to people in Europe, about the nature of our relation to reality and that sort of thing. I have at home a copy of what is probably Jean Wahl's first book in English: *The Philosopher's Way* [1948]. It was written in French and rewritten, with assistance, in English and it moves along quite smoothly. It is a recapitulation of philosophy as a whole. These large views of things, like photographs of lakes and mountains from the terraces of chateaux, are a form of intellecutal tourism. What one wants is much less vast. And it turns out to be (for me, during these last few days) a question of my relation to things about me.
>
> This is, of course, the result of thinking about poetry. Thinking about poetry is the same thing, say, as thinking about painting. The letters of Pissarro to his son Lucien, who lived in England, are full of thinking about painting. These are precious because they are simple, and in a way, final;

that is to say, Pissarro did not improvise. He spoke from long experience and without affectation. The pleasure we feel in Pissarro's pictures may or may not justify them but surely it justifies Pissarro himself. Bonnard, on the other hand, left no text except in his pictures. He did not paint the things he painted in the way he went about it without meaning to do just what he did. These men attach one to real things: closely, actually, without the interventions or excitements of metaphor. One wonders sometimes whether this is not exactly what the whole effort of modern art has been about: the attachment to real things. When people were painting cubist pictures, were they not attempting to get at not the invisible but the visible? They assumed that back of the peculiar reality that we see, there lay a more prismatic one of many facets. Apparently deviating from reality, they were trying to fix it; and so on, through their successors.

While one thinks about poetry as one thinks about painting, the momentum toward abstraction exerts a greater force on the poet than on the painter. I imagine that the tendency of all thinking is toward the abstract and perhaps I am merely saying that the abstractions of the poet are abstracter than the abstractions of the painter. Anyhow, that does not have to be settled this morning. It is enough right now to say that after a month of rain my wife's roses look piercingly bright. I went out alone last evening to look at them and while piercing was the word, it was, after all, a very slight sensation on which to make so much depend. During the day I had received a book on the Jesuit Church at Luzern. Would one rather be in that church at Luzern or in the garden at Hartford and why? Well, the why is not very difficult, even if one stripped the church of every sanction except its physical aspect. But that makes both the same thing although not equal. Two similar creations are no more equal than two similar creatures.

Gide, in his Journal, speaks of redemption of the spirit by work, in this present time of skepticism. Only to work is nonsense in a period of nihilism. Why work? Keeping a journal, however dense the nihilism may be, helps one. And thinking about the nature of our relation to what one sees out of the window, for example, without any effort to see to the bottom of things, may some day disclose a force capable of destroying nihilism. My mind is as full of this at the moment as of anything except unassorted drivel.

Yesterday I received a letter from José in Havana. He speaks of his mother who has been ill. As a girl she went to a nunnery at Pou. She loves the country in Cuba "and knows more about cows, horses and chickens than most people I know***. She wanted to name a newly born colt Platon but I told her that the name was too precious and she said that it was musical and went well with his languid eyes." How much more this mother knows than her son who reads Milosz and Svevo. She is controlled by the force that attaches; he by the force that detaches; and both are puppets on the strings of their relationship to reality. She shrinks from leaving home; he, from returning there.

The Stevenses shrink from everything. This means that we are tired of

> staying home and at the same time do not have a thought of going away. It would be different if we had a place down home. Yet very likely that society of which Martin Luther was once the chief pillar is now sustained by Stalin. How in the world the full moon of these nights can go on looking as if nothing had happened gets me. I do not speak of the sun because we see it too infrequently to know it when we see it. . . . (*L* 601–02)

It is striking that in this late period of feeling the resurgence of his spirit's power the poet again struck blows at religion, as he had done at the moments in the past right before he was about to set out on the voyages that brought him to the shores of new poems. And as this happened—as it had, too, in the past—there was a simultaneous expression of disgust (it "gets me") with the world as it was and the people in it. He projected this intolerance onto the moon, one of the figures for his imagined planetary existence, and he praised those who held simpler values, values he had attributed years before to his German peasant ancestors. Seeing this pattern emerge yet another time suggests that the self Stevens experienced as his true one, the one that was "vigorous" was, in spite of the glossy refinement he had cultivated since his Harvard years, a "peasant," a man "of simple salad-beds and,/ Of honest quilts" (*CP* 27). But he had worn the costumes of the courtier for so long that they seemed to make him who he was—"Sartor Resartus." The emperor wanted to parade his naked, muzzy belly in parade and himself proudly announce that he wore no clothes, but it was too late. The silk dresses he had made out of worms—one of his most beautifully conceived metaphors for the products of his activity as a poet—had shaped him. Clothes made the man.

> . . . so the selfsame sounds
> On my spirit make a music, too.
> (*CP* 89)

Between the lines of his letters to Barbara Church—especially those in which he wrote of Pissarro and Bonnard, cubism and abstraction in connection with "attaching one to real things" as opposed to using "intervening though exciting metaphor"—were the beginnings of the thoughts he would develop into his last essay, "The Relations Between Poetry and Painting." In his coming to focus on the abstract in his own work, in trying to escape evasion by a single metaphor, and in his latest preoccupation with the "central," Stevens was attempting, finally, to be his "plain self." Would he succeed? The difference between his earlier essays with their complex harmonies and "Effects of Analogy" with its plain terms illustrated the force of his will to effect a change in style, which was, in turn, a change in the subject he was. ("A change of style is a change of subject" [*OP* 171].) But this was in prose where the enticement of metaphor was nothing like what it was when he romanced his poetic Muse. Only the lines he would compose from this point on could show whether he would succeed in the final stage of his project: to reach the "ultimate hue"-you.

Stevens closed this letter in which he began to grapple with the ideas of showing his "plain self" with an apology for its formidable stiffness and then contradictorily added that this was intended. To the mind that had always come to know and show itself in hiding, exploring openness would naturally seem strangely constrained. "One must have a mind of winter. . . ."

On June 23, the day after writing to Barbara Church, Stevens wrote to Wilson Taylor in a slightly more sardonic tone than he characteristically used with him. Taking off on a comment Taylor had made to him apropos of having visited James Powers and his family in Oregon and observing that they seemed to enjoy the "fine things of life," Stevens noted that he didn't believe one could find these things in Portland. He went on to reveal through his domestic descriptions the same issues he had raised in a more "professional" way to Barbara Church:

> To enjoy the fine things of life you have to go to 438½ East 78th St., two floors up in the rear, not three floors, and pay $6.00 a pound for Viennese chocolates. One of the men in the office here got talking to me about tea the other day. I asked him what kind of tea he used. Oh, he said, anything that the A. & P. happens to have. I am sure that the beggar walks around the house in his bare feet.
>
> Of course I haven't dug in the garden for years. Some time ago I thought of buying a lot across the street so that I could have someplace to put the two or three house plants that I nourish every winter outdoors during the summer. Every time I try to put one someplace in the garden I find that my wife is intending to plant a rose in that very spot. But even if it were completely otherwise it would make little difference this spring. It has been raining for a month. We have become so accustomed to it that a fair day is irritating just in the same way that in the olden times a rainy day used to be irritating. When I hear a pattering on the roof these mornings I know that it is not the rainfall, because that is now part of my life, but I grind my teeth and realize that it is the doves dropping their damned eggs all over the place. What miseries will Providence not think of next? The other night I looked out the window and was horrified to find there a full moon shining in the cloudless night, but thank God that didn't last long. I was positively dizzy with apprehension when I lay down and, yet, before dawn the dear old mist was around me once again and I realized how able-bodied my guardian angel really is.
>
> And, finally, on the subject of sweet peas: do you realize that they are just beginning to bloom here? I looked at a long row of them in Elizabeth Park last Sunday morning. Although the plants are now more than three feet high, there is not a single flower open on a stretch of possibly fifty yards of them. Sweet peas I love. They change me into a nigger. They are like woodbine. When on a soft summer evening I walk in a place where there are

> sweet peas, or, better still, a place where there is woodbine, I feel that I have laid off all my Aryan habits and that I am a big fat colored person; and I am able to hum again and make plans on how I shall spend the next dollar that I get and feel good because I have only fifteen cents to go. In real life I take a hundred dollars to New York, spend a day and come back broke with nothing to show for the trip except a swell shoe shine. No wonder I cherish your allusion to sweet peas and the Flower Show. My wife and I went to the Flower Show this spring. Tickets were $1.75 each. Each of us bought a bag of cocoanut patties and walked around the place trying the mechanical sprayers. It would have been all right if it hadn't been so expensive.
>
> Mozart is out. It is curious that I have never been able to go for Mozart. He makes me as nervous as a French poodle. I realize that every now and then he gets away from himself, but most of the time he seems to me merely a mechanical toy. Beethoven is my meat. But, as far as that goes, I have bought very few records recently. The last one was one of Mahler's symphonies and that reduced itself to a simple movement. Listening to the same music, I mean to say, keeping on listening to the same music over and over again is about like drinking the same water over and over again or, better, like chewing the same food over and over again, as a cow does. What I want more than anything else in music, painting and poetry, in life and in belief is the thrill that I experienced once in all the things that no longer thrill me at all. I am like a man in a grocery store that is sick and tired of raisins and oyster crackers and who nevertheless is overwhelmed by appetite. (*L* 603–04)

Quite extraordinary here were the contrasting selves Stevens painted: the man who, in his exquisite refinement, nosed out sources of delicacies and sneered at someone who only knew tea as it came in A&P boxes against the man who still felt he changed "into a nigger" smelling sweet peas; the man who happily walked through the flower show eating coconut patties like the simplest peasant against the man who yearned to be satisfied by music, painting, and poetry. Did he, as he closed his letter, realize that the "thrill" he continued to seek and mourned not finding in art or anything at all he had just described still feeling when he walked through summer evenings humming to the smell of his favorite flowers? The contradiction pointed to the essential tension the poet was now resolving, the tension he had experienced all his life between wanting to be "man number one" and knowing that to become him meant forgetting that first and foremost he was simply a man. Now, approaching death, that man was "overwhelmed by appetite."

In the passage describing the normality established by the recent rains, Stevens skirted the reasons for his having become who he was. It was the old theme of *Carlos Among the Candles* and "The Snow Man": We are what is around us. He had become the things he had gathered around him: Beethoven was the "meat" for his Aryan self (a strange word to choose to identify himself in the postwar atmosphere), but he washed it down with delicate English teas;

he went out of his way to get Viennese chocolates but was just as happy with coconut patties. Could a simple man finally emerge from this mass of differences? Over the last few years left to him Stevens restated the theme of being one with his surroundings periodically in letters to various correspondents. It was as though in contemplating it and playing it out, Stevens had come to recognize that, in large part, his voracious hunger for the countless samples of the world—postcards, foods, household items, books, music, paintings—was connected with the fact that he had never satisfied his early wish to extend his actual surroundings, to live on a houseboat in Florida or on a farm in Sweden, a garret in Paris, a bed-sitter in London or a pension in Berlin, truly to become a citizen of the world where his imagination roamed. He had used all the things he acquired and read to make it seem that he was more than the boy from Reading who had gone to Harvard, the insurance man from Hartford who wrote poems. But now it was time for final reckoning, and he knew that no matter how many times he listened to Beethoven's or Mahler's symphonies and no matter how precisely Barbara Church described "blue and white Munich" to him (*L* 605), he had never smelled a German flower, that no matter how many varieties of teas he savored and in spite of his observation that "The tongue is an eye" (*OP* 167), he had never seen or smelled the fields in Assam filled with jasmine flowers. He was still hungry. But what if he had gone knocking about the world" as a young man? What if he had not heeded his father's voice of reason? What if he had not been smitten by a certain pair of blue eyes? What if it had not been so important to make a place for himself on the front bench? And where had he gotten the taste for the fine things of life that, in the end, always left him yearning for something more? The Tal Coat he was waiting for from Mlle. Vidal he hoped would be "bright" enough to satisfy him, at least for a while.

On the same day he wrote to Taylor Stevens wrote teasingly to his French procuress that he had not heard from her in so long he wondered if she had fallen in love. He went on to order more things to read: Colette's *L'Étoile Vesper,* and, curiously, Groethuysen's *Les Origines de l'Esprit Bourgeois.* It was as if the poet wanted to address, at long last, the question of his values—his "practical" values, those that had actually determined the shape of his everyday life. Perhaps he had managed to evade this examination so successfully because ever since his years at Harvard he had concerned himself with "ultimate" values—the value of belief, of God, of poetry, of "Poetry and Manhood," of art for art's sake—and so felt satisfied that he had performed the critical reflection that, according to Socrates, makes life worth living. But had he ever stopped to question why he had found the life W. G. Peckham lived so attractive, why he would wear underwear woven only of the finest Egyptian pima cotton, why he would not tolerate his daughter's pleas to attend other than a small exclusive college for young women, or what any of these preferences had to do with the primary peasant values he extolled? Was his dismissal of Marxism the conclusion of a closely reasoned and informed argument, or could it have been the subtle suggestion that he himself was a pawn in the hands of a capitalist system that prompted an immediate rejection? In any case, the Groethuysen volume was not one of those rare or special editions that the poet ordered to decorate his shelves; when he read it, what did he think?

❧

Even before the volume arrived, Stevens found himself musing on the notion of "value." It is impossible to know if when, on July 12, he accepted Norman Holmes Pearson's invitation to lecture at the English Institute at Columbia University in September and noted that he was thinking about "imagination as value" for his subject, he had anything more in mind than another aesthetic exploration of ultimate goods. But it is certain that by the time he composed his lecture, he had spent a long time looking at his chosen subject in the light cast by its aureole of practical values. "Imagination as Value" was the penultimate phrase in Stevens's apology for himself that was also his defense of poetry, and it pointed out precisely considerations of the kinds of practical and political choices, as well as the absence of choices, that were suggested above to have forced themselves into the poet's consciousness as the auroras of the autumn of his life brightened his descent into darkness.

Certain sentences from this lecture/essay announced themselves as parts of Stevens's defense of his values. Regarded in the frame of the poet's last quizzing of himself, these passages are striking in what they disclose. Halfway through the piece, for example, is this seemingly simple sentence: "Most men's lives are thrust upon them." He followed it with "The existence of aesthetic value in lives that are forced upon them is an improbable sort of thing. There can be lives, nevertheless, which exist by the deliberate choice of those that live them" (*NA* 147). To illustrate this second kind of life, he chose the example of Santayana then living in his convent in Rome, having used his imagination to find a situation that reflected both his beliefs and his need to surround himself with saintly surrogates of his beloved mother. Stevens ended this paragraph of description noting that in examining how imagination functioned, as here, he excluded "from consideration any thought of poverty or wealth, being a *bauer* or being a king, and so on as irrelevant" (*NA* 148).

Many ghostly demarcations sinewed between the lines here. Stevens felt that his life had been thrust upon him, that he had not chosen freely. He had followed what his father had presented as the life of reason rather than take the risk of following the life of imagination. Santayana had followed reason in a more spiritually stringent way in having become a philosopher rather than a poet but at the end of his life finally let himself follow imagination—imagination, which Pascal, whom Stevens cited in opening his essay, called "the mistress of the world," a mistress who deluded and deceived. While on the surface it might have appeared that Stevens saw the old philosopher's imaginative choice in a positive light, it was clear from comments he made concerning Santayana's Roman retirement and eventual death that he regarded him as a tragic figure, one who, because he had not lived his life fully, had resorted to a final fling with his old mistress. Stevens's reflection on his own state at this point showed him that he, too, had been using his escapades with this puissant mistress to escape feeling the powerful consequences of what the life thrust upon him had been. He excluded considerations of poverty or wealth from his dialogue with himself now precisely because there was a voice inside him that whispered that he had sold his birthright for a mess of pottage. In this he was even more tragic than Santayana, whose palliatives had at least included lecture halls and classes filled with the faces of fine young men, more humanly satisfying than the fine things of life that a lifetime of negotiating contracts and claims had bought.

As Stevens went about his cross-examination of himself, where did he find fault? Another set of passages from "Imagination as Value" affixed their beams. In questioning the provenance of an individual's nature and from that the quality of his or her imagination, Stevens once more quoted Freud: "So long as a man's early years are influenced by the religious thought-inhibition . . . as well as by the sexual one, we cannot really say what he is actually like" (*NA* 139). Above and beyond the call for a "science of illusions" to study the products of imagination the poet was addressing what he retrospectively realized to have been his own religious thought and sexual inhibitions. Stevens realized that his external life had been determined by the exquisite trap of the religion in which he had been reared, a religion he thought he had escaped but that through the subtle translation of its power into the work ethic had dominated his choices. His affective life, too, had been shaped by that same religion's repressive attitudes, attitudes strengthened by the collective reaction to Darwin's findings that made Victorians and their American imitators assume whatever disguises were most effective in hiding the fact that they, too, were simply animals without the slightest hope of becoming angels, necessary or unnecessary.

It was not surprising then that in the lecture/essay Stevens struck hard at religion. "Imagination as Value" was the prose commentary illuminating his gnomic aphorism: "God and the imagination are one." This was not a statement of pantheistic union with the all but a stab with a double-edged sword. An individual's imagination was both a function of the God or gods in whom one was taught to believe and, if one finally ever found one's true intelligence beyond the thought inhibitions prescribed by religion, the destroyer, of that God or gods. In mounting his attack, Stevens blamed the imaginative structure this religion had established—a structure that promised the rewards of future paradise for present suffering—for what he saw as the present evil of communism:

> . . . while the reason of a few men may underlie what they do, they act as their imaginations impel them to act. The world may, certainly, be lost to the poet but it is not lost to the imagination. I speak of the poet because we think of him as the orator of the imagination. And I say that the world is lost to him, certainly, because, for one thing, the great poems of heaven and hell have been written and the great poem of the earth remains to be writ-

> ten. I suppose it is that poem that will constitute the true prose of the spirit and that until it is written many lesser things will be so regarded, including conquests that are not unimaginable. One wants to consider the imagination on its most momentous scale. Today this scale is not the scale of poetry, nor of any form of literature or art. It is the scale of international politics and in particular of communism. Communism is not the measure of humanity. But I limit myself to an allusion to it as a phenomenon of the imagination. Surely the diffusion of communism exhibits imagination on its most momentous scale. This is because whether or not communism is the measure of humanity, the words themselves echo back to us that it has for the present taken the measure of an important part of humanity. With the collapse of other beliefs, this grubby faith promises a practicable earthly paradise. The only earthly paradise that even the best of other faiths has been able to promise has been one in man's noblest image and this has always required an imagination that has not yet been included in the fortunes of mankind. (*NA* 142–43)

The imagination required to ignore the temptation of future promises had "not yet been included in the fortunes of mankind" because there was not yet an imagination that had been educated by what Stevens called for in his lecture: the "great poem of earth." The poet recognized himself to be one of the poets to whom "the world [was] lost" because he had been shaped by the "great poems of heaven and hell." Beginning with the Bible, which, he was careful to point out, should no longer determine society's expectations, and stretching through the centuries to Milton, the metaphysical poets of the seventeenth century, Blake, and most recently Eliot, the dominant but hidden image in Western literature was of the soul gridded with profit-and-loss margins, individual success as "a bustling merchant, a money-making lawyer, a soldier, a politician" (*L* 32) or the like being the mark of election, sign of paradise regained. Stevens closed the paragraph in which he laid this out with yet another statement that the imagination should not attach itself to politics but that it should seek to satisfy the "universal mind," that this "would be an imagination that trie[d] to penetrate to basic images, basic emotions, and so to compose a fundamental poetry even older than the ancient world" (*NA* 145). He was envisioning a future time when the figure of the youth as virile poet, having matured free from the religious and sexual thought inhibitions, would be able, as he himself had not been, to go his own way, realizing that politics is not a body of issues to be addressed theoretically and about which positions are assumed, but the accumulation of choices made through a lifetime. As long as imagination remained attached not to "things as they are"—the basic facts, the "basic slate" of nature—but to wishes for things as they could be, there could be no possibility of making even the smallest decision free from the subliminal tallying up of what this meant in the heavenly scale.

Stevens began this lecture/essay using the images of costumes and display as illustrating the delusion that imagination fosters and noting that with these elaborate red robes and ermines in which, for example, Pascal's magistrates "swathe themselves like furry cats" (*NA* 133), individuals find the persuasive authority to enact their power over others. Stevens knew that he wore the trappings of his society's imagination and that he could not have escaped putting them on and at the same time have remained the American of his time that he was. Beyond the influence of his family of "good Puritans," he recognized that Harvard had played its part: "What is the residual effect of the years we spend at a university, the years of imaginative life, if ever in our lives there are such years, on the social form of our own future and on the social form of the future of the world of which we are part, when compared with the effects of our later economic and political years?" (*NA* 146).

Here were the forces that had determined his choices, and what had been the result? He had not been able "to pervade or . . . create a social form" (*NA* 145) with his work as he had desired, and he understood now that this had not been possible precisely because his imagination had not been separate enough from the very forms that had shaped it and that he wanted to transcend. Though the imagination was "the irrepressible revolutionist" (*NA* 152), so long as it paraded itself in clothes that it was used to wear, it could not be an effective molder of a new "universal mind." This would have to wait for a future generation—if it came at all. The only thing the poet himself could hope to do now, when he could at least conceive an intelligence free of thought inhibitions, was to look back at his failure and ahead to a time when the poet could walk "Naked . . . like a savage source" (*CP* 70) without need of the finery that weighed down the wings of meaning.

Stevens had peppered this essay with many allusions to what had most recently struck him as he read his books, journals, and letters from friends: Barbara Church's image of "blue and white Munich" appeared, as did Jean Paulhan's description of the park in Tarbes, France, the town where he lived, and the impression left by the poet's imagining of the Jesuit church at Lucerne. There were references, too, to Poussin, to what Gide wrote of him, and to Vasari on Giorgione. Stevens's involvement with what he considered was immediate, his sentences a mental mapping of the thoughts that scudded like clouds through his mind to gather and rain down in words. The examples he cited all were chosen to illustrate the central importance of seeing the imagination as the instrument of the abnormal, necessary to correct, to balance the normal state of things as they were. The point he returned to once again echoed William James's asking that the "pluralistic hypothesis" in regard to religion be given serious attention if individuals were to find their freedom: "The imagination is the power of the mind over the possibilities of things; but if this constitutes a certain single characteristic, it is the source not of a single value but of as many values as reside in the possibilities of things" (*NA* 136).

The poet saw himself as having exerted very little power during his lifetime over the "possibilities of things." Laying out his defense, his apology, was salutary. If he could not at this late stage change his values, he could question them. But he must have wondered, if he were at least to imagine himself walking nakedly through his last lines, would it be acknowledged, would in be recognized that he was penetrating finally to "basic images, basic emotions," or would all still comment on the richness of his display, the beautiful cut of his garment?

In the poems Stevens composed during this summer of 1948, when he mused on the thoughts that would find expression in "Imagination as Value," he voiced himself more directly than he ever had, as he stripped images from earlier poems of their heavenly costumes. In "The Woman in Sunshine" (*CP* 445) the poet recorded that the warmth and movement of the sun reminded him of the feelings stirred by a "taciturn and yet indifferent" female; here the basic emotions of the child yearning for contact with a seemingly inaccessible mother and of the husband desirous of a wife made unattainable by him and the accidents of circumstance replaced the myriad abstract associations of the sun as "gold flourisher" or pagan source of life. In "Reply to Papini" (*CP* 446–48), the poet announced what he would reiterate in "Imagination as Value": "The way through the world/ Is more difficult to find than the way beyond it (abandon myths about the roads to paradise); ". . . a politics/ Of property is not an area// For triumphals" (the poet shaped by such "a politics" could not write the "great poem of the earth"); the poet he was was "The angry day-son clanging at its maker" (of course, he was angry at what had made him who he was).

In "The Bouquet" Stevens focused a dialogue between the poet as realist and the poet as metaphysician around the controlling image indicated by the title and illustrated that the "basic" value of metaphysical elaborations was to trigger memories ". . . that still cling/ By trivial filaments to the thing intact" (*CP* 450). What was unreal made the real "more acute" by finding the "special hue of origin" in what we feel. Mirroring this perception, the poet included in these lines references to his "farouche" comedian, the "sovereign of symbols," making his "interpretations voluble" (*CP* 451). He recalled the pink and white of carnations in the poem he wrote years before to memorialize one of his visits home to Elsie while they were courting. He demythologized the images of lightning in "Earthy Anecdote" and of the jar in "Anecdote of the Jar"; they were "metaphors," evasions from expressing the "reality of [what] the eye" sees, "Nothing much" (*CP* 448) without recognizing the feelings that infuse what is fixed on with meaning. To regard things without perceiving this "true subject" was to be one of the "meta-men," "Cold with an under impotency that they know,// Now that they know, because they know" (*CP* 449).

Stevens closed this poem with an image of a soldier entering the unlocked house and moving into the room where the bouquet stands on the table; he bumps into it and walks through the rest of the house and leaves while "The bouquet has slopped over the edge and lies on the floor" (*CP* 453). The effect was of the "abnormal" on the "normal," which he was to elucidate more specifically in "Imagination as Value." The poem brought home the realization that the assumed normal reality of the mass of men of whom the soldier was a representative was, in fact, the abnormal that intruded on and ignored the most essentially human activity of perceiving what is around and increasing the "aspects of experience" (*CP* 447) with the light cast through the prism of consciousness, consciousness being nothing more than the crystal forged from the accumulation of memories.

In "World Without Peculiarity" the poet was more open than he had ever been both about the most painful of his memories and about the facts of his continued present:

> The day is great and strong—
> But his father was strong, that lies now
> In the poverty of dirt.
>
> Nothing could be more hushed than the way
> The moon moves toward the night.
> But what his mother was returns and cries on his
>   breast.
>
> The red ripeness of round leaves is thick
> With the spices of red summer.
> But she that he loved turns cold at his light touch.
>
> What good is it that the earth is justified,
> That it is complete, that it is an end,
> That in itself it is enough?
>
> It is the earth itself that is humanity . . .
> He is the inhuman son and she,
> She is the fateful mother, whom he does not know.
>
> She is the day, the walk of the moon
> Among the breathless spices and, sometimes,
> He, too, is human and difference disappears
>
> And the poverty of dirt, the thing upon his breast,
> The hating woman, the meaningless place,
> Become a single being, sure and true.
>
> (*CP* 453–54)

Here the poet counterpointed in each of the first three stanzas what he would have in the past focused on when touched by the sources of these facts of feeling. In doing this, Stevens "deconstructed," as it were, his own strategy; he presented the beginnings of what could easily have become elaborate evasions—the images of the day, the moon, the leaves—the "poetry of the subject," cut by the "true" ones. The question he posed in the fourth stanza, then, because of the irresolution of the preceding stanzas, was equivocally rhetorical, mimicking his state of mind as he looked back on all he had done to find out if it was, in the end, good. In the last three stanzas, having looked back at what he had created over the years, he described what he saw. He was the "inhuman son" who had not visited his mother often enough before she died. To comfort himself, he had made the "earth itself . . . humanity." The "she" who incorporated both the memory of his mother and the "hating woman" who had denied him in his marriage became the elements of the earth with which he had felt secure and which could not reject him. In this universe where inanimate replaced animate the man who had wished to be a "thinking stone" had resided and there "sometimes" felt "human." Stevens was certainly baring himself, but after so many years of lines where "mother" had become "death," "father" the sun itself, the "round leaves" of summer figures for the products of his imagination, how many would now see these terms in their nakedness?

In "Our Stars Come from Ireland" the poet openly delineated the process by which his imagination had transformed reality. His imagination—"mistress of the world"—"loved" the idea of Tom McGreevy in Ireland and transported him with the strength of her feeling to America, where he became one with the intelligence of the poet. In romances such as this one the poet had lost himself countless times, conjuring new lives out of "the ashes of fiery weather" to change his "whole habit of mind" (*CP* 455).

> These bland excursions into time to come,
> Related in romance to backward flights,
> However prodigal, however proud,
> Contained in their afflatus the reproach
> That first drove Crispin to his wandering.
> (*CP* 39)

"The conch/ Of loyal conjuration trumped" (*CP* 102) as Stevens revealed his stratagems, still weighted with his father's reproach for his afflatus.

As the heavy rains of this spring and early summer nourished the earth and brought forth flowering days, Stevens was looking back more than forward. Depending on how moved he was by the "pathos" of what he saw, he shifted between backward glances to a past he could never really see and more lingering looks at the steps of his own passage. Illustrating the first kind of imagined past was a description of the landscape around Lexington, Kentucky, which, as he wrote to Victor Hammer, who considered moving there, he wanted to know more about "because it [was] one of the gateways through which people, and many of [his] own people [had] passed: one hundred and fifty years ago, say" (*L* 607). Illustrating the second kind of recollection was something he wrote to Thomas McGreevy at the end of July apropos of the poem he had imagined around him: ". . . when I look back, I do not really remember myself but the places in which I lived and things there with which I was familiar" (*L* 608). In his retrospection Stevens came to experience the truth of Emerson's image of the self as a "transparent eyeball" itself the particulars of its surroundings. With this did Stevens also feel "erect before Nature," a figure of capable imagination?

Certainly, he did not feel capable in the face of what he saw to be the worsening political reality. While he believed that the recent Republican nomination of Thomas E. Dewey offered a promise of "health and solvency" (*L* 605), Europe seemed to him "to be lying once more under the menace of war." "The thing makes me shudder," he noted in closing his letter to McGreevy. Twelve days later he wrote to Barbara Church in France urging her to go as she planned to Ireland, which he had by this time romanticized as being untroubled by the "enticements of Communism," as he also imagined Aix-en-Provence, which had most recently become real for him quite accidentally:

> . . . how easy it would be, at Aix, without much more effort than that of turning a few corners, to find a peace, a security, a sense of good fortune and of things that change only slowly, so much more certain than a whole era of Communism could ever give. And if that is so how contentedly one could loaf there for a little while merely studying why it is so. Some books came recently wrapped in a Paris newspaper which contained photos of some fountains at Aix, not great things, but enough to make a little sound as one walked by. This makes me think of a wild dove that was sitting high up on a wire near home a few mornings ago cooing about nothing much. I stopped to look at her. She turned around so that she could see me better but went right on with her talk. (*L* 609–10)

Remarkable here was the unselfconscious way Stevens revealed the associative turns of his mind and how effectively these meanderings protected the borders of his consciousness so that he could avoid developing his thoughts around what he stubbornly refused to admit as having "ultimate" importance to his imagination: the political facts that every day intruded themselves into his world. Now that he believed that his work had not in any way been a "social force," he felt more impotent than ever before things as they were. Yet the need to feel himself part of his world remained. In the same letter to Church he described by what means he came to feel that he belonged to America, to the planet:

> It interests me immensely to have you speak of so many places that have been merely names for me. Yet really they have always been a great deal more than names. I practically lived in France when old Mr. Vidal was alive because if I had asked him to procure from an obscure fromagerie in the country some of the cheese with raisins in it of which I read one time, he would have done it and that is almost what living in France or anywhere else amounts to. In what sense do I live in America if I walk to and fro from the office day after day. I wrote the other day to a friend in Oregon and asked him to try to find Kieffer pears for me this autumn and in that sense I live in

> America and not merely in a street that branches off from a street that leads to the office. There are other enlargements. Often instead of walking downtown I walk in the little park through which you drove when you were here. Until quite lately a group of nuns came there each morning to paint water colors especially of the water lilies. Whenever I saw them I thought of the chasteness of the thing like the chasteness of the girl in Oscar Wilde who spent her time looking at photographs of the Alps.
>
> But this morning even these exquisite creatures were no longer there and in addition the tops of the ferns were dry and there were acorns on the path. Hélas! Hélas! Hélas! Next week I expect to go to Boston for a day to see the pictures from the Kaiser Friedrich Museum in Berlin which are there. I saw them in New York but there were far too many for a single visit. Besides I like to go to Boston for the same reason that anyone likes to go to Boston.

While the "enlargements" of his sense of self that came through his various samplings of the fruits of the earth were most valuable in stimulating his imagination (his experience of the nuns in Elizabeth Park, for instance, prompted "Nuns Painting Water Lilies" [*OP* 92], in which he poetically illustrated the value of his "furtive fiction[s]"), they could not provide him with the security that he was anything more than "a pseudo-villain in the drama" (*L* 32) of the life of his time. Stevens's deep need to belong and to be recognized had not yet been satisfied. Ironically, perhaps the primary reason that it had not been was that the elements on which he depended as "enlargements" were, for the most part, the equipage of a "good burgher," things that money could buy to give him tastes of the world's various regions and times, but these things could not resonate with feelings attached to "real facts" of direct experience. Irrespective of any external judgment, Stevens still felt he had not made a place for himself in his world because he was still ashamed at looking at himself without his dress of words and things. In this, he was the antithesis of Walt Whitman, whose greatest excitement came from his delight in his "body electric." The nineteenth-century epic poet had not been reared with a taste for the fine things of life or with the religious and sexual thought inhibitions of the descendants of "good Puritans."

Stevens, who had wanted so much to be the American poet par excellence—the poet of the "epic of disbelief"—was coming to terms, finally, with his limits. His preoccupation with what had for most of his life seemed of value and what was, at bottom, of value kept bringing him up against images and memories of "costumes," a figure for the myriad disguises he had donned, the personae he had taken up so as to be able to speak at all. Another such memory Stevens recalled in a late August letter to McGreevy:

> A man living in a twelfth century stronghold in County Dublin pluming himself on such a title inevitably makes me think of Tommy Collins, a poor thing at home when I was a boy, who rode around town in gorgeous costumes. The people in the livery stable used to lend him a white horse. He

> liked the animal and took good care of it and what a cry would go up when children saw him in the distance coming their way and dressed up say like the Admiral of the Schuylkill and its Convivial Streams. (*L* 611)

Beneath the surface of this recollection, which could have in the past contributed yet one more aspect to "The Emperor of Ice-Cream"—the children's emperor—was a hidden fear that he, too, in all his "gorgeous costumes" was a "poor thing," someone to be laughed at, ridiculed. He had imagined this often enough whenever he thought his "plain self" had revealed itself behind his masks. As requests for new poems continued to come (the most recent was from Archibald MacLeish acting as an intermediary for the Princess Marguerite de Bassiano Caetani), Stevens must have felt the basses of his being throb in apprehension, knowing that editors would naturally expect more of the man who spoke through masks while he was coming to realize that for his last attempts, at least, he was abandoning them. Would they laugh?

He was an old man in a dry month, many months, again, of not drinking. He noted in closing the letter to McGreevy in which he had described the "poor thing" in his "gorgeous costumes" that the current heat wave of the "fag end of the summer" must have been "making the fortunes of the barkeepers, all of whom {were}, however, strangers and Hottentots as far as {he was} concerned" (*L* 612). Perhaps this latest retreat into austere habits to protect his health also had something to do with the seriousness with which he was now regarding himself, "from the point of view of saintly living and saintly dying," as he wrote in his self-mocking manner to Sister Mary Bernetta Quinn at the beginning of September (*L* 612). Gently and ironically suggesting to her, apropos of her religious reading of "Cy Est Pourtraicte, Madame Ste Ursule, et Les Unze Mille Vierges," that "nothing means the same thing to everyone alike," he pointed to the "true subject" he had always hidden beneath the "poetry of the subject" that he was in the process of stripping away. It was the end of summer. He had completed "Imagination as Value" and the poems and had found himself "more truly and more strange" in his spiritual nakedness.

On September 7 he wrote to Barbara Church, back in France, he assumed, after her trip to Ireland. In keeping with his having grappled with the question of values in completing his lecture, he commented that he liked "natives: people in civilized countries whose only civilization is that of their own land." He had never met any, he added; this was simply an idea he enjoyed. He went on to describe the "motionless air, motionless streets" and general emptiness of the Labor Day weekend, the primary satisfaction of which for him had been that the spots in his left eye had seemed to disappear in the limited light of his room one late afternoon. The eye troubled him, though he would not let on how much. The date for his delivering his lecture at Columbia was only a few days away. He had not read at all in preparing "Imagination as Value," he reported, and thinking that he, on the last day of a four-day conference, would have "to set {the audience} on fire" made him want to fortify himself with "that bottle of Jameson [whiskey] of which [she] spoke." Perhaps then he "could really get somewhere," he voiced in the playful way that indicated how heavily the idea weighed on him (*L* 613).

Stevens did not comment, in the letters as they remain, on how his lecture was received, nor have I reports from any people who were present. The complete silence surrounding the event is unusual. All that can be assumed is that he was relieved to have gone through one more test of strength. In the weeks that followed there were, as usual, reinforcements of this strength in the form of additional requests for poems; John Crowe Ransom wrote asking for a contribution from the "venerable" poet. Yet there were signs that Stevens had not fared very well in New York. In mid-September, for example, he closed a letter to Leonard van Geyzel—in which he again expressed his gratitude that there was someone in Ceylon who was so devoted to him and went on to comment about the typical American's reaction to India and Indian art—observing that he was not surprised that he was unknown by a certain naval officer of whom Van Geyzel had written:

> It did not surprise me to find myself unknown in the Navy or even to a man from Hartford. I try to draw a definite line between poetry and business and I am sure that most people here in Hartford know nothing about the poetry and I am equally sure that I don't want them to know because once they know they don't seem to get over it. I mean that once they know they never think of you as anything but a poet and, after all, one is inevitably much more complicated than that. (*L* 615)

How could the "Giant" expect to be known, no less understood, by those who surrounded him every day? It must have been that the poet felt that the specialists in the lore of the language he spoke—the English Institute at Columbia—had not understood him and so transferred his perception that he was too "complicated" to be understood onto his more immediate, if not actual, peers.

The day after writing to Van Geyzel Stevens wrote to Barbara Church. He opened by speaking of *Seelenfriede*—peace of the soul. (Since the end of the war and the beginning of his correspondence with Mrs. Church, who was a native of Bavaria, the poet sprinkled his prose with German words, but not only in writing to her; it was as though his earlier attempts to get beneath the surface of the German spirit had yielded these nominal residues.) He noted that this state of being was "not to be had for the asking." He added that "one has to find it for one's self" and then later went on:

> My own guess is that . . . moments of despair can best be controlled by the regimen of life: exercise, sleep and a will not to see the spots in one's eye. . . . How is one to restore savor to life when life has lost it? . . . By restoring oneself physically? By a gesture of the will? They are all absurd. All the same each one of us has (or probably has) his own personal absurdity,

> by means of which to restore the status quo ante: the state in which one once enjoyed the mere act of being alive. To allow that act to become an act of misery or even, eventually, of terror is easy; to do the opposite is no less easy. (*L* 615)

The poet was wavering; his hand at the helm felt a shudder that might have signaled a weakness in his craft, though it could just as easily have been the effect of the movement of a submerged rogue wave portending a change in the weather—perhaps another storm. Winter was approaching.

❧

Stevens was just two weeks away from the birthday that would mark the beginning of his seventieth year. As he put it to Emma Stevens Jobbins, the only one of his first cousins still alive: "All of last week I was saying that I was approaching my seventieth year. This year it will be the case that I am in it. Next year I shall say I am seventy and the year after I shall say that I am just past seventy. The only thing odd about it is that I should have outlived so long all the other members of my family" (*L* 619). Though he kept trying to pretend that things as they were were as they should be—perhaps remembering some of Alain's advice on how to live, what to do—he also recognized the absurdity of doing so. In "The Novel," a poem that borrowed verbatim a few words from one of José Rodríguez Feo's recent letters to him, Stevens spelled out more of what he felt as the days carried him closer to what he prepared himself to regard as perhaps his last winter—a feeling that was to repeat itself mercilessly for the next five years. Imagining himself drawing up his blanket against an icy draft, he wrote of

> . . . .
> Feeling the fear that creeps beneath the wool,
> Lies on the breast and pierces the heart,
>
> Straight from the Arcadian imagination,
> Its being beating heavily in the veins,
> Its knowledge cold within one as one's own;
>
> And one trembles to be so understood and, at last,
> To understand, as if to know became
> The fatality of seeing things too well.
> (*CP* 458–59)

In this poem illustrating how life imitated art, the almost mythological hero was imitating one of the first Western heroes, an inhabitant of a place near Arcadia, Oedipus, who, as he lost his sight, gained the fatal insight of seeing things too well. As spots disturbed Stevens's vision so that he could no longer enjoy looking at a vase of flowers or the play of light on his piano's polished surface or the flicker of lake wavelets moved by the wind in Elizabeth Park without at the same time being conscious of how "that monster, the body" now asserted its dying strength over the will he had used like a whip to tame it so often in the past, he looked more and more at things he could not see—the fears, motivations, regrets, and hopes from which he had managed for most of his life to distract himself.

Provoking the worst of Stevens's fears—that the poems he had written, were, in fact, not good—John Alden (from the University of Pennsylvania Library, who had requested a contribution), in acknowledging the receipt of "The Novel" and noting that he thought it represented the poet at his "very best," added, rather presumptuously, "if I may be permitted to suggest that there are occasions when you are not that" (September 29, 1948). The gratuitous meanness of the swipe went unremarked by Stevens, who, if he had not felt uncertain about the ultimate value of his work, would no doubt have parried Alden's thrust with one of the piercing repartees for which he was noted in the insurance world—where he was secure. In his reply to Alden the next day Stevens merely changed the first word in the twelfth stanza of his poem from "Three" to "Day's" and observed that the Spanish phrase at the end of the sixth stanza was borrowed from Federico García Lorca. Poor "Giant"—to have to greet the opening of his seventieth year with his most unpleasant feelings bared.

Perhaps to compensate, Stevens ordered a new painting from Mlle. Vidal. His gift to himself this time was a landscape by Eric Detthow, whose work he had come to know in a recent catalog from the Salon d'Automne in Paris. Before it arrived, Stevens was to order another of this painter's canvases, a "blue vase full of yellow and red flowers"; he was in need of "something fresh and clear" (*L* 623) during this period, when he felt "everything [had] been so much disturbed" (October 4, 1948). One of the things he now admitted as being most "disturbing" was the continued existence of Joseph Stalin, as he noted in the letter to Paule Vidal in which he wrote of wanting something by Detthow. In spite of his strong desire to ignore the political scene, he could not. Perhaps this had to do with his more general recognition of the weakening force of his will. The result, in any case, was that his recently expressed hope for the "solvency and health" that the Republican nomination promised notwithstanding, he seems to have reconsidered his position and by the time of the election voted for Truman. At least what he wrote to Mlle. Vidal just after the surprising returns of that day suggested that though he was "of two minds" about Truman, his vote had helped tip the tree that meant his reelection:

> As to Truman: I am of two minds about the results of the election. So far as I am personally concerned his election is probably a misfortune because he is one of those politicians who keep themselves in office by taxing a small class for the benefit of a large class. If I had been able to save during recent years what I have been obliged to pay in taxes, I should be much more secure and so would my family. On the other hand, I recognize that the vast altruism of the Truman party is probably the greatest single force for good in the world

today and while I regret that the situation is such that I have to think twice about buying pictures, still one could not enjoy books and pictures in a world menaced by poverty and enemies. By enemies I mean the Russians, assuming that they are enemies. One never knows. Perhaps they are merely undertakers. (*L* 623)

Here, too, for the first time, Stevens openly questioned if the Russians were really "enemies." What was happening? Could it have been that in confronting the facts about where he had gotten his practical values while he composed his last lecture and then read Groethuysen's book on the sources of the bourgeois spirit, "the whole habit of [his] mind was changed," as he recalled the "starker, barer self" he had paraded in the thirties before he began to quail before things as they were?

A glimpse into the state of mind of the poet as he began this slow turnaround is offered by a letter he wrote five days after his birthday to Thomas McGreevy. Stevens was preoccupied with how he would be remembered after his death, with what, if anything, would be celebrated about his reputation. He had received from his Irish friend news clippings of the elaborate ceremonies surrounding the transport of William Butler Yeats's body from France—where he had died on January 28, 1939, and been buried because the war prevented the return of his remains to Ireland—to Drumcliffe Cemetery, County Sligo, where he had expressed the wish that he be interred. Stevens observed, no doubt recalling the paltry funeral of Stephen Crane that had led him to comment nearly fifty years earlier that in America there were "no hero worshippers. Therefore, no heroes":

In spite of Yeats' contributions to the national spirit, or, say, in spite of his additions to the national nature, it is hard to see how these ceremonies came to take on their public aspect. The transport from France on a corvette of the Navy, the procession from Galway to Sligo, the lying in state were acts of recognition and homage of a public character. Conceding that Yeats was a man of world-wide fame, it is an extraordinary thing in the modern world to find any poet being so honored. Yet the funeral of Paul Valery [*sic*] was a great affair. Moreover, people are as much interested in Rilke as if he was [*sic*] human enough and, in addition, something more. The fact must be that the meaning of the poet as a figure in society is a precious meaning to those for whom it has any meaning at all. If some of those who took part in this episode did so, very likely because of the man's fame, the fact remains that his fame could not be different from his poetry. So that in this event there was a good deal that had to do with human beings both deeply and, likewise, superficially. I shall save the papers. Thanks for sending them. (*L* 617–18)

Between the lines here it is possible to read some of the thoughts that strayed around the poet's imagining of what his own funeral would be like.

Again, he could only conjure the future from what he knew of the past. What could he expect, looking back coolly at what he had achieved, at the vicissitudes of his reputation. Had he, in spite of his career of thirty-odd years as a poet, attained the kind of recognition that Crane, with only the few years of his youthful one, had? Stevens knew that his name was certainly not recognized by more than what—in comparison to those who at the time of his death had recognized Crane's name—was a handful of his fellow Americans and that most of them inhabited the ivy-covered halls of ivory towers. He rationalized his perception by finding it "extraordinary" that in Ireland, France, Germany, "in the modern world . . . any poet [was] so honored." Yet there were these instances he knew, so it must have meant that in those countries the masses of men did read and appreciate the poetry on which the "fame" of these individuals rested. In America, by contrast—he may have gone on thinking to himself—poetry was neither read nor appreciated sufficiently by the few who did read it. Consequently, at his funeral he could not expect there to be more than a handful of people—this, sadly, proved to be true, and of the handful only two or three had anything to do with Stevens the poet—so it was probably not worthwhile to spend time and energy contemplating how he would be perceived. How many cared, even now that he was alive, what Wallace Stevens felt about this or that political figure, about communism, socialism, Truman? The most difficult thing was to be honest with oneself, as he had recently noted to one of his correspondents. And if that was the most difficult thing, then the final test of his strength and character would be to remain true to himself and voice that truth—even if he could do so only by again equivocating: "I am of two minds. . . ." It was no wonder Stevens so often compared himself to the figure of a rabbi, one skilled in talmudic reasoning.

In keeping with this seemingly final commitment to the "real," Stevens became interested during this "early autumn"—"the most moving part of our calendar," full of "cold nights and warm days" (*L* 619)—in the personality and work of Jean Dubuffet, who, as he noted to McGreevy, had been mentioned to him by Barbara Church. He asked her to have the painter send him his "Notice sur la Compagnie de l'Art Brut," a kind of manifesto of what the French painter attempted to reach through his childishly crude style that imitated the true *art brut* of "prisoners, mediums, the insane and other nonprofessionals."[11] Dubuffet had come to appreciate these raw perceptions through his own precarious career as a painter. Born in 1901, he had begun painting at seventeen and had studied briefly in Paris. After living for about seven years in Montparnasse as a painter and reading widely in ethnology, paleography, ancient and modern literatures, he had become first a clerk and then a wine merchant. He had stopped painting but returned to it twice and finally remained with his recalcitrant Muse. He had been unknown as a painter, however, until his first one-man show after the liberation of Paris, in October 1944. Since then he lived, with his wife and children, as a nomad in the North African desert, returning to Paris seasonally. Stevens became intrigued with this man who sought primary contact with the sun and stars and who chose to live without the encumbrances he had been brought up to value, like a good bourgeois.

After coming to know Dubuffet's work and the details of his life, Stevens praised both, commenting especially on the courage and nobility that it took to live in direct contact with nature, with and like the simpler peasants, who knew, without having to think, how to live and what to do. There could be nothing more salutary for art than this essential relationship with the world. Here was a figure—though not quite a youth—of the virile poet, a maker who had gone back to primary sources, who voiced his intentions in terms that echoed those in which the poet had regaled his high-toned old Christian woman more than twenty-five years before:

> The merit which we Occidental nations attribute to art and the attention lavished on it tend to substitute a specious product which is the counterfeit of art. Too highly honored, art is rarely nowadays a free celebration (to which one would rush even if it were forbidden and probably rush even faster because it is forbidden). It has become, instead, a game of ceremonies which leads it far into alien terrain. Its true and only terrain is rapture and delirium; it is extracurricular and doesn't belong in the school schedule. To help art regain its place, it should, I believe, be stripped of all the tinsel, laurels and buskins in which it has been decked, and be seen naked with all the creases of its belly. Once disencumbered, it will doubtless begin again to function—to dance and yell like a madman, which is its function, and stop putting on pretentious airs from its professor's chair.[12]

Stevens could not help recovering a part of the old self who wanted to parade his own muzzy belly as he read Dubuffet's words.

Stevens recognized in Dubuffet the "avant-garde of the avant-garde" purpose he had been aware of in the years when he composed the poems of *Harmonium,* years of constant encouragement to be himself that came from the Arensberg circle. This purpose was something he had almost forgotten at times as he had tried to make his imagination that of the mass of men in the absence of the old friends who had collectively served as a mirror for his iconoclastic self. It was a purpose that had certainly not been admitted in the art world during the Depression and into the years of the Second World War. It was far too threatening to continue quizzing all sounds, all shapes, all everything for everything was in chaos, and only surfaces that bore some resemblance to what was known or formerly known could be tolerated. But to see that purpose, to help people see again with an ignorant eye, was revivifying. It made him realize that what he had originally attempted was not some limited aesthetic aim, but part of a larger need the existence of which he had intuited but which, until now, had not shown itself except in the few instances of "poets that mattered," all of whom, like Marianne Moore, were in some way connected to the circle of initiates he had known. But here was someone unattached, someone who truly lived the "marginal" and "experimental," working with the "potent imagination . . . on the verge of consciousness" (*NA* 115). There was hope.

Looking at the work of Jean Dubuffet gives some idea of the "irrepressible revolutionist" that in his last years Stevens rediscovered himself to be. While his taste for the impressionist style could have been predicted, and his appreciation for abstract line drawings becomes understandable in terms of his commitment to patterns imitating thought, his overwhelmingly positive judgment of Dubuffet's art in terms identifiable with what he sought in his own work is, at first, startling. These canvases and drawings that most closely resemble the attempts of children uneasily wielding recalcitrant brushes to render their apprehension of a reality whose structure they do not understand, Stevens saw as "the most potent things I have seen for a long time; horrible but at the same time potent with the effort of an extraordinarily intelligent man to arrive at the source of art in the mind." This he wrote to José Rodríguez Feo in the middle of December 1948, after seeing Dubuffet's first New York show at the Pierre Matisse Gallery. He went on to describe how the artist lived and what he derived from this adventurous choice: "Jean Dubuffet goes to Africa in the winter and there he and his wife and children, or at least one child, live in the desert in a tent, with the Arabs. A friend of his told me this. And there in the desert he struggles against everything that he has picked up at home in an effort to arrive at what he himself is and what he himself sees, feels and thinks" (December 14, 1948).

Stevens recognized Dubuffet to be actually struggling—not only theoretically contemplating—to find the "central," the "self" in its freedom from the fine things of life that society offers in recompense for taking from each individual who contracts with it the primary satisfactions that come from negotiating directly with nature and with the others on whom existence depends. If only from his long weekend walks as a young man and that all-important hunting trip to British Columbia—the memory of which would return as the comforting refrain of his dreams as he lay dying—Stevens knew what it meant to feel oneself part of the harmony of nature: to be wakened by the song of birds that high up in trees tumbled toward the light just a little before he; to find a mountain pass smoothed by a river in an earlier season; to read lines of clouds to learn how to prepare for the next day's weather; to deal with people without the protective code of manners and dress. To use intelligence to understand the book of nature successfully enough to survive, Stevens knew, made a god of a man. There was no more certain sense of self than that derived from making a place for oneself in the amassing harmony of light and darkness, cold and warmth, wind and weather. To do this was to feel true humility, to experience the sacred—that man cannot control all that is—as the first and foremost law. How different this knowledge of reality from that of the man who rose every day to an alarm clock; walked or rode only on paved sidewalks and highways; read the weather forecast in his morning newspaper; slept every night in a warm, soft bed in a hard-angled room in a house locked up against the dark; dealt only with people who spoke in as well-mannered tones as he and called the rest "barbarians"—just as his models, the Greeks, had called the Persians. From all these evidences it was easy for a man to believe that the world ran along like a fine-oiled machine that he and others like him controlled. If occasionally something went wrong, well, a new part would be made, a switch repaired. And wars: What could be expected from barbarians who did not yet appreciate the wonderful uses to which modern machines could be put? It was just a matter of time and education in the manners of civilization.

Dubuffet brutally reminded Stevens of civilization's discontents and of how complacent he had become. But now the poet could not avoid looking again at the life of his time. His years had spanned the last period when, in America, one could have a direct understanding of what it meant to be part of the intelligence of one's soil. His time had dictated the mass movement away from beloved countrysides to urban centers and the subsequent transformation of countrysides into mechanical imitations of urban strips. These were the consequences of political choices made by his peers and their children. And while he had never learned how to drive an automobile, he did enjoy the view of the fluid landscape rolling by as he was driven through Connecticut in his glass coach. The Hartford executive had been complicitous in the changes, as he well knew, and knew, too, that his place had been prepared for him long before by his father's voice of reason, reason forged in the same crucible as the myth of progress that had produced its inevitable discontents.

Just how sharply Stevens felt these discontents and how far the work of Dubuffet went to lighten some of the despair the poet faced in reviewing his life and his time came through loudly in the following letter, which he wrote to Rodríguez Feo right after he first became curious about Dubuffet through his project for *l'art brut,* but before he came to know his work:

> Dear José:
>
> . . . At the moment I feel completely illiterate, so to speak. I rather think that nature gets at me more thoroughly now than at any other time of the year. One grows used to spring; and summer and winter become bores. But Otonno! How this oozing away hurts notwithstanding the pumpkins and the glaciale of frost and the onslaught of books and pictures and music and people. It is finished, Zarathustra says; and one goes to the Canoe Club and has a couple of Martinis and a pork chop and looks down the spaces of the river and participates in the disintegration, the decomposition, the rapt finale. Murder . . . and adieu; assassination . . . and farewell.
>
> And, somehow, for all the newness in this world in which every familiar thing is being replaced by something unfamiliar, in which all the weak affect to be strong, and all the strong keep silence, one has a sense that the world was never less new than now, never more an affair of routine, never more mechanical and lacking in any potency of fineness. Nicht wahr? It is as

if modern art, modern letters, modern politics had at last demonstrated that they were merely diversions, merely things to be abandoned when the time came to pick up the ancient burden again and carry it on. What I mean is getting rid of all our horrid diction and getting back to the realities of mankind. Perhaps instead of living in an era of man released at last from history, we are living in a period of a lot of damned nonsense. I cannot help feeling that communism, in spite of its organization, in spite of its revolutionary program and detonations, is the bunk: something specious, the refuge of failure.

I am writing, as you detect, in the mood of autumn, the mood in which one sums up and meditates on the actualities of the actual year. What has this last year meant to me as a reasonably intelligent and reasonably imaginative person? What music have I heard that has not been the music of an orchestra of parrots and what books have I read that were not written for money and how many men of ardent spirit and star-scimitar mind have I met? Not a goddam one. And I think it is because the world in general is not really moving forward. There is no music because the only music tolerated is modern music. There is no painting because the only painting permitted is painting derived from Picasso or Matisse. And of course there are very few living individuals because we are all compelled to live in clusters: unions, classes, the West, etc. Only in such pious breasts as yours and mine does freedom still dwell. When I go into a fruit store nowadays and find there nothing but the fruits du jour: apples, pears, oranges, I feel like throwing them at the Greek. I expect, and you expect, sapodillas and South Shore bananas and pineapples a foot high with spines fit to stick in the helmet of a wild chieftain.

You probably asked me a lot of questions in your last letter. I ignore them. Why should I answer questions from young philosophers when I receive perfumed notes from Paris? What I really like to have from you is not your tears on the death of [writer Georges] Bernanos, say, but news about chickens raised on red peppers and homesick rhapsodies of the Sienese look of far away Havana and news about people I don't know, who are more fascinating to me than all the characters in all the novels of Spain, which I am unable to read.

Cordial salutes,
WALLACE STEVENS
(*L* 621-22)

In his beautifully balanced lyric periods, Stevens expressed his total disillusionment with the "horrid fiction" of modern civilization. He voiced his desire to get back to the "realities of mankind" in the same terms Dubuffet used. The painter described the "specious . . . counterfeit . . . game of ceremonies" that substituted for the truly necessary celebratory function of art: to seek out and trumpet the joy of particulars as yet unknown in their rawness, their nakedness—"chickens raised on red peppers." How gratifying it must have been for Stevens after a season of bitterness to have found a man "of ardent spirit and star-scimitar mind"! (And was it without significance that the poet's return to strongly expressed sentiments coincided with another period of once more sipping martinis on the porch of the Canoe Club?)

But before he did find Dubuffet, while the "scene" around him slowly became "ice bound" as winter came nearer, Stevens's despair turned to violence. This expression prefigured the "horrid" quality he would find so "potent" in the painter's work. On December 1 the poet wrote another letter to Rodríguez Feo in which he indulged in a rather lurid fantasy spun around his imagining one of his Cuban friend's neighbors in Havana killing Rodríguez Feo's dog. Stevens used this story to voice his disgust with things as they were. (The only bright note recently had been some French stamps arranged in a Klee-like pattern on an envelope enclosing a letter from Barbara Church.) The poet reported that he was in a period when nothing quite sufficed:

> When I have been busy in the office, suddenly I feel that, important as all that is, I am after all losing time and then I read, and again, suddenly, I feel that reading is not enough and that it is time I collected myself and did a poem or two. Thus, the need for variety of experience asserts itself and the pressure of obscure cravings makes itself felt even here in Hartford, which is presumably an insensitive mass of insensitive people. . . .
>
> Anyhow, I am not much worried right now by the fact that I know almost nothing of the thoughts of the early Christian fathers and expositors of Alexandria and so on. Last week I read a note on Valery [*sic*] in the October number of French Studies, a periodical published by Blackwell in Oxford which I think you ought to look up because it makes Valery's skeleton ring, and yet as I read it I kept saying Who cares? Who the heck cares? One of the great spectacles in the world today is the flood of books coming from nothing and going back to nothing. This is due in part to the subjection of literature to money, in part to the existence of a lettered class to which literature is a form of self-indulgence. The savage assailant of life who uses literature as a weapon just does not exist, any more than the savage lover of life exists. Literature today is largely about nothing but nobodies. Is it not so? What kind of book would that dazzling human animal Consuelo [Rodríguez Feo's Havana neighbor] sit down to read after she had finished washing the blood off her hands and had hidden once more her machete in the piano? Will you write it for her? Sartre or Camus would if they had time.
>
> These stimulating suggestions are most inappropriate to the month of Christmas. Perhaps they are part of the revulsion I feel after looking through the book catalogues that have been coming in. Here one is in a fury to understand and to participate and one realizes that if there is anything to understand and if there is anything in which to participate one will pretty nearly have to make it oneself. . . . I suppose one never really writes about life when it is someone else's life, in the feeble laborious reportage of the

> student and artist. One writes about it when it is one's own life provided one is a good barbarian, a true Cuban, or a true Pennsylvania Dutchman, in the linguistics of that soul which propriety, like another Consuelo, has converted into nothingness. (*L* 623–25)

The poet wanted to be a "good barbarian." He was recovering the sense of himself that he had begun with as the maker of *Harmonium,* the "vigorous warrior" who had occasionally reappeared later to "bang" from reality a "savage blue," to "pick [its] acrid colors out,// To nail [its] thought across the door" (*CP* 166). The idea of *l'art brut,* even before he had seen examples of it, seduced his imagination, the mistress of his world, and made her remember what she once was.

On a trip to New York with Elsie during the first week of December Stevens had intended to go to the Pierre Matisse Gallery to see the Dubuffets but did not. He felt too impatient with galleries. "Salesmen disguised as catalogues or as chairs get on one's nerves," he wrote a few days later to McGreevy. He preferred for the moment the memory of a Thomas Cole landscape exhibit he had just seen in Hartford: "I like to hold on to anything that seems to have a definite American past even though the American trees may be growing by the side of queer Parthenons set, say, in the neighborhood of Niagara Falls. One is so homeless over here in such things and something really American is like meeting a beautiful cousin or, for that matter, even one's mother for the first time" (*L* 626). By the following week, however, he had gone to New York again, seen the Dubuffets, and written to Rodríguez Feo that he ought to make a special point of stopping in New York to see them. The two chords struck in Stevens by Cole and this French painter resounded loudly in the years ahead. Something American was attached to ideas of the "mother," while something barbarian, *brut*al, was attached to ideas of the "potent" father. Around these suggestions Stevens was to spin out the filaments completing his web of words.

The poet ended the year in higher spirits than he was used to for the holiday season. He playfully signed a Christmas note to C. L. Daughtry, "Wallans Santevens" (December 20, 1948), commented appreciatively about the girls in the office dressed up like "Mrs. Astor's goat" for the holiday season (December 21, 1948), considered a proposed idea that he write the script for a puppet play "sparkling" (*L* 627), though he could not think of getting to it before autumn, and voiced a renewed commitment to poetry as his "real job" (*L* 627). This last he expressed to Norman Holmes Pearson, who suggested, as others had, that Stevens do something with his prose pieces. "They are a kind of compost pile and should be kept out on the back lot," the poet observed brusquely, dismissing thoughts about devoting himself again to something that in the end always left him feeling less than himself: "My real job is poetry and not papers about poetry." Perhaps having just received a note from Alfred Knopf announcing the "extremely gratifying" news that the check he would receive by the end of the month would be the largest single one ever mailed to him had given Stevens the strength to name poetry, finally, his "real job"—no longer as "absurd," "lady-like," the "afflatus [that was] not serious" that his father's voice had continued to whisper it was.

❧

As 1949 opened, Stevens had every reason to stride proudly. If he did not now feel confident enough to begin showing his "plain self" without fear, he never would. Indeed, the poet did reveal the barbaric, peasant self directly to Barbara Church in one of his first letters of the new year. He opened by being unusually outspoken in his disagreement with her about the current Arp exhibit at the Curt Valentin Gallery. He did not spare her feelings in expressing his belief that it was "nonsense to speak of [Arp's] integrity as an abstractionist in the same breath with which one [spoke] of Mondrian. Arp [was] a minor stylist. . . ." Nonetheless, the poet would have liked to have had one of the "smoother pebbles," which he found "exquisite . . . freest from eccentricity." Quite in contrast with his experience at this precious little gallery was his visit to the Morgan Library, where there was a Giovanni Piranesi exhibit, ". . . a far greater thing if one is to judge it by its effects on the observer," an "idea" that made him "feel that what really validate[d] modern art [was] not so much its results as its intentions and purposes." To ground himself in "reality" once more, before he went back to Hartford, he stopped, as he noted to Church, at Manganaro's on Ninth Avenue, where "the odor of cheese, fish and Dagos as you go into the store is a little baffling, but, after so much Arp, and so on, it fixed [him] with the greatest of firmness back on the ground" (*L* 628). Certainly Stevens would not have dared, unless he was feeling quite secure, to reveal to Mrs. Church his coarser taste for "Dago things," nor would he have taken the chance of using one of his discriminatory terms, no matter how obviously playful the context.

This letter seemed to set the stage for the rest of the year. In almost all the many letters he wrote during the months to come Stevens found occasion to express at least one strong judgment or to reveal some aspect of his barbaric self. Writing to Thomas McGreevy a few days after this letter to Mrs. Church, Stevens reiterated his opinions about Arp, comparing him unfavorably to Brancusi, whom he praised; went on about how the routine of galleries had reduced the experimentation of modernism to routine as well; and added that at least New York still held the chance of seeing "a few decent looking girls" and of swallowing some oysters in the bar in the tunnel at Grand Central (*L* 630). As he waited for the early return of the birds this spring, which he came to expect from a report that he read and forwarded to Barbara Church, now vacationing in Tucson, Arizona, he wrote to Rodríguez Feo about how much he would appreciate a series of postcards from Madrid if he went as planned in autumn; he commented, too, about the many invitations to lecture that he was declining because he didn't "see the connection between writing poetry and delivering lectures . . . except in cases in which [he] very much want[ed] to." To this he added humorously:

It would be interesting to meet people in colleges, but then one never meets them at a lecture. If, for example, General Eisenhower should ask me to come down to Columbia and have a few highballs with him, that would be worth while. Yet it may be that, even if he did, when I got down there he would want to show me moving pictures of Hitler's funeral or something.

Good luck my tropical amigo. I mean well but a widower with six children or a cat with twelve kittens has nothing on me. (*L* 631)

Two days later, on March 11, he wrote to McGreevy and continued a dialogue they had been having about asceticism and humanism that grew out of exchanges they had had about Giorgione and, more recently, Courbet (after Stevens had sent him a catalog of a current exhibit in New York). Stevens did not equivocate in his present judgment of Baudelaire, whom McGreevy had quoted reverently to him in his preceding letter:

CHEVALIER [McGreevy had won the palm of the Légion d'Honneur]:

Your quotation from Baudelaire made me run through the poems again. I am afraid that B. is beginning to date. Would anyone read him quite naturally today? The poems seem unrelated to anything actual or perhaps it is only that they are so unlike the actuality of this earliest spring weather in Hartford. Thus your line which at first is so evocative soon becomes

I have lived a long time in a porchéd [*sic*] vastness

or something equally rhetorical.

The demand for reality in poetry brings one sooner or later to a point where it becomes almost impossible since a real poetry, that is to say, a poetry that is not poetical or that is not merely the notation of objects in themselves poetic is a poetry divested of poetry. That is what I am trying to get at at the moment. Perhaps I am not young enough for it, or old enough, or should think about it only when Sagittarius is in jeopardy. The bare idea makes everything else seem false and verbose and even ugly. It is from that point of view that

J'ai habité longtemps etc.

becomes repulsive. Alas that such lovely things can become repulsive from any point of view. Perhaps I should have my point of view extracted and roam like a member of the Russian ballet under these vast porches.

A painter like Courbet sharpens this obsession. It is true that it is a common enough obsession, but it is also true that it might at least be called the obsession of Courbet: the Parisian complex. To look at Courbet's things as the accomplishment of an ascetic gives them a value they don't have otherwise. He was an ascetic by virtue of all his rejections and also by virtue of his devotion to the real. Since my last letter to you I found the catalogue of the exhibition of Giorgione which I had mislaid. I suppose it is possible to say, not wholly rightly, that Giorgione represents the exquisite opposite, the humanistic opposite, of Courbet. They were both exquisite, only one never thinks of Courbet as exquisite. Yet his things are full of resistance to the false, the fraudulent. If they are works of aesthetic piety, they are exquisite. Very likely what I am thinking of is that the ascetic is negative and the humanistic affirmative, and that they face in two different ways which would bring them together ultimately at the other side of the world, face to face.

Ghandi [*sic*], alack, has always bored me. I sometimes wondered how long he could keep it up, but it never mattered much. While this is all wrong, still that sense of him comes back when he is spoken of in connection with Buddha and Jesus and, as you say, with Eamon de Valera. I say it is all wrong because Buddha and Jesus are not human figures. They are human figures transposed and seen in their own particular vast porches and, in addition, the still vaster porches of time. Ghandi, however, is without all this Baudelaire. He is as yet a creature of the Associated Press. To be consistent I should ignore Buddha and Jesus and try to preserve the dazzling purity of this contemporary and to understand that although he lacks mythological perspective and rhetorical perspective, he lives a truly living life in the minds and hearts of millions of people whose principal fault is that they are so far away. Yet that is an extremely serious fault for me and I could argue the point if the vessel was not about to sail or the plane to fly. I am, after all, more moved by the first sounds of the birds on my street than by the death of a thousand penguins in Antarctica.

We do not have in this country either ascetics or humanists, unless it should be in Boston. All that belongs to someone else: to the photographs of Cardinal Newman and J. P. Morgan . . . . . .[*sic* punctuation] And just a word about Twó-son and Arizona before I stop. You cannot imagine the size of a place like Arizona and its neighbor, New Mexico nor the effect of that size on the validity of French poets in general. Tucson is about as far from Hartford in one direction as Dublin in another. It is a kind of antipodes where they have no winter and where there is nothing to read. (*L* 631–32)

The vituperative edge in Stevens's voice was sharp; it sliced away at whatever was not central to him. In what might have been taken as his provincial dismissal of Mahatma Gandhi (recently assassinated), the poet was actually expressing that he had finally outgrown all heroes as sentimental inhabitants of "vast porches" in the minds of multitudes. It may have been a "serious fault" of his, but no matter, he was moved by the real sounds of the birds on his street as they announced the return of the season he had at last made his friend. This kind of poetic sensibility could not be appreciated in a country where the actual vastness of spaces made the rhetorical evocation of vastness seem silly and pretentious, a country without either ascetics or humanists, where, outside of perhaps Boston, no one read. Was the poet imagining his own funeral again?

Marking the change in attitude that had come about, Stevens observed to Barbara Church, back in New York after her western sojourn, that this third Thursday in March, when he would as usual be in the city for the annual meeting of the livestock insuring group, would again memorialize the last day he had met with her husband (*L* 633). But he could now think of this coolly as he planned to attend the St. Nicholas Society's Easter celebration, to which he would invite Rodríguez Feo. In his fortified state of mind Stevens remarked to Allen Tate at the very end of March that it was "a happy thought" for him to have proposed Yvor Winters, who had misunderstood Stevens's progress as that of a "hedonist," for membership in the National Institute of Arts and Letters (*L* 633). To Tate's recommendation of Winters as one with the "highest critical standards," Stevens added his own comment: "One of those standards has been to reach his own conclusions. His intelligence is one of the few that is capable of surprising us." He went on to relate his imagined offense to Cleanth Brooks and his wife the year before, asking Tate if he might do something and describing his state on that day as being so disrupted by the "too good" or "too many" cocktails he had downed that he had mistakenly paid cash for his ticket on the train back to Hartford when, all the time, he had had a return ticket in his pocket (*L* 634). He told his story with aplomb as though it were an anecdote about one of his poetic characters, his present attitude about himself and the world not admitting the painful feelings of embarrassment and insecurity that would surface again and eventually prompt his letter of apology to Brooks two years later.

One of the things that helped Stevens continue riding the wave of good feeling that had crested with Knopf's "gratifying" end-of-the-year report was that he was at work on a long poem. Giving attention to one subject over an extended period of time had always pleased him, and never more so than now, when because of the number of requests that he had been receiving, he had had to begin something new two or three times a month. This had been particularly wearing over the last year, as he had noted to one or two correspondents. Musing on "An Ordinary Evening in New Haven," the poem he was to deliver to the Connecticut Academy of Arts and Sciences on November 9, sustained him from the beginning of March and into June. It more than sustained him; it strengthened him. The poet translated both his late commitment to show his "plain self" and his fascination with the idea of *l'art brut* into his study of the subject. As he noted to his newest correspondent, Bernard Heringman (then a graduate student at Columbia, doing his dissertation on Stevens's poetry),[13] who had queried the poet about various influences and intentions:

> At the moment I am at work on a thing called An Ordinary Evening in New Haven. This is confidential and I don't want the thing to be spoken of. But here my interest is to try to get as close as possible to the ordinary, the

> commonplace and the ugly as it is possible for a poet to get. It is not a question of grim reality but of plain reality. The object is of course to purge oneself of anything false. I have been doing this since the beginning of March and intend to keep studying the subject and working on it until I am quite through with it. (*L* 636–37)

The exercise of composing "An Ordinary Evening in New Haven" was a purifying one, announced even in the poem itself:

> "This man abolishes by being himself
> That which is not ourselves: the regalia,
> The attributions, the plume and helmet-ho."
> (*CP* 485)

Stevens was stripping away his fine trappings. He was strong enough to do this now because he accepted the plain earth in its most ordinary guise—dressed in the "eccentric exterior" (*CP* 478) of New Haven—as "inamorata, of loving fame/ Added and added out of a fame-full heart . . ." (*CP* 484), while his own heart was full of the fame celebrated by Knopf's note and check. The renewed power of sight, sound, touch that made the lines of this poem tingle with images like that of "lewd spring com[ing] from winter's chastity" (*CP* 468) or of "Life fix[ing] him, wandering on the stair of glass" (*CP* 483), came from his recognizing that in the final act of the comedy he staged, the disillusion he experienced was itself an illusion—"disillusion as the last illusion" (*CP* 468). He revealed himself openly, though in plurality:

> . . . It is as if
> Men turning into things, as comedy,
> Stood, dressed in antic symbols, to display
>
> The truth about themselves, having lost, as things,
> That power to conceal they had as men,
> . . . .
> (*CP* 470)

The beautiful knowledge that came of this long-postponed confrontation of his "plain self" with the real, as it was in its plainest, ugliest form—not the noble reality of nature or one of its elements, or the imagined reality of a place he had never seen, but of this "simple seeing" of commonplace New Haven—was that his spirit was, indeed, "part of the res itself." He was the breath he had exchanged with the universe for seventy years:

. . . .
Our breath is like a desperate element
That we must calm, the origin of a mother tongue

With which to speak to her [the real]

. . . .
(*CP* 470–71)

He no longer felt his imagination was something added to reality to make life complete but that imagination was reality. Finally the two elements of his being "rolled as one and from the two/ Came fresh transfigurings of freshest blue" (*CP* 102). There was in this "spirit's alchemicana" (*CP* 471) something essential about accepting America as America, as it was, slightly crude in its imitations of European manners, though still desirous—ugly New Haven longing to be New Heaven.[14] There was potency in being able to accept this paltriness as part of the real, equal in beauty to the quivering transparencies of the sea in its "transcendent change" (*CP* 484). Aspects that until now had been separate in the poet merged. Professor Eucalyptus, well hidden for so many years in the leaves of his books, answered plainly after all his baroque evasions—products of abstracting himself into various planetary guises to feel himself one with sun, moon, rainy clouds—that he now sought God "In New Haven with an eye that [did] not look// Beyond the object" (*CP* 475). He also named himself "A figure like Ecclesiast" (*CP* 479), the maker of what could be understood to be an iconoclastic book, focusing the attention of the brethren on the fleeting satisfaction of the here and now rather than on possibilities of future redemption. There was deliverance in the simple recording of repetitions with their shimmering everyday variations—the notations of one human being's passage:

. . . .
. . . .
. . . But there was always one:

A century in which everything was part
Of that century and of its aspect, a personage,
A man who was the axis of his time.
(*CP* 479)

Stevens opened this poem with a reassertion of his attempt to create the "vulgate of experience" that he had last set forth as his intention in "The Man with the Blue Guitar." He had thought during his "dark year of 1947" and well into 1948 that he had failed in this purpose and that any notion of it had to be abandoned. But through the confrontation with his "starker, barer self" in composing "Effects of Analogy" and the starker, barer poems of the summer of 1948, he had come to terms with how he had evaded the "central," his "self" for most of his life. Instead of being built out of things changed on the blue guitar of imagination into powerful instruments used to attack and destroy things as they were, the new vulgate would be built out of the "eye's plain version" (*CP* 465) of things. The products of this shift in consciousness would be instruments of praise for whatever was. What was absent in this "recent imagining of reality" was violence. No clashed edges of words killed any part of the precious present. Only "a second giant" appeared to kill the "first," who had been merciless in his slaughter of anything less than "the makings of the sun" (*CP* 532). Consequently, this "vulgate" would be "A larger poem for a larger audience" (*CP* 465). Stevens's early admonition to himself to "come down" from his Jovian atelier was finally becoming a reality: "We *must* come down, we *must* use tooth and nail, it is the law of nature, 'the survival of the fittest'; providing [*sic*] we maintain at the same time self-respect, integrity and fairness. I believe, as unhesitatingly as I believe in anything, in the efficacy and necessity of fact meeting fact—with a background of the ideal" (*L* 32).

The poet was discovering himself to be more than a man made out of words as he fulfilled the hidden prophecy he had voiced for himself at nineteen. Terms from this past utterance reappeared, though changed, in his poem. "Nail" became the "clou"-clue (*CP* 473), the "pin" on which meaning hung teasingly. And "fact"—fact met fact throughout the poem's lines, though "fact" not realized before. Ironically—and this he himself probably realized as well—the very "fact" that he did fulfill the promise of his words belonged to the deepest structure of the religious thought that had made him who he was. He made of his word God. Was this an inhibition? All things were made by him; and without him was not anything made that was made. It was only through this magnificent eye, partaking like Plotinus of what it was a part, that New Haven appeared in its plainness as desirable as the most divine inamorata. The doublings of the "double-things" of the "enigmatical/ Beauty of each beautiful enigma" (*CP* 472), the paradox of being, was accepted for what it was. The poet's New Haven might have, like Bishop Berkeley's forest, disappeared when he left it, but the memory of what it once was on that ordinary evening stretched like a lazy cat in his mind over months of other ordinary evenings and days, occasionally pawing at images that lay nearby: his favorite flower, the fuschia that appeared like a tremulous earth-star; the "lion of Juda [*sic*]" that came pictured on an Easter card from Sister Mary Bernetta. These trivial things were the *real* "enlargements" that allowed him to know himself as one with the world of which he was a part. These were *facts* tied to actual "looks and feelings" (*CP* 471): a flower he actually smelled and knew in its particularity, not one imagined; a card that came bearing the gift of reverence, not "Bergamo on a postcard" (*CP* 486) without a message, collected to fill a sense of emptiness.

In this poem Stevens took up again the task of elaborating the theory of poetry. The strength he feared had failed him had returned, though changed. In being true to himself, he elaborated the theory as poetry itself—"part of the res itself and not about it," as it necessarily had to be in prose. The theory was Stevens's offering toward the "science of illusion" he proposed in "Effects of Analogy." Using the tools of this science to unlock the mysteries of "the intricate evasions of as" (*CP* 486), one could analyze and thus *see* the difference between "things seen and unseen, created from nothingness,/ The heavens, the hells, the worlds, the longed-for lands" (*CP* 486). It would be like separating light from darkness to understand, from careful attention given to the images themselves, which were attached to real fact and which were not, and through that to understand the complex mechanisms of human evasion: why, when, and how it became necessary. Before which facts of feeling was it almost impossible not to turn away? This apprehension made the theory of poetry the theory of life.

As Stevens studied his subject, formulated his theory in "An Ordinary Evening in New Haven," the sharp shadows of his earlier selves evened into the "shade that traverses/ A dust" (*CP* 489), like the very light of evening itself—the twilight of the god he had made of himself. One of the phrases that he kept in his mind as he set himself to his work was a sentence of Santayana's written in a letter to José Rodríguez Feo, which the Cuban had forwarded to the poet. Returning the letter, Stevens observed, "I love his remark: 'I have always, somewhat sadly, bowed to expediency or fate'" (*L* 635). In the same note to Rodríguez Feo the poet commented on Santayana's "strong mind" and praised the Cuban's "devotion to this superb figure. But in his letter to Bernard Heringman about two weeks later, in which he repeated with a minor but striking variation the sentence that so captured his imagination, as "I have always bowed, however sadly, to expediency or fate," he referred to Santayana as "the decrepit old philosopher," who, for him, was "not a philosopher in any austere sense" (*L* 637). Was the poet being generous to Rodríguez Feo by not disillusioning him with his genuine perception of Santayana, or had he just now in the process of working through the steps of his theory suddenly come to realize the inadequacies of Santayana as a thinker and as a man? In view of the way he had used him as an illustration in "Effects of Analogy," it seems that Stevens was dissembling to Rodríguez Feo and that whatever he had understood in composing "An Ordinary Evening" simply reinforced his earlier perception. What was clear was that Stevens had finally cleared the shadows of his fathers from the skies. His misremembering of Santayana's words mirrored the reduction, changing an utterance weighted with the dignity of stoic acceptance into one bespeaking fatalistic inadequacy. Perhaps Stevens wanted his younger friend to strip his heroes of their regalia without help from him.

Stevens had not set the final period on his long poem before more requests for new things came. He promised the Princess Caetani a few poems for *Botteghe Oscure* by August, and to Alfred Knopf, who again urged him to think of publishing an edition of collected poems, he promised another volume—*The Auroras of Autumn*—by the end of the year. He wanted to complete just one more act in the comedy that had subtly become a drama before he thought about the final shape of "The Whole. . . ." The "Giant" seemed up to any task, including facing the political scene as it was, as he made clear to Rodríguez Feo during the first days of June:

> I cannot say that one is free any longer to go on enjoying the weather in June. Politics is in everything. This morning I received a notice of a meeting of the Phi Beta Kappa. I enclose part of the notice saying who was to be orator and whose name is x'd out. So that the sextons of liberty at Washington horn in even on the meetings of the Phi Beta Kappa. Judith Caplan and Alexander Palmer and Mr. Chambers and Mr. Hiss all give me a prolonged pain in the neck. I wish I could forget all about them when I am taking my walk in the park in the mornings by sitting down and having a little talk with the ducks, but I am sure that the ducks are Russian spies. It would be almost a relief if someone blew hell out of everything. In an effort to prove that everything that has been has been wrong, what really has been accomplished is the establishing of the fact that everything that is is nuts. The Canoe Club was built for just this purpose and I am going there for lunch today. Yet you can see how dreadfully wrong everything is from this: last night we had some strawberries after dinner. They were the most perfect berries in the world but the *only* sugar available was brown *health* sugar. Oh my god! Misericorde and misericorde. (June 9, 1949)

The poet was no longer hiding his impatience with the state of affairs and with those who now began naming names of others suspected to be witches. Everything was "nuts." Having come to accept and voice this, too, was freeing. He wrote to Barbara Church on June 13—responding to her latest letter from aboard the USS *America* on her way back to France with charming fellow passengers, who, as she reported to him, all seemed to be "enthousiastic [*sic*]" about him and his work—that he felt for the first time able to think of giving himself wholly to poetry. The promise he had made to Knopf for a volume by the end of the year would force "steady application" of a sort he had not experienced in his previous "casual and intermittent" flirtations with the Muse. In this new imagining of himself in his confrontation with the real, Stevens paid no attention to the fact that he still gave the greater part of his time to the Hartford. It seems, then, that what had changed was his deepest attitude toward poetry. It was now something he could recognize as the object of his whole devotion since he could unequivocally celebrate the "plain sense of things" as well as "noble accents." Affirming the feeling of completion this brought, he spoke of how much he enjoyed the peace of being able to sit in his room at night watching the fireflies. It was "the feeling that one is back again where one was as a child. Life is so much larger and more continued than it can ever be for people who break it up with incidents" (*L* 639).

Aware of the fullness of his humanity during this late phase, Stevens seems to have become more "human" to the other beings whose lives directly touched his own. This may have been a function of his again experiencing a new life in that of his grandson. Just as his manner with others had changed during the years after Holly's birth when he stretched himself to imagine what she must have been perceiving, so now there were signs that Stevens became more sensitive to the needs and "otherness" of others. Encouraging little Peter's curiosity, the lover of order didn't wink as his grandchild took apart a chocolate cake and smeared it "all over the place" (*L* 639). He made a point of interrupting his "steady application" to work to visit in the hospital Edward Southworth, his fellow officer at the American Bonding Company, an old friend with whom he occasionally had shared dinners in the first years of his marriage when Elsie was away. This friend had always sent him tender Christmas greetings; when he died on September 16, 1949, Stevens saved the news clipping as he had the annual cards of greeting. Perhaps the clearest sign of a change was that he returned to one of the habits that he had abandoned—though not only because of himself—in the early years of his marriage: He again read his poems aloud to Elsie. It is impossible to know the precise moment when Stevens took her once more with him into his "fluent mundo," but it is certain that she was an inhabitant there by the time of his composing "An Ordinary Evening in New Haven." As he related to Louis Martz, apropos of how he made his selection of which stanzas of the long poem he would read at the meeting of the Connecticut Academy of Arts and Sciences—in order not to exceed the time limit—he had read aloud to Elsie each section as he finished it; "as is my custom," Martz remembered Stevens saying. The sections to which Elsie responded by putting her hands over her eyes and saying, "They're not going to understand this," the poet set aside.[15] They would clarify themselves in print on the quiet page together with the others.

Considering the obvious trust to which such an acquiescence to another's judgment attests, it is probably safe to speculate that Stevens again made Elsie a native in his world rather recently as he came to accept the simpler, peasant core of himself around which he had spent so much time spinning webs of delicate evasion. It was he, after all, who had made the deer's head a central feature of their first furnishings forty years before, and it was he who had on more than one occasion when more than "half lit" told bawdy stories, laughing at each phrase while others listened stony-faced. He had probably come to celebrate her acumen as a critic as one of her "perfections" when he recognized how, in fact, Elsie had never judged but loved him, like the Good Shepherd he had wished for in the months before their marriage. If she didn't look up from her rose bed when he proudly announced through the window that he had won another honorary degree, it didn't matter; she was probably too lost in her immediate occupation with the earth to be attentive to words unshaped by breath strained into rhymes and measured by meter. No one gave her honors or awards for her garden, which was, in its order and variety, as much a sacrament of praise to what was as were his poems.

As the summer deepened and the days grew hotter and stickier, Stevens felt the need for "a lot of leisure and space" around him that he would have had were his life truly devoted only to poetry. He wrote of this to Thomas McGreevy in mid-July, when he described how much energy it took to focus on the short things he had to work on again because he had promised both Princess Caetani and John Crowe Ransom poems that he wanted to get out of the way before completing what he wanted to include in *The Auroras of Au-*

tumn; he wanted to add at least one other long poem to the various pieces he already had. He was feeling his age:

> And, now, for the first time, I begin to feel at the end of the day that I am through for that day. It is not that I grow tired but that my elan seems somewhat bent. I should much rather stroll home looking at the girls than anything else. But I suppose that if I were a less disciplined character I should even have a drink when I reach home instead of sitting down in an easy chair with the New York paper and having orange juice—a lot of it. But orange juice is not what I had in mind when I spoke of a drink. (*L* 640)

Feeling pressed and disgruntled at his waning endurance made Stevens on the same day reply rather snappishly to a letter from Samuel French Morse, who had not written for quite some time since asking him for a recommendation for a Guggenheim Fellowship (which he did not get). Stevens seemed to find Morse querying him somewhat intrusively and closed his letter commenting:

> I don't remember saying much of anything to Harry Duncan in letters, etc. and I don't really think that one's offhand remarks should be taken seriously. Some people always know exactly what they think. I am afraid I am not one of those people. The same thing keeps active in my mind and rarely becomes fixed. This is true about politics as it is about poetry. But I suppose that it is really true about everything.
>
> If I can be of any help to you otherwise, I shall be glad to do the best I can although this does not seem to be a very promising start. (*L* 641)

This unusually clipped reply was in keeping with Stevens's new, if late-found, sense of security as a poet. He had begun the year speaking his mind and would continue. The harshness that he had for years before confined to expressing to those in the business world with whom he became impatient he could afford to show now in the literary world as well—perhaps because he felt he no longer had to court it for attention.

By the end of July Stevens had finished about half of the short poems he had promised. He sent "A Half Dozen Small Pieces" ("What We See Is What We Think," "A Golden Woman in a Silver Mirror," "The Old Lutheran Bells at Home," "Questions Are Remarks," "Study of Images I," and "Study of Images II" [*CP* 459–65]) to *Botteghe Oscure.* He was not wholly pleased with these, as he wrote to Barbara Church on July 27:

> These were on such things as came into my head. They pleased me. But after a round of this sort of thing I always feel the need of getting some different sort of satisfaction out of poetry. Often when I am writing poetry I have in mind an image of reading a page of a large book: I mean the large page of a book. What I read is what I like. The things that I have just sent to Rome

> are not the sort of things that one would find on such a page. At least what one ought to find is normal life, insight into the commonplace, reconciliation with every-day reality. The things that it makes me happy to do are things of this sort. However, it is not possible to get away from one's own nature.
>
> I am planning to stick to odds and ends until the end of August. I have been making promises right and left and I want to try to fulfill these. At the moment what I have in mind is a group of things which mean a good deal more than they sound like meaning: for instance, airing the house in the morning; the colors of sunlight on the side of the house; people in their familiar aspects. All this is difficult for me. It is possible that pages of insight and of reconciliation, etc. are merely pages of description. The trouble is that poetry is so largely a matter of transformation. To describe a cup of tea without changing it and without concerning oneself with some extreme aspect of it is not at all the easy thing that it seems to be. (*L* 642–43)

Writing these pieces, he had come up again against his old evasive nature, his inability to stick to the commonplace; he did not feel through them the "reconciliation with every-day reality" he now desired, almost desperately. He had gotten carried away once more with the enchantments of distraction, pure pattern; like a good Arab, he could not utter the name of God or render His image. Under pressure to produce he fell back into what he had learned to do to perfection: Arabesques of sound and shape appeared that he could not resist, because they were so beautiful. In "A Golden Woman in a Silver Mirror"—a brilliant figure for the secondary perfection of the imperfection of the poems he now composed as reflected against his intention—he masterfully pointed to his weakness. He addressed Abba, father of the word, as God, noting that "dark death is the breaking of a glass" (*CP* 460)—a distanced image of the final fact, an image of an inanimate object that could not cry out. He closed with a question: "How long have you lived and looked,/ Ababba, expecting this king's queen to appear?" (*CP* 461). His verbal play could not refrain from transforming and so identifying his progenitor as a rhyme scheme, *ababba;* the pattern for closing a sonnet forever possible still determined him. What more than these deep structures of grammar rearranged to mimic thought and feeling had given him life?

But it was direct contact he wanted, as he enviously listened to his two-year-old grandson ask, "Mother, what is that" (*CP* 462), instead of what he, as an old man asked, "Mother, my mother, who are you" (*CP* 463)—as he nobly recorded in "Questions Are Remarks," there naming "Peter the voyant," who could speak what was in fact. Composing these poems showed Stevens there was still work to be done so that the memory of "The Old Lutheran Bells at Home" would not make him St. Francis or St. Jerome or Don Juan but would force him to speak as the simple man he was. Still, perhaps these evasions had somehow been designed just so he would feel he had work ahead. If and when he finally spoke of things as they were without evasion by a single metaphor, would there be any reason to go on?

There can be nothing more wrenching than final reflections, nothing more painful than tallying the last sums of what has been achieved against the still-remembered projections of what was wanted, desired. Perhaps there are those who successfully avoid the difficulty of this last act by continuing the make-believe that they are young, or by imagining that their children will fulfill whatever dreams they didn't. Stevens knew such individuals, but he knew, too, that he was not one of them. He felt all too keenly with his age that his "interior world [was] in great disorder," as he expressed it to Rodríguez Feo at nearly the end of July, just after observing that he regretted not having come to know better someone, Theodore Spencer, who had recently died of a heart attack in a taxicab. Arrived at his destination, his home, the driver opened the door and Spencer's "big foot fell out": "While I never knew him well, I wish I had. We came from the same part of the world. We must have had much in common. And one is always desperately in need of the fellowship of one's own kind. I don't mean intellectual fellowship, but the fellowship of one's province: membership in a clique, the fellowship of the landsman and compatriot" (*L* 644).

Measuring life in the slow steps he had followed back and forth from the office, in and out of Elizabeth Park, up and down the steps to his room, Stevens had never stopped. One of those on whom his imagination fastened now was Albert Schweitzer, who had just recently visited the United States, probably in connection with the publication of his *The Forest Hospital at Lambaréné.* Stevens would have been hard put to find someone more antithetical to himself. He found him "magnificent: an eminent figure of non-self-seeking in a world in which self-seeking is as prevalent as breathing" (*L* 644). How did he then perceive himself? Was he slipping into another depression, or were these last summations accurate perceptions of who he was?

To comfort himself, he propped on his dresser a postcard from Rodríguez Feo showing Varadero Beach so that every morning he could imagine the surf making Cuban sounds. Was the poet just now beginning to feel the regret of having lived the routine life he led as he realized his deep devotion to poetry? He was certainly not finding satisfaction in the things that he had used in the past to distract him. He wrote to Barbara Church and Thomas McGreevy that he had gone down to New York in August to see an exhibit of new Italian things at the Museum of Modern Art, but that it was hardly worth the trouble. Though it made him more appreciative of the presence of Italian-Americans around him, the "professional modernism" of the museum, which, to his mind, cultivated the idea that everything it displayed, including curtains and plants on the landings, was the "nuts," disgusted him. "The whole of New York was a lemon" (*L* 647). But, he reflected, perhaps his reaction was a function of the way he lived his life: "It is not easy to experience much in the rather routine life that I lead. While one is never sure that it makes much difference, one is equally never sure that it doesn't" (*L* 647–48).

The anxiety Stevens was experiencing about himself he also felt about the world: "One's sense of anxiety about the future, which everything seems to exploit, does not grow less" (*L* 648). He reported this to Barbara Church in mid-September, preparing himself to write what he thought would be his last long poem since he had finished the other short poems that he had promised. As it turned out, there was no last long poem. "The Rock" would be composed of fragments of what was.

Luckily, by the end of the month the Tal Coat still life had arrived, as though presenting itself as a gift for his seventieth birthday. Stevens found it "fascinating," "full of contrariness and sophistication," its colors rich and fresh. He knew it would give him a great deal of pleasure. Within a few days he gave it his own title, *Angel Surrounded by Peasants:* "The angel is the Venetian glass bowl in the left with the little spray of leaves in it. The peasants are the terrines, bottles and the glasses that surround it. This title alone tames it as a lump of sugar might tame a lion" (*L* 650). Within the week he had composed a poem around and to it, "Angel Surrounded by Paysans" (*Q* 496), which he sent off to Nicholas Moore (now dissociated from the publishing enterprise with which Knopf had had so many difficulties) for *Poetry London* (in which it appeared in the January 1950 issue). It is not hard to imagine Stevens studying his new painting, seeing the changing light of day transfigure its shapes, turning his shoulder quickly to find that the angel he had just seen in a scene transformed from the simple still life was gone. Within a few days more he had sent the poem off to Victor Hammer (the private printer who ran the Anvil Press) in the hope that he would print it specially in some fine old type and get someone—Stevens thought of Fritz Kredel, a contemporary German artist whose drawing Stevens liked—to illustrate it. The idea of commemoration seems to have been in Stevens's mind. Did he see himself as the angel surrounded by peasants, the "necessary angel of earth" (*CP* 496) in whose sight the earth is seen again? Or was the necessary angel a spirit of the earth itself and the poet one of the peasants simple and uncomplicated enough to perceive it?

In the weeks surrounding his birthday there were the usual round of letters from friends and professional acquaintances. Barbara Church wrote of the hurricane that met her ship before it reached New York, asked the poet whether he could say something to help advance the interests of St.-John Perse in America; Stevens had to refuse, he responded, because in order to do what she asked, he would have to read all of the French poet's work in the original and he needed all the time he could manage for his own work (he recommended she ask St.-John Perse's friend Allen Tate or Archibald MacLeish for help instead). She also recommended that Stevens read Xavier de Maistre's *Le Voyage Autour de Ma Chambre,* and he did, as he observed to her, appropriately costumed in a nightcap he had not worn for years (*L* 653). Sister Mary Bernetta Quinn faithfully sent her birthday greeting with news that the *Sewanee Review* had accepted her piece on him. Stevens answered her note and news, reporting: "At seventy one ought to be a venerable wreck, with a bottle of medicine in one hand and a prayer book in the other. But . . . this morning I said to my wife, 'I am off for eighty'" (October 10, 1949). About Sister Mary Bernetta's observation concerning the "Supreme Fiction," the poet gently guided her away from a reading that would be "religious" in her sense: "My interest in *A Supreme Fiction* is certainly not to create an object for worship, whatever else may be said about it. At the moment I am not particularly interested even in that because one passes from one thing to another. It is curious how people try to fix one as if a man of seventy is going to be seventy even at seventy-one" (October 17, 1949).[16]

Then, too, as the brewing political crucible was being fueled even more, concerned writers petitioned and protested certain "intolerable" offenses. One such occasion involved the *Saturday Review*'s suggested adumbration of a fascist grouping of particular writers as a result of Robert Hillyer's outrage over the Bollingen's being awarded to Ezra Pound. Allen Tate wrote to Stevens and asked him to sign a letter expressing opposition to this kind of interference in the world of letters. Stevens's response was characteristic of his manner when he felt strong and secure:

> Dear Allen:
>
> I don't see the Saturday Review and, even if I did, I should skip anything it might contain by Benet [*sic*] and/or Hillyer. So that 1. I know nothing about this: 2. care less; 3. do not believe that the Saturday Review or Benet or Hillyer, jointly or severally, or both, could possibly harm the cause of letters; 4. prefer to keep out of this; and 5. intend to do just that.
>
> In spite of all this, I am happy to hear from you and particularly to hear from you in Princeton, which I believe that you like.
>
> Everything goes well up here. I have recently decided to live to be a hundred. One of the ways of doing that is not to jump into bonfires.
>
> Yours sincerely
>
> (October 20, 1949)

Stevens expressed himself without any attempt to protect Tate's feelings, yet the humorous tone of the closing neutralized the judgment his recipient might make. The technique was not different from that Stevens used in his poems, especially the early *Harmonium* pieces: There were unpleasant things to address, to describe, and one had to face them, but they could always somehow be set in the broader frame of the human comedy.

Stevens continued until the end of the year with the same determination to do as much as he possibly could. In addition to preparing the typescript for his last volume for Knopf, he made time to write a catalog introduction for the paintings of Marcel Gromaire, "the Rubens of the coal mines," for the Carré Gallery in New York. The terms he chose to describe the essence of the man as he perceived him through his work could have just as easily been used to describe himself:

> These oddly hallucinatory tableaux (in the English sense) are the pictures of a determined man, somewhat possessed, predestined and, because of these characteristics, also rebellious. Being rebellious is being oneself and being oneself is not being one of the automata of one's time. Gromaire's appearances come to us, one by one, as he experiences them but not as part of the day's great, common flocks and herds and shoals of things alike. (*OP* 290)

These echoes of how Stevens had seen himself in the portrait of Henry Church suggest that as the poet grew older, he opened his being. The ability that had shown itself even in his adolescence of imagining himself in a harmonious movement with trees, stars, mountains, and the countless other tongues and fingers of nature now extended itself to human beings besides those he imagined as second selves. As he drew closer to the ultimate cause of the "pathos" of the human condition, he could not hide from his feelings; he no longer turned away from what in his youth would have bathed him in tears. The poet would not die a stranger on the earth.

It was curious how many times over the months following the arrival of the Tal Coat Stevens mentioned it to his different correspondents. The poet had invested it with the presence of his protecting "necessary angel"; it accompanied him in his thoughts. He spoke of its "solidity and burliness" (*L* 654), its "virile . . . naturalness" (*L* 656), its "violence" (*L* 653). In it he found his own qualities, actual and wished for. The painting, together with a few other things, sustained him through the winter. He was pleased by the news and the idea of Delmore Schwartz's marriage because it suggested to him that the younger poet had not lost a sense for the nourishing institutions of the past (*L* 651). He delighted in reading the correspondence of Romain Rolland. He looked forward to tasting the Bahri dates he had asked Wilson Taylor to find for him. He enjoyed thinking of his niece Jane's little girl, Susan, now two years old with thick golden braids like those Elsie had once had. He was pleased, too, that William Van O'Connor had found a publisher for a scholarly study of his poems. There was also the annual Yale-Harvard game and the St. Nicholas Society Christmas dinner. He described his feelings of participation in his life now to Barbara Church in a letter dated November 18. After noting that he would be in New York on December 6 for the St. Nicholas bash, he went on: "The cumbersome routine of my year moves more or less in a fixed orbit. What a bore. And yet how all this keeps things going round and round and round in a world in which things seem to prefer to go sidewise. So much is waiting in New York—the Van Gogh show included. Tomorrow three of us are going to the Yale-Harvard game in New Haven, just to keep young, but hardly to look it." But he found the game "dismal," he reported, except for one "bright spot," he noted in a letter to Wilson Taylor: ". . . a very charming couple that sat in the next row but one in front of me. She kept her head on his shoulder throughout the game and every now and then he would turn towards her and they would stay that way for minutes at a time—oh boy" (November 26, 1949). How far Stevens had come from being the "prim letter writer in a wig." Now that he no longer hid his feelings, he appreciated finding others who could express theirs. This, he observed to Rodríguez Feo, was why he was enjoying reading Rolland:

> Of course Rolland was not a man of strong ideas. He was a man of feeling. His reactions to the artistic Goethe, the laborious Schiller, elaboration of the mass on special occasions, aspects of Rome, aspects of the Mediterranean, Mounet, etc., seem to me to be just the sort of thing that I have been greatly in need of. The letters extricated me from contemporary life and placed me in close contact with a man who was not in any sense a big man but who was one of the most interesting men of the last generation or two. (*L* 657)

Luckily for Stevens, the weather as Christmas drew near felt more like spring than winter. Together with his thinking about gifts for Peter this helped lift the usual pall that covered him during the holiday season. Largely because of the mildness, he had enjoyed his recent visit to New York more than he had in a long time. He walked through Fifth Avenue crowds to F.A.O. Schwarz, went to the Pierre for a haircut (*L* 658)—as though commemorating one of his first indulgences in the New York of 1900 when he had emerged from the barber's feeling like "an embalmèd [*sic*] sweet"—bought cakes and cookies at Dean's, and visited the New York Public Library, as he had done often when a young man. When he wrote to Barbara Church on his return to Hartford to thank her for the wonderful evening at her place, he disclosed his yearning for the renewal that the springlike weather suggested:

> New York was stimulating all round. I enjoyed the warm weather—running about in the sunshine, with errands to do—even an errand to the catalogue room of the Public Library to see what was listed under and in respect to Malwida von Meysenbug [a correspondent of Rolland's]. Hélas, what dreary things yesterday's revolutionaries were, particularly the conversational, letter-writing ones. In any event, the catalogue room is a place full of the lesser voices of the past. More and more, one wants the voices of one's contemporaries—*today's* music, painting, poetry, thinking. I don't mean the voices of mere experimentalists, but the actual voices of our actual spirits . . [*sic* punctuation] When I was able to sit in a room full of the paintings of Raoul Dufy: not ambitious or pretentious things, my chief pleasure was in the companionship of Dufy himself, without any factitious chic. It was possible really to see things as he sees them . . [*sic* punctuation] Now that I am back home, we have to content ourselves with snow and fog—and the rockpile [the office]. If I could afford it I should throw away everything I have, each autumn, but particularly this one, and start all over with all the latest inventions: radiant heating ci-inclus, fresh walls, new pictures—and possibly a goat. One would always like to bring home a goat from New York, for the

> humanity of it. I think you must feel this way, too, because your apartment is always a bit different and better: more comfortable, more genial.
>
> The house is already full of Xmas. This is an occasion I never quite rise to and, absurd as it is to say so, I experience a variety of pangs. The hugeness of it abashes me—the upheaval, all the sad little carols bawled out all over the place and all the loving-kindness metamorphosed into incredible things. But so it is. And somehow people do rise to it. Holly and Peter, for example. I took a box of cookies from Dean's to Peter the morning after my return—(Xmas trees etc.) and he came to the door holding a package and said "I have a package." He has, at least, the idea. (*L* 659)

Peter was learning to participate in the ritual cycle of returns and repetitions created by human beings to protect themselves, however slightly, from the knowledge that nothing was ever the same. Stevens was touched; the gesture marked the edge of one of many circles, spheres within spheres. A few days later, on December 19, the poet wrote a return Christmas greeting to Helen Head Simons about how he had come to adjust to the changes around him. She had noted to him that her daughter Sylvia had married a man interested in lizards. Stevens responded that "it was just one of those things. Holly who really [came] from the ~~land of~~ [*sic*] pays de porcelaine [had] turned up at home yesterday with a pair of ski pants with a fur lined overcoat. One just has to grow used to this, that and the other" (December 19, 1949, excised from letter as it appears in *L* 660).

So the year ended. But before its last days Stevens received a note from William Carlos Williams praising his introduction to the Gromaire exhibit as "one of the most impressive pieces of writing . . . that [he had] ever encountered" (December 15, 1949). The *Auroras of Autumn* was finished; Stevens sent off the typescript on the twenty-eighth with a note to Knopf indicating that he wanted more space around each of the poems than had been allowed for those in *Transport to Summer*. The shadows cast in the long twilight of his northern fall needed space to be seen.

❧

The new year was hardly three days old before Stevens sent Mlle. Vidal a heavy book order; it was winter, his season for reading. He couldn't have known at the time he sent his letter how very much he would welcome the things that came. Around the middle of the month the "Giant" had a spill on the ice that injured his ankle. He had to stay home for a few weeks. When he finally began going back to the office, he had to taxi back and forth. As he wrote to Barbara Church on February 1, the month past had been the longest and dreariest he could remember. He had been wholly unable to think or to write. The only "happy thing" about being at home had been being with Elsie—a "true angel" (*L* 663–64). How ironic that after forty years of marriage this was the first extended time he had spent at home with his wife and that it happened around a circumstance that fulfilled one of the strangest wishes he had had for her, as he had expressed in one of the letters of their courtship: that she be his nurse.

Just before his accident—an event that made him acutely aware of the perverse trick of "that monster, the body" to become a highly sensitive detector of change just at the point when what was desired most was a sense of ease, a suggestion of permanence—there had been other reminders of the final inevitability. A favorite aunt of Elsie's had died and Elsie had gone to Pennsylvania for the funeral. Stevens's friend Arthur Powell had written a late Christmas greeting (in response to Elsie's card); he described the effects of the osteoporosis from which he now suffered, commenting good-humoredly but sadly on the ravages of time passing, seemingly ever more quickly. And as though there were indeed some strange connection between these facts of reality and the imagination, by the end of January Stevens had to put his "angel of reality" on the shelf; the idea of the plaquette for "Angel Surrounded by Paysans" had to be abandoned. As he noted regretfully to Victor Hammer, "you and Mr. Kredel can no more be expected to interest yourselves in things that are against the nature of things for you—your nature of things—than I can be. Sincere thanks to both of you" (*L* 662–63).

Steven's state of mind was not helped by the bleak chill of this winter's weather, which seemed like retribution from some malevolent god for the balminess of December. The poet commented on it in almost every one of the many letters he wrote through the icy months. The combination of his physical condition and the cold, dismal days contributed to the way he saw himself as he looked back over his life and at what he had done. In mid-February he wrote to McGreevy:

> I don't know whether or not I have told you that I am expecting to have another book in the early autumn which will contain one or two things with which you are familiar. I shall send you a copy. There is a possibility that the book may go better than any book that I have ever had. And, yet, for my own part, I feel that it is something of an improvisation and not at all what I should like it to be. However, at my age one cannot move in the circles of spaciousness in quite the grand way that one moved a generation ago. If Beethoven could look back on what he had accomplished and say that it was a collection of crumbs compared to what he had hoped to accomplish, where should I ever find a figure of speech adequate to size up the little that I have done compared to that which I had once hoped to do. Of course, I have had a happy and well-kept life. But I have not even begun to touch the spheres within spheres that might have been possible if, instead of devoting the principal amount of my time to making a living, I had devoted it to thought and poetry. Certainly it is as true as it ever was that whatever means most to one should receive all of one's time and that has not been true in my case. But, then, if I had been more determined about it, I might now be looking back not with a mere sense of regret but at some actual devastation. To be cheerful about it, I am now in the happy position of being able to say

> that I don't know what would have happened if I had had more time. This is very much better than to have had all the time in the world and have found oneself inadequate.
>
> Well, I see that the bad weather has got into this last paragraph to some extent. (*L* 668–69)

Earlier in the month there had been brighter notes: William Carlos Williams had been elected to the National Institute of Arts and Letters, and Stevens was genuinely pleased, and pleased, too, by his old rival's invitation to him to visit and stay at Rutherford (*L* 665); e. e. cummings was being considered for the Bollingen, and Stevens was delighted to be asked to be one of his sponsors (*L* 667); Bernard Heringman was fulfilling one of the poet's old dreams and going to live for a while in Paris—to this news Stevens responded: "I suppose that if I ever go to Paris the first person I meet will be myself since I have been there in one way or another for so long" (*L* 665)—and the *Botteghe Oscure* number (autumn 1949) containing his "Half Dozen Small Pieces" arrived and the poet found it "extraordinary" (February 14, 1950). He also was looking forward to getting to know James Johnson Sweeney, another habitué of Barbara Church's circle, who within the next two years would become director of the Guggenheim Museum. But in spite of the vicarious and secondary satisfactions these things offered, the poet still felt in need "desperately for Liberty and Sunshine" (February 17, 1950).

With the beginning of spring things brightened. Just after hearing of Thomas McGreevy's appointment to the directorship of the Irish National Gallery in Dublin and celebrating with him by imaginatively accompanying him on a European tour that included prolonged stays in Rome (and an audience with the pope) and Aix-en-Provence—which prompted this aside from the poet: "On my death there will be found carved in my heart, along with the initials of lots of attractive girls that I have known, the name of Aix-en-Provence" (*L* 671)—Stevens was himself duly honored with the Bollingen Prize for 1949. A series of congratulatory letters and notes followed. Arthur Powell wrote long and appreciatively of how much he had been moved by his friend's lines, even with his own layman's knowledge of poetry and the arts in general. Eleanor Stevens Sauer (Stevens's niece), in keeping with the "simple ways" of Reading, congratulated her uncle on winning $1,000. How much in contrast, Stevens must have thought, was her attitude from that of Arthur Powell's daughter, whose note was penned on the back of a postcard reproduction of a painting of St. John at Patmos. Delmore Schwartz's letter was particularly touching; paraphrasing Eliot's remark presumably about Yeats that a "great poet was one who wrote good poetry at seventy," Schwartz commented that for him, Stevens came to mind as the poet fitting this category. (He also made a point of asking Stevens to visit him and his new wife in New York whenever and if ever he felt like it.) Alfred Knopf, of course, communicated his heartfelt congratulations, inviting the poet to a celebration at his convenience; Stevens responded that fall would be best. Now, too, it was William

Carlos Williams's turn to shower praise upon the "Giant," which he did in a sprawling note attesting to the sincerity of his feelings:

> DEAR WALLACE:
>
> This time it's my time (as e.e.c. might say) to congratulate. Don't spend it all on candied violets.
>
> It's nice to see the old men coming in. Can you tell me why you work so hard to earn a living? Encourage me. I want to quit but everyone warns me that if I do I shall lose my ingenuity or (since that sounds bad) my pristine purity as an amateur. I wonder. In fact I don't wonder at all; I think it's a lot of crap.
>
> It's been a long time coming. All I can add as counsel will be what the colored gal said to her lover: (quote) A little lower. No, a little higher. That's just right, now enjoy yourself.
>
> With the best wishes I have to offer,
>
> Yours as ever, BILL
> (March 28, 1950).

In addition to these and other notes from those who were in one way or another connected with Stevens's "literary life," there were letters from individuals long lost to the poet. One such came from Oscar T. Stager, a contemporary of Stevens who had lived a few doors away from him in Reading until 1892. In answer to his warm congratulations the poet commented: "One of the real advantages of winning a thing like the Bollingen Award is that the publicity that goes with it, which in most respects is a nuisance, has led a number of old friends from whom I had not heard in years to write to me and this is a most agreeable experience" (*L* 675). He went on to observe, sadly, to this old friend he imagined to be "about the same age" as he that until "only a few months ago [he] used to say that [he] felt as if [he were] still 28 or 30," but that since his ankle injury this was no longer the case. He also remembered—or thought he remembered—that one day more than forty years earlier Stager's sister Bess had gotten in touch with him in Cambridge and that they might have gone to a football game together. How strange, the poet must have thought, not quite to remember if one remembered.

All these acknowledgments of fame and success might have made someone less practical-minded walk on air for weeks, but not Stevens. One of his first reactions to the news of the award was to ask Manning Heard, one of his assistants at the Hartford, to investigate whether the $1,000 was taxable. On April 3 Heard was happy to answer that it was not since it was determined to be in recompense for "services promoting the public welfare" (April 3, 1950). These descriptive terms must have tickled Stevens as much as anything else. But did he find himself adequate to any of this bravura?

From the evidence of a letter he wrote to Philip Blair Rice, acting editor of the *Kenyon Review* (John Crowe Ransom was on leave at Indiana University), who had written in mid-April asking the poet for another contribution, it seems that none of the recent celebrations, including the burgeoning of spring, had helped bring Stevens any closer to the Muse. He reported to Rice that he had no new poems and that whatever he might write between then and the end of May was already promised to Renato Poggioli for *Inventario* (April 20, 1950).

But at least Stevens was now moving around more comfortably. He had been to New York on the third Thursday in March for the annual meeting of the livestock insuring group. And sometime during the first two weeks of April he had joined Barbara Church and some other friends on a visit to the Sweeneys' (James Johnson) one evening after having spent a "good time" with Alfred Knopf in the afternoon. Certainly, on these two last occasions, after the news of his recent award, Stevens must have been properly feted, and if he had not still been a victim of his own misgivings about himself, he could have come away from both feeling wholly gratified. But as usual, the poet was "afraid [he had] enjoyed [him]self inordinately" the evening at the Sweeneys' and was "frightfully worried the next day," as he wrote to Barbara Church on April 13, asking her to convey, nonetheless, to the Sweeneys how much he had enjoyed them and their apartment, which he had kept "thinking about ever since" no doubt because of the display of both the latest and the best modernist examples. He also mentioned to Mrs. Church in the same note that he had just returned the script of a Voice of America broadcast he had been asked to do which, he felt, made "much more of an owl of [him] than he [was]." (I have not located this script; it is not "Connecticut," another Voice of America broadcast the poet prepared in 1955 [*OP* 294].)

There seemed to be no escaping the *dis-ease* Stevens felt in himself. It was still as though he examined himself through a monocle, unable to adjust two images of himself that constantly presented themselves.

This feeling found expression in what the poet wrote to William Van O'Connor after reading his just published book, *The Shaping Spirit: A Study of Wallace Stevens*. Though he found the whole thing generally "very well done," he had had a hard time beginning: "The only part of it that was difficult for me was the first chapter. Reading this was like looking over a batch of negatives from the photographer" (*L* 697). It was no wonder. The first chapter, entitled "Stevens as Legend," was built around the perception that "Stevens the man and the poet became a legend because in him the complex pattern of alienation found a personification."[17] It is doubtful that Stevens had ever thought of "alienation" in terms of his relationship to the world; it is doubtful that "alienation" as a term was part of his vocabulary. Nonetheless, seeing how he was perceived through the eyes of someone who was both a careful student of his poems and a scholar attentive to all the details then available about him and his work, Stevens could not deny that there were "objective" grounds for his being seen this way. The effect, for him, was like looking at a photographer's negatives because none of the shadows and colors of the actual scene, his life, were developed. Yet he himself, as indicated by many of the anecdotes O'Connor related, was the one responsible for this. O'Connor's observations gave Stevens pause. Had he perhaps been too successful in keeping "personality hidden before the world," so that in the end the legend of the personality that emerged was one that would detract from the primary purpose of his poetry: to describe the actual "relation between a man and his world"? Ruminating on this split in the way his personality was understood, after a few months Stevens found himself far less pleased with *The Shaping Spirit* than he had originally been. As he wrote in mid-June to Barbara Church, he came, finally, to the conclusion that O'Connor was too purely following the "new critical" attitude, and while things of this sort might please academicians, he was afraid "the whole lot [led] to confusion, and it [was] the duty of anyone who want[ed] to enjoy life to skip them entirely" (*L* 682).

In spite of this judgment, the idea of himself as a legend seems to have contributed to the way Stevens came to shape "The Rock," the poem he worked on through the first half of spring and then sent to Poggioli. It was from a legendary point of view that he looked back on the relation he had had with the world and spoke now "Seventy Years Later"—the title of the first section. Here the notion of the transparent "negative" was translated into the images of "illusion," "shadows," and "nothingness" that came to promise the "birth of sight":

> It is an illusion that we were ever alive,
> Lived in the houses of mothers, arranged ourselves
> By our own motions in a freedom of air.
>
> Regard the freedom of seventy years ago.
> It is no longer air. The houses still stand,
> Though they are rigid in rigid emptiness.
>
> Even our shadows, their shadows, no longer remain.
> The lives these lived in the mind are at an end.
> They never were . . . The sounds of the guitar
>
> Were not and are not. Absurd. The words spoken
> Were not and are not. It is not to be believed.
> The meeting at noon at the edge of the field seems
> like
>
> An invention, an embrace between one desperate
> clod
> And another in a fantastic consciousness,
> In a queer assertion of humanity:
>
> A theorem proposed between the two—
> Two figures in a nature of the sun,
> In the sun's design of its own happiness,

As if nothingness contained a métier,
A vital assumption, an impermanence
In its permanent cold, an illusion so desired

That the green leaves came and covered the high
  rock,
That the lilacs came and bloomed, like a blindness
  cleaned,
Exclaiming bright sight, as it was satisfied,

In a birth of sight. The blooming and the musk
Were being alive, an incessant being alive,
A particular of being, that gross universe.
(*CP* 525–26)

Paradoxically what the poet named as seeming like "An invention, an embrace between one desperate clod/ And another . . ." grounded the lines in reality, developed the empty images with the colors and shadows of feeling. In the next section, then "The Poem as Icon," a figure for the legend as legend beginning

It is not enough to cover the rock with leaves.
We must be cured of it by a cure of the ground
Or a cure of ourselves, that is equal to a cure.
(*CP* 526)

the ambiguous uses of the first and second "It" and "it," at first as nebulous, as uncertain as impressions on negatives, take on precise definition only by our looking back at the assertion of what "It" is in the opening line of the first section: "It is an illusion. . . ." The second "it" then "[w]e must be cured of . . . by a cure of the ground," mirroring what the poet achieved in the previous section by *ground*ing it with the image of the "desperate *clod*." In order to understand what Stevens was laying out here, we must look back at the previous section, just as he was looking back over his life. "The poem is part of the res itself and not about it": The process of unlocking meaning from the darkly lucid negatives of words re-creates the feeling of what the poet himself was doing. Out of this "embrace" between "one desperate clod," the poet, and "another," the reader, "in a fantastic consciousness" come the buds and blooms, the "engenderings of sense" (*CP* 527)—the only paradise we shall ever know.

Looking back on the relation he had had to the world more than forty years before, when still preoccupied with the idea of physical love, he wrote, "It comes, it blooms, it bears its fruit and dies" (*CP* 16), the poet contrasted his present relation. He understood now that there was "nothing else" but illusion, including that of love, but that if grounded in the real, these illusions "bud and bloom and bear their fruit without change" (*CP* 527). Stevens had come to know that what was true was what could not be forgotten, as the Greeks knew in their very voicing of their word for truth, "α'λήθειă." These flowerings from

"The body quickened and the mind in root" (*CP* 527)—images like that of budding, blooming, bearing fruit—that did return again and again, the memories that came back with certainty (not those that trembled nervously outside the stage door of consciousness, rehearsing lines that might make them seem real, like Stevens's uncertain memory of Oscar Stager's sister) were the only evidences that it was not "an illusion that we were ever alive."

In his recognition of these final facts Stevens understood the truth of Socrates' final words in the *Phaedrus,* in which, as William Gass has recently and brilliantly pointed out:

> . . . energy and feeling are joined to order and idea to produce a metaphysical climax not entirely lacking its own passionate outcry and genital spasm. Here, the mind cares; the mind comes.
>
> The word is like the soul itself, that intermediary thing which moves between the realms of Being and Becoming; and if my additions to the myth are not altogether unseemly, then it will be the lower parts of the *logos* as well as the *psyche* that remember the world, and the upper one which gazes on or connects itself to the Forms; and unless these separate aspects of ourselves and our language speak to one another, respond to one another, there will be no match of "thing" to the Form it is said to resemble, no string will stretch from significance to subject, for I argued that such resemblance could not be read from the thing itself, nor predicted from the Form in its featureless silence.[18]

Stevens knew the *Phaedrus* very well. (He used Plato "as a sort of buoy" not only in his youth.) He built, for example, "The Noble Rider and the Sound of Words" around the dialogue's controlling figure, which he quoted in opening his lecture (*NA* 3). Considering the direction Stevens pointed out by making this allusion, it would be difficult to avoid drawing the connections between the poet's images of his buds and blooms and Socrates' "words which instead of remaining barren contain a seed whence new words grow up in new characters whereby the seed is vouchsafed immortality."[19] It would be equally difficult to ignore those between Socrates' sexually charged references and Stevens's of "The body quickened" or in "Things of August" (*CP* 489)—the last longish poem Stevens wrote before "The Rock"—his proposing a "new aspect" of considering the "spirit's sex" and the "sex of its voices." And in the same poem his evocation of "locusts" and "crickets" (*CP* 489) (as in "Le Monocle de Mon Oncle" and in many other earlier poems) reminds us of Socrates' description of their origin in the *Phaedrus* as well:

> The story is that once upon a time these creatures were men—men of an age before there were any Muses—and that when the latter came into the world, and music made its appearance, some of the people of those days were so thrilled with pleasure that they went on singing, and quite forgot to eat and drink until they actually died without noticing it. From them in due course sprang the race of cicadas, to which the Muses have granted the boon of needing

> no sustenance right from their birth, but of singing from the very first, without food or drink, until the day of their death, after which they go and report to the Muses how they severally are paid honor among mankind, and by whom.[20]

Stevens's final poems were proclamations of potency, of eternally possible "engenderings." A "silent rhapsodist," he went back and picked up stitches of meaning and reference; with these he sewed his consciousness to that of his readers. As a result, for each of the years since his death there have been at least as many words as he ever wrote spilled like new seeds themselves in an ongoing rebirth of meaning. In accomplishing this, his "curious fate," Stevens satisfied his desire to be "man number one." In these paper embraces, his readers exquisitely aroused, exhilarated by the movement they give to the lines in which they lose themselves, the poet could disclose himself as lover, unembarrassed by "that monster, the body."

While he had managed to recover his strength and to walk his two miles and more to and from the office during the spring—he had again needed the grounding of his own rhythm meeting the earth to compose his last lines—Stevens was preoccupied with the essential weakness of old age: being unable to avoid the ultimate loneliness of individual existence. Had he really been aware of this all his life, and was this what O'Connor meant by "alienation"? Stevens projected his feeling. In mid-April, returning Arthur Powell's letter of congratulation, he attempted to solace his friend for what he had perceived as his "loneliness." Powell felt compelled to write back assuring Stevens that he was not "experiencing loneliness" (April 24, 1950). Later, in mid-May, hearing from Norman Holmes Pearson the details surrounding the suicide of F. O. Matthiessen, Stevens replied and interpreted Matthiessen's wish to be buried near his mother as the desire "of a man left alone and intensely hurt by it. . . ." He added, ". . . when a man's trouble comes down to the final intimacy he just doesn't give anyone access to it . . ." (*L* 679). Sensing his own loneliness more intensely as he looked back made it increasingly difficult for him to write poetry; this he told Thomas McGreevy on June 1 (*L* 680). The difficulty did not ease. He wrote to Joseph Bennett, editor of the *Hudson Review,* in early December, voicing his regret that though he wished he could send something to him, he had not been writing lately. The reason he gave: "I know what it is that I want to write about. The trouble is that I have not particularly felt like writing about it" (*L* 701).

But the very uttering of his difficulty seems to have freed him from it, at least for the moment; three days later he sent Bennett "Final Soliloquy of the Interior Paramour" (*CP* 524) and followed it up at the end of January 1951 with "The Course of a Particular" (*OP* 96). Before this, however, there were months of painful false starts, broken only by intermittent callings, some of which he did manage to shape into poems.

In mid-July Stevens sent six poems to *Wake*—"As at a Theatre," "The Desire to Make Love in a Pagoda," "Nuns Painting Water-lilies," "The Role of the Idea in Poetry," "Americana," and "The Souls of Women at Night" (*OP* 91–95)—with a note to the editor indicating that since the volume of *The Auroras of Autumn* would be his last, these pieces would probably appear only in some future general collection after their publication in his magazine. The poet was deeply disturbed about completing his last volume. For the man who had lived his life "on paper," such finality spelled death. Stevens did not include any of these six poems in *The Collected Poems*. The voice was a ghost's. It was appropriate that they would appear in *Opus Posthumous*.

These last six poems were forced out of the being already become "the rock," unfeeling. He had escaped the devastating sensation attached to coming to grips with the fact that there were no more chances to change, to show himself, by, as it were, going to "the theatre," as he had done so often as a young man when beset by one of his dark moods. In "As at a Theatre," he conjured "A universe without life's limp and lack," inhabited by "an image of himself"—a shade:

> Even as a vine on her dry pole I support myself now
> on a staff and death calls me to Hades.
>
> (*OP* 91)

It was easier to imagine himself already dead and in Hades than to continue feeling his spirit limp.

In "The Desire to Make Love in a Pagoda" Stevens even emptied desire of desire. After evoking the feeling and place he had known with ferocious intensity in the years of his courtship, when he would have liked nothing more than to take Elsie up Mount Penn to the wonderfully fanciful pagoda and there in the midst of still summer, find a quiet corner at the top of "green green's apogee" where he could undress her slowly, kissing, as he unbuttoned each of the forty buttons down the back of her high-necked Victorian dress, the bit of flesh revealed, the poet conjured not the "second self" that Elsie was but one of his own, so that he remained, in effect, "alone," seeing from the peak and murmuring lines that strangely echoed another shade, John Keats.

In "Nuns Painting Water-lilies" he memorialized the loss he had written about in a letter a year or so earlier with feeling, now without it. In "The Role of the Idea in Poetry" he coldly acknowledged having been "Determined . . . by his father's ghost. . . . The father who does not come to adorn the chant" (*OP* 93). In "Americana" he spelled out as clearly as he could the feeling of not feeling:

> (. . . like
>
> A man that looks at himself in a glass and finds
> It is the man in the glass that lives, not he.
> He is the image, the second, the unreal,

> The abstraction. He inhabits another man,
> Other men, and not this grass, this valid air.
> He is not himself. He is vitally deprived . . .)
>
> These things he thinks of, as the buckskin hoop-la,
> In a returning, a seeming of return,
> Flaunts that first fortune, which he wanted so much.
> (*OP* 94)

And in "The Souls of Women at Night," he spoke directly in the voice of a ghost: "Now, being invisible, I walk without mantilla" (*OP* 94). In this "blindness . . . seeing would be false" (*OP* 95); how could he write more, then, of what he saw? The months ahead were most trying.

The world situation only reinforced Stevens's desperation. As the Korean War became a reality, the poet reread the *Iliad* (*L* 688), looking for some way of transforming the collective madness into nobility. He came to blame the madness as openly on religion as on communisn—"Religion, I am afraid, is part of it. Russia is making a fortune out of life's poverty but she is giving a fury of belief and a fury of hope in return. For my own part, I think that both furies are the results of deception and an incredible control . . ." (*L* 684–85). While he thought "It would be fatal not to stand up to" Russia, he felt he, in fact, belonged to "a vast element that [was] simply not interested one way or the other, but want[ed] to lie in the sun or sleep in the shade" (*L* 687). He had retreated once more, playing dead to the world of politics. As he did, a biting cynicism replaced the usual sardonic cast of his humor in letters. On August 15 he wrote to Rodríguez Feo announcing that *The Auroras of Autumn* had come out, that it was very well done, and that he was having a copy sent, but the publication of the volume did not seem to give him joy. He went on in the letter to ask Rodríguez Feo about the promised photographs of Cuba:

> Where are they? I need some such thing in the dead center of summer and not a particularly pleasant summer either meteorologically or otherwise, except in Korea where it is possible to shoot Communists. Yet I continue to receive occasional messages from Europe which indicate that the mania of Marxism has not yet seized the whole world. Weather or no weather, people still lunch on the terraces of Paris and drink Chablis; and they still travel in Spain; and the lakes of Switzerland are still blue and the little steamers on them toot-toot-toot (in Swiss). (*L* 687)

What had happened to his recent commitment to the real, to getting beyond the distractions offered by dreaming of Switzerland? He knew how many had been undone by death, but he had not thought the idea of death could undo him.

That it had was clear.

The next day he wrote to Barbara Church that this "Summer . . .

drag[ged] along like the days of a woman without any taste regarding what she ought to wear," and he didn't quite know what to do with himself. He was feeling, he noted to her, "a bit low." He thought of going to New York once or twice but somehow couldn't motivate himself to get there. The neighborhood in Hartford was "as quiet as an attic," he reported—the expected "tomb" no doubt playing on the tip of his tongue—and he liked it that way, he commented, with all the children and dogs, signs of life, away on holiday: ". . . if one wakes up at night there is neither breath nor sound. All this is discouraging. Going to bed at nine and getting up at six will soon appear to be great virtues, as no doubt they are" (*L* 689).

Stevens entered death before dying. He had spent his life imagining himself in places he had never seen ("I had . . . looked forward to a particularly busy summer running around all over Europe [in other people's shoes] . . ." [*L* 689]); it would have taken extraordinary effort not to develop from the "microfilm of the imagination" the myriad negatives stored over the years into images of death as, say, possibly, the "negatives" of everything he had ever known.

As Stevens's imagination became involved with death, it finally detached itself from one of its most constant habitations. An inversion, like a last sea change, was taking place, as the poet dissolved his ancient self. On August 25 he wrote to Thomas McGreevy:

> After all, would one really go to Europe to enjoy life if one had the choice nowadays? I don't mean pictures or books of Paris. Wouldn't one just as lief go to some of the blesseder spots over here where there would be no risk of being suddenly ossified by the stare of an Englishman? I believe that my own curiosity about Europe would very easily be satisfied and that the microfilm of the imagination would attach itself a good deal more significantly to some of our own things. Europe is something that for most of us exists as part of our mass notion of things. Conceding that the generations of people there have not lived in vain, it is still probably true that there are infinitely more meanings for Americans in America. The vernal migration to Europe does not disprove this. It proves nothing more than that the mass of people exist [*sic*] in the mass notion of things. (*L* 691)

The transition had been quick, and there were other evidences that the being now conceived was the inverse of the one who had existed up until only a few months before. He wrote to Renato Poggioli on August 23, as he corrected the page proofs of "The Rock," that the last part, which he had liked most when he wrote the poem, he now liked least (*L* 690).

But the poet who began as a child thinking that things proceeded by the opposition of contrasts was used to the movement up and down, and so, even in this period of what seemed to be one of almost total rejection of all that had once been sustaining, he found, as the weather crisped toward the first days of autumn, something "new" that, in turn, touched something old. On September 18 he wrote to Barbara Church: "One of my friends came in the morning [the day before]. We went to visit a part of the country that was new to me. It was like seeing Connecticut as it *was* and I had the same feeling that one has when one is in the woods and is alive to the fact that there are all sorts of things living and moving around" (*L* 692). He had also been to New York during the last week; just sitting on the train and looking out the window, he noted, often helped get him over "periods of restlessness." On his return, however, it was not the outside scene or the promise of the "glitter and gusto of October" lying ahead that stirred him. "There was a pretty girl in a new cloche hat on the train and I enjoyed looking at such pride and pleasure as much as anything" (*L* 692). Was the "Giant" coming to life again? He was trying, but the best he could do was by Christmas "to pretend that [things were] as good as they [were] ever going to be" (*L* 702). Having expressed to Joseph Bennett what his "trouble" had been—that he knew what it was he wanted to write about but had not felt like facing it—had at least allowed him to reach a point of pretense. The intervening months had brought his seventy-first birthday; the day of the Yale-Harvard game when he visited Richard Eberhart and remembered Sybil Gage, "that angel"; Knopf's announcement that he would reissue all the poet's earlier volumes, an honor for which Stevens felt most grateful; the letters of praise for *The Auroras of Autumn* (especially welcome were those from Delmore Schwartz and Norman Holmes Pearson, who both lauded him as the only poet writing major poetry in America, poetry that resolved the "terrifying" [November 12, 1950] dichotomy between the individual and things that were outside); Bernard Heringman's beautiful *explication de texte* that Stevens found the work of a "right reader" (*L* 695), for unlike O'Connor, Heringman focused on the poet as the perfect representative of everyman, not as an "alienated" late symbolist.[21] But none of these events or evidences of his power had helped him. He noted to Emma Stevens Jobbins that only the routine of the office and the mountains of reading at home that he would never have time to get to were "blessings," and they were because they distracted him. Stevens could not get back to the "central." It was finished, it seemed. His last volume had appeared.

As might be expected, Christmas this year was more trying than it had ever been, and Holly's and Peter's being away for the holiday season made it worse. As he wrote to Barbara Church on the day after Christmas—when "an everyday sorrow becomes unbearable"—he felt like "shutting the day and all its feelings out." He wanted to "read all the books," he noted, paraphrasing Mallarmé, to put off experiencing the sadness of his flesh. He was working on the lecture he had been invited to give at the Museum of Modern Art on January 18, "The Relations Between Poetry and Painting," but felt inadequate to the task. He had "to read all the books," too, before he could "think." But then, rather than read what he believed he should read, he read a book on elephants that he had sent away for to England because Peter was interested in elephants, and he listened over and over again to Ernst von Dohnányi's *Variations on a Nursery Song* (*L* 703–04). Peter and the music as he played it were part "Of that which is always beginning, over and over" (*CP* 530). The poet preferred to be obsessed by repetitions to feeling the slice of the "central." What made Christmas "all emotion" was that it was and is one of those days on which the spinning top of time stops and falls, when memories of all past Christmases meet and make the day one that pulls us to the core. Why couldn't Stevens write of this "In verses wild with motion, full of din" (*CP* 16)? While he would have answered, simply, that it was part of his temperament to shrink from Christmas as from loud noises, he would have known, too, that this was an evasion and that he had never adequately answered the "central" question of what had made that temperament.

❧

It was most fortunate that from its very first days 1951 brought Stevens good fortune. News came that on January 18—during the evening after his lecture at the Museum of Modern Art—the Poetry Society of America would award him its gold medal. The lecture itself was, according to Monroe Wheeler, "an immense success . . . old and young said it was the finest in the series" (January 1, 1951), and Wheeler urged the poet to publish this and his other prose pieces. Later in the month Stevens read at the YMHA. When he received a petulant note from Alfred Knopf a few days later complaining of having learned of the previous events only in the newspapers—"Perhaps you'll take me into your confidence one of these days" (January 29, 1951)—Stevens was delighted. He wrote back to Knopf that his note had given him as much pleasure as anything in the last two weeks and added about the gold medal he had received that it was "really swagger" and that he was "proud to have it" (January 30, 1951). He also promised the publisher that in the future he would make a point of seeing him when he was in New York.

The uncertain young man who had argued so vituperatively against what should be expected of "gold medal boys" more than forty years earlier had fulfilled the promise he feared could not be fulfilled. From this point on Stevens lived as one of the heroic shades in Hades. He found that he, in fact, had made a noble reputation out of words "on paper." The fears that had stretched from the time of Henry Church's death until only recently, when he had gone on to McGreevy about the Yeats ceremony, were ungrounded. While this was deeply gratifying, it also meant that the rationalizations Stevens had offered himself about his reputation being mediocre had to be thrown out. What he said would be given attention. Consequently, the most prudent tack in relationship to political matters was to fall back into at least feigned indifference.

For the next two years the poet's life was an almost constant round of being asked to speak on one occasion or another when honors and awards would be offered—instead of blood, as appropriate to his secular time—for the privilege of hearing him. There was no time left for brooding, for Janus to look back. So demanding was the schedule of events that began this January that the poet almost forgot that he was dying. But he did use something as a charm, just in case. He resisted Knopf's repeated urgings that he put together an edition of collected poems. Then in 1954 it was almost as though he had a premonition that he could put it off no longer. (This premonition had been fed by intimations of impending mortality in the form of his no longer being able to eat first this, then the other.)

During these last years there were periods when it seemed that nothing of his old self remained. In the rush of events, with almost every day demanding that he give attention to the figure of the poet he had created, the old movement up and down stopped. Things as they had been all his life changed. Indeed, the last instance of the painful insecurity that belonged to his dark moods occurred early in January 1951 just as there began the whirl of activity in which his spirit would spin and flit over the next few years. This was the letter to Cleanth Brooks apologizing for his imagined offense at the Pearsons' years before. Stevens's sending off this letter now belonged to his last depression, which had reached its depth around Christmas. Attesting to the shift that started to occur as January brought its rewards, when the poet wrote to Norman Holmes Pearson on February 6 and related that he had sent his note to Brooks, he added that he felt "quite relieved":

> . . . at least until another bugaboo took the place of that one. I went to New York and after a reading went to a little party at which I was to meet a number of people whom I was very much interested in meeting. After three cocktails I asked them if they had ever heard the story of the man who etc., etc., etc. After making quite sure they all wanted to hear it, I told it. It is the funniest story in the world, but, curiously, I was the only person that really laughed and I have been worried to death ever since, that is to say, until recently, when I said the hell with it. (*L* 707)

The same old scene had been staged once again, but for the first time the poet could simply dismiss it—"the hell with it." (What the poet did not relate to Pearson—perhaps because he did not remember—was that in addition to the story about the man who, etc., he had given a blow-by-blow description of the fight with Hemingway years before and that in this account the "Giant" came out the hero; this was more than likely the real "bugaboo," the thing repressed that Stevens did not want returned.)

No sooner was the jaunt through January over than February promised a renewed fury of activity. Before the first week was out, Stevens learned that Bard College wanted to award him an honorary degree of Doctor of Letters on March 16. In his February 6 note to Pearson the poet nervously inquired about the etiquette involving caps and gowns: Was he expected to have his own, or would the college provide what was necessary? Within another few days Alfred Knopf, carefully heeding Monroe Wheeler's advice, wrote a letter strongly urging Stevens to put together a volume of his prose. The poet set to work immediately to write "Honors and Acts" (*OP* 238–41), his acceptance speech at Bard. No sooner was the ink dry than he would have to compose another, for on the twenty-third Knopf informed him that he had won the National Book Award (*L* 708). Even before this, Stevens had begun to feel the effects of what this final phase of his life as a full-fledged man of letters was to mean. He wrote to Barbara Church on February 19: "There has been a great deal more literary activity than I care for recently. The more active other people are on one's account, the more one stands still on one's own account" (*L* 707). He had stopped revolving, except in the crystal of his fame.

Realizing that after the National Book Award, the "literary activity" would not diminish, Stevens devised strategies for dealing with the nervousness he continued to experience each time he presented himself in public. "These things must be done as well as one can do them. If I can walk for a few hours beforehand and make myself physically tired, this almost completely eliminates nerves," he wrote again to Barbara Church. He noted, too, that it was a good thing that he was "well-disposed to a reasonable amount of drinking" (*L* 709) to ease the awkwardness he felt at the usual post-lecture/reading/award gatherings. Something else that Stevens did was order from Mlle. Vidal André Siegfried's *Savoir Parler en Public* (*sic* in Stevens's letter to Vidal and on the bit of scrap paper where he had jotted down the title). This touching detail begins to suggest how profoundly committed he was to living up to the image that he had labored so diligently to perfect for so many years. But what had ever happened to the supremely self-possessed boy of seventeen who had won prizes as much for the eloquence of his persuasive delivery as for the power of his argument and images? Beyond the fears about how his physical presence was perceived, could it have been that the erosion of his self-confidence was connected to how deeply he felt inhabited by the spirit of his age? In 1897 it was possible for a properly well-bred young man to speak proudly and certainly about values and truth, about how industry, thrift, and sobriety would help ensure those values and truth. But each year that followed had removed one more block from the edifice of pride and certainty that had been the habitation America had carefully constructed for its idea of civilization. How could the poet who felt himself vibrate with the voices of a million on one string, who returned to his generation what he derived from his generation—as he stated in his acceptance speech for the National Book Award (*OP* 245)—not tremble with trepidation when he presented an image of nobility after the vast devastations that had occurred in his time?

In the midst of fulfilling his obligations to the mythological self he had created, it wasn't surprising that there were moments of private self-doubt as well as public uneasiness. Stevens wrote to Sister Mary Bernetta at the end of March: ". . . I am beginning to feel that publicity is definitely a thing that degrades one" (*L* 711). Nonetheless, he had made himself out of words and now had to live up to them, and so he continued in his rounds, even when it meant being "run ragged." These requests came from the "vast world of other people" (*OP* 245) who now came forward to acknowledge that indeed he did speak for them.

By the end of March, too, Stevens had agreed to put together the prose volume for Knopf within a month or so. However, he refused to include his recent comments at the National Book Awards despite Knopf's and

Weinstock's praise for them; the poet maintained that these remarks were not up to being included in a text that he now foresaw as being used in college classrooms. Within another few weeks he was to accept an invitation to speak at the College English Association meeting to be held at Mount Holyoke College on April 28. For this he would compose "Two or Three Ideas" (*OP* 202–16); in addition, during the same period he would be writing the Introduction to the essays for *The Necessary Angel.* While he set himself to "clearing his mind"—as he put it to Barbara Church—in putting these ideas down, he learned that in June he would have not only his fiftieth reunion clambake at Harvard to look forward to but also the awarding of another honorary degree. This really "set him up," he commented; it was a more than fitting completion to the career he had begun in the college's hallowed halls fifty-four years before as a "special student."

With almost each day bringing more evidence of his stature, Stevens was able to address himself and things as they had been in his time more directly than he ever had. When he presented his "Two or Three Ideas" at Mount Holyoke, he described why and how he had lost the cool assurance of that "special student":

> To see the gods dispelled in mid-air and dissolve like clouds is one of the great human experiences. It is not as if they had gone over the horizon to disappear for a time; nor as if they had been overcome by other gods of greater power and profounder knowledge. It is simply that they came to nothing. Since we have always shared all things with them and have always had a part of their strength and, certainly, all of their knowledge, we shared likewise this experience of annihilation. It was their annihilation, not ours, and yet it left us feeling that in a measure, we, too, had been annihilated. It left us feeling dispossessed and alone in a solitude, like children without parents, in a home that seemed deserted, in which the amical rooms and halls had taken on a look of hardness and emptiness. What was most extraordinary is that they left no mementoes behind, no thrones, no mystic rings, no texts either of the soil or of the soul. It was as if they had never inhabited the earth. There was no crying out for their return. They were not forgotten because they had been a part of the glory of the earth. At the same time, no man ever muttered a petition in his heart for the restoration of those unreal shapes. There was always in every man the increasingly human self, which instead of remaining the observer, the non-participant, the delinquent, became constantly more and more all there was or so it seemed; and whether it was so or merely seemed so still left it for him to resolve life and the world in his own terms. (*OP* 206–07)

While Stevens's sensitivity to the deepest problems of his age should not be underestimated, it is important to remember that the poet had never had in his most intimate relationship the kind of mirroring of the noble self he presented "on paper." Though he had accommodated himself to the eccentricities of his wife's personality, for which he was, in part, responsible and even found in them "perfections," it was clear that the aspects of his being that she reflected were not those that could have helped him gain a measure of public security. The parts that she nurtured were private in the most profound sense. The wish that he had repeatedly expressed to her during their courtship—that their relationship remain "secret" before the world—proved to have been a form of prophecy. Whatever he shared with her, whatever the communication, could not be shared outside. Keeping these parts of himself and her hidden meant that he could never be wholly comfortable, could never show his whole self, so he would be uneasy in public.

One of the last instances of this occurred on the day of the Mount Holyoke lecture, when Stevens was picked up by two members of the college's faculty, Elizabeth Green and Joyce Horner, who were to drive him to the college. On their arrival at Westerly Terrace the poet was not quite ready. While waiting for him, they exchanged a few words with Elsie, who was dressed in a pink housedress and looked, as one of the visitors recorded, "thin and faded, *blanched* . . . as if she had been hiding in the house." Then Stevens appeared:

> JOYCE HORNER: We had a very curious conversation. She said, "What do you teach? My ancestors were concerned with education." Here there was an interruption from Wallace Stevens, who had come in. "Need we go into that?" She went on. She said, "I never went to college, but I made good marks in composition and art, and I got an A in composition."
> ELIZABETH GREEN: I think this was in the fourth grade; I'm sure it was in elementary school.
> JOYCE HORNER: I thought perhaps there was some glow of remembering that she got an A on her own, but "glow" is too strong a word. As if she remembered that she had glowed before she met the man who was too clever for her. She gave us cocoa and biscuits. Wallace Stevens said, "What dry biscuits." She did not say "It is in the nature of biscuits to be dry," but something like it. Then Elizabeth said, "I'd like to hear about your ancestors." She said they were Swiss schoolmasters, the first schoolmasters in Berks County. Well, at that point Wallace Stevens got up, impatiently. "He doesn't like me to talk about myself," she said, "but I do like people to know that I am interested in something besides cooking and cleaning. Oh, dear, you haven't finished your cocoa!" He certainly gave the impression of being dominant. What I surmised, probably most unjustly, was that she had been different earlier, that maybe after childbirth she had changed. She gave the impression of naïveté, beyond any normal adult, in the language, in the sentences she spoke."[22]

The "Giant" had kept Elsie his "Little Girl." His impatient embarrassment that others might discover the more than rational distortion of his image that Elsie's being mirrored was understandable. This was an awareness he could not avoid. The poet could also not have helped being occasionally disturbed by the worry that he himself might be a bit mad, that he didn't have to wait to break down as his father and brother had. Doesn't living with someone who exhibits irrational behavior mean that you, too, become irrational, insofar as there is communication? But, then, for the man who wrote about the value, the potency of the irrational element in poetry, it could have been most useful to test out whether or not it was present in his work by the way this creature reacted. Had this been why he had begun reading his poems to her again?

The drive to Mount Holyoke began with the poet's announcing that he had a sore throat and would not speak at all on the trip. He then talked nonstop. He left his two chauffeurs saying, "I'll tell my wife neither of you made any passes at me."[23] The comedian's one-liners were to distract attention from earlier stings.

With the increased public demands Stevens kept up the old pace of seeing and writing to friends and acquaintances. There were the usual visits to Barbara Church, lunches with James Powers and his son (now at Yale), invitations to Bernard Heringman to accompany him on trips to lecture just so they would have some time to speak. There were even new correspondents added to his list of worthy regulars: Peter Lee, a Korean poet and student of literature to whom the poet was as helpful and forthcoming as he had been and continued to be with Rodríguez Feo and now, too, Heringman. In his very first letter to Lee it was clear that Stevens had adopted him as one of his ephebes: "Isn't it the function of every poet, instead of repeating what has been said before, however skillfully he may be able to do that, to take his station in the midst of the circumstances in which people actually live and to endeavor to give them, as well as himself, the poetry that they need in those very circumstances?" (*L* 711). "The great machine of life goes round and round and round," Stevens wrote to McGreevy in mid-April, adding, now that he had no time for the reflection out of which his poems used to grow, "and little comes of it, except that one is able to hold on" (*L* 715). This was something to be thankful for, and the poet knew it. William Carlos Williams, he heard, had just recently suffered a stroke and would not speak at the College English Association meeting together with Stevens as planned. Stevens wrote him a warm note after the event, full of encouragement in the face of old age and with a wish that it would be possible to see him. Williams tenderly answered with the first letter he typed after his stroke; he commented that though either of them might "croak" at any minute, he agreed that they were not old. His penned, broken "Bill" closing the letter showed the force of his determination to believe just that.

In the letter to McGreevy in which Stevens described his present orbit, he noted his renewed deliberate turning away from politics and the current scene; he spoke as a son of Emerson:

> I want very much to live quietly this summer, writing as may be but in any case turning my back on politics. It may be necessary sooner or later to

> emigrate to some region where there are no radios, newspapers etc. and where the natural man can be himself, saying his prayers in the dark without fear of being slugged. Over here it is just as if there was a war going on, vast crowds of young men in training camps, restrictions on this, that and the other. (*L* 716)

And in a letter to Barbara Church on April 22 in which he described how a walk to the office in spring seemed to restore his "innocence—almost the lost innocence of the U.S.A.," he curiously invoked the name of God three times in different contexts: twice as parts of well-worn expressions (about Henri Pourrat, "God bless him"); about himself in connection to his plans about attending her next party on May 10 ("I must add God willing"); and as part of a French quotation celebrating spring ("Ah, mon dieu"). In the absence of the makings of his imagination, this word, the idea of which had been filled by his imagination—"God and the imagination are one"—returned as a synecdochal charm to ensure that all was well, a shorthand notation, as it were, of a poem.

That there was no time for poetry did not mean that the activity of Stevens's imagination ceased. It simply attached itself to different things. Two magnificent yet very different instances of this were a particular letter to Barbara Church and another to the company that manufactured the undershirts the "Giant" wore. Written within a week of each other, they exhibited in their "style"—which, Stevens had pointed out in his "Two or Three Ideas," was equivalent to "a poem," "a man," or "a god" interchangeably—two of the most characteristic features of his imagination. In the first, written as the poet conjured Barbara Church preparing to leave for France, Stevens composed the scene behind a scene behind a scene he had never seen: the steamship that would carry Mrs. Church back across the Atlantic approaching New York while those preparing to sail on her themselves were approaching New York from different quarters; the voyage Mrs. Church would make in the company of these various fellow travelers, who before that moment had had nothing in common except their convergence on the point of departure; the house at Ville-d'Avray being prepared for her as she sailed. He had, in fact, made his imagination that of Barbara Church, the ship, the house, the other passengers. But as though realizing this was a kind of runaway use of the imagination that he would have preferred, for reasons of value that were ultimately "moral"—something he now expressed belonged to his poetry (*OP* 206)—to be attached elsewhere, he added the term "alienation" to his vocabulary in describing how he would feel in a country where there was a difference of language.

The second instance can be appreciated only directly. It was the last in an exchange of letters that had begun the previous December, when questioning, like the best of lawyers, the meaning of an ambiguous clause—". . . we can make them to any length that you desire" (December 22, 1950)—in one of the letters of the Deimel Linen Mesh Company the poet wanted to know, like the thrifty Puritan he was reared to be, if when undershirts had shrunk, it was possible to send them back to the company to be lengthened by the weaving in of an additional panel. The company, admitting that it was indeed possible to misinterpret the clause, responded that unfortunately this miracle was not yet possible. The poet finally sent the following:

> GENTLEMEN:
>
> Will you please make for me a half dozen undershirts of your lightest weight cotton mesh. I believe this is your 100 weight, but I could be wrong. In one of your letters you refer to my last measurements as those covered by your invoice of January 14, 1949, CI5408. I measured one of my shirts yesterday. The length from the center of the back on the top edge to the edge at the bottom of the back is 39″. From the center of the front to the edge at the bottom of the front in 33½″. Since your material shrinks a good deal, it may be you can find a set of measurements which are larger than the 39″ and 33½″ measurements which I have just spoken. Those would be the ones I want because I find that I have another half dozen of your shirts which are too short for me. I am not trying to buy a necklace, but undershirts. In other words, if you should find that you have measurements something like 40″ by 35″, those would be the ones I want. But I don't want to get them too long. Perhaps when your shirts grow old they stretch instead of shrink. Anyhow, 39 by 33½ at least.
>
> (May 14, 1951)

Stevens's imagination delighted in the idea of how the recipient of his letter would react to his sentence about necklaces. Imagining this effect was like imagining the effects he expected to draw from particular moments of illumination in poems—"angelic hilarity"—moments when through veils of words, sentences arranged, thought following thought in careful measurement of perception, one human actor in the comedy of life recognized another, his muzzy belly parading itself beneath a too-short shirt.

By the beginning of June Stevens had committed himself for more public duty by agreeing to give the Moody Lecture at the University of Chicago in mid-November. At the same time he was accepted for membership in the Century Association, which pleased him greatly, he noted, because now he would have someplace gracious to stop for fresh springwater on days in New York when he found himself panting in the crowds and still unwilling to drink tap water from coffee shops like the rest of mere mortals. By midsummer he was diligently preparing "A Collect of Philosophy" (*OP* 183–201) for the Moody Lecture by gathering from Jean Wahl and Jean Paulhan—the latter at Barbara Church's suggestion—their thoughts on the subject of which philosophical ideas were inherently poetic. While Wahl's lengthily scrawled indications of sources were offered in the best spirit and Paulhan's were insightful, they missed the point as far as Stevens was concerned (*L* 725). But Paulhan had contributed at least the major perception of Max Planck as one of the great figures in the world whose idea of the world was inherently poetic:

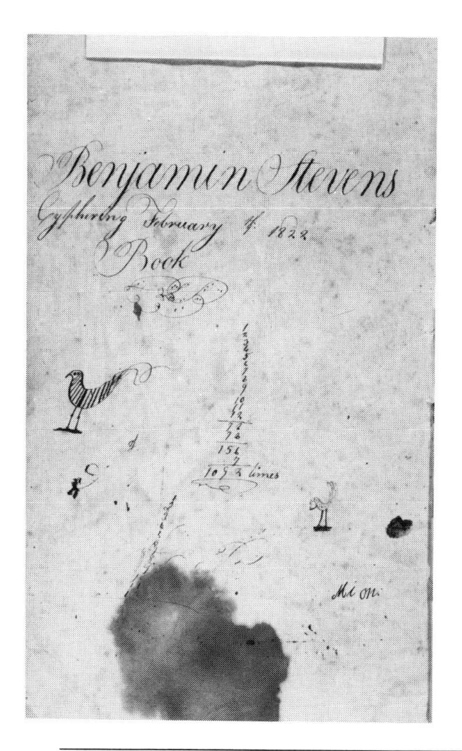

The theatre is filled with flying birds,
Wild wedges, as of a volcano's smoke, palm-eyed
And vanishing, a web in a corridor

Or massive portico. A capitol,
It may be, is emerging or has just
Collapsed. The denouement has to be postponed . . .

This is nothing until in a single man contained,
Nothing until this named thing nameless is
And is destroyed. He opens the door of his house

On flames. The scholar of one candle sees
An Arctic effulgence flaring on the frame
Of everything he is. And he feels afraid.

THE AURORAS OF AUTUMN

Pages from the cyphering book of Benjamin Stevens, Wallace Stevens's paternal grandfather.

Angry men and furious machines
Swarm from the little blue of the horizon
To the great blue of the middle height.
Men scatter throughout clouds.
The wheels are too large for any noise.

And you, my semblables, in sooty residence
Tap skelton drums inaudibly.

There are shouts and voices.
There are men shuffling on foot in air.
Men are moving and marching
And shuffling lightly, with the heavy lightness
Of those that are marching, many together.

And you, my semblables—the old flag of Holland
Flutters in tiny darkness.

DUTCH GRAVES IN BUCKS COUNTY

The original Dutch burial ground in Feasterville, in Bucks County, where Wallace Stevens's ancestors, John Stevens and his wife, Saartje Stoothof, are buried.

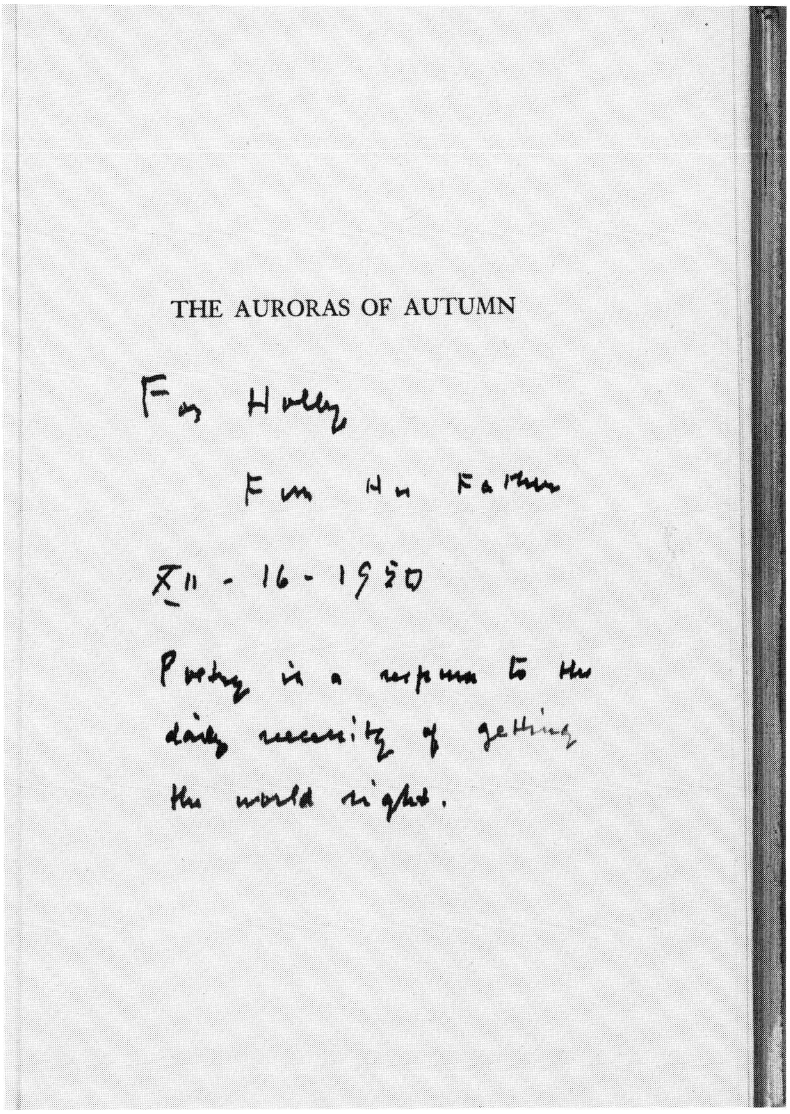

THE AURORAS OF AUTUMN

For Holly

From Her Father

XII - 16 - 1950

Poetry is a response to the daily necessity of getting the world right.

The title page of *Auroras of Autumn* inscribed by the poet for his daughter. The inscription reads:

"For Holly
From Her Father
XII–16–1950

Poetry is a response to the
daily necessity of getting
the world right."

November 12, 1951

Mr. Herbert Weinstock,
c/o Alfred A. Knopf Incorporated,
501 Madison Avenue,
New York 22, N. Y.

Dear Mr. Weinstock:

Here is a list of selections which I think is representative. It is based on a different theory from the theory that was at the bottom of the selection I made for you some time ago. It is not a list of things that are what "the author wishes to preserve." It should not be advertised that way; it is representative.

The books have been mentioned to facilitate reference. The index should not mention the books.

In the case of An Ordinary Evening I desire to use only the short form of that poem as in the enclosed pamphlet, of which I can supply other copies if needed.

At the end of the list there are some poems to be added or deleted as the paging of the book requires.

I shall be passing through New York on November 15th on the way to Chicago and will give you a ring to find out if everything is as you wish it. I shall not be in the office after Wednesday until next Monday. My stenographer will not be able to take on any home work, after she returns to the office, for some little time. Accordingly, if it is part of my obligation to furnish a manuscript text, please have the job done in New York and send me the bill.

Your copy of The Necessary Angel is on the way back.

Sincerely yours,

P.S. Angel Surrounded By Paysans was first printed in Poetry in London, which will no doubt consent to its use.

W.S.

1.

Book	Title of Poem	Length
Harmonium	Earthy Anecdote	1 page
	In The Carolinas	1/2
	The Paltry Nude ..	1
	The Plot Against The Giant	1
	Infanta Marina	1
	Domination of Black	1 1/2
	The Snow Man	1/2
	Le Monocle de Mon Oncle	6 1/2
	Ploughing On Sunday	1
	Cy Est Pourtraicte ..	1 1/2
	Fabliau of Florida	1/2
	Another Weeping Woman	1/2
	From the Misery of Don Joost	1/2
	The Worms At Heaven's Gate	1/2
	Of the Manner of Addressing Clouds	1/2
	Of Heaven Considered As A Tomb	1/2
	A High-Toned Old Christian Woman	1
	Depression Before Spring	1/2
	The Emperor of Ice-Cream	1/2
	Tea at the Palaz of Hoon	1/2
	Disillusionment of Ten O'Clock	1/2
	Sunday Morning	6
	The Virgin Carrying A Lantern	1/2
	Bantams in Pine Woods	1/2
	Anecdote of the Jar	1/2
	The Bird with the Coppery, Keen Claws	1

2

Book	Title of Poem	Length
	Life Is Motion	1/2
	To the One of Fictive Music	1 1/2
	Hymn From A Watermelon Pavilion	1
	Peter Quince At the Clavier	3 1/2
	Thirteen Ways of Looking At A Blackbird	3 1/2
	Nomad Exquisite	1/2
	Sea Surface Full of Clouds	4 1/2
	Tea	1/2
The Man With the Blue Guitar	The Man With the Blue Guitar	28
	The Men That Are Falling	1 1/2
Ideas of Order	Sad Strains of A Gay Waltz	1 1/2
	The Idea of Order At Key West	2 1/2
	The Sun This March	1/2
	Evening Without Angels	2
Parts of A World	Dry Loaf	1 1/2
	Country Words	1 1/2
	A Rabbit As King of the Ghosts	1 1/2
	Asides on the Oboe	2 1/2
	Metamorphosis	1
Transport to Summer	~~[illegible]~~	~~[illegible]~~
	Flyer's Fall	1/2
	Late Hymn from the Myrrh Mountain	1/2
	A Completely New Set of Objects	1/2
	Men Made Out of Words	1/2
	The House was Quiet and the World was Calm	1
	Extraordinary References	1/2

3

Book	Title of Poem	Length
	Credences of Summer	7 1/2
	Notes Toward A Supreme Fiction	32
The Auroras of Autumn	Large Red Man Reading	1 1/2
	This Solitude of Cataracts	1 1/2
	A Primitive Like An Orb	6
	An Ordinary Evening In New Haven	12
	Angel Surrounded By Paysans	1 1/2

Adjustments

Add at	1	Invective Against Swans	1
	2	Auroras of Autumn	15
	3	Things of August	10
Delete		Infanta Marina	1
		A Primitive Like An Orb	6

"The selections for the Faber book were made by myself. Mr. Weinstock of Knopf's office seems to think it was a good selection. He has had a lot of experience with just that sort of thing and he ought to know. My own choice would not be likely to be what others would choose. Nevertheless, I tried to choose what I thought would be representative" (*Letters,* p. 750).

A letter from Stevens to his editor at Knopf concerning the Faber and Faber edition of his *Selected Poems*. Stevens enclosed his handwritten list and plan for the volume.

Receive Mt. Holyoke Honors DN
6/2/52

South Hadley, June 2—Honorary degrees were awarded to two persons as Mount Holyoke College held its 115th annual commencement today. Recipients were Emma Perry Carr and Wallace Stevens, shown left to right.

"I don't know whether Marianne Moore told you [Barbara Church] about Mt. Holyoke. They gave me a degree up there a few days before the affair at Columbia. At Mt. Holyoke there was a feeling of friendliness and of being human, which women seem to create. The Commencement exercises were typical Americana. The address was given by Dr. Frederick Eliot, the president of the American Unitarian Society, who is a first cousin of T. S. Eliot: their fathers were brothers—a very simple address, neither a sermon nor an oration . . ." (*Letters,* p. 756).

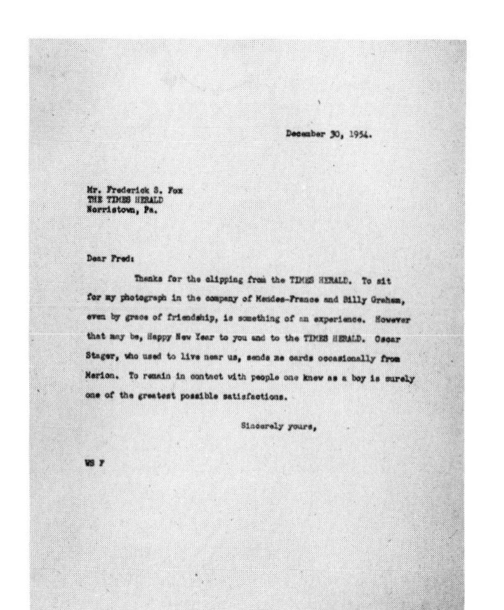

December 30, 1954.

Mr. Frederick S. Fox
THE TIMES HERALD
Norristown, Pa.

Dear Fred:

Thanks for the clipping from the TIMES HERALD. To sit for my photograph in the company of Mendes-France and Billy Graham, even by grace of friendship, is something of an experience. However that may be, Happy New Year to you and to the TIMES HERALD. Oscar Stager, who used to live near us, sends me cards occasionally from Marion. To remain in contact with people one knew as a boy is surely one of the greatest possible satisfactions.

Sincerely yours,

WS F

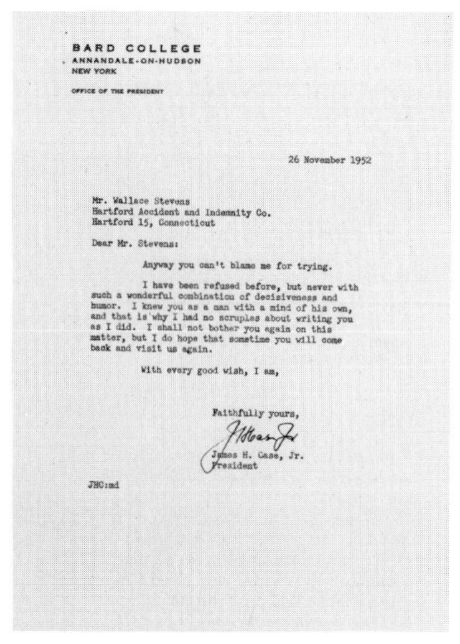

BARD COLLEGE
ANNANDALE-ON-HUDSON
NEW YORK

OFFICE OF THE PRESIDENT

26 November 1952

Mr. Wallace Stevens
Hartford Accident and Indemnity Co.
Hartford 15, Connecticut

Dear Mr. Stevens:

Anyway you can't blame me for trying.

I have been refused before, but never with such a wonderful combination of decisiveness and humor. I knew you as a man with a mind of his own, and that is why I had no scruples about writing you as I did. I shall not bother you again on this matter, but I do hope that sometime you will come back and visit us again.

With every good wish, I am,

Faithfully yours,

James H. Case, Jr.
President

JHC:md

An exchange of letters typical of Stevens's later years when he dealt with the details of reality more and more as a comedian.

8

The Times Herald

"An American Newspaper Since 1799"

Entered at Post Office Norristown Pa., July 21, 1923, under the Act of March 3, 1879 as second class matter Published every afternoon except Sunday by Norristown Herald, Inc., Markley, Ann to Airy Sts. Phone NO 8-2500 Frederick S. Fox, President and Editor; William H. Shelton, Vice President and General Manager.

Terms of Subscription: Single copy, 7c. Weekly by Carrier 42c. Subscription rates by mail, United States outside of Norristown.

1 Year	6 Months	3 Months	1 Month
$21.00	$10.50	$5.25	$1.75

Payable in advance. For other rates apply Circulation Department.

The Associated Press is entitled exclusively to the use for republication of all news dispatches credited to it or not otherwise credited to this paper and local news of spontaneous origin published herein. Right of republication of all other matters herein is also reserved.

NORRISTOWN, PA., MONDAY, DEC. 27, 1954

Conducted under the true Federal principles laid down to us by the Political saviour of his country, the immortal Washington. — From the Norristown HERALD, June 15, 1799.

TOP NEWS OF THE YEAR

THIS is the season for picking the ten biggest news stories and personalities of the year. Annually the Associated Press asks member papers to make their selections of the top events and then tabulates them.

In an informal score keeping game, we kept our nominations to check against the concensus of other editors. Here is the comparison.

We picked the ten best news stories in the following order: 1—McCarthy hearings and censure case; 2—Supreme Court outlawing of public school segregation; 3—Five congressmen shot by Puerto Ricans; 4—East Coast hurricanes; 5—Fall of Dien Bien Phu; 6—Oppenheimer case; 7—Democrats win House and Senate; 8—Sheppard murder trial; 9—Death of Vishinsky; 10—Explosion on the U. S. Carrier Bennington.

The Associated Press consensus was: 1—McCarthy; 2—Segregation; 3—Congressmen shot; 4—Democrats win; 5—Signing of pacts to rearm Germany; 6—Fall of Dien Bien Phu; 7—Geneva Conference and Indo-China settlement; 8—East Coast hurricanes; 9—Korean war prisoner exchange completed; 10—Atoms for Peace plan.

We were probably so close to Hurricane Hazel it made an overall appraisal of its news value difficult, but are still unconvinced that Vishinsky's death and the blast on the Bennington in which 100 American sailors were killed don't rate in the top ten events. We felt that the Korean prisoner exchange was a continuing story from 1953. So were the A-bomb developments and the foreign negotiations.

Our choices for the personalities of the year were: Man of the Year, John Foster Dulles; Foreign Affairs, Mendes-France; Religion, Billy Graham; Labor, Walter Reuther; Science, Dr. Enrico Fermi; Literature, Wallace Stevens; Sports, Roger Bannister; Entertainment, George Gobel.

The Associated Press selections: Man of the Year, Mendes-France; Foreign Affairs, John Foster Dulles; Religion, Billy Graham; Labor, Walter Reuther; Science, Dr. Jonas Salk; Literature, Ernest Hemingway; Sports, Roger Bannister; Entertainment, George Gobel.

Hemingway and Salk were honored for what they did in previous years rather than 1954. Our selection of Wallace Stevens may have been influenced by a personal friendship and admiration for the poet-business executive, whose omnibus book of poems was published this year. Hemingway belonged in last year's list and we picked him at that time.

Ere the year is out we shall publish our own annual reviews of local, general and sports events.

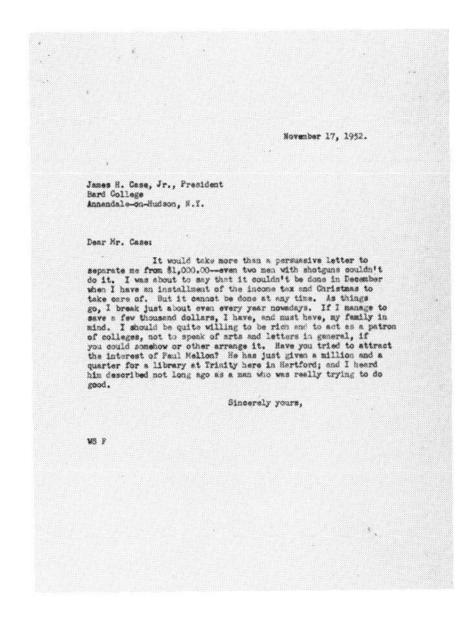

November 17, 1952.

James H. Case, Jr., President
Bard College
Annandale-on-Hudson, N.Y.

Dear Mr. Case:

It would take more than a persuasive letter to separate me from $1,000.00—even two men with shotguns couldn't do it. I was about to say that it couldn't be done in December when I have an installment of the income tax and Christmas to take care of. But it cannot be done at any time. As things go, I break just about even every year nowadays. If I manage to save a few thousand dollars, I have, and must have, my family in mind. I should be quite willing to be rich and to act as a patron of colleges, not to speak of arts and letters in general, if you could somehow or other arrange it. Have you tried to attract the interest of Paul Mellon? He has just given a million and a quarter for a library at Trinity here in Hartford; and I heard him described not long ago as a man who was really trying to do good.

Sincerely yours,

WS F

Another example of the poet as comedian.

Called 'Best Least-Known Poet'

Wallace Stevens, 75, Dies; Insurance Official and Poet

Special to the Herald Tribune

HARTFORD, Conn., Aug. 2.—Wallace Stevens, seventy-five, one of the most distinguished of contemporary American poets and vice-president of the Hartford Accident and Indemnity Co., died today at St. Francis Hospital.

Mr. Stevens had undergone an operation in April and re-entered the hospital on July 21 for further treatment. His home was at 18 Westerly Terrace in Hartford.

When Mr. Stevens was awarded an honorary degree by Yale University last June, he was cited as one in whom "the two worlds of practical affairs and art have found a perfect marriage." He led his double life far from the limelight of publicity, his name coming to the fore only when he received one of the many honors heaped upon him in recent years. He was, in fact, as one critic put it, "the country's best least-known poet."

Herald Tribune—United Press

Wallace Stevens

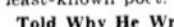

Told Why He Wrote

"Poetry," Mr. Stevens once explained, "is my way of making the world palatable. It's the way of making one's experience, almost wholly inexplicable, acceptable."

To one critic, Mr. Stevens was "the most finished poet of his age." To another, his poetry was "a strangely fastidious and hermetic art." To a third, his perspective was "that of the man of art, the museum—and concert-goer, the student of French Poetry . . . the esthete in the best sense of the word."

To Mr. Stevens—who composed his poetry as the urge seized him, often on scraps of paper brought to his office for his secretary to transcribe—his "unromantic" life was important.

"It gives a man character as a poet to have this daily contact with a job," Mr. Stevens himself said. "I doubt whether I've lost a thing by leading an exceedingly regular and disciplined life."

Attended Harvard

He was born in Reading, Pa., where his father, Garrett Barcalow Stevens, was a lawyer. He attended Harvard, where he specialized in English and began to write poetry. For a year he was a reporter on the "New York Tribune." After graduation from New York Law School in 1904, he worked for several law firms and in 1916 joined Hartford Accident and Indemnity as head of its surety claims department. He became a vice-president of the company in 1934.

So shy a person was he that critics wondered that he ever published any of his works. For some reason, however, in 1914, at the age of thirty-five, he submitted four poems for the $100 prize offered by the late Harriet Monroe, then editor of "Poetry" magazine. Miss Monroe had her November, 1914, "War Number" all made up, but tore it apart to make room for "Phases," as the then unknown poet named his work.

The following year "Poetry" again awarded him $100, this for a one-act play in free verse called "Three Travelers Watch a Sunrise," which was produced at the Provincetown Theater in New York in 1920. A second playlet "Carlos Among the Candles," was presented in Milwaukee and later in New York's Neighborhood Playhouse, but neither was published.

It was not until 1923 that Carl Van Vechten persuaded Alfred A. Knopf to publish Mr. Stevens' first book, "Harmonium," although before, as after, its appearance his poems appeared in anthologies. Nine more volumes followed and last fall, "The Collected Poems of Wallace Stevens" appeared to mark his seventy-fifth birthday and earn him this year the Pulitzer Prize for poetry and his second National Book Awards gold medal.

Recognition came quickly in the past decade. In 1945, with such volumes as "Ideas of Order," "Owl's Clover," "The Man with the Blue Guitar" and "Notes Toward a Supreme Fiction" published, he became a member of the National Institute of Arts and Letters. The following year he received the Harriet Monroe Poetry Award and in 1951 the gold medal of the Poetry Society of America. His later works included "Transport to Summer," "Three Academic Pieces," "The Auroras of Autumn" and "The Necessary Angel."

Held Honorary Degrees

He held honorary degrees from Harvard, Columbia, Wesleyan, Mount Holyoke and Bard as well as Yale. The role of a poet, he said earlier this year when he received his second National Book Award, "is simply to remind him, in the midst of all his hopes for poetry that he lives in the world of Darwin and not in the world of Plato. He does not accept them as a true satisfaction because there is no true satisfaction for the poet but poetry itself."

Surviving, besides his wife are a daughter, Mrs. Holly B Stevens, and a grandson. A funeral service will be held at 3 p. m. Thursday at the Pratt Funeral Home in Hartford.

And blue broke on him from the sun,
A bullioned blue, a blue abulge,

Like daylight, with time's bellishings,
And sensuous summer stood full-height.

The master of the spruce, himself,
Became transformed. But his mastery

Left only the fragments found in the grass,
From his project, as finally magnified.

He left half a shoulder and half a head
To recognize him in after time.

These marbles lay weathering in the grass
When the summer was over, when the change

Of summer and of the sun, the life
Of summer and of the sun, were gone.

He had said that everything possessed
The power to transform itself, or else,

And what meant more, to be transformed.
He discovered the colors of the moon

In a single spruce, when, suddenly,
The tree stood dazzling in the air

TWO ILLUSTRATIONS THAT THE WORLD
IS WHAT YOU MAKE OF IT

WALLACE STEVENS, NOTED POET, DEAD

1955 Pulitzer Prize Winner, Vice President of Hartford Insurance Companies

STRESSED IMAGINATION

Sought to 'Make the World Palatable' Through Works Challenging Intelligence

The New York Times, 1951

Wallace Stevens

Special to The New York Times.

HARTFORD, Aug. 2—Wallace Stevens, vice president of the Hartford Accident and Indemnity Company and a Pulitzer Prize winner for poetry this year, died in St. Francis Hospital today. He was 75 years old.

Mr. Stevens joined the local insurance company in 1916 as head of the Surety Claims Department. He was named a vice president in 1934. He also was a vice president of the Hartford Livestock Insurance Company.

A native of Reading, Pa., Mr. Stevens attended Harvard and received a law degree from New York Law School.

He is survived by his widow, Mrs. Elsie V. Kachel Stevens, and a daughter, Miss Holly B. Stevens, also of Hartford.

His Work Reviewed

Wallace Stevens was a weaver whose threads were words. He spun webs to trap his moods.

"Hence, unpleasant as it is to record such a conclusion, the very remarkable work of Wallace Stevens cannot endure," wrote Percy Hutchison, the late poetry editor of The New York Times.

Mr. Hutchison had just reviewed the new edition of the poet's "Harmonium." That was in 1931, eight years after the volume first appeared. The poetry editor described the poems as closest to pure poetry. He explained that such works depended for their effectiveness on the rhythms and tonal values of words used with only the remotest link to ideational content.

He remarked that the poems were "stunts" in which rhythms, vowels and consonants were substituted for musical notes. But this achievement is not poetry, Mr. Hutchison said before adding:

"From one end of the book to the other there is not an idea that can vitally affect the mind, there is not a word that can arouse emotion."

Yet Mr. Stevens would not compromise with the imagination that in his poems was reality.

He was 44 years old when "Harmonium," his first book, was published in 1923. It contained the four poems that appeared in a special 1914 wartime number of Poetry Magazine.

He had begun writing poems upon his graduation from New York Law School in 1904, when he took a job as a reporter on The New York Tribune before beginning his law practice.

In "The Collected Poems of Wallace Stevens," which appeared in 1954 to mark his seventy-fifth birthday, came the realization that he had, in fact, twisted an idea or two into his poetic yarn without dulling the shimmer of the finished product. His earlier illusions were now positive beliefs expressed freely in verse.

When his poems sometimes seemed obscure, he explained:
"The poem must resist the intelligence
Almost successfully."

However, in his personal and business life there was a very clear discipline. "It gives a man character as a poet to have this daily contact with a job," Mr. Stevens told a newspaper reporter five years ago in an interview.

He said that he composed his poems just about anywhere. Usually, he said on another occasion, he got most of his ideas when on a walk.

Mr. Stevens said that poetry was his way of making the world palatable. "It's the way of making one's experience, almost wholly inexplicable, acceptable," he said.

Defined Poet's Role

In recent years he felt a sense of imminent tragedy in the world, and to this situation a poet addresses himself, he said. "What he gets is not necessarily a solution but some defense against it," Mr. Stevens remarked.

In "The Necessary Angel," a book of his essays published in 1951, the poet said:

"My final point, then, is that imagination is the power that enables us to perceive the normal in the abnormal, the opposite of chaos in chaos."

His volumes of poems include "Ideas of Order" and "Owl's Clover" in 1936, "The Man With the Blue Guitar" in 1937, "Parts of a World" in 1942, "The Auroras of Autumn" in 1950. He won a National Book Award in 1950 and again in 1954.

Columbia University gave him an honorary degree in 1952. Harvard University had conferred a similar honor on him the year before. And in 1949 he received the Bollingen Prize in Poetry from Yale University. He also received the 1951 Gold Medal of the Poetry Society of America.

"The quantum theory to which he refers is not a thing to be assimilated offhand" (*L* 725).

By the end of June the poet had received his honorary degree from Harvard—". . . for me . . . the highest prize I can ever win," he noted to Barbara Church, now traveling though postwar Europe in a brand-new Cadillac that, she thought, people stopped agape to look at because it was an American car bearing French plates. (Her husband's humble habits had obviously not infected her, the poet may have thought.) Stevens was especially tickled that the award was conferred in the presence of his class gathered for their fiftieth reunion. With his "morale up to an all-time high" (*L* 720), the "Giant" felt able to tackle even what he was most hesitant about: the philosophic ideas that he had thought he was "too erratic and inconsequential a thinker" with a "bad memory" to handle; hence, the project for "A Collect of Philosophy."

Before he had completed the first working draft of his lecture, Stevens learned of the death of Arthur Powell. Unlike his reactions to the news of the deaths of other important people in his life, the poet seemed hardly to stop in his tracks with this loss. It was almost as though since he had himself been living as his own shade in the glory of his reputation, he had lost sight of what loss of body and breath meant. Was this what he had meant when he wrote to Sister Mary Bernetta about being "degraded" by publicity?

While Stevens wrote to McGreevy that he should like to go back "home"—"chez moi"—for a holiday because doing so when he was young had always been like going back to "mother earth" and made him feel "rather furiously set up and independent," he did not. He doubted whether he "would pick up any such restoration nowadays" (*L* 728). What was there to restore? we might ask. Could he feel any more powerful and independent than he felt now? Or any more degraded and alienated, so that renewal seemed impossible?

The summer came to an end, and fall began with more and more evidences of his fame. Vincent Persichetti wrote, introducing himself as the composer of a song cycle built around twenty of the poems, ending on "Thirteen Ways" as the synoptic mirror of all. The poet was intrigued and pleased by Persichetti's implicit recognition of his own project for "The Whole of Harmonium." Arriving as if to celebrate his seventy-second birthday, the first copies of *The Necessary Angel* showed themselves to be, to the poet's mind, "très coquet," which was his translation of Elsie's simple observation that "everything [was] all right" (October 9, 1951). He did not seem to notice how she again shrank from the public recognition of his potency. Within a few days of this Herbert Weinstock wrote that Faber and Faber (under the direction of T. S. Eliot), at the suggestion of Marianne Moore, wanted, as was long overdue, to publish an edition of his selected poems. At about the same time Stevens was also asked to serve as a judge for the next year's National Book Award in poetry. It might be expected that with all this he would have been able to celebrate his victory. But things had not changed that much. As he wrote to Barbara Church on his birthday, nothing mattered much—except, he added, one thing, Holly's divorce, now final. He paid the $1,980 lawyer's bill happily as he continued to pay his daughter's rent, to send her a monthly stipend with, usually, a delightful note and, often, "a little bit more." This expense was a small price to pay for the possibility of her happiness and the privilege of being able to stop and see her and Peter occasionally on his way back from the office. The relationship that evolved between them in these last years could alone have accounted for stopping the old movement up and down.

Though at Christmas this year Stevens felt his usual desire to shut out what it made him feel, he was finally able to locate the source of his "sensation" about the holiday: It was in the mechanical crudeness of the way this day, which should have been devoted, he noted to Rodríguez Feo (*L* 735–36), to renewing old friendships, writing letters, and visiting friends, had come to be celebrated. For the first time he expressed nostalgia for the Christmases of his childhood, as he wrote to Barbara Church (December 17, 1951), when the things of "feeling and delicacy" that truly made it a "precious holiday" (*L* 735) still existed. Stevens's ability to recollect and voice the loss he experienced marked the real change that had come about. Paralleling this coming to terms with things as they had become, the poet made a kind of profession of faith in response to a question about his belief in God put to him by Sister Mary Bernetta: "I am not an atheist although I do not believe to-day in the same God in whom I believed when I was a boy. But to talk to you about God is like explaining French to a Frenchman" (*L* 735). While his answer was gently evasive, it also revealed his willingness to expose himself. The reply was not encoded in some theoretical framework pointing away from the self to poetry—such as "God and the imagination are one"—but was a direct, if negative, declaration. He had also just recently formulated in "Two or Three Ideas" that God, man, and poetry were interchangeable terms identifiable in the "style" each one exhibited in making the immanent perfections of existence apparent. "Let be be finale of seem/ The only emperor is the emperor of ice-cream"—a very slippery character. It isn't surprising that in feeling his own power there were days when he felt "like an assassin" (*L* 734). The one poem that remained in his folder for 1951 was "Madame La Fleurie":

> Weight him down, O side-stars, with the great weightings of
> the end.
> Seal him there. He looked in a glass of the earth and thought
> he lived in it.
> Now, he brings all that he saw into the earth, to the waiting
> parent.
> His crisp knowledge is devoured by her, beneath a dew.
>
> Weight him, weight, weight him with the sleepiness of the
> moon.

It was only a glass because he looked in it. It was nothing he
could be told.
It was a language he spoke, because he must, yet did not know.
It was a page he had found in the handbook of heartbreak.

The black fugatos are strumming the blacknesses of black . . .
The thick strings stutter the finial gutturals.
He does not lie there remembering the blue-jay, say the jay.
His grief is that his mother should feed on him, himself and
what he saw,
In that distant chamber, a bearded queen, wicked in her dead light.
(*CP* 507)

Mother, oh, Mother, is it you who will punish me?

❧

Another year began: 1952. It would be as busy as, if not busier than, the one just passed. On the third Stevens received a note confirming the arrangements for a reading he was to give at Wellesley College on the fourteenth. Later in the month he was in New Haven for a meeting of the Bollingen committee, on which he had agreed to serve for the awarding of the current prize, which went to Marianne Moore for her *Collected Poems*. (Later the same year Moore would also win the National Book Award—for which Stevens was again one of the judges, another of his many commitments—and the Pulitzer Prize for the same volume.) Unfortunately, within the same few days Stevens received word that "A Collect of Philosophy" had been rejected by Paul Weiss, to whom he had sent a copy for the *Review of Metaphysics*. Feeling a stab to the potent being he had in the past months conjured himself to be, the poet refused to consider resubmitting it for publication elsewhere. The paper he had been so pleased with as disclosing "modern man as one to be measured by the greatness of poetry or rather by the idea of the greatness of poetry" (*L* 734–35) he now did "not really think well of" (*L* 736). But he took the death of this figure in his stride as well. "It is hard to get away from the machinery once it has started to go round," he wrote to Barbara Church on January 28 (*L* 738), and the great machine was working to keep alive what was alive; no use stopping it to mourn over what could not be. Perhaps he truly was an erratic and inconsequential thinker. Did it matter given the obvious greatness of his poetry? Or the greatness of poetry itself? In this spirit he sent his congratulatory wire to Marianne Moore for the National Book Award:

I knock this morning at your door
To bow and say Forever! Moore!
(*L* 738)

But there was at least one sign that the "Giant" had been unsettled by what he thought the rejection of his piece indicated. He again fell into using a discriminatory cliché, this time in a public situation where its effect was quite shocking. It happened during the meeting of the National Book Award committee that gave the poetry prize to Marianne Moore. While waiting for Peter Viereck, the last of the judges, delayed by a snowstorm, to arrive, the other five (Winfield Townley Scott, Selden Rodman, Conrad Aiken, Wallace Stevens, and William Cole) passed the time looking at photographs of previous meetings of National Book Award judges. Gwendolyn Brooks appeared in one of these. On seeing the photo, Stevens remarked, "Who's the coon?" (The meeting, it should be noted, took place after lunch, which for the poet had probably begun with two healthy martinis and continued with a fine bottle of wine.) Noticing the reaction of the group to his question, he added, "I know you don't like to hear people call a lady a coon, but who is it?" What was going on here? Was the poet simply revealing his barbaric self unguardedly under the effect of his "lunch"? Or was the comedian at work, shocking the group with his remark and restated question. The play on the category mistake in his follow-up question suggests that perhaps Stevens did simply want to disturb his fellow judges and enjoy the effect. He then went on to tell one of his jokes: "Pat and Mike were on the trolley car, and a nun came in and sat down. Mike said to Pat, 'What's that?' And Mike said, 'That's a nun.' Pat said, 'Why's she called a nun?' 'Because she never had none and will never get none!'" His last contribution was to the group's discussion concerning bad language in poetry; he observed, "There is this poem that mentions a womb. I can't even pronounce the filthy thing." The business done, his attempts at punning finished, the "Giant" excused himself early, noting as he put on his topcoat that he had a date with a lady[24]—no doubt an appointment for cocktails at Barbara Church's. "Thus, our bawdiness/ Unpurged by epitaph, indulged at last,/ Is equally converted into palms" (*CP* 59).

In the spirit of converting everything into palms, Stevens continued to support others who would contribute to the greatness of poetry—for example, Richard Wilbur, whom, since their first meeting at the Poetry Society awards the year before, Stevens had been actively nurturing.[25] He had recommended him for a Guggenheim and on January 24 communicated to Norman Holmes Pearson that he wanted to have Wilbur considered for the next Bollingen should he not win the Guggenheim. With Wilbur himself he exchanged ideas that were, to his mind, germane to the understanding of poetry and the imagination, as on February 19, when in connection to the younger poet's observations on the work of Gaston Bachelard, Stevens noted: "G. Bachelard is upside down. The great part of the imaginative life of people is both created and enjoyed in polar circumstances. However, I suppose that without being contrary, one can say that the right spot is the middle spot between the polar and the anti-polar. It is the true center always that is unapproachable or, rather, extremely difficult to approach" (*L* 740). The "true center," where one came to know oneself without evasion by a single metaphor—that was the place for the figure of the poet as virile youth to approach.

On the same day Stevens also wrote to Rodríguez Feo and described his feeling as spring drew near, now that he was the shade of his old self:

> Tomorrow I am going to New York to do a number of errands and otherwise nothing at all. Perhaps I shall have my hair cut. I know almost no one there any more, so that I am like a ghost in a cemetery reading epitaphs. I am going to visit a bookbinder, a dealer in autographs, Brook's about pajamas, try to find a copy of Revue de Paris for December because of an article about Alain that it contains, visit a baker, a fruit dealer and, as it may be, a barber. An ordinary day like that does more for me than an extraordinary day: the bread of life is better than any souffle. I have joined a club down there in order to rescue a place from the placeless.
>
> I suppose the coming on of spring has much to do with this state of mind. It is almost as if everything was going to be all right again—as if the boards were to be taken down, the windows washed, fresh curtains put up, all on account of the arrival of a rich aunt who before she leaves will whisper in my ear that she intends to leave everything to me, including her chic little villa in Almendares, next door to the blackest eyes in Cuba. Ah! Mon Dieu, how nice it is to drop fifty years in the waste-basket. It is the same thing as writing a poem all night long and then finding in the morning that it is so much the best thing one has ever done—something to make them ring the chimes. (*L* 740–41)

Meanwhile, as always, more things continued to arrive from Mlle. Vidal to keep him abreast of the news in Paris; yet another composer, Ian Wisse, wrote and sent the poet, this time, a copy of a cantata composed around "Thirteen Ways"; Peter Lee sent an offering of a beautiful scroll that the poet found to have the "impression of something venerable, true and quiet" that also belonged to the best poetry (*L* 742); and there was news of yet another death, Livy's. The poet mounted the obituary notice of Edwin Stanton Livingood, the friend with whom he had walked often through the woods around Reading, reciting poetry aloud. There must have been moments now of willingly believing in a fiction where after death the shades of noble souls met and again walked together and spoke of the great poem of earth.

March came roaring with words of more awards. The president of Columbia University wrote first, inviting Stevens to accept another honorary degree at that year's commencement on June 5; this was followed by an invitation from Mount Holyoke, where the degree would be conferred on June 2. The poet seemed to recover his old self. Between the end of January and March 24 he composed six poems, which he sent (to be followed by three others before they all appeared in the *Hudson Review*) to Joseph Bennett. On the same day he wrote to Barbara Church, apropos of her recent remarks about *Der Rosenkavalier,* that he had been trying to reproduce the effects of its haunting chords. But while he again found voice "on paper," he backed away from speaking publicly as he had been doing so often the past year. In his return letter to the president of Mount Holyoke, he expressed how moved he was by the news of the honor but refused the invitation to speak. Perhaps some answer to this latest curious inversion lay in the words of the poems he composed as he composed himself for his final voyage. Now, after his imaginary sojourn in Hades, where he had, as it were, spoken with Tiresias, this passage did not seem so frightening. Something had changed, so much so that in sharp contrast with three or four months before, when nothing had seemed to matter, now everything did: the smell of cookies—"Elsie's bakeing, backing, baking, or whatever it is . . ."—filling the house when he arrived home from his third Thursday in New York with the livestock group and then, later, Barbara Church and Marianne Moore (*L* 743); Peter's wide-eyed wonder as he sat in his grandfather's lap listening to stories about elephants with two trunks, one bass and one tenor (*L* 744); the calls of robins in early mornings and evenings (*L* 744); two large willow trees on the side of the slope nearby that "really [got him]" (April 21, 1952). Everything was deepened with meanings that the words of his poems disclosed.

The group of poems that Stevens sent off on March 25—"To an Old Philosopher in Rome," "The Poem That Took the Place of a Mountain," "Vacancy in the Park," "Two Illustrations That the World Is What You Make of It," and "Prologues to What Is Possible" (*CP* 508–17)—announced the poet's return to earth; he had gotten over having finished his "last volume" and had committed himself to loving as fully as possible whatever time remained. He would not look away from any fact but meet it directly—not as a shade but as the old animal he was. The first step in this dance with death was taken not alone, however, but in company with the imagined figure of Santayana, whom he conjured in his room in Rome hearing the same music as he. His spiritual-surrogate father of years before would take the lead on the "threshold of heaven" (*CP* 508). Of course, what Stevens perceived about the "old philosopher" he knew in himself: the desire "to escape/ From fire"—from the myth of hell—"and be part only of that of which// Fire is the symbol"—sun, light, intelligence, pure spirit; the necessity now that he "[s]peak to [his] pillow as if it was [him]self" (*CP* 509), "speak . . . without speech" (*CP* 510)—"Whereof one cannot speak, thereof one must be silent." Each day that passed made it more difficult to speak as each day was now passed with the full consciousness of what it meant to be about to die.

In this group of poems it was as though death itself walked across the snow, its silent footsteps inescapable in the cold, still nights. The most constant aspects of Stevens's surroundings—the arbor in Elizabeth Park that he had seen change through forty-six years, the "certain house" where he had lived his days—began to seem to him unreachable, unfathomable, mysterious. In "Vacancy in the Park" the poet shaped these feelings into some of the simplest but most powerful lines he had ever written. Feeling the rightness of the metaphor

> It is like a boat that has pulled away
> From a shore at night and disappeared
> (*CP* 511)

he must have mused on whether this description of what it was like to die was apt because things as they are were that way or whether it seemed apt because of all he had read and remembered over so many years about crossing the river Styx.

In "Prologues to What Is Possible" he developed the metaphor as though it were his alone. His lines rolled like long sea waves; his craft became the magical weightless crystal he described, the art that carried him to brilliant transcendence. Through a series of subtle transformations the poet entered the craft that was of rocks that became crystal that was himself still attempting to penetrate the first and last "syllable without any meaning" (*CP* 516) that stood beyond the alphabet of his days. The watery syllable that in middle age outdid him would now, if he entered it, shatter him. But in his having become himself the rock, the crystal, shattering would mean bursting into countless fragments of light so that at the same time as the metaphor stirred his fear, it increased "all of his hereditary lights" and he felt the "puissant flick" (*CP* 517) that spawned new engenderings—"fragments . . ./ From his project . . . finally magnified" (*CP* 515).

The comedian was completing his voyage; after so many years his craft became him. He rounded up into the wind of words that moved him, making adjustments for his final course, remembering what could not be forgotten, the truth of lines that he had learned to handle from others, and he recorded what he did and saw in these poems as in a log. As though realizing, in the process of developing the metaphor of the boat leaving shore, that indeed the images that were preparing him for death came from Greek mythology, before the summer was out, Stevens composed "The World as Meditation," in which he named Ulysses as one of the figures his imagination had been following. Like him, he had paid his visit to Hades before his time for the final passage arrived, and it had given him the strength to return to his patiently waiting Muse.

The other poems of the group were equally triumphant. "The Poem That Took the Place of a Mountain" proclaimed the power he felt. He surveyed himself and all he saw from what he himself had created. At peace atop himself he beheld the sea-C-see, his "unique and solitary home" (*CP* 512). He was "Removed from any shores, from any man or woman, and needing none" (*CP* 516). Lines from these different poems rushed together, met, and separated like the currents of the sea itself, but he no longer had to stem their verboseness; he had become one with them. No explanations were necessary. The terms that appeared now needed none. He had made himself transparent. Anyone who had read his poems all along the way would not need any more words to see him through these. Hence he would not speak at Mount Holyoke and planned never to speak again before a public audience. (Only his unprecedented second National Book Award in 1955 for *The Collected Poems* would break this silence.) As for poetry, there was one reading at Harvard to which he was already committed; he thought it would be his last.

On May 1, back again in Cambridge, his voice weakened now as much by age as by anything else, the poet slowly spoke his shaped syllables. As he noted to Bernard Heringman, his reading had been taped without his knowledge, but he wasn't disturbed. This was both ironic and lucky. The regular sound system in the overfull auditorium was not working, so almost all who were there—with the exception of Richard Wilbur, who had introduced him and was also onstage, and a few others nearby—could not hear a word. Out of deference for the poet, however, all remained in their seats without complaint during what was, according to Wilbur, a beautiful reading. Stevens was disgruntled on learning of this later, but then had an enjoyable evening at "Jack Sweeney's (brother of Jim)" in the company of Wilbur, William James's son William, and others. He was pleased his reading had been preserved. He spoke easily and at length about his time at Harvard with Royce and Santayana and came away without being afraid he had offended anyone.

Spring and summer passed quickly with work at the office, the usual exchange of letters, and additional responses to at least some of the increasing number of people who wrote. Here and there, in answer to a particular question, the poet voiced a carefully modulated political view—to Barbara Church about Henri Pétain, for example, whose difficult position he understood (*L* 747), and to Norman Holmes Pearson about the London *Nation,* which, he noted, he had read for years until it got so socialistic that there was no other point of view expressed. To Sister Mary Bernetta, Samuel French Morse, and the other essentially literary correspondents, he clarified certain points concerning himself and his work and praised aspects of theirs. Though he continued to receive new things to read from Mlle. Vidal, he found himself reading less and less. By the end of summer, all the poems for the *Hudson Review* finished and sent off, Stevens again felt oppressed by the pressure of events, so much so that as he expressed it to Barbara Church, this was the first summer he had not liked:

> This has been the first summer that I have ever disliked. Summer has always made me happy. This year it did not belong to us and was like a foreign oppressor and this has made me low-spirited and blank: or perhaps I should say reduced me to a state of unrelieved realism. I saw a report the other day that only thirty pianos had been sold in Austria last year. Over here the presidential election, so far as the New Deal is concerned, is based on the idea that the poorer people were never so well off as they are now. How well off they are remains to be seen with bankruptcy facing the country unless there is a change of policy . . [*sic* punctuation]. My own corner in this great advicus is concerned only with poetry. There is going to be a *Selected Poems* published in London shortly. I returned the proofs yesterday. The book seemed rather slight and small to me—and unbelievably irrelevant to our actual world. It may be that all poetry has seemed like that at all times and always will. The close approach to reality has always been the supreme difficulty of any art: the communication of actuality, as [poetics?], has been not only impossible, but has never appeared to be worth while because it loses

> identity as the event passes. Nothing in the world is deader than yesterday's political (or realistic) poetry. Nevertheless the desire to combine the two things, poetry and reality, is a constant desire. The next *Hudson Review* will contain a number of my things and I look forward to its appearance. As one grows older, one's own poems begin to read like the poems of some one else. (*L* 760)

A few days later Stevens heard of the death of Santayana in Rome and was grieved. His feelings, opened up through the last months of involvement with the Muse, did not allow him to regard it coolly, as he seemed to have regarded Arthur Powell's death during the period when he himself moved like a shade. He mourned that the old philosopher had kept "reason" as his only "jealous mistress." He knew what privation this meant from his own involvement with "the law, which is only a form of the reason," as he noted to Barbara Church (*L* 761).

By the time of his birthday Stevens felt "as blank as one of the ponds which in [the] weather at [that] time of year [were] motionless" (*L* 762). He was nearing the "ultimate slate," the "final hue." About a week later he wrote to Thomas McGreevy about what he felt he would like to be able to do in the face of his "blankness": "At my age it would be nice to be able to read more and think more and be myself more and to make up my mind about God, say, before it is too late, or at least before he makes up his mind about me. And I should like to walk more and be in the air more and get around more. But it is all incompatible with paying taxes and trying to save a little money" (*L* 763). He went on to McGreevy, Sister Mary Bernetta, and others about how busy the work at the office kept him but now communicated not so much the saving grace of routine it offered as the sense of pressure he felt to work enough so that he could leave behind what would be necessary for Elsie, for Holly and Peter, beyond what the increasing taxes consumed. The slight tone of bitterness at the way things were was understandable. The "Giant" was tired. And now that he had found his voice again, he would have liked more time. He still dreamed of the long poem. The group of seven short poems he sent on November 12 to Margaret Marshall for the *Nation* comprised only 115 lines ("An Old Man Asleep," "The Irish Cliffs of Moher," "The Plain Sense of Things," "One of the Inhabitants of the West," "Lebensweisheitspielerei," "The Hermitage at the Center," and "The Green Plant" [*CP* 501–06]). How had this come about? Stevens must have questioned himself. Did everything become its inverse as one neared the end? Up until now it had always been short poems that were trying and this had led him to prefer prolonged attention to one thing. Now there were only short poems, new beginnings. It was a matter of time.

And these poems—he might have expected, after the last burst of reveling in the revelations of transcendence, more. But the summer had not nourished him. He felt disturbed about his age—"as if [he] stood outside the destiny common to people" (*L* 759)—about the weather, politics; even the strawberries he so loved disturbed his digestion. These poems were of the "effete vocabulary of [a] summer [that]/ No longer [said] anything" (*CP* 506). He was dying again with the season, but now with his feelings as well as his imagination tied to the process of decay. He was angry. In spite of what might remain—the "green plant" that glared, "outside of the legend, with the barbarous green/ Of the harsh reality of which it [was] part" (*CP* 506)—he would not. "The shadows of the trees/ [seemed] like wretched umbrellas" during this autumn, this fall into nothingness. Through these seven poems the poet walked with death. For the first time he openly searched for his father as he had for his mother almost all his life: "Who is my father in this world, in this house,/ At the spirit's base" (*CP* 501). He was trying to solve the problems he had described to McGreevy, trying to settle his accounts with God before it was too late. The greatest problem of his age—the will to believe—was the greatest problem of his age now, as the days dwindled into "two worlds . . . asleep" (*CP* 501). A dumb sense possessed him in a kind of solemnity.

The sense of what it was for him to live these days—each one broken by his knowing that as it passed it could be his last—is perhaps best expressed by "Lebensweisheitspielerei." While its title suggested that this passage into wisdom, too, should be regarded as a game, another neat trick of the comedian's, its lines paced out the denying end of repetitions:

> Weaker and weaker, the sunlight falls
> In the afternoon. The proud and the strong
> Have departed.
>
> Those that are left are the unaccomplished,
> The finally human,
> Natives of a dwindled sphere.
>
> Their indigence is an indigence
> That is an indigence of the light,
> A stellar pallor that hangs on the threads.
>
> Little by little, the poverty
> Of autumnal space becomes
> A look, a few words spoken.
>
> Each person completely touches us
> With what he is and as he is,
> In the stale grandeur of annihilation.
>
> (*CP* 504–05)

The old master of irony returned to rehearse his own funeral.

Though he tried as in "The Hermitage at the Center" to transform the cold dry noise of the leaves on the macadam into an image of the desired, as of old—

> The leaves on the macadam make a noise—
> How soft the grass on which the desired
> Reclines in the temperature of heaven—
> (*CP* 505)

it was impossible. Nothing was sustaining. Suddenly and repeatedly all was dissolved and gone.

There was not even a mention of Christmas this year.

❧

Only after almost two weeks of the new year had passed did the "Giant" refer to the holiday. "You might think that Christmas in itself would be a diversion," he began a letter to José Rodríguez Feo, but "after seventy-three of them Christmas, too, is part of the normality of the normal" (*L* 766). Perhaps because of what he had seen in writing his last group of poems, Stevens once more took a sharp turn away from everything but the routine of the office, as he went on to express to Rodríguez Feo in the letter referred to above, a letter characterized in its first half by the movement of his imagination through its lines as through a poem. Just as when during the previous spring he had not been writing poetry his letters to Barbara Church and the undershirt company exhibited characteristics that usually found their way into poems, so now, too:

> The sudden, sleek, sliding of the Rio Yayabo [which the poet's Cuban friend had mentioned in his previous letter, primarily, as he later reported, to delight Stevens with the sound of its name] is truly a wand.
>
> Are you visiting some new scene? A young man in a new scene, a new man in a young scene, a young man in a young scene—excuse my guitar. Up here the guitars are stacked along the attic walls for a while.
>
> We have had a really winter week-end—snow, sleet, rain. I wanted to stay in bed and make for myself a week-end world far more extraordinary than the one that most people make for themselves. But the habitual, customary, has become, at my age, such a pleasure in itself that it is coming to be that that pleasure is at least as great as any. It is a large part of the normality of the normal. And, I suppose, that projecting this idea to its ultimate extension, the time will arrive when just to *be* will take in everything without the least *doing* since even the least doing is irrelevant to pure being. When the time comes when just to be does in fact take in everything, I may just do my being on the banks of the Rio Yayabo.
>
> You will already have observed the abstract state of my mind. This is in part due to the fact that I have done little or no reading, little or no writing or walking or thinking. I have not been to New York. In short, I have been working at the office, nothing else: complaining a little about it but content, after all, that I have that solid rock under my feet, and enjoying the routine without minding too much that I have to pay a respectable part of my income to the government in order that someone else representing the government may sit at the Cafe X at Aix or go to lectures at the Sorbonne.

The Democrats, if they are Democrats, have gone to incredible lengths in introducing their conception of things into American life and practice; and just to think of things as they were twenty-five years ago makes one feel like William Cullen Bryant's great, great grandfather, to use an expression that someone else used not long ago. Perhaps the only actual piece of bad luck that I have had is to allow myself to become conscious of my age. A correspondent in Paris takes a more cheerful attitude and writes:

"Ne me parlez plus de vieillesse. Le destin des artistes et des poètes est précisement de ne pas vieiller."*

It is a good deal truer than one thinks that one's age is largely a matter of paying attention to it or of not paying attention to it. I am beginning to feel that it is quite necessary no longer to pay attention to it.

The only news that I have is the awarding of the Bollingen prizes. Last year was not a conspicuously good year for poetry in this country. The most respectable book published was MacLeish's volume of collected poems. There was a difference of opinion, however, about the awarding of the prize because, while William Carlos Williams had not published a volume of poetry last year, his position is such that there is a feeling that he ought to have a prize because of his general value to poetry. The result of all this was that the Bollingen people awarded two prizes. Williams is said to be in bad physical condition. I believed that he had had a stroke. But I did not know that he had in fact had three strokes and is unable to use his right side. Moreover, since he is now almost 70, I imagined that when he retired he did so because he was able to live modestly without being active. This appears to be untrue. He was invited to act as consultant in poetry to the Library of Congress, some time ago, and agreed to take on the job. I don't know how much it pays but not a great deal. Then the rumors began to circulate that he was a Communist and the people in Washington have never allowed him to occupy his chair, so to speak. Of course, I have no idea whether or not he is a Communist. But, since he is a man who is interested in anything new that may be going around, the chances are that he has interested himself in the subject and I suppose that the only way to interest yourself in such a subject is to associate with Communists. So far as Williams himself is concerned, he is the least subversive man in the world. The question in his case is not what he would do but what his associates would do. I am told that this experience is causing him a great deal of anxiety. As I say, I have not the slightest knowledge of what the facts are but I infer from the attitude of the people in Washington that something has been discovered, which I regret because Williams is one of the few people in this country that really has an active and constant interest in writing. Now, if something has been discovered and if his record is not clear, one wonders what effect this may

* "Do not speak to me anymore of old age. The destiny of artists and poets is precisely not to grow old."

> have on the Bollingen Prize which is already involved on Pound's account. But I think that the Bollingen people and the government occupy different positions. I don't see how the government could be expected to countenance any man who is committed to throw bricks at it. Of all people, Williams would be the least justified in throwing bricks at it anyhow because his case is typical of the philosophy with which America treats those who come to it from elsewhere. It is true that he was born in this country but neither one of his parents were, unless I am mistaken. (*L* 766–68)

Rodríguez Feo must have delighted in seeing the poet's process of verbal play at work, as in the second paragraph above in which Stevens presented his Cuban friend with the gift of elucidating one of his key metaphors. As he showed here, the movement of his mind through language, through a sentence, and playing with the qualifying terms was like playing variations on the guitar. Out of this kind of improvisation came new accords. It was out of this semantic juggling that he had created the title "Dry Birds Are Fluttering in Blue Leaves" and countless other images that reflected his mind's kaleidoscopically turning a phrase, a perception, to see how many times it could be done before the phrase was no longer recognizable, before the perception lost its integrity, its truth. Here was a basic lesson for a "right reader" in how to read the man of many tropes: Think of any poem as one or a series of images in the mind's kaleidoscope, the images like cubistic arabesques, all variations on one beginning fact, and the scene observed through the kaleidoscope that then gets turned and turned and turned. The game is to find the basic scene, perception, image—the "central"—through the variations. This was an iconic analogue of musical process: "All art should aspire to a condition of music." The fundamental lesson of art for art's sake had not been lost on the poet.

The letter went on to open doors both on the past and on the future. The wish that opened the third paragraph was to re-create the world of R. L. Stevenson's hero of counterpane atop his blanket-mountain surveying the sprawling landscape of his imagination. The return of this figure, in which the poet had recognized himself and which he had developed brilliantly to his own ends in the past long gone, was revealing, especially since it was followed by a wish for the future that he would simply *be*—when he would have stopped revolving even in the crystal of his mind. To be in that way, to stop, represented the wish not to die.

The poet went on, unable to separate his comments and puns—on "X-Aix"—on politics from his concern with age. He lost himself finally in thoughts about Williams and the Communist witch-hunt. Stevens no doubt silently commended himself on his prudence through the last few years, though there was probably at least a twinge of regret that things were the way they were, for it would have been most valuable for him, too, to learn of what was new more directly than he had been able to from all his reading.

Another measuring against a different poet had opened the year and could have predisposed Stevens to feel that he wanted to stop where he was and remain seventy-three forever. On January 7 the poet wrote to Bernard Heringman, responding to his New Year's greeting and to a question about an edition of collected poems:

> Knopf's collected edition, which may actually come to be called a selected edition, is something for 1954, when I shall become 75, if I am still around. When I consider the excitement that is being caused by Carl Sandburg's 75th birthday, I am embarrassed. They are having a big party for him in Chicago. Governor Stevenson has declared this week, I believe, to be Carl Sandburg Week. They are going to give him a gold medal shortly in New York, and, with a shrewd eye to business, that becomes any poet, he has just issued the first volume of an autobiography which it appears can be added to indefinitely. I dread to think that on the occasion of my own birthday they will probably ask me down to Washington to address a joint session of Congress and mount guard day and night in front of my house here in Hartford. Carl raises goats. They produce something like forty gallons of milk a day, which makes it seem either that they are very large goats or that he has a lot of them. This is the last straw. I shall have to take up raising ducks, or some such thing. But, of course, the long and short of Carl Sandburg is that he is an enormously popular person, who likes everybody and whom everybody likes, in turn. On several occasions when he was in Hartford he brought his guitar out to the house and sang for us. Such warmth and friendliness are their own reward. (*L* 765)

Beyond his irony and humor the poet seemed to be protesting too loudly. In response to the pomp and ceremony surrounding Yeats, Rilke, and Valéry that he had written to McGreevy about just over four years before, he had taken the sting out of his projection that he would never be so publicly regaled by rationalizing that in America, largely because of its vastness and the differences between various regions, the general recognition of the importance of a poet was impossible. But now here was all this hoopla about Sandburg; the only rationalization possible at this point was that the Chicago poet was "an enormously popular person who like[d] everybody and whom everybody like[d]." How awful it must have been for the man who so wanted to become "man number one" to think that on his seventy-fifth birthday there would be nothing like the party there had been for this other "gold medal boy." (That these thoughts were truly disturbing and that Stevens was being at least unconsciously disingenuous in his "embarrassment" for Sandburg are supported by the evidence of his reaction to a different kind of public acknowledgment of a brother poet. The bust of Robert Frost gracing the rare book library at Harvard had almost the same effect on Stevens as the Commendatore's statue on Don Giovanni. These markers of a stature he had not reached himself plucked the chord that sounded his father's old "afflatus" theme, which, interestingly, reappeared in connection with poetry once more in "To an Old Philosopher in

Rome," in which a father's presence was evoked: ". . . misery, the afflatus of ruin,/ Profound poetry of the poor and of the dead" [*CP* 509.]) The feeling of not measuring up to Sandburg, who used to bring his guitar to serenade the "Giant" and Elsie, perhaps was behind the poet's aside to Rodríguez Feo: "Up here the guitars are stacked along the attic walls for a while."

As Stevens declared to Barbara Church, he had suffered more than the usual struggle to get through January's thirty-one days this year (*L* 769). He was withdrawing more and more. He no longer read at all at night or in the evening; he sometimes listened to music or more often just sat in the dark thinking things over. His concern with the outside world—apart from the necessary attention to things at the office—shrank to what touched him immediately. He was disturbed to think of Holly and Peter traveling cross-country this coming summer, as she planned, but how else was one going to see the Blue Grass State or the Grand Canyon? He thought and read a bit more about Léon Paul Fargue in response to Barbara Church's ongoing interest in him. In some way it seemed that Stevens was trying to discover a lasting value in the work of this poet, who had been a student of Mallarmé and close, too, to Valéry. Stevens had, after all, done paraphrases of three of Fargue's pieces that he had read (after his own things) by way of introducing him to an American audience in 1951 at the Poetry Society, and he had done this while not thinking very highly of the work itself, as he had written to Barbara Church around the time he first began reading him. Had he done this simply to please her? His preoccupation now had to do with trying to see in the French poet what others saw, and he was pleased to discover that Fargue, in the eyes of one of his critics, "wasn't much of a human being." The poet was trying to get things straight.

Though he had removed himself from the round of readings, lectures, and conferences out of "a desire to be at home and to be quiet there" (*L* 777), there were still the enormous number of things "on paper" that had to be attended to, besides the work at the office. One such was rather problematic. In February 1953 Herbert Weinstock of Knopf alerted Stevens to the appearance of Dennis Williamson's unauthorized Fortune Press selection of his poems. (Knopf had originally contracted with the Fortune Press for an English edition but later canceled the contract, preferring to deal with Faber and Faber.) Enlisting the help of John Sweeney, Stevens managed to procure a copy as the greater part of the edition (except for reviewers' copies that had already been sent out) was being destroyed, by agreement with the Fortune Press, which did not welcome the idea of a lawsuit.

There were also the myriad requests from young poets asking to be heard. As Stevens described it to Sister Mary Bernetta, handling these situations was often difficult, especially when he did not find the genuine note in the work sent him and the poets persisted, sometimes by phone, in trying to make him understand exactly what they meant. One delightful exception was a pony-tailed young Norwegian woman studying at Yale who had none of the affectations of the "poet." She visited Stevens one day at his home. As he went on to note to Sister Mary Bernetta, though he did not understand a word of what she read to him, "the definiteness of sounds and the expression of her feeling in the sounds showed how completely she was a poet" (*L* 774). The noble rider of the sounds of words offered his correspondent another key to unlocking his own meanings.

Then, too, there were still the almost sacred third Thursdays in March in New York. After this year's livestock meeting there was a particularly lively party to look forward to at Jack Sweeney's since the Guggenheim, of which he had been chosen director, had only opened on February 6, and the celebrations continued whenever Mr. Sweeney had occasion to invite those, like Stevens, who had been unable to make the opening festivities. To this Thursday evening gathering Barbara Church and Marianne Moore, who had, by now, become almost constant companions, were also invited. Stevens had one of his rather boisterous times but did not "*wallow* in contrition" (*L* 772) inordinately afterward. As he wrote to Mrs. Church (though promising a week later to "stick chiefly to the anchovies in the future" [*L* 772]): "The Martinis at the Sweeneys pushed me around a bit. But I enjoyed being with all of you so greatly that I am not in the mood to take the veil because of the Martinis. You looked particularly well. And Mrs. Sweeney looked younger. When I reached home Hartford was wet with an all day rain—and cold—but I was glad to be home in the quiet after a riotous and most agreeable party." And to Miss Moore, now "Marianne" both at parties and "on paper": "I was in rather a chaotic state when we separated the other evening and may have been doggone informal. Your note tells me, in effect, that you have no grudge. The web of friendship between poets is the most delicate thing in the world—and the most precious. Your note does me immense good" (*L* 771).

Stevens's desire to be quiet at home had to do with his desire to write more poems. As he expressed to Mlle. Vidal on April 2, after reporting on the weather (March had been the rainiest on record) and the general melancholy, which for him was occasionally relieved by the "refreshing" packages she sent from Paris, he realized that he was probably not any busier at the office than he had ever been, but the mark of his age was that a full day there now absolutely precluded "the concentration of poetry, which require[d] ease and strength" (*L* 773). There was also the expenditure of energy as he exerted his will not to dwell on thoughts of death. This he did not describe to Vidal, but in a note to C. L. Daughtry. On hearing from him of the death of another business associate, he wrote: "The older one gets the more frequently this sort of thing happens and the more definitely one's own will to survive seems to protect one" (April 7, 1953). To keep his will exercised on the now sporadic occasions when he did read early in the morning, he went back to Alain as to a source of strength. He found his *Definitions,* "really something precious" (April 10, 1953) and continued to order from Vidal whichever of the French philosopher's titles he did not already have (*L* 777).

Even at the office these days, between taking care of the necessary business and sending off a series of letters to Renato Poggioli, who was about to embark on the project of translating a group of Stevens's poems for an Italian edition—with this, as noted earlier, the poet was most helpful, explicating in detail whatever lines or poems Poggioli asked about—there were long moments of withdrawal. He described these to Mrs. Church in a note accompanying a photo of him with his grandson:

> Speaking of living in the present: the boy in the striped jersey is Peter. On his birthday he took five of his friends to the Circus, here in Hartford, six-shooters and all . . [*sic* punctuation] It has been raining ever since you sailed and right now it is ready to start all over again, after an early morning thunder-shower. How fortunate I am in such weather, to have the office, where one lives in a sort of vacuum, containing nothing but the pastime of work. The great building is like a neutral zone, invulnerable to the weather. The leaves outdoors seen through the windows, belong to a perishable landscape, come from nowhere. My pen and my inkwell and my blotter and memorandum pads are what count. Every now and then, a colored boy places fresh mail on my desk, like a planet passing at night and casting its light on objects, but with more meanings than any planet. (*L* 776)

But one thing that the poet did commit himself to in this period of gathering himself was to serve again on the Bollingen committee. The greater good of poetry could not be abandoned. In any case the manuscripts would not arrive for a while, and the meeting of the judges would not be until January. This gave him the time he needed, because he was working again, now on "The River of Rivers in Connecticut."

In this poem, having realized in writing the penultimate group the hold that Greek mythology still had on his imaginings of death, Stevens attempted to distinguish his Connecticut River from that other river in "Stygia." In so doing, he tried to purge the mythology of his region of the last leftovers, the last weak whisperings of his studious ghosts. He was soon to join them himself, and it was only fitting that he do so with his territory clearly staked out. The river did not delimit any two separate realms but was simply a "third commonness with light and air" and "flow[ed] nowhere, like a sea," like time itself. Moreover, it could not "be seen beneath the appearances/ That [told] of it" (*CP* 533). It was, in short, an American river—a practical, secular, democratic, common, great, monumental river—but it was only a river. It was what it was, a natural phenomenon, nothing more. Beneath the surface of this seemingly simple poem, Stevens was presenting the final lineaments of the fiction in which he had chosen to believe and showing its inextricable ties to his soil. Behind this poem were thoughts of how absurd it was for an American poet to attempt to write haikus like the Japanese, epigrams or tragedies like the Greeks. Each form had its *real* place. Just as, for example, the Japanese built houses of rice paper around frames and beams lashed with rope—the most efficient construction in a place of frequent earthquakes—so gradually extending this sensibility bound to the transient, they created in their poetry fleeting gestures of the floating world of their islands. These forms were abstractions—"drawn off from"—their actual lives. How absurd, then, to expect, in America, the continent of majestic permanence, awe-inspiring heights, and spaces that seemed always to have been and always to be, that subtle gestures could easily be noticed. Only something equally vast in scope, expressed in high diction suited to monumentality, and at the same time familiar in its pentameter rhythms—as appropriate to a democracy—would do. It had not been an accident that "The Whole of Harmonium: The Grand Poem" had taken the shape it had or that its last section was called "The Rock"—solid, permanent, common, and echoing with associations to what had made America what it was: the Puritans landing at Plymouth Rock with their biblical memory of certain words, "On this rock I shall build my. . ." What had Stevens made?

The river he would figuratively cross in death would lead "nowhere"; on its banks there were no "shadows," no shades; but the flowing of its water, like the sounds of his words, would remain "a gayety," as he joined the "commonness" of air, water, fire, earth that was all there was. The sounds of his words were no different from the songs of birds or the babbling of the river—voicings of participation in the universe. The faith he founded on this rock was in nothing more than that. God: nature, the order and variations of the universe itself. In his time of quiet Stevens had answered his last questions. As he told Barbara Church at around the same time, what "set [him] up" nowadays was not reading in the morning but looking out the window at the changes in the garden. He had tried recently to reread the aphorisms of Matthew Arnold, now collected in their entirety, but couldn't: "I started to read them as I once read the lesser volume but lost interest. One good saying is a great deal; but ten good sayings are not anything at all. Anyhow, it may be that I don't belong to that church anymore, or that I don't care for conversation with that particular set of gods; nor, perhaps, with any" (*L* 780).

But soon the poet would write to John Zimmerman Harner, who was collecting funds for the restoration of the Amityville Cemetery, where some of Stevens's ancestors had been buried, that he was supportive and pleased by his efforts which would "bring the people buried there back to life in a way . . . keep them alive in at least the memory of the families to which they belong" (*L* 782). In the end all that mattered was memory; the Greeks had been right. In setting down their epics on the gift of papyrus made by the Egyptians, they had discovered themselves in history. Words that had before evaporated in air now lingered to be pondered and remembered. In this they had discovered the importance of memory. Stevens realized that his own words had become part of this rock of memory, and he was pleased; it was good that the rocks marking the graves of those from whom he had sprung be preserved.

Though Stevens now prized above all the "sense of permanence and calm and continuity" he found at home—where, beyond the "rush" of "neverending changes . . . fixed things move[d] about [him], obscurely: [a] memory of summers fifty and sixty years [before], when there was no end to the possibilities of experience, before one realized that, in reality, it would finally be an achievement to come down to dinner and find a fresh bouquet on the table" (*L* 798)—he did go out of his way one day in late June to visit John Gruen and his wife, Jane Wilson, in their Greenwich Village apartment. The poet walked through memories that his old Bohemia's streets bore like signs. Gruen had asked Stevens to come and hear him sing some of the songs he had composed around the poems. Gruen and Wilson expected, from the poetry itself, someone who looked like the "poet" and were very surprised to see the rotund, well-dressed "Giant" climbing the stairs to their rooms above the Bleecker Street shoe repair shop. Stevens was protectively gracious with the younger people, not even complaining about the two black cats that crawled and purred all over him as he tried to concentrate on listening to Gruen's songs. The composer and his wife remembered him speaking very slowly and deliberately in a very low voice: "A kind of monotone and a kind of heaviness, which was his bearing in general. A kind of even, measured speech that was impressive."[26] Gruen remembered, too, the poet's saying that he didn't have "a good ear," which the composer took to mean that he didn't have an ear for music. But what Stevens was revealing was that he didn't hear in one ear, no doubt expecting that a musician interested in his poetry would translate that fact into his reading. The poet was offering another key. He chose not one St. Peter to keep all the keys to his kingdom but distributed them variously here and there—one to Sister Mary Bernetta, another to Heringman, another to Poggioli, another to Rodríguez Feo—an extension of the game begun long ago at the Arensbergs.

Gruen's and Wilson's recollections of being struck by the quality and manner of Stevens's speech is important because it suggests that beyond whatever reticent nervousness the poet experienced about speaking in public, there was a physiological source of his difficulty. Whether Stevens's slow, low monotone was connected to his deafness in one ear—a compensatory mechanism against speaking too loudly—or whether it was the result of the progress of his acromegalic condition (as a consequence of the gradual changes in the bones of the auditory passage and the maxilla), the poet's experience of his condition must also have had a great deal to do with his fear of being ridiculed. The knowledge that there were organic reasons for what in the case of a poet amounts to a disability lends particular poignancy to Stevens's response to the woman at one of his lectures who asked him to speak more loudly: "I'll try, lady. I'll try." (Since Stevens did not attempt to correct his deafness with a hearing aid, it is probably the case that he believed that the slowing and heaviness of his speech had to do with his acromegaly and that beyond the reasons of vanity that might have prevented his getting a device, the situation would not be greatly improved were he to get one.)

After his outing to the Gruens, and a stop at the Fifty-seventh Street fruit store, where he loaded up on exotics, Stevens did not again go down to New York all summer. One thing that made the season in Hartford more pleasing than usual was the proximity of James Powers, who had bought an old farm in nearby Cornwall, Connecticut, where the poet visited the family several times. The enjoyment he derived from this contact with one of his oldest younger friends stood out in sharp relief against the general pattern of his days. As he noted to Barbara Church in early August, "Personally, I nourish myself on books, nature, this and that, music—so rarely on the good friendships of men and women . . [*sic* punctuation]" (*L* 795). He went on to tell her that he was expecting to vary his diet soon as he was negotiating through Mlle. Vidal for something new to take the place of the Tal Coat where it hung. He commented on his contentedness at home and on a speech of Eisenhower's that he had heard the night before that made him see the president as "a builder, not of the future, but of the present" in contrast with Roosevelt, who "was always casting out devils." About the news that his old friend Ed Bechtel was not well he observed, ". . . if he should put his shoes in the hall for good, it would hurt." He closed his letter with a sentence suggesting that he was again thinking more about death than life: "Anyhow, this is the state of affairs within my shadow" (*L* 796).

The torrid heat wave of this summer contributed to the "indifference" Stevens again began to feel (*L* 798). Though he responded at length, as usual, to his worthy correspondents, there was an increasing evasiveness that showed itself particularly in connection with personal questions of ultimate value and belief. In answer to Bernard Heringman's query about his religious feelings, for example, Stevens offered only "I dismiss your question by saying that I am a dried-up Presbyterian, and let it go at that because my activities are not religious." In closing the same letter, he tauntingly balanced his skirting with ". . . I believe in pure explication de texte. This may in fact be my principal form of piety" (*L* 792–93). The message: Seek me and you shall find me in my words. And to Heringman's later question about whether in his thesis he could quote from a particular letter, the poet noted in his typically sphingine manner: "If this should be inconsistent with something that I have said elsewhere, it would not matter because one often says contradictory things" (*L* 798). The man of many tropes was as much a Zen master shouting *katsu* to one of his disciples as he was anything else.

Though Stevens did not travel farther than Farmington, Connecticut—to visit the Swans (parents of the wife of Philip Rahv) and the Rahvs one Sunday afternoon—and to Cornwall to visit the Powerses that summer, he not only made it possible for Holly and Peter to range far and wide but also helped finance a trip back to Reading (with a three-day stopover in Hartford) for his niece Jane and her family. The "Giant" was obviously happy in his role as provider. It was most clearly evidenced in the thoughtful and spontaneous generosity that prompted him to write an extra check to Holly that she would find with an accompanying note when she returned from one of her holidays—"Nothing like finding $500 under the door when you come home broke" (April 23, 1954). His "good Puritan" habits, despite the constraints they had imposed on him, had served him well on this account, and in this sense he truly was a man of fortune greeting heirs—something that he was not certain of being for the literary generations to come:

> If the present generation likes the mobile-like arrangement of lines to be found in the work of William Carlos Williams or the verbal conglomerates of e. e. cummings, what is the next generation to be like? Pretty much the bare page, for that alone would be new. . . . Some day we may have a really new world not the mere variations of an old world that constitute what is new to-day. If only the desire for what is new was not so fundamental, so unquestioned and unquestionable. (*L* 801)

As fall began, Stevens was still not keen on moving far from home. He at first even refused the invitation to Barbara Church's autumn gathering on October 15 but changed his mind when it turned out that Holly could drive him down and back. He was opening his seventy-fourth year quietly. He had celebrated his birthday, "a suave afternoon-like day . . . sitting outdoors and watching the grass grow and the heavens roll" (*L* 799). As though to commemorate his seventy-fifth year, the current *Vogue* magazine was running a piece on the poet, who must have been amused when his niece Jane, as part of her birthday greeting, complimented him on his photo in the glossy rather than on his poems. Perhaps extending the celebration of his years, he had taken Richard Eberhart and Samuel French Morse to lunch at the Canoe Club.

But by the beginning of November Stevens had again made plans to go here and there. In spite of his decision earlier in the year not to read in public again, on the third he accepted an invitation from Horace Taylor of Columbia University to deliver the Phi Beta Kappa poem the following June. On November 23 the poet flew to Boston to see an exhibition of Japanese pictures. The viewing, unfortunately, was not possible because the museum was closed; instead he went to the Fogg in Cambridge to recover bits of time captured in certain tones, lines, and figures of the pieces he had begun to love as a young man. On the next day he flew to New York, where he attended to a few errands and had lunch, together with Holly, at the apartment of Mrs. Church, and later, dinner, alone with Holly, at "the Black Angus on E. 50th St. where they [had] things for the youthful appetite" (*L* 804). They then drove back to Hartford.

One of the invitations the poet declined during November was to speak at a memorial meeting for Dylan Thomas. Though he excused himself on the grounds that he did not speak well in public and that, in addition, an *oraison funebre* was not up his alley, he really refused, he reported to Barbara Church, because he thought Thomas was "an utterly improvident person," who kept on coming to America as long as there "was any money to be picked up" (*L* 802). Stevens had no respect for Thomas "as a man," he noted. How could he? The Irish poet could not have been more antithetical to the man Stevens had shaped himself to be. The letter in which he expressed this to Barbara

Church opened with the poet's observing that while it was autumn, and he might be expected to be blue, he just felt "cross." He at first blamed his eyes for this; after reading steadily for several hours, he had to sit still and compose himself for ten to fifteen minutes before doing anything else. But he was probably "cross," too, that there was going to be a memorial honoring the profligate poet; it was just one more sign that things as they were were not as they should be.

By the beginning of December there were a few new things to look forward to as the weather chilled and drove the poet and his gardening wife indoors. One was a new volume of poems by Richard Eberhart; another was the coming visit of Thomas McGreevy to the United States, where he would spend at least one night in Hartford; yet another was the painting to replace the Tal Coat. There was also some new reading in store. Stevens ordered Maurice Merleau-Ponty's *Étage de la Philosophie,* one of the many titles that had intrigued him from his now regular reading of the *Nouvelle Revue Française.*

In connection with the Eberhart volume (*Undercliff: Poems 1946–1953*), something happened that was most uncharacteristic of Stevens, who all through his life had, even when ambivalent about or displeased with something he read, not hesitated to express his feelings, albeit graciously. Here for the first time (that I have been able to determine) he on one day led Eberhart to believe that the book had given him "much pleasure" (*L* 803), while on the next day he described his disappointment with it as "a miscellany without an axis"—though not mentioning the author or title—to Barbara Church (*L* 804). From the contact he had had with Eberhart before reading his work, Stevens had conjured him to be like a "modern, poetic Cicero" (*L* 804), "an author to be read by every man of taste" (*L* 802), but after reading the poems, he was "shocked by his lack of care and feeling" (*L* 804). Why then did he write precisely the opposite to the younger poet?

> DEAR EBERHART:
>
> I had an opportunity yesterday to read UNDERCLIFF and to get to know your nature and perhaps to understand the habit of your mind better than before. To speak only of the quality that interested me most, I was struck by your sincerity. By this I don't mean so much that you mean what you say as that what you say is free from self-consciousness. There is more good than bad in this. But there is bad in it. This quality alone makes you right in my own way of thinking of things, although I am not too sure that my own way of thinking of things is right, particularly when I come across the universal acceptance of Bill Williams, for instance, who rejects the idea that meaning has the slightest value and describes a poem as a structure of little blocks. I am merely using Williams as an illustration. There are many things to say about your own poems which I shall try to remember the next time we meet. This is merely to say how much pleasure the book gave me. (*L* 803)

Stevens wanted to protect Eberhart's feelings and, probably, their friendship. There were so few people, especially in his "literary life," with whom the "Giant" had more than paper relationships. Here was someone who was a poet but who had also had experience outside the world of letters, with whom Stevens had shared football games and memories, who lived fairly close by, whom he had treated with the respect attached to his imaginings of him as a modern-day Cicero. How could he again face him if he had written his actual perceptions? Perhaps Stevens preferred relationships on paper precisely because he knew that in less distanced situations he was unable to voice what he truly felt or thought when he feared that it might injure another. Perhaps this was also the hidden reason behind his having wanted to keep Elsie his "Little Girl" always. As such in his mind, she was dependent and shared his views. Consequently, he would not have to worry about hurting her, since, in theory at least, differences should not have arisen. If they did, they could be attributed to childish recalcitrance, and she could be ignored, cajoled, or punished.

One paper relationship that was about to take on real life—if only for a short time—was that with Thomas McGreevy. Stevens must have been touched by his Irish friend's describing to him in one of his last letters before they were to meet his nervousness about coming face-to-face. He was afraid that Stevens might "not find it such a grand thing for a happy correspondent [to] turn into just another old human" (December 1, 1953). How perceptive Stevens had been in sensing McGreevy to be another version of his "second self." While originally Stevens had unusually extended an invitation to McGreevy to stay at Westerly Terrace—apologizing in advance, no doubt ironically and metaphorically, for the "dust on the piano"—by the time of the actual visit in January, McGreevy had made other arrangements at a local hotel, much to the relief of both men. It would be easier to confine their contact to the drawing-room atmosphere of Barbara Church's apartment.

By Christmas Stevens was, as he put it in a December 21 letter to James Powers, "nursing his usual grudge against" the holiday. He went on to be more specific about his feelings:

> Somehow, it makes me sore to see all those Christmas cards. Last night there was a man on Yale Interprets the News, a local radio program on which members of the Yale Faculty talk every Sunday evening for a short time. Last night's man talked on the loss of all religious significance in respect to Christmas. I don't mean to say that I miss the religious significance of Christmas, or of any other time, but when I feel sore about Christmas cards and someone gets on the air and talks about the Incarnation and its practical value for all of us, I clap my hands and stamp my feet and say Bravo, Bravo! Perhaps that only goes to show how queer you become if you remain in New England long enough. (*L* 805)

The American business machine had done its job, robbing the myth of the last bit of transcendence. In spite of his feelings that an anthropomorphic God was no more than an exalted expression of egotism, Stevens felt that the myth was to be preferred to purely practical commercialism. A society that had no sense of the magical power of symbolic metamorphoses could not be expected to be sensitive to the poet's transformations of things as they were. Too, this expression of hostility to the secularizing process of the Calvinist ethic whispered that Stevens still had not quite resolved the feelings attached to his having followed his father's very reasonable advice about the shape his life had taken. He now, together with the rest of his society, was "out on a limb," as he put it. There was no room in the world as it was for considerations of value, belief. Though there was a desperate need for each individual to entertain these questions and arrive at his or her own "supreme fiction" in answer to them, most people simply ignored content entirely, preferring to deal with form alone.

For the poet the year ended with an eerily prophetic sense of the hidden meanings of things. As he wrote to his cousin Emma—after reporting the details of family news, as far as he knew them, now that Reading had again become distant with his sense that the younger generation (with the exception of Jane) regarded him as they would "pictures on the wall"—"I shall be 75 next October and intend to stay 75 for some years after that" (*L* 807).

V

IT MUST GIVE PLEASURE

1954–1955

ARIEL WAS GLAD HE HAD WRITTEN HIS POEMS.
THEY WERE OF A REMEMBERED TIME
OR OF SOMETHING SEEN THAT HE LIKED.

—"Planet on the Table,"
The Collected Poems (p. 532)

> The final belief is to believe in a fiction, which you know to be a fiction, there being nothing else. The exquisite truth is to know that it is a fiction and that you believe in it willingly.
>
> —"Adagia," *Opus Posthumous* (p. 163)

"The process of growing old accelerates the longer it continues, so that one seems to grow old faster today than one did yesterday" (*L* 856). So 1954 passed, the poet repeating the theme of his age with increasing frequency as he neared the day that marked what he called "the beginning of his last quarter" (*L* 846). The planetary metaphor served him well: He would never reach fullness. He had not made the $1 million he had set out to make, he noted ironically to Peter Lee, nor had he, as he had reported to Thomas McGreevy earlier, brought to completion the idea he had had in mind when he had set out to fashion the "Supreme Fiction." He still liked a few things in *Harmonium* better than anything he had done since (*L* 807) and knew that in the grayness of his years he could not strike any more of a hullabaloo among the spheres than he had.

In the same way that a celestial orb spins faster and faster in its final plunging back into the sun of which it was originally a part, Stevens's consciousness of moments of himself in time past, present, and future spun ever more quickly in his mind's eye as he sat in the quiet evenings, more unwilling than unable to read anything but the lines of memory that presented themselves like prismatic streaks of light. Was his mind still quick enough to catch them before they passed into blackness? It was these morsels it needed to nourish itself now, translating them into words he could turn and savor, but he had to catch them. . . . "Only, here and there, an old sailor,/ Drunk and asleep in his boots,/ Catches tigers/ In red weather" (*CP* 66).

As though with the full awareness that his prophecy for remaining seventy-five was truth, as though this were an integral aspect of his supreme fiction for himself (did the poet know that the Etruscans, too, had set the limit for the life of their civilization and had quietly died out as a people upon reaching it?), Stevens attempted during his last phase to fulfill again as many public obligations as he could. He seemed to have needed the respite of the past year to regain some strength to do this. In addition to the Bollingen gathering in January, he accepted invitations to read both at Vassar and at the Poetry Center of the YMHA in New York in the fall. He also agreed to tape something on the idea of the American concept of the free man at Amherst and to make a record for the Harvard Library. Things he thought he would never do and things he thought he would not do again, he did. Now, too, it was time for the collected poems.

On April 22 Stevens answered Knopf's annual reminder with a note saying he was ready; it couldn't be put off any longer. It "put an end to things," but he didn't have a "choice"; it was a necessary part of "good housekeeping." He trimmed earlier volumes and added last touches of the new old reality he experienced now to make as perfect an anthology as he could, a volume that would resolve the striking chords of his early years into the final tones of accord. He wanted to leave behind the impression of something venerable, quiet, and true. The shearsman snipped "a few rather stuffy things" (*L* 832)—"Owl's Clover," "Life on a Battleship," "The Woman Who Had More Babies Than That"—and set the very last adornments to "The Rock": "The River of Rivers in Connecticut," "The Planet on the Table," "Not Ideas About the Thing but the Thing Itself." He had wanted to name that last group of poems "Amber Umber," mimicking the transformation of his auroral flickerings into lullaby notations preceding slumber. Unfortunately, the phrase had been used, just recently by Christopher Fry in *Venus Observed.* (Stevens must have wondered whether he had somehow picked up these gentle words in passing, perhaps from a review or quotation. One couldn't be sure at so much more than seventy: "a scrawny cry from outside/ Seemed like a sound in his mind" [*CP* 534].)

As he shaped the volume that would take the place of the mountain he conjured himself to be—an integral part of the intelligence of his soil—Stevens seems to have remembered something he had read years before about what for the "old Chinese" constituted the perfect anthology. In Witter Bynner's and Kiang Kang-Hu's Introduction to *The Jade Mountain: A Chinese Anthology,* he had learned that the Chinese considered about 300 poems to be the ideal number for an anthology. This was based on an old saying that "By reading thoroughly three hundred T'ang poems, one will write verse without learning."[1] Such a volume would be an integral part of any household and would be read from every day in the ongoing attempt to harmonize human experience with the tremors and changes of nature. The perfect Chinese anthology was dealt with as a secular sacred book. To those members of a household who could not read, the poems would be read aloud. Memory's echoes of his mother's voice intoning the phrases of Bible stories while he prepared to enter the world of dreams mixed with his recollection of this odd bit of Chinese cultural history. Was it accidental that the number of his collected poems circled 300? Was the youthful prankster turned sleight of hand man playing with the idea of a delightful puzzle that a future reader would someday unlock after finding through him a way, too, to *The Jade Mountain*? "The Whole of Harmonium: The Grand Poem" was still the title Stevens desired for his "anthology." Playing its pieces, reading through it thoroughly and repeatedly with the seasons of the year, one could write verse without learning. This was a script for a human, not a divine, comedy. The slightly vulgar sound of the harmonium set the tone for his time and place. The comedian had not forgotten his mission: "Begin, ephebe, by perceiving the idea/ Of this invention . . ." (*CP* 380). (To the poet's regret, Knopf, with his better business sense, persuaded him that the simpler, more direct title of *The Collected Poems* was more fitting.)

In keeping with his continued desire to preserve his relationship with Knopf, Stevens did something else he had, except in rare instances, declined and agreed to write a jacket blurb for a fellow author. Luckily he found Randall Jarrell's *Pictures from an Institution* rich and rewarding. As he noted to Barbara Church, "Jarrell is a poet. We have lots of poets in this country who also write criticism, but not nearly so many who, in addition to writing criticism, write fiction that is really good prose fiction. Jarrell's book is exceptionally good" (*L* 818). It was only in rare cases now that the poet extended himself beyond the spheres within spheres which he chose and created for himself and in which he circled ever more quickly toward the center. In addition to the Jarrell volume, he ordered and read William Carlos Williams's *Paterson* as it existed so far, perhaps wanting to fill in more of the details of the mythology of the region they had shared at a distance throughout their lives. And, too, there was the new painting, Jean Jules Cavaillès' view of the port of Cannes, which seemed to him to "have been painted with melted candy" (*L* 830) and which he found "it was necessary for him to believe in" (*L* 833) before he could determine whether it depicted morning or evening light. He gave himself to this as he wanted others to give themselves to his work. This gave pleasure.

There had also been one or two occasions that spring of getting to New York—once to see an exhibition of Indian things at the Modern and for the annual livestock meeting. There were the usual visits with Barbara Church, who by now had become almost a member of the family. Stevens was gratified that she, too, approved of Holly's new friend Elias Mengel, who was also to visit Mrs. Church during his stay in Europe, which he planned for later in the year. The poet was pleased that his daughter now moved comfortably in his world and that there was a young man who seemed both sensitive and worthy. The old man could begin to rest in peace.

There was also another trip to New York planned primarily for Elsie to see the eye doctor she used to have when they were first married. In the softening of age the "Giant" wanted to indulge her need for a past sense of security. On that trip, too, he hoped to stop in again at what he called "Sweeney's museum" (the Guggenheim) to have a better look at a new Cézanne his friend had acquired to grace Frank Lloyd Wright's twisting walls (*L* 828). But what gave the poet most pleasure still, as he noted in his Easter greeting to Sister Mary Bernetta, was nature—the birds around his house and in the park and his desire, as he put it, to "réaliser the weather" (*L* 828). The closer he could come to "realizing" these parts of his world, the easier the final transition would be.

As he opened more and more to these feelings of slow dissolution, he composed the poem he would read for the Phi Beta Kappa address at Columbia on May 31. In "The Sail of Ulysses" (*OP* 99–105), Stevens disclosed himself: the equation of the "central" with the "self"; the propelling "need" and "poverty" that had led him to create like "a child asleep in its own life" his "fluent mundo" within the world; the pain he now felt at looking back like an old woman looking down the road. Memories welled up and carried him in his imagination's craft out to middle ocean's emptiness—Ulysses, "symbol of the seeker," on his last voyage. Stevens's experience of reading the poem to his audience, hearing his syllables intoning his "old shape/ Worn and leaning to nothingness" was so intense that afterward, in spite of praise and requests to publish it, he adamantly refused. He wrote to Babette Deutsch, to whom he at first seems to have said that he would throw the poem away, that though he promised not to—on her insistence—he would certainly not use the poem in its present form or let anyone see it (*L* 834). He repeated this about a week later to Columbia University's Horace Taylor, noting that he would not let the poem out of his hands. As he described it in the poem's opening lines, this was a reading of "his own mind," nothing more. Was he frightened by what he saw? Could it have been that now, with *The Collected Poems* soon to appear—"A book that contains everything that one has done in a lifetime does not reassure one" (*L* 839)—he had translated all the doubts and fears that still remained into this symbolically last poem? The poet seemed unable to let go of the poem in more than a physical sense. Lines from it, such as "A child asleep in its own life," extended themselves into titles or lines for other poems in a kind of compressed recursiveness. It was as though the process of returning to a particular phrase that in the past had stretched over years now occurred with the same increased speed as he had described his days passing.

With this intensified, accelerated sense, Stevens experienced the various elements of his life more sharply. As he observed to Barbara Church in thanking her for the series of postcards she had sent from her most recent tour through Spain on her way, via Bordeaux, to Ville-d'Avray, "I have often seen Seville before but never smelled the heavy fragrance of its orange blossoms. And I have seen Granada but never felt the noise of its mountain water. Also, I have been in Madrid but this time it was a change to get away from the Prado and to go to restaurants and sit by the door and look out at the 18th century. I liked to stop at Bordeaux where other friends of mine have lived" (*L* 837). Unfortunately, however, not all the elements were pleasant. He wrote to Leonard van Geyzel near the end of June:

> Here the newspapers from time to time say that the feeling about the Communists is much less hysterical than it was. Personally, I have no sense of its ever having been hysterical at all. I think that newspapers, and people on the radio, use words about as inexactly as they possibly can be used. President Eisenhower is probably right in saying that the general state of affairs may continue for another forty years. The truth is, however, that I find such a

> period of time incomprehensible. It is easy to imagine a difference in things a year or two from now. But it is not easy to imagine such a thing at forty years from now. One thing that this remark involves is that we have to take everything that is going on in our stride. I cannot say that there is any way to adapt myself to the idea that I am living in the Atomic Age and I think it a lot of nonsense to try to adapt oneself to such a thing. The exhaustion of Europe is a great menace both to Europe and ourselves. It looks to us and also to you.
>
> I shall be 75 in October. Knopf will publish a volume of collected poems about that time. It will contain all of the *Auroras of Autumn* and I shall send you a copy. I look forward to the appearance of this volume rather dismally. . . . Then, the fact that I am 75 begins to seem like the most serious thing that has ever happened to me. Perhaps the way to evade all these considerations is to be like an old Swedish woman who lives in my general neighborhood. She is 90. I don't believe she has ever really thought of the Atomic Age. She just goes on growing older and remaining cheerful. (*L* 838–39)

The man who had struggled throughout his life to make language a tool precise enough to measure the verve of earth was naturally perturbed by the inexactness with which words were used. Beneath the surface of his perception was the same awareness George Orwell had expressed in "Politics and the English Language": There was a connection between living in the intolerable situation of the atomic age as though it were tolerable and the imprecise use of language. But the poet had "finished [his] combat with the sun;/ And [his] body, the old animal,/ [knew] nothing more" (*CP* 46). It was not surprising that he looked forward "dismally" to the appearance of his final offering.

The young man who at the turn of the century mourned the passing of America's pastoral way of life before advancing urbanization and industrialization could not have imagined that even clouds would become reminders of the constant threat of total annihilation. He could not have conceived then, as he freed himself from the strictures of the religion in which he had been reared to believe in an all-powerful anthropomorphic God, that within his lifetime, with the disappearance of that God, human beings would invent and inflict the punishment they would have expected from that God for no longer believing in him. In the face of collective disillusion and fear, Stevens, no matter how successful he had been in completing his life and touching at least a few others through his poetry, could not possibly look back and say, "It was good."

Nonetheless, with the perseverance he had always attributed to his Dutch forebears, he went on. Putting aside "The Sail of Ulysses" because it was not quite time for the final setting out, the poet, this summer, attempted to cultivate "the leisure and space of far niente," as he wrote to Barbara Church, to compose a few more poems. He had come full circle. At twenty-one being in a state of "far niente" had been bitterly disturbing; the voice of his father urging him to make something of himself then resounded too loudly inside him. Now, with only a little time left, that voice finally quieted, he found himself free and wondered:

> . . . have I lived a skeleton's life,
> As a disbeliever in reality [?]
>
> (*OP* 117)

These lines from "As You Leave the Room"—one of the poems he wrote during this period after "Reality Is an Activity of the Most August Imagination," "Solitaire Under the Oaks," "Local Objects," "Artificial Populations," and "A Clear Day with No Memories" (*OP* 110–13)—reflected the purity of confrontation with things as they were that he had come to attain. These poems were neither paeans nor elegies, but direct transcriptions of the fleeting, like perfect descriptions of satori states. The contrasting senses of good and evil, hope and despair, seeming and being all were gone. The poet continued in this spirit into the autumn weather, recording the simplest experiences, as "On the Way to the Bus," in language made crystalline under the pressure of more than fifty years of gradual transformation. He was now a

> Transparent man in a translated world,
> In which he [fed] on a new known,
>
> In a season, a climate of morning, of elucidation
> . . . .
>
> (*OP* 116)

In the meantime, as always, there was the unending exchange of letters with Peter Lee, Barbara Church, Thomas McGreevy, and others. He still nourished himself on their adventures, one of the most satisfying of late being Lee's stay in Fribourg, Switzerland, where Stevens hoped that the young Korean would attend one of Martin Heidegger's lectures: ". . . even [if you only] see him, tell me about him because it will help to make him real" (*L* 839). Similarly, he also wanted to make Paul Klee more real, ordering from Blackwell's an analysis of the mind and work of the painter with whom, as with Heidegger, he shared the desire to get at the spare lineaments of reality's prism.

By the time of his seventy-fifth birthday celebration on October 1 at the Harmonie Club in New York (a place Knopf must have chosen for its name to add one more delight for the poet) Stevens had reached a plateau of jovial serenity. The poems he had composed had brought him here, as he reported to Wilson Taylor a few days after the party, where Carl Van Vechten, Delmore Schwartz, James Merrill and many others had gathered to honor him. Finding that he was "still able to write poetry [was] a great thing" (October 6, 1954). From this point on his strength would not be shaken, even by something that must have made him bristle as he was visited by the last ironic scraping of his father's spirit.

In a seeming carryover of the feelings of rivalry attached to the childhood years of Stevens's brother John, John Stevens, Jr., on October 5, as part of his birthday greeting to his uncle, noted that the following week the *Reading Eagle* would publish a piece on Garrett Sr.'s efforts as a poet; he also enclosed an October 3 clipping from the same newspaper by Leonard Harris entitled "Off-Beat Jottings" which briefly discussed *The Necessary Angel* under the subheading of "Freud Criticized." Completely misreading Stevens's acknowledgment of Freud's contribution, Harris misrepresented the poet's text, as he wrote that "in the book [Stevens] says that Freud [had] done more than anyone else during the past 100 years to 'cut the throat' of poetry.'" It is not difficult to imagine what Stevens must have thought as he considered that those who most closely shared the intelligence of his soil should turn his words in a way that made him reflect their own parochial point of view.

It is also not difficult to imagine what he felt after his nephew John had forwarded the following week's article on Garrett Sr.'s gifts as a poet. In this piece Harris, thanking John Stevens, Jr., for the information on which he based his perceptions, not so subtly attempted to deflate Stevens of the "afflatus" his father had thought "not serious" by suggesting that in the end there was no difference between the talents of father and son. Harris opened his piece with "Wallace Stevens may be the most illustrious poet in his family, but he is by no means the first and only one. Like his father. . ." He went on: "The primary difference between the two men (they are alike in so many ways) lies in the fact that the work of the son is so much better known. And that is, perhaps, because the son learned his craft so expertly from his father." He gave the particulars of Garrett's publishing, noting that his poems began appearing anonymously—as part of the game he played with a few other local poets—in the region's newspapers in 1906 and that they were later collected and reprinted in 1911 and 1912 after his death by Lewis Kershner, one of his friends. Harris made a point, too, of commenting on Garrett Sr.'s ingenious use of Pennsylvania Dutch words and his masterful use of other verbal plays, quietly suggesting in each instance that these tricks had been learned by his son.

In the short note John, Jr., sent along with this clipping he offered to forward his uncle a copy of Kershner's book. "I will be happy to send it to you," he wrote, probably not entirely unconscious of getting back at the successful poet by properly carrying over his long-dead father's competition with his brother. To this Stevens coolly responded:

> DEAR JOHN,
>
> I think that I have seen the Kershner book. In any case, don't send it over here. I shall take a look at it some time when I am in Reading. You get to a point where you don't ever want to see poetry again and just at the moment I am at that point. However, that is not the whole story. I have

made it a point of my own discipline to read very little of other people's poetry.

Jane wrote a pleasant letter.

Sincerely,
(October 15, 1954)

His last sentence said all there was to be said in the subtle contrast it set up between what John had sent as his birthday greeting and Jane's "pleasant letter," which she had closed tenderly with "and so, my favorite uncle. . ."

The boy who had so wanted to make a place of praise for himself within the family where he had grown up moving up and down between his two brothers arrived at the edge of death having made a place on the "front bench" but still not with the heirs of his ghosts. "Mother, oh, my mother, who are you" had not been an empty voicing. As if sensing his need, though it is possible that Stevens mentioned the details of this "birthday gift" from John to her, Barbara Church, on seeing the current issue of *Vogue* magazine, which published another poem and photo of the poet, commented in a note to her friend that his mother would have been proud to see him so honored, that she herself was happy to be in possession of the magazine, and that she thought him a "brilliant and successful man" (October 14, 1954).

Fortunately, as November came, there were other deeply gratifying tributes to the poet. On the sixth he read at the Poetry Center of the YMHA in New York, and the room was "filled up to the roof." Although not too many people came up afterward to ask him to sign their copies of the just published *Collected Poems,* it was clear to the poet that he and his work had been appreciated; he attributed the small number of people who had the book in hand simply to the fact that it was an expensive volume. His next reading at Vassar College on the twelfth was even more successful. After it, he received one of the most specifically appreciative letters of homage from Helen Lockwood, the chairperson of the English Department. She focused on the music of the poems and how it had stimulated the students to want to go on reading more of his work. She mentioned a young professor, generally "scornful in the main of twentieth-century writing," who was "so moved that he would not go up to [Stevens] afterwards—'When some one has opened such imagination and life to you,' he said, 'what can you say? I haven't anything to say. I just want to go home and think about it.'" She went on to add that she herself came away renewed, having experienced a "whole new dimension" (November 16, 1954). This occasion had been especially beautiful for Stevens, too, because he had been accompanied and appreciated by Holly, who, in a note to Barbara Church a few days later, described the drive down to Poughkeepsie for the reading in terms that seemed to forecast the significance of this day and season with her father: "When we drove to Poughkeepsie on Friday afternoon we had a magnificent sunset before us all the way, perceptibly darkening until we reached our destination, and then it went out. This is a most wonderful autumn in my life" (November 16, 1954).

As the end of the year came near, the poet continued to receive acknowledgments of his importance. Various individuals praised *The Collected Poems.* Ebba Dalin from Sweden wrote that the volume gave her "the quiet sense of a tender spirit communing with itself in the green grove" (November 29, 1954). Archibald MacLeish extended the invitation that Stevens be the Charles Eliot Norton professor at Harvard for 1955–1956. A special issue of *Perspectives* (autumn 1954) appeared, wholly dedicated to Stevens. And Jackson Mathews wrote asking the poet to do the introductions to one of the volumes of the collected works of Paul Valéry for the Bollingen Series. Stevens considered this last request for about two weeks before deciding to accept; he would focus on "Eupalinos" and "L'Âme et la Danse." This last stretching into the imaginary world of another seems, at first, to have been an unusual undertaking at this point for the poet who had come to rest in his "central." Yet perhaps it was precisely because he knew that he had found what he had been seeking that he felt free to open himself to another strong voice. The experience itself would be an illustration of one of the themes he explored as his soul danced with that of Valéry.

Just after committing himself to this task, Stevens received a tender and charming note of late birthday congratulations and an appreciation of his *Collected Poems* from Witter Bynner. He opened his letter with an address to "Dear Pete," for such he had been at Harvard, and closed reminding his friend of the incident of "Copey's" asking him, just before he left Cambridge, what he was going to be and on hearing "a poet," exclaiming, "Jesus Christ!" (December 11, 1954). This note made Stevens "happy," as he wrote back to Bynner. It was a necessary part of the "central" that its unity in time be perceived, intention meeting itself in extension—the dance of the soul through life.

In this spirit Stevens went through his last Christmas season. This blues that always gripped him he transformed into sparkling greetings. The one perhaps most characteristic of his feelings was an ingeniously delightful postcard reproduction of a Modigliani seated woman which he sent, cut in half in two envelopes, to C. L. Daughtry. As he noted on the back, there was such a mountain of things to attend to on his desk that he hardly had had time to do what he ought, which was to run and get extra Christmas cards at the museum, and that is what he had done. He went on to comment playfully that this was "a picture of one of the girls in the office" but that it wouldn't fit into one of the Hartford's "niggardly envelopes," so he had cut it in half. "Please keep one half and give the other half to Mr. Wilkins, [a co-worker in Daughtry's office]," he wrote before signing off, probably chuckling to himself like the best Santa Claus.

Atop the mountain of things that had to be attended to was, as he put it, "an avalanche of cards"—from the growing number of people he had never met but who now knew him through his words. While the year before Christmas cards had made him particularly bilious, this year, because they evidenced his success and acceptance, he was pleased. He wrote to Wilson Taylor that it had been "a warm and brilliant holiday." The weather of his spirit mimicked the weather outside, and it was not because he had forgotten about death. As he commented on January 4 to Barbara Church in his late letter of holiday greeting to her, after noting that he would be in New Haven again for the awarding of the Bollingen Prize at the end of the week, "I have no present digressions in mind beyond this. But it is precisely the blank into and through which the horseman suddenly rides. Who can tell?" (*L* 866). But he was happy, strangely happy. He observed to Peter Lee on the same day, no doubt looking forward to the warmer days ahead, ". . . my idea of a happy life: to be able to grow old and fat and lie outdoors under the trees thinking about people and things and things and people. What else is there that it is worth while to do, except, of course, to eat and drink and chase girls?" His life had become "like an old book full of associations of which [he was] the possessor" (*L* 865).

❧

As soon as Stevens finished sending off the last of his holiday letters to his long-devoted friends, he set to work preparing the introductions to the Valéry dialogues; these were to be ready by April 1. Not satisfied that his French was good enough—in spite of his perception of French and English as a single language—he wrote to Thomas McGreevy asking him to help him get hold of a particularly good translation. Within days of sending off this letter, the poet received word of two more honors: Yale was to award him an honorary degree on June 13 (he was to keep this "greatest prize for a Harvard man" confidential until the formal announcement was made months later), and he was again to win the National Book Award for his *Collected Poems* (the ceremony was to be on January 25). Sadly, just as the letters bearing these tidings arrived, Elsie suffered a stroke (on January 14).

Accompanied by Holly, Stevens received his second National Book Award, an unprecedented honor. His brief acceptance speech focused not on the satisfactions of the award, which, he observed, belonged to "the world of Darwin . . . not the world of Plato," but on the satisfactions of the act of writing poetry. Indeed, even now, unexpectedly facing his wife's mortality more pressingly than his own, it was almost as if his faith in the life of poetry itself had carried him through. There were no notes of despair when he commented on her illness. He had confidence that her will "to exorcise the devil by not recognizing him, or, rather, to expel him by turning her back on [her condition]" would ensure her full recovery. He commented to Barbara Church on this and on how Elsie was "cheerful and courageous as women so often are in the face of illness" (*L* 874). He no doubt remembered his mother with her indomitable spirit as she lay dying and silently prepared himself to show equal fortitude when his time arrived, even though he did not share the faith these two women had in the life hereafter. Sharing Elsie's "main force," which she exerted to act as if there were nothing wrong—in spite of her needing a nurse for months afterward—Stevens attended to his work at the office and on Valéry (though, under the circumstances, it was difficult for him to "stick to it") and celebrated the first signs of spring as the "great event" it was. He stayed at home as much as possible, tending his Elsie as she had tended him through that period five years before, when he had learned how pleasant it was to be at home with her.

Through all this he did not lose any of the strength and serenity that he had come to enjoy. He felt himself more certain than ever before, so certain that he could write to Peter Lee apropos of the young man's not understanding aspects of the poetry: "No one tries to be more lucid than I do. If I do not always succeed, it is not a question of my English, nor of yours, but I should say of something not communicated because not shared" (*L* 873). The burden was on the other: The ideal reader would stretch himself or herself by adventuring through his words, searching out the thoughts and feelings behind them. Similarly, in passing a judgment on a volume of poetry he had been sent, he was equally straightforward. He observed that the poet "had not mastered her life" and for that reason "had not mastered her own poetry." He came away from reading the poems muttering, "la malheureuse." The "Giant" was finally sure of his way.

By March 24 Stevens had finished the introductions to the Valéry dialogues. Especially in that for "Eupalinos" all the threads that had been running through the last seven years of his life were woven together into a testament of praise not so much for Valéry as for the act of the maker who shaped the imperfections of life into perfect forms. Stevens stressed the magnificent way Valéry had solved the primary formal constraint he faced of producing a text of exactly 115,800 characters (because it was to accompany a collection of engravings and plans, and the number of letters and spaces had to conform precisely to the decoration and pagination of the work) by deciding on the dialogue as a vehicle since an insignificant rejoinder could be deleted or added finally as required. Echoes of Alain were heard. Through the pages of his Introduction the poet imagined walking through the Elysian fields in the company of the figures he named: Socrates, Phaedrus, Eupalinos, Mallarmé, Valéry, Alain. He selected quotations that focused on death as the mother of beauty. The maker put himself in the place of God by creating himself "above his own nature" through his attention to form. What moved him in Valéry were perceptions he had recognized himself:

> If, then, the universe is the effect of some act; that act itself, the effect of a Being, and of a need, a thought, a knowledge, and a power which belong to that Being, it is then by an act that you can rejoin the grand design, and undertake the imitation of that which has made all things. And that is to put oneself in the most natural way in the very place of God.
>
> Now of all acts the most complete is that of constructing.[2]

He agreed with Valéry that "of all the indicators of thought the most sensitive were poets, first because they take risks a little further than logic permits; also because the rule they adopt always carries them a little beyond what they hoped for."[3]

Stevens had recently explained to Robert Pack, who had sent the poet a copy of a paper on his work, that there was one thing he felt ought to be changed. Pack had concluded that Stevens got "nowhere in particular," which Stevens strongly corrected by noting that he did "arrive at the end of [his own] logic" (*L* 861). As he had also subtly suggested to Lee, it was the job of the good reader to enter into a dance with the form in order to be able to understand the poet's individual logic and language. Stevens, in his last year, was sure of the milk within the saltiest spurge of his imagination. But he seemed to know that this sense of completeness, the perfecting of his spirit, meant that his death was near. Just before closing his Introduction, he called up the shade of Rilke and noted that the German had "read 'Eupalinos' when it came out in the *Nouvelle Revue Française,* and that his translation of it was the last work he did before he died."[4] There was really no reason for Stevens to mention this, except for what it revealed about what he knew, or thought he knew, about himself. He had constructed this Introduction with as much care to its form as to anything else to which he had devoted himself, and he took very seriously the passage about this that he quoted from the dialogue: "By dint of constructing, . . . I truly believe that I have constructed myself. . . . To construct oneself, to know oneself—are these two distinct acts or not?"[5]

Stevens was saying farewell in many ways without having to actually say so. He expressed it here, and his *Collected Poems* expressed it, as he noted to Sister Mary Bernetta in his Easter greeting to her during the first week of April. He had already been to see a local doctor, at the insistence of Anthony Sigmans, to whom he had confided one day at the office that he had not been feeling himself; the first tests run by Dr. James Moher, which included an X ray and barium enema, showed nothing amiss. By April 13 the poet wrote the first letter indicating that he was "not well"; it was to Joseph Bennett, to whom he apologized that he would not be able to send him anything. The next day he wrote both to Richard Eberhart and Samuel French Morse, canceling a luncheon date they had. Stevens was feeling worse and on April 19 was to undergo the gastrointestinal series that revealed a very bloated stomach in addition to diverticulitis and a gallstone. The poet had wanted to see Eberhart before his next test date because he knew, though the younger poet did not yet know, that Eberhart had won the current Harriet Monroe Poetry Award; Stevens had been one of the judges but had not, as was consistent with his true evaluation of *Undercliff,* put Eberhart in first place (his choice was Randall Jarrell). Still, Stevens was happy for his friend. In his note to him, he wrote of his condition: "The only thing that seems to do any good is to remain absolutely quiet and completely abstemious" (April 14, 1955). On the same day, obviously in a weakened state and probably also in great discomfort, the poet wrote again to Robert Pack. But to this young man, with whom he did not have to break an appointment, he mentioned nothing of his illness. He simply went on with the business at hand, being as helpful and warmly protective as he usually was with one of his ephebes. "One must go on pretending that things as they are are as they should be."

Just before Stevens entered St. Francis Hospital, where he would be for more than three weeks with no visitors allowed, Barbara Church sent him a letter in which she commented sadly on the death of Albert Einstein, whom she and her husband had known both in Munich and Princeton. "He was a romantic, a great intelligence and a Bavarian" (April 18, 1955) she proudly announced (perhaps disingenuously ignoring the fact that he also happened to be a Jew). If Stevens had the chance of reading this letter before entering the hospital, it may have made him wonder how and to whom Mrs. Church would celebrate his reputation once he, too, had died.

The last piece of business the poet attended to before leaving for the hospital was to make sure that Holly and her rent would be taken care of through July 1. The "Giant" remained prudent and practical even now. The last thing he had written before his condition made it too difficult for him to concentrate was his piece "Connecticut" (*OP* 294–96), which he had been asked to do for another Voice of America broadcast. There he began by speaking of the "strength of character" which had developed in the people of this region in their response to the "many hardships" they had faced; he was part of the intelligence of this soil, and he exemplified it.

Surgery took place on April 26. It disclosed that the cancer that had been eating away at his stomach was too far advanced to be removed. The doctors advised and Holly agreed that it would be best not to tell her father of his condition. The surgeon had performed a gastroenterostomy above the cancer which would allow some food to pass through the stomach and so relieve the constipation and discomfort Stevens had been experiencing for about a month before and attributing to the change in routine and diet that Elsie's illness had caused; he thought the total lack of exercise, because he had not been walking, in his desire to stay with Elsie as much as possible, had caused his sluggish bowels. Nominally believing that the operation had been a success (Holly remains uncertain whether her father dissembled), by the beginning of May the poet had begun sending short notes to the many who had sent their best wishes to him in the hospital. On May 2 he wrote to Barbara Church that he expected to be soon on his feet for a long time to come after a period of recuperation at home, where he hoped he would be in about a week. The next day the poet received word from Alfred Knopf that he had been awarded the Pulitzer Prize; in his response to Grayson Kirk, Stevens voiced his deep appreciation and gratitude along with his regret that he had to limit himself to only a few words. Two days later he noted to Charles Burns, one of his Canoe Club acquaintances, that he was feeling better every day and looked forward to being back on the club's porch in no time at all, sipping lemonade instead of martinis. The following day the poet wrote to his nephew John and his niece Eleanor thanking them for their flowers and voicing his sadness that he had again become cut off from Reading; John's birthday gibe at his uncle had been forgiven.

Once he was home, however, it became clear just after a few days that his situation put too much of a strain on Elsie, who tried to take complete care of him while not yet wholly recovered herself. And so on the twentieth of the month Stevens removed himself to the Avery Convalescent Hospital across the way on Westerly Terrace. He wanted to be certain to be in shape to go to the Yale ceremonies, now only three weeks away; he eagerly anticipated the conferring of this "precious" award. He wrote to Reuben A. Holden of Yale that under the circumstances he did not plan to attend the dinner the evening before but would drive to New Haven with Holly on the Saturday morning of the commencement and would stay through lunch; he also explained that because Elsie had been ill earlier in the year, she would not be able to attend—not that she had ever attended any of the ceremonies honoring her husband, who had always, like the boy who cried wolf, used the excuse that she had not been well to account for her absence.

One of the things that gave Stevens an extra boost as he prepared for the thirteenth was the news that came from Knopf during the first days of June that *The Collected Poems* was already in its third edition. This, in addition to winning the Pulitzer, "really set [him] up," he wrote back to his publisher (June 7, 1955). There could be nothing more gratifying than knowing that the spirit he had shaped "on paper" had its own life now that that old animal of a body seemed to be giving up its combat with the sun and accepting its need to return, like a child exhausted by its playing at the end of a long summer day, to rest in the embrace of its mother, the earth. This knowledge and the fresh roses Elsie cut from her garden every day and sent to him with Holly were enough. When friends and associates from the Hartford came by to visit, he teased them smilingly, as he always had, and delighted in showing them his favorite places on the well-kept spacious grounds. He taught his nurses to listen for and then spot the different birds that hid themselves in thick leaves. Once a late scarlet tanager surprised him and made him think of those the "comedian" had seen, their color changed back to green in the tropics where he arrived.

On June 9, Stevens had his first outing from the convalescent hospital; it was like a rehearsal for the big day coming up on the thirteenth. This was to the Hartt School of Music, where he received yet another honorary degree. Holly brought Peter along to this ceremony, and when the poet received his black hood trimmed with brilliant red, the boy exclaimed, "Grandfather is the best of all!" Stevens was delighted by this, as he reported to Barbara Church on June 24 in the first long letter he had composed since his illness (*L* 887). It was as though his grandson had spontaneously discovered the *summum bonum* in his grandfather's mimicking the colors of the red-winged blackbird.

June 13 having arrived, the poet and his daughter set out at eight, driven down to New Haven by one of the Hartford's drivers in "a good, big, comfortable car" (*L* 886–87). He was feeling in "very good shape" and was happy that during the ceremonies no one would have noticed anything unusual except, perhaps, his loss of weight. At lunch the strawberries especially enticed him, and he ate about "ten big ones"—one of the last times he was to enjoy them. After lunch and returning to Hartford, to the Avery, he still felt strong enough to dictate a longish letter to his niece Eleanor, returning her note of the eighth, in which he described his improving condition—that he now had an appetite for breakfast and almost one for lunch—and Elsie's progress. He focused far more on Elsie and the expectation he and Holly had for her total recovery than on himself; it seemed he believed he was "clear for a long time to come."

Once back at home Stevens returned to the office immediately. He planned to spend only a few hours there each day until his full strength returned. But after four days and "at least one terrific battle with strawberries," which he found so difficult to resist, he felt like going back to the hospital for two more months (June 24, 1955). Concentration was almost impossible. He had already come to terms with the fact that he could not muster the concentration that was necessary to write any more poems—the last had been "Of Mere Being" and "A Mythology Reflects Its Region" (*OP* 117–18), which were written before he entered the hospital, the second poem composed almost as a companion piece to "Connecticut"—but now he felt that he would not be able to manage even the attention required for at least some of his practical business. He spent most of his time answering personal mail and seeing people; he was also determined to fulfill his obligation to the Hartford, in spite of the fact that earlier in the year some of his responsibilities had been transferred to another section—something that had angered him into the second bellowing tantrum he had indulged in while at work.[6] (It was shortly after this that Stevens began experiencing the symptoms of his condition.) Back at the office, he was more than occasionally in great pain but refused to admit it or to leave earlier than one-thirty, the time he had set for himself. As some of his associates recalled, there were periods now when obviously suffering, Stevens simply and stoically just rested his head on his hand and closed his eyes until he could recover himself.

While he continued to do what he had to for the Hartford, there was no question in his mind that absolutely everything else from now on had to be refused. When Henry Kissinger, then executive director of the International Seminar at Harvard, wrote to the poet on June 27, asking him to give an address, Stevens more than once expressed his regret that he would be unable to do this, adding, sadly and ironically, in closing, that besides having no energy because of his recent illness and surgery, he had "no voice" at all. Though he noted that he did not know about the future, it was clear that only words "on paper" would have to do from now on.

Stevens persisted at the office for several weeks, using his long afternoons in the garden with Elsie, where he felt that the pressure of time was a little delayed, to prepare himself again for the next day's demands. In his quiet times of lying beneath the trees and looking at the sky, he again found himself dreaming of living on a farm in Sweden or on a mountaintop in Switzerland, as he wrote in another letter to his niece Eleanor (June 27, 1955). While the days passed, the man who had loved to feast on capon and fresh peach pie had greater and greater difficulty keeping food down. On one of the first days of July Holly took her father to a restaurant where he ordered a vegetable salad. When it arrived, it appeared to him like "an offering to Ceres," so daunting did the amount of food seem. He was able to manage only "a few peas and a slice of carrot and a mouthful of cauliflower" (July 5, 1955).

Though he weakened every day and couldn't eat even half of what Elsie religiously offered him, Stevens kept maintaining in various notes he sent that he was "getting better day by day" (July 8, 1955) and that in spite of feeling "completely played out . . . [he had] reason to believe that by autumn he [would] have recovered [his] strength" (July 6, 1955). Stevens's resolve to make things seem the way he wanted them to be, even now, was an exercise learned from William James, who, in a central example in *The Will to Believe,* offered the case of an individual who comes to a point in a mountain pass where, for whatever reason, it is impossible to turn back and is now faced with leaping across a chasm. Life depends on the leap. While it is possible that the individual might not be successful in the jump, unless he or she believes that it is possible to make it across, there is no chance at all. The argument was the same for Pascal's choice to believe in God.

By July 15 Stevens could no longer concentrate even on reading. He returned briefly to the Avery Convalescent Hospital, where he expected he would be able to keep food down as he had the month before. But by the twenty-first he had been vomiting up to five times a day and was taken back to St. Francis, where he was fed intravenously. By now cancer had spread through his liver. But Stevens did not lose his spirit. He entertained nurses by reciting Longfellow, one of Elsie's old favorite poets. Did he feel that they, like her, educated in simpler ways, would be more familiar with and so delight in these lines, or was he again playing pranks, thinking that since they knew he was a poet, they would believe that these were his lines? Herbert Schoen remembered this on one of his visits to the hospital where he did not expect to see the man who had been so gnarled by pain on his last days at the office appear, as he did, "cherubic," acting like the perfect Santa Claus to those around him.[7]

With Father Arthur Hanley, the chaplain at St. Francis, the poet continued reminiscing, as he had recently with Elias Mengel during his stay at the Avery, about Harvard, Santayana, and Catholicism. He also spoke about the many times he had sat quietly meditating in the sweet darkness of St. Patrick's Cathedral during his early years in New York and on later visits. Did the priest take the poet's curiosity for a late profession of faith? Was Stevens insuring himself as Pascal had? Father Hanley reported later the steps, including the poet's desire to have a St. Christopher's medal pinned on one side of his pillow balancing the crucifix that lay on the other, leading to the poet's conversion, which the priest and the attendant, Sister Philomena, decided at the time to keep secret.[8]

Holly Stevens reports that her father complained to her that he was being bothered by visits from the priest but was too weak to protest.[9] Which are we to believe? Is it possible that a man of the cloth would manufacture words and details in order to claim a soul for the church? Is it possible that Holly misinterpreted her father? He spoke to her of many things in and out of his day sleep (he did not need sedation because he was so weak): the trip to British Columbia returned again and again (the paleness of the cold sky before dawn, the mountain cat, the rattlesnake, the movement of things that could never be seen in the dark of the night woods—all memories circling the figure of the man from whom he had learned so much of how to live and what to do, whose signature imitated the sharp movement of pits and tips of snowy mountains); his concern that Peter learn to swim properly (he was so fearless; it was important that he learn well; what freedom it had been when he himself had learned, how piercing the water in the canals at home on the first days of summer); Elsie, Elsie had to be looked after well, she would need her. Of these and many other things he whispered to his child.

Is it possible that as his final prank the comedian had led both Father Hanley and Holly to believe two different things, that the poet did, in fact, ask for Communion and Extreme Unction as part of the final act of his comedy without telling Holly, so that we now still wonder how he resolved the greatest problem of his age, the will to believe? It would make sense against the sky of America, spangled with a plurality of religions like stars, following Thomas Jefferson's profoundly moving argument: If the good God saw fit to create so many varieties of trees, creatures, everything, who are we to say that there should be one way? The poet's commitment to his country grew out of a well-researched understanding of what it meant to his forebears to find a place free of the persecution they had suffered. To offer the same possibility of freedom to believe would have been the end of his own logic. He respected the difference in William Carlos Williams's approach to poetry in the same way. The pluralistic hypothesis had to be entertained in all things. It is the belief, not the fiction, that matters.

❧

After lapsing in and out of a coma during his last two days, Wallace Stevens died on the morning of August 2. His last words were his "Good night" to Holly and Peter in a quietly lucid moment the evening before. Two days later the funeral services and interment secured the poet's bond to all that dust.

NOTES

INTRODUCTION

1. New York: Random House, 1987, p. 222.

CHAPTER I. *The Sea of Spuming Thought 1923–1933*

1. Ludwig Wittgenstein, *Tractatus Logico-Philosophicus,* tr. C. K. Ogden (London, Boston, Melbourne, and Henley: Routledge & Kegan Paul, 1983, (2d paperback edition), p. 89–the closing of the volume. The parallels between Wittgenstein's perceptions, as phrased in the *Tractatus,* and many of Stevens's perceptions, phrased both in poems and in his "Adagia" as well as informally in letters in which he explained his "theory" of poetry is remarkable and worth study.

2. H. Stuart Hughes, *Consciousness and Society: The Reconstruction of European Social Thought, 1870–1930* (New York: Vintage, 1961), p. 393.

3. Ibid., p. 394.

4. As distinct from C. S. Peirce's "pragmatism," later modified by him to "pragmaticism" to distinguish it from James's coinage, originally borrowed from him.

5. Hughes, op. cit., p. 396.

6. *Historical Review of Berks County,* Vol. XXIV (fall 1959), p. 112.

7. *The Timetables of History,* compiled by Bernard Grun (New York: Simon & Schuster, 1982), p. 479.

8. In "Poets Without Laurels," *The World's Body* (Baton Rouge: Louisiana State University Press, 1968), pp. 55–75.

9. For this reading, see my article, "A Reading of 'Sea Surface Full of Clouds,'" in *The Wallace Stevens Journal,* Vol. 6, Nos. 3 and 4 (fall 1982), pp. 60–68.

10. See Harold Bloom, *Wallace Stevens: The Poems of Our Climate* (Ithaca and London: Cornell University Press, 1977), p. 38, on the "no, no"; see also Milton Bates, "Stevens in Love, The Woman Won, The Woman Lost,"

English Literary History, Vol. 48 (1981), p. 254, on including a reading of "Red Loves Kit" as a companion to "Le Monocle."

11. Clive Bell, *Poems* (Richmond: Hogarth, 1921); John Millington Synge, *Poems and Translations* (Dublin: Maunsel & Roberts, 1921), which Stevens acquired on October 14, 1924; and Harriet Monroe, *The Difference and Other Poems* (Chicago: Covici & McGee, 1924) are included here.

12. From Thomas Mann, *Death in Venice,* tr. Kenneth Burke, *Dial,* Vol. LXXVI (March 1924), pp. 215–16.

13. The volume in Stevens's library, now at the Huntington, published in 1924 by the Hogarth Press, p. 10; the page numbers for following quotations from the novella will be in parentheses or brackets within the text.

14. Peter Brazeau notes two later occasions when Stevens avoided MacLeish: *Parts of a World: Wallace Stevens Remembered* (New York: Random House, 1983), pp. 26 and 119.

15. It has been suggested to me that the thyroid and pituitary disturbances in Stevens's family could be connected with mineral leaching into the Reading water supply, as is common in the Appalachians.

16. From a letter dated September 7, 1927, in the Bienecke Library, Yale University.

17. George Lensing has wonderfully reproduced Stevens's notebook entitled "From Pieces of Paper" in the *Southern Review,* Vol. 15, No. 4 (October 1979), pp. 877–920; he has added valuable comments linking these recordings to later poems and essays. More recently these have been reproduced in his *Wallace Stevens: A Poet's Growth* (Baton Rouge: Louisiana State University Press, 1987).

18. Brazeau, op. cit., p. 16.

19. This volume, part of Stevens's library, is now in the Special Collections of the University of Massachusetts Library at Amherst; it was translated by W. D. Robson-Scott and published by the Hogarth Press in 1928. This quotation is from p. 44; others will appear in parentheses or brackets within the text.

20. These are "The Man Whose Pharynx Was Bad" (1921); "The Death of a Soldier," "Negation," "Lunar Paraphrase" (from the "Lettres d'Un Soldat" group, 1918); "The Surprises of the Superhuman" (1918); and "New England Verses" (submitted to and rejected by the *New Republic* in 1922). The dating of "The Revolutionists Stop for Orangeade" is uncertain.

21. This volume, containing "Mademoiselle de Scudery" and "Salvatore Rosa" (Paris: no publisher, 1929), is also at the University of Massachusetts at Amherst; Stevens noted on the jacket that he read the book at Atlantic City, September 4–11, 1930, his daughter's first trip to the seashore.

22. Hi Simons, "The Vicissitudes of Reputation," *Harvard Advocate,* Vol. CXXVII (December 1940), p. 39.

23. Vol. V, pp. 223–55; reprinted in *The Achievement of Wallace Stevens,* eds. Ashley Brown and Robert S. Haller (Philadelphia and New York: Lippincott, 1962), pp. 52–80.

24. These were: John Gould Fletcher, "Some Contemporary American Poets," *Chapbook,* Vol. II (May 1920), pp. 1–31; Harriet Monroe, "A Cavalier of Beauty," *Poetry,* Vol. XXIII (March 1924), pp. 322–27, and "The Free-Verse Movement in America," *English Journal,* Vol. XIII (December 1924), pp. 69–75; Marianne Moore's review, "Well-Moused Lion," *Dial,* Vol. LXXVI (January 1924), pp. 84–91; Gorham Munson, "The Dandyism of Wallace Stevens," *Dial,* Vol. LXXIX (November 1925), pp. 413–17; Llewelyn Powys, "The Thirteenth Way," *Dial,* Vol. LXXVII (July 1924), pp. 45–50; Allen Tate, "American Poetry Since 1920," *Bookman,* Vol. LXVIII (January 1929), pp. 503–08; Edmund Wilson, "Wallace Stevens and e. e. cummings," *New Republic,* Vol. XXXVIII (March 19, 1924), pp. 102–03.

25. Simons, "Vicissitudes," loc. cit., p. 40.

26. *New York Herald Tribune Books* (September 27, 1931), p. 28.

27. In "American Poetry Since 1920," see Note 24 above.

CHAPTER II. *A Great Order Is a Disorder 1933–1942*

1. Later, however, by the end of this period, in late 1941 and early 1942, when he was composing "The Noble Rider and the Sound of Words," Stevens referred directly to *The Future of an Illusion,* paraphrasing its central argument and even quoting one of the sentences that had particular resonance for him in shaping one of his later lines; as noted earlier, this was "The voice of the intellect is a soft one, but it does not rest until it has gained a hearing" (*NA* 15). Stevens did not mention Freud's use of Ananke here.

2. This is described in Kiang Kang-Hu's Introduction (following Witter Bynner's) to *The Jade Mountain: A Chinese Anthology* (New York: Vintage, 1957; first published in 1929 by Knopf), pp. xxvi–vii. Stevens's connections with the view of poetry described here will be taken up in Chapter V.

3. See, for example, letters to Henri Amiot (*L* 480), William Carlos Williams (*L* 716), and Sister Mary Bernetta Quinn (*L* 612).

4. See Eleanor Cook, "Riddles, Charms, and Fictions in Wallace Stevens," *Centre and Labyrinth: Essays in Honor of Northrop Frye,* eds. Eleanor Cook, Chaviva Hošek, Jay MacPherson, Patricia Parker, and Julian Patrick (Toronto: University of Toronto Press, 1983), for particulars on Stevens's use of puzzles, riddles, and charms, and Northrop Frye on "Charms and Riddles" generally in his essay of that title collected in *Spiritus Mundi: Essays on Literature, Myth, and Society* (Bloomington and London: Indiana University Press, 1976), pp. 123–47, to which Cook also refers.

5. Though asked to contribute a statement about Stevens for the special issue of the *Harvard Advocate* (December 1940), Eliot declined, saying he was not familiar enough with Stevens's work.

6. Edward Albert Filene (1860–1937), president of William Filene's Sons in Boston, not only was a pioneer in applying scientific methods to business but applied his labors to important social causes, especially peace. In 1919 he founded the Cooperative League, which later became the Twentieth Century

Fund. He also planned and helped organize the Boston Chamber of Commerce and the Chamber of Commerce of the United States and was chairman, during the First World War, of the War Shipping Committee (*Columbia Encyclopedia* [New York: Columbia University Press], p. 674). His commitment was to a redistribution of both power and wealth.

7. New York: Penguin Books, 1976, p. 189.

8. Ibid., pp. 153–54.

9. Brazeau, op. cit., p. 90.

10. Ibid., p. 79. Since Stevens had a very well-stocked wine cellar that he proudly displayed on at least one occasion to dinner guests (ibid., p. 49) and bought wine by the case not only in New York but at the package store in Hartford and would have it picked up and delivered by his driver from the insurance company, it seems that Elsie's negative reactions were intermittent, perhaps corresponding to her own varying inner states or, perhaps, belonging to times when she knew her husband was under doctor's orders not to indulge in spirits of any kind.

11. Brazeau, op. cit., p. 98 n.

12. Ibid., p. 98.

13. Ernest Hemingway, *Selected Letters, 1917–1961,* ed. Carlos Baker (New York: Charles Scribner's Sons, 1981), pp. 438–40, as also noted by Brazeau, op. cit., p. 98 n.

14. Brazeau, p. 98 n.

15. Ibid., p. 191.

16. It, he added, reminded him of the "duck for dinner" he, May, and others had *not* had one night in Florida. Here was the source of the sense of absence informing the "Duck for Dinner" sections of *Owl's Clover,* in which it became a metaphor for what, under the present political and social conditions, the masses, including the poet, could not have. Holly Stevens also notes this connection (*L* 307 n.).

17. Brazeau, op. cit., p. 243.

18. Baker's review is reprinted in *The Achievement of Wallace Stevens,* loc. cit., pp. 81–96.

19. This point about the tie between Stevens and Bacon is also made by Beverly Coyle, *A Thought to Be Rehearsed: Aphorism in Wallace Stevens's Poetry* (Ann Arbor: UMI Research Press, 1974), pp. 13–14.

20. These fragments of experience remembered by Holly Stevens have been recorded in various sources: *Souvenirs and Prophecies,* itself an expansion of "Bits of Remembered Time," which appeared in the *Southern Review,* Vol. VII (July 1971), pp. 651–57; notes and comments in *Letters;* and her "Holidays in Reality," *Wallace Stevens: A Celebration,* eds. Frank Doggett and Robert Buttel (Princeton: Princeton University Press, 1980), pp. 105–13.

21. This is evident on the manuscript in the Huntington Library.

22. Marguerite Flynn died even before Peter Brazeau began taping the interviews on which he based his *Parts of a World.* She did, however, leave in

writing a record of what she did for Mr. Stevens although she did not keep the scraps of paper from which she typed fair copies of his poems.

23. The Huntington has assigned the dates 1932–1953 for these two notebooks. A. Walton Litz, in "Particles of Order: The Unpublished *Adagia,*" *Celebration,* loc. cit., pp. 57–77, has partially reproduced portions of these two and the "Materia Poetica" notebooks.

24. Vol. 12, p. 204, as Stevens noted.

25. "Sur Plusieurs Beaux Sujets," Vol. I, p. 15, apropos of an observation of Graham Bell's about Cézanne.

26. In November 1938 issue of *Apollo,* p. 226.

27. There was an illustrated weekly from Ceylon that Van Geyzel sent (*L* 337). There was also another volume about Ceylon that Stevens himself ordered that turned out to have some of the best photographs he had seen of the place: Angus Holden, 3rd baron Holden: *Ceylon* (New York: Macmillan, 1939).

28. Holly Stevens, "Holidays in Reality," loc. cit., p. 110.

29. Brazeau, op. cit., p. 246.

30. Holly Stevens, "Holidays in Reality," loc. cit., p. 113.

31. Brazeau, "A Trip in a Balloon: A Sketch of Stevens' Later Years in New York," *Celebration,* loc. cit., pp. 114–29, and Brazeau, *Parts of a World,* loc. cit.

32. Stevens's observation here parallels that made by T. S. Eliot in closing *The Three Voices of Poetry* (New York: Cambridge University Press, 1954), p. 38: "If you complain that a poet is obscure, and apparently ignoring you, the reader, or that he is speaking only to a limited circle of initiates from which you are excluded—remember that what he may have been trying to do, was to put something into words which could not be said in any other way, and therefore in a language which may be worth the trouble of learning."

33. In "Holidays in Reality," loc. cit., p. 109, Holly Stevens records her memories of this day trip; later she notes that this was the summer her father wrote "Variations on a Summer Day" but does not connect it directly with the experience on the ferry.

34. This extraordinarily valuable distinction between the "real" and "reality" has recently been drawn by William Gass, *Habitations of the Word* (New York: Simon & Schuster, 1985), pp. 39–40, in which he uses it to point out the differences between the essayist's (like Emerson's) approach to seeing things as they are and the philosopher's.

35. Peter Brazeau, "'Hepped on Family Ties': Wallace Stevens in the 1940's," in *The Motive for Metaphor: Essays on Modern Poetry,* eds. Francis C. Blessington and Guy Rotella (Boston: Northeastern University Press, 1983), p. 41; and Brazeau, *Parts of World,* loc. cit., p. 234 n.

36. Holly Stevens, "Holidays in Reality," loc. cit., p. 111.

37. Brazeau, *Parts of World,* loc. cit., p. 143.

38. For a wonderful portrait of Christian Gauss, whom Stevens came to

know through his contact with Henry Church and the Princeton circle, see Edmund Wilson, *The Shores of Light: A Literary Chronicle of the 1920's and 1930's* (New York: Farrar, Straus, Giroux, 1979), pp. 3–26.

39. From the notes and markings in Stevens's copy of *Folios of New Writing: Autumn, 1940* (London: Hogarth [1940])—in Virginia Woolf, "The Leaning Tower," and Stephen Spender, "Creative Imagination in the World Today"—it is clear that there was much food for the poet's thought. Stevens's focus on the "pressure of external fact" in relationship to poetry echoed, for example, this sentence from Spender which he underlined, as well as those following to the end of the paragraph which it opens: "Poets are faced with the problem of transforming into the comprehensible terms of the imagination the chaos of this politically obsessed world" (pp. 147–48). Similarly, many of Virginia Woolf's observations paralleled his own: "Thinking should be based on facts" (p. 15), for example. Stevens marked passages particularly where Woolf spoke about the importance of education in the life of the writer and that the education her generation of writers had received did not adequately prepare them for the necessary change that had to come in the social order; the "tower" was her metaphor for education, and it was now leaning because the foundations on which it had stood until the Great War had been since then gradually eroding. There are other overlays of Stevens/Spender and Stevens/Woolf as well—too numerous to be developed here. The volume is at the University of Massachusetts Library at Amherst.

40. This edition (the fifth), now at the Huntington (London: Hogarth, 1931), was sent to the poet by Leonard van Geyzel (*L* 331 n.).

41. These are either at the Huntington or at Amherst; specific bibliographic information for those cited here following will be indicated at the appropriate point; information on the others can be found by consulting Milton J. Bates, "Stevens' Books at the Huntington: An Annotated Checklist," *The Wallace Stevens Journal,* Vol. 2, Nos. 3 and 4 (fall 1978), pp. 45–61, and Vol. 3, Nos. 1 and 2 (Spring 1979), pp. 15–33, and "Stevens' Books at the Huntington: Errata," *The Wallace Stevens Journal,* Vol. 3, Nos. 3 and 4 (Fall 1979), p. 70; and Peter Brazeau, "Wallace Stevens at the University of Massachusetts: Checklist of an Archive," *Wallace Stevens Journal,* Vol. 2, Nos. 1 and 2 (Spring 1978), pp. 50–54.

42. Ibid.

43. These are too numerous to list here; see Bates, "Stevens' Books at the Huntington," loc. cit. I shall mention or discuss in the text only those items that seem to have contributed to Stevens's thinking out of the poetic or historical problems he was threading through at the time, as well as items that seem to have contributed to the aureole of meaning he created around images in poems or essays on which he was working.

44. *The Life and Writings of Giambattista Vico* (London: Allen & Unwin, 1935); at Amherst.

45. Leon Roth, *Descartes' Discourse on Method* (Oxford: Clarendon, 1937),

p. 56, quoting Bacon; at Amherst. Following page references indicated in text.

46. Benedetto Croce, *The Defense of Poetry: Variations on a Theme of Shelley,* tr. E. F. Carritt (Oxford: Clarendon, 1933), p. 30; at Amherst. Following page references indicated in text.

47. He was perhaps reminded of this by his reading of F. L. Lucas, *The Criticism of Poetry* (London: H. Milford, 1933)—also at Amherst—in which on p. 4, we find:

> To the Greek in his best days good poetry meant, above all, poetry that bred good men. The Muses were the daughters of Omniscience. The God of Poetry was the God also of Prophecy and of Healing, the divine voice that spoke at the Delphic centre of the earth. How to plough, how to fight, how to live, how to die—the poets taught all these. The boy who got by heart the great speech of Sarpedon, the girl who heard recited the farewell of Hector to Andromache, might learn, so the Greek believed, how themselves to face hereafter the breaking-points of life.

We can better imagine Stevens's reaction to reading this when we recall how when still a young man and hearing of a death, he wrote to an acquaintance that the man who can quotes Latin on such an occasion.

48. Brazeau, *Parts of World,* loc. cit., pp. 66–67; Brazeau also notes that the occasion of John's funeral marked a turning point in Stevens's relations with his family.

49. New York: Vintage Books, 1979; page references for following quotations in the text will be indicated in parentheses.

50. In addition to Vico, Croce, Virginia Woolf, I. A. Richards on Coleridge, Bateson, Mauron, and Freud, Stevens noted Vilfredo Pareto, Robert Wolseley, Feruccio Busoni's *Letters to His Wife,* a recent translation of Kierkegaard, Boileau on Descartes, Rostrevor Hamilton, recent reviews of painting exhibitions, as well as rereadings of Plato, Wordsworth, and Bergson in his lecture.

51. He had sent Stevens a pamphlet entitled *The Essence of Buddha's Teaching.*

CHAPTER III. *It Must Be Abstract 1942–1947*

1. This phrase is borrowed from the title of Stephen Kern's *The Culture of Time and Space* (Cambridge: Harvard University Press, 1983). In connection with what the coming of flight meant, Kenneth Burke, *Attitudes Toward History,* 3d ed. (Berkeley: University of California Press, 1984), pp. 27–28, notes that "Marinetti became remade [as he reported], during a trip in an airplane, an event that seems to have startled him by a secular vision of 'the pit.'" Burke then expands on similar perceptions in Faulkner, in Thomas Mann, and

Muriel Rukeyser, *Theory of Flight,* in which the poet is piloted above "the modern Chamber of Horrors, as Virgil guided Dante through hell. . . ."

In another connection, tying himself to Stevens in terms of the way the political world was perceived, Burke notes:

> Nonetheless, critics must persist in their attempts to spread and perfect a "comic" interpretation of human motives, aware that, whatever avalanches of heroic euphemism of the Hitler or Mussolini variety may fall upon the world at times, the movement towards the humane and civilized is maintained precisely insofar as the austere self-consciousness of comedy is "implemented" by the accumulated body of comic shrewdness. (p. 79 n.)

First published in 1937, the "attitudes" expressed by Burke, here and throughout the text, closely parallel those of Stevens during the same period.

2. Brazeau, *Parts of World,* loc. cit., p. 87.

3. Dated February 11, 1942, this letter is also quoted by Brazeau, ibid., p. 87 n.

4. Ibid., p. 246.

5. Ibid., pp. 250–51.

6. Ibid., pp. 231–35.

7. I am indebted for this information to various members of the Study Group in the History of Psychiatry Section of the Payne Whitney Clinic in New York City, especially to Dr. Eric T. Carlson, who searched out and sent me photocopies of a description of acromegaly from a medical text in the library at the clinic.

8. Brazeau, *Parts of World,* loc. cit., p. 85.

9. New York: Doubleday, Image, 1978, pp. 504–05.

10. From an interview with Mr. Schoen, December 17, 1982.

11. Stevens owned a set of Flaubert's complete works in French; perhaps he did not think that they had to be rebound (they are now at the Huntington). He ordered that Stendhal's *Chartreuse de Parme (Charterhouse of Parma)* be specially bound. It was one of his favorite novels, as he expressed in an early letter; it has not remained as part of his library at the Huntington, nor is it at Amherst.

12. From a Biographical Note to Alain's *The Gods,* tr. Richard Pevear (New York: New Directions, 1974), p. 183.

13. Foreword, ibid., p. 6.

14. Ibid., p. 3.

15. Ibid., p. 2.

16. From Alain, Introduction, *The Gods,* loc. cit., pp. 9–10.

17. Ibid., pp. 10–11.

18. Ibid., p. 184.

19. For the full account of what Jones remembered, see Brazeau, *Parts of World,* loc. cit., pp. 123–32.

20. In connection with Stevens's love of his garden and of Elizabeth Park,

which he tried to walk through every day on his way to and from the office, the photographer Eugène Atget, another lover of gardens, observed that no gardener ever came twice to the same garden, a properly Heraclitan note characterizing both his spirit and the poet's. The observation was recorded on an accompanying plaque to a series of Atget's photographs on exhibit at the Museum of Modern Art in New York during April 1985.

21. Brazeau, *Parts of World,* loc. cit., pp. 268–70.

22. Dewey's piece was "Anti-Naturalism in Extremis," *Partisan Review,* Vol. X (January–February 1943), pp. 24–39; Hook's, "The New Failure of Nerve," ibid., pp. 2–23. The only Laski title remaining in Stevens's library (now, I believe, in Holly Stevens's) was *The Danger of Being a Gentleman and Other Essays* (London: Allen & Unwin, 1939) (*L* 441 n.).

23. This was the second summer that the Entretiens de Pontigny Conference was held in America.

> The poets responsible for them were invited by M. Jean Wahl, who had charge of the week whose mornings were devoted to the discussion of poetry. The afternoons were given over to talk on politics. The initiative to hold these conferences, modelled on the famous Decades which until 1940 were conducted by Paul Desjardins at the Cistercian monastery at Pontigny in Burgundy, was, however due, primarily to the great French medieval scholar, Gustave Cohen, formerly of the Sorbonne and now Dean of the Faculty of Literature of the École Libre des Hautes Études. He had the aid of a number of his colleagues at the school, which is in essence a French university, founded by exiles, after the fall of France, in the city of New York. The conferences were made possible by the support of Miss Helen Patch, chairman of the French Department at Mount Holyoke College, who saw that one could not do better in time of war than to provide a place where ideas could be exchanged on the immediate issues of the war, in so far as they are things of the mind, as well as on those permanent concerns of men, who, though driven out of their countries by an enemy whose weakness and strength is that he has always wanted to be either more or less than mankind, are determined to remain within the human domain. . . .
>
> The whole point of the conferences at Pontigny, whether held on the borders of Burgundy or on the western edge of Massachusetts, is that there is a continuity of thought which must at all costs be maintained. There are bound to be interruptions, the dull ones of daily occurrence, the more deadly and dreadful ones of war. They cannot be ignored; but, short of death, the silence they impose need never be permanent.
>
> France had fallen; we were surrounded by exiles from France and other countries occupied by the German armies; some had come after fighting; some from prisons and concentration camps; some had been deprived of their homes, robbed of their books, despoiled of the records of a lifetime of study; all had come from defeat. None had succumbed. . . .

From John Peale Bishop, "Entretiens de Pontigny: 1943; I. Introduction," by John Peale Bishop, *Sewanee Review,* Vol. LII, No. 4, pp. 493–529. (This was Bishop's last literary work.)

24. The many little magazines that he had such affection for, as expressed to Frank Jones in the interview referred to earlier in this chapter, and the small presses like the Cummington.

25. Also noted in Brazeau, *Parts of World,* loc. cit., p. 265, and in his "Hepped on Family Ties," loc. cit., p. 37.

26. See Roy Harvey Pearce, "The Cry and Its Occasion: 'Chocorua to Its Neighbor,'" *Southern Review,* Vol. 15, No. 4 (October 1979), pp. 777–91.

27. Collected in Yvor Winters, *In Defense of Reason,* 3d ed. (Chicago: Swallow Press, 1947), pp. 431–59.

28. For a full discussion of this, see "Yvor Winters: The Case of the Wincing Widow," Chapter 7 of my dissertation, "By Their Fruits: Wallace Stevens, His Poetry, His Critics" (CUNY, 1977), pp. 257–315.

29. The reference to "Durand-Ruel's" was perhaps prompted by a postcard Stevens received from Walter Pach in Mexico, dated January 27, 1943, laid into the poet's copy of Henri Focillon's *The Life of Forms in Art* (Huntington). It reads:

> DEAR WALLACE
>
> I have just looked your letter again, and it says you want post cards of "true things." Well, what are they? It is true (or I see in the paper) that Durand-Ruel has been showing a Bouguereau—but it is as false as ever though two critics mention it with Renoir. This church (over [picture on postcard]) even; they stuck a false front on it. I painted it, and so I know it.
>
> Yours
>
> WALTER PACH

The church pictured is a sprawling mixture of brickwork in a kind of Mexican-Romanesque style overlaid with the heaviest of baroque façades.

30. "Artists, Soldiers, Positivists," *Kenyon Review,* Vol. VI (spring 1944), pp. 276–77.

31. On D-Day Stevens sent a memo typed in the shape of a cross to one of his associates, reporting that the idea was his secretary's.

32. This quotation, also used in an earlier chapter in another context is from a line of William Butler Yeats's "Leda and the Swan," *The Collected Poems of . . .* (Toronto: Macmillan, 1969), p. 212.

33. Brazeau, *Parts of World,* loc. cit., p. 275.

34. See Lewis Thomas, "The Unforgettable Fire," *Late Night Thoughts on Listening to Mahler's Ninth Symphony* (New York: Viking, 1983), pp. 6–7. Thomas is one of the many scientists who have recently quoted from or made reference to the work of Stevens, as though in implicit acknowledgment that the poet in fact did understand something "true" about the structure of reality.

35. Kern, op. cit., p. 68.

36. In *The Life of Forms in Art,* trs. C. Beecher Hogan and George Kubler (New Haven: Yale University Press, 1942); in Amherst.

37. Looking at this watercolor perhaps contributed to Stevens's putting together of "Someone Puts a Pineapple Together," the central one of the "Three Academic Pieces." These "Pieces" were first published in the *Partisan Review,* Vol. XIV, No. 3 (May–June 1947), pp. 243–53, after their delivery as a lecture at Harvard; they will be discussed in detail later in this chapter.

38. Stevens's interest was spurred even more after speaking with Walter Pach, whom he saw in New York at the end of February 1945. As the poet reported to Rodríguez Feo, Pach was full of admiration for things Latin American, especially since returning from his recent trip to Mexico. In closing his note to his Cuban friend, Stevens added, ". . . after listening to Walter, I couldn't wait to reach Hartford, where I immediately sent off an order for some of Sr. Reyes' books. True, I shall not be able to read them, but I shall get something out of them" (*L* 490).

39. As he wrote to Rodríguez Feo on February 26, 1945, he defined the "major man" in "Paisant Chronicle" and intended to communicate the same idea as that behind his earlier statement to Henry Church that "Il faut être paysan d'être poète."

40. There has been a good deal of scholarship on Stevens's use of "major man" as a figure; see Edelstein, op. cit., and MLA Bibliography following 1971; see most recently, too, Milton J. Bates, *Wallace Stevens: A Mythology of Self* (Berkeley: University of California Press, 1985).

41. Translated by George Bull (New York: Penguin, 1967), pp. 179–80; I am indebted to John Hollander for this find.

42. *Voices,* No. 121 (spring 1945).

43. As Holly Stevens notes (*L* 506 n.), this is from F. O. Matthiessen, *Henry James: The Major Phase* (New York: Oxford University Press, 1944), p. 10.

44. Among the many authors and books Stevens and Rodríguez Feo exchanged opinions about around this period were: Richard Blackmur and Morton Dauwen Zabel (*L* 484–85); Hemingway, John Malcolm Brinnin, and Robert Penn Warren, with whom Stevens felt he shared feelings (*L* 489–90); Roger Caillois, *Les Impostures de la Poésie* (Paris: Gallimard, 1945); Robert Lowell and Randall Jarrell (both of whose work Stevens said he did not read because he did not want to pick up anything [*L* 490–91]), as he also reported feeling about the later Eliot; Flaubert and Stendhal (*L* 505); Thomas Barbour, *A Naturalist in Cuba* (Boston: Little, Brown, 1945) (*L* 525); Elizabeth Bishop and William Carlos Williams (*L* 544), as discussed later in the text (p. 277). Early in their correspondence, Rodríguez Feo had noted one of his "discoveries" to Stevens; this was Pierre de Bourdeilles, seigneur de Brantôme, *Vie des Dames Galantes.* The young Cuban observed: "This pornographic book tells the inside stories of the great princes and princesses of the age of Francis the First and really puts to shame Mr. Connolly's and Mr. Miller's attempts"

(March 23, 1945). This had to have provided Stevens with another moment of recognizing the identity between his young friend and himself, when he remembered his own delightful discovery of the same text twenty-three years earlier. As he reported then to Harriet Monroe in an observation not dissimilar from Rodríguez Feo's, this book "knocks Plutarch hollow" (*L* 230).

45. Vol. LIII (autumn 1945), pp. 566–79; reprinted in *Wallace Stevens: A Collection of Critical Essays,* ed. Marie Borroff (Englewood Cliffs, N.J.: Prentice-Hall Twentieth Century Views, 1963), pp. 43–53.

46. Ransom's early judgment never detracted from the way Stevens perceived him. Rather, he found him, as he noted to Church, "very American and therefore very valuable" (*L* 518).

47. Though it is impossible to know whether the three-year-old Stevens would have witnessed a particularly striking meteorological event involving a display of "Brilliant auroras," whether because of the time they occurred or the clearness of the sky or other more banal considerations, it is nonetheless interesting to note the following, as reported in the "100 Years Ago" column of the *Scientific American,* Vol. 246, No. 12 (December 1982), p. 10:

> Last month was characterized by many wide-spread electrical disturbances, which culminated in intensity on November 17. On that day telegraphic communication was more or less interrupted over the northern half of the United States, and much damage was done to switch boards and other telegraphic apparatus. The disturbance extended across the sea, interfering seriously with the work of the cables, and made itself felt in many parts of the European continent. Brilliant auroras [both abroad and in the United States] were generally seen where the sky was clear. The appearance of exceptionally large sun spots is believed to have more than an accidental connection with these disturbances of the earth's electric equilibrium.

Even if the young Stevens did not witness the effects of this disturbance, it seems that like the great New York blackout, it was one of those events that the adults around him would have referred to either in dating other less striking happenings or simply in reminiscing. The connection with Stevens is particularly intriguing because of his major uses of the images of the "aurora," the sun—the events on its surface accounting for disequilibrium of the planet—and the poet's "movement up and down" between sun and moon.

48. *Sewanee Review,* Vol. LIV (winter 1946), pp. 156–61.

49. Noted by David Franklin in his review of Barton Gilman, *Contending with Kennan: Toward a Philosophy of American Power* (New York: Praeger, 1985), *New York Times Book Review* (May 12, 1985), p. 31.

50. *Complete Works,* ed. Oscar Leng, tr. Ludovici, 18 vols. (London: 1909–15), Vol. 22, p. 16.

51. Among others these requests came from Randall Jarrell for the *Nation* (to whom Stevens first sent "A Pastoral Nun" with reservations with which Jarrell agreed and so did not publish; he later sent "The Beginning," which

appeared in the October 18, 1947, issue [Vol. CLXV, No. 16], p. 412) and from José García Villa for *Viva* (later *Wake*), to whom Stevens sent "Credences of Summer," though it never appeared there.

52. Brazeau, *Parts of World,* loc. cit., pp. 285 and 310 n.

53. Ibid., p. 268.

54. In terms of the kinds of puzzles that this kind of musing can present to the mind and that Stevens no doubt enjoyed, it is interesting to see that Douglas Hofstadter has recently explored this same relation in "Metafont, Mathematics, and Metaphysics: Comments on Donald Knuth's Article 'The Concept of Meta-Font,'" which appeared originally in the August 1982 issue of the *Scientific American,* reprinted in *Metamagical Themas: Questing for the Essence of Mind and Pattern* (New York: Basic Books, 1985), pp. 260–96.

55. In the same letter he noted that he had "a taste for Braque and a purse for Bombois," yet, as Holly Stevens adds, among her father's papers was one of the first color lithographs of Braque which the artist pulled himself, *Nature Morte: Verre et Fruit* (1921). The poet "had never had it framed and it is not known when or where he obtained it" (*L* 545 n.).

56. *Princeton Encyclopedia of Poetry and Poetics,* eds. Alex Preminger, Frank J. Warnke, and O. B. Hardison, Jr. (Princeton: Princeton University Press, 1974), p. 258.

57. *Encyclopédie de la Pléiade: Histoire des Littératures,* 3 vols., ed. Raymond Queneau (Paris: Gallimard, 1968), Vol. 2, p. 65.

58. Ibid., p. 372.

59. *Princeton Encyclopedia,* loc. cit., pp. 258–59.

60. Notably in *The Comedy of Errors, Two Gentlemen of Verona, Love's Labor Lost,* and, most obviously in *Henry IV, Part I* (Act 2, Scene 4), *Princeton Encyclopedia,* loc. cit., p. 259.

61. At the Rosenbach Library in Philadelphia.

CHAPTER IV. *It Must Change 1947–1954*

1. As reported by Brazeau, *Parts of World,* loc. cit. (from the Hartford Accident and Indemnity Company's Employee's Record Card), Stevens's annual salary with the date of each raise is as follows: March 15, 1916, $3,000; April 1, 1917, $3,600; April 1, 1918, $3,900; April 1, 1919, $4,400; January 1, 1920, $4,840; April 1, 1920, $6,000; September 1, 1920, $7,500; February 1, 1922, $8,400; May 1, 1923, $10,000; January 1, 1926, $11,000; January 1, 1927, $13,000; January 1, 1928, $14,000; January 1, 1929, $15,000; July 1, 1932, $13,500; February 1, 1934, $17,500; May 15, 1935, $20,000; November 1, 1945, $22,000; February 1, 1948, $24,000 (p. 231).

2. Ibid., p. 277.

3. Samuel French Morse, *Wallace Stevens: Life as Poetry* (New York: Pegasus, 1970), p. 33.

4. Ian Hamilton, *Robert Lowell: A Biography* (New York: Random House, 1982), pp. 197 and 206.

5. Brazeau, *Parts of World,* loc. cit., p. 172.

6. Ibid., p. 174 n.

7. Ibid., p. 172.

8. Ibid., p. 173.

9. *The Timetables of History,* loc. cit., p. 530.

10. The Fargue title Stevens read was *Portraits de Famille;* he also read Georges Bernanos, *La France Contre les Robots* during this period (*L* 594–95).

11. "Jean Dubuffet Catalogue," Pierre Matisse Gallery, in the Wallace Stevens Collection, Huntington Library (Catalog No. 448270), p. 21.

12. Ibid., p. 17.

13. This and other pieces of Bernard Heringman's criticism—"Wallace Stevens: The Reality of Poetry," Ph.D. dissertation, Columbia University, 1955; "The Poetry of Synthesis," *Perspective,* Vol. VII (autumn 1954), pp. 167–74; "Two Worlds and Epiphany," *Bard Review,* Vol. II (May 1948), pp. 156–59; "Wallace Stevens: The Use of Poetry," *English Literary History,* Vol. XVI (December 1949), pp. 325–36 (also in Pearce and Miller)—Stevens found good analyses and precise examples of fine *explication de texte.*

14. John Hollander reported to me that another critic, Eleanor Cook, reads "New Haven" as "New Heaven."

15. Brazeau, *Parts of World,* loc. cit., p. 175.

16. The original of this and the previous note to Sister Mary Bernetta Quinn are at the Dartmouth Library.

17. William Van O'Connor, *The Shaping Spirit: A Study of Wallace Stevens* (Chicago: Henry Regnery, 1950), p. 13.

18. Gass, op. cit., p. 259.

19. *Plato: Collected Critical Dialogues,* eds. Edith Hamilton and Huntington Cairns, Bollingen Series, LXXI (Princeton: Princeton University Press, 1978), p. 522.

20. Ibid., p. 504.

21. Heringman, "The Use of Poetry," loc. cit.

22. Brazeau, *Parts of World,* loc. cit., p. 187.

23. Ibid., p. 188.

24. Ibid., p. 196.

25. On the occasion of this first meeting Wilbur reports: ". . . in the midst of all this gaiety, he leaned forward towards me, and he said with absolute seriousness, indeed something approaching grimness—the look of an abbot talking to a novice—'Now, Wilbur, you're good, but you must stop publishing in *The New Yorker.*' Well, I was very flustered—and happy to have him use the word 'good' to me. I confusedly defended myself. I said that I didn't have any money, and that they paid the best of all the magazines. Also, that to be published in *The New Yorker* meant that you got a pretty good wide readership, and apparently reached even Wallace Stevens. He said, 'That doesn't matter. Money doesn't matter. If you're a poet, you must be prepared

to be poor, if that's necessary. You must be like a monk. You must sacrifice yourself to your work.' Now of course I'm not able to repeat what he said in his words, but he did say he felt it would be impossible for me to write over a period of years for a chic magazine that carried advertisements for Black Starr Frost and Gorham without adapting myself to their expectations." This account is in Brazeau, *Parts of World,* loc. cit., p. 197.

26. Ibid., p. 207.

CHAPTER V: *It Must Give Pleasure 1954–1955*

1. *The Jade Mountain: A Chinese Anthology,* loc. cit., p. xxvi.

2. Paul Valéry, *Dialogues,* tr. William McCausland Stewart, with Two Prefaces by Wallace Stevens, Bollingen Series, XLV–4 (New York: Pantheon, 1956), p. xiii.

3. Ibid.

4. Ibid., p. xvi.

5. Ibid., p. xiii.

6. Brazeau, *Parts of World,* loc. cit., pp. 292–93.

7. Ibid., p. 293.

8. Ibid., p. 295.

9. Ibid., p. 310 n.

INDEX